A BUDGET FOR

AMERICA'S FUTURE

ANALYTICAL PERSPECTIVES

BUDGET OF THE U.S. GOVERNMENT

FISCAL YEAR 2021

THE BUDGET DOCUMENTS

Budget of the United States Government, Fiscal Year 2021 contains the Budget Message of the President, information on the President's priorities, and summary tables.

Analytical Perspectives, Budget of the United States Government, Fiscal Year 2021 contains analyses that are designed to highlight specified subject areas or provide other significant presentations of budget data that place the budget in perspective. This volume includes economic and accounting analyses, information on Federal receipts and collections, analyses of Federal spending, information on Federal borrowing and debt, baseline or current services estimates, and other technical presentations.

Appendix, Budget of the United States Government, Fiscal Year 2021 contains detailed information on the various appropriations and funds that constitute the budget and is designed primarily for the use of the Appropriations Committees. The *Appendix* contains more detailed financial information on individual programs and appropriation accounts than any of the other budget documents. It includes for each agency: the proposed text of appropriations language; budget schedules for each account; legislative proposals; narrative explanations of each budget account; and proposed general provisions applicable to the appropriations of entire agencies or group of agencies. Information is also provided on certain activities whose transactions are not part of the budget totals.

Major Savings and Reforms, Fiscal Year 2021, which accompanies the President's Budget, contains detailed information on major savings and reform proposals. The volume describes both major discretionary program eliminations and reductions and mandatory savings proposals.

GENERAL NOTES

1. All years referenced for budget data are fiscal years unless otherwise noted. All years referenced for economic data are calendar years unless otherwise noted.

2. At the time the Budget was prepared, the United States-Mexico- Canada Agreement Implementation Act (Public Law 116-113) had not yet been signed into law. As a result, the Budget includes a Government-wide allowance to represent the discretionary appropriations included in this proposal, which the Administration transmitted to the Congress on December 13, 2019, the House passed on December 19, 2019, and the Senate passed on January 16, 2020.

3. Detail in this document may not add to the totals due to rounding.

ISBN: 978-1-64143-460-7

TABLE OF CONTENTS

LIST OF CHARTS AND TABLES

LIST OF CHARTS AND TABLES

LIST OF CHARTS

LIST OF TABLES

Federal Receipts

Special Topics

Technical Budget Analyses

*Available on the internet at *http://www.whitehouse.gov/omb/analytical-perspectives/*

*Available on the internet at *http://www.whitehouse.gov/omb/analytical-perspectives/*

INTRODUCTION

1. INTRODUCTION

The *Analytical Perspectives* volume presents analyses that highlight specific subject areas or provide other significant data that place the President's 2021 Budget in context and assist the public, policymakers, the media, and researchers in better understanding the Budget. This volume complements the main *Budget* volume, which presents the President's Budget policies and priorities, and the Budget *Appendix* volume, which provides appropriations language, schedules for budget expenditure accounts, and schedules for selected receipt accounts.

Presidential Budgets have included separate analytical presentations of this kind for many years. The 1947 Budget and subsequent budgets included a separate section entitled *Special Analyses and Tables* that covered four, and later more, topics. For the 1952 Budget, the section was expanded to 10 analyses, including many subjects still covered today, such as receipts, investment, credit programs, and aid to State and local governments. With the 1967 Budget this material became a separate volume entitled *Special Analyses*, and included 13 chapters. The material has remained a separate volume since then, with the exception of the Budgets for 1991–1994, when all of the budget material was included in one volume. Beginning with the 1995 Budget, the volume has been named *Analytical Perspectives*.

In addition to the information included in this volume, supplemental tables and other materials that are part of the *Analytical Perspectives* volume are available at *http://www.whitehouse.gov/omb/analytical-perspectives*. All of the supplemental information included at this link was previously included on the Budget CD-ROM, which is no longer made available. Tables included at this link are shown in the List of Tables in the front of this volume with an asterisk instead of a page number.

Overview of the Chapters

Economic and Budget Analyses

Economic Assumptions and Overview. This chapter reviews recent economic developments; presents the Administration's assessment of the economic situation and outlook; compares the economic assumptions on which the 2021 Budget is based with the assumptions for last year's Budget and those of other forecasters; provides sensitivity estimates for the effects on the Budget of changes in specified economic assumptions; and reviews past errors in economic projections.

Long-Term Budget Outlook. This chapter assesses the long-term budget outlook under current policies and under the Budget's proposals. It focuses on 25-year projections of Federal deficits and debt to illustrate the long-term impact of the Administration's proposed policies, and shows how alternative long-term budget assumptions affect the results. It also discusses the uncertainties of the long-term budget projections and discusses the actuarial status of the Social Security and Medicare programs.

Federal Borrowing and Debt. This chapter analyzes Federal borrowing and debt and explains the budget estimates. It includes sections on special topics such as trends in debt, debt held by the public net of financial assets and liabilities, investment by Government accounts, and the statutory debt limit.

Management

Strengthening the Federal Workforce. This chapter presents summary data on Federal employment and compensation, and discusses the approach the Administration is taking with Federal human capital management.

Payment Integrity. This chapter addresses proposals aimed at bolstering payment integrity by taking steps intended to help prevent improper payments, through initiatives such as increasing data access, providing needed authorities to correct known mistakes prior to payment, increasing use of analytics, improving pre-payment reviews, and simplifying program access to reduce complicated eligibility requirements. If adopted, the proposals will help shape a Budget that improves mission support and enhances mission accomplishment while providing better stewardship of taxpayer resources.

Federal Real Property. This chapter provides background on the Government-wide real property portfolio, summarizes recent actions taken to improve governance and management of the program, and addresses proposals to optimize the Government's real property portfolio for mission effectiveness and cost efficiency.

Budget Concepts and Budget Process

Budget Concepts. This chapter includes a basic description of the budget process, concepts, laws, and terminology, and includes a glossary of budget terms.

Coverage of the Budget. This chapter describes activities that are included in budget receipts and outlays (and are therefore classified as "budgetary") as well as those activities that are not included in the Budget (and are therefore classified as "non-budgetary"). The chapter also defines the terms "on-budget" and "off-budget" and includes illustrative examples.

Budget Process. This chapter discusses proposals to improve budgeting, fiscal sustainability, and transparency within individual programs as well as across Government.

Federal Receipts

Governmental Receipts. This chapter presents information on estimates of governmental receipts, which consist of taxes and other compulsory collections. It includes descriptions of tax-related legislation enacted in the last year and describes proposals affecting receipts in the 2021 Budget.

Offsetting Collections and Offsetting Receipts. This chapter presents information on collections that offset outlays, including collections from transactions with the public and intragovernmental transactions. In addition, this chapter presents information on "user fees," charges associated with market-oriented activities and regulatory fees. The user fee information includes a description of each of the user fee proposals in the 2021 Budget. A detailed table, "Table 12–5, Offsetting Receipts by Type" is available at the internet address cited above.

Tax Expenditures. This chapter describes and presents estimates of tax expenditures, which are defined as revenue losses from special exemptions, credits, or other preferences in the tax code.

Special Topics

Aid to State and Local Governments. This chapter presents crosscutting information on Federal grants to State and local governments. The chapter also includes a table showing historical grant spending, and a table with budget authority and outlays for grants in the Budget. Tables showing State-by-State spending for major grant programs are available at the internet address cited above.

Information Technology. This chapter addresses Federal information technology (IT), highlighting initiatives to improve IT management through modern solutions to enhance service delivery. The Administration will invest in modern, secure technologies and services to drive enhanced efficiency and effectiveness. This will include undertaking complex Government-wide modernization efforts, driving improved delivery of citizen-facing services, and improving the overall management of the Federal IT portfolio. The Administration will also continue its efforts to further build the Federal IT workforce and strategically reduce the Federal Government's cybersecurity risk.

Federal Investment. This chapter discusses federally financed spending that yields long-term benefits. It presents information on annual spending on physical capital, research and development, and education and training.

Research and Development. This chapter presents a crosscutting review of research and development funding in the Budget.

Credit and Insurance. This chapter provides crosscutting analyses of the roles, risks, and performance of Federal credit and insurance programs and Government-sponsored enterprises (GSEs). The chapter covers the major categories of Federal credit (housing, education, small business and farming, energy and infrastructure, and international) and insurance programs (deposit insurance, pension guarantees, disaster insurance, and insurance against terrorism-related risks). Five additional tables address transactions including direct loans, guaranteed loans, and GSEs. These tables are available at the internet address cited above.

Cybersecurity Funding. This chapter displays enacted and proposed cybersecurity funding for Federal Departments and Agencies, and includes analysis of broad cybersecurity trends across Government.

Federal Drug Control Funding. This chapter displays enacted and proposed drug control funding for Federal Departments and Agencies.

Technical Budget Analyses

Current Services Estimates. This chapter discusses the conceptual basis of the Budget's current services, or "baseline," estimates, which are generally consistent with the baseline rules in the Balanced Budget and Emergency Deficit Control Act of 1985 (BBEDCA). The chapter presents estimates of receipts, outlays, and the deficit under this baseline. Two detailed tables addressing factors that affect the baseline and providing details of baseline budget authority and outlays are available at the internet address cited above.

Trust Funds and Federal Funds. This chapter provides summary information about the two fund groups in the Budget—Federal funds and trust funds. In addition, for the major trust funds and certain Federal fund programs, the chapter provides detailed information about income, outgo, and balances.

Comparison of Actual to Estimated Totals. This chapter compares the actual receipts, outlays, and deficit for 2019 with the estimates for that year published in the 2019 Budget, published in February 2018.

The following materials are available at the internet address cited above.

Detailed Functional Table

Detailed Functional Table. Table 24–1, "Budget Authority and Outlays by Function, Category, and Program," displays budget authority and outlays for major Federal program categories, organized by budget function (such as healthcare, transportation, or national defense), category, and program.

Federal Budget by Agency and Account

Federal Budget by Agency and Account. Table 25–1, "Federal Budget by Agency and Account," displays budget authority and outlays for each account, organized by agency, bureau, fund type, and account.

Budgets of the Federal Statistical Agencies

Budgets of the Federal Statistical Agencies. Table 26-1, "Budgets of the Federal Statistical Agencies," displays the budgets of the Principle Statistical Agencies recognized by OMB, organized by agency.

Calfed Bay-Delta Program Federal Budget Crosscut

Calfed Bay-Delta Program Crosscut. The Calfed Bay-Delta Program interagency budget crosscut report provides an estimate of Federal funding by each of the participating Federal Agencies with authority and programmatic responsibility for implementing this program, fulfilling the reporting requirements of section 106(c) of Public Law 108–361.

Columbia River Basin Federal Budget Crosscut

Columbia River Basin Federal Budget Crosscut. The Columbia River interagency budget crosscut report includes an estimate of Federal funding by each of the participating Federal agencies to carry out restoration activities within the Columbia River Basin, fulfilling the reporting requirements of section 123 of the Clean Water Act (33 U.S.C. 1275).

ECONOMIC AND BUDGET ANALYSES

2. ECONOMIC ASSUMPTIONS AND OVERVIEW

This chapter presents the economic assumptions that underlie the Administration's 2021 Budget.[1] It outlines an overview of the recent performance of the American economy, provides the Administration's projections for key macroeconomic variables, contrasts them with forecasts prepared by other prominent institutions, and discusses the unavoidable uncertainty inherent in providing an eleven-year forecast.

The American economy continues the longest expansion in its recorded history. The unemployment rate reached its deepest level in half a century. Prime-age labor force participation has hit decade highs. Real wages sustained their rise. Deregulation has removed over seven substantial regulations for each one added. The Tax Cut and Jobs Act (TCJA) expanded the capital base and encouraged multinational enterprises to repatriate nearly $1 trillion previously invested abroad.

Discordant elements perturbed this harmonious expansion. The Federal Government's deficit swelled as large spending increases were approved. Poor performance in the global economy, industrial turmoil at flagship U.S. companies, and international trade uncertainty subdued business confidence, investment growth, and manufacturing output. In order for 2020 to extend the economic expansion of the past three years, continued implementation of the Administration's pro-growth agenda is imperative.

This chapter proceeds as follows:

The first section provides an overview of the recent functioning of the U.S. economy, examining the performance of a broad array of key economic indicators.

The second section provides a detailed exposition of the Administration's economic assumptions behind the 2021 Budget, discussing how key macroeconomic variables are expected to evolve over the years 2020 to 2030.

The third section compares the forecast of the Administration with those of the Congressional Budget Office, the Federal Open Market Committee of the Federal Reserve, and the Blue Chip panel of private sector forecasters.

The fourth section discusses the sensitivity of the Administration's projections of Federal receipts and outlays to fluctuations in macroeconomic variables.

The fifth section considers the errors and possible biases[2] in past Administration forecasts, comparing them with the errors in forecasts produced by the Congressional Budget Office (CBO) and the Blue Chip panel of private professional forecasters.

The sixth section uses information on past accuracy of Administration forecasts to provide understanding and insight into the uncertainty associated with the Administration's current forecast of the budget balance.

Recent Economic Performance[3]

The U.S. economy expanded steadily but unevenly. Real gross domestic product (GDP) grew at an average of 2.4 percent growth during the first three quarters of 2019. This compares to the 4-quarter growth of 2.5 percent in 2018 and 2.8 percent in 2017; which were well above both the current law expectations of the CBO and the observed yearly average of 2.2 percent between 2010 and 2016. Disaggregating the demand components of GDP during the first three quarters of 2019, private consumption contributed 2.0 percentage points (p.p.) of growth and Government purchases contributed 0.5 p.p., while stagnating private investment diminished growth by -0.1 p.p. and net exports failed to contribute anything. On the supply side, productivity growth measured by annualized nonfarm business sector real output per hour increased by an average of 1.9 percent in the first three quarters of 2019. This is elevated from an average of 0.8 percent growth between 2010 and 2016, 1.4 in 2017 and 1.0 in 2018, indicating a sustained acceleration in productivity and far outpacing other advanced nations: the non-U.S. G7+Australia averaged productivity growth of -0.2 percent for Q4:2017-Q3:2019.

A sundering occurred this year between the manufacturing and agricultural sectors and the rest of the economy. Manufacturing and agriculture are highly exposed to international markets, so global stagnation and trade frictions have outsized impacts in these sectors. Impactful economic events this year included a global growth slowdown, trade uncertainty, a Federal Government shutdown, a worker strike at General Motors, and ongoing issues at Boeing. These factors prompted lower output and damaged business confidence, with real output in the manufacturing sector falling in Q1 and Q2 of 2019, though there was some recovery in Q3. The resolution of these affairs will generate higher growth in future quarters. The U.S. Government has pledged to provide assistance of $28 billion, equivalent to a fifth of all U.S. agricultural exports in 2018, to farmers in order to compensate for the damage caused by trade actions.

The Labor Market

Overview—The U.S. labor market has exceeded expectations, fostering the best climate for job seekers in

---

[1] Economic performance, unless otherwise specified, is discussed in terms of calendar years (January-December). Budget figures are discussed in terms of fiscal years (October-September).

[2] As discussed later in this chapter, "bias" here is defined in the statistical sense and refers to whether previous Administrations' forecasts have tended to make positive or negative forecast errors on average.

[3] The statistics in this section are based on information available in December 2019.

generations. The civilian unemployment rate continued to decline, descending from 4.7 percent at the end of 2016 to 3.5 percent in November 2019, the lowest rate since November 1969 (when over three million individuals were serving in the military—compared with 1.3 million today), and remaining well below the post-war average of 5.8 percent. There were 7.3 million job openings in October 2019, exceeding the number of unemployed by 1.4 million. A labor market with more openings than job seekers is an unprecedented situation and has been maintained for 20 consecutive months. The labor force participation rate reached 63.2 percent in November 2019, continuing its climb upwards from a crevasse of 62.4 percent in September 2015. Prime-age labor force participation, 82.8 percent in November 2019, is up from a low of 80.6 percent in September 2015, but is still below the 84.6 percent recorded in January 1999. This cannot be blamed on baby boomer retirements and is partially explained by the opioid epidemic, indicating the importance of the Administration's efforts to treat those suffering from addiction and interdict further illegal imports of opiates.[4]

The Workforce—The state of the labor market is especially impressive when it is framed by the rapid aging of the average American. The percent of the population above 65 has increased from 14.9 in 2015 to 16.0 in 2018. To illustrate, the first of the baby boomers turned 65 in 2011, and the corresponding drags on the labor force participation rate and fiscal path from their retirement has only accelerated. The last of the baby boomers will turn 65 in 2029. These demographic shifts will generate additional downward pressure on the labor force participation rate over the next decade.

This must be mitigated by greater opportunities for marginalized individuals to leave the sidelines of the economy. Health improvements and less physically demanding jobs should increase participation among traditional retirement-age individuals, which could be decisive in allowing the United States to thrive despite this demographic challenge. Continuing to recoup the losses from retirement with additional prime-age participation is critical for an adequate labor force supply that can meet employer demands.

There are other positive trends: the percent of the population receiving Social Security Disabled worker benefits has fallen with the improving economy, from 5.8 percent in 2015 to 5.5 percent in 2018. However, this is still elevated from 3.7 percent in 2000. The proportion of college graduates has continued to rise, from 34.1 percent of 25-34 year olds in 2015 to 36.2 in 2018. Furthermore, the percentage of total graduate degrees that are science and engineering has also increased from 15.0 percent to 16.9 percent over the same period.

Wages—In Q3:2019 average hourly earnings had improved 3.1 percent and median weekly real earnings had increased by 1.4 percent from one-year prior, benefiting workers by creating a higher standard of living. Wage growth for production workers is elevated above wage growth for supervisors. Wage growth for lower earning

individuals is elevated above wage growth for higher earning individuals. Wage growth for those without a college degree is elevated above those with a college degree. Wage growth for African Americans is elevated above wage growth for Whites. These phenomenon reverse trends from earlier in this economic expansion, and have contributed to a fall in the poverty rate, from 13.5 percent in 2015 to 11.8 percent in 2018.

Unemployment and Underemployment—The number of individuals employed part-time for economic reasons has fallen to 4.3 million in November 2019, well below a peak of over 9 million during the Great Recession. Furthermore, the share of the unemployed that have been job-hunting for longer than 27 weeks has fallen to 20.8 percent in November 2019, from a pinnacle of nearly half the unemployed during the Great Recession.

The portion of the labor force working part-time for economic reasons and the portion unemployed for more than 27 weeks have finally recovered to pre-Great Recession ranges, as have the shares of the working-age population marginally attached to the labor force or too discouraged to look for work. However, these critical indicators are still elevated compared to the late 1990s. Even with this improved employment picture, there remains space for further ascent.

Gross Domestic Product

Consumption—Real consumer spending increased by 2.6 percent over the four quarters ending 2019:Q3. This was driven by increased purchases of a variety of goods and services, including recreational goods and vehicles (12 percent), transportation services (3 percent), food and beverages (3 percent), furnishings (3 percent), clothing and footwear (2 percent), and healthcare (2 percent). The personal savings rate reached 7.9 percent in November 2019, above its 20-year average of 6.1 percent, and household debt service payments have fallen to 9.7 percent of disposable income in 2019:Q2, from a peak of 13.2 percent in 2007:Q4. This heightened savings rate suggests that the pace of consumption growth is driven by the observed real wage gains rather than an unsustainable increase of personal debt.

Investment—Real nonresidential fixed investment increased by 1.4 percent over the four quarters ending 2019:Q3. Equipment investment increased 1.0 percent, investment in structures decreased 6.7 percent, and investment in intellectual property products increased 7.6 percent. Overall, real private fixed investment (residential and nonresidential) grew 0.9 percent over the four quarters ending 2019:Q3, compared with 3.5 percent in 2018, 5.1 percent in 2017 and 2.8 percent in 2016.

The rapid growth of investment during 2017 and 2018 was encouraged by substantial reductions in the cost of capital from the Tax Cut and Jobs Act (TCJA), enacted in December 2017 but retroactive to 2017:Q4. However, this momentum has faltered, due primarily to falling business confidence, generated by global growth and trade concerns. Despite these countervailing factors, the TCJA raised investment and real disposable personal income

---

[4] Dionissi Aliprantis, Kyle Fee, and Mark E. Schweitzer, 2019, "Opioids and the Labor Market," Federal Reserve Bank of Cleveland.

above pre-TCJA expectations. This resulted from both productivity gains and lower tax liability. Investment was 4.5 percent higher in 2018 and 3.3 percent higher in 2019 than the Blue Chip panel's pre-TCJA forecast[5].

Government—Real Government purchases (consumption and gross investment) increased 2.2 percent over the four quarters ending in Q3:2019. State and local government purchases increased 1.4 percent, while Federal purchases increased 3.7 percent. Federal defense spending rose 4.6 percent, and non-defense spending increased 2.4 percent. The Federal deficit as a percentage of GDP increased to 4.6 percent in fiscal year 2019 from 3.8 in fiscal year 2018 and 3.5 percent in fiscal year 2017. As the deficit rises, a greater percentage of the budget must be diverted to debt servicing, creating a vicious spiral that is difficult to break.

Trade—Exports of goods and services increased 0.2 percent in the four quarters ending 2019:Q3, generated by an increase of 0.8 percent in goods and a decrease of 0.9 percent in services. Imports increased 0.9 percent over the same period, generated by an increase of 0.1 percent in goods and an increase of 4.3 percent in services. While cheap imports benefit the American consumer, this worsening trade imbalance is not sustainable.

Key Factors

Monetary Policy—After holding the nominal Federal funds rate near zero for seven years, the Federal Open Market Committee of the Federal Reserve began raising the Federal funds rate target range at the end of 2015. This range steadily increased to 2.25-2.5 percent by January of 2019. This year the Fed reversed course, cutting interest rates three times to reach a rate range of 1.5-1.75 percent in December 2019. Inflation remains low and stable, defying predictions that labor market tightness would drive up prices. The increase in labor force participation indicates there was more slack in the labor market than was readily apparent.

Environment and Energy—Forty-six years after President Nixon announced Project Independence the United States has finally achieved its goal of ending net oil imports. Gross greenhouse gas emissions are falling in the United States, from 7,339.0 teragrams CO_2 equivalent in 2005 to 6,456.7 in 2017, the latest year data is available. Between 2010 and 2019:Q3, the nominal price of natural gas decreased 60 percent, crude oil decreased 20 percent, coal increased by 6 percent, solar decreased by 77 percent, off-shore wind decreased by 20 percent and on-shore wind decreased by 35 percent.[6] As energy costs are effectively a tax on production, lower energy costs have been a boon for this economic expansion. New technologies that continue to lower the complete costs of energy while maintaining high standards of environmental quality for all Americans will promote greater abundance.

Housing—2019 was a year of steady growth in the housing market. After the breathtaking crash of 2007-

2012, housing prices have continued a return to normalcy, growing 4.6 percent in the year prior to Q3:2019. Increases in home building have followed, buoyed by lower interest rates, with new private starts up 13.6 percent in the 12 months ending November 2019. These trends reduce America's housing shortage, which is reaching epidemic proportions in restrictive high-density areas.

External Sector—Internationally, economic prospects are bleak. According to the International Monetary Fund's World Economic Outlook, October 2019, global growth for 2019 is estimated at 3.0 percent, its lowest level since the Great Recession. Additionally, growth in 2020 is forecast to increase just 3.4 percent, a downward revision of 0.2 p.p. from the previous report. The Euro area is projected to grow by 1.4 percent in 2020, up from 1.2 percent in 2019. In Asia, annual growth is projected to decrease in Japan from 0.9 percent in 2019 to 0.5 percent in 2020 and China from 6.1 to 5.8 percent. Overall, any growth reversal among trading partners will create difficulties for U.S. exporters, notably the agriculture sector, and depress U.S. growth, while additional foreign growth will have the opposite effect.

Risks—The largest risk to the current U.S. economic expansion is a crisis of confidence, especially in the manufacturing sector. The Organization for Economic Co-operation and Development manufacturing composite index has declined 2.2 percent in the past year and the Chicago Federal Reserve measurement of business conditions remains gloomy. When business owners are pessimistic about the future, they fail to invest in capital and labor, and their cloudy outlook becomes self-fulfilling. To reverse this, the atmosphere of uncertainty must be dispelled by the dawn of trade deals and reforms that attract more high-skilled workers to fill job openings across the Nation.

In the medium to long term, the rise of debt is concerning. The Federal Debt Held by the Public of the United States as a percentage of Gross Domestic Product has increased steadily since 2001, rising from 32 percent in 2001 to 80 percent in 2019. To comprehend the complete depiction of the financial situation of the United States it is necessary to understand the effects of today's budget on future generations (generational accounting[7]), including Federal debt and the fiscal gap, which is the difference between the forecasted net present value of future Government spending and tax receipts. As a measure of this fiscal gap, the "Long-Term Budget Outlook" chapter shows that, under current law, the 25-year fiscal gap above the average postwar ratio of debt held by the public to GDP of 45 percent is 1.3 percent of GDP per year, with the fiscal gap for Gross Federal Debt to GDP being even larger. This is untenable. The fact that Government debt has failed to fall in this period of historic growth indicates that a change in the current fiscal approach is required to keep the Nation solvent.

Educational expenses are rising rapidly. Student loan debt grew 5.1 percent in the 12 months ending October

---

[5] October 2016

[6] Renewable price estimates made by the International Renewable Energy Agency.

[7] Alan J. Auerbach, Jagadeesh Gokhale, and Laurence J. Kotlikoff. 1994. "Generational Accounting: A Meaningful Way to Evaluate Fiscal Policy." Journal of Economic Perspectives, 8 (1): 73-94.

Table 2–1.   ECONOMIC ASSUMPTIONS[1]
(Calendar Years, Dollar Amounts In Billions)

	Actual 2018	Projections											
		2019	2020	2021	2022	2023	2024	2025	2026	2027	2028	2029	2030
Gross Domestic Product (GDP):													
Levels, Dollar Amounts in Billions:													
Current Dollars	20,580	21,437	22,494	23,645	24,849	26,113	27,442	28,822	30,242	31,719	33,269	34,893	36,598
Real, Chained (2012) Dollars	18,638	19,077	19,619	20,219	20,829	21,458	22,106	22,760	23,410	24,070	24,749	25,447	26,165
Chained Price Index (2012=100), Annual Average ...	110	112	115	117	119	122	124	127	129	132	134	137	140
Percent Change, Fourth Quarter over Fourth Quarter:													
Current Dollars	4.9	4.2	5.2	5.1	5.1	5.1	5.1	5.0	4.9	4.9	4.9	4.9	4.9
Real, Chained (2012) Dollars	2.5	2.5	3.1	3.0	3.0	3.0	3.0	2.9	2.8	2.8	2.8	2.8	2.8
Chained Price Index (2012=100)	2.3	1.8	2.0	2.0	2.0	2.0	2.0	2.0	2.0	2.0	2.0	2.0	2.0
Incomes, Billions of Current Dollars:													
Domestic Corporate Profits	1,573	1,554	1,699	1,821	1,917	2,010	2,095	2,182	2,231	2,271	2,319	2,343	2,417
Employee Compensation	10,928	11,500	12,094	12,725	13,414	14,127	14,885	15,673	16,492	17,347	18,250	19,199	20,199
Wages and Salaries	8,889	9,370	9,844	10,348	10,915	11,493	12,110	12,752	13,416	14,115	14,838	15,611	16,415
Nonwage Personal Income	5,276	5,431	5,601	5,817	6,077	6,349	6,652	7,002	7,365	7,771	8,129	8,474	8,828
Consumer Price Index (All Urban)[3]:													
Level (1982-1984 = 100), Annual Average ...	251	256	261	267	273	280	286	292	299	306	313	320	327
Percent Change, Fourth Quarter over Fourth Quarter ...	2.2	1.9	2.3	2.3	2.3	2.3	2.3	2.3	2.3	2.3	2.3	2.3	2.3
Unemployment Rate, Civilian, Percent:													
Annual Average	3.9	3.7	3.5	3.6	3.8	4.0	4.0	4.0	4.0	4.0	4.0	4.0	4.0
Interest Rates, Percent:													
91-Day Treasury Bills[2]	1.9	2.1	1.4	1.5	1.5	1.6	1.7	2.0	2.2	2.4	2.5	2.5	2.5
10-Year Treasury Notes	2.9	2.2	2.0	2.2	2.5	2.7	3.0	3.1	3.1	3.1	3.2	3.2	3.2

[1] Based on information available as of mid-November 2019
[2] Average rate, secondary market (bank discount basis)
[3] Seasonally Adjusted

2019, outpacing nominal GDP by over a percentage point. Curbing the soaring cost of a quality education is critical to producing a highly skilled workforce capable of investing in their future.

The continued rise of non-financial corporate debt, approaching $6.6 trillion, begs questions of viability.

Additional industrial turmoil arising from manufacturing or labor issues remain a threat to growth, The halting of production of the 737 MAX at Boeing is forecast to reduce annualized GDP growth by half a percentage point in Q1:2020.

Finally, 2020 is an election year, and there is the risk that this will distract from implementation of the necessary policies required for continued increases in prosperity.

Economic Projections for Current Law and Administration Policies

The Administration forecast was finalized on November 4, with data available as of that date. The forecast informs the 2021 Budget and rests on the central assumption of full implementation of all the Administration's policy proposals. The Administration's projections are reported in Table 2-1 and summarized below. The current law forecast incorporates the TCJA, passed in 2017, and previous Administration efforts to remove unhelpful regulations, which has supported a growth rate of GDP well above the rate forecasted by CBO. Moreover, as can be seen, the enactment of additional Administration policies would contribute to even higher growth rates of GDP, emphasizing the importance of these policies to the American economy.

Real GDP—In early November, when the forecast was finalized, the Administration projected that real GDP growth would achieve a four-quarter percent change of 2.5 in 2019. The pace of growth is projected to increase to 3.1 percent in 2020 before declining slightly to 2.8 percent at the end of the forecast window. The Administration is building on the pro-growth impact of criminal justice amnesty, tax reform, opportunity zones, historic deregulation, and a variety of trade deals. The enactment of additional Administration policies, such as reducing the burden of unnecessarily complex regulation, creating useful and cost-efficient infrastructure, streamlining the immigration process, lowering barriers to trade, and increasing labor force participation, are expected to improve the trajectory of the U.S. economy and hit these high growth rate targets.

Table 2–2. COMPARISON OF ECONOMIC ASSUMPTIONS IN THE 2020 AND 2021 BUDGETS

(Calendar Years)

	2018	2019	2020	2021	2022	2023	2024	2025	2026	2027	2028	2029
Real GDP (Percent Change)[1]:												
2020 Budget Assumptions	3.1	3.2	3.1	3.0	3.0	3.0	3.0	2.9	2.8	2.8	2.8	2.8
2021 Budget Assumptions	2.5	2.5	3.1	3.0	3.0	3.0	3.0	2.9	2.8	2.8	2.8	2.8
GDP Price Index (Percent Change)[1]:												
2020 Budget Assumptions	2.1	2.0	2.0	2.0	2.0	2.0	2.0	2.0	2.0	2.0	2.0	2.0
2021 Budget Assumptions	2.3	1.8	2.0	2.0	2.0	2.0	2.0	2.0	2.0	2.0	2.0	2.0
Consumer Price Index (All-Urban; Percent Change)[1]:												
2020 Budget Assumptions	2.3	2.2	2.3	2.3	2.3	2.3	2.3	2.3	2.3	2.3	2.3	2.3
2021 Budget Assumptions	2.2	1.9	2.3	2.3	2.3	2.3	2.3	2.3	2.3	2.3	2.3	2.3
Civilian Unemployment Rate (Percent)[1]:												
2020 Budget Assumptions	3.9	3.6	3.6	3.7	3.9	4.0	4.1	4.2	4.2	4.2	4.2	4.2
2021 Budget Assumptions	3.9	3.7	3.5	3.6	3.8	4.0	4.0	4.0	4.0	4.0	4.0	4.0
91-Day Treasury Bill Rate (Percent)[2]:												
2020 Budget Assumptions	1.9	2.7	3.1	3.2	3.2	3.1	3.0	3.0	3.0	3.0	3.0	3.0
2021 Budget Assumptions	1.9	2.1	1.4	1.5	1.5	1.6	1.7	2.0	2.2	2.4	2.5	2.5
10-Year Treasury Note Rate (Percent)[2]:												
2020 Budget Assumptions	2.9	3.4	3.6	3.8	3.8	3.7	3.7	3.7	3.7	3.7	3.7	3.7
2021 Budget Assumptions	2.9	2.2	2.0	2.2	2.5	2.7	3.0	3.1	3.1	3.1	3.2	3.2

[1] % Change 4Q
[2] Calendar Year Average

Unemployment—As of November 2019, the unemployment rate stood at 3.5 percent. The Administration expects the unemployment rate to remain low as a result of increasing business investment and higher real GDP growth even as more people enter the labor force, maintaining an average of 3.5 percent through 2020. As technology becomes more pervasive and the population becomes more mobile, with a 35 percent increase in moving for a new job between 2010-2011 and 2018-2019, the rate of non-cyclical unemployment will decrease, with job seekers matching with employers at an accelerated rate.

Interest Rates—The 91-day and 10-year Treasuries are expected to continue to decline until 2020, at which point they will rise to their forecasted long-term values of 2.5 and 3.2 percent, respectively. Demand for a safe haven and low economic growth rates worldwide have generated increased purchases of U.S. Government debt that will continue for the near future. The negative yields in Europe and Japan make the relatively higher interest rates in the U.S. attractive.

General Inflation—The Administration expects the Consumer Price Index for all Urban Consumers (CPI-U) to rise to 2.3 percent in 2020 (on a fourth quarter-over-fourth quarter basis). Little to no inflation is preferable to facilitate certainty about future costs for employers and workers, which benefits overall economic activity and avoids a deflationary spiral, in which no one wants to spend money today because his or her dollar will be worth more tomorrow.

Changes in Economic Assumptions from Last Year's Budget—Table 2-2 compares the Administration's forecast for the 2021 Budget with that from the 2020 Budget. Compared with the previous forecast, the Administration expects future real output growth to be essentially unchanged. Both forecasts are predicated on the full implementation of the Administration's policies designed to boost productivity and labor force participation. The Administration's expectations for inflation differ little from the previous forecast. The forecast for the unemployment rate is the first major deviation. The Administration now expects a lower long-run rate of unemployment, reflecting technological advances that result in increased mobility and faster matching of job seekers and employers, greater dynamism resulting from opportunity zones, reduced occupational licensing and worker training, and the rising value of labor generated by increased investment. The 2021 Budget predicts lower interest rates in the near term and longer term, as U.S. debt continues to be in high demand because it is a safe haven for savings amidst global turmoil.

The Current Law Economic Forecast—Chart 2-1 shows the importance of Administration policy to the real GDP growth forecast. The current law forecast incorporates the TCJA, passed in 2017, and previous Administration efforts to remove unhelpful regulations. As can be seen, without the enactment of additional Administration policies into law, the growth rate of GDP will be substantially lower, emphasizing the importance of these policies to the American economy.

Labor Market Policies—A key Administration labor market policy is altering the current immigration process into a simpler, merit-based system. Immigrants will bring the most benefit to America when they possess highly demanded skills and manifest strong labor force

Chart 2-1. Forecast of Q4 over Q4 Growth Rate

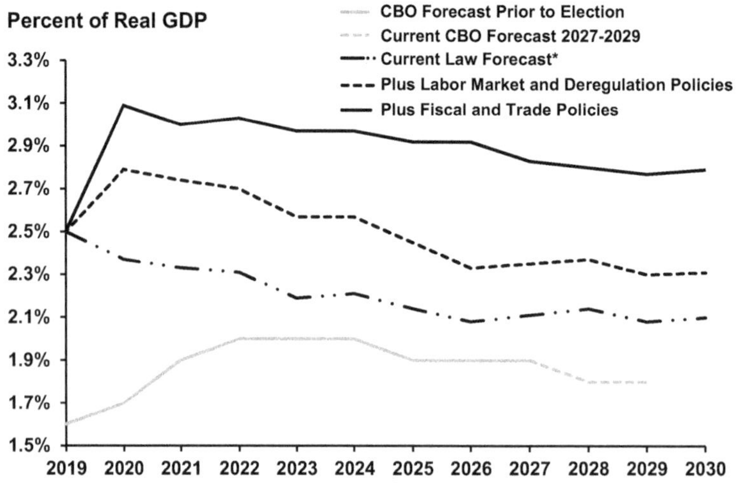

Percent of Real GDP

- CBO Forecast Prior to Election
- Current CBO Forecast 2027-2029
- Current Law Forecast*
- Plus Labor Market and Deregulation Policies
- Plus Fiscal and Trade Policies

*Includes TCJA, Deregulation prior to 2020, Global Trade Environment, etc.

Sources: Bureau of Economic Analysis, Bureau of Labor Statistics, Department of the Treasury, Office of Management and Budget, Council of Economic Advisors and Congressional Budget Office.

Note: Forecast is based on information available as of November 4, 2019.

participation.[8] Other labor market policies, such as work requirements for receiving social assistance, are also expected to improve labor force participation and output. The estimates for the growth impact of labor market policies are derived from the Administration's internal modeling.

Deregulation Policies—The Administration is continuing to declutter unnecessary and counter-productive regulations. In addition, the Administration is setting a high criterion for adding additional regulations, removing an ongoing drag on economic growth. The Administration has estimated that these policies have substantially improved the economic growth rate.[9]

Trade Policies—The Administration is pursuing reciprocal fair trade deals with a variety of partners, with the eventual ambition of achieving free trade: a world of zero tariffs, zero non-tariff barriers, and zero subsidies. A reduction of trade barriers will allow for robust competition, greater productivity and improved consumer welfare. The USMCA, KORUS, and US-JPN trade agreements are but the first steps in a comprehensive overhaul of the existing trade architecture. The shortcomings of previous systems has limited the incredible gains achieved through reciprocal free trade.

Fiscal Policies—Enacting comprehensive infrastructure investment increases is a core fiscal policy of the Administration. Using input estimates from a variety of sources[10], the Administration evaluated the growth impacts of the Administration's proposed infrastructure investment increase. After 2025, the Administration also forecasts an extension of those TCJA provisions that will benefit economic growth, encourage physical investment and improve productivity and wages.

The President's Budget calls for a reduction in Government outlays compared with the baseline over the next decade. Recent research[11] has shown that a plan based around reducing outlays assists fiscal stabilization via a positive impact on output growth, as confidence in the Government's fiscal path increases and uncertainty about future tax increases is dispelled. In addition, there will be a reduction in the cost of debt financing brought about by a decline in the perceived risk of holding Government bonds. Currently there is a low risk premium, as the Federal Government is perceived as a reliable borrower. That can change if the United States continues to spend more than it taxes indefinitely. In addition, eliminating deficit spending could curtail the trade deficit, as if there is a reduction in U.S. debt available for purchase in the capital account (the transfer of asset ownership), the current account (the transfer of goods and services) may reach balance.

[8] George J. Borjas, 2019. "Immigration and Economic Growth," NBER Working Papers 25836, National Bureau of Economic Research, Inc.

[9] The Council of Economic Advisers, 2019. "The Economic Effects of Federal Deregulation since January 2017: An Interim Report."

[10] Pedro R.D. Bom and Jenny E. Ligthart. 2014. "What Have We Learned From Three Decades Of Research On The Productivity Of Public Capital?," Journal of Economic Surveys, Wiley Blackwell, vol. 28(5), pages 889-916, December. Congressional Budget Office, 2016. "The Macroeconomic and Budgetary Effects of Federal Investment." Jeffrey M. Stupak, 2018. "Economic Impact of Infrastructure Investment," Congressional Research Service.

[11] Alberto Alesina, Carlo Favero, and Francesco Giavazzi, 2019. "Austerity: When It Works and When It Doesn't," Princeton; Oxford: Princeton University Press.

Table 2–3. COMPARISON OF ECONOMIC ASSUMPTIONS

(Calendar Years)

	2019	2020	2021	2022	2023	2024	2025	2026	2027	2028	2029	2030
Real GDP (Year-over-Year, Percent Change):												
2021 Budget	2.4	2.8	3.1	3.0	3.0	3.0	3.0	2.9	2.8	2.8	2.8	2.8
CBO	2.6	2.1	1.8	1.7	1.7	1.7	1.8	1.7	1.8	1.8	1.8	N/A
Blue Chip [1]	2.3	1.7	1.8	1.9	2.0	2.0	2.0	2.0	2.0	2.0	2.0	2.0
Federal Reserve [2]	2.2	2.0	1.9	1.8	1.9	1.9	1.9	1.9	1.9	1.9	1.9	1.9
Consumer Price Index (All-Urban, Percent Change):												
2021 Budget	1.9	2.3	2.3	2.3	2.3	2.3	2.3	2.3	2.3	2.3	2.3	2.3
CBO	1.9	2.4	2.5	2.5	2.4	2.4	2.3	2.3	2.3	2.3	2.3	N/A
Blue Chip [1]	1.8	2.1	2.1	2.2	2.2	2.2	2.2	2.2	2.2	2.2	2.2	2.2
Federal Reserve [2,3]	1.8	1.9	2.0	2.0	2.0	2.0	2.0	2.0	2.0	2.0	2.0	2.0
Civilian Unemployment Rate (Percent):												
2021 Budget	3.7	3.5	3.6	3.8	4.0	4.0	4.0	4.0	4.0	4.0	4.0	4.0
CBO	3.7	3.7	3.9	4.2	4.5	4.7	4.7	4.8	4.7	4.7	4.6	N/A
Blue Chip [1]	3.7	3.7	4.0	4.1	4.1	4.1	4.1	4.1	4.1	4.1	4.1	4.1
Federal Reserve [2]	3.7	3.7	3.8	3.9	4.2	4.2	4.2	4.2	4.2	4.2	4.2	4.2
Interest Rates:												
91-Day Treasury Bills (Discount Basis, Percent):												
2021 Budget	2.1	1.4	1.5	1.5	1.6	1.7	2.0	2.2	2.4	2.5	2.5	2.5
CBO	2.2	2.1	2.3	2.3	2.3	2.4	2.4	2.4	2.5	2.5	2.5	N/A
Blue Chip [1]	2.1	1.5	1.7	2.0	2.1	2.2	2.3	2.4	2.4	2.4	2.4	2.4
10-Year Treasury Notes (Percent):												
2021 Budget	2.2	2.0	2.2	2.5	2.7	3.0	3.1	3.1	3.1	3.2	3.2	3.2
CBO	2.3	2.2	2.5	2.9	3.0	3.1	3.1	3.1	3.2	3.2	3.2	N/A
Blue Chip [1]	2.1	1.8	2.2	2.6	2.8	2.9	3.0	3.1	3.1	3.1	3.1	3.1

Sources: Administration; CBO, The Budget and Economic Outlook: 2019 to 2029, August 2019; October 2019 Blue Chip Economic Indicators, Aspen Publishers, Inc.; Federal Reserve Open Market Committee, September 18, 2019

[1] 2026-2030 are 5 year averages
[2] Median Projection
[3] PCE Inflation
N/A = Not Available

Comparison with Other Forecasts

For some additional perspective on the Administration's forecast, this section compares it with forecasts prepared at the same time by the CBO, the Federal Open Market Committee of the Federal Reserve (FOMC), and the Blue Chip panel of private-sector forecasters. There are important differences that must inform such a comparison.

The most important difference between these forecasts is that they make different assumptions about the implementation of the Administration's policies. As already noted, the Administration's forecast assumes full implementation of these proposals. At the opposite end of the spectrum, CBO produces a forecast that assumes no changes to current law. It is not clear to what extent FOMC participants and Blue Chip panelists incorporate policy implementation in their respective outlooks. The Blue Chip panel, in particular, compiles a large number of private-sector forecasts, which are marked by considerable heterogeneity across individual forecasters and their policy expectations.

A second difference is the publication dates of the various forecasts. While the forecast published by the Administration is based on data available in November, the Blue Chip long-term forecast is based on their October Survey, the FOMC projections were released in September, and the CBO forecast was published in August.

In spite of these differences, the forecasts share several attributes. All of them project a further short-run plateau in the unemployment rate, followed by a rise back toward a rate consistent with long-term labor market fundamentals. They all forecast a rise in inflation, followed by a stable path at its long-run rate. Finally, they all foresee a gradual rise in interest rates over the course of the forecast horizon. What separates the Administration's forecast is its views on real output growth. See Table 2-3 for a comparison.

Real GDP—The Administration forecasts a higher path for real GDP growth compared with the CBO, FOMC, and Blue Chip forecasts throughout the forecast period, with a year-over-year growth rate 0.7 p.p faster than the next fastest forecast in 2020 and 0.8 p.p. faster than the next fastest forecast at the end of the forecast window. This reflects the Administration's expectation of full implementation of its policy proposals, while other forecasters vary in their outlooks regarding implementation of these policies. The CBO in particular is constrained to assume a continuation of current law in its forecast.

Unemployment—On the unemployment rate, the Administration's expectations are largely aligned with those of the other forecasters. Along with the Administration, all forecasters expect unemployment to remain below 4.0 in 2020. After 2020, all forecasters project a gradual uptick in the unemployment rate to their respective estimates of the long-term rate (4.0 percent for the Administration, 4.6 percent for the CBO, 4.2 percent for the FOMC, and 4.1 percent for the Blue Chip panel).

Interest Rates—The Administration's 91-day interest rate forecast is lower than other forecasts for 2022-2025. Another deviation of note is the CBO's 2020-2022 forecast for 91-day Treasury Bills, which is higher than Blue Chip and the Administration's forecasts. For both short- and long-term rates, all forecasters agree that they will tend to gradually rise, the Treasury bill rate is expected to rise to a steady-state level of around 2.5 percent and the 10-year Treasury note yield is expected to lie around 3.2 percent.

General Inflation—Expectations for inflation are similar across the Administration, the CBO, and the Blue Chip. The Blue Chip Panel expects a CPI-U inflation rate of 2.2 percent in the long run, while the Administration and CBO expect a 2.3 percent long-run rate. The Federal Reserve predicts it will hit its target of 2.0 percent for Personal Consumption Expenditure (PCE) inflation, which tends to be lower than inflation measured by the CPI-U.

Sensitivity of the Budget to Economic Assumptions

Federal spending and tax collections are heavily influenced by developments in the economy. Tax receipts are a function of growth in incomes for households and firms. Spending on social assistance programs may rise when the economy enters a downturn, while increases in nominal spending on Social Security and other programs are dependent on consumer price inflation. A robust set of projections for macroeconomic variables assists in Budget planning, but unexpected developments in the economy have ripple effects for Federal spending and receipts. This section seeks to provide an understanding of the magnitude of the effects that unforeseen changes in the economy can have on the Budget.

To make these assessments, the Administration relies on a set of heuristics that can predict how certain spending and receipt categories will react to a change in a given subset of macroeconomic variables, holding almost everything else constant. These provide a sense of the broad changes one would expect after a given development, but they cannot anticipate how policy makers would react and potentially change course in such an event. For example, if the economy were to suffer an unexpected recession, tax receipts would decline and spending on programs such as unemployment insurance would go up. In such a situation, however, policy makers might cut tax rates to

stimulate the economy, leading to secondary and tertiary changes that are difficult to predict.

Another caveat is that it is often unrealistic to suppose that one macroeconomic variable might change while others would remain constant. Most macroeconomic variables interact with each other in complex and subtle ways. These are important considerations to bear in mind when examining Table 2-4.

For real GDP growth and employment:

- The first panel in the table illustrates the effect on the deficit resulting from a one percentage point reduction in real GDP growth, relative to the Administration's forecast, in 2020 that is followed by a subsequent recovery in 2021 and 2022. The unemployment rate is assumed to be half a percentage point higher in 2020 before returning to the baseline level in 2021 and 2022.

- The next panel in the table reports the effect of a reduction of one percentage point in real GDP growth in 2020 that is not subsequently made up by faster growth in 2021 and 2022. Consistent with this output path, the rate of unemployment is assumed to rise by half a percentage point relative to that assumed in the Administration's forecasts.

- The third panel in the table shows the impact of a GDP growth rate that is permanently reduced by one percentage point, while the unemployment rate is not affected. This is the sort of situation that would arise if, for example, the economy were hit by a permanent decline in productivity growth.

For inflation and interest rates:

- The fourth panel in Table 2-4 shows the effect on the Budget in the case of a one percentage point higher rate of inflation and a one percentage point higher nominal interest rate in 2020. Both inflation and interest rates return to their assumed levels in 2021. This would result in a permanently higher price level and nominal GDP level over the course of the forecast horizon.

- The fifth panel in the table illustrates the effects on the Budget deficit of a one percentage point higher inflation rate and interest rate than projected in every year of the forecast.

- The sixth panel reports the effect on the deficit resulting from an increase in interest rates in every year of the forecast, with no accompanying increase in inflation.

- The seventh panel in the table reports the effect on the Budget deficit of a one percentage point higher inflation rate than projected in every year of the forecast window, while the interest rate remains as forecast.

- Finally, the table shows the effect on the Budget deficit if the Federal Government were to borrow an

Table 2–4. SENSITIVITY OF THE BUDGET TO ECONOMIC ASSUMPTIONS

(Fiscal Years; In Billions of Dollars)

Budget Effect	2020	2021	2022	2023	2024	2025	2026	2027	2028	2029	2030	Total of Budget Effects: 2020-2030
Real Growth and Employment:												
Budgetary effects of 1 percentage point lower real GDP growth:												
(1) For calendar year 2020 only, with real GDP recovery in 2021–2030:[1]												
Receipts	−15.6	−24.5	−12.4	−1.9	0.2	0.2	0.2	0.2	0.2	0.2	0.2	−53.1
Outlays	9.9	20.2	9.0	1.8	1.6	1.9	2.1	2.3	2.5	2.6	2.7	56.6
Increase in deficit (+)	25.5	44.7	21.5	3.6	1.4	1.7	2.0	2.1	2.3	2.4	2.5	109.8
(2) For calendar year 2020 only, with no subsequent recovery:[1]												
Receipts	−15.6	−32.6	−38.1	−40.1	−42.2	−44.3	−46.8	−49.1	−51.3	−53.7	−56.2	−470.2
Outlays	9.9	24.6	25.0	25.5	26.7	28.7	31.9	35.4	38.7	42.5	46.3	335.4
Increase in deficit (+)	25.5	57.1	63.1	65.7	69.0	73.1	78.7	84.5	90.1	96.3	102.5	805.5
(3) Sustained during 2020–2030, with no change in unemployment:												
Receipts	−15.6	−48.6	−89.0	−133.4	−181.9	−234.2	−292.8	−354.7	−420.1	−490.5	−565.9	−2,826.6
Outlays	0.0	0.2	0.9	2.4	4.0	6.9	11.0	16.9	23.6	31.3	40.0	137.2
Increase in deficit (+)	15.6	48.8	90.0	135.9	185.9	241.0	303.8	371.5	443.6	521.7	605.9	2,963.8
Inflation and Interest Rates:												
Budgetary effects of 1 percentage point higher rate of:												
(4) Inflation and interest rates during calendar year 2020 only:												
Receipts	16.8	32.8	34.7	35.1	36.9	38.7	40.8	42.8	44.7	46.8	48.9	418.9
Outlays	39.6	63.0	49.8	48.9	47.4	48.6	47.7	48.8	49.4	50.2	52.2	545.5
Increase in deficit (+)	22.8	30.2	15.1	13.8	10.5	9.9	6.8	6.0	4.6	3.4	3.4	126.6
(5) Inflation and interest rates, sustained during 2020–2030:												
Receipts	16.8	50.4	88.4	129.3	174.5	224.0	280.1	340.0	404.1	474.0	549.8	2,731.4
Outlays	38.5	108.5	170.8	231.6	288.7	352.3	416.5	484.6	564.1	627.6	714.5	3,997.9
Increase in deficit (+)	21.8	58.1	82.4	102.3	114.3	128.3	136.5	144.6	160.0	153.6	164.7	1,266.5
(6) Interest rates only, sustained during 2020–2030:												
Receipts	1.3	2.8	3.4	3.6	3.8	4.1	4.4	4.7	5.0	5.3	5.5	43.8
Outlays	24.8	70.5	104.5	133.7	158.3	182.0	203.3	223.8	242.2	260.3	276.2	1,879.7
Increase in deficit (+)	23.5	67.7	101.1	130.1	154.5	178.0	198.9	219.0	237.2	255.0	270.7	1,835.9
(7) Inflation only, sustained during 2020–2030:												
Receipts	15.4	47.6	84.9	125.6	170.5	219.7	275.4	334.9	398.7	468.3	543.7	2,684.8
Outlays	13.6	37.8	66.2	97.9	131.0	171.3	215.0	263.6	325.7	372.2	444.6	2,138.8
Decrease in deficit (–)	−1.8	−9.8	−18.8	−27.6	−39.5	−48.4	−60.4	−71.3	−73.0	−96.1	−99.2	−545.9
Interest Cost of Higher Federal Borrowing:												
(8) Outlay effect of 100 billion increase in borrowing in 2020	0.8	1.5	1.6	1.7	1.9	2.2	2.5	2.8	3.0	3.1	3.2	24.3

[1] The unemployment rate is assumed to be 0.5 percentage point higher per 1 percent shortfall in the level of real GDP.

additional $100 billion in 2020, while all of the other projections remain constant.

- These simple approximations that inform the sensitivity analysis are symmetric. This means that the effect of, for example, a one percentage point higher rate of growth over the forecast horizon would be of the same magnitude as a one percentage point reduction in growth, though with the opposite sign.

Forecast Errors for Growth, Inflation, and Interest Rates

As with any forecast, the Administration's projections will not be fully accurate. It is impossible to foresee every eventuality over a one–year horizon, much less ten or more years. This section evaluates the historical accuracy of the past administration forecasts for real GDP growth, inflation, and short-term interest rates from 2002 to present day, especially as compared with the accuracy

Table 2–5. FORECAST ERRORS, 2002-PRESENT

REAL GDP ERRORS

2-Year Average Annual Real GDP Growth	Administration	CBO	Blue Chip
Mean Error	0.9	0.5	0.1
Mean Absolute Error	1.0	0.8	0.3
Root Mean Square Error	1.5	1.3	0.4
6-Year Average Annual Real GDP Growth			
Mean Error	1.2	1.0	0.6
Mean Absolute Error	1.3	1.3	0.8
Root Mean Square Error	1.9	1.9	1.4

INFLATION ERRORS

2-Year Average Annual Change in the Consumer Price Index	Administration	CBO	Blue Chip
Mean Error	-0.1	-0.1	0.0
Mean Absolute Error	0.7	0.5	0.1
Root Mean Square Error	1.0	0.8	0.1
6-Year Average Annual Change in the Consumer Price Index			
Mean Error	0.1	-0.0	0.2
Mean Absolute Error	0.8	0.7	0.6
Root Mean Square Error	1.1	1.0	0.9

INTEREST RATE ERRORS

2-Year Average 91-Day Treasury Bill Rate	Administration	CBO	Blue Chip
Mean Error	0.7	0.6	0.0
Mean Absolute Error	0.9	0.7	0.1
Root Mean Square Error	1.4	1.3	0.1
6-Year Average 91-Day Treasury Bill Rate			
Mean Error	1.8	1.5	1.0
Mean Absolute Error	2.0	1.6	1.1
Root Mean Square Error	2.5	2.5	1.8

of forecasts produced by the CBO or Blue Chip panel. For this exercise, forecasts produced by all three entities are compared with realized values of these variables.

The results of this exercise are reported in Table 2-5 and contain three different measures of accuracy. The first is the average forecast error. When a forecaster has an average forecast error of zero, it may be said that the forecast has historically been unbiased, in the sense that realized values of the variables have not been systematically above or below the forecasted value. The second is the average absolute value of the forecast error, which offers a sense of the magnitude of errors. Even if the past forecast errors average to zero, the errors may have been of a very large magnitude, with both positive and negative values. Finally, the table reports the square root of the mean of squared forecast error (RMSE). This metric applies a harsher penalty to forecasts showing large errors. The table reports these measures of accuracy at both the 2-year and the 6-year horizons, thus evaluating the relative success of different forecasts in the short run and in the medium term.

Past administrations have forecast 2-year higher growth and interest rates then were actually realized by 0.9 p.p. and 0.7 p.p. respectively. This is related to the assumption detailed above - that all administration policies are enacted - which has not always been the case.

The 2-year forecast error for inflation is smaller, -0.1 p.p., and has a slightly negative bias, and is in line with other forecasts.

Uncertainty and the Deficit Projections

This section assesses the accuracy of past Budget forecasts for the deficit or surplus, measured at different time horizons. The results of this exercise are reported in Table 2-6, where the average error, the average absolute error, and the RMSE are reported.

In the table, a negative number means that the Federal Government ran a greater surplus than was expected, while a positive number in the table indicates a smaller surplus or a larger deficit. In the current year in which the Budget is published, the Administration has tended to understate the surplus (or, equivalently, overstate the deficit) by –0.7 percent of GDP. For the budget year, however, the historical pattern has been for the Budget deficit to be larger than the administration expected by 0.2 percent of GDP.[12] One possible reason for this is that past administrations' policy proposals have not all been implemented. The forecast errors tend to grow with the

---

[12] Additionally, CBO has on average underestimated the deficit in their forecasts.

Table 2–6.   DIFFERENCES BETWEEN ESTIMATED AND ACTUAL SURPLUSES OR DEFICITS FOR FIVE-YEAR BUDGET ESTIMATES SINCE 1985

(As a Percent of GDP)

	Current Year Estimate	Budget Year Estimate	Estimate for Budget Year Plus:			
			One Year (BY + 1)	Two Years (BY + 2)	Three Years (BY + 3)	Four Years (BY + 4)
Mean Error	−0.7	0.2	1.1	1.6	2.0	2.3
Mean Absolute Error	1.0	1.3	2.1	2.6	3.1	3.4
Root Mean Squared Error	1.2	1.9	2.9	3.5	3.8	4.0

time horizon, which is not surprising given that there is much greater uncertainty in the medium run about both the macroeconomic situation and the specific details of policy enactments.

It is possible to construct a probabilistic range of outcomes for the deficit. This is accomplished by taking the RMSE of previous forecast errors and assuming that these errors are drawn from a normal distribution. This exercise is undertaken at every forecast horizon from the current Budget year to five years into the future. Chart 2-2 displays the projected range of possible deficits. In the chart, the middle line represents the Administration's expected Budget balance and represents the 50th percentile outcome. The rest of the lines in the chart may be read in the following fashion. The top line reports the 95th percentile of the distribution of outcomes over 2020 to 2025, meaning that there is a 95 percent probability that the actual balance in those years will be more negative than expressed by the line. Similarly, there is a 95 percent probability that the balance will be more positive than suggested by the bottom line in the chart.

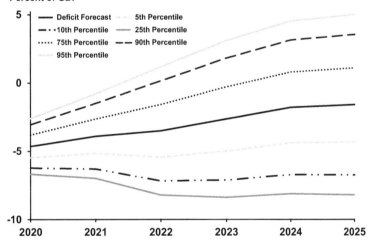

Chart 2-2. Range of Uncertainty for the Budget Deficit

3. LONG-TERM BUDGET OUTLOOK

The 2021 President's Budget improves the Federal Government's long-term fiscal picture by responsibly controlling spending and increasing efficiencies Government-wide. This chapter demonstrates the positive impact of the Administration's policies by comparing long-term budget forecasts under current policy (baseline projections) with forecasts based on the 2021 Budget proposals (policy projections). Baseline projections indicate that the deficit and debt held by the public will continue at elevated levels beyond the 10-year window. Conversely, policy projections indicate that enacting the Budget's proposed reforms could reduce deficits and publicly held debt as a percentage of GDP.

Chart 3-1 shows the path of debt as a percent of GDP under continuation of current policy, *without* the proposed changes in the President's Budget, as well as the debt trajectory under the President's policies. Under current policy, the ratio of debt to GDP is about the same in 2020 (80.5 percent) as in 2030 (80.4 percent). In contrast, the debt ratio is projected to be 66.1 percent in 2030 under the proposed policy changes. By the end of the 25-year horizon, there is a notable difference in the debt burden—68.4 percent of GDP under current policy compared to 23.3 percent of GDP under Budget policy. The savings proposed by the Administration from 2021-2030 are a significant down payment toward reducing the debt and reaching a balanced budget by 2035.

The projections in this chapter are highly uncertain. Small changes in economic or other assumptions can cause large differences to the results, especially for projections over longer horizons. For instance, the 2018

Financial Report of the U.S. Government presents long-run projections using different assumptions.[1]

The chapter is organized as follows:

- The first section details the assumptions used to create the baseline projections and analyzes the long-term implications of leaving current policies in place. This forecast serves as a point of comparison against the proposals in the 2021 Budget in the second section.

- The second section demonstrates how the Administration's policies will alter the current trajectory of the Federal budget by reducing deficits and debt, and balancing the budget by 2035 under a long-term term extension of the Budget's policies.

- The third section discusses alternative assumptions about the evolution of key variables and uncertainties in the resulting projections.

- The fourth section discusses the actuarial projections for Social Security and Medicare.

- The appendix provides further detail on data sources, assumptions, and other methods for estimation.

Long-Run Projections under Continuation of Current Policies

For the 10-year budget window, the Administration produces both baseline projections, which show how deficits and debt would evolve under current policies, and projections showing the impact of proposed policy changes. Like

---

[1] Available here: *https://fiscal.treasury.gov/reports-statements/financial-report/*.

Chart 3-1. Comparison of Publicly Held Debt

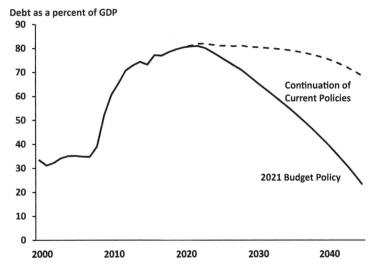

the budget baseline more generally, long-term projections should provide policymakers with information about the Nation's expected fiscal trajectory in the absence of spending and tax changes. Consistent with the methodology used in the 2018 and 2019 Budgets, the 2021 long term extension uses separate economic assumptions for baseline and policy projections to ensure the policy projections account for the anticipated economic feedback resulting from proposed Administration policies. For more information about the baseline and policy economic assumptions, see Chapter 2, "Economic Assumptions and Overview."

The baseline long-term projections assume that current policy continues for Social Security, Medicare, Medicaid, other mandatory programs, and revenues.[2] Projections for all mandatory programs maintain consistency with other Federal agency projections, and grow at an average annual nominal rate of about 5 percent from 2021-2045. For discretionary spending, it is less clear how to project a continuation of current policy. After the expiration of the statutory caps in 2021, both the Administration's and CBO's 10-year baselines assume that discretionary funding levels generally grow slightly above the rate of inflation (about 2.4 percent per year) per statutory baseline rules. Thereafter, the baseline long-run projections assume that per-person discretionary funding remains constant.

Over the next 10 years, debt in the baseline projections rises from 80.5 percent of GDP in 2020 to 81.1 percent of GDP in 2025 and then falls back to 80.4 percent of GDP in 2030. Beyond the 10-year horizon, debt continues to decrease slowly, reaching 68.4 percent of GDP by 2045, the end of the 25-year projection window. As discussed in the "Economic Assumptions and Overview" chapter, elevated levels of debt that are higher than the historical postwar average of 45 percent of GDP could pose a risk to economic growth.

Implementation of Administration policies.—The baseline reflects the implementation of some Administration policies, such as the TCJA and deregulation efforts, which improve the economic outlook in the 25-year window. Regulatory burden reductions and permanent corporate income tax cuts, along with other tax reforms in the TCJA, have promoted job creation and will help partially offset the effects of rapid healthcare cost growth.

Aging Population.—In the past several years, an aging population has put significant pressure on the Budget. Consistent with the demographic assumptions in the 2019 Medicare and Social Security Trustees' reports, U.S. population growth slows during the 25-year window while baby boomers retire through the mid-2030s. This slowdown drove baseline projections in past Budgets, as

Social Security costs relative to GDP grew. Social Security costs relative to GDP have plateaued in baseline projections, and no longer contribute significantly to changes in the debt-to-GDP ratio over the 25-year window.

Health Costs.—Healthcare costs per capita have risen much faster than per-capita GDP growth for decades, thus requiring both public and private spending on healthcare to increase as a share of the economy. While in recent years spending per enrollee has grown roughly in line with, or more slowly than, per-capita GDP in both the public and private sectors, this slower per-enrollee growth is not projected to continue.

Based on projections of Medicare enrollment and expenditures included in the 2019 Medicare Trustees Report, the projections here assume that Medicare per-beneficiary spending growth will increase, with the growth rate averaging about 1.0 percentage point above the growth rate of GDP over the next 25 years. (This average growth rate is still below the historical average for the last 25 years.)

Revenues and Discretionary Spending.—The increase in revenues as a percent of GDP occurs primarily because individuals' real, inflation-adjusted incomes grow over time, and so a portion of their income falls into higher tax brackets. (Bracket thresholds are indexed for inflation but do not grow in real terms.) This restrains deficits relative to GDP, partially offsetting the pressure from increases in spending for health programs.

The Impact of 2021 Budget Policies on the Long-Term Fiscal Outlook

The impact of the 2021 Budget is projected using economic assumptions that account for the economic feedback of the Administration's policies. In addition to successfully negotiated free trade agreements, the policy economic assumptions assume full achievement of the Administration's policy agenda with respect to deregulation, infrastructure, fiscal consolidation, and labor market policies designed to incentivize higher labor force participation.

To show the long-term effects of implementing new policies, expenditures and revenues are extended through the 25-year timeframe. The President's 2021 Budget proposals reduce deficits by decreasing non-defense discretionary and mandatory spending over the next 10 years while protecting or increasing funding for border security, addressing the opioid crisis, law enforcement, childcare, veterans' healthcare, infrastructure, and workforce development. Beyond the 10-year window, most categories of mandatory spending grow at the same rates as under the baseline projections, discretionary outlays grow with inflation and population, and revenues continue to rise as the result of a growing economy. Details about the assumptions are available in the appendix.

As shown in Chart 3-2, 2021 Budget policies reduce the deficit to 0.7 percent of GDP by 2030 and ultimately lead to a balanced budget by 2035. At the end of the 25-year horizon, the debt ratio would be the lowest since before

---

[2] The long-run baseline projections are consistent with the Budget's baseline concept, which is explained in more detail in Chapter 21, "Current Services Estimates," in this volume. The projections assume extension of the individual income tax and estate tax provisions of the Tax Cuts and Jobs Act beyond their expiration in 2025, and also assume full payment of scheduled Social Security and Medicare benefits without regard to the projected depletion of the trust funds for these programs. Additional baseline assumptions beyond the 10-year window are detailed in the appendix to this chapter.

Chart 3-2. Comparison of Annual Surplus/Deficit

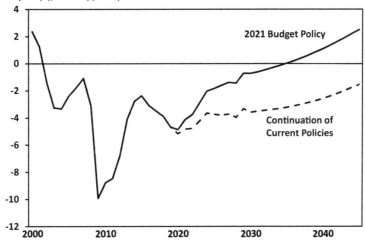

1981, representing significant progress in reducing the Federal debt burden.

One way to quantify the size of the Nation's long-term fiscal challenges is to determine the size of the increase in taxes or reduction in non-interest spending needed to reach a target debt-to-GDP ratio over a given period. There is no one optimal debt ratio, but one illustrative target is reaching the average postwar debt ratio of 45 percent. Policy adjustments of about 1.3 percent of GDP would steer the debt ratio to the postwar average by the end of the 25-year horizon. In comparison, the President's Budget policies are projected to decrease the debt ratio within the 10-year window and reduce it to the postwar average by 2039, more than satisfying the definition of fiscal sustainability as a declining debt-to-GDP ratio over the long term.

The Budget achieves these fiscal goals through promoting economic growth and security while improving the efficiency of the Federal Government. For example, the President's Budget includes the economic benefits of a more expansive trade deal with China while continuing reductions of regulatory burden will promote job creation and extending tax reform will allow families to keep more of their earnings. In addition, the Budget proposes streamlining Medicare to make it a better deal for seniors and the Government. Eliminating fraud, waste, and abuse from Medicare contributes to a lower debt and deficit in the long run.

Uncertainty and Alternative Assumptions

Future budget outcomes depend on a host of unknowns: changing economic conditions, unforeseen international developments, unexpected demographic shifts, and unpredictable technological advances. The longer budget projections are extended, the more the uncertainties increase. These uncertainties make even accurate short-run budget forecasting quite difficult. For example, the Budget's projection of the deficit in five years is 1.9 percent of GDP, but a distribution of probable outcomes

ranges from a deficit of 7.0 percent of GDP to a surplus of 3.3 percent of GDP, at the 10th and 90th percentiles, respectively. Results from the following alternatives are presented in Table 3-1.

Productivity and Interest Rates.—The rate of future productivity growth has a major effect on the long-run budget outlook (see Chart 3-3). Higher productivity growth improves the budget outlook, because it adds directly to the growth of the major tax bases while having a smaller effect on outlay growth. Productivity growth is also highly uncertain. For much of the last century, output per hour in nonfarm business grew at an average rate of around 2.2 percent per year, but there were long periods of sustained productivity growth at notably higher and lower rates than the long-term average. The base case long-run projections assume that real GDP per hour worked will grow at an average annual rate of 2.3 percent per year and assume interest rates on 10-year Treasury securities of 3.2 percent. The alternative scenarios illustrate the effect of raising and lowering the projected productivity growth rate by 0.25 percentage point and changing interest rates commensurately. At the end of the 25-year

Table 3–1. 25–YEAR DEBT PROJECTIONS UNDER ALTERNATIVE BUDGET SCENARIOS
(Percent of GDP)

2021 Budget Policy	23.3
Health:	
Excess cost growth averages 1.5%	39.7
Discretionary Outlays:	
Grow with GDP	29.2
Revenues:	
Revenues steady as a share of GDP, with bracket creep	27.0
Productivity and Interest:[1]	
Productivity grows by 0.25 percentage point per year faster than the base case	9.4
Productivity grows by 0.25 percentage point per year slower than the base case	41.6

[1] Interest rates adjust commensurately with increases or decreases in productivity.

Chart 3-3. Alternative Productivity and Interest Assumptions

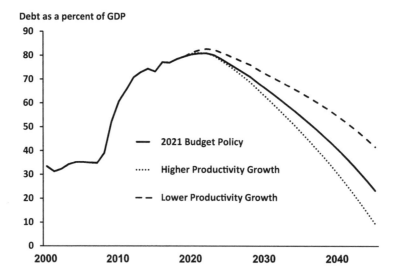

horizon, the public debt ranges from 9.4 percent of GDP in the high productivity scenario to 41.6 percent of GDP in the low productivity scenario. This variation highlights the importance of investment and smart tax policy, which can contribute to higher productivity.

Health Spending.—Healthcare cost growth represents another major source of uncertainty in the long-term budget projections. As noted above, the baseline projections follow the Medicare Trustees in assuming that Medicare per-beneficiary costs grow an average of about 1.0 percentage point faster than GDP growth over the next 25 years. However, in the past, especially prior to 1990, healthcare costs grew even more rapidly. Over the last few years, per-enrollee healthcare costs have grown roughly in line with or more slowly than GDP, with particularly slow growth in Medicare and Medicaid.

Chart 3-4 shows the large impacts that faster healthcare cost growth would have on the budget. If healthcare cost growth averaged 1.5 percentage points faster than GDP growth, the debt ratio in 25 years would increase

from 23.3 percent of GDP under the base case Budget policy to 39.7 percent of GDP.

Policy Assumptions.—As evident from the discussion of the 2021 Budget proposals, policy choices will also have a large impact on long-term budget deficits and debt. The base case policy projections for discretionary spending assumes that after 2030, discretionary outlays grow with inflation and population (see Chart 3-5). An alternative assumption is to grow discretionary spending with GDP only. At the end of the 25-year horizon, the debt ratio ranges from 23.3 percent of GDP in the base case to 29.2 percent of GDP if discretionary spending grows with GDP.

In the base case policy projections, revenues gradually increase with rising real incomes. Chart 3-6 shows an alternative receipts assumption in which receipts remain a constant percent of GDP after the budget window. At the end of the 25-year horizon, the debt ratio increases from 23.3 percent of GDP in the base case to 27.0 percent of GDP in the alternative case.

Chart 3-4. Alternative Health Care Costs

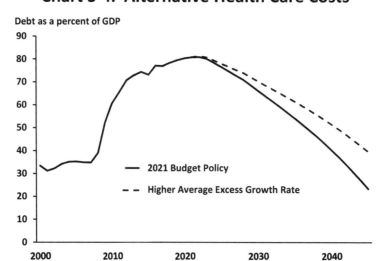

Chart 3-5. Alternative Discretionary Assumptions

Debt as a percent of GDP

—— 2021 Budget Policy: Discretionary Spending Grows with Inflation and Population

– – Discretionary Spending Grows with GDP

Finally, Chart 3-7 shows how uncertainties compound over the forecast horizon. As the chart shows, under the base case Budget policy projections, debt declines to 23.3 percent of GDP in 2045. Alternatively, assuming a combination of slower productivity growth and faster healthcare cost growth results in less debt reduction, with the debt ratio reaching 59.0 percent by the end of the window. Meanwhile, assuming a combination of higher productivity growth and slower healthcare cost growth results in the debt ratio reaching 4.4 percent in 2045.

Despite considerable uncertainties, long-term projections are helpful in highlighting some of the budget challenges on the horizon, especially the impact of healthcare costs. In addition, the wide range of the projections highlight the need for policy awareness of key drivers of future budgetary costs and potential action to address them.

Actuarial Projections for Social Security and Medicare

While the Administration's long-run projections focus on the unified budget outlook, Social Security and Medicare Hospital Insurance benefits are paid out of trust funds financed by dedicated payroll tax revenues. Projected trust fund revenues fall short of the levels necessary to finance projected benefits over the next 75 years.

The Social Security and Medicare Trustees' reports feature the actuarial balance of the trust funds as a summary measure of their financial status. For each trust fund, the balance is calculated as the change in receipts or program benefits (expressed as a percentage of taxable payroll) that would be needed to preserve a small positive balance in the trust fund at the end of a specified time period. The estimates cover periods ranging in length from 25 to 75 years.

Under the Medicare Modernization Act (MMA) of 2003, the Medicare Trustees must issue a "warning" when two consecutive Trustees' reports project that the

Chart 3-6. Alternative Revenue Assumptions

Debt as a percent of GDP

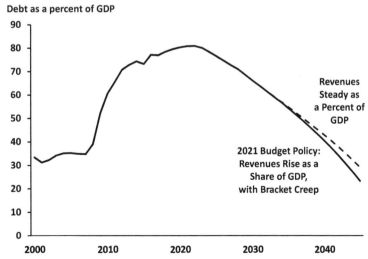

Revenues Steady as a Percent of GDP

2021 Budget Policy: Revenues Rise as a Share of GDP, with Bracket Creep

Chart 3-7. Long Term Uncertainties

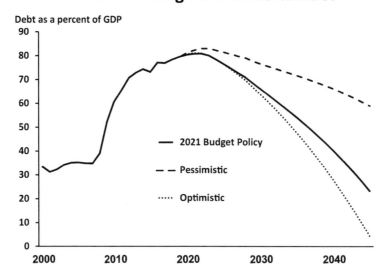

share of Medicare funded by general revenues will exceed 45 percent in the current year or any of the subsequent six years. Like the 2017 and 2018 Trustees' Report, the 2019 Trustees' Report made a determination of excess revenues and therefore issued a Medicare funding warning. The MMA requires that, because a Medicare funding warning has been issued, the President submit proposed legislation responding to that warning, within 15 days of submitting the Budget. In accordance with the Recommendations Clause of the Constitution and as the Executive Branch has noted in prior years, the Executive Branch considers a requirement to propose specific legislation to be advisory.

Table 3-2 shows the projected income rate, cost rate, and annual balance for the Medicare HI and combined OASDI trust funds at selected dates under the Trustees' intermediate assumptions in the 2019 reports. There is a continued imbalance in the long-run projections of the HI program due to demographic trends and continued high

per-person costs. According to the 2019 Trustees' report the HI trust fund is projected to become insolvent in 2026.

As a result of reforms legislated in 1983, Social Security ran an annual cash surplus with taxes exceeding costs through 2009. This surplus in the Social Security trust fund helped to hold down the unified budget deficit. The last year of annual cash surplus was 2009; in 2010, the trust fund began using a portion of its interest earnings to cover benefit payments. The 2019 Social Security Trustees' report projects that under current law, the trust fund will not return to annual cash surplus and that the program will start to experience an overall deficit starting in 2020. After that, Social Security will begin to draw on its trust fund balances to cover current expenditures. Over time, as the ratio of workers to retirees falls, costs are projected to rise further while revenues excluding interest are projected to rise less rapidly. In the process, the Social Security trust fund reserves, which were built up since 1983, would be drawn down and eventually be ex-

Table 3–2.   INTERMEDIATE ACTUARIAL PROJECTIONS FOR OASDI AND HI, 2019 TRUSTEES' REPORTS

	2018	2020	2030	2040	2090
	Percent of Payroll				
Medicare Hospital Insurance (HI):					
Income Rate	3.3	3.4	3.6	3.8	4.4
Cost Rate	3.4	3.5	4.4	4.9	5.3
Annual Balance	−0.1	−0.2	−0.7	−1.1	−0.9
Projection Interval:			25 years	50 years	75 years
Actuarial Balance			−0.8	−0.9	−0.9
	Percent of Payroll				
Old Age Survivors and Disability Insurance (OASDI):					
Income Rate	12.7	12.9	13.2	13.3	13.4
Cost Rate	13.8	13.9	15.8	16.6	17.4
Annual Balance	−1.1	−1.1	−2.6	−3.3	−4.0
Projection Interval:			25 years	50 years	75 years
Actuarial Balance			−1.7	−2.4	−2.8

hausted in 2035. These projections assume that benefits would continue to be paid in full despite the projected exhaustion of the trust fund reserves to show the long-run cost of maintaining current benefit formulas. Under current law, not all scheduled benefits could be paid after the trust funds reserves are exhausted. However, ben-

efits could still be partially funded from current revenues. According to the 2019 Trustees' report, beginning in 2035, 80 percent of projected Social Security scheduled benefits would be funded. This percentage would eventually decline to 75 percent by 2093.

TECHNICAL NOTE: SOURCES OF DATA AND METHODS OF ESTIMATING

The long-run budget projections are based on actuarial projections for Social Security and Medicare as well as demographic and economic assumptions. A simplified model of the Federal budget, developed at OMB, is used to compute the budgetary implications of these assumptions.

Demographic and Economic Assumptions.—For the years 2020-2030, the assumptions are drawn from the Administration's economic projections used for the 2021 Budget. The economic assumptions are extended beyond this interval by holding the inflation rate, interest rates, and the unemployment rate constant at the levels assumed in the final year (2030) of the budget forecast. Population growth and labor force growth are extended using the intermediate assumptions from the 2019 Social Security Trustees' report. The projected rate of growth for real GDP is built up from the labor force assumptions and an assumed rate of productivity growth. Productivity growth, measured as real GDP per hour, is assumed to equal its average annual rate of growth in the Budget's economic assumptions—2.3 percent per year.

Under Budget policies, the CPI inflation rate is held constant at 2.3 percent per year, the unemployment rate is held constant at 4.0 percent, the yield to maturity on 10-year Treasury notes is constant at 3.2 percent, and the 91-day Treasury bill rate is kept at 2.5 percent. Consistent with the demographic assumptions in the Trustees' reports, U.S. population growth slows from an average of just over 0.7 percent per year during the budget window to about three-quarters of that rate by 2040, and slower rates of growth beyond that point. By the end of the 25-year projection period total population growth is slightly below 0.5 percent per year. Real GDP growth is projected to be less than its historical average of around

2.8 percent per year because the slowdown in population growth and the increase in the population over age 65 reduce labor supply growth. In these projections, real GDP growth averages between 2.6 percent and 2.8 percent per year for the period following the end of the 10-year budget window.

The economic and demographic projections described above are set exogenously and do not change in response to changes in the budget outlook. This makes it easier to interpret the comparisons of alternative policies.

Budget Projections.—For the period through 2030, receipts and outlays in the baseline and policy projections follow the 2021 Budget's baseline and policy estimates respectively. Discretionary spending grows at the rate of growth in inflation and population outside the budget window. Long-run Social Security spending is projected by the Social Security actuaries using this chapter's long-run economic and demographic assumptions. Medicare benefits are projected based on a projection of beneficiary growth and excess healthcare cost growth from the 2019 Medicare Trustees' report current law baseline. For the policy projections, these assumptions are adjusted based on the Budget proposal to streamline Medicare. Medicaid outlays are based on the economic and demographic projections in the model, which assume average excess cost growth of approximately 0.9 percentage point above growth in GDP per capita after 2030. For the policy projections, these assumptions are adjusted based on the Budget proposals to reform Medicaid funding. Other entitlement programs are projected based on rules of thumb linking program spending to elements of the economic and demographic projections such as the poverty rate.

4. FEDERAL BORROWING AND DEBT

Debt is the largest legally and contractually binding obligation of the Federal Government. At the end of 2019, the Government owed $16,801 billion of principal to the individuals and institutions who had loaned it the money to fund past deficits. During that year, the Government paid the public approximately $423 billion of interest on this debt. At the same time, the Government also held financial assets, net of financial liabilities other than debt, of $1,906 billion. Therefore, debt held by the public net of financial assets was $14,894 billion.

In addition, at the end of 2019 the Department of the Treasury had issued $5,869 billion of debt to Government accounts. As a result, gross Federal debt, which is the sum of debt held by the public and debt held by Government accounts, was $22,669 billion. Interest on the gross Federal debt was $573 billion in 2019. Gross Federal debt is discussed in more detail later in the chapter.

The $16,801 billion debt held by the public at the end of 2019 represents an increase of $1,051 billion over the level at the end of 2018. This increase is the result of the $984 billion deficit in 2019 and other financing transactions that increased the need to borrow by $67 billion. Debt held by the public grew from 77.4 percent of Gross Domestic Product (GDP) at the end of 2018 to 79.2 percent of GDP at the end of 2019. The deficit is estimated to increase to $1,083 billion in 2020, and then to fall to $966 billion in 2021. After 2021, the deficit is projected to continue to decrease, declining to $261 billion in 2030. Debt held by the public is projected to grow to $17,881 billion at the end of 2020 and $18,912 billion at the end of 2021. Debt held by the public as a percent of GDP is projected to increase to 80.5 percent at the end of 2020 and 81.0 percent at the end of 2021. After 2022, debt held by the public as a percent of GDP is projected to begin to decline, falling to 66.1 percent in 2030. Debt held by the public net of financial assets is expected to similarly grow to 71.9 percent of GDP at the end of 2020 and to 72.6 percent at the end of 2021, then to begin to decline in 2023, falling to 59.7 percent of GDP at the end of 2030.

Trends in Debt Since World War II

Table 4–1 depicts trends in Federal debt held by the public from World War II to the present and estimates from the present through 2030. (It is supplemented for earlier years by Tables 7.1–7.3 in the Budget's *Historical Tables*, available as supplemental budget material.[1]) Federal debt peaked at 106.1 percent of GDP in 1946, just after the end of the war. From that point until the 1970s, Federal debt as a percentage of GDP decreased almost every year because of relatively small deficits, an expanding economy, and unanticipated inflation. With households borrowing large amounts to buy homes and consumer durables, and with businesses borrowing large amounts to buy plant and equipment, Federal debt also decreased almost every year as a percentage of total credit market debt outstanding. The cumulative effect was impressive. From 1950 to 1975, debt held by the public declined from 78.6 percent of GDP to 24.6 percent, and from 53.3 percent of credit market debt to 17.9 percent. Despite rising interest rates during this period, interest outlays became a smaller share of the budget and were roughly stable as a percentage of GDP.

Federal debt relative to GDP is a function of the Nation's fiscal policy as well as overall economic conditions. During the 1970s, large budget deficits emerged as spending grew faster than receipts and as the economy was disrupted by oil shocks and rising inflation. The nominal amount of Federal debt more than doubled, and Federal debt relative to GDP and credit market debt stopped declining for several years in the middle of the decade. Federal debt started growing again at the beginning of the 1980s, and increased to almost 48 percent of GDP by 1993. The ratio of Federal debt to credit market debt also rose during this period, though to a lesser extent. Interest outlays on debt held by the public, calculated as a percentage of either total Federal outlays or GDP, increased as well.

The growth of Federal debt held by the public was slowing by the mid-1990s. In addition to a growing economy, three major budget agreements were enacted in the 1990s, implementing spending cuts and revenue increases and significantly reducing deficits. The debt declined markedly relative to both GDP and total credit market debt, with the decline accelerating as budget surpluses emerged from 1997 to 2001. Debt fell from 47.9 percent of GDP in 1993 to 31.5 percent of GDP in 2001. Over that same period, debt fell from 26.2 percent of total credit market debt to 17.3 percent. Interest as a share of outlays peaked at 16.5 percent in 1989 and then fell to 8.9 percent by 2002; interest as a percentage of GDP fell by a similar proportion.

The progress in reducing the debt burden stopped and then reversed course beginning in 2002. The attacks of September 11, 2001, a recession, two major wars, and other policy changes all contributed to increasing deficits, causing debt to rise, both in nominal terms and as a percentage of GDP. Following the most recent recession, which began in December 2007, the deficit began increasing rapidly in 2008 and 2009, as the Government intervened in the potential collapse of several major corporations and financial institutions as well as enacting a major "stimulus" bill. Since 2008, debt as a percent of GDP has more than doubled, increasing from 35.2 percent at the end of 2007 to 79.2 percent in 2019.

---

[1] The *Historical Tables* are available at *https://www.whitehouse. gov/omb/historical-tables/*.

Table 4–1.   TRENDS IN FEDERAL DEBT HELD BY THE PUBLIC AND INTEREST ON THE DEBT HELD BY THE PUBLIC
(Dollar amounts in billions)

Fiscal Year	Debt held by the public		Debt held by the public as a percent of		Interest on the debt held by the public [3]		Interest on the debt held by the public as a percent of [3]	
	Current dollars	FY 2019 dollars [1]	GDP	Credit market debt [2]	Current dollars	FY 2019 dollars [1]	Total outlays	GDP
1946	241.9	2,602.8	106.1	N/A	4.2	45.0	7.6	1.8
1950	219.0	1,904.1	78.6	53.3	4.8	42.1	11.4	1.7
1955	226.6	1,731.7	55.8	42.1	5.2	39.6	7.6	1.3
1960	236.8	1,603.9	44.3	33.1	7.8	52.9	8.5	1.5
1965	260.8	1,655.1	36.8	26.4	9.6	60.8	8.1	1.4
1970	283.2	1,497.9	27.1	20.3	15.4	81.3	7.9	1.5
1975	394.7	1,537.8	24.6	17.9	25.0	97.4	7.5	1.6
1980	711.9	1,928.5	25.5	18.4	62.8	170.0	10.6	2.2
1985	1,507.3	3,111.9	35.3	22.2	152.9	315.7	16.2	3.6
1990	2,411.6	4,277.8	40.9	22.5	202.4	359.0	16.2	3.4
1995	3,604.4	5,639.2	47.7	26.3	239.2	374.2	15.8	3.2
2000	3,409.8	4,916.0	33.7	18.7	232.8	335.7	13.0	2.3
2005	4,592.2	5,925.1	35.8	17.1	191.4	246.9	7.7	1.5
2010	9,018.9	10,540.4	60.8	25.1	228.2	266.7	6.6	1.5
2015	13,116.7	14,048.7	72.5	30.4	260.6	279.2	7.1	1.4
2016	14,167.6	15,041.1	76.4	31.3	283.8	301.3	7.4	1.5
2017	14,665.4	15,298.4	76.0	31.3	309.9	323.2	7.8	1.6
2018	15,749.6	16,054.3	77.4	31.8	371.4	378.6	9.0	1.8
2019	16,800.7	16,800.7	79.2	32.4	423.3	423.3	9.5	2.0
2020 estimate	17,881.2	17,535.5	80.5	N/A	430.9	422.6	9.0	1.9
2021 estimate	18,912.1	18,183.1	81.0	N/A	435.2	418.5	9.0	1.9
2022 estimate	19,890.7	18,746.5	81.0	N/A	454.5	428.3	9.1	1.9
2023 estimate	20,688.3	19,115.1	80.2	N/A	485.9	449.0	9.5	1.9
2024 estimate	21,283.7	19,277.3	78.5	N/A	518.3	469.5	10.0	1.9
2025 estimate	21,848.3	19,399.4	76.7	N/A	560.8	497.9	10.3	2.0
2026 estimate	22,361.9	19,463.3	74.8	N/A	603.5	525.3	10.7	2.0
2027 estimate	22,826.4	19,476.7	72.8	N/A	649.2	554.0	11.0	2.1
2028 estimate	23,327.4	19,511.9	71.0	N/A	685.4	573.3	11.0	2.1
2029 estimate	23,603.7	19,354.6	68.5	N/A	709.8	582.0	11.3	2.1
2030 estimate	23,892.2	19,205.6	66.1	N/A	732.2	588.6	11.0	2.0

N/A = Not available.

[1] Amounts in current dollars deflated by the GDP chain-type price index with fiscal year 2019 equal to 100.

[2] Total credit market debt owed by domestic nonfinancial sectors. Financial sectors are omitted to avoid double counting, since financial intermediaries borrow in the credit market primarily in order to finance lending in the credit market. Source: Federal Reserve Board flow of funds accounts. Projections are not available.

[3] Interest on debt held by the public is estimated as the interest on Treasury debt securities less the "interest received by trust funds" (subfunction 901 less subfunctions 902 and 903). The estimate of interest on debt held by the public does not include the comparatively small amount of interest paid on agency debt or the offsets for interest on Treasury debt received by other Government accounts (revolving funds and special funds).

Under the proposals in the Budget, the deficit is projected to grow to $1,083 billion in 2020. The deficit is projected to begin to decline in 2021, falling to $261 billion, or 0.7 percent of GDP, in 2030. Gross Federal debt is projected to increase to 107.6 percent of GDP in 2020 and then begin to decline, falling to 84.6 percent of GDP in 2030. Debt held by the public as a percent of GDP is estimated to be 80.5 percent at the end of 2020, to increase slightly in 2021 and 2022, and then to begin to decline, falling to 66.1 percent of GDP by 2030. Debt held by the public net of financial assets as a percent of GDP is estimated to similarly grow to 71.9 percent of GDP at the end of 2020, grow gradually through 2022, and then begin to fall, reaching 59.7 percent of GDP by the end of 2030.

Debt Held by the Public and Gross Federal Debt

The Federal Government issues debt securities for two main purposes. First, it borrows from the public to provide for the Federal Government's financing needs, including both the deficit and the other transactions requiring financing, most notably disbursements for direct student loans and other Federal credit programs.[2] Second, it issues debt to Federal Government accounts, primarily trust funds, that accumulate surpluses. By law, trust fund surpluses must generally be invested in Federal securities. The gross Federal debt is defined to consist of both the debt held by the public and the debt held by Government accounts. Nearly all the Federal debt has been issued by the Treasury and is sometimes called "public debt," but a small portion has been issued by other Government agencies and is called "agency debt."[3]

Borrowing from the public, whether by the Treasury or by some other Federal agency, is important because it represents the Federal demand on credit markets. Regardless of whether the proceeds are used for tangible or intangible investments or to finance current consumption, the Federal demand on credit markets has to be financed out of the saving of households and businesses, the State and local sector, or the rest of the world. Federal borrowing thereby competes with the borrowing of other sectors of the domestic or international economy for financial resources in the credit market. Borrowing from the public thus affects the size and composition of assets held by the private sector and the amount of saving imported from abroad. It also increases the amount of future resources required to pay interest to the public on Federal debt. Borrowing from the public is therefore an important concern of Federal fiscal policy as it tends to crowd out private sector economic activity and impact Governmental budget priorities. Borrowing from the public, however, is an incomplete measure of the Federal impact on credit

markets. Different types of Federal activities can affect the credit markets in different ways. For example, under its direct loan programs, the Government uses borrowed funds to acquire financial assets that might otherwise require financing in the credit markets directly. (For more information on other ways in which Federal activities impact the credit market, see the discussion at the end of this chapter.) By incorporating the change in direct loan and other financial assets, debt held by the public net of financial assets adds useful insight into the Government's financial condition.

Issuing debt securities to Government accounts performs an essential function in accounting for the operation of these funds. The balances of debt represent the cumulative surpluses of these funds due to the excess of their tax receipts, interest receipts, and other collections over their spending. The interest on the debt that is credited to these funds accounts for the fact that some earmarked taxes and user fees will be spent at a later time than when the funds receive the monies. The debt securities are assets of those funds but are a liability of the general fund to the funds that hold the securities, and are a mechanism for crediting interest to those funds on their recorded balances. These balances generally provide the fund with authority to draw upon the U.S. Treasury in later years to make future payments on its behalf to the public. Public policy may result in the Government's running surpluses and accumulating debt in trust funds and other Government accounts in anticipation of future spending.

However, issuing debt to Government accounts does not have any of the current credit market effects of borrowing from the public. It is an internal transaction of the Government, made between two accounts that are both within the Government itself. Issuing debt to a Government account is not a current transaction of the Government with the public; it is not financed by private savings and does not compete with the private sector for available funds in the credit market. While such issuance provides the account with assets—a binding claim against the Treasury— those assets are fully offset by the increased liability of the Treasury to pay the claims, which will ultimately be covered by the collection of revenues or by borrowing. Similarly, the current interest earned by the Government account on its Treasury securities does not need to be financed by other resources.

The debt held by Government accounts may differ from the estimated amount of the account's obligations or responsibilities to make future payments to the public. For example, if the account records the transactions of a social insurance program, the debt that it holds does not necessarily represent the actuarial present value of estimated future benefits (or future benefits less taxes) for the current participants in the program; nor does it necessarily represent the actuarial present value of estimated future benefits (or future benefits less taxes) for the current participants plus the estimated future participants over some stated time period. The future transactions of Federal social insurance and employee retirement programs, which own 90 percent of the debt held by Government accounts,

---

[2] For the purposes of the Budget, "debt held by the public" is defined as debt held by investors outside of the Federal Government, both domestic and foreign, including U.S. State and local governments and foreign governments. It also includes debt held by the Federal Reserve.

[3] The term "agency debt" is defined more narrowly in the budget than customarily in the securities market, where it includes not only the debt of the Federal agencies listed in Table 4–4, but also certain Government-guaranteed securities and the debt of the Government-sponsored enterprises listed in Table 18–7 in the supplemental materials to the "Credit and Insurance" chapter. (Table 18–7 is available on the internet at: *https://www.whitehouse.gov/omb/analytical-perspectives/*.)

Table 4–2. FEDERAL GOVERNMENT FINANCING AND DEBT

(In billions of dollars)

	Actual 2019	Estimate										
		2020	2021	2022	2023	2024	2025	2026	2027	2028	2029	2030
Financing:												
Unified budget deficit	984.2	1,083.4	966.1	919.8	746.3	551.9	526.5	481.2	435.4	474.9	250.0	261.2
Other transactions affecting borrowing from the public:												
Changes in financial assets and liabilities:[1]												
Change in Treasury operating cash balance	−2.2	2.5	....	....	....	....	....	....	....	....	....	....
Net disbursements of credit financing accounts:												
Direct loan accounts	42.9	−15.6	67.2	62.8	54.5	46.2	40.6	35.3	33.0	31.0	27.3	27.2
Guaranteed loan accounts	27.7	11.9	−1.0	−2.2	−1.8	−1.4	−1.2	−1.5	−2.8	−3.9	−*	0.8
Troubled Asset Relief Program equity purchase accounts	−*	−*	−*	−*	−*	....	....	....	....	....	....	....
Subtotal, net disbursements	70.6	−3.7	66.3	60.6	52.7	44.8	39.4	33.8	30.2	27.1	27.2	28.0
Net purchases of non-Federal securities by the National Railroad Retirement Investment Trust	−1.2	−1.5	−1.1	−1.4	−1.1	−1.1	−1.0	−1.0	−0.9	−0.7	−0.6	−0.4
Net change in other financial assets and liabilities[2]	0.4	....	....	....	....	....	....	....	....	....	....	....
Subtotal, changes in financial assets and liabilities	67.6	−2.7	65.1	59.2	51.6	43.7	38.4	32.8	29.4	26.4	26.6	27.6
Seigniorage on coins	−0.5	−0.3	−0.3	−0.3	−0.3	−0.3	−0.3	−0.3	−0.3	−0.3	−0.4	−0.4
Total, other transactions affecting borrowing from the public	67.0	−3.0	64.8	58.9	51.3	43.4	38.1	32.5	29.0	26.1	26.3	27.3
Total, requirement to borrow from the public (equals change in debt held by the public)	1,051.2	1,080.4	1,030.9	978.7	797.6	595.3	564.6	513.7	464.5	501.0	276.3	288.5
Changes in Debt Subject to Statutory Limitation:												
Change in debt held by the public	1,051.2	1,080.4	1,030.9	978.7	797.6	595.3	564.6	513.7	464.5	501.0	276.3	288.5
Change in debt held by Government accounts	156.0	150.3	146.3	103.3	122.8	163.8	102.9	100.7	−1.0	−86.9	91.9	−46.3
Less: change in debt not subject to limit and other adjustments	4.6	2.6	1.7	1.6	1.8	2.0	0.9	1.0	1.6	1.4	1.1	0.2
Total, change in debt subject to statutory limitation	1,211.8	1,233.4	1,178.8	1,083.6	922.2	761.1	668.4	615.3	465.1	415.5	369.3	242.4
Debt Subject to Statutory Limitation, End of Year:												
Debt issued by Treasury	22,646.6	23,878.4	25,056.1	26,138.4	27,059.4	27,819.6	28,488.0	29,103.0	29,567.2	29,981.8	30,350.5	30,592.9
Less: Treasury debt not subject to limitation (−)[3]	−9.3	−7.7	−6.5	−5.3	−4.1	−3.2	−3.2	−2.8	−2.0	−1.1	−0.5	−0.5
Agency debt subject to limitation	*	*	*	*	*	*	*	*	*	*	*	*
Adjustment for discount and premium[4]	49.3	49.3	49.3	49.3	49.3	49.3	49.3	49.3	49.3	49.3	49.3	49.3
Total, debt subject to statutory limitation[5]	22,686.6	23,920.0	25,098.9	26,182.5	27,104.6	27,865.8	28,534.2	29,149.5	29,614.6	30,030.1	30,399.4	30,641.8
Debt Outstanding, End of Year:												
Gross Federal debt:[6]												
Debt issued by Treasury	22,646.6	23,878.4	25,056.1	26,138.4	27,059.4	27,819.6	28,488.0	29,103.0	29,567.2	29,981.8	30,350.5	30,592.9
Debt issued by other agencies	22.9	21.8	21.4	21.0	20.4	19.4	18.4	17.8	17.0	16.5	16.0	15.8
Total, gross Federal debt	22,669.5	23,900.2	25,077.4	26,159.4	27,079.8	27,838.9	28,506.5	29,120.8	29,584.2	29,998.3	30,366.5	30,608.7
As a percent of GDP	106.9%	107.6%	107.4%	106.6%	105.0%	102.7%	100.1%	97.4%	94.4%	91.3%	88.1%	84.6%
Held by:												
Debt held by Government accounts	5,868.7	6,019.1	6,165.3	6,268.7	6,391.4	6,555.3	6,658.2	6,758.9	6,757.8	6,670.9	6,762.8	6,716.5
Debt held by the public[7]	16,800.7	17,881.2	18,912.1	19,890.7	20,688.3	21,283.7	21,848.3	22,361.9	22,826.4	23,327.4	23,603.7	23,892.2
As a percent of GDP	79.2%	80.5%	81.0%	81.0%	80.2%	78.5%	76.7%	74.8%	72.8%	71.0%	68.5%	66.1%

*$50 million or less.

[1] A decrease in the Treasury operating cash balance (which is an asset) is a means of financing a deficit and therefore has a negative sign. An increase in checks outstanding (which is a liability) is also a means of financing a deficit and therefore also has a negative sign.

[2] Includes checks outstanding, accrued interest payable on Treasury debt, uninvested deposit fund balances, allocations of special drawing rights, and other liability accounts; and, as an offset, cash and monetary assets (other than the Treasury operating cash balance), other asset accounts, and profit on sale of gold.

[3] Consists primarily of debt issued by the Federal Financing Bank.

[4] Consists mainly of unamortized discount (less premium) on public issues of Treasury notes and bonds (other than zero-coupon bonds) and unrealized discount on Government account series securities.

[5] Legislation enacted August 2, 2019, (P.L. 116-37) temporarily suspends the debt limit through July 31, 2021.

[6] Treasury securities held by the public and zero-coupon bonds held by Government accounts are almost all measured at sales price plus amortized discount or less amortized premium. Agency debt securities are almost all measured at face value. Treasury securities in the Government account series are otherwise measured at face value less unrealized discount (if any).

[7] At the end of 2019, the Federal Reserve Banks held $2,113.3 billion of Federal securities and the rest of the public held $14,687.4 billion. Debt held by the Federal Reserve Banks is not estimated for future years.

are important in their own right and need to be analyzed separately. This can be done through information published in the actuarial and financial reports for these programs.[4]

This Budget uses a variety of information sources to analyze the condition of Social Security and Medicare, the Government's two largest social insurance programs. The excess of future Social Security and Medicare benefits relative to their dedicated income is very different in concept and much larger in size than the amount of Treasury securities that these programs hold.

While gross Federal debt is important because it represents obligations imposed on households and businesses and is used to determine the debt subject to a limit, debt held by the public and debt held by the public net of financial assets are often considered to be better gauges of the direct influence of Federal debt on current credit markets.

Government Deficits or Surpluses and the Change in Debt

Table 4–2 summarizes Federal borrowing and debt from 2019 through 2030.[5] In 2019 the Government borrowed $1,051 billion, increasing the debt held by the public from $15,750 billion at the end of 2018 to $16,801 billion at the end of 2019. The debt held by Government accounts grew by $156 billion, and gross Federal debt increased by $1,207 billion to $22,669 billion.

Debt held by the public.—The Federal Government primarily finances deficits by borrowing from the public, and it primarily uses surpluses to repay debt held by the public.[6] Table 4–2 shows the relationship between the Federal deficit or surplus and the change in debt held by the public. The borrowing or debt repayment depends on the Government's expenditure programs and tax laws, on the economic conditions that influence tax receipts and outlays, and on debt management policy. The sensitivity of the budget to economic conditions is analyzed in Chapter 2, "Economic Assumptions and Overview," in this volume.

The total or unified budget consists of two parts: the on-budget portion; and the off-budget Federal entities, which have been excluded from the budget by law. Under present law, the off-budget Federal entities are the two Social Security trust funds (Old-Age and Survivors Insurance and Disability Insurance) and the Postal Service Fund.[7] The on-budget and off-budget surpluses or deficits are added together to determine the Government's financing needs.

Over the long run, it is a good approximation to say that "the deficit is financed by borrowing from the public" or "the surplus is used to repay debt held by the public." However, the Government's need to borrow in any given year has always depended on several other factors besides the unified budget surplus or deficit, such as the change in the Treasury operating cash balance. These other factors—"other transactions affecting borrowing from the public"—can either increase or decrease the Government's need to borrow and can vary considerably in size from year to year. The other transactions affecting borrowing from the public are presented in Table 4–2 (where an increase in the need to borrow is represented by a positive sign, like the deficit).

In 2019 the deficit was $984 billion while these other factors increased the need to borrow by $67 billion, or 6 percent of total borrowing from the public. As a result, the Government borrowed $1,051 billion from the public. The other factors are estimated to reduce borrowing by $3 billion (less than 1 percent of total borrowing from the public) in 2020, and increase borrowing by $65 billion (6 percent) in 2021. In 2022–2030, these other factors are expected to increase borrowing by annual amounts ranging from $26 billion to $59 billion.

Three specific factors presented in Table 4–2 have historically been especially important.

Change in Treasury operating cash balance.—The cash balance decreased by $2 billion in 2019, to $382 billion. In some years, the change in cash balance is much larger. The cash balance decreased by $194 billion in 2017, to $159 billion, and increased by $225 billion in 2018, to $385 billion. The large 2017 and 2018 changes were primarily related to actions that Treasury took to continue to finance Federal Government operations while at the debt ceiling and to unwind those actions following the debt limit suspension. (The debt limit suspensions are discussed in further detail elsewhere in this chapter.) For risk management purposes, Treasury seeks to maintain a cash balance roughly equal to one week of Government outflows, with a minimum balance of about $150 billion. The operating cash balance is projected to increase by $3 billion, to $385 billion, at the end of 2020. Changes in the operating cash balance, while occasionally large, are inherently limited over time. Decreases in cash—a means of financing the Government—are limited by the amount of past accumulations, which themselves required financing when they were built up. Increases are limited because it is generally more efficient to repay debt.

Net financing disbursements of the direct loan and guaranteed loan financing accounts.—Under the Federal Credit Reform Act of 1990 (FCRA), the budgetary program account for each credit program records the estimated subsidy costs—the present value of estimated net

---

[4] Extensive actuarial analyses of the Social Security and Medicare programs are published in the annual reports of the boards of trustees of these funds. The actuarial estimates for Social Security, Medicare, and the major Federal employee retirement programs are summarized in the *Financial Report of the United States Government*, prepared annually by the Department of the Treasury in coordination with the Office of Management and Budget, and presented in more detail in the financial statements of the agencies administering those programs.

[5] For projections of the debt beyond 2030, see Chapter 3, "Long-Term Budget Outlook."

[6] Treasury debt held by the public is measured as the sales price plus the amortized discount (or less the amortized premium). At the time of sale, the book value equals the sales price. Subsequently, it equals the sales price plus the amount of the discount that has been amortized up to that time. In equivalent terms, the book value of the debt equals the principal amount due at maturity (par or face value) less the unamortized discount. (For a security sold at a premium, the definition is symmetrical.) For inflation-protected notes and bonds, the book value includes a periodic adjustment for inflation. Agency debt is generally recorded at par.

[7] For further explanation of the off-budget Federal entities, see Chapter 9, "Coverage of the Budget."

losses—at the time when the direct or guaranteed loans are disbursed. The individual cash flows to and from the public associated with the loans or guarantees, such as the disbursement and repayment of loans, the default payments on loan guarantees, the collection of interest and fees, and so forth, are recorded in the credit program's non-budgetary financing account. Although the non-budgetary financing account's cash flows to and from the public are not included in the deficit (except for their impact on subsidy costs), they affect Treasury's net borrowing requirements.[8]

In addition to the transactions with the public, the financing accounts include several types of intragovernmental transactions. They receive payment from the credit program accounts for the subsidy costs of new direct loans and loan guarantees and for any upward reestimate of the costs of outstanding direct and guaranteed loans. They also receive interest from Treasury on balances of uninvested funds. The financing accounts pay any negative subsidy collections or downward reestimate of costs to budgetary receipt accounts and pay interest on borrowings from Treasury. The total net collections and gross disbursements of the financing accounts, consisting of transactions with both the public and the budgetary accounts, are called "net financing disbursements." They occur in the same way as the "outlays" of a budgetary account, even though they do not represent budgetary costs, and therefore affect the requirement for borrowing from the public in the same way as the deficit.

The intragovernmental transactions of the credit program, financing, and downward reestimate receipt accounts do not affect Federal borrowing from the public. Although the deficit changes because of the budgetary account's outlay to, or receipt from, a financing account, the net financing disbursement changes in an equal amount with the opposite sign, so the effects are cancelled out. On the other hand, financing account disbursements to the public increase the requirement for borrowing from the public in the same way as an increase in budget outlays that are disbursed to the public in cash. Likewise, receipts from the public collected by the financing account can be used to finance the payment of the Government's obligations, and therefore they reduce the requirement for Federal borrowing from the public in the same way as an increase in budgetary receipts.

Borrowing due to credit financing accounts was $71 billion in 2019. In 2020 credit financing accounts are projected to reduce borrowing by $4 billion. After 2020, the credit financing accounts are expected to increase borrowing by amounts ranging from $27 billion to $66 billion over the next 10 years.

In some years, large net upward or downward reestimates in the cost of outstanding direct and guaranteed loans may cause large swings in the net financing disbursements. In 2020, upward reestimates for student loans are partly offset by downward reestimates for Federal Housing Administration (FHA) guarantees, re-

sulting in a net upward reestimate of $51.2 billion. In 2019, there was a net upward reestimate of $9.6 billion.

Net purchases of non-Federal securities by the National Railroad Retirement Investment Trust (NRRIT).— This trust fund, which was established by the Railroad Retirement and Survivors' Improvement Act of 2001, invests its assets primarily in private stocks and bonds. The Act required special treatment of the purchase or sale of non-Federal assets by the NRRIT trust fund, treating such purchases as a means of financing rather than as outlays. Therefore, the increased need to borrow from the public to finance NRRIT's purchases of non-Federal assets is part of the "other transactions affecting borrowing from the public" rather than included as an increase in the deficit. While net purchases and redemptions affect borrowing from the public, unrealized gains and losses on NRRIT's portfolio are included in both the "other transactions" and, with the opposite sign, in NRRIT's net outlays in the deficit, for no net impact on borrowing from the public. In 2019, net decreases, including redemptions and losses, were $1.2 billion. A $1.5 billion net decrease is projected for 2020 and net annual decreases ranging from $0.4 billion to $1.4 billion are projected for 2021 and subsequent years.[9]

Debt held by Government accounts.—The amount of Federal debt issued to Government accounts depends largely on the surpluses of the trust funds, both on-budget and off-budget, which owned 89 percent of the total Federal debt held by Government accounts at the end of 2019. Net investment may differ from the surplus due to changes in the amount of cash assets not currently invested. In 2019, the total trust fund surplus was $113 billion, while trust fund investment in Federal securities increased by $114 billion. The remainder of debt issued to Government accounts is owned by a number of special funds and revolving funds. The debt held in major accounts and the annual investments are shown in Table 4–5.

Debt Held by the Public Net of Financial Assets and Liabilities

While debt held by the public is a key measure for examining the role and impact of the Federal Government in the U.S. and international credit markets and for other purposes, it provides incomplete information on the Government's financial condition. The U.S. Government holds significant financial assets, which can be offset against debt held by the public and other financial liabilities to achieve a more complete understanding of the Government's financial condition. The acquisition of those financial assets represents a transaction with the credit markets, broadening those markets in a way that is analogous to the demand on credit markets that borrowing entails. For this reason, debt held by the public is also an incomplete measure of the impact of the Federal Government in the United States and international credit markets.

---

[8] The FCRA (sec. 505(b)) requires that the financing accounts be non-budgetary. They are non-budgetary in concept because they do not measure cost. For additional discussion of credit programs, see Chapter 18, "Credit and Insurance," and Chapter 8, "Budget Concepts."

[9] The budget treatment of this fund is further discussed in Chapter 8, "Budget Concepts."

Table 4–3.   DEBT HELD BY THE PUBLIC NET OF FINANCIAL ASSETS AND LIABILITIES

(Dollar amounts in billions)

	Actual 2019	Estimate										
		2020	2021	2022	2023	2024	2025	2026	2027	2028	2029	2030
Debt Held by the Public:												
Debt held by the public	16,800.7	17,881.2	18,912.1	19,890.7	20,688.3	21,283.7	21,848.3	22,361.9	22,826.4	23,327.4	23,603.7	23,892.2
As a percent of GDP	79.2%	80.5%	81.0%	81.0%	80.2%	78.5%	76.7%	74.8%	72.8%	71.0%	68.5%	66.1%
Financial Assets Net of Liabilities:												
Treasury operating cash balance	382.5	385.0	385.0	385.0	385.0	385.0	385.0	385.0	385.0	385.0	385.0	385.0
Credit financing account balances:												
Direct loan accounts	1,414.8	1,399.3	1,466.5	1,529.3	1,583.8	1,629.9	1,670.5	1,705.9	1,738.9	1,769.9	1,797.1	1,824.4
Guaranteed loan accounts	32.5	44.4	43.4	41.2	39.4	38.1	36.9	35.4	32.6	28.7	28.7	29.4
Troubled Asset Relief Program equity purchase accounts	*	*	*	*	–*	–*	–*	–*	–*	–*	–*	–*
Subtotal, credit financing account balances	1,447.4	1,443.6	1,509.9	1,570.5	1,623.2	1,668.0	1,707.4	1,741.2	1,771.5	1,798.6	1,825.8	1,853.8
Government-sponsored enterprise preferred stock	112.1	112.1	112.1	112.1	112.1	112.1	112.1	112.1	112.1	112.1	112.1	112.1
Non-Federal securities held by NRRIT	24.4	23.0	21.8	20.4	19.3	18.3	17.3	16.3	15.5	14.8	14.2	13.8
Other assets net of liabilities	–59.9	–59.9	–59.9	–59.9	–59.9	–59.9	–59.9	–59.9	–59.9	–59.9	–59.9	–59.9
Total, financial assets net of liabilities	1,906.4	1,903.7	1,968.9	2,028.1	2,079.7	2,123.5	2,161.9	2,194.7	2,224.1	2,250.5	2,277.2	2,304.8
Debt Held by the Public Net of Financial Assets and Liabilities:												
Debt held by the public net of financial assets	14,894.3	15,977.4	16,943.2	17,862.6	18,608.6	19,160.2	19,686.4	20,167.2	20,602.3	21,076.9	21,326.5	21,587.4
As a percent of GDP	70.2%	71.9%	72.6%	72.8%	72.2%	70.7%	69.1%	67.5%	65.7%	64.1%	61.9%	59.7%

*$50 million or less.

One transaction that can increase both borrowing and assets is an increase to the Treasury operating cash balance. When the Government borrows to increase the Treasury operating cash balance, that cash balance also represents an asset that is available to the Federal Government. Looking at both sides of this transaction—the borrowing to obtain the cash and the asset of the cash holdings—provides much more complete information about the Government's financial condition than looking at only the borrowing from the public. Another example of a transaction that simultaneously increases borrowing from the public and Federal assets is Government borrowing to issue direct loans to the public. When the direct loan is made, the Government is also acquiring an asset in the form of future payments of principal and interest, net of the Government's expected losses on the loan. Similarly, when NRRIT increases its holdings of non-Federal securities, the borrowing to purchase those securities is offset by the value of the asset holdings.

The acquisition or disposition of Federal financial assets very largely explains the difference between the deficit for a particular year and that year's increase in debt held by the public. Debt held by the public net of financial assets is a measure that is conceptually closer to the measurement of Federal deficits or surpluses; cumulative deficits and surpluses over time more closely equal the debt held by the public net of financial assets than they do the debt held by the public.

Table 4–3 presents debt held by the public net of the Government's financial assets and liabilities. Treasury debt is presented in the Budget at book value, with no adjustments for the change in economic value that results

from fluctuations in interest rates. The balances of credit financing accounts are based on projections of future cash flows. For direct loan financing accounts, the balance generally represents the net present value of anticipated future inflows such as principal and interest payments from borrowers. For guaranteed loan financing accounts, the balance generally represents the net present value of anticipated future outflows, such as default claim payments net of recoveries, and other collections, such as program fees. NRRIT's holdings of non-Federal securities are marked to market on a monthly basis. Government-sponsored enterprise (GSE) preferred stock is measured at market value.

Due largely to the $71 billion increase in net credit financing account balances, net financial assets grew by $66 billion, to $1,906 billion, in 2019. This $1,906 billion in net financial assets included a cash balance of $382 billion, net credit financing account balances of $1,447 billion, and other assets and liabilities that aggregated to a net asset of $77 billion. At the end of 2019, debt held by the public was $16,801 billion, or 79.2 percent of GDP. Therefore, debt held by the public net of financial assets was $14,894 billion, or 70.2 percent of GDP. As shown in Table 4–3, the value of the Government's net financial assets is projected to fall slightly, to $1,904 billion in 2020, principally due to the value of the credit financing accounts. While debt held by the public is expected to increase from 79.2 percent to 80.5 percent of GDP during 2020, debt held by the public net of financial assets is expected to increase from 70.2 percent to 71.9 percent of GDP.

Debt securities and other financial assets and liabilities do not encompass all the assets and liabilities of the Federal Government. For example, accounts payable occur in the normal course of buying goods and services; Social Security benefits are due and payable as of the end of the month but, according to statute, are paid during the next month; and Federal employee salaries are paid after they have been earned. Like debt securities sold in the credit market, these liabilities have their own distinctive effects on the economy. The Federal Government also has significant holdings of non-financial assets, such as land, mineral deposits, buildings, and equipment. The different types of assets and liabilities are reported annually in the financial statements of Federal agencies and in the *Financial Report of the United States Government*, prepared by the Treasury in coordination with OMB.

Treasury Debt

Nearly all Federal debt is issued by the Department of the Treasury. Treasury meets most of the Federal Government's financing needs by issuing marketable securities to the public. These financing needs include both the change in debt held by the public and the refinancing—or rollover—of any outstanding debt that matures during the year. Treasury marketable debt is sold at public auctions on a regular schedule and, because it is very liquid, can be bought and sold on the secondary market at narrow bid-offer spreads. Treasury also sells to the public a relatively small amount of nonmarketable securities, such as savings bonds and State and Local Government Series securities (SLGS).[10] Treasury nonmarketable debt cannot be bought or sold on the secondary market.

Treasury issues marketable securities in a wide range of maturities, and issues both nominal (non-inflation-protected) and inflation-protected securities. Treasury's marketable securities include:

Treasury Bills—Treasury bills have maturities of one year or less from their issue date. In October 2018, Treasury introduced an 8-week bill, issued on a weekly basis, to complement its existing suite of 4-, 13-, and 26-week bills issued each week. In addition to the regular auction calendar of bill issuance, Treasury issues cash management bills on an as-needed basis for various reasons such as to offset the seasonal patterns of the Government's receipts and outlays.

Treasury Notes—Treasury notes have maturities of more than one year and up to 10 years.

Treasury Bonds—Treasury bonds have maturities of more than 10 years. The longest-maturity securities issued by Treasury are 30-year bonds.

Treasury Inflation-Protected Securities (TIPS)—Treasury inflation-protected—or inflation-indexed—securities are coupon issues for which the par value of the security rises with inflation. The principal value is adjusted daily to reflect inflation as measured by changes in the Consumer Price Index (CPI-U-NSA, with a two-month lag). Although the principal value may be adjusted downward if inflation is negative, at maturity, the securities will be redeemed at the greater of their inflation-adjusted principal or par amount at original issue.

Floating Rate Securities—Floating rate securities have a fixed par value but bear interest rates that fluctuate based on movements in a specified benchmark market interest rate. Treasury's floating rate notes are benchmarked to the Treasury 13-week bill. Currently, Treasury is issuing floating rate securities with a maturity of two years.

Historically, the average maturity of outstanding debt issued by Treasury has been about five years. The average maturity of outstanding debt was 70 months at the end of 2019.

In addition to quarterly announcements about the overall auction calendar, Treasury publicly announces in advance the auction of each security. Individuals can participate directly in Treasury auctions or can purchase securities through brokers, dealers, and other financial institutions. Treasury accepts two types of auction bids: competitive and noncompetitive. In a competitive bid, the bidder specifies the yield. A significant portion of competitive bids are submitted by primary dealers, which are banks and securities brokerages that have been designated to trade in Treasury securities with the Federal Reserve System. In a noncompetitive bid, the bidder agrees to accept the yield determined by the auction.[11] At the close of the auction, Treasury accepts all eligible noncompetitive bids and then accepts competitive bids in ascending order beginning with the lowest yield bid until the offering amount is reached. All winning bidders receive the highest accepted yield bid.

Treasury marketable securities are highly liquid and actively traded on the secondary market, which enhances the demand for Treasuries at initial auction. The demand for Treasury securities is reflected in the ratio of bids received to bids accepted in Treasury auctions; the demand for the securities is substantially greater than the level of issuance. Because they are backed by the full faith and credit of the United States Government, Treasury marketable securities are considered to be credit "risk-free." Therefore, the Treasury yield curve is commonly used as a benchmark for a wide variety of purposes in the financial markets.

Whereas Treasury issuance of marketable debt is based on the Government's financing needs, Treasury's issuance of nonmarketable debt is based on the public's demand for the specific types of investments. Decreases in outstanding balances of nonmarketable debt, such as occurred in 2019, increase the need for marketable borrowing.[12]

Agency Debt

A few Federal agencies other than Treasury, shown in Table 4–4, sell or have sold debt securities to the public and, at times, to other Government accounts. Currently, new debt is issued only by the Tennessee Valley Authority

---

[10] Under the SLGS program, the Treasury offers special low-yield securities to State and local governments and other entities for temporary investment of proceeds of tax-exempt bonds.

[11] Noncompetitive bids cannot exceed $5 million per bidder.

[12] Detail on the marketable and nonmarketable securities issued by Treasury is found in the *Monthly Statement of the Public Debt,* published on a monthly basis by the Department of the Treasury.

(TVA) and the Federal Housing Administration; the remaining agencies are repaying past borrowing. Agency debt was $22.9 billion at the end of 2019. Agency debt is less than one-quarter of one percent of Federal debt held by the public. Primarily as a result of TVA activity, agency debt is estimated to fall to $21.8 billion at the end of 2020 and to $21.4 billion at the end of 2021.

The predominant agency borrower is TVA, which had borrowings of $22.8 billion from the public as of the end of 2019, or over 99 percent of the total debt of all agencies other than Treasury. TVA issues debt primarily to finance capital projects.

TVA has traditionally financed its capital construction by selling bonds and notes to the public. Since 2000, it has also employed two types of alternative financing methods, lease financing obligations and prepayment obligations. Under the lease financing obligations method, TVA signs long-term contracts to lease some facilities and equipment. The lease payments under these contracts ultimately secure the repayment of third-party capital used to finance construction of the facility. TVA retains substantially all of the economic benefits and risks related to ownership of the assets.[13] Under the prepayment obligations method, TVA's power distributors may prepay a portion of the price of the power they plan to purchase in the future. In return, they obtain a discount on a specific quantity of the future power they buy from TVA. The quantity varies, depending on TVA's estimated cost of borrowing.

OMB determined that each of these alternative financing methods is a means of financing the acquisition of assets owned and used by the Government, or of refinancing debt previously incurred to finance such assets. They are equivalent in concept to other forms of borrowing from the public, although under different terms and conditions. The budget therefore records the upfront cash proceeds from these methods as borrowing from the

public, not offsetting collections.[14] The budget presentation is consistent with the reporting of these obligations as liabilities on TVA's balance sheet under generally accepted accounting principles. Table 4–4 presents these alternative financing methods separately from TVA bonds and notes to distinguish between the types of borrowing. At the end of 2019, lease financing obligations were $1.5 billion and there were no outstanding obligations for prepayments.

Although the FHA generally makes direct disbursements to the public for default claims on FHA-insured mortgages, it may also pay claims by issuing debentures. Issuing debentures to pay the Government's bills is equivalent to selling securities to the public and then paying the bills by disbursing the cash borrowed, so the transaction is recorded as being simultaneously an outlay and borrowing. The debentures are therefore classified as agency debt.

A number of years ago, the Federal Government guaranteed the debt used to finance the construction of buildings for the National Archives and the Architect of the Capitol, and subsequently exercised full control over the design, construction, and operation of the buildings. These arrangements are equivalent to direct Federal construction financed by Federal borrowing. The construction expenditures and interest were therefore classified as Federal outlays, and the borrowing was classified as Federal agency borrowing from the public.

Several Federal agencies borrow from the Bureau of the Fiscal Service (Fiscal Service) or the Federal Financing

---

[13] This arrangement is at least as governmental as a "lease-purchase without substantial private risk." For further detail on the current budgetary treatment of lease-purchase without substantial private risk, see OMB Circular No. A–11, Appendix B.

[14] This budgetary treatment differs from the treatment in the *Monthly Treasury Statement of Receipts and Outlays of the United States Government* (Monthly Treasury Statement) Table 6 Schedule C, and the *Combined Statement of Receipts, Outlays, and Balances of the United States Government* Schedule 3, both published by the Treasury. These two schedules, which present debt issued by agencies other than Treasury, exclude the TVA alternative financing arrangements. This difference in treatment is one factor causing minor differences between debt figures reported in the Budget and debt figures reported by Treasury. The other factors are adjustments for the timing of the reporting of Federal debt held by NRRIT and treatment of the Federal debt held by the Securities Investor Protection Corporation and the Public Company Accounting Oversight Board.

Table 4–4. AGENCY DEBT

(In millions of dollars)

	2019 Actual		2020 Estimate		2021 Estimate	
	Borrowing/ Repayment(–)	Debt, End-of-Year	Borrowing/ Repayment(–)	Debt, End-of-Year	Borrowing/ Repayment(–)	Debt, End-of-Year
Borrowing from the public:						
Housing and Urban Development:						
Federal Housing Administration	....	19	....	19	....	19
Architect of the Capitol	–11	69	–11	58	10	16
National Archives	–27	*	–*	....	....	....
Tennessee Valley Authority:						
Bonds and notes	–1,329	21,367	–972	20,395	–209	20,186
Lease financing obligations	–124	1,451	–105	1,346	–242	1,104
Prepayment obligations	–10	....	....	....	....	....
Total, borrowing from the public	**–1,501**	**22,906**	**–1,088**	**21,817**	**–464**	**21,354**
Total, agency borrowing	**–1,501**	**22,906**	**–1,088**	**21,817**	**–464**	**21,354**

* $500,000 or less.

Table 4–5.   DEBT HELD BY GOVERNMENT ACCOUNTS [1]

(In millions of dollars)

Description	Investment or Disinvestment (–)			Holdings, End of 2021 Estimate
	2019 Actual	2020 Estimate	2021 Estimate	
Investment in Treasury debt:				
Commerce:				
Public safety trust fund	1,318	139	200	7,900
Defense—Military:				
Host nation support fund for relocation	354	136	–530	1,333
Energy:				
Nuclear waste disposal fund [1]	1,681	1,221	1,184	43,004
Uranium enrichment decontamination fund	–780	–800	910	1,799
Health and Human Services:				
Federal hospital insurance trust fund	–4,180	–9,109	201	189,717
Federal supplementary medical insurance trust fund	6,519	895	–3,450	102,161
Vaccine injury compensation fund	99	135	144	4,128
Child enrollment contingency fund	....	15,044	–5,002	10,042
Homeland Security:				
Aquatic resources trust fund	51	9	10	2,016
Oil spill liability trust fund	298	57	92	7,004
National flood insurance reserve fund	793	386	–305	1,606
Housing and Urban Development:				
Federal Housing Administration mutual mortgage insurance capital reserve	23,626	17,378	9,059	77,038
Guarantees of mortgage-backed securities	–509	1,271	1,988	19,043
Interior:				
Bureau of Land Management permanent operating funds	73	63	158	1,182
Abandoned mine reclamation fund	–27	–9	–45	2,625
Federal aid in wildlife restoration fund	–82	64	–38	2,046
Environmental improvement and restoration fund	23	23	22	1,563
Natural resource damage assessment fund	258	336	350	2,450
Justice:				
Assets forfeiture fund	–2,826	27	2	2,135
U.S. victims of State sponsored terrorism fund	–121	–540	....	500
Labor:				
Unemployment trust fund	11,786	13,549	12,800	110,710
Pension Benefit Guaranty Corporation	5,053	5,924	7,067	49,704
State:				
Foreign service retirement and disability trust fund	134	142	138	19,598
Transportation:				
Airport and airway trust fund	806	10	386	15,414
Highway trust fund	–13,019	–14,192	–12,950	1,050
Aviation insurance revolving fund	43	25	39	2,357
Treasury:				
Exchange stabilization fund	311	577	542	23,741
Treasury forfeiture fund	–399	204	80	1,428
Gulf Coast Restoration trust fund	261	203	160	1,908
Comptroller of the Currency assessment fund	134	10	10	1,991
Veterans Affairs:				
Servicemembers' group life insurance fund	300	811	836	1,948
National service life insurance trust fund	–558	–633	–427	1,396
Veterans special life insurance fund	–129	–148	–174	1,035
Corps of Engineers:				
Harbor maintenance trust fund	138	1,071	1,099	11,452
Other Defense-Civil:				
Military retirement fund [1]	83,993	68,181	93,200	988,795

Table 4–5. DEBT HELD BY GOVERNMENT ACCOUNTS [1]—Continued

(In millions of dollars)

Description	Investment or Disinvestment (–)			Holdings, End of 2021 Estimate
	2019 Actual	2020 Estimate	2021 Estimate	
Medicare-eligible retiree health care fund [1]	13,994	8,421	15,184	277,781
Education benefits fund	18	–55	–82	941
Environmental Protection Agency:				
Hazardous substance superfund	333	184	190	5,625
General Services Administration:				
Civil service retirement and disability trust fund	....	....	978,227	978,227
Postal Service retiree health benefits fund	....	....	38,949	38,949
Employees life insurance fund	....	....	51,088	51,088
Employees and retired employees health benefits fund	....	....	31,904	31,904
International Assistance Programs:				
Overseas Private Investment Corporation	47	–5,864	....	....
Development Finance Corporation corporate capital account	....	5,991	185	6,176
Office of Personnel Management:				
Civil service retirement and disability trust fund	16,709	18,908	–958,611	....
Postal Service retiree health benefits fund	–2,534	–2,553	–42,058	....
Employees life insurance fund	1,582	1,483	–49,682	....
Employees and retired employees health benefits fund	433	2,573	–30,375	....
Social Security Administration:				
Federal old-age and survivors insurance trust fund [2]	3,142	11,842	–6,494	2,809,744
Federal disability insurance trust fund [2]	3,119	–1,734	3,191	97,977
District of Columbia: Federal pension fund	102	60	48	3,906
Farm Credit System Insurance Corporation: Farm Credit System Insurance fund	238	284	289	5,505
Federal Communications Commission: Universal service fund	–2,574	–308	....	....
Federal Deposit Insurance Corporation: Deposit insurance fund	7,584	6,654	6,006	116,675
National Credit Union Administration: Share insurance fund	381	893	915	17,084
Postal Service fund [2]	–1,152	823	1,256	11,420
Railroad Retirement Board trust funds	68	137	–384	2,374
Securities Investor Protection Corporation [3]	230	194	45	3,619
United States Enrichment Corporation fund	47	25	–1,728	....
Other Federal funds	262	–183	191	4,815
Other trust funds	124	107	258	4,479
Unrealized discount [1]	–1,565	....	....	–14,777
Total, investment in Treasury debt [1]	**156,011**	**150,342**	**146,269**	**6,165,331**
Total, investment in Federal debt [1]	**156,011**	**150,342**	**146,269**	**6,165,331**
Memorandum:				
Investment by Federal funds (on-budget)	45,196	55,620	34,873	718,722
Investment by Federal funds (off-budget)	–1,152	823	1,256	11,420
Investment by trust funds (on-budget)	107,271	83,791	113,442	2,542,246
Investment by trust funds (off-budget)	6,262	10,108	–3,303	2,907,721
Unrealized discount [1]	–1,565	....	....	–14,777

* $500 thousand or less.

[1] Debt held by Government accounts is measured at face value except for Treasury zero-coupon bonds, which are recorded at market or redemption price; and the unrealized discount on Government account series, which is not distributed by account. In 2019, zero-coupon bonds were held only by the Nuclear waste disposal fund. If recorded at face value, at the end of 2019 the debt figure would be $13.4 billion higher for the Nuclear waste disposal fund than recorded in this table. In 2020, zero-coupon bonds were purchased by the Military retirement fund and the Medicare-eligible retiree health care fund. Changes are not estimated in the unrealized discount.

[2] Off-budget Federal entity.

[3] Amounts on calendar-year basis.

Bank (FFB), both within the Department of the Treasury. Agency borrowing from the FFB or the Fiscal Service is not included in gross Federal debt. It would be double counting to add together (a) the agency borrowing from the Fiscal Service or FFB and (b) the Treasury borrowing from the public that is needed to provide the Fiscal Service or FFB with the funds to lend to the agencies.

Debt Held by Government Accounts

Trust funds, and some special funds and public enterprise revolving funds, accumulate cash in excess of current needs in order to meet future obligations. These cash surpluses are generally invested in Treasury securities.

The total investment holdings of trust funds and other Government accounts increased by $156 billion in 2019. Net investment by Government accounts is estimated to be $150 billion in 2020 and $146 billion in 2021, as shown in Table 4–5. The holdings of Federal securities by Government accounts are estimated to increase to $6,165 billion by the end of 2021, or 25 percent of the gross Federal debt. The percentage is estimated to decrease gradually over the next 10 years.

The Government account holdings of Federal securities are concentrated among a few funds: the Social Security Old-Age and Survivors Insurance (OASI) and Disability Insurance (DI) trust funds; the Medicare Hospital Insurance (HI) and Supplementary Medical Insurance (SMI) trust funds; and four Federal employee retirement funds. These Federal employee retirement funds include two trust funds, the Military Retirement Fund and the Civil Service Retirement and Disability Fund (CSRDF), and two special funds, the uniformed services Medicare-Eligible Retiree Health Care Fund (MERHCF) and the Postal Service Retiree Health Benefits Fund (PSRHBF). At the end of 2021, these Social Security, Medicare, and Federal employee retirement funds are estimated to own 89 percent of the total debt held by Government accounts. During 2019–2021, the Military Retirement Fund has a large surplus and is estimated to invest a total of $245 billion, 54 percent of total net investment by Government accounts. Some Government accounts are projected to have net disinvestment in Federal securities during 2019–2021.

Technical note on measurement.—The Treasury securities held by Government accounts consist almost entirely of the Government account series. Most were issued at par value (face value), and the securities issued at a discount or premium are traditionally recorded at par in the OMB and Treasury reports on Federal debt. However, there are two kinds of exceptions.

First, Treasury issues zero-coupon bonds to a very few Government accounts. Because the purchase price is a small fraction of par value and the amounts are large, the holdings are recorded in Table 4–5 at par value less unamortized discount. The only Government account that held zero-coupon bonds during 2019 is the Nuclear Waste Disposal Fund in the Department of Energy. The unamortized discount on zero-coupon bonds held by the Nuclear Waste Disposal Fund was $13.4 billion at the

end of 2019. In 2020, the Military Retirement Fund and MERHCF purchased zero-coupon bonds.

Second, Treasury subtracts the unrealized discount on other Government account series securities in calculating "net Federal securities held as investments of Government accounts." Unlike the discount recorded for zero-coupon bonds and debt held by the public, the unrealized discount is the discount at the time of issue and is not amortized over the term of the security. In Table 4–5 it is shown as a separate item at the end of the table and not distributed by account. The amount was $14.8 billion at the end of 2019.

Debt Held by the Federal Reserve

The Federal Reserve acquires marketable Treasury securities as part of its exercise of monetary policy. For purposes of the Budget and reporting by the Department of the Treasury, the transactions of the Federal Reserve are considered to be non-budgetary, and accordingly the Federal Reserve's holdings of Treasury securities are included as part of debt held by the public.[15] Federal Reserve holdings were $2,113 billion (13 percent of debt held by the public) at the end of 2019. Over the last 10 years, the Federal Reserve holdings have averaged 16 percent of debt held by the public. The historical holdings of the Federal Reserve are presented in Table 7.1 in the Budget's *Historical Tables*. The Budget does not project Federal Reserve holdings for future years.

Limitations on Federal Debt

Definition of debt subject to limit.—Statutory limitations have usually been placed on Federal debt. Until World War I, the Congress ordinarily authorized a specific amount of debt for each separate issue. Beginning with the Second Liberty Bond Act of 1917, however, the nature of the limitation was modified in several steps until it developed into a ceiling on the total amount of most Federal debt outstanding. This last type of limitation has been in effect since 1941. The limit currently applies to most debt issued by the Treasury since September 1917, whether held by the public or by Government accounts; and other debt issued by Federal agencies that, according to explicit statute, is guaranteed as to principal and interest by the U.S. Government.

The third part of Table 4–2 compares total Treasury debt with the amount of Federal debt that is subject to the limit. Nearly all Treasury debt is subject to the debt limit.

A large portion of the Treasury debt not subject to the general statutory limit was issued by the Federal Financing Bank. The FFB is authorized to have outstanding up to $15 billion of publicly issued debt. The FFB has on occasion issued this debt to CSRDF in exchange for equal amounts of regular Treasury securities. The FFB securities have the same interest rates and maturities as the Treasury securities for which they were exchanged. The FFB issued: $14 billion of securities to the CSRDF on November 15, 2004, with maturity dates ranging from

---

[15] For further detail on the monetary policy activities of the Federal Reserve and the treatment of the Federal Reserve in the Budget, see Chapter 9, "Coverage of the Budget."

June 30, 2009, through June 30, 2019; $9 billion to the CSRDF on October 1, 2013, with maturity dates from June 30, 2015, through June 30, 2024; and $3 billion of securities to the CSRDF on October 15, 2015, with maturity dates from June 30, 2026, through June 30, 2029. The outstanding balance of FFB debt held by CSRDF was $9 billion at the end of 2019 and is projected to be $7 billion at the end of 2020.

The other Treasury debt not subject to the general limit consists almost entirely of silver certificates and other currencies no longer being issued. It was $479 million at the end of 2019 and is projected to gradually decline over time.

The sole agency debt currently subject to the general limit, $209 thousand at the end of 2019, is certain debentures issued by the Federal Housing Administration.[16]

Some of the other agency debt, however, is subject to its own statutory limit. For example, the Tennessee Valley Authority is limited to $30 billion of bonds and notes outstanding.

The comparison between Treasury debt and debt subject to limit also includes an adjustment for measurement differences in the treatment of discounts and premiums. As explained earlier in this chapter, debt securities may be sold at a discount or premium, and the measurement of debt may take this into account rather than recording the face value of the securities. However, the measurement differs between gross Federal debt (and its components) and the statutory definition of debt subject to limit. An adjustment is needed to derive debt subject to limit (as defined by law) from Treasury debt. The amount of the adjustment was $49 billion at the end of 2019 compared with the total unamortized discount (less premium) of $73 billion on all Treasury securities.

Changes in the debt limit.—The statutory debt limit has been changed many times. Since 1960, the Congress has passed 85 separate acts to raise the limit, revise the definition, extend the duration of a temporary increase, or temporarily suspend the limit.[17]

The seven most recent laws addressing the debt limit have each provided for a temporary suspension followed by an increase in an amount equivalent to the debt that was issued during that suspension period in order to fund commitments requiring payment through the specified end date. The Bipartisan Budget Act of 2018 suspended the $20,456 billion debt ceiling from February 9, 2018, through March 1, 2019, and then raised the debt limit on March 2, 2019, by $1,532 billion to $21,988 billion. The Bipartisan Budget Act of 2019 suspended the $21,988 billion debt ceiling from August 2, 2019, through July 31, 2021.

At many times in the past several decades, including 2018 and 2019, the Government has reached the statutory debt limit before an increase has been enacted. When this has occurred, it has been necessary for the Treasury to take "extraordinary measures" to meet the Government's obligation to pay its bills and invest its trust funds while remaining below the statutory limit.

---

[16] At the end of 2019, there were also $18 million of FHA debentures not subject to limit.

[17] The Acts and the statutory limits since 1940 are listed in Table 7.3 of the Budget's *Historical Tables*, available at *https://www.whitehouse.gov/omb/historical-tables/*.

Table 4–6. FEDERAL FUNDS FINANCING AND CHANGE IN DEBT SUBJECT TO STATUTORY LIMIT

(In billions of dollars)

Description	Actual 2019	Estimate										
		2020	2021	2022	2023	2024	2025	2026	2027	2028	2029	2030
Change in Gross Federal Debt:												
Federal funds deficit	1,096.9	1,195.5	1,064.5	977.3	824.0	670.7	583.8	539.0	389.1	341.4	295.8	167.8
Other transactions affecting borrowing from the public—Federal funds [1]	68.2	–1.5	66.0	60.3	52.4	44.5	39.1	33.5	29.9	26.7	26.9	27.7
Increase (+) or decrease (–) in Federal debt held by Federal funds	44.0	56.4	36.1	45.7	45.1	45.1	45.6	42.9	45.3	46.5	46.1	47.2
Adjustments for trust fund surplus/deficit not invested/disinvested in Federal securities [2]	–0.4	–19.7	10.6	–1.4	–1.1	–1.1	–1.0	–1.0	–0.9	–0.7	–0.6	–0.4
Change in unrealized discount on Federal debt held by Government accounts	–1.6	....	....	....	....	....	....	....	....	....	....	....
Total financing requirements	1,207.2	1,230.8	1,177.2	1,082.0	920.4	759.2	667.5	614.3	463.4	414.0	368.2	242.2
Change in Debt Subject to Limit:												
Change in gross Federal debt	1,207.2	1,230.8	1,177.2	1,082.0	920.4	759.2	667.5	614.3	463.4	414.0	368.2	242.2
Less: increase (+) or decrease (–) in Federal debt not subject to limit	–3.0	–2.6	–1.7	–1.6	–1.8	–2.0	–0.9	–1.0	–1.6	–1.4	–1.1	–0.2
Less: change in adjustment for discount and premium [3]	–1.5	....	....	....	....	....	....	....	....	....	....	....
Total, change in debt subject to limit	1,211.8	1,233.4	1,178.8	1,083.6	922.2	761.1	668.4	615.3	465.1	415.5	369.3	242.4
Memorandum:												
Debt subject to statutory limit [4]	22,686.6	23,920.0	25,098.9	26,182.5	27,104.6	27,865.8	28,534.2	29,149.5	29,614.6	30,030.1	30,399.4	30,641.8

[1] Includes Federal fund transactions that correspond to those presented in Table 4–2, but that are for Federal funds alone with respect to the public and trust funds.

[2] Includes trust fund holdings in other cash assets and changes in the investments of the National Railroad Retirement Investment Trust in non-Federal securities.

[3] Consists of unamortized discount (less premium) on public issues of Treasury notes and bonds (other than zero-coupon bonds).

[4] Legislation enacted August 2, 2019, (P.L. 116–37) temporarily suspends the debt limit through July 31, 2021.

One such extraordinary measure is the partial or full suspension of the daily reinvestment of the Thrift Savings Plan (TSP) Government Securities Investment Fund (G-Fund).[18] The Treasury Secretary has statutory authority to suspend investment of the G-Fund in Treasury securities as needed to prevent the debt from exceeding the debt limit. Treasury determines each day the amount of investments that would allow the fund to be invested as fully as possible without exceeding the debt limit. The TSP G-Fund had an outstanding balance of $251 billion at the end of December 2019. The Treasury Secretary is also authorized to suspend investments in the CSRDF and to declare a debt issuance suspension period, which allows him or her to redeem a limited amount of securities held by the CSRDF. The Postal Accountability and Enhancement Act of 2006 provides that investments in the Postal Service Retiree Health Benefits Fund shall be made in the same manner as investments in the CSRDF.[19] Therefore, Treasury is able to take similar administrative actions with the PSRHBF. The law requires that when any such actions are taken with the G-Fund, the CSRDF, or the PSRHBF, the Treasury Secretary is required to make the fund whole after the debt limit has been raised by restoring the forgone interest and investing the fund fully. Another measure for staying below the debt limit is disinvestment of the Exchange Stabilization Fund. The outstanding balance in the Exchange Stabilization Fund was $23 billion at the end of December.

As the debt has neared the limit, including in 2019, Treasury has also suspended the issuance of SLGS to reduce unanticipated fluctuations in the level of the debt. At times, Treasury has also adjusted the schedule for auctions of marketable securities.

In addition to these steps, Treasury has previously exchanged Treasury securities held by the CSRDF with borrowing by the FFB, which, as explained above, is not subject to the debt limit. This measure was most recently taken in October 2015.

The debt limit has always been increased prior to the exhaustion of Treasury's limited available administrative actions to continue to finance Government operations when the statutory ceiling has been reached. Failure to enact a debt limit increase before these actions were exhausted would have significant and long-term negative consequences. The Federal Government would be forced to delay or discontinue payments on its broad range of obligations, including Social Security and other payments to individuals, Medicaid and other grant payments to States, individual and corporate tax refunds, Federal employee salaries, payments to vendors and contractors, principal and interest payments on Treasury securities, and other obligations. If Treasury were unable to make timely interest payments or redeem securities, investors would cease to view U.S. Treasury securities as free of credit risk and Treasury's interest costs would increase. Because interest rates throughout the economy are benchmarked

to the Treasury rates, interest rates for State and local governments, businesses, and individuals would also rise. Foreign investors would likely shift out of dollar-denominated assets, driving down the value of the dollar and further increasing interest rates on non-Federal, as well as Treasury, debt.

The debt subject to limit is estimated to increase to $23,920 billion by the end of 2020 and to $25,099 billion by the end of 2021. The Budget anticipates timely congressional action to address the statutory limit as necessary before exhaustion of Treasury's extraordinary measures.

Federal funds financing and the change in debt subject to limit.—The change in debt held by the public, as shown in Table 4–2, and the change in debt held by the public net of financial assets are determined primarily by the total Government deficit or surplus. The debt subject to limit, however, includes not only debt held by the public but also debt held by Government accounts. The change in debt subject to limit is therefore determined both by the factors that determine the total Government deficit or surplus and by the factors that determine the change in debt held by Government accounts. The effect of debt held by Government accounts on the total debt subject to limit can be seen in the second part of Table 4–2. The change in debt held by Government accounts results in 11 percent of the estimated total increase in debt subject to limit from 2020 through 2030.

The Budget is composed of two groups of funds, Federal funds and trust funds. The Federal funds, in the main, are derived from tax receipts and borrowing and are used for the general purposes of the Government. The trust funds, on the other hand, are financed by taxes or other receipts dedicated by law for specified purposes, such as for paying Social Security benefits or making grants to State governments for highway construction.[20]

A Federal funds deficit must generally be financed by borrowing, which can be done either by selling securities to the public or by issuing securities to Government accounts that are not within the Federal funds group. Federal funds borrowing consists almost entirely of Treasury securities that are subject to the statutory debt limit. Very little debt subject to statutory limit has been issued for reasons except to finance the Federal funds deficit. The change in debt subject to limit is therefore determined primarily by the Federal funds deficit, which is equal to the difference between the total Government deficit or surplus and the trust fund surplus. Trust fund surpluses are almost entirely invested in securities subject to the debt limit, and trust funds hold most of the debt held by Government accounts. The trust fund surplus reduces the total budget deficit or increases the total budget surplus, decreasing the need to borrow from the public or increasing the ability to repay borrowing from the public. When the trust fund surplus is invested in Federal securities, the debt held by Government accounts increases, offsetting the decrease in debt held by the public by an equal amount. Thus, there is no net effect on gross Federal debt.

---

[18] The TSP is a defined contribution pension plan for Federal employees. The G-Fund is one of several components of the TSP.

[19] Both the CSRDF and the PSRHBF are administered by the Office of Personnel Management.

[20] For further discussion of the trust funds and Federal funds groups, see Chapter 22, "Trust Funds and Federal Funds."

Table 4–6 derives the change in debt subject to limit. In 2019 the Federal funds deficit was $1,097 billion, and other factors increased financing requirements by $68 billion. The net financing disbursements of credit financing accounts increased financing requirements by $71 billion, partly offset by the change in the Treasury operating cash balance and other Federal fund factors, which together reduced financing requirements by $2 billion. In addition, special funds and revolving funds, which are part of the Federal funds group, invested a net of $44 billion in Treasury securities. Small adjustments are also made for the difference between the trust fund surplus or deficit and the trust funds' investment or disinvestment in Federal securities (including the changes in NRRIT's investments in non-Federal securities) and for the change in unrealized discount on Federal debt held by Government accounts. As a net result of all these factors, $1,207 billion in financing was required, increasing gross Federal debt by that amount. Since Federal debt not subject to limit fell by $3 billion and the adjustment for discount and premium changed by $2 billion, the debt subject to limit increased by $1,212 billion, while debt held by the public increased by $1,051 billion.

Debt subject to limit is estimated to increase by $1,233 billion in 2020 and by $1,179 billion in 2021. The projected increases in the debt subject to limit are caused by the continued Federal funds deficit, supplemented by the other factors shown in Table 4–6. While debt held by the public increases by $7,091 billion from the end of 2019 through 2030, debt subject to limit increases by $7,955 billion.

Foreign Holdings of Federal Debt

Foreign holdings of Federal debt are presented in Table 4–7. During most of American history, the Federal debt was held almost entirely by individuals and institutions within the United States. In the late 1960s, foreign holdings were just over $10 billion, less than 5 percent of the total Federal debt held by the public. Foreign holdings began to grow significantly in the early 1970s, and then remained about 15–20 percent of total Federal debt until the mid-1990s. During 1995–97, growth in foreign holdings accelerated, reaching 33 percent by the end of 1997. Since 2004, foreign holdings of Federal debt have represented around 40 percent or more of outstanding debt. Foreign holdings increased to 48 percent by the end of 2008 and then remained relatively stable through 2015. After 2015, foreign holdings began to decline as a percent of total Federal debt held by the public, falling from 47 percent at the end of 2015 to 40 percent at the end of 2018.

By the end of 2019, foreign holdings of Treasury debt had grown to $6,779 billion, remaining at 40 percent of

Table 4–7. FOREIGN HOLDINGS OF FEDERAL DEBT
(Dollar amounts in billions)

Fiscal Year	Debt held by the public			Change in debt held by the public [2]	
	Total	Foreign [1]	Percentage foreign	Total	Foreign
1965	260.8	12.2	4.7	3.9	0.3
1970	283.2	14.0	4.9	5.1	3.7
1975	394.7	66.0	16.7	51.0	9.1
1980	711.9	126.4	17.8	71.6	1.3
1985	1,507.3	222.9	14.8	200.3	47.3
1990	2,411.6	463.8	19.2	220.8	72.0
1995	3,604.4	820.4	22.8	171.3	138.4
2000	3,409.8	1,038.8	30.5	-222.6	-242.6
2005	4,592.2	1,929.6	42.0	296.7	135.1
2010	9,018.9	4,316.0	47.9	1,474.2	745.4
2011	10,128.2	4,912.1	48.5	1,109.3	596.1
2012	11,281.1	5,476.1	48.5	1,152.9	564.0
2013	11,982.7	5,652.8	47.2	701.6	176.7
2014	12,779.9	6,104.0	47.8	797.2	451.2
2015	13,116.7	6,105.9	46.6	336.8	1.9
2016	14,167.6	6,155.9	43.5	1,050.9	50.0
2017	14,665.4	6,301.9	43.0	497.8	146.0
2018	15,749.6	6,225.9	39.5	1,084.1	-76.0
2019	16,800.7	6,779.2	40.4	1,051.2	553.3

[1] Estimated by Department of the Treasury. These estimates exclude agency debt, the holdings of which are believed to be small. The data on foreign holdings are recorded by methods that are not fully comparable with the data on debt held by the public. Projections of foreign holdings are not available.

[2] Change in debt held by the public is defined as equal to the change in debt held by the public from the beginning of the year to the end of the year.

the total debt held by the public.[21] The dollar increase in foreign holdings was about 53 percent of total Federal borrowing from the public in 2019 and 17 percent over the last five years. Increases in foreign holdings have been almost entirely due to decisions by foreign central banks, corporations, and individuals, rather than the direct marketing of these securities to foreign investors. All of the foreign holdings of Federal debt are denominated in dollars.

In 2019, foreign central banks and other foreign official institutions owned 61 percent of the foreign holdings of Federal debt; private investors owned the rest. At the end of 2019, the nations holding the largest shares of U.S. Federal debt were Japan, which held 17 percent of all foreign holdings, and China, which held 16 percent.

Foreign holdings of Federal debt are around 20-25 percent of the foreign-owned assets in the United States, depending on the method of measuring total assets. The foreign purchases of Federal debt securities do not measure the full impact of the capital inflow from abroad on the market for Federal debt securities. The capital inflow supplies additional funds to the credit market generally, and thus affects the market for Federal debt. For example, the capital inflow includes deposits in U.S. financial intermediaries that themselves buy Federal debt.

---

[21] The debt calculated by the Bureau of Economic Analysis is different, though similar in size, because of a different method of valuing securities.

Federal, Federally Guaranteed, and Other Federally Assisted Borrowing

The Government's effects on the credit markets arise not only from its own borrowing but also from the direct loans that it makes to the public and the provision of assistance to certain borrowing by the public. The Government guarantees various types of borrowing by individuals, businesses, and other non-Federal entities, thereby providing assistance to private credit markets. The Government is also assisting borrowing by States through the Build America Bonds program, which subsidizes the interest that States pay on such borrowing. In addition, the Government has established private corporations—Government-sponsored enterprises—to provide financial intermediation for specified public purposes; it exempts the interest on most State and local government debt from income tax; it permits mortgage interest to be deducted in calculating taxable income; and it insures the deposits of banks and thrift institutions, which themselves make loans.

Federal credit programs and other forms of assistance are discussed in Chapter 18, "Credit and Insurance," in this volume. Detailed data are presented in tables accompanying that chapter.

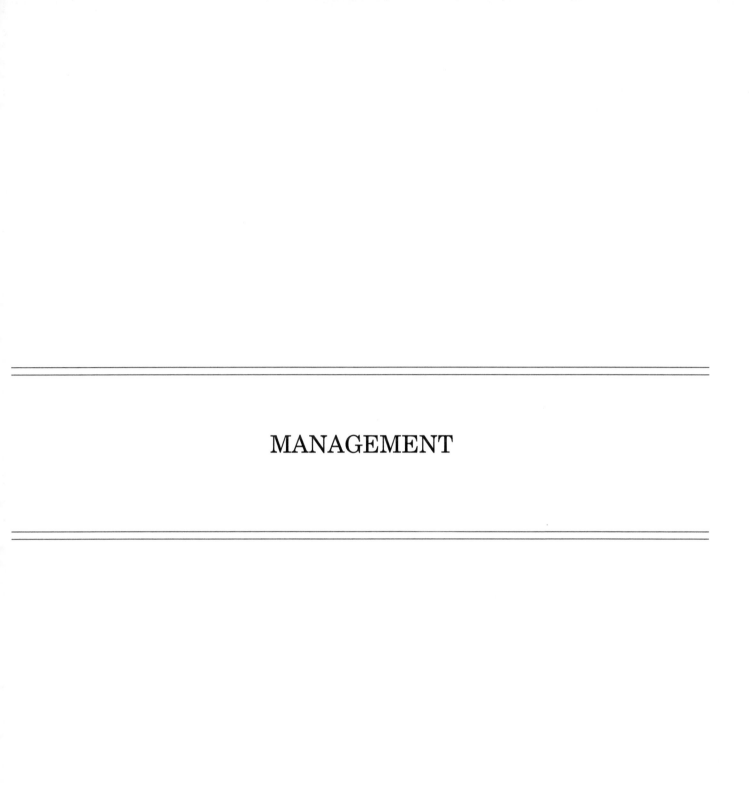

MANAGEMENT

5. STRENGTHENING THE FEDERAL WORKFORCE

The President's Management Agenda (PMA) identifies the Federal workforce, along with information technology (IT) and data, as one of the three key drivers of Government transformation. These three drivers should function as interlocking gears that together enable a Government that operates at the high level that its citizens expect and deserve. As the private sector demonstrates daily, modernized information technology systems that put the best available data in the hands of well-trained and well-managed employees can produce exponential increases in organizational productivity. With the mission as the priority and the feedback of the customer as guidance, the Federal enterprise must accelerate the pace of transformation toward a vision of the future where managers and employees work in new ways, supported by technology and data and rewarded for innovation and excellence.

The workforce is critical to the mission. The vast and varied work of the Federal Government is largely carried out by its 2.1 million member civilian workforce. Inevitably, the Government's effectiveness and efficiency hinges in no small part on their collective performance. As the President expressed in his recent holiday letter to Executive Branch employees, the vast majority of Federal workers, whether they are Veterans Affairs doctors or Border Patrol officers, are dedicated to the mission of public service.

Unfortunately, the personnel system these men and women work within is structured for stability not agility. The legislative framework for the civil service was crafted in another era, for a different workforce, doing a different type of work. Recent, rapid changes in the nature of work have prompted resilient private sector employers to respond with nimbleness and agility, overhauling hiring practices, job descriptions, compensation packages, and work arrangements to stay competitive. Federal personnel practices have remained comparatively static. The underlying framework of the General Schedule (the civil service personnel system in which most Federal workers are employed) has proven to be neither nimble nor agile. Its job classification system becomes more archaic with each passing year. Both hiring and dismissal processes are lengthy and byzantine. Stellar performance is inadequately recognized and poor performance insufficiently addressed. The lack of mobility frustrates managerial efforts to restructure and employee ambitions to excel. Considering these factors, it is remarkable that so many Federal workers continue to pursue and attain excellence.

While critical aspects of this workforce system are entrenched in law, the Administration has taken the initiative to use its available discretion to implement a series of changes designed to increase flexibility and inject accountability. The Administration has proposed statutory changes that would instigate more systemic change toward agility in the workforce, operations, and service delivery of the Federal enterprise.

Federal Workforce Demographics

The Federal civilian workforce represents an annual taxpayer investment of approximately $350 billion. The Administration continues its successful efforts to realign that investment in ways that maximize the ability of the workforce to support the American people. This commitment requires optimizing workforce skills, capabilities, and compensation based on mission needs and labor market dynamics, while leveraging leading market practices. To that end, the President signed into law a paid parental leave benefit for Federal civilian employees. Since the Federal Government employs more Americans than any other entity, this benefit may spur other employers in the public and private sectors to follow suit.

The total workforce comprises approximately 2.1 million non-postal civilian workers and 1.4 million active duty military, as well as approximately one million military reserve personnel serving throughout the Nation and the world. The postal workforce includes an additional 580,000 employees. Approximately 85 percent of the non-postal civilian workforce, or 1.7 million people, live outside of the Washington, D.C., metropolitan area. About 36 percent of these employees live in rural communities outside of a metropolitan area. Notably, an even larger "indirect" workforce carries out much of the work paid for by Federal funds. This includes Federal contractors and State, local, and educational institutions, and nonprofit employees whose jobs are funded by Federal contracts, grants, or transfer payments.

As mission, service, and stewardship needs should drive the optimal size of the Federal workforce, the Administration does not set targets for full-time equivalent (FTE) levels for each agency. While some agencies may choose to reduce FTEs, in many areas, the Administration seeks to increase the workforce protecting the Nation domestically and abroad. Table 5–1 shows actual Federal civilian FTE levels in the Executive Branch by agency for 2018 and 2019, and estimates for 2020 and 2021, Table 5–2 contains the total Federal employment, including the uniformed military, Postal Service, and Judicial and Legislative branches.

The total workforce size was 2,085,000 in 2019, and 2,061,000 in 2018, with increases in staffing that primarily occurred at the Departments of Defense (DOD), Homeland Security, and Veterans Affairs being partially offset by reductions in personnel at other civilian agencies. The size of the Federal civilian workforce grew from 2018 to 2019, with a coming one-year surge in 2020 to conduct the Census. Agencies focused on defense, home-

Chart 5-1. Masters Degree or Above by Year for Federal and Private Sectors

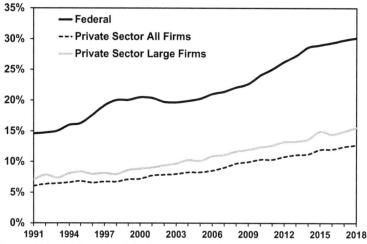

Source: 1992–2019 Current Population Survey, Integrated Public Use Microdata Series.

Notes: Federal excludes the military and Postal Service, but includes all other Federal workers. Private Sector excludes the self-employed. Neither category includes State and local government workers. Large firms have at least 1,000 workers. This analysis is limited to full-time, full-year workers, i.e. those with at least 1,500 annual hours of work and presents five-year averages. Industry is from the year preceding the year on the horizontal axis.

land security, and veterans' affairs increased, and will continue to do so with the Budget.

Agencies continue to examine their workforces to determine the functions needed to accomplish their missions in light of technological changes that automate transactional processes, such as artificial intelligence to streamline compliance and regulatory processes, online and telephone chat-bots to improve customer service, and other tools to reduce agency personnel needs. Several agencies are already using shared-service models for mission-support positions, which may also reduce the need for full-time employees. Changes in Federal procurement, real-estate utilization, and administrative processes may also reduce personnel needs.

According to February 2019 Office of Personnel Management (OPM) data (the most recent available), the

Chart 5-2. High School Graduate or Less by Year for Federal and Private Sectors

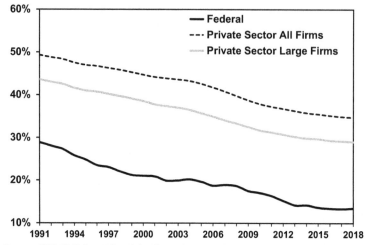

Source: 1992–2019 Current Population Survey, Integrated Public Use Microdata Series.

Notes: Federal excludes the military and Postal Service, but includes all other Federal workers. Private Sector excludes the self-employed. Neither category includes State and local government workers. Large firms have at least 1,000 workers. This analysis is limited to full-time, full-year workers, i.e. those with at least 1,500 annual hours of work and presents five-year averages. Industry is from the year preceding the year on the horizontal axis.

Chart 5-3. Average Age by Year for Federal and Private Sectors

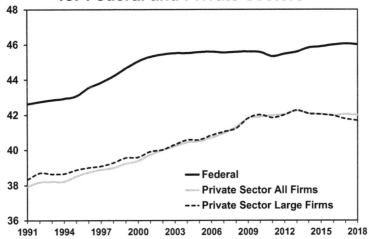

Source: 1992–2019 Current Population Survey, Integrated Public Use Microdata Series.

Notes: Federal excludes the military and Postal Service, but includes all other Federal workers. Private Sector excludes the self-employed. Neither category includes State and local government workers. Large firms have at least 1,000 workers. This analysis is limited to full-time, full-year workers, i.e. those with at least 1,500 annual hours of work and presents five-year averages. Industry is from the year preceding the year on the horizontal axis.

Chart 5–4. GOVERNMENT-WIDE ON-BOARD U.S. DISTRIBUTION 10–1–1978

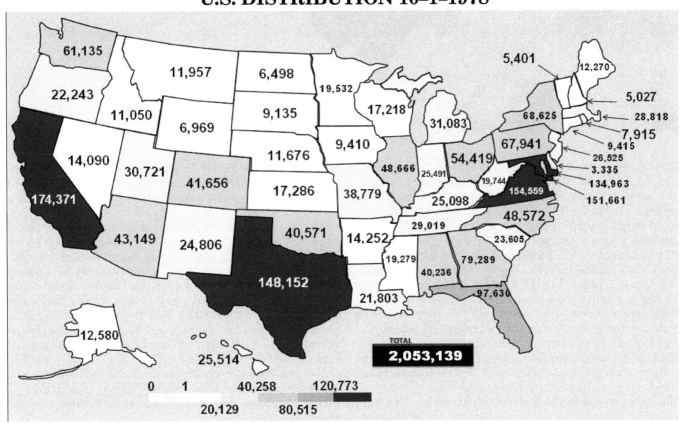

Source: Office of Personnel Management.

Chart 5–5. GOVERNMENT-WIDE ON-BOARD
U.S. DISTRIBUTION 2–28–2019

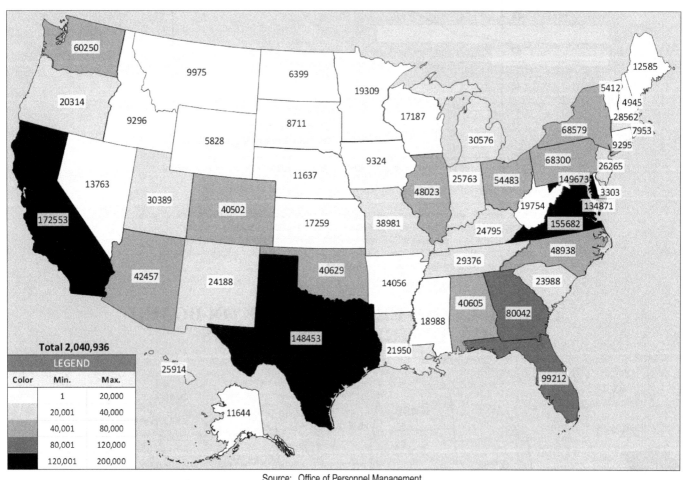

Source: Office of Personnel Management.

Federal civilian workforce self-identifies as 61.3 percent White, 18.1 percent Black, 9.1 percent Hispanic of all races, 6.5 percent Asian/Pacific Islander, 1.6 percent Native American/Alaska Native, and 1.8 percent more than one race. Men make up 56.1 percent of all permanent Federal employees and women are 43.8 percent. Veterans currently constitute 31.5 percent of the workforce, which represents a slight increase from a year ago. This includes the 11.7 percent of the workforce who are veterans receiving disability compensation as of August 2018. By comparison, veterans represent only 5.7 percent of the private sector non-agricultural workforce. About 9.2 percent of all Federal employees self-identify as having a disability, which includes the approximately 1 percent who have a "targeted disability" such as blindness and are hired through a streamlined hiring process.

The average age in the Federal workforce is older than the Nation's broader working population. About 28.8 per-cent (604,000) of Federal employees are older than 55. At the other end of the spectrum, only 7.3 percent (154,000) are younger than 30, compared to 23 percent of private sector workers.

Using data from the Bureau of Labor Statistics on full-time, full-year workers, Table 5–3 breaks out all Federal and private sector jobs into 22 occupational groups to demonstrate the differences in composition between the Federal and private workforces. Charts 5–1 and 5–2 present trends in educational levels for the Federal and private sector workforces over the past two decades. Chart 5–3 shows the trends in average age in both the Federal and private sectors. Chart 5–4 and Chart 5–5 show the location of Federal employees in 1978 and 2019. Chart 5–6 shows the growing age disparity in the information technology sector since 2010, when Federal internships and hiring programs for recent graduates became subject to new restrictions.

Chart 5-6. Potential Retires to Younger than 30 Employees: Federal IT Workforce Vs. Federal Workforce

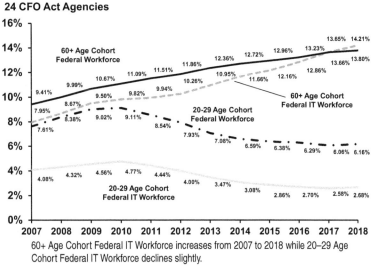

24 CFO Act Agencies

60+ Age Cohort Federal IT Workforce increases from 2007 to 2018 while 20–29 Age Cohort Federal IT Workforce declines slightly.

Source: FedScope FY2007-FY2018, CFO Act Agencies Only.

Developing a Modern Civil Service System

The Administration is committed to the development of a civil service framework to enable Federal employees to carry out successfully the missions of Government. The PMA is pursuing structural alterations through both statutory changes and administrative actions. The Administration is working within existing statutes to become more agile while adhering to merit system principles, the foundation of our Federal civil service. Over the past 70 years, position classification and related staffing rules have become compliance focused rather than the means to ensure a competitive, effective workforce. The existing system places obstacles to many who would consider a career in public service. For instance, the Administration intends to eliminate degree requirements for Federal jobs when not inherently necessary to perform the duties of a position, and to identify other instances where degrees are used as a poor proxy for specific competencies sought in job candidates. Over-reliance on degrees can be a barrier to entry into Federal service, and it can also prevent current civil servants who possess relevant skills, training or experience from transitioning into emerging fields within the Federal sector.

Streamlining and Eliminating Complex Rules

Reports from the National Academy of Public Administration, the Government Accountability Office, and other observers have concluded that the civil service system is increasingly weighed down by burdensome rules that incentivize rigid compliance instead of strategic workforce management. The Administration remains committed to streamlining bureaucratic human resources processes.

Pay and Compensation Reform

A modern civil service system requires flexible pay and compensation that is sensitive to labor market dynamics. A Congressional Budget Office (CBO) report issued in April 2017 found that, based on observable characteristics, Federal employees on average received a combined 17 percent higher wage and benefits package than the private sector average over the 2011–2015 period. The difference is realized on the benefits side. CBO found that Federal employees receive, on average, 47 percent higher benefits levels and 3 percent higher wages than counterparts in the private sector. In CBO's analysis, these differences reflect higher Federal compensation paid to individuals with a bachelor's degree or less, with Federal employees with professional degrees undercompensated relative to private sector peers (Chart 5–7). Table 5–4 summarizes total Federal compensation.

The 2021 Budget re-proposes several reforms from the 2020 Budget that reflect difficult choices in light of fiscal realities including:

- Increasing employee payments to the Federal Employees Retirement System (FERS) defined benefit plan, so that employees and their employing agency pay an equal share of the employee's annuity cost (phased in at a one-percent increase each year); and reducing or eliminating cost of living adjustments for existing and future retirees.

- Basing annuity calculations on employees' "High–5" salary years instead of "High–3" salary years (a common private sector practice) and the elimination of the FERS Special Retirement Supplement for those

Table 5–1.   FEDERAL CIVILIAN EMPLOYMENT IN THE EXECUTIVE BRANCH

(Civilian employment as measured by full-time equivalents (FTE) in thousands, excluding the Postal Service)

Agency	Actual		Estimate		Change: 2020 to 2021	
	2018	2019	2020	2021	FTE	Percent
Cabinet agencies						
Agriculture	84.1	81.4	85.1	84.3	–0.8	–1.0%
Commerce	40.2	45.0	96.3	42.9	–53.5	–55.5%
Defense--Military Programs	730.3	741.5	774.9	773.6	–1.3	–0.2%
Education	3.8	3.6	3.8	4.0	0.2	5.1%
Energy	14.2	14.0	15.3	15.4	0.1	0.6%
Health and Human Services	73.1	73.0	75.7	76.1	0.4	0.5%
Homeland Security	186.4	192.4	197.1	192.9	–4.3	–2.2%
Housing and Urban Development	7.6	7.4	7.7	7.8	0.1	1.5%
Interior	63.1	61.6	62.4	60.9	–1.5	–2.4%
Justice	113.0	111.9	116.1	117.7	1.6	1.4%
Labor	15.3	14.8	15.2	15.4	0.2	1.5%
State	26.3	25.3	25.7	25.7	*	*
Transportation	53.9	53.1	54.9	55.1	0.1	0.2%
Treasury	88.5	88.0	90.3	101.8	11.5	12.8%
Veterans Affairs	363.4	375.8	389.9	404.9	15.0	3.9%
Other agencies -- excluding Postal Service						
Bureau of Consumer Financial Protection	1.6	1.5	1.6	1.4	–0.2	–11.6%
Corps of Engineers--Civil Works	22.7	23.2	23.6	23.6	....	....
Environmental Protection Agency	14.2	13.6	14.0	12.8	–1.3	–9.1%
Equal Employment Opportunity Commission	2.0	2.1	1.9	1.7	–0.2	–9.7%
Federal Communications Commission	1.5	1.4	1.4	1.4	....	....
Federal Deposit Insurance Corporation	6.1	5.9	5.9	5.9	....	....
Federal Trade Commission	1.1	1.1	1.1	1.1	....	....
General Services Administration	11.1	11.0	11.5	14.0	2.5	21.4%
International Assistance Programs	5.3	5.3	5.5	5.4	–0.1	–1.4%
National Aeronautics and Space Administration	17.0	17.2	16.9	16.9	*	*
National Archives and Records Administration	2.8	2.6	2.7	2.6	–0.1	–2.1%
National Credit Union Administration	1.1	1.1	1.2	1.2	....	....
National Labor Relations Board	1.3	1.3	1.3	1.3	–*	–1.6%
National Science Foundation	1.4	1.4	1.4	1.4	–*	–0.1%
Nuclear Regulatory Commission	3.1	2.9	3.0	2.9	–0.1	–3.4%
Office of Personnel Management **	5.5	5.5	2.4	....	–2.4	–100.0%
Securities and Exchange Commission	4.5	4.4	4.5	4.6	0.1	2.9%
Small Business Administration	5.6	4.2	3.3	3.3	*	0.3%
Smithsonian Institution	5.0	5.1	5.3	5.2	–0.1	–1.6%
Social Security Administration	60.9	61.2	61.7	61.4	–0.2	–0.4%
Tennessee Valley Authority	10.0	10.0	10.0	10.0	....	....
U.S. Agency for Global Media	1.6	1.6	1.6	1.5	–0.1	–7.3%
All other small agencies	13.1	13.0	13.7	14.2	0.6	4.2%
Total, Executive Branch civilian employment	2,061.2	2,085.5	2,206.1	2,172.4	–33.7	–1.5%

* 50 or less.

** Includes transfer of functions to the General Services Administration.

employees who retire before their Social Security eligibility age.

- Modifying the G Fund, an investment vehicle available only through the Thrift Savings Plan (TSP), the defined contribution plan for Federal employees. G Fund investors benefit from receiving a medium-term Treasury bond rate of return on what is essentially a short-term security. The Budget would instead base the G Fund yield on a short-term T-bill rate.

The members of the Federal workforce underserved by the existing hybrid retirement system are the roughly 70,000 term employees who are hired for an initial period of up to four years. The existing system discourages term hires, because their terms will fall short of the five years necessary to become vested in the defined benefit program. Term hiring is attractive to individuals who may not want to make a career of Government service, but who still want to serve in specific areas of interest for a limited time (e.g., STEM fields; medicine, biological science,

Table 5–2. TOTAL FEDERAL EMPLOYMENT
(As measured by Full-Time Equivalents)

Description	2019 Actual	2020 Estimate	2021 Estimate	Change: 2020 to 2021	
				FTE	PERCENT
Executive Branch Civilian:					
All Agencies, Except Postal Service	2,085,496	2,206,137	2,172,433	–33,704	–1.6%
Postal Service [1]	583,573	585,682	578,984	–6,698	–1.2%
Subtotal, Executive Branch Civilian	2,669,069	2,791,819	2,751,417	–40,402	–1.5%
Executive Branch Uniformed Military:					
Department of Defense [2]	1,363,348	1,350,264	1,356,861	6,597	0.5%
Department of Homeland Security (USCG)	42,588	50,230	50,511	281	0.6%
Commissioned Corps (DOC, EPA, HHS)	6,480	6,532	6,626	94	1.4%
Subtotal, Uniformed Military	1,412,416	1,407,026	1,413,998	6,972	0.5%
Subtotal, Executive Branch	4,081,485	4,198,845	4,165,415	–33,430	–0.8%
Legislative Branch [3]	31,182	31,877	32,221	344	1.1%
Judicial Branch	32,973	33,716	34,143	427	1.3%
Grand Total	4,145,640	4,264,438	4,231,779	–32,659	–0.8%

[1] Includes the U.S. Postal Service Office of Inspector General and Postal Regulatory Commission.
[2] Includes activated Guard and Reserve members on active duty. Does not include Full-Time Support (Active Guard & Reserve (AGRSs)) paid from Reserve Component appropriations.
[3] FTE data not available for the Senate (positions filled were used for actual year and extended at same level).

health science, and emergency management). To address the existing disincentive to term hires, the Budget includes a proposal under which term employees would receive an expanded defined contribution benefit through the TSP, in lieu of the defined benefit annuity that offers them little value.

Federal employee sick and annual leave benefits are also managed differently than in the private sector. All Federal employees receive 10 paid holidays and up to 13 sick days annually, as well as 13 to 26 vacation days, depending on tenure. The 2021 Budget proposes to transition the existing civilian leave system to a model used in the private sector to grant employees maximum flexibility by combining all leave into one paid time off category. While the total leave days would be reduced, the proposal adds a short term disability insurance policy to protect

employees. Beginning this October, many employees will also benefit from additional leave days due to a recently-enacted paid parental leave benefit for Federal employees.

The Administration proposes a one percent pay increase for Federal civilian employees for calendar year 2021, while also increasing funds available for on-the-spot and ratings-based performance awards. The Administration has attempted to make pay more flexible and performance-based, since across-the-board pay increases have long-term fixed costs and fail to address existing pay disparities or to target mission-critical recruitment and retention goals. A more targeted approach that rewards the top performers with the most critical skills is needed. The Administration believes in aligning pay with an employee's performance where possible. The existing Federal salary structure rewards longevity over

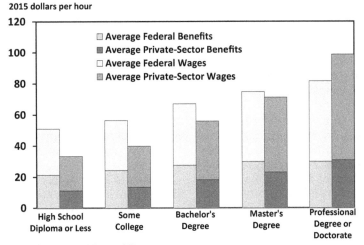

Chart 5-7. Average Compensation of Federal and Private-Sector Workers by Educational Attainment

Source: Congressional Budget Office.

Table 5–3.   OCCUPATIONS OF FEDERAL AND PRIVATE SECTOR WORKFORCES

(Grouped by Average Private Sector Salary)

Occupational Groups	Percent	
	Federal Workers	Private Sector Workers
Highest Paid Occupations Ranked by Private Sector Salary		
Lawyers and judges	3%	1%
Engineers	4%	2%
Scientists and social scientists	5%	1%
Managers	12%	14%
Pilots, conductors, and related mechanics	3%	0%
Doctors, nurses, psychologists, etc.	8%	6%
Miscellaneous professionals	17%	10%
Administrators, accountants, HR personnel	7%	3%
Inspectors	1%	0%
Total Percentage	**60%**	**37%**
Medium Paid Occupations Ranked by Private Sector Salary		
Sales including real estate, insurance agents	1%	6%
Other miscellaneous occupations	3%	5%
Automobile and other mechanics	2%	3%
Law enforcement and related occupations	9%	1%
Office workers	2%	5%
Social workers	2%	1%
Drivers of trucks and taxis	1%	3%
Laborers and construction workers	3%	10%
Clerks and administrative assistants	12%	10%
Manufacturing	2%	7%
Total Percentage	**35%**	**51%**
Lowest Paid Occupations Ranked by Private Sector Salary		
Other miscellaneous service workers	2%	6%
Janitors and housekeepers	2%	2%
Cooks, bartenders, bakers, and wait staff	1%	4%
Total Percentage	**4.5%**	**12.0%**

Source: 2015–2019 Current Population Survey, Integrated Public Use Microdata Series.

Notes: Federal workers exclude the military and Postal Service, but include all other Federal workers in the Executive, Legislative, and Judicial Branches. However, the vast majority of these employees are civil servants in the Executive Branch. Private sector workers exclude the self-employed. Neither category includes State and local government workers. This analysis is limited to full-time, full-year workers, i.e. those with at least 1,500 annual hours of work.

performance. This is most evident in the tenure-based "step-increase" promotions that most Federal employees receive on a fixed, periodic schedule without regard to whether they are performing at an exceptional or merely passable level (granted 99.7 percent of the time). The Budget proposes to slow the frequency of these step increases, while increasing performance-based pay for workers in mission-critical areas.

The Budget directs agencies to use their performance awards funding to finance more strategic and innovative approaches to meeting critical recruitment, retention, and reskilling needs across Government. Currently, agencies spend approximately one percent of their salary spending on awards. However, awards funding is often spent in a non-strategic manner. In recent Federal Employee Viewpoint Surveys (FEVS), both managers and nonsupervisory workers report that the awards structure does not adequately provide an incentive to perform or reward

the best employee. Office of Management and Budget guidance to agencies released in 2019 directed the use of awards funding to reward high-performing, critical employees. In addition to lifting the cap on the amount of salary devoted to awards, the 2021 Budget includes funding for agencies to spend an additional one percentage point of their salary budget on awards for their high performing employees and those with critical skillsets. This increase in awards spending will allow agencies to effect an awards and recognition program that drives positive behavior; provides opportunities for employees to develop, grow, and enhance their careers; and recognizes accomplishments in a timely way. The increase also ensures that agencies have sufficient funding to differentiate among levels of performance and maintain an appropriate distribution between performance awards and individual contribution awards.

To ensure the top performers are indeed rewarded, the performance management system must effectively measure performance. Instead, it is often a rote exercise with inconsistent definitions that do not differentiate levels of performance. In every FEVS, employees report that performance does not relate to compensation. To start the necessary culture change needed to support a meaningful appraisal system, the Administration released guidance in 2019 defining what each performance level must include for employees to attain specific rating levels. This practice will increase consistency and transparency.

President's Management Agenda 21st Century Workforce Goal

The PMA defines a framework for change that has the Federal workforce at its core, namely the Cross Agency Priority (CAP) Goal focused on "Developing the 21st Century Workforce." This CAP Goal has three focus areas: (1) actively managing the workforce based on performance; (2) developing agile operations, to include efforts to reskill and redeploy current Federal employees toward higher value work; and (3) transforming processes to acquire top talent.

Actively Managing the Workforce Based on Performance

The Senior Executive Service (SES), comprising roughly 7,000 of the highest-ranking Federal managers, are the most critical career positions in the Government. SES members are disproportionately retirement-eligible. To mitigate the effects of the aging workforce, the Administration is continuing efforts to modernize policies and practices governing the SES, including creating a more robust and effective SES succession pipeline and more recruitment outreach to the private sector. As a complement to efforts to increase the external SES succession pipeline, OPM developed the Federal Supervisor Assessment, an online assessment of competencies critical for supervisors, which will increase the talent level of the internal SES succession pipeline by improving agencies' ability to select highly capable managers and supervisors. During the past year, OPM has modernized a range of SES processes, including performance appraisal programs, the Presidential Rank Awards program, SES allocations, and SES assessment and interview processes. In 2020, OPM will offer the new Executive Assessments to assist agencies in identifying the top applicants for SES positions using assessment tools comparable to those used in the private sector.

Employee engagement indicators continued to hold steady in the first survey after the lapse in appropriations, a testament to the resiliency of the workforce and vastly improved management communication practices. Almost all of the approximately 600,000 FEVS respondents reported willingness to put in extra effort to get the job done and seek ways to do their jobs better. However, fewer than 40 percent believe that pay raises depend on job performance, promotions are based on merit, and managers recognize differences in performance and take steps to address poor performers.

Regarding the latter concern of Federal workers, the President responded in May 2018 by issuing Executive Order 13839, "Promoting Accountability and Streamlining Removal Procedures Consistent with Merit System Principles." OPM will be issuing regulations to implement that Order this year. The President also instructed a new Interagency Labor Relations Working Group to address labor-management relations in the Executive Branch, and to recommend to him improvements in the organization, structure, and functioning of labor relations programs across agencies. In addition, OPM has developed a publicly available online database of collective bargaining agreements (CBAs) established between agencies and unions. Approximately 57 percent of the non-Postal Executive Branch workforce is covered by policies and procedures in CBAs. This work represents a significant step forward in making the arrangements under which Federal employees work transparent to the public they serve.

Preparing the Federal Workforce for the Future of Government

Emerging technologies are fundamentally changing both the nature of work and the delivery of Government services across the Nation. As a result, the Federal workforce must be positioned to meet the evolving needs of the citizens we serve and changing demands to promote improved mission outcomes and agency effectiveness. The 2021 Budget directs agencies to increase awards spending. Importantly, agencies have the flexibility to direct part of this spending toward strategic workforce development initiatives that close current or projected skills gaps in emerging areas such as data analytics, human centered design, and artificial intelligence. More broadly, the Administration intends to provide training opportunities for 400,000 Federal employees, in keeping with the Pledge to America's Workers sponsored by the President's National Council for the American Worker.

Developing Agile Operations and Reskilling

As agencies implement new technology and processes, the Administration will invest in reskilling its workforce to meet current needs. Certain transactional work is going away as fewer Federal forms are submitted in a paper format requiring manual processing. Employees responsible for processing paper forms can shift their attention to other responsibilities, including customer-facing roles. This shift is part of a broader trend in which existing employees will move from legacy positions to emerging fields where the Government faces staffing shortages, such as data analysis, cybersecurity, and other information technology disciplines. OPM is partnering with agencies to develop a Federal Robotic Process Automation (RPA) Reskilling Academy to train and mentor Federal employees whose jobs are being affected by RPA. These employees will learn how to conduct process mapping and develop and deploy "bots" without the need for extensive information technology training. The Administration is also putting

Table 5–4. PERSONNEL PAY AND BENEFITS

(In millions of dollars)

Description	2019 Actual	2020 Estimate	2021 Estimate	Change: 2020 to 2021	
				Dollars	Percent
Civilian Personnel Costs:					
Executive Branch (excluding Postal Service):					
Pay	204,045	212,087	216,857	4,770	2.2%
Benefits	89,217	93,281	95,959	2,678	2.9%
Subtotal	293,262	305,368	312,816	7,448	2.4%
Postal Service:					
Pay	38,874	39,662	39,873	211	0.5%
Benefits	15,724	15,383	15,590	207	1.3%
Subtotal	54,598	55,045	55,463	418	0.8%
Legislative Branch:					
Pay	2,295	2,464	2,670	206	8.4%
Benefits	769	831	931	100	12.0%
Subtotal	3,064	3,295	3,601	306	9.3%
Judicial Branch:					
Pay	3,368	3,538	3,676	138	3.9%
Benefits	1,129	1,186	1,213	27	2.3%
Subtotal	4,497	4,724	4,889	165	3.5%
Total, Civilian Personnel Costs	355,421	368,432	376,769	8,337	2.3%
Military Personnel Costs					
Department of Defense--Military Programs:					
Pay	103,608	107,349	111,364	4,015	3.7%
Benefits	48,645	51,489	58,053	6,564	12.7%
Subtotal	152,253	158,838	169,417	10,579	6.7%
All other Executive Branch uniform personnel:					
Pay	3,495	3,651	3,815	164	4.5%
Benefits	734	795	814	19	2.4%
Subtotal	4,229	4,446	4,629	183	4.1%
Total, Military Personnel Costs	156,482	163,284	174,046	10,762	6.6%
Grand total, personnel costs	**511,903**	**531,716**	**550,815**	**19,099**	**3.6%**
ADDENDUM					
Former Civilian Personnel:					
Pensions	90,457	93,571	96,957	3,386	3.6%
Health benefits	13,131	13,658	14,190	532	3.9%
Life insurance	42	43	44	1	2.3%
Subtotal	103,630	107,272	111,191	3,919	3.7%
Former Military Personnel:					
Pensions	63,166	65,412	67,227	1,815	2.8%
Health benefits	10,600	11,278	11,877	599	5.3%
Subtotal	73,766	76,690	79,104	2,414	3.1%
Total, Former Personnel	177,396	183,962	190,295	6,333	3.4%

this idea into practice. In 2021, the Administration will build on the success of efforts to grow the Federal cybersecurity workforce through reskilling. The 2021 Budget invests in training personnel with an aptitude for cybersecurity to fill these critically needed roles.

Transforming the Hiring Process

The Government must compete for talent in the labor markets. This effort requires effective hiring practices; however, the Federal hiring process is slow and awkward, typically requiring at least 14 steps. The process frustrates hiring managers and potential employees and causes agencies to lose qualified candidates, who frequently abandon their pursuit of a Federal job during the course of the lengthy process. During OMB-led strategic review meetings last year, a majority of agencies identified hiring top talent as one of the most significant risks to achieving their mission and goals.

While the Administration will focus on using the statutory flexibilities the Congress has already provided, it will also seek further statutory flexibilities to improve hiring and performance management. Reflecting both the needs of Government and preferred career paths of top talent, these new authorities would: (1) enable the temporary hire of highly qualified experts; (2) create an industry exchange similar to that which allows nonprofit employees and academics to serve temporarily on Government projects; (3) expand the limits of temporary and term hires; and (4) modernize qualification requirements.

Throughout the past 20 years, applicant assessment has been regularly identified as the weakest link in the Federal hiring process by the Merit Systems Protection Board, the Partnership for Public Service, and others. To address this noted weakness and to reinforce the use of effective assessments, OPM issued a memorandum in 2019, "Improving Federal Hiring through the Use of Effective Assessment Strategies to Advance Mission Outcomes." The memorandum provides guidance to enable simple and strategic hiring by: (1) analyzing and improving methods of assessing applicant quality; (2) involving subject matter experts in the assessment process; and (3) applying more rigor to determine minimum qualifications. The memo highlights a process that was successfully piloted by two agencies in 2019 and will be used by at least six agencies in 2020, including a multi-agency, Government-wide hiring effort. Rather than using self-assessment questionnaires, the pilots deployed subject matter experts to conduct structured interviews before determining an applicant qualified and applying preference. All 24 Chief Financial Officer (CFO) Act agencies have been briefed on the process, and additional guidance and templates will be issued in 2020 to support agency implementation Government-wide.

The Administration inherited an excessive background investigation inventory that led to challenges in quickly staffing critical mission areas, such as cybersecurity. Background investigations are necessary for onboarding the Federal workforce, including the granting of security clearances. The large volume of investigations slowed workforce onboarding by overwhelming existing resources and processes. Since reaching its peak of 725,000 in April 2018, the inventory has dropped substantially due to the Administration's efforts. The Security Executive Agent (Office of the Director of National Intelligence, ODNI) and the Suitability and Credentialing Executive Agent (OPM) chartered a new Trusted Workforce 2.0 (TW 2.0) initiative to modernize and transform the personnel vetting framework. Reforms under TW 2.0 dramatically reduced the inventory to under 250,000 cases in December 2019, which reflects a progress rate of 91 percent toward the Administration's goal of 200,000. The Administration achieved this success while simultaneously transferring OPM's background investigation function from OPM's National Background Investigations Bureau (NBIB) to DOD by establishing the Defense Counterintelligence and Security Agency (DCSA) within DOD. The DCSA creates economies of scale to perform investigations, simplifies leveraging of DOD's existing enterprise IT capabilities, and provides an opportunity to incorporate truly transformational reform. The Security Clearance, Suitability, and Credentialing Performance Accountability Council, which includes OMB, ODNI, OPM, and DOD, continues to provide overall accountability in pursuing personnel vetting reform across the Executive Branch.

6. PAYMENT INTEGRITY

The Administration has made protecting taxpayer money a top priority, which includes making sure the money is serving its intended purpose. This chapter describes proposals aimed at bolstering Federal payment integrity and public trust in Government by reducing improper payments that result in a monetary loss. The strategic vision of the Administration is to get payments right by taking appropriate actions at the front end to prevent improper payments from being made.

The proposals in this chapter are intended to significantly reduce Government-wide improper payments through increased data access, additional legal and regulatory authorities, increased use of analytic tools and shared solutions, improved pre-payment reviews, and simplification of eligibility determination requirements. If adopted, these proposals will improve the effectiveness of Federal programs while providing better stewardship of taxpayer resources.

Maintaining integrity of Federal programs is essential to sustaining public trust in Government. Accordingly, the Administration supports a number of legislative and administrative reforms to help prevent improper payments with priority given to the prevention of improper payments that result in a monetary loss. Specifically, the Budget includes concrete payment integrity proposals to save $182 billion over 10 years (see Table 6–1).

I. IMPROPER PAYMENT PREVENTION

The proposals detailed in this chapter include significant reforms to ensure that taxpayer dollars are spent correctly by expanding oversight and enforcement activities in the largest Federal benefit programs such as Child Nutrition, Earned Income Tax Credit (EITC), Federal Employees' Compensation Act (FECA), Medicaid, Medicare, Pell Grants, Social Security, Supplemental Nutrition Assistance Program (SNAP), and Unemployment Insurance (UI). These proposals seek to maximize savings to the Government, while also considering and balancing costs, risks, and program performance in establishing a tolerable level of improper payments.

In addition, the Administration will continue to identify areas where it can work with the Congress to further enhance efforts to detect, prevent, and recover improper payments, to include identifying ways to improve the Federal Government's capacity to validate individual and entity identities and to improve entitlement verification methods.

Monetary Loss Prevention

While Government and other reports about improper payments in Federal programs can erode citizens' trust in Government, not all reported improper payments result from fraud and some of the payments reported as improper do actually represent payments that should have been made. The term "improper payment" consists of two main components (1) improper payments resulting in a monetary loss to the Government and (2) improper payments that do not result in a monetary loss to the Government. Monetary loss occurs when payments are made to the wrong recipient and/or in the wrong amount. Improper payments that do not result in a monetary loss include underpayments and payments made to the right recipient for the right amount, but the payment was not made in strict accordance with statute or regulation.

Although working to reduce all improper payments is an important goal, the Administration has made the prevention of improper payments resulting in a monetary loss its highest priority. The Office of Management and Budget (OMB) released the Getting Payments Right[1] Cross Agency Priority (CAP) goal as part of the President's Management Agenda in March 2018. This CAP goal is focused on reducing monetary loss by making payments correctly the first time. Establishment of this CAP goal led to exceptional collaboration across the Federal Government by sharpening the focus of the Government efforts to prevent improper payments resulting in monetary loss. During 2019, this CAP goal improved the prevention of improper payments through five main strategies: (1) clarifying and streamlining requirements, (2) identifying true root causes of the monetary loss, (3) strategic data use for pre-payment eligibility validation, (4) scaling successful mitigation strategies, and (5) strengthening partnerships with States. Notable accomplishments include improving the transparency of payment integrity data on paymentaccuracy.gov, identifying 160 new data sets currently being used by Federal Programs for pre-check of payment eligibility, identification of root causes of monetary losses across 57 programs, and identification of eight mitigation strategies with the potential for broad impact across multiple programs.

---

[1] https://www.performance.gov/CAP/CAP_goal_9.html

II. PROPOSALS FOR GOVERNMENT-WIDE PAYMENT INTEGRITY IMPROVEMENT

Historically, and for a variety of reasons, the Federal Government addressed improper payments broadly, placing similar efforts toward addressing process errors that do not result in a payment to the wrong recipient or in the wrong amount as those payments that result in a monetary loss. Agencies responded to numerous improper payment requirements – often to comply with prescriptive laws and regulations or in response to audit reports and other questions about reported improper payments. In some cases, agencies spent more time complying with low-value activities than researching the underlying causes of improper payments and building the capacity to help prevent future improper payments. The Getting Payments Right CAP goal is geared toward improving payment integrity by preventing improper payments that result in monetary loss. Proposals that impact the prevention of improper payments across multiple agencies are a critical part of the 2021 Budget. Implementation of these proposals will significantly improve agency capacity to prevent improper payments and thus bolster the integrity of Federal programs.

Reducing improper payment reporting burden through changes to the Improper Payments Information Act of 2002 (IPIA), as amended.— Focusing on the prevention of monetary loss, using compliance criteria to drive desired behaviors and outcomes, and improving transparency and reporting will reduce improper payments and improve payment integrity in the Federal Government. The 2021 Budget proposes making explicit changes to existing improper payment laws intended to have agencies re-direct resources from complying with low-value activities to activities that will prevent improper payments resulting in monetary loss. Through the reinvestment of resources available as a result of the risk-based approach for burden reduction, agencies will strategically focus on implementing measures that directly address the prevention of improper payments resulting in monetary loss. Examples of changes that will improve burden reduction and allow agencies to redirect resources to improving prevention of improper payments resulting in monetary loss include:

- ***Target risk assessment resources for highest risk programs.*** Specifically, under the Improper Payments Elimination and Recovery Act of 2010 (IPERA) Section 2, reduce the burden for low risk programs by including a threshold for the periodic review of all programs and activities. Currently agencies expend too many resources assessing payments that have a minimal impact on enhancing payment integrity. Revising the threshold for improper payments review to any program or activity with an annual outlay over $100 million would reduce the number of risk assessments Government-wide by 60 percent and yet only reduce the dollar amount of payments assessed by one percent. This proposal is estimated to save $121 million over 10 years.

- ***Clarify the definition of improper payments.*** The Budget proposes isolating the items with documentation or procedural errors as control deficiencies and including a provision addressing program statutes that cause otherwise proper payment to be classified as improper. Agencies are currently required to place too much emphasis and effort on

reporting improper payments that do not result in a monetary loss, such as payments that simply lacked complete documentation but would have been made regardless of those errors. In addition, an improper payment should not include any overpayment that is the result of a statutory requirement to pay benefits or to continue to pay benefits by a specified period when all necessary information has not been received due to statutory barriers. This would give agencies the ability to wait to count a payment as proper or improper until after the statutory due process specified in the program has occurred. This proposal is estimated to save $978 million over 10 years.

- ***Streamline reporting requirements to reduce burden.*** Specifically, the Budget proposes changes to the IPERA Section 2 to change an annual November 1 report so that the information can be included in an Agency Annual Financial Report or Performance and Accountability Report (which is typically November 15) to eliminate the need for agencies to produce two separate reports. This proposal is estimated to save $14 million over 10 years.

- ***Remove reporting of aging and disposition of recaptured amounts.*** Under IPERA Section 2, the Budget proposes removing the requirement for agencies to report an aging schedule of the amount of identified improper payments outstanding and a summary of how the recovered amounts have been disposed of. Reporting this information is burdensome and does not drive the prevention of improper payments. This proposal is estimated to save $88 million over 10 years.

- ***Remove requirement to set recovery audit targets.*** Under IPERA Section 2, the Budget proposes removing the requirement for reporting targets for recovered amounts as the reported information does not drive the prevention of improper payments and is a burdensome requirement that is often outside of the immediate agency control. This proposal is estimated to save $5 million over 10 years.

- ***Allow reporting to adapt to needs of Government and the public.*** Under IPERA Section 2, allow for reporting of payment integrity information to adapt to the changing needs of the Government and public for reporting transparency by removing the specific mandate that the information must be reported in the annual financial statement. This allows agencies to eliminate duplicative reporting requirements and ensure that the information is reported in a manner that provides the most transparency and easy accessibility. This proposal is estimated to save $249 million over 10 years.

- ***Clarify compliance requirements for IPERA to improve improper payment prevention and reduction.*** Specifically, the Budget proposes to remove burdensome compliance criteria under IPERA Section 3 that do not drive the appropriate behavior for prevention of improper payments resulting in monetary loss such as the compliance criteria to; publish an annual financial statement, conduct a risk assessments , and reported an estimate below an arbitrary number of 10 percent. Under IPERA Section 3, we propose the criteria to set and meet a reduction target should be modified so that that the program will be considered compliant if it is demonstrating improvement. This moves the requirement away from an estimation exercise and toward driving for improved improper payment rates. This proposal is estimated to save $63 million over 10 years.

- *Reduce risk assessment burden by clarifying assessment method type.* Specifying under IPIA Section 2 clarifying that the risk factors are only for programs and activities performing a qualitative risk assessments. This is an important distinction as the programs and activities that perform a quantitative risk assessment will be developing an improper payment estimate to determine whether the program is susceptible to significant improper payments under statute (which is the main goal of the risk assessment). Requiring programs and activities to also consider and document the other numerous factors is burdensome and unnecessary. This proposal is estimated to save $53 million over 10 years.

- *Specify which programs should be assessed for compliance annually by the Office of Inspectors General (OIG) and the compliance review frequency.* The Budget proposes changing IPERA Section 3 to require OIGs to evaluate only programs and activities that are susceptible to significant improper payments by statute for compliance with the law. This will reduce burden for both OIGs and agencies. The rationale is that programs and activities below the statutory threshold for susceptibility to significant improper payments are not required to be reporting improper payments estimates, therefore finding a program non-compliant because they missed a reduction target when they are already below the acceptable threshold established under statute is counterproductive and creates extra burden for the OIG and the agency. This will ensure agencies and OIGs are focusing resources on the areas that have the highest risk to the Government. Additionally, under IPERA Section 3, the Budget proposes allowing the OIGs to evaluate for compliance on an every other fiscal year basis for programs that have been compliant with the law requirements for two consecutive years. This will allow resources to be directed to improving the compliance of non-compliant programs rather than spending resources to annually review programs that are at low risk for improper payments. This proposal is estimated to save $87 million over 10 years.

- *Increase interagency collaboration and reduce burden of duplicate working groups.* The Budget proposes replacing requirements for narrowly focused working groups such as that required in the Fraud Reduction and Data Analytics Act of 2015 with a requirement for an interagency payment integrity working group. This change allows for sharing and collaborating about payment integrity rather than narrowly focusing on fraud or other topics from a narrow perspective. This change will allow for statutorily required working groups to modify their focus and structure so that they are better equipped to strengthen overall payment integrity and take a more holistic view of improper payments and fraud. Creating narrowly defined working groups legislatively, while well intended, increases burden and prohibits agencies from taking a more risk based approach to the problem and adapting the strategy to address emerging areas needing attention. This proposal is estimated to save $19 million over 10 years.

- *Increase the threshold of significant improper payments.* Giving the Office of Management and Budget the authority to adjust the dollar threshold of "significant" every five years for inflation to ensure that the threshold remains relevant. This proposal is estimated to save $408 million over 10 years.

- *Reduce the burden of Recovery Audit Assessments.* Under IPERA Section 2, the Budget proposes to increase the recovery audit threshold from $1 million to $100 million or more if conducting the audits would be cost effective. This increase will reduce the amount of time and resources programs are currently spending on documenting that the recovery audits with programs below this threshold are not cost-effective. This proposal is estimated to save $25 million over 10 years.

- *Direct improper payment recoveries to prevention activities.* Under IPERA Section 2, the Budget proposes to strike the current disposition of recaptured funds allocation requirements and replace them with a requirement to use improper payment recoveries to specifically improve the prevention of improper payments resulting in monetary loss. It is most cost effective for the law to be structured so that agencies will prioritize the prevention of improper overpayments rather than providing incentives for recovering overpayments. This proposal is estimated to save $2 billion over 10 years.

- *Improve accountability and transparency for material programs.* To improve accountability and transparency in programs, the Budget proposes adding a requirement for managers of high-priority Federal programs to meet with the Director of the Office of Management and Budget at least once a year to discuss actions taken or planned to prevent improper payments within their programs.

Improve access to data for the Do Not Pay (DNP) Business Center.—Government-wide efforts to improve payment accuracy include increased access to data and better matching services to help detect, prevent, and recover improper payments. Agencies making Federal payments currently do not have the same capacity or access to information needed to prevent, identify, and recover improper payments due to the fragmented nature of Federal mission support functions. The Administration continues to pursue opportunities to reduce improper payments through improving information sharing among agencies and by developing or enhancing policy guidance, ensuring privacy protection, and developing legislative proposals to leverage available information and technology to help validate recipient identity and benefit eligibility. The Budget proposes legislation to enhance the Government's capacity to identify, detect, and prevent fraud and improper payments across all Federal programs and activities. Collectively the DNP proposals below will identify an estimated $21.06 billion of improper payments over 10 years. Examples of efforts that will improve data analytics for payment integrity improvement include:

- ***Provide the DNP Business Center the authority to include publicly available data sources for review.*** The Budget proposes providing the DNP initiative the authority under the Improper Payments Elimination and Recovery Improvement Act of 2012 (IPERIA) Section 5, to expedite designating publicly available data sources for the purposes of identifying, preventing, and reducing improper payments. This would shorten the timeframe between a request for designation and the acquisition of publicly available data sources and increase the identification and prevention of improper payments across

the initiative. This proposal is estimated to increase the improper payments identified by $35 million over 10 years.

- ***Eliminate constraints on the DNP Business Center to work with States on improper payments.*** This effort would allow the DNP Business Center to work with Federally funded State administered programs, State auditors, or other State entities that play a role in preventing and detecting improper payments in these programs. This proposal is estimated to increase the improper payments identified by $21 billion over 10 years.

- ***Allow the DNP Business Center full access to the Social Security Administration (SSA) full death file.*** This proposal would include the Department of the Treasury (Treasury) and the SSA working together to determine the most efficient manner to make full death information available for use in preventing improper payment and fraud. Outcomes of this work could range from obtaining authority for Treasury to serve as a central repository for such information to crafting the required legislative language to ensure the SSA can share its full file of death information—including State-reported death data—with Federal law enforcement agencies, and with Treasury's DNP Business Center. This proposal is estimated to increase the improper payments identified by $25.3 million over 10 years.

III. PROPOSALS FOR PROGRAM-SPECIFIC PAYMENT INTEGRITY IMPROVEMENT

In addition to including proposals that will reach across the Government-wide enterprise to tackle the improper payment problem, it is also critical to pursue program specific proposals aimed at preventing improper payments.

Department of Agriculture

The 2021 Budget demonstrates the Administration's commitment to reducing payment error and ensuring the Department of Agriculture's (USDA) nutrition assistance benefits go to the intended recipients. The Budget proposes increasing and improving verification of information reported on household applications for benefits, and strengthening use of technology to prevent improper payments in the SNAP and Child Nutrition Programs. Administrative application processing errors and errors in household reporting are the most common causes of improper payments in these programs. The proposals would result in more than $1.5 billion in savings over 10 years.

Supplemental Nutrition Assistance Program.—

- ***Improve income verification.*** The Budget is requesting an additional $380 million in administrative funding to implement a nationwide contract for electronic income verification in SNAP. This proposal builds upon the 2020 Budget request to evaluate and implement best practices related to electronic data matching through existing data sources, such as the Work Number. The Budget requests administrative funds to implement the contract at the Federal level in order to achieve standardized pricing and economies of scale, however the proposal overall is expected to reduce improper payments and lead to a reduction in mandatory outlays of $787 million, resulting in a net savings of $407 million over 10 years.

- ***Implement National Accuracy Clearinghouse nationwide.*** In order to prevent duplicate participation in SNAP, the Budget requests $23 million to implement an interstate data system known as the National Accuracy Clearinghouse (NAC). Building upon the success of the 5-State NAC pilot as well as the support included in the 2020 appropriations, this nationwide system would allow for real-time data matching of SNAP applicant and participant information in order to prevent the issuance of benefits in more than one State simultaneously. This proposal is estimated to have a net savings of $658 million over 10 years due to the anticipated reduction in improper payments associated with use of the Clearinghouse.

Child Nutrition Programs.—

- **Increase school meal verification to eight percent.** The Budget proposes increasing the number of household applications for free and reduced price meal benefits that schools participating in the National School Lunch and School Breakfast Programs must annually verify. Currently, the Richard B. Russell National School Lunch Act limits verification to a maximum of three percent of all applications or 3,000 "error prone" applications. This limit restricts the ability of USDA, States, and LEAs to identify and reduce payment error. This proposal would increase the verification limit to eight percent of applications with reduced requirements for high performing schools. This proposal saves $464 million over 10 years.

Department of Education

The 2021 Budget supports ongoing efforts and builds on recent legislative success to identify and prevent improper payments in the Pell Grant program. The President recently signed the Fostering Undergraduate Talent by Unlocking Resources for Education (FUTURE) Act, which will help ensure the accuracy of income information used for determining Pell Grant eligibility. One of the primary causes of improper payments in the Pell Grant program is failure to accurately verify financial data. The FUTURE Act provides an exception to the Department of Education from restrictions of Section 6103 of the Internal Revenue Code to allow the Department to more easily receive income tax data from the IRS, thereby simplifying and improving the accuracy of Free Application for Federal Student Aid filing by prepopulating certain fields. This exception will also allow borrowers to more easily recertify their income to stay enrolled in Income Driven Repayment plans. The FUTURE Act closely reflects the proposal to reduce improper payments put forth in the 2020 Budget.

The Department of Education will also continue to utilize sophisticated statistical techniques to more efficiently target student aid recipients for verification of eligibility for aid as well as target its program compliance reviews at schools with the greatest risks of improper payments. Pell Grant improper payments that result in monetary loss are most frequently the result of administrative errors by schools, including distribution of funds to ineligible students or in incorrect amounts based on a students' eligibility. In addition to the ongoing administrative actions Education is taking, the Budget proposes to:

- **Improve Pell fraud prevention.** The Budget proposes to bar someone from receiving another Pell Grant if they have been awarded three consecutive Pell Grants without earning any credits. This will prevent the fraudulent practice of people going from school to school, enrolling long enough to receive a

reimbursement but not pursuing any credits. This proposal would reduce discretionary program costs by $164 million and mandatory outlays by $38 million over 10 years.

Department of Health and Human Services

The Budget includes a robust package of Medicare, Medicaid, Children's Health Insurance Program (CHIP), and Child Care Development Fund payment integrity proposals to help prevent fraud and abuse before they occur; detect fraud and abuse as early as possible; provide greater flexibility to the Secretary of Health and Human Services to implement program integrity activities that allow for efficient use of resources and achieve high return on investment; and promote integrity in Federal-State financing. For example, the Budget includes several proposals aimed at strengthening the authorities and tools that the Centers for Medicare & Medicaid Services (CMS) has to ensure that the Medicare program only pays those providers and suppliers who are eligible and who furnish items and services that are medically necessary to the care of beneficiaries. The package of payment integrity proposals will help prevent inappropriate payments, eliminate wasteful Federal and State spending, protect beneficiaries, and reduce time-consuming and expensive "pay and chase" activities. Together, the CMS payment integrity legislative and administrative proposals would net approximately $48.6 billion in savings over 10 years. Finally, the Budget proposes to continue investments in Health Care Fraud and Abuse Control (HCFAC) program, which will provide CMS with the resources and tools to combat waste, fraud, and abuse and promote high-quality and efficient healthcare. Additional information can be found in the Budget Process chapter in this volume.

Medicare Fee for Service Program.—

- **Expand prior authorization to additional Medicare fee-for-service items at high risk of fraud, waste, and abuse.** The Budget proposes expanding the Medicare program's authority to conduct prior authorization on certain items or services that are prone to high improper payments, such as inpatient rehabilitation services. The proposal would reduce improper payments and save taxpayer dollars from paying for Medicare services that are not medically necessary by ensuring that the right payment goes to the right provider for the appropriate service. This proposal saves $13.7 billion over 10 years.

- **Prevent fraud by applying penalties on providers and suppliers who fail to update enrollment records.** The Budget proposes increasing CMS' authority to enforce appropriate reporting of changes in provider enrollment information through civil monetary penalties or other intermediate sanctions to mitigate the associated risk. This proposal will ensure CMS has the most up-to-date data as it continues to monitor for fraud and abuse. This proposal saves $32 million over 10 years.

- *Require reporting on clearinghouses and billing agents when Medicare providers and suppliers enroll in the program.* This proposal would provide CMS with the necessary organizational information to remove providers or suppliers from the Medicare program if clearinghouses and billing agents, acting on behalf of the provider or supplier, engage in abusive or potentially fraudulent billing practices.

- *Assess a penalty on physicians and practitioners who order services or supplies without proper documentation.* This proposal allows the Secretary to assess an administrative penalty on providers for claims that have not been properly documented for high risk and high cost items and services.

- *Address improper payments of chiropractic services through targeted medical review.* Under this administrative proposal, CMS will test whether prior authorization review is an effective tool at addressing improper payments in chiropractic services.

- *Address excessive billing for durable medical equipment (DME) that requires refills on serial claims.* Under this administrative proposal, CMS would test whether creating a DME benefits manager for serial claims, such as for non-emergency oxygen supplies, results in more appropriate utilization and lower improper payments. The benefits manager would be responsible for ensuring beneficiaries receive the correct quantity of supplies or services for the appropriate time period by contacting the ordering physician directly to obtain documentation.

Medicare Advantage Program (Medicare Part C) and Medicare Prescription Drugs Program (Medicare Part D).—

- *Implement targeted risk-adjustment pre-payment review in Medicare Advantage.* The Budget proposes requiring MA plans to submit medical record documentation to support the risk-adjustment diagnosis for plans, diagnoses, beneficiaries, or other indicators that pose an elevated risk of improper payments.

- *Require providers and suppliers to produce Part B records to support Part D investigations or audits.* The Budget proposes requiring Part B providers and suppliers to submit Part B records to CMS in support of a Part D investigation or audit. This proposal would provide CMS with additional patient information not available in Part B records, enhancing CMS' ability to investigate and determine abusive prescribing patterns.

- *Improve efficiency and strengthen program integrity efforts in Medicare Parts C and D.*

The Budget proposes removing the requirement that the Secretary enter into contracts with Parts C and D recovery audit contractors (RACs) and replace it with the flexibility to enter into contracts with RACs. The Secretary has never entered into a contract with a Part C RAC because the contingency payment arrangement is unfavorable to RACs, and the Part D RAC has had a low return on investment. The Budget also proposes to expand on Section 6063 of the SUPPORT Act to require the submission of data on incidents of fraud and abuse related to the inappropriate prescribing of prescription drugs and to give the Secretary discretion on the platform Part D plans would use to report potential fraudulent or abusive prescribing.

Medicaid and the Children's Health Insurance Program.—

- *Address Medicaid payments to States for ineligible beneficiaries and strengthen CMS's ability to recoup Medicaid improper payments.* Through both statutory and regulatory changes, the Budget proposes strengthening CMS's ability to partner with States to address improper payments and ensure Federal recovery of incorrect eligibility determinations, an area of concern identified by the HHS OIG. These proposals save $5.6 billion over 10 years.

- *Strengthen Medicaid eligibility process program integrity.* The Budget proposes to allow States flexibility to more frequently assess beneficiary eligibility, while clarifying data matching requirements to ensure taxpayer resources are not supporting ineligible beneficiaries. This administrative proposal saves $17.1 billion over 10 years.

- *Strengthen and clarify State provider screening, enrollment, and termination requirements.* Noncompliance with provider screening, enrollment, revalidation, and National Provider Identifier requirements are the largest drivers of Medicaid improper payments; however, there are no penalties for States that do not comply with current law. The Budget proposes to enact financial penalties for States not complying with current laws and regulations related to provider screening and enrollment. The Budget also proposes CMS conduct all eligibility screenings for Medicaid and CHIP providers, as it does for Medicare.

- *Improve processes for recovering Federal and State overpayments.* The Budget offers new flexibilities to help States recover Federal and State Medicaid overpayments and to target resources to activities that are most effective in returning funds to the taxpayer. States will have the option to partner with the Department of the Treasury to recover debts owed to Medicaid and CHIP. State participation in the Medicaid recovery audit contractor program will also be optional. This proposal saves $988 million over 10 years.

- **Implement pre-payment controls to prevent inappropriate personal care services (PCS) payments.** The Budget proposes to require States to implement claims edits to automatically deny unusual PCS payments such as duplicative services, services provided by unqualified providers, or services provided to those no longer eligible for Medicaid, as recommended by the HHS OIG. This proposal saves $11.1 billion over 10 years.

Medicare and Medicaid programs (crosscutting proposals).—

- **Expand the provisional period of enhanced oversight statutory authority for new providers and suppliers to further stem fraud, waste, and abuse.** The Budget proposes to give the Secretary more flexibility in using his oversight to ensure that bad actors are not able to abuse CMS programs. This would also permit the Secretary to target oversight actions on providers that may be more risky to the program, thus reducing the burden on providers and suppliers complying with Medicare and Medicaid policies.

- **Improve Open Payments Reporting and strengthen the Healthcare Fraud Prevention Partnership (HFPP).** The Budget includes several proposals to clarify the authority of the HFPP, require reporting of physician-owned distributorships in Open Payments Reporting, and to extend flexibility in the deadline for Open Payments Reporting. This will improve information available to address waste, fraud, and abuse in health programs.

- **Require annual certification of National Provider Identifier.** The Budget includes proposals to expand the Secretary's discretion for enhanced oversight of new providers and would require annual certification of the National Provider Identifier. The provisional period of enhanced oversight statutory authority for new providers and suppliers to further stem fraud, waste, and abuse. This will enable the Secretary to target resources on higher-risk providers.

Child Care Development Fund.—

- **Mandatory set-aside and incentive structure for monitoring and improper payments activities.** This proposal includes a set-aside for monitoring and improper payment activities, as well as incentives for states to recoup improper payments to be used for improving management and administration of the Child Care Development Fund program through error and fraud prevention, identification, and recovery.

Department of Labor

The 2021 Budget includes proposals aimed at improving integrity in the Department of Labor's UI program. The proposals would result in approximately $500 million in savings subject to the Pay-As-You-Go Act of 2010 (PAYGO) over 10 years, and would result in more than $1.9 billion in non-PAYGO savings. The PAYGO and non-PAYGO savings include a reduction in State unemployment taxes, which would reduce revenues for State accounts within the Unemployment Insurance Fund. The Department of Labor has also established an Agency Priority Goal to focus its implementation efforts, committing to decrease unemployment insurance improper payments to under 10 percent by September 30, 2021.

Unemployment Insurance Program.—

- **Expand State use of the Separation Information Data Exchange System.** This proposal improves program integrity by allowing States and employers to exchange information on reasons for a claimant's separation from employment and thereby helping States to determine UI eligibility.

- **Mandate the use of the National Directory of New Hires to conduct cross-matches for program integrity purposes.** This proposal would require State UI agencies to use the National Directory of New Hires to better identify individuals continuing to claim unemployment compensation after returning to work, which is one of the leading root causes of UI improper payments.

- **Allow the Secretary to set corrective action measures for poor State performance.** This proposal would allow the Secretary of Labor to require States to implement corrective action measures for poor State performance in the UI program, helping to reduce improper payments in States with the higher improper payment rates.

- **Require States to cross-match claimants against the Prisoner Update Processing System (PUPS).** Under current law, State UI agencies' use of this cross-match is permissible and the Social Security Administration's PUPS is currently only used by some States for UI verification. Requiring States to cross-match claims against the PUPS or other repositories of prisoner information will help identify those individuals ineligible for benefits due to incarceration and reduce improper payments.

- **Allow States to retain five percent of overpayment and tax investigation recoveries to fund program integrity activities.** This proposal would allow States to retain up to five percent of overpayment recoveries to fund additional program integrity activities in each State's UI program. This provides an incentive to States to increase detection and recovery of improper payments and provides necessary resources to carry out staff-intensive work to validate cross-match hits as required by law.

- **Require States to implement the UI integrity center of excellence's integrated data hub.** This proposal would require States to implement the Integrated Data Hub as a program integrity tool, allowing them to identify fraud schemes and conduct cross-matches that will help them reduce improper payments.

- **Implement Reemployment Services and Eligibility Assessments (RESEA) cap adjustment.** The Budget also includes $200 million in discretionary funding for RESEA, including $117 million in base funding and $83 million in program integrity cap adjustment funding, as authorized in the Balanced Budget and Emergency Deficit Control Act of 1985 (as amended by the Bipartisan Budget Act of 2018). Research, including a random-assignment evaluation, shows that a combination of eligibility reviews and reemployment services reduces the time on UI, increases earnings, and reduces improper payments to claimants who are not eligible for benefits. Additional detail about the cap adjustment can be found in the Budget Process chapter in this volume.

Federal Employees' Compensation Act program.—

- **Reform Federal Employees' Compensation Act (FECA).**—The Budget incorporates longstanding Government Accountability Office, Congressional Budget Office, and Labor OIG recommendations to improve and update the FECA. The reform package includes changes that generate cost savings by simplifying FECA benefit rates, introducing controls to prevent fraud and limit improper payments, and modernizing benefit administration. The provisions would prevent retroactive selection of FECA benefits after claimants have declined them in favor of Federal retirement benefits; apply a consistent waiting period for compensation for all covered employees; suspend payments to indicted medical providers; and make other changes to improve program integrity and reduce improper payments. This proposal saves an estimated $212 million over 10 years.

Department of the Treasury

The Department of the Treasury and the Internal Revenue Service (IRS) proposals will save an estimated $86 billion over 10 years by increasing IRS enforcement efforts, increasing the accuracy of tax returns filed by paid preparers, providing IRS additional authority to correct errors on a taxpayer's tax return, ensure that only those eligible for refundable tax credits receive them, improving wage and information reporting, and increasing the recovery of unclaimed assets and collection of non-tax debts.

Tax Administration.—

- **Increase oversight of paid tax return preparers.** This proposal would give the IRS the statutory authority to increase its oversight of paid tax return preparers. Paid tax return preparers have an important role in tax administration because they assist taxpayers in complying with their obligations under the tax laws. Increasing the quality of paid preparers lessens the need for after-the-fact enforcement of tax laws and increases the amount of revenue that the IRS can collect. This proposal saves $479 million over 10 years.

- **Provide more flexible authority for the Internal Revenue Service to address correctable errors.** The Budget proposes giving the IRS expanded authority to correct errors on taxpayer returns. Current law only allows the IRS to correct errors on returns in certain limited instances, such as basic math errors or the failure to include the appropriate Social Security Number or Taxpayer Identification Number. This proposal would expand the instances in which the IRS could correct a taxpayer's return. For example, with this new authority, the IRS could deny a tax credit that a taxpayer had claimed on a tax return if the taxpayer did not include the required paperwork, where Government databases showed that the taxpayer-provided information was incorrect, where the taxpayer had exceeded the lifetime limit for claiming a deduction or credit, or where the taxpayer had failed to include with the tax return documentation that was required to be included or attached to the return. This proposal saves $17 billion over 10 years.

- **Improve clarity in worker classification and information reporting requirements.** The Budget would require that Form 1099-K be filed by January 31 and would expand electronic wage reporting. Under current law, the Form 1099-K must be furnished to the recipient by January 31 and filed with IRS by March 31. The proposal would change the filing requirement to January 31. The IRS would also eliminate the regulations that allow for an automatic 30-day filing extension. This would allow IRS to receive information about some sources of self-employment income earlier in the filing season. This proposal costs $9 million over 10 years and includes an existing proposal to improve clarity in worker classification and information reporting requirements.

- **Implement tax enforcement program integrity cap adjustment.** The Budget proposes to establish and fund a new adjustment to the discretionary caps for program integrity activities related to IRS program integrity operations starting in 2020. The IRS base appropriation funds current tax administration activities, including all tax enforcement and compliance program activities, in the Enforcement and Operations Support accounts. The additional $400 million cap adjustment in 2021 funds new and continuing investments in expanding and improving the effectiveness and efficiency of the IRS's tax enforcement program. The activities are estimated to generate $79 billion in additional revenue over 10 years and cost approximately $15 billion resulting in an estimated net savings of $64 billion. Once the new enforcement staff are trained and become fully operational these initiatives are expected to generate roughly $5 in additional revenue for every $1 in IRS expenses. Notably, the return on investment is likely understated because it only includes amounts received; it does not reflect the effect enhanced enforcement has on deterring noncompliance. This indirect deterrence helps to ensure the continued payment of $3.6 trillion in taxes paid each year without direct enforcement measures. Additional detail about the cap adjustment can be found in the Budget Process chapter in this volume.

- ***Require a Social Security Number (SSN) that is valid for employment to claim the EITC.*** As part of a broader proposal, the Budget includes a proposal to require an SSN that is valid for employment in order to claim the EITC. While this is already current law for the EITC, the proposal fixes an administrative gap to strengthen enforcement of this provision. This proposal ensures that only individuals who are authorized to work in the United States are able to claim this credit. This proposal saves roughly $3 billion over 10 years.

- ***Increase and streamline recovery of unclaimed assets.*** This proposal would increase and streamline recovery of unclaimed assets owed to the United States by authorizing Treasury to locate and recover these assets and to retain a portion of amounts collected to pay for the costs of recovery. States and other entities hold assets in the name of the United States or in the name of departments, agencies, and other subdivisions of the Federal Government. Many agencies are not recovering these assets due to lack of expertise and funding. While unclaimed Federal assets are generally not considered to be delinquent debts, Treasury's debt collection operations personnel have the skills and training to recover these assets. This proposal saves $62 million over 10 years.

- ***Expand the Treasury Offset Program to increase debt collections.*** This proposal would allow the offset of Federal tax refund payments to collect State debts to encourage State participation in the State Reciprocal program (SRP) and increase Federal debt collections. Currently, under the SRP, States can collect their debts through the offset of Federal non-tax payments in exchange for Treasury to collect Federal non-tax debts through the offset of State payments. For States participating in the SRP, State payments subject to levy under this proposal could include State tax refunds, vendor payments, and payments to Medicaid service providers. This proposal has estimated recoveries between $960 million over 10 years.

Office of Personnel Management

The 2021 Budget demonstrates the Office of Personnel Management's (OPM) commitment to improving the identification and prevention of improper payments in the Federal Employees Health Benefits Program (FEHB). In particular, through increasing the resources devoted to investigating and preventing potential fraud committed against the FEHB program.

Federal Employees Health Benefits.—

- ***Provide additional investigative resources to the OIG for improper payment prevention.*** The Budget would allow the OIG to increase focusing on conducting comprehensive audits on activities where its actions most effectively reduce Government waste, fraud, and abuse. The Budget will allow the OPM OIG to improve its oversight of opioid-related fraud and improve its audit function of fraud against the FEHB. The OIG estimates that for every $1 in funding provided, it is able to recover $4 through its audits. The audit findings improve future controls which in turn prevent the fraud from occurring.

Social Security Administration

Overall, the Budget proposes legislation and administrative approaches that would avert close to $23.6 billion in improper payments in Social Security over 10 years. Much of this savings is considered off-budget and would be non-PAYGO, and includes administrative actions to reduce improper payments that would result in $11 billion in outlay savings over 10 years. The Budget proposes to continue investments in Social Security Administration (SSA) dedicated program integrity funding, as well as continuing an Agency Priority Goal to focus efforts on improving the Agency's Supplemental Security Income (SSI) payment accuracy rates. SSA uses this funding to conduct continuing disability reviews and SSI redeterminations to confirm that participants remain eligible to receive benefits. These funds also support anti-fraud cooperative disability investigation units and special attorneys for fraud prosecutions. Additional information can be found in the Budget Process chapter in this volume.

Old-Age, Survivors Disability Insurance (OASDI) and Supplemental Security Income.—

- ***Reduce improper payments caused by barriers for beneficiaries to report income and assets.*** The Budget proposes to reduce improper payments in disability programs by targeting administrative resources to the development of a uniform system of reporting in mySocialSecurity. This is in addition to instituting a holistic view that provides all beneficiaries' data, including income and assets, in one electronic location, while simultaneously developing a network of automated processes across other IT platforms for work-related benefit payment adjustments, work continuing disability reviews, redeterminations, and payments to Ticket to Work providers. In addition, future related legislative changes to address the root causes of these improper payments could include requiring suspension of benefits when beneficiaries neglect to report wages and resources, and instituting mandatory training for beneficiaries on reporting requirements prior to receipt of their first benefit checks. These administrative actions would result in $11 billion in outlay savings over 10 years.

- *Hold fraud facilitators liable for overpayments.* The Budget proposes holding fraud facilitators liable for overpayments by allowing SSA to recover the overpayment from a third party if the third party was responsible for making fraudulent statements or providing false evidence that allowed the beneficiary to receive payments that should not have been paid. This proposal results in an estimated $10 million in savings over 10 years.

- *Allow Government-wide use of Custom and Border Protection (CBP) Entry/Exit data to prevent improper payments.* The Budget proposes the use of CBP Entry/Exit data to prevent improper OASDI and SSI payments. Generally, U.S. citizens can receive benefits regardless of residence. Non-citizens may be subject to additional residence requirements depending on the country of residence and benefit type. However, an SSI beneficiary who is outside the United States for 30 consecutive days is not eligible for benefits for that month. These data have the potential to be useful across the Government to prevent improper payments. This proposal results in an estimated $29 million in savings over 10 years.

- *Increase the overpayment collection threshold for OASDI.* The Budget would change the minimum monthly withholding amount for recovery of Social Security benefit overpayments to reflect the increase in the average monthly benefit since SSA established the current minimum of $10 in 1960. By changing this amount from $10 to 10 percent of the monthly benefit payable, SSA would recover overpayments more quickly and better fulfill its stewardship obligations to the combined Social Security Trust Funds. The SSI program already utilizes the 10 percent rule. Debtors could still pay less if the negotiated amount would allow for repayment of the debt in 36 months. If the beneficiary cannot afford to have his or her full benefit payment withheld because he or she cannot meet ordinary and necessary living expenses, the beneficiary may request partial withholding. To determine a proper partial withholding amount, SSA negotiates (as well as re-negotiates at the overpaid beneficiary's request) a partial with-

holding rate. This proposal saves almost $1.7 billion over 10 years.

- *Authorize SSA to use all collection tools to recover funds in certain scenarios.* The Budget proposes allowing SSA a broader range of collection tools when someone improperly receives a benefit after the beneficiary has died. Currently, if a spouse cashes a benefit payment (or does not return a directly deposited benefit) for an individual who has died and the spouse is also not receiving benefits on that individual's record, SSA has more limited collection tools available than would be the case if the spouse also receives benefits on the deceased individual's earning record. The Budget proposal would end this disparate treatment of similar types of improper payments and results in an estimated $50 million in savings over 10 years.

- *Simplify administration of the SSI program.* The Budget proposes changes to simplify the SSI program by incentivizing support from recipients' family and friends, reducing SSA's administrative burden, and streamlining requirements for applicants. SSI benefits are reduced by the amount of food and shelter, or in-kind support and maintenance, a beneficiary receives. The policy is burdensome to administer and is a leading source of SSI improper payments. The Budget proposes to replace the complex calculation of in-kind support and maintenance with a flat rate reduction for adults living with other adults to capture economies of scale. The Budget also proposes to eliminate dedicated accounts for past due benefits and to eliminate the administratively burdensome consideration whether a couple is holding themselves out as married. This proposal costs $13 million over 10 years.

- *Improve collection of pension information from States and localities.* The Budget proposes a data collection approach designed to provide seed money to the States for them to develop systems that will enable them to report pension payment information to SSA. The proposal would improve reporting for non-covered pensions by including up to $70 million for administrative expenses, $50 million of which would be available to the States, to develop a mechanism so that SSA can enforce the current law offsets for the Windfall Elimination Provision and Government Pension Offset, which are a major source of improper payments. This proposal saves $10.5 billion over 10 years.

- *Provide additional debt collection authority for SSA civil monetary penalties (CMP) and assessments.* This proposal would assist SSA with ensuring the integrity of its programs and increase SSA recoveries by establishing statutory authority for the SSA to use the same debt collection tools available for recovery of delinquent overpayments toward recovery of delinquent CMP and assessments.

- **Exclude SSA debts from discharge in bankruptcy.** Debts due to an overpayment of Social Security benefits are generally dischargeable in bankruptcy. The Budget includes a proposal to exclude such

debts from discharge in bankruptcy, except when it would result in an undue hardship. This proposal would help ensure program integrity by increasing the amount of overpayments SSA recovers and would save $283 million over 10 years.

Table 6–1. PAYMENT INTEGRITY PROPOSALS

(Deficit increases (+) or decreases (–) in millions of dollars)

	2021	2022	2023	2024	2025	2026	2027	2028	2029	2030	10-year total
Government Wide:											
Target risk assessment resources for highest risk programs	–7	–8	–10	–11	–12	–13	–13	–15	–15	–17	–121
Clarify the definition of improper payments	–59	–68	–78	–88	–98	–103	–108	–117	–122	–137	–978
Streamline reporting requirements to reduce burden	–1	–1	–1	–1	–1	–1	–1	–2	–2	–2	–14
Remove reporting of aging and disposition of recaptured amounts	–5	–6	–7	–8	–9	–9	–10	–11	–11	–12	–88
Remove requirement to set recovery audit targets	–0	–0	–0	–0	–1	–1	–1	–1	–1	–1	–5
Allow reporting to adapt to needs of government and the public	–15	–17	–20	–22	–25	–26	–27	–30	–31	–35	–249
Clarify complliance requirements for IPERA to improve improper payment prevention and reduction	–4	–4	–5	–6	–6	–7	–7	–8	–8	–9	–63
Reduce risk assessment burden by clarifying assessment method type	–3	–4	–4	–5	–5	–6	–6	–6	–7	–7	–53
Specify which programs should be assessed for compliance annually by the OIG and the compliance review frequency	–5	–6	–7	–8	–9	–9	–10	–10	–11	–12	–87
Increase interagency collaboration and reduce burden of duplicate working groups	–1	–1	–1	–2	–2	–2	–2	–2	–2	–3	–19
Increase the threshold of significant improper payments	–24	–29	–33	–37	–41	–43	–45	–49	–51	–57	–408
Reduce the burden of Recovery Audit Assessments	–2	–2	–2	–2	–3	–3	–3	–3	–3	–4	–25
Direct Improper Payment Recoveries to Prevention Activities	–126	–147	–169	–190	–211	–221	–232	–253	–263	–295	–2,107
Improve accountability and transparency for material programs	....	....	....	....	....	....	....	....	....	....	....
Improve access to data for the DNP Business Center	....	....	....	....	....	....	....	....	....	....	....
Total, Government-Wide	–253	–295	–337	–379	–422	–443	–464	–506	–527	–590	–4,216
Agriculture:											
Supplemental Nutrition Assistance Program											
Improve income verification	38	–49	–49	–49	–49	–49	–49	–49	–49	–49	–407
Implement National Accuracy Clearinghouse nationwide	1	–20	–34	–53	–68	–90	–91	–98	–101	–103	–658
Child Nutrition Programs											
Increase school meal verification to 8%	0	0	–27	–57	–59	–61	–63	–64	–66	–68	–464
Total, Agriculture	39	–70	–110	–159	–177	–200	–203	–212	–217	–220	–1,529
Education:											
Pell Grants[1]											
Improve Pell fraud prevention	–2	–4	–4	–4	–4	–4	–4	–4	–4	–4	–38
Total, Education	–2	–4	–4	–4	–4	–4	–4	–4	–4	–4	–38
Health and Human Services:											
Medicare Fee for Service											
Expand prior authorization to additional Medicare fee-for-service items at high risk of fraud, waste, and abuse	–730	–870	–780	–790	–820	–1,650	–1,850	–1,960	–2,050	–2,160	–13,660
Prevent fraud by applying penalties on providers and suppliers who fail to update enrollment records	–2	–2	–3	–3	–3	–3	–4	–4	–4	–4	–32
Require reporting on clearinghouses and billing agents when Medicare providers and suppliers enroll in the program	....	....	....	....	....	....	....	....	....	....	....
Assess a penalty on physicians and practitioners who order services or supplies without proper documentation	....	....	....	....	....	....	....	....	....	....	....
Address improper payments of chiropractic services through targeted medical review	....	....	....	....	....	....	....	....	....	....	....
Address excessive billing for durable medical equipment that requires refills on serial claims	....	....	....	....	....	....	....	....	....	....	....
Medicare Parts C (Medicare Advantage) and D (Prescription Drugs)											
Implement targeted risk-adjustment pre-payment review in Medicare Advantage	....	....	....	....	....	....	....	....	....	....	....

Table 6–1. PAYMENT INTEGRITY PROPOSALS—Continued

(Deficit increases (+) or decreases (–) in millions of dollars)

	2021	2022	2023	2024	2025	2026	2027	2028	2029	2030	10-year total
Require providers and suppliers to produce Part B records to support Part D investigations or audits	....	....	....	....	....	....	....	....	....	....	....
Improve efficiency and strengthen program integrity efforts in Medicare Parts C and D	....	....	....	....	....	....	....	....	....	....	....
Medicaid and Children's Health Insurance Program											
Strengthen CMS's ability to recoup Medicaid improper payments	....	–470	–500	–530	–560	–590	–630	–670	–710	–750	–5,410
Address Medicaid payments to States for ineligible beneficiaries[2]	....	–20	–20	–20	–20	–20	–30	–30	–30	–30	–220
Strengthen Medicaid eligibility process program integrity[2]	–500	–1,000	–1,600	–1,700	–1,800	–1,900	–2,000	–2,100	–2,200	–2,300	–17,100
Strengthen and clarify State provider screening, enrollment, and termination requirements	....	....	....	....	....	....	....	....	....	....	....
Improve processes for recovering Federal and State overpayments	–75	–79	–85	–90	–95	–100	–106	–113	–119	–126	–988
Implement pre-payment controls to prevent inappropriate personal care services payments	–900	–940	–980	–1,030	–1,080	–1,130	–1,180	–1,240	–1,300	–1,360	–11,140
Medicare and Medicaid programs (crosscutting proposals)											
Expand the provisional period of enhanced oversight statutory authority for new providers and suppliers to further stem fraud, waste, and abuse	....	....	....	....	....	....	....	....	....	....	....
Improve Open Payments Reporting and strengthen the Healthcare Fraud Prevention Partnership	....	....	....	....	....	....	....	....	....	....	....
Require annual certification of National Provider Identifier	....	....	....	....	....	....	....	....	....	....	....
Child Care Development Fund											
Mandatory set-aside and incentive structure for monitoring and improper payments activities	....	....	....	....	....	....	....	....	....	....	....
Total, Health and Human Services	–2,207	–3,381	–3,968	–4,163	–4,378	–5,393	–5,800	–6,117	–6,413	–6,730	–48,550
Labor:											
Unemployment Insurance											
Improve UI program integrity	–111	–234	–268	–269	–277	–317	–277	–235	–310	–238	–2,536
Federal Employees' Compensation Act											
Reform the Federal Employees' Compensation Act	–31	–24	–28	–16	–17	–17	–19	–19	–21	–20	–212
Total, Labor	–142	–258	–296	–285	–294	–334	–296	–254	–331	–258	–2,748
Treasury:											
Tax administration											
Increase oversight of paid tax return preparers	–5	–23	–39	–43	–48	–53	–58	–63	–70	–77	–479
Provide more flexible authority for the Internal Revenue Service to address correctable errors	–1,048	–1,551	–1,599	–1,657	–1,709	–1,763	–1,830	–1,902	–1,979	–2,073	–17,111
Improve clarity in worker classification and information reporting requirements	29	37	10	–3	–8	–6	–4	–8	–10	–28	9
Implement tax enforcement program integrity cap adjustment	–264	–542	–3,106	–5,158	–7,356	–9,682	–12,005	–12,974	–13,813	–14,495	–79,395
Increase discretionary outlays from tax enforcement program integrity cap adjustment	353	757	1,110	1,459	1,810	1,948	1,971	1,983	1,992	2,002	15,385
Require a Social Security Number that is valid for work in order to claim the Earned Income Tax Credit	0	–324	–327	–322	–319	–327	–328	–329	–337	–338	–2,951
Other payment integrity proposals											
Increase and streamline recovery of unclaimed assets	–6	–6	–6	–6	–6	–6	–6	–6	–7	–7	–62
Expand the Treasury Offset Program to increase debt collections	–96	–96	–96	–96	–96	–96	–96	–96	–96	–96	–960
Total, Treasury	–1,390	–2,505	–5,163	–7,285	–9,542	–11,933	–14,327	–15,378	–16,312	–17,114	–100,949
Office of Personnel Management:											
Federal Employees' Health Benefits											
Provide additional investigative resources to the OIG for improper payment prevention	2	....	....	....	....	....	....	....	....	....	2
Total, Office of Personnel Management	2	....	....	....	....	....	....	....	....	....	2
Social Security Administration:											
Old -Age, Survivors Disability Insurance and Supplemental Security Income											

Table 6–1. PAYMENT INTEGRITY PROPOSALS—Continued
(Deficit increases (+) or decreases (–) in millions of dollars)

	2021	2022	2023	2024	2025	2026	2027	2028	2029	2030	10-year total
Reduce improper payments caused by barriers for beneficiaries to report income and assets [2]	....	–500	–800	–1,100	–1,100	–1,500	–1,500	–1,500	–1,500	–1,500	–11,000
Hold fraud facilitators liable for overpayments	....	....	....	–2	–2	....	....	–1	–2	–3	–10
Allow Government-wide use of custom and Border Protection entry/exit data to prevent improper payments	....	....	–1	–2	–3	–3	–4	–5	–5	–6	–29
Increase overpayment collection threshold for Old Age, Survivors, and Disability Insurance	–13	–84	–109	–120	–148	–175	–198	–259	–277	–275	–1,658
Authorize Social Security Administration to use all collection tools to recover funds in certain scenarios	....	–2	–3	–4	–6	–6	–6	–7	–7	–9	–50
Simplify administration of the Supplemental Security Income program	....	–335	–20	4	25	40	54	74	76	95	13
Improve collection of pension information from States and localities	18	28	24	–521	–1,246	–1,843	–1,910	–1,811	–1,702	–1,572	–10,535
Provide additional debt collection authority for SSA civil monetary penalties and assessments	....	....	....	....	....	....	....	....	....	....	....
Exclude Social Security Administration debts from discharge in bankruptcy	–4	–13	–20	–26	–30	–34	–36	–38	–40	–42	–283
Total, Social Security	1	–906	–929	–1,771	–2,510	–3,521	–3,600	–3,547	–3,457	–3,312	–23,552
Total, Payment Integrity	**–3,952**	**–7,419**	**–10,808**	**–14,046**	**–17,326**	**–21,828**	**–24,694**	**–26,018**	**–27,261**	**–28,229**	**–181,580**

[1] In addition to the mandatory savings shown here, the Pell Grant payment integrity proposals also reduce discretionary program costs. Over 10 years, Improve Pell fraud prevention reduces these costs by $164 million (discretionary estimates from the 2021 Budget).

[2] Represents baseline outlay savings resulting from administrative actions to reduce improper payments.

7. FEDERAL REAL PROPERTY

The Federal Government owns and leases an extensive portfolio of real property to support execution of the Federal missions, and it is critical that Federal Agencies effectively manage those assets. The updated real property agenda expands the Government's focus to-date on managing the real property portfolio to include obtaining key data on assets to ensure that the right investment and divestment decisions are made. Aligned with the President's Management Agenda, this real property agenda provides a roadmap for agencies to strengthen stewardship, improve service to the taxpayer, and leverage real property. To achieve these objectives, agencies will increase focus on creating standard business processes and data definitions in the real property arena, identifying opportunities to share common business application tools, and improving the overall management of the portfolio.

The Federal portfolio of real property assets is diverse, has an average age of more than 47 years, and as with any portfolio, requires significant upkeep. Agencies invest billions of dollars in the operation, repair and alteration of existing assets and construction of new assets necessary to meet Federal mission requirements. It is important to reinvest in the Federal portfolio at the appropriate level. Deferring necessary maintenance and repair can result in higher outyear costs. Deteriorated condition or the failure of Federal real property can affect the efficiency of agencies' capability to deliver their missions and could potentially inhibit economic growth and lead to divestiture. The Administration's initiatives will ensure that agencies have the information necessary to make the right decisions to maintain their assets and have the right type and amount of assets in place to ensure mission capability, manage costs, and serve taxpayers.

Overview of the Federal Inventory

The Federal inventory of buildings contains a wide range of assets—office buildings, warehouses, hospitals, service buildings, and land ports of entry, among several other building types required to implement agencies' missions. The Department of Defense manages the largest domestic building portfolio, followed by the Department of Veterans Affairs and the Department of Energy. The General Service Administration (GSA) manages approximately 50 percent of the office space in the portfolio, providing office space for most Federal Agencies.

The largest building type—office space—comprises 21 percent of the total square footage of the building space. Of the total office inventory, leased office space comprises 36 percent (on a square foot basis) of all office space and is 67 percent of total reported office building expenditures. By continuing to emphasize capital planning, improving

data quality, and implementing legislative reforms, the Federal Government could better optimize leased and owned building space to improve mission support and reduce costs, as discussed later in this chapter.

The Government's real property inventory also includes structures, the most numerous of which are utility systems, roads and bridges, navigation and traffic aids, miscellaneous military structures, and parking structures. Divestiture, through sale or demolition where operationally feasible, is often the most appropriate method to control the cost of the structure portfolio.

Fifteen Years of Progress and Improvement

Over the last 15 years, the Federal Government has made significant strides in identifying the full range of real property within the Federal inventory, improving the asset management planning process, measuring performance of the assets, leveraging assets to reduce the Federal footprint, and disposing of assets that no longer meet the Federal need.

In February 2004, Executive Order 13327, "Federal Real Property Asset Management," tasked agencies with creating the first, detailed Government-wide inventory of buildings and structures under Federal control. Prior to that, the best estimation of the number and value of Federal assets was garnered from Government-wide financial audit property, plant, and equipment reporting. Much of the high-value, easy-to-dispose real property assets have largely left the Federal inventory. During the 2004-2009 timeframe, the Office of Management and Budget (OMB) utilized a Management Agenda "scorecard" methodology to measure agency success in achieving the Administration's management agenda. In the area of real property, OMB expected agencies to achieve milestones that included the use of data and achievement of disposal targets. Between 2004 and 2009, agencies completed the first inventory of assets, established agency-specific asset management plans, and disposed of thousands of assets with an aggregate replacement value of more than $5 billion. The vast majority of these disposals were demolitions of assets on Federal campuses for which there was no marketable return, so the main benefit was reduced operating costs.

From 2013-2015, agencies disposed of 24.7 million square feet under the "Freeze the Footprint" policy. This averages to approximately 8.3 million square feet annually, with an estimated gross cost avoidance of about $100 million per year. The "Reduce the Footprint" (RTF) policy, in effect since 2015, resulted in the disposal of an additional 16.3 million square feet from 2016 through 2018. Executing identified disposals is largely predicated on availability of discretionary agency funds necessary to complete remediation, relocation, and disposition, and enactment of necessary statutory fixes to aid in the disposal of unneeded assets. To aid in achieving these ongoing goals, the Administration proposes legislative fixes to streamline the disposal of unneeded assets. For example, current statutory prohibitions on the disposal of certain pieces of property mean that the Government must continue to pay to maintain assets it no longer needs. In other instances, the Government wishes to dispose of property, but local stakeholders have impeded disposal for years.

In the early years of these more aggressive real property efforts, agencies were successful in disposing of the "low-hanging fruit": those assets without high-cost environmental contamination requiring remediation, those without stakeholder interests prohibiting disposition, and those empty facilities with private sector marketability. High value disposals, such as San Francisco's Presidio via transfer, were completed early in the effort to improve focus on real property. However, GSA, the Government's disposal agent by statute, generated an average of only $53 million in annual gross proceeds through public and negotiated sales of both GSA's and other agencies' property during 2009—2013. To increase annual sales proceeds, the Government would need to identify and sell larger, difficult-to-market, and politically contentious properties.

In recent years, agencies have expanded their focus on managing their entire portfolios strategically to gain efficiencies and improve mission performance. Agencies have established agency-specific design standards for space utilization, set explicit targets to reduce the amount of unneeded real property that agencies retain, and developed and implemented new analytical tools.

Administration Initiatives to Optimize the Portfolio to Achieve the Mission and Manage Costs

The Administration's multi-pronged approach continues to build on the historic progress made over the last 15 years to improve the management of Federal real property, while also recognizing that new, transformative authorities and reform initiatives are necessary to achieve the next level of accomplishments and achieve an optimized portfolio. The Administration is taking necessary administrative action, as well as proposing legislation, to enable the optimization of the Federal real property portfolio. Under this leadership, agencies are making smart decisions to reduce their square footage and consolidate into federally owned space, such as the Immigration and Customs Enforcement consolidation into the Varick Federal Building proposed in the 2021 Budget, resulting in $13 million in reduced lease payments to the private sector and $7 million in annual agency rent savings. The ongoing administrative initiatives and legislative proposals reflected in the 2021 Budget include:

Federal Real Property Council. OMB issued Memorandum M–18-21, "Designation and Responsibilities of Agency Senior Real Property Officers," in July 2018 to reconstitute the Federal Real Property Council (FRPC), comprised of agency Senior Real Property Officers and empowered to provide comprehensive program governance Government-wide.

The FRPC's objective is to provide the Administration with recommendations on the strategic direction over the Government-wide approach to optimizing the real property portfolio to support mission success, manage costs, and help Federal managers provide the best value for the Government and taxpayer. The FRPC is also working to implement the requirements of recently enacted legislation, including the Federal Assets Sale and Transfer Act (P.L. 114–287) and the Federal Real Property Management and Reform Act (P.L. 114–318).

Issuance of OMB Capital Planning Policy. In November 2019, OMB, in coordination with the FRPC, issued Memorandum M-20-3, Implementation of Agency-wide Real Property Capital Planning, to ensure that agencies consistently implement sound capital planning practices to optimize the portfolio to achieve the mission cost-efficiently. The Memorandum also provides detailed guidance to assist agencies in implementing the Capital Programming Guide in OMB Circular A-11. The capital planning requirement provides a standard that agencies will use for establishing a consistent, repeatable methodology for allocating financial resources to optimize the portfolio and to achieve mission cost-efficiently. The desired outcome of the Memorandum is to elevate visibility and improve planning for real property so capital plans will be based on clearly articulated requirements and objective analysis of life-cycle options, including disposition of unneeded assets, so that the Federal Government has the right type of property, in the right amount, at the right location, at the right cost, and in the right condition to support the diverse mission requirements of the agencies.

Revisions to OMB Circular A-45 Rental and Construction of Government Housing. On November 25, 2019, OMB released OMB Circular A-45, Rental and Construction of Government Housing, which outlines Government-wide policy for civilian Federal employee housing. This was the first update to the Circular since 1993. The two primary objectives of the revision are moving the program toward financial sustainability and ensuring the right housing is built as the demographic composition of the Federal workforce changes. These changes will ensure the housing stock effectively and cost efficiently houses Federal employees.

Revised National Strategy for Real Property. OMB issued the National Strategy for the Efficient Use of Real Property in 2015 to build upon OMB's Freeze the Footprint policy's success in reducing agency portfolios and reducing costs. The RTF policy, focused solely on office and warehouse facilities, reduced the baseline by 16.3 million square feet from 2016 through 2018. In line with the President's Management Agenda, the FRPC provided OMB with recommendations to revise the National Strategy to emphasize the application of a consistent Government-wide real property capital planning process, creating standard business processes and data definitions in line with the Administration's Cross-Agency Priority Goal on Sharing Quality Services and improved transparency, and addressing other issues identified in audit reports. OMB expects to issue a revised Strategy early in calendar year 2020.

Federal Capital Revolving Fund. The Administration's proposal to establish a Federal Capital Revolving Fund is a new and innovative way to budget for the largest civilian real property capital construction projects, valued at more than $250 million. The Budget includes $10 billion in mandatory resources to seed the Fund to execute these vital efforts. This Fund will provide the necessary upfront amounts to execute projects and then require agencies to repay those funds over 15 years, similar to how State capital budgeting occurs, while conforming to a Federal cash budget environment. Without enactment of the Fund, agencies will continue to turn to more costly solutions to meet some of these large requirements, including operating leases, to avoid the upfront cost requirement associated with Federal construction. Further, since projects executed via the new Fund would be paid through annual operations over a 15-year period, Federal decision-makers are incentivized to fund only those projects with the highest return on investment and mission priority to protect taxpayers. Providing budget resources through the Fund will enable agencies to prioritize real property actions that result in lower long-term costs for taxpayers. The 2021 Budget again proposes using $288 million from the new fund for the renovation and expansion of a key National Institute of Science and Technology facility in Boulder, Colorado, as the priority project. The Administration transmitted to the Congress in June 2018 a legislative proposal to establish the Fund and looks forward to working with the Congress to enact this implementing legislation.

Disposing Government Property Directly to the Market. The current process for disposing of unneeded Federal real property is long, convoluted, and results in diminished returns to taxpayers. Title 40 of the U.S. Code requires agencies to screen property disposals for at least 12 discrete public benefit conveyance requirements prior to taking assets to market for sale. The average disposal timeframe is more than 12 months, unnecessarily long and at a time where the Government continues to carry the operating costs. Additionally, certain nonprofit institutions and State and local government can obtain Federal property at no cost or at a substantial discount if they use the property for various types of public uses. Such transfers divert Federal taxpayer funds from deficit reduction and services provided to citizens. The Administration supports streamlining the disposal process by eliminating all of the public benefit conveyances and taking all excess Federal real property directly to sale, thereby maximizing the return to taxpayers. The Administration is supporting two disposal-related efforts as part of the 2021 Budget.

- The Administration supports expanding existing an authority to allow GSA to assist other Federal Agencies in preparing unneeded properties for disposition. The Administration will transmit a legislative proposal to expand the allowable uses of GSA's Disposal Fund to support Executive Agencies in the disposal of unneeded Federal real property. This expansion would further streamline and accelerate the disposal process, allowing GSA to be reimbursed from the sale proceeds rather than requiring agencies to dedicate appropriated budgetary resources up front.

- The Administration also supports the efforts of the newly-established Public Buildings Reform Board (Board), whose members were sworn-in in May 2019. The Board, established under the Federal Assets Sales and Transfer Act of 2016 (P.L. 114–287), is working to identify, and propose to OMB, Federal assets suitable for disposition and consolidation. The law allows for three rounds of disposition actions. The first round of dispositions that identified high-value assets was approved by OMB recently and will seed activities for future disposal actions. The Board has identified several unique opportunities to dispose of Federal assets for future private use, where the proceeds from the disposition will assist the Government in disposing of and consolidating additional real property for which funds were previously unavailable or insufficient. For example, the disposal of GSA's Auburn Federal Complex has been delayed because of a lack of funding to relocate the current Federal tenants. Disposition of other properties under this initiative, together with an appropriation of the proceeds, would allow for the execution of likely several future consolidation and disposition actions such as this example.

Conclusion

The Administration continues to pursue opportunities to optimize the Federal portfolio of real property by disposing of unneeded assets, investing in mission-critical assets, bringing the delivery of the Federal mission closer to the populations serviced, and proposing necessary legislative action to support the real property agenda. The efforts of the Administration are positioning agencies to make informed decisions on their portfolios, executing missions, and serving taxpayers.

For more details on the agency real property inventory see the following website: https://www.gsa.gov/cdnstatic/FY_2016_Open_Data_Set.xlsx.

BUDGET CONCEPTS AND BUDGET PROCESS

8. BUDGET CONCEPTS

The budget system of the United States Government provides the means for the President and the Congress to decide how much money to spend, what to spend it on, and how to raise the money they have decided to spend. Through the budget system, they determine the allocation of resources among the agencies of the Federal Government and between the Federal Government and the private sector. The budget system focuses primarily on dollars, but it also allocates other resources, such as Federal employment. The decisions made in the budget process affect the Nation as a whole, State and local governments, and individual Americans. Many budget decisions have worldwide significance. The Congress and the President enact budget decisions into law. The budget system ensures that these laws are carried out.

This chapter provides an overview of the budget system and explains some of the more important budget concepts. It includes summary dollar amounts to illustrate major concepts. Other chapters of the budget documents discuss these concepts and more detailed amounts in greater depth.

The following section discusses the budget process, covering formulation of the President's Budget, action by the Congress, budget enforcement, and execution of enacted budget laws. The next section provides information on budget coverage, including a discussion of on-budget and off-budget amounts, functional classification, presentation of budget data, types of funds, and full-cost budgeting. Subsequent sections discuss the concepts of receipts and collections, budget authority, and outlays. These sections are followed by discussions of Federal credit; surpluses, deficits, and means of financing; Federal employment; and the basis for the budget figures. A glossary of budget terms appears at the end of the chapter.

Various laws, enacted to carry out requirements of the Constitution, govern the budget system. The chapter refers to the principal ones by title throughout the text and gives complete citations in the section just preceding the glossary.

THE BUDGET PROCESS

The budget process has three main phases, each of which is related to the others:

1. Formulation of the President's Budget;

2. Action by the Congress; and

3. Execution of enacted budget laws.

Formulation of the President's Budget

The Budget of the United States Government consists of several volumes that set forth the President's fiscal policy goals and priorities for the allocation of resources by the Government. The primary focus of the Budget is on the budget year—the next fiscal year for which the Congress needs to make appropriations, in this case 2021. (Fiscal year 2021 will begin on October 1, 2020, and end on September 30, 2021.) The Budget also covers the nine years following the budget year in order to reflect the effect of budget decisions over the longer term. It includes the funding levels provided for the current year, in this case 2020, which allows the reader to compare the President's Budget proposals with the most recently enacted levels. The Budget also includes data on the most recently completed fiscal year, in this case 2019, so that the reader can compare budget estimates to actual accounting data.

In a normal year, the President begins the process of formulating the budget by establishing general budget and fiscal policy guidelines, usually by late spring of each year. Based on these guidelines, the Office of Management and Budget (OMB) works with the Federal agencies to establish specific policy directions and planning levels to guide the preparation of their budget requests.

During the formulation of the budget, the President, the Director of OMB, and other officials in the Executive Office of the President continually exchange information, proposals, and evaluations bearing on policy decisions with the Secretaries of the Departments and the heads of the other Government agencies. Decisions reflected in previously enacted budgets, including the one for the fiscal year in progress, reactions to the last proposed budget (which the Congress is considering at the same time the process of preparing the forthcoming budget begins), and evaluations of program performance all influence decisions concerning the forthcoming budget, as do projections of the economic outlook, prepared jointly by the Council of Economic Advisers, OMB, and the Department of the Treasury.

In early fall, agencies submit their budget requests to OMB, where analysts review them and identify issues that OMB officials need to discuss with the agencies. OMB and the agencies resolve many issues themselves. Others require the involvement of White House policy officials and the President. This decision-making process is usually completed by late December. At that time, the final stage of developing detailed budget data and the preparation of the budget documents begins.

The decision-makers must consider the effects of economic and technical assumptions on the budget estimates. Interest rates, economic growth, the rate of inflation, the unemployment rate, and the number of people eligible for various benefit programs, among other factors, affect Government spending and receipts. Small changes in these assumptions can alter budget estimates by many billions of dollars. (Chapter 2, "Economic Assumptions and Overview," provides more information on this subject.)

Thus, the budget formulation process involves the simultaneous consideration of the resource needs of individual programs, the allocation of resources among the agencies and functions of the Federal Government, and the total outlays and receipts that are appropriate in light of current and prospective economic conditions.

The law governing the President's Budget requires its transmittal to the Congress on or after the first Monday in January but not later than the first Monday in February of each year for the following fiscal year. The budget is usually scheduled for transmission to the Congress on the first Monday in February, giving the Congress eight months to act on the budget before the fiscal year begins. In years when a Presidential transition has taken place, this timeline for budget release is commonly extended to allow the new administration sufficient time to take office and formulate its budget policy. While there is no specific timeline set for this circumstance, the detailed budget is usually completed and released in April or May. However, in order to aid the congressional budget process (discussed below), new administrations often release a budget blueprint that contains broad spending outlines and descriptions of major policies and priorities in February or March.

Congressional Action[1]

The Congress considers the President's Budget proposals and approves, modifies, or disapproves them. It can change funding levels, eliminate programs, or add programs not requested by the President. It can add or eliminate taxes and other sources of receipts or make other changes that affect the amount of receipts collected.

The Congress does not enact a budget as such. Through the process of adopting a planning document called a budget resolution, the Congress agrees on targets for total spending and receipts, the size of the deficit or surplus, and the debt limit. The budget resolution provides the framework within which individual congressional committees prepare appropriations bills and other spending and receipts legislation. The Congress provides funding for specified purposes in appropriations acts each year. It also enacts changes each year in other laws that affect spending and receipts.

In making appropriations, the Congress does not vote on the level of outlays (spending) directly, but rather on budget authority, or funding, which is the authority provided by law to incur financial obligations that will result in outlays. In a separate process, prior to making appropriations, the Congress usually enacts legislation that authorizes an agency to carry out particular programs, authorizes the appropriation of funds to carry out those programs, and, in some cases, limits the amount that can be appropriated for the programs. Some authorizing legislation expires after one year, some expires after a specified number of years, and some is permanent. The Congress may enact appropriations for a program even though there is no specific authorization for it or its authorization has expired.

The Congress begins its work on its budget resolution shortly after it receives the President's Budget. Under the procedures established by the Congressional Budget Act of 1974, the Congress decides on budget targets before commencing action on individual appropriations. The Act requires each standing committee of the House and Senate to recommend budget levels and report legislative plans concerning matters within the committee's jurisdiction to the Budget Committee in each body. The House and Senate Budget Committees then each design and report, and each body then considers, a concurrent resolution on the budget. The congressional timetable calls for the House and Senate to resolve differences between their respective versions of the congressional budget resolution and adopt a single budget resolution by April 15 of each year.

In the report on the budget resolution, the Budget Committees allocate the total on-budget budget authority and outlays set forth in the resolution to the Appropriations Committees and the other committees that have jurisdiction over spending. These committee allocations are commonly known as "302(a)" allocations, in reference to the section of the Congressional Budget Act that provides for them. The Appropriations Committees are then required to divide their 302(a) allocations of budget authority and outlays among their subcommittees. These subcommittee allocations are known as "302(b)" allocations. There are procedural hurdles associated with considering appropriations bills that would breach or further breach an Appropriations subcommittee's 302(b) allocation. Similar procedural hurdles exist for considering legislation that would cause the 302(a) allocation for any committee to be breached or further breached. The Budget Committees' reports may discuss assumptions about the level of funding for major programs. While these assumptions do not bind the other committees and subcommittees, they may influence their decisions.

Budget resolutions may include "reserve funds," which permit adjustment of the resolution allocations as necessary to accommodate legislation addressing specific matters, such as healthcare or tax reform. Reserve funds are most often limited to legislation that is deficit neutral, including increases in some areas offset by decreases in others. The budget resolution may also contain "reconciliation directives" (discussed further below).

Since the concurrent resolution on the budget is not a law, it does not require the President's approval. However, the Congress considers the President's views in prepar-

---

[1]   For a fuller discussion of the congressional budget process, see Bill Heniff Jr., *Introduction to the Federal Budget Process* (Congressional Research Service Report 98–721), and Robert Keith and Allen Schick, *Manual on the Federal Budget Process* (Congressional Research Service Report 98–720, archived).

ing budget resolutions, because legislation developed to meet congressional budget allocations does require the President's approval. In some years, the President and the joint leadership of Congress have formally agreed on plans to reduce the deficit or balance the budget. These agreements were then reflected in the budget resolution and legislation passed for those years.

If the Congress does not pass a budget resolution, the House and Senate typically adopt one or more "deeming resolutions" in the form of a simple resolution or as a provision of a larger bill. A deeming resolution may serve nearly all functions of a budget resolution, except it may not trigger reconciliation procedures in the Senate.

Once the Congress approves the budget resolution, it turns its attention to enacting appropriations bills and authorizing legislation. The Appropriations Committee in each body has jurisdiction over annual appropriations. These committees are divided into subcommittees that hold hearings and review detailed budget justification materials prepared by the Executive Branch agencies within the subcommittee's jurisdiction. After a bill has been drafted by a subcommittee, the full committee and the whole House, in turn, must approve the bill, sometimes with amendments to the original version. The House then forwards the bill to the Senate, where a similar review follows. If the Senate disagrees with the House on particular matters in the bill, which is often the case, the two bodies form a conference committee (consisting of some Members of each body) to resolve the differences. The conference committee revises the bill and returns it to both bodies for approval. When the revised bill is agreed to, first in the House and then in the Senate, the Congress sends it to the President for approval or veto.

Since 1977, when the start of the fiscal year was established as October 1, there have been only three fiscal years (1989, 1995, and 1997) for which the Congress agreed to and enacted every regular appropriations bill by that date. When one or more appropriations bills has not been agreed to by this date, the Congress usually enacts a joint resolution called a "continuing resolution" (CR), which is an interim or stop-gap appropriations bill that provides

authority for the affected agencies to continue operations at some specified level until a specific date or until the regular appropriations are enacted. Occasionally, a CR has funded a portion or all of the Government for the entire year.

The Congress must present these CRs to the President for approval or veto. In some cases, Congresses have failed to pass a CR or Presidents have rejected CRs because they contained unacceptable provisions. Left without funds, Government agencies were required by law to shut down operations—with exceptions for some limited activities—until the Congress passed a CR the President would approve. Shutdowns have lasted for periods of a day to several weeks.

The Congress also provides budget authority in laws other than appropriations acts. In fact, while annual appropriations acts fund the majority of Federal programs, they account for only about a third of the total spending in a typical year. Authorizing legislation controls the rest of the spending, which is commonly called "mandatory spending." A distinctive feature of these authorizing laws is that they provide agencies with the authority or requirement to spend money without first requiring the Appropriations Committees to enact funding. This category of spending includes interest the Government pays on the public debt and the spending of several major programs, such as Social Security, Medicare, Medicaid, unemployment insurance, and Federal employee retirement. Almost all taxes and most other receipts also result from authorizing laws. Article I, Section 7, of the Constitution provides that all bills for raising revenue shall originate in the House of Representatives. In the House, the Ways and Means Committee initiates tax bills; in the Senate, the Finance Committee has jurisdiction over tax laws.

The budget resolution often includes reconciliation directives, which require authorizing committees to recommend changes in laws that affect receipts or mandatory spending. They direct each designated committee to report amendments to the laws under the committee's jurisdiction that would achieve changes in the levels of receipts or reductions in mandatory spending controlled

BUDGET CALENDAR

The following timetable highlights the scheduled dates for significant budget events during a normal budget year:

Between the 1st Monday in January and the 1st Monday in February	President transmits the budget
Six weeks later..	Congressional committees report budget estimates to Budget Committees
April 15..	Action to be completed on congressional budget resolution
May 15...	House consideration of annual appropriations bills may begin even if the budget resolution has not been agreed to.
June 10	House Appropriations Committee to report the last of its annual appropriations bills.
June 15	Action to be completed on "reconciliation bill" by the Congress.
June 30	Action on appropriations to be completed by House
July 15	President transmits Mid-Session Review of the Budget
October 1..	Fiscal year begins

by those laws. These directives specify the dollar amount of changes that each designated committee is expected to achieve, but do not specify which laws are to be changed or the changes to be made. However, the Budget Committees' reports on the budget resolution frequently discuss assumptions about how the laws would be changed. Like other assumptions in the report, they do not bind the committees of jurisdiction but may influence their decisions. A reconciliation instruction may also specify the total amount by which the statutory limit on the public debt is to be changed.

The committees subject to reconciliation directives draft the implementing legislation. Such legislation may, for example, change the tax code, revise benefit formulas or eligibility requirements for benefit programs, or authorize Government agencies to charge fees to cover some of their costs. Reconciliation bills are typically omnibus legislation, combining the legislation submitted by each reconciled committee in a single act.

Such a large and complicated bill would be difficult to enact under normal legislative procedures because it usually involves changes to tax rates or to popular social programs, generally to reduce projected deficits. The Senate considers such omnibus reconciliation acts under expedited procedures that limit total debate on the bill. To offset the procedural advantage gained by expedited procedures, the Senate places significant restrictions on the substantive content of the reconciliation measure itself, as well as on amendments to the measure. Any material in the bill that is extraneous or that contains changes to the Federal Old-Age and Survivors Insurance and the Federal Disability Insurance programs is not in order under the Senate's expedited reconciliation procedures. Non-germane amendments are also prohibited. The House does not allow reconciliation bills to increase mandatory spending in net, but does allow such bills to increase deficits by reducing revenues. Reconciliation acts, together with appropriations acts for the year, are usually used to implement broad agreements between the President and the Congress on those occasions where the two branches have negotiated a comprehensive budget plan. Reconciliation acts have sometimes included other matters, such as laws providing the means for enforcing these agreements.

Budget Enforcement

The Federal Government uses three primary enforcement mechanisms to control revenues, spending, and deficits. First, the Statutory Pay-As-You-Go Act of 2010, enacted on February 12, 2010, reestablished a statutory procedure to enforce a rule of deficit neutrality on new revenue and mandatory spending legislation. Second, the Budget Control Act of 2011 (BCA), enacted on August 2, 2011, amended the Balanced Budget and Emergency Deficit Control Act of 1985 (BBEDCA) by reinstating limits ("caps") on the amount of discretionary budget authority that can be provided through the annual appropriations process. Third, the BCA also created a Joint Select Committee on Deficit Reduction that was instruct-

ed to develop a bill to reduce the Federal deficit by at least $1.5 trillion over a 10-year period, and imposed automatic spending cuts to achieve $1.2 trillion of deficit reduction over nine years after the Joint Committee process failed to achieve its deficit reduction goal.

BBEDCA divides spending into two types—discretionary spending and direct or mandatory spending. Discretionary spending is controlled through annual appropriations acts. Funding for salaries and other operating expenses of Government agencies, for example, is generally discretionary. Mandatory spending (also referred to as direct spending), is controlled by permanent laws. Medicare and Medicaid payments, unemployment insurance benefits, and farm price supports are examples of mandatory spending. Receipts are included under the same statutory enforcement rules that apply to mandatory spending because permanent laws generally control receipts.

Discretionary cap enforcement. BBEDCA specifies spending limits ("caps") on discretionary budget authority for 2012 through 2021. Similar enforcement mechanisms were established by the Budget Enforcement Act of 1990 and were extended in 1993 and 1997, but expired at the end of 2002. The caps originally established by the BCA were divided between security and nonsecurity categories for 2012 and 2013, with a single cap for all discretionary spending established for 2014 through 2021. The security category included discretionary budget authority for the Departments of Defense, Homeland Security, Veterans Affairs, the National Nuclear Security Administration, the Intelligence Community Management account, and all budget accounts in the international affairs budget function (budget function 150). The nonsecurity category included all discretionary budget authority not included in the security category. As part of the enforcement mechanisms triggered by the failure of the BCA's Joint Committee process, the security and nonsecurity categories were redefined and established for all years through 2021. The "revised security category" includes discretionary budget authority in the defense budget function 050, which primarily consists of the Department of Defense. The "revised nonsecurity category" includes all discretionary budget authority not included in the defense budget function 050. The redefined categories are commonly referred to as the "defense" and "non-defense" categories, respectively, to distinguish them from the original categories.

BBEDCA requires OMB to adjust the caps each year for: changes in concepts and definitions; appropriations designated by the Congress and the President as emergency requirements; and appropriations designated by the Congress and the President for Overseas Contingency Operations/Global War on Terrorism. BBEDCA also specifies cap adjustments (which are limited to fixed amounts) for: appropriations for continuing disability reviews and redeterminations by the Social Security Administration; the healthcare fraud and abuse control program at the Department of Health and Human Services; appropriations designated by the Congress as being for disaster relief; appropriations for reemployment services and eligibility assessments; appropriations for wildfire suppression at the Department of Agriculture and the Department of the Interior; and, for 2020 only, appropriations provided for the 2020 Census at the Department of Commerce.

BBEDCA requires OMB to provide cost estimates of each appropriations act in a report to the Congress within seven business days after enactment of such act and to publish three discretionary sequestration reports: a "preview" report when the President submits the Budget; an "update" report in August, and a "final" report within 15 days after the end of a session of the Congress.

The preview report explains the adjustments that are required by law to the discretionary caps, including any changes in concepts and definitions, and publishes the revised caps. The preview report may also provide a summary of policy changes, if any, proposed by the President in the Budget to those caps. The update and final reports revise the preview report estimates to reflect the effects of newly enacted discretionary laws. In addition, the update report must contain a preview estimate of the adjustment for disaster funding for the upcoming fiscal year.

If OMB's final sequestration report for a given fiscal year indicates that the amount of discretionary budget authority provided in appropriations acts for that year exceeds the cap for that category in that year, the President must issue a sequestration order canceling budgetary resources in nonexempt accounts within that category by the amount necessary to eliminate the breach. Under sequestration, each nonexempt account within a category is reduced by a dollar amount calculated by multiplying the enacted level of sequestrable budgetary resources in that account by the uniform percentage necessary to eliminate a breach within that category. BBEDCA specifies special rules for reducing some programs and exempts some programs from sequestration entirely. For example, any sequestration of certain health and medical care accounts is limited to 2 percent. Also, if a continuing resolution is in effect when OMB issues its final sequestration report, the sequestration calculations will be based on the annualized amount provided by that continuing resolution. During the 1990s and so far under the BCA caps, the threat of sequestration proved sufficient to ensure compliance with the discretionary spending limits. In that respect, discretionary sequestration can be viewed first as an incentive for compliance and second as a remedy for noncompliance.

Supplemental appropriations can also trigger spending reductions. From the end of a session of the Congress through the following June 30, a within-session discretionary sequestration of current-year spending is imposed if appropriations for the current year cause a cap to be breached. In contrast, if supplemental appropriations enacted in the last quarter of a fiscal year (i.e., July 1 through September 30) cause the caps to be breached, the required reduction is instead achieved by reducing the applicable spending limit for the following fiscal year by the amount of the breach, because the size of the potential sequestration in relation to the unused funding remaining for the current year could severely disrupt agencies' operations.

Since the Joint Committee sequestration that was ordered on March 1, 2013, the Congress and the President have enacted four consecutive two-year agreements—the Bipartisan Budget Acts (BBA) of 2013, 2015, 2018, and 2019—to increase the caps on discretionary programs over what would have been available under the Joint Committee enforcement mechanisms. The increases to the caps in the 2013 and 2015 agreements were paid for, largely from savings in mandatory spending, while the 2018 and 2019 agreements only partially offset the increases.

Direct spending enforcement. The Statutory Pay-As-You-Go Act of 2010 requires that new legislation changing mandatory spending or revenue must be enacted on a "pay-as-you-go" (PAYGO) basis; that is, that the cumulative effects of such legislation must not increase projected on-budget deficits. Unlike the budget enforcement mechanism for discretionary programs, PAYGO is a permanent requirement, and it does not impose a cap on spending or a floor on revenues. Instead, PAYGO requires that legislation reducing revenues must be fully offset by cuts in mandatory programs or by revenue increases, and that any bills increasing mandatory spending must be fully offset by revenue increases or cuts in mandatory spending.

This requirement of deficit neutrality is not enforced on a bill-by-bill basis, but is based on two scorecards that tally the cumulative budgetary effects of PAYGO legislation as averaged over rolling 5- and 10-year periods, starting with the budget year. Any impacts of PAYGO legislation on the current year deficit are counted as budget year impacts when placed on the scorecard. Like the discretionary caps, PAYGO is enforced by sequestration. Within 14 business days after a congressional session ends, OMB issues an annual PAYGO report. If either the 5- or 10-year scorecard shows net costs in the budget year column, the President is required to issue a sequestration order implementing across-the-board cuts to nonexempt mandatory programs by an amount sufficient to offset those net costs. The PAYGO effects of legislation may be directed in legislation by reference to statements inserted into the *Congressional Record* by the chairmen of the House and Senate Budget Committees. Any such estimates are determined by the Budget Committees and are informed by, but not required to match, the cost estimates prepared by the Congressional Budget Office (CBO). If this procedure is not followed, then the PAYGO effects of the legislation are determined by OMB. Provisions of mandatory spending or receipts legislation that are designated in that legislation as an emergency requirement are not scored as PAYGO budgetary effects.

The PAYGO rules apply to the outlays resulting from outyear changes in mandatory programs made in appropriations acts and to all revenue changes made in appropriations acts. However, outyear changes to mandatory programs as part of provisions that have zero net outlay effects over the sum of the current year and the next five fiscal years are not considered PAYGO.

The PAYGO rules do not apply to increases in mandatory spending or decreases in receipts that result automatically under existing law. For example, mandatory spending for benefit programs, such as unemployment insurance, rises when the number of beneficiaries rises, and many benefit payments are automatically increased for inflation under existing laws.

The Senate imposes points of order against consideration of tax or mandatory spending legislation that would violate the PAYGO principle, although the time periods covered by the Senate's rule and the treatment of previously enacted costs or savings may differ in some respects from the requirements of the Statutory Pay-As-You-Go Act of 2010. The House, in contrast, imposes points of order on legislation increasing mandatory spending in net, whether or not those costs are offset by revenue increases, but the House rule does not constrain the size of tax cuts or require them to be offset.

Joint Committee reductions. The failure of the Joint Select Committee on Deficit Reduction to propose, and the Congress to enact, legislation to reduce the deficit by at least $1.2 trillion triggered automatic reductions to discretionary and mandatory spending in fiscal years 2013 through 2021. The reductions are implemented through a combination of sequestration of mandatory spending and reductions in the discretionary caps. These reductions have already been ordered to take effect for 2013 through 2020, with some modifications as provided for in the American Taxpayer Relief Act of 2012, and the BBAs of 2013, 2015, 2018, and 2019. Unless any legislative changes are enacted, further reductions will be implemented by pro rata reductions to the discretionary caps in 2021, which would be reflected in OMB's discretionary sequestration preview report for those years, and by a sequestration of non-exempt mandatory spending for 2021 onward, which would be ordered when the President's Budget is transmitted to the Congress and would take effect beginning October 1 of the upcoming fiscal year.

OMB is required to calculate the amount of the deficit reduction required for 2021 as follows:

- The $1.2 trillion savings target is reduced by 18 percent to account for debt service.

- The resulting net savings of $984 billion is divided by nine to spread the reductions in equal amounts across the nine years, 2013 through 2021.

- The annual spending reduction of $109.3 billion is divided equally between the defense and non-defense functions.

- The annual reduction of $54.7 billion for each functional category of spending is divided proportionally between discretionary and direct spending programs, using as the base the discretionary cap, redefined as outlined in the discretionary cap enforcement section above, and the most recent baseline estimate of non-exempt mandatory outlays.

- The resulting reductions in defense and non-defense direct spending are implemented through a sequestration order released with the President's Budget and taking effect the following October 1. The reductions in discretionary spending are applied as reductions in the discretionary caps, and are enforced through the discretionary cap enforcement procedures discussed earlier in this section.

The mandatory sequestration provisions were extended beyond 2021 by the BBA of 2013, which extended sequestration through 2023; P.L. 113-82, commonly referred to as the Military Retired Pay Restoration Act, which extended sequestration through 2024; the BBA of 2015, which extended sequestration through 2025; the BBA of 2018, which extended sequestration through 2027; and the BBA of 2019, which extended sequestration through 2029. Sequestration during these years will use the same percentage reductions for defense and non-defense as calculated for 2021 under the procedures outlined above.[2]

Budget Execution

Government agencies may not spend or obligate more than the Congress has appropriated, and they may use funds only for purposes specified in law. The Antideficiency Act prohibits them from spending or obligating the Government to spend in advance or in excess of an appropriation, unless specific authority to do so has been provided in law. Additionally, the Antideficiency Act requires the President to apportion the budgetary resources available for most executive branch agencies. The President has delegated this authority to OMB. Some apportionments are by time periods (usually by quarter of the fiscal year), some are by projects or activities, and others are by a combination of both. Agencies may request OMB to reapportion funds during the year to accommodate changing circumstances. This system helps to ensure that funds do not run out before the end of the fiscal year.

During the budget execution phase, the Government sometimes finds that it needs more funding than the Congress has appropriated for the fiscal year because of unanticipated circumstances. For example, more might be needed to respond to a severe natural disaster. Under such circumstances, the Congress may enact a supplemental appropriation.

On the other hand, the President may propose to reduce a previously enacted appropriation, through a "rescission" or "cancellation" of those funds. How the President proposes this reduction determines whether it is considered a rescission or a cancellation. A rescission is a reduction in previously enacted appropriations proposed following the requirements of the Impoundment Control Act (ICA). The ICA allows the President, using the specific authorities in that Act, to transmit a "special message" to the Congress to inform them of these proposed rescissions, at which time the funding can be withheld from obligation for up to 45 days on the OMB-approved apportionment. Agencies are instructed not to withhold funds without the prior approval of OMB. If the Congress does not act to rescind these funds within the 45 day period, the funds

---

[2] The BBA of 2019 specified that, notwithstanding the 2 percent limit on Medicare sequestration in the BCA, in extending sequestration into 2029 the reduction in the Medicare program should be 4.0 percent for the first half of the sequestration period and zero for the second half of the period.

are made available for obligation. In May of 2018, the President proposed the largest single ICA rescissions package by sending a request to permanently reduce approximately $15 billion of budget authority.

The President can also propose reductions to previously enacted appropriations outside of the ICA; in these cases, these reductions are referred to as cancellations. Cancellation proposals are not subject to the requirements and procedures of the ICA and amounts cannot be withheld from obligation. The 2021 President's Budget includes $18 billion in proposed cancellations.

COVERAGE OF THE BUDGET

Federal Government and Budget Totals

The budget documents provide information on all Federal agencies and programs. However, because the laws governing Social Security (the Federal Old-Age and Survivors Insurance and the Federal Disability Insurance trust funds) and the Postal Service Fund require that the receipts and outlays for those activities be excluded from the budget totals and from the calculation of the deficit or surplus, the budget presents on-budget and off-budget totals. The off-budget totals include the Federal transactions excluded by law from the budget totals. The on-budget and off-budget amounts are added together to derive the totals for the Federal Government. These are sometimes referred to as the unified or consolidated budget totals.

It is not always obvious whether a transaction or activity should be included in the budget. Where there is a question, OMB normally follows the recommendation of the 1967 President's Commission on Budget Concepts to be comprehensive of the full range of Federal agencies, programs, and activities. In recent years, for example, the budget has included the transactions of the Affordable Housing Program funds, the Universal Service Fund, the Public Company Accounting Oversight Board, the Securities Investor Protection Corporation, Guaranty Agencies Reserves, the National Railroad Retirement Investment Trust, the United Mine Workers Combined Benefits Fund, the Federal Financial Institutions Examination Council, Electric Reliability Organizations (EROs) established pursuant to the Energy Policy Act of 2005, the Corporation for Travel Promotion, and the National Association of Registered Agents and Brokers.

In contrast, the budget excludes tribal trust funds that are owned by Indian tribes and held and managed by the Government in a fiduciary capacity on the tribes' behalf. These funds are not owned by the Government, the Government is not the source of their capital, and the Government's control is limited to the exercise of fiduciary duties. Similarly, the transactions of Government-sponsored enterprises, such as the Federal Home Loan Banks, are not included in the on-budget or off-budget totals. Federal laws established these enterprises for public policy purposes, but they are privately owned and operated corporations. Nevertheless, because of their public charters, the budget discusses them and reports summary financial data in the budget *Appendix* and in some detailed tables.

The budget also excludes the revenues from copyright royalties and spending for subsequent payments to copyright holders where (1) the law allows copyright owners and users to voluntarily set the rate paid for the use of protected material, and (2) the amount paid by users of copyrighted material to copyright owners is related to the frequency or quantity of the material used. The budget excludes license royalties collected and paid out by the Copyright Office for the retransmission of network broadcasts via cable collected under 17 U.S.C. 111 because these revenues meet both of these conditions. The budget includes the royalties collected and paid out for license fees for digital audio recording technology under 17 U.S.C. 1004, since the amount of license fees paid is unrelated to usage of the material.

The *Appendix* includes a presentation for the Board of Governors of the Federal Reserve System for information only. The amounts are not included in either the on-budget or off-budget totals because of the independent status of the System within the Government. However, the Federal Reserve System transfers its net earnings to the Treasury, and the budget records them as receipts.

Chapter 9 of this volume, "Coverage of the Budget," provides more information on this subject.

Table 8-1. TOTALS FOR THE BUDGET AND THE FEDERAL GOVERNMENT
(In billions of dollars)

	2019 Actual	Estimate	
		2020	2021
Budget authority:			
Unified	4,704	4,908	5,040
On-budget	3,794	3,944	4,016
Off-budget	910	965	1,023
Receipts:			
Unified	3,464	3,706	3,863
On-budget	2,550	2,739	2,852
Off-budget	914	967	1,011
Outlays:			
Unified	4,448	4,790	4,829
On-budget	3,542	3,830	3,811
Off-budget	907	960	1,018
Deficit (–) / Surplus (+):			
Unified	–984	–1,083	–966
On-budget	–992	–1,091	–959
Off-budget	8	7	–7

Functional Classification

The functional classification is used to organize budget authority, outlays, and other budget data according to the major purpose served—such as agriculture, transportation, income security, and national defense. There are 20 major functions, 17 of which are concerned with broad areas of national need and are further divided into subfunctions. For example, the Agriculture function comprises the subfunctions Farm Income Stabilization and Agricultural Research and Services. The functional classification meets the Congressional Budget Act requirement for a presentation in the budget by national needs and agency missions and programs. The remaining three functions—Net Interest, Undistributed Offsetting Receipts, and Allowances—enable the functional classification system to cover the entire Federal budget.

The following criteria are used in establishing functional categories and assigning activities to them:

- A function encompasses activities with similar purposes, emphasizing what the Federal Government seeks to accomplish rather than the means of accomplishment, the objects purchased, the clientele or geographic area served (except in the cases of functions 450 for Community and Regional Development, 570 for Medicare, 650 for Social Security, and 700 for Veterans Benefits and Services), or the Federal agency conducting the activity (except in the case of subfunction 051 in the National Defense function, which is used only for defense activities under the Department of Defense—Military).

- A function must be of continuing national importance, and the amounts attributable to it must be significant.

- Each basic unit being classified (generally the appropriation or fund account) usually is classified according to its primary purpose and assigned to only one subfunction. However, some large accounts that serve more than one major purpose are subdivided into two or more functions or subfunctions.

In consultation with the Congress, the functional classification is adjusted from time to time as warranted. Detailed functional tables, which provide information on Government activities by function and subfunction, are available online at *https://www.whitehouse.gov/omb/analytical-perspectives/* and on *OMB's website*.

Agencies, Accounts, Programs, Projects, and Activities

Various summary tables in the *Analytical Perspectives* volume of the Budget provide information on budget authority, outlays, and offsetting collections and receipts arrayed by Federal agency. A table that lists budget authority and outlays by budget account within each agency and the totals for each agency of budget authority, outlays, and receipts that offset the agency spending totals is available online at: *https://www.whitehouse.gov/omb/analytical-perspectives/* and on *OMB's website*. The *Appendix* provides budgetary, financial, and descriptive information about programs, projects, and activities by account within each agency.

Types of Funds

Agency activities are financed through Federal funds and trust funds.

Federal funds comprise several types of funds. Receipt accounts of the ***general fund***, which is the greater part of the budget, record receipts not earmarked by law for a specific purpose, such as income tax receipts. The general fund also includes the proceeds of general borrowing. General fund appropriations accounts record general fund expenditures. General fund appropriations draw from general fund receipts and borrowing collectively and, therefore, are not specifically linked to receipt accounts.

Special funds consist of receipt accounts for Federal fund receipts that laws have designated for specific purposes and the associated appropriation accounts for the expenditure of those receipts.

Public enterprise funds are revolving funds used for programs authorized by law to conduct a cycle of business-type operations, primarily with the public, in which outlays generate collections.

Intragovernmental funds are revolving funds that conduct business-type operations primarily within and between Government agencies. The collections and the outlays of revolving funds are recorded in the same budget account.

Trust funds account for the receipt and expenditure of monies by the Government for carrying out specific purposes and programs in accordance with the terms of a statute that designates the fund as a trust fund (such as the Highway Trust Fund) or for carrying out the stipulations of a trust where the Government itself is the beneficiary (such as any of several trust funds for gifts and donations for specific purposes). ***Trust revolving funds*** are trust funds credited with collections earmarked by law to carry out a cycle of business-type operations.

The Federal budget meaning of the term "trust," as applied to trust fund accounts, differs significantly from its private-sector usage. In the private sector, the beneficiary of a trust usually owns the trust's assets, which are managed by a trustee who must follow the stipulations of the trust. In contrast, the Federal Government owns the assets of most Federal trust funds, and it can raise or lower future trust fund collections and payments, or change the purposes for which the collections are used, by changing existing laws. There is no substantive difference between a trust fund and a special fund or between a trust revolving fund and a public enterprise revolving fund.

However, in some instances, the Government does act as a true trustee of assets that are owned or held for the benefit of others. For example, it maintains accounts on behalf of individual Federal employees in the Thrift Savings Fund, investing them as directed by the individual employee. The Government accounts for such funds in *deposit funds*, which are not included in the budget. (Chapter 22 of this volume, "Trust Funds and Federal Funds," provides more information on this subject.)

Budgeting for Full Costs

A budget is a financial plan for allocating resources—deciding how much the Federal Government should spend in total, program by program, and for the parts of each program and deciding how to finance the spending. The budgetary system provides a process for proposing policies, making decisions, implementing them, and reporting the results. The budget needs to measure costs accurately so that decision makers can compare the cost of a program with its benefits, the cost of one program with another, and the cost of one method of reaching a specified goal with another. These costs need to be fully included in the budget up front, when the spending decision is made, so that executive and congressional decision makers have the information and the incentive to take the total costs into account when setting priorities.

The budget includes all types of spending, including both current operating expenditures and capital invest-

ment, and to the extent possible, both are measured on the basis of full cost. Questions are often raised about the measure of capital investment. The present budget provides policymakers the necessary information regarding investment spending. It records investment on a cash basis, and it requires the Congress to provide budget authority before an agency can obligate the Government to make a cash outlay. However, the budget measures only costs, and the benefits with which these costs are compared, based on policy makers' judgment, must be presented in supplementary materials. By these means, the budget allows the total cost of capital investment to be compared up front in a rough way with the total expected future net benefits. Such a comparison of total costs with benefits is consistent with the formal method of cost-benefit analysis of capital projects in government, in which the full cost of a capital asset as the cash is paid out is compared with the full stream of future benefits (all in terms of present values). (Chapter 16 of this volume, "Federal Investment," provides more information on capital investment.)

RECEIPTS, OFFSETTING COLLECTIONS, AND OFFSETTING RECEIPTS

In General

The budget records amounts collected by Government agencies two different ways. Depending on the nature of the activity generating the collection and the law that established the collection, they are recorded as either:

Governmental receipts, which are compared in total to outlays (net of offsetting collections and offsetting receipts) in calculating the surplus or deficit; or

Offsetting collections or *offsetting receipts*, which are deducted from gross outlays to calculate net outlay figures.

Governmental Receipts

Governmental receipts are collections that result from the Government's exercise of its sovereign power to tax or otherwise compel payment. Sometimes they are called receipts, budget receipts, Federal receipts, or Federal revenues. They consist mostly of individual and corporation income taxes and social insurance taxes, but also include excise taxes, compulsory user charges, regulatory fees, customs duties, court fines, certain license fees, and deposits of earnings by the Federal Reserve System. Total receipts for the Federal Government include both on-budget and off-budget receipts (see Table 11–1, "Totals for the Budget and the Federal Government," which appears earlier in this chapter.) Chapter 11 of this volume, "Governmental Receipts," provides more information on governmental receipts.

Offsetting Collections and Offsetting Receipts

Offsetting collections and offsetting receipts are recorded as offsets to (deductions from) spending, not as additions on the receipt side of the budget. These amounts are recorded as offsets to outlays so that the budget totals represent governmental rather than market activity and reflect the Government's net transactions with the public. They are recorded in one of two ways, based on interpretation of laws and longstanding budget concepts and practice. They are offsetting collections when the collections are authorized by law to be credited to expenditure accounts and are generally available for expenditure without further legislation. Otherwise, they are deposited in receipt accounts and called offsetting receipts; many of these receipts are available for expenditure without further legislation.

Offsetting collections and offsetting receipts result from any of the following types of transactions:

- *Business-like transactions or market-oriented activities with the public*—these include voluntary collections from the public in exchange for goods or services, such as the proceeds from the sale of postage stamps, the fees charged for admittance to recreation areas, and the proceeds from the sale of Government-owned land; and reimbursements for damages. The budget records these amounts as *offsetting collections from non-Federal sources* (for offsetting collections) or as *proprietary receipts* (for offsetting receipts).

- *Intragovernmental transactions*—collections from other Federal Government accounts. The budget records collections by one Government account from another as *offsetting collections from Federal sources* (for offsetting collections) or as *intragovernmental receipts* (for offsetting receipts). For example, the General Services Administration rents office space to other Government agencies and records their rental payments as offsetting collections from Federal sources in the Federal Buildings Fund. These transactions are exactly offsetting and do not affect the surplus or deficit. However, they are an important accounting mechanism for allocating costs to the programs and activities that cause the Government to incur the costs.

- *Voluntary gifts and donations*—gifts and donations of money to the Government, which are treated as offsets to budget authority and outlays.

- *Offsetting governmental transactions*—collections from the public that are governmental in nature and should conceptually be treated like Federal revenues and compared in total to outlays (e.g., tax receipts, regulatory fees, compulsory user charges, custom duties, license fees) but required by law or longstanding practice to be misclassified as offsetting. The budget records amounts from non-Federal sources that are governmental in nature as *offsetting governmental collections* (for offsetting collections) or as *offsetting governmental receipts* (for offsetting receipts).

Offsetting Collections

Some laws authorize agencies to credit collections directly to the account from which they will be spent and, usually, to spend the collections for the purpose of the account without further action by the Congress. Most revolving funds operate with such authority. For example, a permanent law authorizes the Postal Service to use collections from the sale of stamps to finance its operations without a requirement for annual appropriations. The budget records these collections in the Postal Service Fund (a revolving fund) and records budget authority in an amount equal to the collections. In addition to revolving funds, some agencies are authorized to charge fees to defray a portion of costs for a program that are otherwise financed by appropriations from the general fund and usually to spend the collections without further action by the Congress. In such cases, the budget records the offsetting collections and resulting budget authority in the program's general fund expenditure account. Similarly, intragovernmental collections authorized by some laws may be recorded as offsetting collections and budget authority in revolving funds or in general fund expenditure accounts.

Sometimes appropriations acts or provisions in other laws limit the obligations that can be financed by offsetting collections. In those cases, the budget records budget authority in the amount available to incur obligations, not in the amount of the collections.

Offsetting collections credited to expenditure accounts automatically offset the outlays at the expenditure account level. Where accounts have offsetting collections, the budget shows the budget authority and outlays of the account both gross (before deducting offsetting collections) and net (after deducting offsetting collections). Totals for the agency, subfunction, and overall budget are net of offsetting collections.

Offsetting Receipts

Collections that are offset against gross outlays but are not authorized to be credited to expenditure accounts are credited to receipt accounts and are called offsetting receipts. Offsetting receipts are deducted from budget authority and outlays in arriving at total net budget authority and outlays. However, unlike offsetting collections credited to expenditure accounts, offsetting receipts do not offset budget authority and outlays at the account level. In most cases, they offset budget authority and outlays at the agency and subfunction levels.

Proprietary receipts from a few sources, however, are not offset against any specific agency or function and are classified as undistributed offsetting receipts. They are deducted from the Government-wide totals for net budget authority and outlays. For example, the collections of rents and royalties from outer continental shelf lands are undistributed because the amounts are large and for the most part are not related to the spending of the agency that administers the transactions and the subfunction that records the administrative expenses.

Similarly, two kinds of intragovernmental transactions—agencies' payments as employers into Federal employee retirement trust funds and interest received by trust funds—are classified as undistributed offsetting receipts. They appear instead as special deductions in computing total net budget authority and outlays for the Government rather than as offsets at the agency level. This special treatment is necessary because the amounts are so large they would distort measures of the agency's activities if they were attributed to the agency.

User Charges

User charges are fees assessed on individuals or organizations for the provision of Government services and for the sale or use of Government goods or resources. The payers of the user charge must be limited in the authorizing legislation to those receiving special benefits from, or subject to regulation by, the program or activity beyond the benefits received by the general public or broad segments of the public (such as those who pay income taxes or customs duties). Policy regarding user charges is established in OMB Circular A–25, "User Charges." The term encompasses proceeds from the sale or use of Government goods and services, including the sale of natural resources (such as timber, oil, and minerals) and proceeds from asset sales (such as property, plant, and equipment). User charges are not necessarily dedicated to the activity they finance and may be credited to the general fund of the Treasury.

The term "user charge" does not refer to a separate budget category for collections. User charges are classified in the budget as receipts, offsetting receipts, or offsetting collections according to the principles explained previously.

See Chapter 12, "Offsetting Collections and Offsetting Receipts," for more information on the classification of user charges.

BUDGET AUTHORITY, OBLIGATIONS, AND OUTLAYS

Budget authority, obligations, and outlays are the primary benchmarks and measures of the budget control system. The Congress enacts laws that provide agencies with spending authority in the form of budget authority. Before agencies can use these resources—obligate this budget authority—OMB must approve their spending plans. After the plans are approved, agencies can enter into binding agreements to purchase items or services or to make grants or other payments. These agreements are recorded as obligations of the United States and deducted from the amount of budgetary resources available to the agency. When payments are made, the obligations are liquidated and outlays recorded. These concepts are discussed more fully below.

Budget Authority and Other Budgetary Resources

Budget authority is the authority provided in law to enter into legal obligations that will result in immediate or future outlays of the Government. In other words, it is the amount of money that agencies are allowed to commit to be spent in current or future years. Government officials may obligate the Government to make outlays only to the extent they have been granted budget authority.

In deciding the amount of budget authority to request for a program, project, or activity, agency officials estimate the total amount of obligations they will need to incur to achieve desired goals and subtract the unobligated balances available for these purposes. The amount of budget authority requested is influenced by the nature of the programs, projects, or activities being financed. For current operating expenditures, the amount requested usually covers the needs for the fiscal year. For major procurement programs and construction projects, agencies generally must request sufficient budget authority in the first year to fully fund an economically useful segment of a procurement or project, even though it may be obligated over several years. This full funding policy is intended to ensure that the decision-makers take into account all costs and benefits at the time decisions are made to provide resources. It also avoids sinking money into a procurement or project without being certain if or when future funding will be available to complete the procurement or project, as well as saddling future agency budgets with must-pay bills to complete past projects.

Budget authority takes several forms:

- **Appropriations**, provided in annual appropriations acts or authorizing laws, permit agencies to incur obligations and make payment;

- **Borrowing authority**, usually provided in permanent laws, permits agencies to incur obligations but requires them to borrow funds, usually from the general fund of the Treasury, to make payment;

- **Contract authority**, usually provided in permanent law, permits agencies to incur obligations in advance of a separate appropriation of the cash for payment or in anticipation of the collection of receipts that can be used for payment; and

- **Spending authority from offsetting collections**, usually provided in permanent law, permits agencies to credit offsetting collections to an expenditure account, incur obligations, and make payment using the offsetting collections.

Because offsetting collections and offsetting receipts are deducted from gross budget authority, they are referred to as negative budget authority for some purposes, such as Congressional Budget Act provisions that pertain to budget authority.

Authorizing statutes usually determine the form of budget authority for a program. The authorizing statute may authorize a particular type of budget authority to be provided in annual appropriations acts, or it may provide one of the forms of budget authority directly, without the need for further appropriations.

An appropriation may make funds available from the general fund, special funds, or trust funds, or authorize the spending of offsetting collections credited to expenditure accounts, including revolving funds. Borrowing authority is usually authorized for business-like activities where the activity being financed is expected to produce income over time with which to repay the borrowing with interest. The use of contract authority is traditionally limited to transportation programs.

New budget authority for most Federal programs is normally provided in annual appropriations acts. However, new budget authority is also made available through permanent appropriations under existing laws and does not require current action by the Congress. Much of the permanent budget authority is for trust funds, interest on the public debt, and the authority to spend offsetting collections credited to appropriation or fund accounts. For most trust funds, the budget authority is appropriated automatically under existing law from the available balance of the fund and equals the estimated annual obligations of the funds. For interest on the public debt, budget authority is provided automatically under a permanent appropriation enacted in 1847 and equals interest outlays.

Annual appropriations acts generally make budget authority available for obligation only during the fiscal year to which the act applies. However, they frequently allow budget authority for a particular purpose to remain available for obligation for a longer period or indefinitely (that is, until expended or until the program objectives have been attained). Typically, budget authority for current operations is made available for only one year, and budget authority for construction and some research projects is available for a specified number of years or indefinitely. Most budget authority provided in authorizing statutes, such as for most trust funds, is available indefinitely. If budget authority is initially provided for a limited period of availability, an extension of availability would require enactment of another law (see "Reappropriation" later in this chapter).

Budget authority that is available for more than one year and not obligated in the year it becomes available is carried forward for obligation in a following year. In some cases, an account may carry forward unobligated budget authority from more than one prior year. The sum of such amounts constitutes the account's **unobligated balance**. Most of these balances had been provided for specific uses such as the multiyear construction of a major project and so are not available for new programs. A small part may never be obligated or spent, primarily amounts provided for contingencies that do not occur or reserves that never have to be used.

Amounts of budget authority that have been obligated but not yet paid constitute the account's **unpaid obligations**. For example, in the case of salaries and wages, one to three weeks elapse between the time of obligation and the time of payment. In the case of major procurement and construction, payments may occur over a period of several years after the obligation is made. Unpaid obligations (which are made up of accounts payable and undelivered orders) net of the accounts receivable and unfilled customers' orders are defined by law as the **obligated balances**. Obligated balances of budget authority at the end of the year are carried forward until the obligations are paid or the balances are canceled. (A general law provides that the obligated balances of budget authority that was made available for a definite period is automatically cancelled five years after the end of the period.) Due to such flows, a change in the amount of budget authority available in any one year may change the level of obligations and outlays for several years to come. Conversely, a change in the amount of obligations incurred from one year to the next does not necessarily result from an equal change in the amount of budget authority available for that year and will not necessarily result in an equal change in the level of outlays in that year.

The Congress usually makes budget authority available on the first day of the fiscal year for which the appropriations act is passed. Occasionally, the appropriations language specifies a different timing. The language may provide an **advance appropriation**—budget authority that does not become available until one year or more beyond the fiscal year for which the appropriations act is passed. **Forward funding** is budget authority that is made available for obligation beginning in the last quarter of the fiscal year (beginning on July 1) for the financing of ongoing grant programs during the next fiscal year. This kind of funding is used mostly for education programs, so that obligations for education grants can be made prior to

the beginning of the next school year. For certain benefit programs funded by annual appropriations, the appropriation provides for **advance funding**—budget authority that is to be charged to the appropriation in the succeeding year, but which authorizes obligations to be incurred in the last quarter of the current fiscal year if necessary to meet benefit payments in excess of the specific amount appropriated for the year. When such authority is used, an adjustment is made to increase the budget authority for the fiscal year in which it is used and to reduce the budget authority of the succeeding fiscal year.

Provisions of law that extend into a new fiscal year the availability of unobligated amounts that have expired or would otherwise expire are called reappropriations. Reappropriations of expired balances that are newly available for obligation in the current or budget year count as new budget authority in the fiscal year in which the balances become newly available. For example, if a 2018 appropriations act extends the availability of unobligated budget authority that expired at the end of 2017, new budget authority would be recorded for 2018. This scorekeeping is used because a reappropriation has exactly the same effect as allowing the earlier appropriation to expire at the end of 2017 and enacting a new appropriation for 2018.

For purposes of BBEDCA and the Statutory Pay-As-You-Go Act of 2010 (discussed earlier under "Budget Enforcement"), the budget classifies budget authority as **discretionary** or **mandatory**. This classification indicates whether an appropriations act or authorizing legislation controls the amount of budget authority that is available. Generally, budget authority is discretionary if provided in an annual appropriations act and mandatory if provided in authorizing legislation. However, the budget authority provided in annual appropriations acts for certain specifically identified programs is also classified as mandatory by OMB and the congressional scorekeepers. This is because the authorizing legislation for these programs entitles beneficiaries—persons, households, or other levels of government—to receive payment, or otherwise legally obligates the Government to make payment and thereby effectively determines the amount of budget authority required, even though the payments are funded by a subsequent appropriation.

Sometimes, budget authority is characterized as current or permanent. Current authority requires the Congress to act on the request for new budget authority for the year involved. Permanent authority becomes available pursuant to standing provisions of law without appropriations action by the Congress for the year involved. Generally, budget authority is current if an annual appropriations act provides it and permanent if authorizing legislation provides it. By and large, the current/permanent distinction has been replaced by the discretionary/mandatory distinction, which is similar but not identical. Outlays are also classified as discretionary or mandatory according to the classification of the budget authority from which they flow (see "Outlays" later in this chapter).

The amount of budget authority recorded in the budget depends on whether the law provides a specific amount or employs a variable factor that determines the amount. It is considered **definite** if the law specifies a dollar amount (which may be stated as an upper limit, for example, "shall not exceed ..."). It is considered **indefinite** if, instead of specifying an amount, the law permits the amount to be determined by subsequent circumstances. For example, indefinite budget authority is provided for interest on the public debt, payment of claims and judgments awarded by the courts against the United States, and many entitlement programs. Many of the laws that authorize collections to be credited to revolving, special, and trust funds make all of the collections available for expenditure for the authorized purposes of the fund, and such authority is considered to be indefinite budget authority because the amount of collections is not known in advance of their collection.

Obligations

Following the enactment of budget authority and the completion of required apportionment action, Government agencies incur obligations to make payments (see earlier discussion under "Budget Execution"). Agencies must record obligations when they enter into binding agreements that will result in immediate or future outlays. Such obligations include the current liabilities for salaries, wages, and interest; and contracts for the purchase of supplies and equipment, construction, and the acquisition of office space, buildings, and land. For Federal credit programs, obligations are recorded in an amount equal to the estimated subsidy cost of direct loans and loan guarantees (see "Federal Credit" later in this chapter).

Outlays

Outlays are the measure of Government spending. They are payments that liquidate obligations (other than most exchanges of financial instruments, of which the repayment of debt is the prime example). The budget records outlays when obligations are paid, in the amount that is paid.

Agency, function and subfunction, and Government-wide outlay totals are stated net of offsetting collections and offsetting receipts for most budget presentations. (Offsetting receipts from a few sources do not offset any specific function, subfunction, or agency, as explained previously, but only offset Government-wide totals.) Outlay totals for accounts with offsetting collections are stated both gross and net of the offsetting collections credited to the account. However, the outlay totals for special and trust funds with offsetting receipts are not stated net of the offsetting receipts. In most cases, these receipts offset the agency, function, and subfunction totals but do not offset account-level outlays. However, when general fund payments are used to finance trust fund outlays to the public, the associated trust fund receipts are netted against the bureau totals to prevent double-counting budget authority and outlays at the bureau level.

The Government usually makes outlays in the form of cash (currency, checks, or electronic fund transfers).

However, in some cases agencies pay obligations without disbursing cash, and the budget nevertheless records outlays for the equivalent method. For example, the budget records outlays for the full amount of Federal employees' salaries, even though the cash disbursed to employees is net of Federal and State income taxes withheld, retirement contributions, life and health insurance premiums, and other deductions. (The budget also records receipts for the amounts withheld from Federal employee paychecks for Federal income taxes and other payments to the Government.) When debt instruments (bonds, debentures, notes, or monetary credits) are used in place of cash to pay obligations, the budget records outlays financed by an increase in agency debt. For example, the budget records the acquisition of physical assets through certain types of lease-purchase arrangements as though a cash disbursement were made for an outright purchase. The transaction creates a Government debt, and the cash lease payments are treated as repayments of principal and interest.

The budget records outlays for the interest on the public issues of Treasury debt securities as the interest accrues, not when the cash is paid. A small portion of Treasury debt consists of inflation-indexed securities, which feature monthly adjustments to principal for inflation and semiannual payments of interest on the inflation-adjusted principal. As with fixed-rate securities, the budget records interest outlays as the interest accrues. The monthly adjustment to principal is recorded, simultaneously, as an increase in debt outstanding and an outlay of interest.

Most Treasury debt securities held by trust funds and other Government accounts are in the Government account series. The budget normally states the interest on these securities on a cash basis. When a Government account is invested in Federal debt securities, the purchase price is usually close or identical to the par (face) value of the security. The budget generally records the investment at par value and adjusts the interest paid by Treasury and collected by the account by the difference between purchase price and par, if any.

For Federal credit programs, outlays are equal to the subsidy cost of direct loans and loan guarantees and are recorded as the underlying loans are disbursed (see "Federal Credit" later in this chapter).

The budget records refunds of receipts that result from overpayments by the public (such as income taxes withheld in excess of tax liabilities) as reductions of receipts, rather than as outlays. However, the budget records payments to taxpayers for refundable tax credits (such as earned income tax credits) that exceed the taxpayer's tax liability as outlays. Similarly, when the Government makes overpayments that are later returned to the Government, those refunds to the Government are recorded as offsetting collections or offsetting receipts, not as governmental receipts.

Not all of the new budget authority for 2020 will be obligated or spent in 2020. Outlays during a fiscal year may liquidate obligations incurred in the same year or in prior years. Obligations, in turn, may be incurred against budget authority provided in the same year or against unobligated balances of budget authority provided in prior years. Outlays, therefore, flow in part from budget authority provided for the year in which the money is spent and in part from budget authority provided for prior years. The ratio of a given year's outlays resulting from budget authority enacted in that or a prior year to the original amount of that budget authority is referred to as the outlay rate for that year.

As shown in the accompanying chart, $3,764 billion of outlays in 2021 (78 percent of the outlay total) will be made from that year's $5,040 billion total of proposed new budget authority (a first-year outlay rate of 75 percent). Thus, the remaining $1,065 billion of outlays in 2021 (22 percent of the outlay total) will be made from budget authority enacted in previous years. At the same time, $1,275 billion of the new budget authority proposed for 2021 (25 percent of the total amount proposed) will not lead to outlays until future years.

As described earlier, the budget classifies budget authority and outlays as discretionary or mandatory. This classification of outlays measures the extent to which actual spending is controlled through the annual appropriations process. About 30 percent of total outlays in 2019 ($1,338 billion) were discretionary and the remaining 70 percent ($3,111 billion in 2019) were mandatory spending and net interest. Such a large portion of total spending is mandatory because authorizing rather than appropriations legislation determines net interest ($375 billion in 2019) and the spending for a few programs with large amounts of spending each year, such as Social Security ($1,038 billion in 2019) and Medicare ($644 billion in 2019).

The bulk of mandatory outlays flow from budget authority recorded in the same fiscal year. This is not necessarily the case for discretionary budget authority and outlays. For most major construction and procurement projects and long-term contracts, for example, the budget authority covers the entire cost estimated when the projects are initiated even though the work will take place and

outlays will be made over a period extending beyond the year for which the budget authority is enacted. Similarly, discretionary budget authority for most education and job training activities is appropriated for school or program years that begin in the fourth quarter of the fiscal year. Most of these funds result in outlays in the year after the appropriation.

FEDERAL CREDIT

Some Government programs provide assistance through direct loans or loan guarantees. A ***direct loan*** is a disbursement of funds by the Government to a non-Federal borrower under a contract that requires repayment of such funds with or without interest and includes economically equivalent transactions, such as the sale of Federal assets on credit terms. A ***loan guarantee*** is any guarantee, insurance, or other pledge with respect to the payment of all or a part of the principal or interest on any debt obligation of a non-Federal borrower to a non-Federal lender. The Federal Credit Reform Act of 1990, as amended (FCRA), prescribes the budgetary treatment for Federal credit programs. Under this treatment, the budget records obligations and outlays up front, for the net cost to the Government (subsidy cost), rather than recording the cash flows year by year over the term of the loan. FCRA treatment allows the comparison of direct loans and loan guarantees to each other, and to other methods of delivering assistance, such as grants.

The cost of direct loans and loan guarantees, sometimes called the "subsidy cost," is estimated as the present value of expected payments to and from the public over the term of the loan, discounted using appropriate Treasury interest rates.[3] Similar to most other kinds of programs,

---

[3]   Present value is a standard financial concept that considers the time-value of money. That is, it accounts for the fact that a given sum of money is worth more today than the same sum would be worth in the future because interest can be earned.

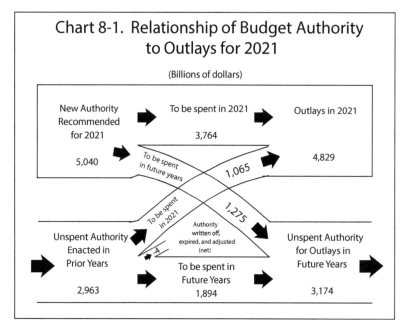

Chart 8-1. Relationship of Budget Authority to Outlays for 2021

(Billions of dollars)

New Authority Recommended for 2021 — 5,040
To be spent in 2021 — 3,764
To be spent in future years
Outlays in 2021 — 4,829
1,065
1,275
To be spent in 2021
Unspent Authority Enacted in Prior Years — 2,963
Authority written off, expired, and adjusted (net) — 4
To be spent in Future Years — 1,894
Unspent Authority for Outlays in Future Years — 3,174

agencies can make loans or guarantee loans only if the Congress has appropriated funds sufficient to cover the subsidy costs, or provided a limitation in an appropriations act on the amount of direct loans or loan guarantees that can be made.

The budget records the subsidy cost to the Government arising from direct loans and loan guarantees—the budget authority and outlays—in *credit program accounts*. When a Federal agency disburses a direct loan or when a non-Federal lender disburses a loan guaranteed by a Federal agency, the program account disburses or outlays an amount equal to the estimated present value cost, or subsidy, to a non-budgetary credit *financing account*. The financing accounts record the actual transactions with the public. For a few programs, the estimated subsidy cost is negative because the present value of expected Government collections exceeds the present value of expected payments to the public over the term of the loan. In such cases, the financing account pays the estimated subsidy cost to the program's negative subsidy receipt account, where it is recorded as an offsetting receipt. In a few cases, the offsetting receipts of credit accounts are dedicated to a special fund established for the program and are available for appropriation for the program.

The agencies responsible for credit programs must reestimate the subsidy cost of the outstanding portfolio of direct loans and loan guarantees each year. If the estimated cost increases, the program account makes an additional payment to the financing account equal to the change in cost. If the estimated cost decreases, the financing account pays the difference to the program's downward reestimate receipt account, where it is recorded as an offsetting receipt. The FCRA provides permanent indefinite appropriations to pay for upward reestimates.

If the Government modifies the terms of an outstanding direct loan or loan guarantee in a way that increases the cost as the result of a law or the exercise of administrative discretion under existing law, the program account records obligations for the increased cost and outlays the amount to the financing account. As with the original subsidy cost, agencies may incur modification costs only if the Congress has appropriated funds to cover them. A modification may also reduce costs, in which case the amounts are generally returned to the general fund, as the financing account makes a payment to the program's negative subsidy receipt account.

Credit financing accounts record all cash flows arising from direct loan obligations and loan guarantee commitments. Such cash flows include all cash flows to and from the public, including direct loan disbursements and re-

payments, loan guarantee default payments, fees, and recoveries on defaults. Financing accounts also record intragovernmental transactions, such as the receipt of subsidy cost payments from program accounts, borrowing and repayments of Treasury debt to finance program activities, and interest paid to or received from the Treasury. The cash flows of direct loans and of loan guarantees are recorded in separate financing accounts for programs that provide both types of credit. The budget totals exclude the transactions of the financing accounts because they are not a cost to the Government. However, since financing accounts record all credit cash flows to and from the public, they affect the means of financing a budget surplus or deficit (see "Credit Financing Accounts" in the next section). The budget documents display the transactions of the financing accounts, together with the related program accounts, for information and analytical purposes.

The budgetary treatment of direct loan obligations and loan guarantee commitments made prior to 1992 was grandfathered in under FCRA. The budget records these on a cash basis in *credit liquidating accounts*, the same as they were recorded before FCRA was enacted. However, this exception ceases to apply if the direct loans or loan guarantees are modified as described above. In that case, the budget records the subsidy cost or savings of the modification, as appropriate, and begins to account for the associated transactions under FCRA treatment for direct loan obligations and loan guarantee commitments made in 1992 or later.

Under the authority provided in various acts, certain activities that do not meet the definition in FCRA of a direct loan or loan guarantee are reflected pursuant to FCRA. For example, the Emergency Economic Stabilization Act of 2008 (EESA) created the Troubled Asset Relief Program (TARP) under the Department of the Treasury, and authorized Treasury to purchase or guarantee troubled assets until October 3, 2010. Under the TARP, Treasury purchased equity interests in financial institutions. Section 123 of the EESA provides the Administration the authority to treat these equity investments on a FCRA basis, recording outlays for the subsidy as is done for direct loans and loan guarantees. The budget reflects the cost to the Government of TARP direct loans, loan guarantees, and equity investments consistent with the FCRA and Section 123 of EESA, which requires an adjustment to the FCRA discount rate for market risks. Similarly, Treasury equity purchases under the Small Business Lending Fund are treated pursuant to the FCRA, as provided by the Small Business Jobs Act of 2010.

BUDGET DEFICIT OR SURPLUS AND MEANS OF FINANCING

When outlays exceed receipts, the difference is a deficit, which the Government finances primarily by borrowing. When receipts exceed outlays, the difference is a surplus, and the Government automatically uses the surplus primarily to reduce debt. The Federal debt held by the public is approximately the cumulative amount of borrowing to

finance deficits, less repayments from surpluses, over the Nation's history.

Borrowing is not exactly equal to the deficit, and debt repayment is not exactly equal to the surplus, because of the other transactions affecting borrowing from the public, or other means of financing, such as those discussed in this section. The factors included in the other means of financing can either increase or decrease the Government's borrowing needs (or decrease or increase its ability to repay debt). For example, the change in the Treasury operating cash balance is a factor included in other means of financing. Holding receipts and outlays constant, increases in the cash balance increase the Government's need to borrow or reduce the Government's ability to repay debt, and decreases in the cash balance decrease the need to borrow or increase the ability to repay debt. In some years, the net effect of the other means of financing is minor relative to the borrowing or debt repayment; in other years, the net effect may be significant.

Borrowing and Debt Repayment

The budget treats borrowing and debt repayment as a means of financing, not as receipts and outlays. If borrowing were defined as receipts and debt repayment as outlays, the budget would always be virtually balanced by definition. This rule applies both to borrowing in the form of Treasury securities and to specialized borrowing in the form of agency securities. The rule reflects the common-sense understanding that lending or borrowing is just an exchange of financial assets of equal value—cash for Treasury securities—and so is fundamentally different from, say, paying taxes, which involve a net transfer of financial assets from taxpayers to the Government.

In 2019, the Government borrowed $1,051 billion from the public, bringing debt held by the public to $16,801 billion. This borrowing financed the $984 billion deficit in that year, as well as the net impacts of the other means of financing, such as changes in cash balances and other accounts discussed below.

In addition to selling debt to the public, the Department of the Treasury issues debt to Government accounts, primarily trust funds that are required by law to invest in Treasury securities. Issuing and redeeming this debt does not affect the means of financing, because these transactions occur between one Government account and another and thus do not raise or use any cash for the Government as a whole.

(See Chapter 4 of this volume, "Federal Borrowing and Debt," for a fuller discussion of this topic.)

Exercise of Monetary Power

Seigniorage is the profit from coining money. It is the difference between the value of coins as money and their cost of production. Seigniorage reduces the Government's need to borrow. Unlike the payment of taxes or other receipts, it does not involve a transfer of financial assets from the public. Instead, it arises from the exercise of the Government's power to create money and the public's desire to hold financial assets in the form of coins. Therefore, the budget excludes seigniorage from receipts and treats it as a means of financing other than borrowing from the public. The budget also treats proceeds from the sale of gold as a means of financing, since the value of gold is determined by its value as a monetary asset rather than as a commodity.

Credit Financing Accounts

The budget records the net cash flows of credit programs in credit financing accounts. These accounts include the transactions for direct loan and loan guarantee programs, as well as the equity purchase programs under TARP that are recorded on a credit basis consistent with Section 123 of EESA. Financing accounts also record equity purchases under the Small Business Lending Fund consistent with the Small Business Jobs Act of 2010. Credit financing accounts are excluded from the budget because they are not allocations of resources by the Government (see "Federal Credit" earlier in this chapter). However, even though they do not affect the surplus or deficit, they can either increase or decrease the Government's need to borrow. Therefore, they are recorded as a means of financing.

Financing account disbursements to the public increase the requirement for Treasury borrowing in the same way as an increase in budget outlays. Financing account receipts from the public can be used to finance the payment of the Government's obligations and therefore reduce the requirement for Treasury borrowing from the public in the same way as an increase in budget receipts.

Deposit Fund Account Balances

The Treasury uses non-budgetary accounts, called deposit funds, to record cash held temporarily until ownership is determined (for example, earnest money paid by bidders for mineral leases) or cash held by the Government as agent for others (for example, State and local income taxes withheld from Federal employees' salaries and not yet paid to the State or local government or amounts held in the Thrift Savings Fund, a defined contribution pension fund held and managed in a fiduciary capacity by the Government). Deposit fund balances may be held in the form of either invested or uninvested balances. To the extent that they are not invested, changes in the balances are available to finance expenditures without a change in borrowing and are recorded as a means of financing other than borrowing from the public. To the extent that they are invested in Federal debt, changes in the balances are reflected as borrowing from the public (in lieu of borrowing from other parts of the public) and are not reflected as a separate means of financing.

United States Quota Subscriptions to the International Monetary Fund (IMF)

The United States participates in the IMF primarily through a quota subscription. Financial transactions with the IMF are exchanges of monetary assets. When the IMF temporarily draws dollars from the U.S. quota, the United States simultaneously receives an equal, offsetting, interest-bearing, Special Drawing Right (SDR)-denominated claim in the form of an increase in the U.S. reserve position in the IMF. The U.S. reserve position in the IMF increases when the United States makes deposits in its account at the IMF when the IMF temporarily uses members' quota resources to make loans and decreases when the IMF returns funds to the United States as borrowing countries repay the IMF (and the cash flows from the reserve position to the Treasury letter of credit).

The U.S. transactions with the IMF under the quota subscriptions do not increase the deficit in any year, and the budget excludes these transfers from budget outlays and receipts, consistent with the budgetary treatment for exchanges of monetary assets recommended by the President's Commission on Budget Concepts in 1967. The only exception is that interest earnings on U.S. deposits in its IMF account are recorded as offsetting receipts. Other exchanges of monetary assets, such as deposits of cash in Treasury accounts at commercial banks, are likewise not included in the Budget. However, the Congress has historically expressed interest in showing some kind of budgetary effect for U.S. transactions with the IMF.[4]

---

[4] For a more detailed discussion of the history of the budgetary treatment of U.S. participation in the quota and New Arrangements to Borrow (NAB), see pages 139-141 in the *Analytical Perspectives* volume of the 2016 Budget. As discussed in that volume, the budgetary treatment of the U.S. participation in the NAB is similar to the quota. See pages 85-86 of the *Analytical Perspectives* volume of the 2018 Budget for a more complete discussion of the changes made to the budgetary presentation of quota increases in Title IX of the Department of State, Foreign Operations, and Related Programs Appropriations Act, 2016.

FEDERAL EMPLOYMENT

The budget includes information on civilian and military employment. It also includes information on related personnel compensation and benefits and on staffing requirements at overseas missions. Chapter 5 of this volume, "Strengthening the Federal Workforce," provides employment levels measured in full-time equivalents (FTE). Agency FTEs are the measure of total hours worked by an agency's Federal employees divided by the total number of one person's compensable work hours in a fiscal year.

BASIS FOR BUDGET FIGURES

Data for the Past Year

The past year column (2019) generally presents the actual transactions and balances as recorded in agency accounts and as summarized in the central financial reports prepared by the Department of the Treasury for the most recently completed fiscal year. Occasionally, the budget reports corrections to data reported erroneously to Treasury but not discovered in time to be reflected in Treasury's published data. In addition, in certain cases the Budget has a broader scope and includes financial transactions that are not reported to Treasury (see Chapter 23 of this volume, "Comparison of Actual to Estimated Totals," for a summary of these differences).

Data for the Current Year

The current year column (2020) includes estimates of transactions and balances based on the amounts of budgetary resources that were available when the budget was prepared. In cases where the budget proposes policy changes effective in the current year, the data will also reflect the budgetary effect of those proposed changes.

Data for the Budget Year

The Budget year column (2021) includes estimates of transactions and balances based on the amounts of budgetary resources that are estimated to be available, including new budget authority requested under current authorizing legislation, and amounts estimated to result from changes in authorizing legislation and tax laws.

The budget *Appendix* generally includes the appropriations language for the amounts proposed to be appropriated under current authorizing legislation. In a few cases, this language is transmitted later because the exact requirements are unknown when the budget is transmitted. The *Appendix* generally does not include appropriations language for the amounts that will be requested under proposed legislation; that language is usually transmitted later, after the legislation is enacted. Some tables in the budget identify the items for later transmittal and the related outlays separately. Estimates of the total requirements for the budget year include both the amounts requested with the transmittal of the budget and the amounts planned for later transmittal.

Data for the Outyears

The budget presents estimates for each of the nine years beyond the budget year (2022 through 2030) in order to reflect the effect of budget decisions on objectives and plans over a longer period.

Allowances

The budget may include lump-sum allowances to cover certain transactions that are expected to increase or decrease budget authority, outlays, or receipts but are not, for various reasons, reflected in the program details. For example, the budget might include an allowance to show the effect on the budget totals of a proposal that would affect many accounts by relatively small amounts, in order to avoid unnecessary detail in the presentations for the individual accounts.

Baseline

The budget baseline is an estimate of the receipts, outlays, and deficits or surpluses that would occur if no changes were made to current laws and policies during the period covered by the budget. The baseline assumes that receipts and mandatory spending, which generally are authorized on a permanent basis, will continue in the future consistent with current law and policy. The baseline assumes that the future funding for most discretionary programs, which generally are funded annually, will equal the most recently enacted appropriation, adjusted for inflation.

Baseline outlays represent the amount of resources that would be used by the Government over the period covered by the budget on the basis of laws currently enacted.

The baseline serves several useful purposes:

- It may warn of future problems, either for Government fiscal policy as a whole or for individual tax and spending programs.

- It may provide a starting point for formulating the President's Budget.

- It may provide a "policy-neutral" benchmark against which the President's Budget and alternative proposals can be compared to assess the magnitude of proposed changes.

The baseline rules in BBEDCA provide that funding for discretionary programs is inflated from the most recent enacted appropriations using specified inflation rates. Because the resulting funding would exceed the discretionary caps, the Administration's baseline includes adjustments that reduce overall discretionary funding to levels consistent with the caps. (Chapter 21 of this volume, "Current Services Estimates," provides more information on the baseline.)

PRINCIPAL BUDGET LAWS

The Budget and Accounting Act of 1921 created the core of the current Federal budget process. Before enactment of this law, there was no annual centralized budgeting in the Executive Branch. Federal Government agencies usually sent budget requests independently to congressional committees with no coordination of the various requests in formulating the Federal Government's budget. The Budget and Accounting Act required the President to coordinate the budget requests for all Government agencies and to send a comprehensive budget to the Congress. The Congress has amended the requirements many times and portions of the Act are codified in Title 31, United States Code. The major laws that govern the budget process are as follows:

Article 1, section 8, clause 1 of the Constitution, which empowers the Congress to collect taxes.

Article 1, section 9, clause 7 of the Constitution, which requires appropriations in law before money may be spent from the Treasury and the publication of a regular statement of the receipts and expenditures of all public money.

Antideficiency Act (codified in Chapters 13 and 15 of Title 31, United States Code), which prescribes rules and procedures for budget execution.

Balanced Budget and Emergency Deficit Control Act of 1985, as amended, which establishes limits on discretionary spending and provides mechanisms for enforcing mandatory spending and discretionary spending limits.

Chapter 11 of Title 31, United States Code, which prescribes procedures for submission of the President's budget and information to be contained in it.

Congressional Budget and Impoundment Control Act of 1974 (Public Law 93–344), as amended. This Act comprises the:

- *Congressional Budget Act of 1974*, as amended, which prescribes the congressional budget process; and

- *Impoundment Control Act of 1974*, as amended, which controls certain aspects of budget execution.

- *Federal Credit Reform Act of 1990,* as amended (2 USC 661–661f), which the Budget Enforcement Act of 1990 included as an amendment to the Congressional Budget Act to prescribe the budget treatment for Federal credit programs.

Chapter 31 of Title 31, United States Code, which provides the authority for the Secretary of the Treasury to issue debt to finance the deficit and establishes a statutory limit on the level of the debt.

Chapter 33 of Title 31, United States Code, which establishes the Department of the Treasury as the authority for making disbursements of public funds, with the authority to delegate that authority to executive agencies in the interests of economy and efficiency.

Government Performance and Results Act of 1993 (Public Law 103–62, as amended*)* which emphasizes managing for results. It requires agencies to prepare strategic plans, annual performance plans, and annual performance reports.

Statutory Pay-As-You-Go Act of 2010, which establishes a budget enforcement mechanism generally requiring that direct spending and revenue legislation enacted into law not increase the deficit.

GLOSSARY OF BUDGET TERMS

Account refers to a separate financial reporting unit used by the Federal Government to record budget authority, outlays and income for budgeting or management information purposes as well as for accounting purposes.

All budget (and off-budget) accounts are classified as being either expenditure or receipt accounts and by fund group. Budget (and off-budget) transactions fall within either of two fund group: (1) Federal funds and (2) trust funds. (Cf. Federal funds group and trust funds group.)

Accrual method of measuring cost means an accounting method that records cost when the liability is incurred. As applied to Federal employee retirement benefits, accrual costs are recorded when the benefits are earned rather than when they are paid at some time in the future. The accrual method is used in part to provide data that assists in agency policymaking, but not used in presenting the overall budget of the United States Government.

Advance appropriation means appropriations of new budget authority that become available one or more fiscal years beyond the fiscal year for which the appropriation act was passed.

Advance funding means appropriations of budget authority provided in an appropriations act to be used, if necessary, to cover obligations incurred late in the fiscal year for benefit payments in excess of the amount specifically appropriated in the act for that year, where the budget authority is charged to the appropriation for the program for the fiscal year following the fiscal year for which the appropriations act is passed.

Agency means a department or other establishment of the Government.

Allowance means a lump-sum included in the budget to represent certain transactions that are expected to increase or decrease budget authority, outlays, or receipts but that are not, for various reasons, reflected in the program details.

Balanced Budget and Emergency Deficit Control Act of 1985 (BBEDCA) refers to legislation that altered the budget process, primarily by replacing the earlier fixed targets for annual deficits with a Pay-As-You-Go requirement for new tax or mandatory spending legislation and with caps on annual discretionary funding. The Statutory Pay-As-You-Go Act of 2010, which is a standalone piece of legislation that did not directly amend the BBEDCA, reinstated a statutory pay-as-you-go rule for revenues and mandatory spending legislation, and the Budget Control Act of 2011, which did amend BBEDCA, reinstated discretionary caps on budget authority.

Balances of budget authority means the amounts of budget authority provided in previous years that have not been outlayed.

Baseline means a projection of the estimated receipts, outlays, and deficit or surplus that would result from continuing current law or current policies through the period covered by the budget.

Budget means the Budget of the United States Government, which sets forth the President's comprehensive financial plan for allocating resources and indicates the President's priorities for the Federal Government.

Budget authority (BA) means the authority provided by law to incur financial obligations that will result in outlays. (For a description of the several forms of budget authority, see "Budget Authority and Other Budgetary Resources" earlier in this chapter.)

Budget Control Act of 2011 refers to legislation that, among other things, amended BBEDCA to reinstate discretionary spending limits on budget authority through 2021 and restored the process for enforcing those spending limits. The legislation also increased the statutory debt ceiling; created a Joint Select Committee on Deficit Reduction that was instructed to develop a bill to reduce the Federal deficit by at least $1.5 trillion over a 10-year period; and provided a process to implement alternative spending reductions in the event that legislation achieving at least $1.2 trillion of deficit reduction was not enacted.

Budget resolution—see concurrent resolution on the budget.

Budget totals mean the totals included in the budget for budget authority, outlays, receipts, and the surplus or deficit. Some presentations in the budget distinguish on-budget totals from off-budget totals. On-budget totals reflect the transactions of all Federal Government entities except those excluded from the budget totals by law. Off-budget totals reflect the transactions of Government entities that are excluded from the on-budget totals by law. Under current law, the off-budget totals include the Social Security trust funds (Federal Old-Age and Survivors Insurance and Federal Disability Insurance Trust Funds) and the Postal Service Fund. The budget combines the on- and off-budget totals to derive unified (i.e. consolidated) totals for Federal activity.

Budget year refers to the fiscal year for which the budget is being considered, that is, with respect to a session of Congress, the fiscal year of the Government that starts on October 1 of the calendar year in which that session of the Congress begins.

Budgetary resources mean amounts available to incur obligations in a given year. The term comprises new budget authority and unobligated balances of budget authority provided in previous years.

Cap means the legal limits for each fiscal year under BBEDCA on the budget authority and outlays (only if applicable) provided by discretionary appropriations.

Cap adjustment means either an increase or a decrease that is permitted to the statutory cap limits for each fiscal year under BBEDCA on the budget authority and outlays (only if applicable) provided by discretionary appropriations only if certain conditions are met. These conditions may include providing for a base level of funding, a designation of the increase or decrease by the Congress, (and in some circumstances, the President) pursuant to a section of the BBEDCA, or a change in concepts and definitions of funding under the cap. Changes in concepts and definitions require consultation with the Congressional Appropriations and Budget Committees.

Cash equivalent transaction means a transaction in which the Government makes outlays or receives collections in a form other than cash or the cash does not accurately measure the cost of the transaction. (For examples, see the section on "Outlays" earlier in this chapter.)

Collections mean money collected by the Government that the budget records as a governmental receipt, an offsetting collection, or an offsetting receipt.

Concurrent resolution on the budget refers to the concurrent resolution adopted by the Congress to set budgetary targets for appropriations, mandatory spending legislation, and tax legislation. These concurrent resolutions are required by the Congressional Budget Act of 1974, and are generally adopted annually.

Continuing resolution means an appropriations act that provides for the ongoing operation of the Government in the absence of enacted appropriations.

Cost refers to legislation or administrative actions that increase outlays or decrease receipts. (Cf. savings.)

Credit program account means a budget account that receives and obligates appropriations to cover the subsidy cost of a direct loan or loan guarantee and disburses the subsidy cost to a financing account.

Current services estimate—see Baseline.

Debt held by the public means the cumulative amount of money the Federal Government has borrowed from the public and not repaid.

Debt held by the public net of financial assets means the cumulative amount of money the Federal Government has borrowed from the public and not repaid, minus the current value of financial assets such as loan assets, bank deposits, or private-sector securities or equities held by the Government and plus the current value of financial liabilities other than debt.

Debt held by Government accounts means the debt the Department of the Treasury owes to accounts within the Federal Government. Most of it results from the surpluses of the Social Security and other trust funds, which are required by law to be invested in Federal securities.

Debt limit means the maximum amount of Federal debt that may legally be outstanding at any time. It includes both the debt held by the public and the debt held by Government accounts, but without accounting for offsetting financial assets. When the debt limit is reached, the Government cannot borrow more money until the Congress has enacted a law to increase the limit.

Deficit means the amount by which outlays exceed receipts in a fiscal year. It may refer to the on-budget, off-budget, or unified budget deficit.

Direct loan means a disbursement of funds by the Government to a non-Federal borrower under a contract that requires the repayment of such funds with or without interest. The term includes the purchase of, or participation in, a loan made by another lender. The term also includes the sale of a Government asset on credit terms of more than 90 days duration as well as financing arrangements for other transactions that defer payment for more than 90 days. It also includes loans financed by the Federal Financing Bank (FFB) pursuant to agency loan guarantee authority. The term does not include the acquisition of a federally guaranteed loan in satisfaction of default or other guarantee claims or the price support "loans" of the Commodity Credit Corporation. (Cf. loan guarantee.)

Direct spending—see mandatory spending.

Disaster funding means a discretionary appropriation that is enacted that the Congress designates as being for disaster relief. Such amounts are a cap adjustment to the limits on discretionary spending under BBEDCA. The total adjustment for this purpose cannot exceed a ceiling for a particular year that is defined as the total of the average funding provided for disaster relief over the previous 10 years (excluding the highest and lowest years) and the unused amount of the prior year's ceiling (excluding the portion of the prior year's ceiling that was itself due to any unused amount from the year before). Disaster relief is defined as activities carried out pursuant to a determination under section 102(2) of the Robert T. Stafford Disaster Relief and Emergency Assistance Act.

Discretionary spending means budgetary resources (except those provided to fund mandatory spending programs) provided in appropriations acts. (Cf. mandatory spending.)

Emergency requirement means an amount that the Congress has designated as an emergency requirement. Such amounts are not included in the estimated budgetary effects of PAYGO legislation under the requirements of the Statutory Pay-As-You-Go Act of 2010, if they are mandatory or receipts. Such a discretionary appropriation that is subsequently designated by the President as an emergency requirement results in a cap adjustment to the limits on discretionary spending under BBEDCA.

Entitlement refers to a program in which the Federal Government is legally obligated to make payments or provide aid to any person who, or State or local government that, meets the legal criteria for eligibility. Examples include Social Security, Medicare, Medicaid, and the Supplemental Nutrition Assistance Program (formerly Food Stamps).

Federal funds group refers to the moneys collected and spent by the Government through accounts other than those designated as trust funds. Federal funds include general, special, public enterprise, and intragovernmental funds. (Cf. trust funds group.)

Financing account means a non-budgetary account (an account whose transactions are excluded from the budget totals) that records all of the cash flows resulting from post-1991 direct loan obligations or loan guarantee commitments. At least one financing account is associated with each credit program account. For programs that make both direct loans and loan guarantees, separate financing accounts are required for direct loan cash flows and for loan guarantee cash flows. (Cf. liquidating account.)

Fiscal year means the Government's accounting period. It begins on October 1 and ends on September 30, and is designated by the calendar year in which it ends.

Forward funding means appropriations of budget authority that are made for obligation starting in the last quarter of the fiscal year for the financing of ongoing grant programs during the next fiscal year.

General fund means the accounts in which are recorded governmental receipts not earmarked by law for a specific purpose, the proceeds of general borrowing, and the expenditure of these moneys.

Government-sponsored enterprises mean private enterprises that were established and chartered by the Federal Government for public policy purposes. They are classified as non-budgetary and not included in the Federal budget because they are private companies, and their securities are not backed by the full faith and credit of the Federal Government. However, the budget presents statements of financial condition for certain Government sponsored enterprises such as the Federal National Mortgage Association. (Cf. off-budget.)

Intragovernmental fund—see Revolving fund.

Liquidating account means a budget account that records all cash flows to and from the Government resulting from pre-1992 direct loan obligations or loan guarantee commitments. (Cf. financing account.)

Loan guarantee means any guarantee, insurance, or other pledge with respect to the payment of all or a part of the principal or interest on any debt obligation of a non-Federal borrower to a non-Federal lender. The term does not include the insurance of deposits, shares, or other withdrawable accounts in financial institutions. (Cf. direct loan.)

Mandatory spending means spending controlled by laws other than appropriations acts (including spending for entitlement programs) and spending for the Supplemental Nutrition Assistance Program, formerly food stamps. Although the Statutory Pay-As-You-Go Act of 2010 uses the term direct spending to mean this, mandatory spending is commonly used instead. (Cf. discretionary spending.)

Means of financing refers to borrowing, the change in cash balances, and certain other transactions involved in financing a deficit. The term is also used to refer to the debt repayment, the change in cash balances, and certain other transactions involved in using a surplus. By definition, the means of financing are not treated as receipts or outlays and so are non-budgetary.

Obligated balance means the cumulative amount of budget authority that has been obligated but not yet outlayed. (Cf. unobligated balance.)

Obligation means a binding agreement that will result in outlays, immediately or in the future. Budgetary resources must be available before obligations can be incurred legally.

Off-budget refers to transactions of the Federal Government that would be treated as budgetary had the Congress not designated them by statute as "off-budget." Currently, transactions of the Social Security trust funds and the Postal Service are the only sets of transactions that are so designated. The term is sometimes used more broadly to refer to the transactions of private enterprises that were established and sponsored by the Government, most especially "Government-sponsored enterprises" such as the Federal Home Loan Banks. (Cf. budget totals.)

Offsetting collections mean collections that, by law, are credited directly to expenditure accounts and deducted from gross budget authority and outlays of the expenditure account, rather than added to receipts. Usually, they are authorized to be spent for the purposes of the account without further action by the Congress. They result from business-like transactions with the public, including payments from the public in exchange for goods and services, reimbursements for damages, and gifts or donations of money to the Government and from intragovernmental transactions with other Government accounts. The au-

thority to spend offsetting collections is a form of budget authority. (Cf. receipts and offsetting receipts.)

Offsetting receipts mean collections that are credited to offsetting receipt accounts and deducted from gross budget authority and outlays, rather than added to receipts. They are not authorized to be credited to expenditure accounts. The legislation that authorizes the offsetting receipts may earmark them for a specific purpose and either appropriate them for expenditure for that purpose or require them to be appropriated in annual appropriation acts before they can be spent. Like offsetting collections, they result from business-like transactions or market-oriented activities with the public, including payments from the public in exchange for goods and services, reimbursements for damages, and gifts or donations of money to the Government and from intragovernmental transactions with other Government accounts. (Cf. receipts, undistributed offsetting receipts, and offsetting collections.)

On-budget refers to all budgetary transactions other than those designated by statute as off-budget. (Cf. budget totals.)

Outlay means a payment to liquidate an obligation (other than the repayment of debt principal or other disbursements that are "means of financing" transactions). Outlays generally are equal to cash disbursements, but also are recorded for cash-equivalent transactions, such as the issuance of debentures to pay insurance claims, and in a few cases are recorded on an accrual basis such as interest on public issues of the public debt. Outlays are the measure of Government spending.

Outyear estimates mean estimates presented in the budget for the years beyond the budget year of budget authority, outlays, receipts, and other items (such as debt).

Overseas Contingency Operations/Global War on Terrorism (OCO/GWOT) means a discretionary appropriation that is enacted that the Congress and, subsequently, the President have so designated on an account by account basis. Such a discretionary appropriation that is designated as OCO/GWOT results in a cap adjustment to the limits on discretionary spending under BBEDCA. Funding for these purposes has most recently been associated with the wars in Iraq and Afghanistan.

Pay-as-you-go (PAYGO) refers to requirements of the Statutory Pay-As-You-Go Act of 2010 that result in a sequestration if the estimated combined result of new legislation affecting direct spending or revenue increases the on-budget deficit relative to the baseline, as of the end of a congressional session.

Public enterprise fund—see Revolving fund.

Reappropriation means a provision of law that extends into a new fiscal year the availability of unobligated amounts that have expired or would otherwise expire.

Receipts mean collections that result from the Government's exercise of its sovereign power to tax or otherwise compel payment. They are compared to outlays in calculating a surplus or deficit. (Cf. offsetting collections and offsetting receipts.)

Revolving fund means a fund that conducts continuing cycles of business-like activity, in which the fund charges for the sale of products or services and uses the proceeds to finance its spending, usually without requirement for annual appropriations. There are two types of revolving funds: Public enterprise funds, which conduct business-like operations mainly with the public, and intragovernmental revolving funds, which conduct business-like operations mainly within and between Government agencies. (Cf. special fund and trust fund.)

Savings refers to legislation or administrative actions that decrease outlays or increase receipts. (Cf. cost.)

Scorekeeping means measuring the budget effects of legislation, generally in terms of budget authority, receipts, and outlays, for purposes of measuring adherence to the Budget or to budget targets established by the Congress, as through agreement to a Budget Resolution.

Sequestration means the cancellation of budgetary resources. The Statutory Pay-As-You-Go Act of 2010 requires such cancellations if revenue or direct spending legislation is enacted that, in total, increases projected deficits or reduces projected surpluses relative to the baseline. The Balanced Budget and Emergency Deficit Control Act of 1985, as amended, requires annual across-the-board cancellations to selected mandatory programs through 2029 and would require cancellations if discretionary appropriations exceed the statutory limits on discretionary spending.

Special fund means a Federal fund account for receipts or offsetting receipts earmarked for specific purposes and the expenditure of these receipts. (Cf. revolving fund and trust fund.)

Statutory Pay-As-You-Go Act of 2010 refers to legislation that reinstated a statutory pay-as-you-go requirement for new tax or mandatory spending legislation. The law is a standalone piece of legislation that cross-references BBEDCA but does not directly amend that legislation. This is a permanent law and does not expire.

Subsidy means the estimated long-term cost to the Government of a direct loan or loan guarantee, calculated on a net present value basis, excluding administrative costs and any incidental effects on governmental receipts or outlays.

Surplus means the amount by which receipts exceed outlays in a fiscal year. It may refer to the on-budget, off-budget, or unified budget surplus.

Supplemental appropriation means an appropriation enacted subsequent to a regular annual appropriations act, when the need for additional funds is too urgent to be postponed until the next regular annual appropriations act.

Trust fund refers to a type of account, designated by law as a trust fund, for receipts or offsetting receipts dedicated to specific purposes and the expenditure of these receipts. Some revolving funds are designated as trust funds, and these are called trust revolving funds. (Cf. special fund and revolving fund.)

Trust funds group refers to the moneys collected and spent by the Government through trust fund accounts. (Cf. Federal funds group.)

Undistributed offsetting receipts mean offsetting receipts that are deducted from the Government-wide totals for budget authority and outlays instead of being offset against a specific agency and function. (Cf. offsetting receipts.)

Unified budget includes receipts from all sources and outlays for all programs of the Federal Government, including both on- and off-budget programs. It is the most comprehensive measure of the Government's annual finances.

Unobligated balance means the cumulative amount of budget authority that remains available for obligation under law in unexpired accounts. The term "expired balances available for adjustment only" refers to unobligated amounts in expired accounts.

User charges are charges assessed for the provision of Government services and for the sale or use of Government goods or resources. The payers of the user charge must be limited in the authorizing legislation to those receiving special benefits from, or subject to regulation by, the program or activity beyond the benefits received by the general public or broad segments of the public (such as those who pay income taxes or custom duties).

9. COVERAGE OF THE BUDGET

The Federal budget is the central instrument of national policy making. It is the Government's financial plan for proposing and deciding the allocation of resources to serve national objectives. The budget provides information on the cost and scope of Federal activities to inform decisions and to serve as a means to control the allocation of resources. When enacted, it establishes the level of public goods and services provided by the Government.

Federal Government activities can be either "budgetary" or "non-budgetary." Those activities that involve direct and measurable allocation of Federal resources are budgetary. The payments to and from the public resulting from budgetary activities are included in the budget's accounting of outlays and receipts. Federal activities that do not involve direct and measurable allocation of Federal resources are non-budgetary and are not included in the budget's accounting of outlays and receipts. More detailed information about outlays and receipts may be found in Chapter 8, "Budget Concepts," of this volume.

The budget documents include information on some non-budgetary activities because they can be important instruments of Federal policy and provide insight into the scope and nature of Federal activities. For example, the budget documents show the transactions of the Thrift Savings Program (TSP), a collection of investment funds managed by the Federal Retirement Thrift Investment Board (FRTIB). Despite the fact that the FRTIB is budgetary and one of the TSP funds is invested entirely in Federal securities, the transactions of these funds are non-budgetary because current and retired Federal employees own the funds. The Government manages these funds only in a fiduciary capacity.

The budget also includes information on cash flows that are a means of financing Federal activity, such as for credit financing accounts. However, to avoid double-counting, means of financing amounts are not included in the estimates of outlays or receipts because the costs of the underlying Federal activities are already reflected in the deficit.[1] This chapter provides details about the budgetary and non-budgetary activities of the Federal Government.

Budgetary Activities

The Federal Government has used the unified budget concept—which consolidates outlays and receipts from Federal funds and trust funds, including the Social Security trust funds—since 1968, starting with the 1969 Budget. The 1967 President's Commission on Budget Concepts (the Commission) recommended the change to include the financial transactions of all of the Federal Government's programs and agencies. Thus, the budget includes information on the financial transactions of all 15 Executive Departments, all independent agencies (from all three branches of Government), and all Government corporations.[2]

The budget shows outlays and receipts for on-budget and off-budget activities separately to reflect the legal distinction between the two. Although there is a legal distinction between on-budget and off-budget activities, conceptually there is no difference between them. Off-budget Federal activities reflect the same kinds of governmental roles as on-budget activities and result in outlays and receipts. Like on-budget activities, the Government funds and controls off-budget activities. The "unified budget" reflects the conceptual similarity between on-budget and off-budget activities by showing combined totals of outlays and receipts for both.

Many Government corporations are entities with business-type operations that charge the public for services at prices intended to allow the entity to be self-sustaining, although some operate at a loss in order to provide subsidies to specific recipients. Often these entities are more independent than other agencies and have limited exemptions from certain Federal personnel requirements to allow for flexibility.

All accounts in Table 25-1, "Federal Budget by Agency and Account," in the supplemental materials to this volume are budgetary.[3] The majority of budgetary accounts are associated with the Departments or other entities that are clearly Federal agencies. Some budgetary accounts reflect Government payments to entities that the Government created or chartered as private or non-Federal entities. Some of these entities receive all or a majority of their funding from the Government. These include the Corporation for Public Broadcasting, Gallaudet University, Howard University, the Legal Services Corporation, the National Railroad Passenger Corporation (Amtrak), the Smithsonian Institution, the State Justice Institute, and the United States Institute of Peace. A related example is the Standard Setting Board, which is not a Federally created entity but since 2003

---

[1] For more information on means of financing, see the "Budget Deficit or Surplus and Means of Financing" section of Chapter 8, "Budget Concepts," in this volume.

[2] Government corporations are Government entities that are defined as corporations pursuant to the Government Corporation Control Act, as amended (31 U.S.C. 9101), or elsewhere in law. Examples include the Commodity Credit Corporation, the Export-Import Bank of the United States, the Federal Crop Insurance Corporation, the Federal Deposit Insurance Corporation, the Millennium Challenge Corporation, the Overseas Private Investment Corporation, the Pension Benefit Guaranty Corporation, the Tennessee Valley Authority, the African Development Foundation (22 U.S.C. 290h-6), the Inter-American Foundation (22 U.S.C. 290f), the Presidio Trust (16 U.S.C. 460bb note), and the Valles Caldera Trust (16 U.S.C. 698v-4).

[3] Table 25-1 can be found at: *https://www.whitehouse.gov/omb/analytical-perspectives*.

Table 9–1.   COMPARISON OF TOTAL, ON-BUDGET, AND OFF-BUDGET TRANSACTIONS[1]

(In Billions Of Dollars)

Year	Receipts			Outlays			Surplus or deficit (–)		
	Total	On-budget	Off-budget	Total	On-budget	Off-budget	Total	On-budget	Off-budget
1981	599.3	469.1	130.2	678.2	543.0	135.3	–79.0	–73.9	–5.1
1982	617.8	474.3	143.5	745.7	594.9	150.9	–128.0	–120.6	–7.4
1983	600.6	453.2	147.3	808.4	660.9	147.4	–207.8	–207.7	–.1
1984	666.4	500.4	166.1	851.8	685.6	166.2	–185.4	–185.3	–.1
1985	734.0	547.9	186.2	946.3	769.4	176.9	–212.3	–221.5	9.2
1986	769.2	568.9	200.2	990.4	806.8	183.5	–221.2	–237.9	16.7
1987	854.3	640.9	213.4	1,004.0	809.2	194.8	–149.7	–168.4	18.6
1988	909.2	667.7	241.5	1,064.4	860.0	204.4	–155.2	–192.3	37.1
1989	991.1	727.4	263.7	1,143.7	932.8	210.9	–152.6	–205.4	52.8
1990	1,032.0	750.3	281.7	1,253.0	1,027.9	225.1	–221.0	–277.6	56.6
1991	1,055.0	761.1	293.9	1,324.2	1,082.5	241.7	–269.2	–321.4	52.2
1992	1,091.2	788.8	302.4	1,381.5	1,129.2	252.3	–290.3	–340.4	50.1
1993	1,154.3	842.4	311.9	1,409.4	1,142.8	266.6	–255.1	–300.4	45.3
1994	1,258.6	923.5	335.0	1,461.8	1,182.4	279.4	–203.2	–258.8	55.7
1995	1,351.8	1,000.7	351.1	1,515.7	1,227.1	288.7	–164.0	–226.4	62.4
1996	1,453.1	1,085.6	367.5	1,560.5	1,259.6	300.9	–107.4	–174.0	66.6
1997	1,579.2	1,187.2	392.0	1,601.1	1,290.5	310.6	–21.9	–103.2	81.4
1998	1,721.7	1,305.9	415.8	1,652.5	1,335.9	316.6	69.3	–29.9	99.2
1999	1,827.5	1,383.0	444.5	1,701.8	1,381.1	320.8	125.6	1.9	123.7
2000	2,025.2	1,544.6	480.6	1,789.0	1,458.2	330.8	236.2	86.4	149.8
2001	1,991.1	1,483.6	507.5	1,862.8	1,516.0	346.8	128.2	–32.4	160.7
2002	1,853.1	1,337.8	515.3	2,010.9	1,655.2	355.7	–157.8	–317.4	159.7
2003	1,782.3	1,258.5	523.8	2,159.9	1,796.9	363.0	–377.6	–538.4	160.8
2004	1,880.1	1,345.4	534.7	2,292.8	1,913.3	379.5	–412.7	–568.0	155.2
2005	2,153.6	1,576.1	577.5	2,472.0	2,069.7	402.2	–318.3	–493.6	175.3
2006	2,406.9	1,798.5	608.4	2,655.1	2,233.0	422.1	–248.2	–434.5	186.3
2007	2,568.0	1,932.9	635.1	2,728.7	2,275.0	453.6	–160.7	–342.2	181.5
2008	2,524.0	1,865.9	658.0	2,982.5	2,507.8	474.8	–458.6	–641.8	183.3
2009	2,105.0	1,451.0	654.0	3,517.7	3,000.7	517.0	–1,412.7	–1,549.7	137.0
2010	2,162.7	1,531.0	631.7	3,457.1	2,902.4	554.7	–1,294.4	–1,371.4	77.0
2011	2,303.5	1,737.7	565.8	3,603.1	3,104.5	498.6	–1,299.6	–1,366.8	67.2
2012	2,450.0	1,880.5	569.5	3,526.6	3,019.0	507.6	–1,076.6	–1,138.5	61.9
2013	2,775.1	2,101.8	673.3	3,454.9	2,821.1	633.8	–679.8	–719.2	39.5
2014	3,021.5	2,285.9	735.6	3,506.3	2,800.2	706.1	–484.8	–514.3	29.5
2015	3,249.9	2,479.5	770.4	3,691.9	2,948.8	743.1	–442.0	–469.3	27.3
2016	3,268.0	2,457.8	810.2	3,852.6	3,077.9	774.7	–584.7	–620.2	35.5
2017	3,316.2	2,465.6	850.6	3,981.6	3,180.4	801.2	–665.4	–714.9	49.4
2018	3,329.9	2,475.2	854.7	4,109.0	3,260.5	848.6	–779.1	–785.3	6.2
2019	3,464.2	2,549.9	914.3	4,448.3	3,541.7	906.6	–984.2	–991.8	7.7
2020 estimate	3,706.3	2,739.3	967.1	4,789.7	3,829.9	959.8	–1,083.4	–1,090.7	7.3
2021 estimate	3,863.3	2,852.3	1,011.0	4,829.4	3,811.1	1,018.2	–966.1	–958.9	–7.2
2022 estimate	4,085.7	3,021.0	1,064.7	5,005.4	3,920.5	1,084.9	–919.8	–899.5	–20.2
2023 estimate	4,359.1	3,243.4	1,115.7	5,105.3	3,951.4	1,153.9	–746.3	–708.0	–38.2
2024 estimate	4,656.5	3,482.1	1,174.4	5,208.5	3,983.2	1,225.3	–551.9	–501.0	–50.9
2025 estimate	4,924.3	3,690.5	1,233.8	5,450.8	4,150.1	1,300.6	–526.5	–459.7	–66.8

[1] Off-budget transactions consist of the Social Security Trust funds and the Postal Service fund.

has received a majority of funding through a federally mandated assessment on public companies under the Sarbanes-Oxley Act. Although the Federal payments to these entities are budgetary, the entities themselves are non-budgetary.

Whether the Government created or chartered an entity does not alone determine its budgetary status. The Commission recommended that the budget be comprehensive but it also recognized that proper budgetary classification required weighing all relevant factors regarding establishment, ownership, and control of an entity while erring on the side of inclusiveness. Generally, entities that are primarily Government owned or controlled are classified as budgetary. OMB determines the budgetary classification of entities in consultation with the Congressional Budget Office (CBO) and the Budget Committees of the Congress.

One recent example of a budgetary classification was for the Puerto Rico Financial Oversight Board, created in June 2016 by the Puerto Rico Oversight, Management, and Economic Stability Act (P.L. 114–187). By statute, this oversight board is not a department, agency, establishment, or instrumentality of the Federal Government, but is an entity within the territorial government financed entirely by the territorial government. Because the flow of funds from the territory to the oversight board is mandated by Federal law, the budget reflects the allocation of resources by the territorial government to the territorial entity as a receipt from the territorial government and an equal outlay to the oversight board, with net zero deficit impact. Because the oversight board itself is not a Federal entity, its operations are not included in the budget.

Another example involved the National Association of Registered Agents and Brokers (NARAB). NARAB allows for the adoption and application of insurance licensing, continuing education, and other nonresident producer qualification requirements on a multi-State basis. In other words, NARAB streamlines the ability of a non-resident insurer to become a licensed agent in another State. In exchange for providing enhanced market access, NARAB collects fees from its members. The Terrorism Risk Insurance Reauthorization Act of 2015 established the association. In addition to being statutorily established—which in itself is an indication that the entity is governmental—NARAB has a board of directors appointed by the President and confirmed by the Senate. It must also submit bylaws and an annual report to the Department of the Treasury and its primary function involves exercising a regulatory function.

Off-budget Federal activities.—Despite the Commission's recommendation that the budget be comprehensive, every year since 1971 at least one Federal program or agency has been presented as off-budget because of a legal requirement.[4] The Government funds such off-budget Federal activities and administers them according to Federal legal requirements. However, their net costs are excluded, by law, from the rest of the budget totals, also known as the "on-budget" totals.

Off-budget Federal activities currently consist of the U.S. Postal Service and the two Social Security trust funds: Old-Age and Survivors Insurance and Disability Insurance. Social Security has been classified as off-budget since 1986 and the Postal Service has been classified as off-budget since 1990.[5] Other activities that had been designated in law as off-budget at various times before 1986 have been classified as on-budget by law since at least 1985 as a result of the Balanced Budget and Emergency Deficit Control Act of 1985 (P.L. 99–177). Activities that were off-budget at one time but that are now on-budget are classified as on-budget for all years in historical budget data.

Social Security is the largest single program in the unified budget and it is classified by law as off-budget; as a result, the off-budget accounts constitute a significant part of total Federal spending and receipts. Table 9–1 divides total Federal Government outlays, receipts, and the surplus or deficit between on-budget and off-budget amounts. Within this table, the Social Security and Postal Service transactions are classified as off-budget for all years to provide a consistent comparison over time.

Non-Budgetary Activities

The Government characterizes some important Government activities as non-budgetary because they do not involve the direct allocation of resources.[6] These activities can affect budget outlays or receipts even though they have non-budgetary components.

Federal credit programs: budgetary and non-budgetary transactions.—Federal credit programs make direct loans or guarantee private loans to non-Federal borrowers. The Federal Credit Reform Act of 1990 (FCRA), as amended by the Balanced Budget Act of 1997, established the current budgetary treatment for credit programs. Under FCRA, the budgetary cost of a credit program, known as the "subsidy cost," is the estimated lifetime cost to the Government of a loan or a loan guarantee on a net present value basis, excluding administrative costs.

---

[4] While the term "off-budget" is sometimes used colloquially to mean non-budgetary, the term has a meaning distinct from non-budgetary. Off-budget activities would be considered budgetary, absent legal requirement to exclude these activities from the budget totals.

[5] See 42 U.S.C. 911, and 39 U.S.C. 2009a, respectively. The off-budget Postal Service accounts consist of the Postal Service Fund, which is classified as a mandatory account, and the Office of the Inspector General and the Postal Regulatory Commission, both of which are classified as discretionary accounts. The Postal Service Retiree Health Benefits Fund is an on-budget mandatory account with the Office of Personnel Management. The off-budget Social Security accounts consist of the Federal Old-Age and Survivors Insurance trust fund and the Federal Disability Insurance trust fund, both of which have mandatory and discretionary funding.

[6] Tax expenditures, which are discussed in Chapter 13 of this volume, are an example of Government activities that could be characterized as either budgetary or non-budgetary. Tax expenditures refer to the reduction in tax receipts resulting from the special tax treatment accorded certain private activities. Because tax expenditures reduce tax receipts and receipts are budgetary, tax expenditures clearly have budgetary effects. However, the size and composition of tax expenditures are not explicitly recorded in the budget as outlays or as negative receipts and, for this reason, tax expenditures might be considered a special case of non-budgetary transactions.

Outlays equal to the subsidy cost are recorded in the budget up front, as they are incurred—for example, when a loan is made or guaranteed. Credit program cash flows to and from the public are recorded in non-budgetary financing accounts and the information is included in budget documents to provide insight into the program size and costs. For more information about the mechanisms of credit programs, see Chapter 8 of this volume, "Budget Concepts." More detail on credit programs is in Chapter 18 of this volume, "Credit and Insurance."

Deposit funds.—Deposit funds are non-budgetary accounts that record amounts held by the Government temporarily until ownership is determined (such as earnest money paid by bidders for mineral leases) or held by the Government as an agent for others (such as State income taxes withheld from Federal employees' salaries and not yet paid to the States). The largest deposit fund is the Government Securities Investment Fund, also known as the G-Fund, which is part of the TSP, the Government's defined contribution retirement plan. The Federal Retirement Thrift Investment Board manages the fund's investment for Federal employees who participate in the TSP (which is similar to private-sector 401(k) plans). The Department of the Treasury holds the G-Fund assets, which are the property of Federal employees, only in a fiduciary capacity; the transactions of the Fund are not resource allocations by the Government and are therefore non-budgetary.[7] For similar reasons, Native American-owned funds that are held and managed in a fiduciary capacity are also excluded from the budget.

Government-Sponsored Enterprises (GSEs).—GSEs are privately owned and therefore distinct from Government corporations. The Federal Government has chartered GSEs such as the Federal National Mortgage Association (Fannie Mae), the Federal Home Loan Mortgage Corporation (Freddie Mac), the Federal Home Loan Banks, the Farm Credit System, and the Federal Agricultural Mortgage Corporation to provide financial intermediation for specified public purposes. Although Federally chartered to serve public-policy purposes, GSEs are classified as non-budgetary because they are intended to be privately owned and controlled—with any public benefits accruing indirectly from the GSEs' business transactions. Estimates of the GSEs' activities can be found in a separate chapter of the Budget *Appendix*, and their activities are discussed in Chapter 18 of this volume, "Credit and Insurance."

In September 2008, in response to the financial market crisis, the director of the Federal Housing Finance Agency (FHFA)[8] placed Fannie Mae and Freddie Mac into conservatorship for the purpose of preserving the assets and restoring the solvency of these two GSEs. As conservator, FHFA has broad authority to direct the operations of these GSEs. However, these GSEs remain private companies with boards of directors and management responsible for their day-to-day operations. The Budget continues to treat these two GSEs as non-budgetary private entities in conservatorship rather than as Government Agencies. By contrast, CBO treats these GSEs as budgetary Federal Agencies. Both treatments include budgetary and non-budgetary amounts.

While OMB reflects all of the GSEs' transactions with the public as non-budgetary, the payments from the Treasury to the GSEs are recorded as budgetary outlays and dividends received by the Treasury are recorded as budgetary receipts. Under CBO's approach, the subsidy costs of Fannie Mae's and Freddie Mac's past credit activities are treated as having already been recorded in the budget estimates; the subsidy costs of future credit activities will be recorded when the activities occur. Lending and borrowing activities between the GSEs and the public apart from the subsidy costs are treated as non-budgetary by CBO, and Treasury payments to the GSEs are intragovernmental transfers (from Treasury to the GSEs) that net to zero in CBO's budget estimates.

Overall, both the budget's accounting and CBO's accounting present Fannie Mae's and Freddie Mac's gains and losses as Government receipts and outlays—which reduce or increase Government deficits. The two approaches, however, reflect the effect of the gains and losses in the budget at different times.

Other federally created non-budgetary entities.—In addition to the GSEs, the Federal Government has created a number of other entities that are classified as non-budgetary. These include federally funded research and development centers (FFRDCs), non-appropriated fund instrumentalities (NAFIs), and other entities; some of these are non-profit entities and some are for-profit entities.[9]

FFRDCs are entities that conduct agency-specific research under contract or cooperative agreement. Some FFRDCs were created to conduct research for the Department of Defense but are administered by colleges, universities, or other non-profit entities. Despite this

---

[7] The administrative functions of the Federal Retirement Thrift Investment Board are carried out by Government employees and included in the budget totals.

[8] FHFA is the regulator of Fannie Mae, Freddie Mac, and the Federal Home Loan Banks.

[9] Although most entities created by the Federal Government are budgetary, the Congress and the President have chartered, but not necessarily created, approximately 100 non-profit entities that are non-budgetary. These include patriotic, charitable, and educational organizations under Title 36 of the U.S. Code and foundations and trusts chartered under other titles of the Code. Title 36 corporations include the American Legion, the American National Red Cross, Big Brothers—Big Sisters of America, Boy Scouts of America, Future Farmers of America, Girl Scouts of the United States of America, the National Academy of Public Administration, the National Academy of Sciences, and Veterans of Foreign Wars of the United States. Virtually all of the non-profit entities chartered by the Government existed under State law prior to the granting of a Government charter, making the Government charter an honorary rather than governing charter. A major exception to this is the American National Red Cross. Its Government charter requires it to provide disaster relief and to ensure compliance with treaty obligations under the Geneva Convention. Although any Government payments (whether made as direct appropriations or through agency appropriations) to these chartered non-profits, including the Red Cross, would be budgetary, the non-profits themselves are classified as non-budgetary. On April 29, 2015, the Subcommittee on Immigration and Border Security of the Committee on the Judiciary in the U.S. House of Representatives adopted a policy prohibiting the Congress from granting new Federal charters to private, non-profit organizations. This policy has been adopted by every subcommittee with jurisdiction over charters since the 101st Congress.

non-budgetary classification, many FFRDCs receive direct resource allocation from the Government and are included as budget lines in various agencies. Examples of FFRDCs include the Center for Naval Analysis and the Jet Propulsion Laboratory.[10] Even though FFRDCs are non-budgetary, Federal payments to the FFRDC are budget outlays. In addition to Federal funding, FFRDCs may receive funding from non-Federal sources.

Non-appropriated fund instrumentalities (NAFIs) are entities that support an agency's current and retired personnel. Nearly all NAFIs are associated with the Departments of Defense, Homeland Security (Coast Guard), and Veterans Affairs. Most NAFIs are located on military bases and include the Armed Forces exchanges (which sell goods to military personnel and their families), recreational facilities, and childcare centers. NAFIs are financed by proceeds from the sale of goods or services and do not receive direct appropriations; thus, they are characterized as non-budgetary but any agency payments to the NAFIs are recorded as budget outlays.

A number of entities created by the Government receive a significant amount of non-Federal funding. Non-Federal individuals or organizations significantly control some of these entities. These entities include Gallaudet University, Howard University, Amtrak, and the Universal Services Administrative Company, among others.[11] Most of these entities receive direct appropriations or other recurring payments from the Government. The appropriations or other payments are budgetary and included in Table 25-1. However, many of these entities are themselves non-budgetary. Generally, entities that receive a significant portion of funding from non-Federal sources but are not controlled by the Government are non-budgetary.

Regulation.—Federal Government regulations often require the private sector or other levels of government to make expenditures for specified purposes that are intended to have public benefits, such as workplace safety and pollution control. Although the budget reflects the Government's cost of conducting regulatory activities, the costs imposed on the private sector as a result of regulation are treated as non-budgetary and not included in the budget. The annual Regulatory Plan and the semi-annual Unified Agenda of Federal Regulatory and Deregulatory Actions describe the Government's regulatory priorities and plans.[12] OMB has published the estimated costs and benefits of Federal regulation annually since 1997.[13]

Monetary policy.—As a fiscal policy tool, the budget is used by elected Government officials to promote economic growth and achieve other public policy objectives. Monetary policy is another tool that governments use to promote economic policy objectives. In the United States, the Federal Reserve System—which is composed of a Board of Governors and 12 regional Federal Reserve Banks—conducts monetary policy. The Federal Reserve Act provides that the goal of monetary policy is to "maintain long-run growth of the monetary and credit aggregates commensurate with the economy's long run potential to increase production, so as to promote effectively the goals of maximum employment, stable prices, and moderate long-term interest rates."[14] The Full Employment and Balanced Growth Act of 1978, also known as the Humphrey-Hawkins Act, reaffirmed the dual goals of full employment and price stability.[15]

By law, the Federal Reserve System is a self-financing entity that is independent of the Executive Branch and subject only to broad oversight by the Congress. Consistent with the recommendations of the Commission, the effects of monetary policy and the actions of the Federal Reserve System are non-budgetary, with exceptions for the transfer to the Treasury of excess income generated through its operations. The Federal Reserve System earns income from a variety of sources including interest on Government securities, foreign currency investments and loans to depository institutions, and fees for services (e.g., check clearing services) provided to depository institutions. The Federal Reserve System remits to Treasury any excess income over expenses annually. For the fiscal year ending September 2019, Treasury recorded $52.8 billion in receipts from the Federal Reserve System. In addition to remitting excess income to Treasury, current law requires the Federal Reserve to transfer a portion of its excess earnings to the Consumer Financial Protection Bureau (CFPB).[16]

The Board of Governors of the Federal Reserve is a Federal Government Agency, but because of its independent status, its budget is not subject to Executive Branch review and is included in the Budget *Appendix* for informational purposes only. The Federal Reserve Banks are subject to Board oversight and managed by boards of directors chosen by the Board of Governors and member banks, which include all National banks and State banks that choose to become members. The budgets of the regional Banks are subject to approval by the Board of Governors and are not included in the Budget *Appendix*.

---

[10] The National Science Foundation maintains a list of FFRDCs at *www.nsf.gov/statistics/ffrdc*.

[11] Under section 415(b) of the Amtrak Reform and Accountability Act of 1997, (49 U.S.C. 24304 and note), Amtrak was required to redeem all of its outstanding common stock. Once all outstanding common stock is redeemed, Amtrak will be wholly-owned by the Government and, at that point, its non-budgetary status may need to be reassessed.

[12] The most recent Regulatory Plan and introduction to the Unified Agenda issued by the General Services Administration's Regulatory Information Service Center are available at *www.reginfo.gov* and at *www.gpo.gov*.

[13] In the 2018, 2019, and 2020 draft report, OMB indicates that for the five rules for which monetized costs and benefits were estimated in 2019, the issuing agencies estimated a total of $0.2 to $3.7 billion in annual benefits and up to $0.6 billion in annual costs, in 2018 dollars.

These totals include only the benefits and costs for the minority of rules for which both those categories of impacts were estimated. The most recent draft report is available at *https://www.whitehouse.gov/omb/information-regulatory-affairs/reports/#ORC*.

[14] See 12 U.S.C. 225a.

[15] See 15 U.S.C. 3101 et seq.

[16] See section 1011 of Public Law 111-203 (12 U.S.C. 5491).

10. BUDGET PROCESS

This chapter addresses several broad categories of budget process—enforcement, presentation, and reforms issues. First, the chapter discusses proposals to improve budget enforcement. These proposals include: an extension of the spending reductions required by the Joint Select Committee on Deficit Reduction and what comes after the expiration of the discretionary caps in 2021; program integrity initiatives both enacted and proposed within budget law; funding requests for disaster relief and wildfire suppression; reforms to the budgetary treatment of disaster assistance funding; limits on changes in mandatory programs in appropriations Acts; limits on advance appropriations; a discussion of the system under the Statutory Pay-As-You-Go Act of 2010 (PAYGO) of scoring legislation affecting receipts and mandatory spending; and administrative PAYGO actions affecting mandatory spending.

Second, this chapter describes proposals in budget presentation. The proposals include a discussion of the differences in the baseline presentation of revenues and spending in the Highway Trust Fund and the associated reauthorization proposal; adjustments in the BBEDCA baseline that extend certain expiring tax laws; proposals for the Pell Grant program; improvements to how Joint Committee sequestration is shown in the Budget; the budgetary treatment of the housing Government-sponsored enterprises and the United States Postal Service; and using fair value as a method of estimating the cost of credit programs.

Third, this chapter describes reform proposals to improve budgeting and fiscal sustainability with respect to individual programs as well as across Government. These proposals include: discretionary spending caps; changes to capital budgeting for large civilian Federal capital projects; budgetary treatment of Federal employee cost reforms; an extension and increase in the U.S. Government's participation in the International Monetary Fund's New Arrangements to Borrow; accounting for debt service in cost estimates; and reform ideas to rein in Government spending.

These proposals combine fiscal responsibility with measures to provide citizens with a more transparent, comprehensive, and accurate measure of the reach of the Federal budget. Together, the reforms and presentations discussed create a budget more focused on core Government functions and more accountable to the taxpayer.

I. BUDGET ENFORCEMENT PROPOSALS

Joint Committee Enforcement

In August 2011, as part of the Budget Control Act of 2011 (BCA; Public Law 112-25), bipartisan majorities in both the House and Senate voted to establish the Joint Select Committee on Deficit Reduction to recommend legislation to achieve at least $1.5 trillion of deficit reduction over the period of fiscal years 2012 through 2021. The failure of the Congress to enact such comprehensive deficit reduction legislation to achieve the $1.5 trillion goal triggered a sequestration of discretionary and mandatory spending in 2013, led to reductions in the discretionary caps for 2014 through 2020, and forced additional sequestrations of mandatory spending in each of fiscal years 2014 through 2020. A further sequestration of mandatory spending is scheduled to take effect beginning on October 1, 2020 based on the order released with the 2021 Budget.

To date, various laws have changed the annual reductions required to the discretionary spending limits set in the BCA through 2021. Most recently, the Bipartisan Budget Act of 2019 (BBA of 2019; Public Law 116-37) adjusted these discretionary spending limits for fiscal years 2020 and 2021, the last years of the BCA caps. The 2021 caps remain at the levels enacted in this Act and are reflected in the sequestration preview report issued with this Budget. Looking ahead, future reductions to mandatory programs are to be implemented by a sequestration of non-exempt mandatory budgetary resources in each of fiscal years 2021 through 2029, which are triggered by the transmittal of the President's Budget for each year and take effect on the first day of the fiscal year. The Budget proposes to continue mandatory sequestration into 2030 to generate an additional $16.7 billion in deficit reduction.

For discretionary programs, the 2021 caps, as noted, remain at the BBA levels of $671.5 billion for defense and $626.5 billion for non-defense. For 2021, the President's Budget requests funding up to the current law defense cap while funding non-defense programs at a level of $590 billion—which is the original BCA cap level for non-defense in 2021 before Joint Committee enforcement and the BBA of 2019. This non-defense level is five percent below the 2020 cap level in the BBA of 2019. The Administration has long articulated its view that spending caps should be treated as ceilings for spending and not floors. By funding non-defense programs at the original BCA level, the Administration is instituting much-needed spending discipline. After 2021, the Administration proposes levels that would increase defense programs by about 2 percent each year through 2025 and then hold spending flat for the remaining five years in the budget window. Non-defense programs will be reduced by 2 percent each year.

In addition to these base levels, the 2021 Budget proposes $69 billion for the Overseas Contingency Operations budget, which is consistent with the levels specified in the BBA of 2019. In total, this would provide $740.5 billion in defense funding to support the 2018 National Defense Strategy and to protect America's vital national interests.

After 2021, the Administration supports new base caps for defense and non-defense programs through 2025 at the levels included in the 2021 Budget. After 2025, the Congress should again set discretionary spending caps, at levels that are appropriate given national security needs and the need to control Federal deficits and debt. The Budget leaves in place placeholder levels that project current policies with defense programs frozen at the 2025 level while non-defense programs continue to be reduced by two percent annually. See Table S–7 in the main *Budget* volume for the proposed annual discretionary caps.

Discretionary Cap Adjustment Funding

Discretionary Funding for Program Integrity Cap Adjustments

All Federal programs must be run efficiently and effectively. There is compelling evidence that investments in administrative resources can significantly decrease the rate of improper payments and recoup many times their initial investment for certain programs. In such programs, the Administration continues to support using discretionary dollars to make significant investments in activities that ensure that taxpayer dollars are spent correctly. Using cap adjustment funding on program integrity activities allows for the expansion of oversight and enforcement activities in the largest benefit programs including Social Security, Unemployment Insurance, Medicare and Medicaid, where return on investment using discretionary dollars is proven. Additionally, the Administration supports increasing investments in tax compliance related to Internal Revenue Service tax enforcement.

The following sections explain the benefits and budget presentation of the enacted and proposed adjustments to the discretionary caps for program integrity activities. The Administration proposes legislative and administrative reforms that support several other program integrity efforts. Chapter 6, Payment Integrity, provides a comprehensive discussion of these proposals.

Enacted Adjustments Pursuant to BBEDCA.— The Balanced Budget and Emergency Deficit Control Act of 1985, as amended (BBEDCA), recognizes that a multiyear strategy to reduce the rate of improper payments, commensurate with the large and growing costs of the programs administered by the Social Security Administration (SSA), the Department of Health and Human Services (HHS) and the Department of Labor, is a laudable goal. To support the overall goal, BBEDCA provides for adjustments to the discretionary spending limits through 2021 to allow for additional funding for specific program integrity activities to reduce improper payments in the Social Security programs, in the Medicare and Medicaid programs and more recently, in Unemployment Insurance programs. Because the additional funding is classified as discretionary and the savings as mandatory, the savings cannot be offset against the funding for budget enforcement purposes. These adjustments to the discretionary caps are made only if appropriations bills increase funding for the specified program integrity purposes above specified minimum, or base levels. This method ensures that the additional funding amounts

TABLE 10–1.   PROGRAM INTEGRITY DISCRETIONARY CAP ADJUSTMENTS, INCLUDING MANDATORY SAVINGS

(Budget authority and outlays in millions of dollars)

	2021	2022	2023	2024	2025	2026	2027	2028	2029	2030	10-year Total
Social Security Administration (SSA) Program Integrity:											
Discretionary Budget Authority (non add)[1]	1,302	1,585	1,624	1,813	1,761	1,805	1,866	1,914	1,917	1,968	17,555
Discretionary Outlays[1]	1,273	1,579	1,623	1,808	1,762	1,804	1,865	1,913	1,917	1,967	17,511
Mandatory Savings[2]	–17	–1,738	–3,190	–3,971	–5,241	–6,187	–7,150	–8,495	–8,798	–10,080	–54,867
Net Savings	1,256	–159	–1,567	–2,163	–3,479	–4,383	–5,285	–6,582	–6,881	–8,113	–37,356
Health Care Fraud and Abuse Control Program:											
Discretionary Budget Authority/Outlays[1]	496	514	532	552	571	592	613	635	658	682	5,845
Mandatory Savings[2,3]	–955	–1,013	–1,073	–1,138	–1,178	–1,219	–1,262	–1,310	–1,357	–1,407	–11,912
Net Savings	–459	–499	–541	–586	–607	–627	–649	–675	–699	–725	–6,067
Unemployment Insurance (UI) Program Integrity:											
Discretionary Costs[1]	83	133	258	433	533	608	633	646	659	672	4,658
Mandatory Savings[2]	–178	–256	–461	–723	–796	–694	–516	–568	–620	–617	–5,429
Net Savings	–95	–123	–203	–290	–263	–86	117	78	39	55	–771

[1] The discretionary costs are equal to the outlays associated with the budget authority levels authorized for cap adjustments in BBEDCA through 2021. For SSA, the costs for 2022 through 2030 reflect the costs to complete the anticipated dedicated program integrity workloads for SSA; for HCFAC the costs for each of 2022 through 2030 are equal to the outlays associated with the budget authority levels inflated from the 2021 level for HCFAC, using the 2021 Budget assumptions. The UI levels for 2022 through 2027 are equal to the amounts authorized for congressional enforcement, while 2028, 2029, and 2030 are inflated from the 2027 level. For each program the levels in the baseline are equal to the 2021 Budget policy levels. The Budget proposes discretionary caps and cap adjustments through 2025 and levels from 2026 through 2030.

[2] The mandatory savings from the cap adjustment funding are included in the baselines for Social Security, Medicare, Medicaid, and UI programs. For SSA, amounts are based on SSA's Office of the Chief Actuary's estimates of savings. For UI amounts are based on the Department of Labor's Division of Fiscal and Actuarial Services' estimates of savings.

[3] These savings are based on estimates from the HHS Office of the Actuary for return on investment (ROI) from program integrity activities.

authorized in BBEDCA do not supplant other Federal spending on these activities and that such spending is not diverted to other purposes. The Budget continues to support full funding of the authorized cap adjustments for these programs in 2021. The Budget proposes to extend those funding levels through 2030 at the rate of inflation assumed in the Budget for the current services baseline for Medicare, Medicaid and Unemployment Insurance, and assumes cap adjustments levels supporting the full program integrity workload volumes for SSA. The 2021 Budget shows the baseline and policy levels at equivalent amounts throughout the 10 year window. Accordingly, savings generated from such funding levels in the baseline for program integrity activities are reflected in the baselines for Social Security programs, Medicare, Medicaid, and Unemployment Insurance.

SSA Medical Continuing Disability Reviews (CDRs) and Non-Medical Redeterminations of SSI Eligibility.—For SSA, the Budget's proposed discretionary amount of $1,575 million ($273 million in base funding and $1,302 million in cap adjustment funding, pursuant to BBEDCA) will allow SSA to conduct 690,000 full medical CDRs and approximately 2.0 million Supplemental Security Income (SSI) non-medical redeterminations of eligibility. The Social Security Act requires that SSA conducts Medical CDRs, which are periodic reevaluations to determine whether disabled Old-Age, Survivors, and Disability Insurance (OASDI) or SSI beneficiaries continue to meet SSA's standards for disability. Redeterminations are periodic reviews of non-medical eligibility factors, such as income and resources, for the means-tested SSI program and can result in a revision of the individual's benefit level. As noted, the Budget reflects the full funding necessary to support the projected CDRs occurring during the Budget window, which increases the projected cap adjustment levels needed by approximately $2.1 billion more than straight inflation from 2022-2030. The increase includes $1.8 billion associated with the CDR Notice of Proposed Rulemaking in 2022-2030, which increases CDRs by a net of 1.2 million full medical reviews and about 1.5 million CDR mailer reviews. Revised unit costs of performing CDR and redetermination workloads adds approximately $300 million. SSA calculates the fully loaded administrative costs for dedicated program integrity workloads consistent with its procedures for allocating administrative costs across programs.

As a result of the discretionary funding requested in 2021, as well as the fully funded base and continued funding of cap adjustment amounts in 2022 through 2030, the OASDI, SSI, Medicare and Medicaid programs would recoup about $77 billion in gross Federal savings, including approximately $55 billion from access to cap adjustments amounts, with additional savings after the 10-year period, according to estimates from SSA's Office of the Chief Actuary and the Centers for Medicare and Medicaid Services' Office of the Actuary. Access to increased cap adjustment amounts and SSA's commitment to fund the fully loaded costs of performing the requested CDR and redetermination volumes would produce net deficit savings of approximately $37 billion in the 10-year window,

and additional savings in the outyears. These costs and savings are reflected in Table 10-1.

SSA is required by law to conduct medical CDRs for all beneficiaries who are receiving disability benefits under the OASDI program, as well as all children under age 18 who are receiving SSI. SSI redeterminations are also required by law. SSA achieved currency in its CDR workload in 2018 and is currently processing all CDRs in the fiscal year they come due. SSA uses predictive models to prioritize the completion of redeterminations based on likelihood of change in non-medical factors. The frequency of CDRs and redeterminations is constrained by the availability of funds to support these activities. The mandatory savings from the base funding in every year and the enacted discretionary cap adjustment funding assumed for 2020 are included in the BBEDCA baseline, consistent with the levels adopted by the Bipartisan Budget Act of 2015 (BBA of 2015), because the baseline assumes the continued funding of program integrity activities. The BBA of 2015 increased the level of such adjustments for Social Security programs by a net $484 million over the 2017-2021 period, and it expanded the uses of cap adjustment funds to include cooperative disability investigation (CDI) units, and special attorneys for fraud prosecutions. To support these important anti-fraud activities, the Budget provides for SSA to transfer up to $11.2 million, $1.2 million over last year, to the SSA Inspector General to fund CDI unit team leaders. This anti-fraud activity is an authorized use of the cap adjustment funding.

The Budget shows the savings that would result from the increase in CDRs and redeterminations made possible by the discretionary cap adjustment funding requested in 2021 through 2025 with the supporting levels continuing through 2030. With access to the amounts proposed, SSA is on track to remain current with program integrity workloads throughout the budget window.

Current estimates indicate that CDRs conducted in 2021 will yield a return on investment (ROI) of about $8 on average in net Federal program savings over 10 years per $1 budgeted for dedicated program integrity funding, including OASDI, SSI, Medicare and Medicaid program effects. Similarly, SSA estimates indicate that non-medical redeterminations conducted in 2021 will yield a ROI of about $3 on average of net Federal program savings over 10 years per $1 budgeted for dedicated program integrity funding, including SSI and Medicaid program effects. The Budget assumes the full cost of performing CDRs to ensure that sufficient resources are available. The savings from one year of program integrity activities are realized over multiple years because some results find that beneficiaries are no longer eligible to receive OASDI or SSI benefits.

However, the schedule of savings resulting from redeterminations will be different for the base funding and the cap adjustment funding levels in 2021 through 2030. This is because redeterminations of eligibility can uncover underpayment errors as well as overpayment errors. SSI recipients are more likely to initiate a redetermination of eligibility if they believe there are underpayments, and these recipient-initiated redeterminations are included in the base program amounts provided annually. The estimated savings per dollar spent on CDRs and non-medical redeterminations in the baseline reflects an interaction with the State option to expand Medicaid coverage for individuals under age 65 with income less than 133 percent of poverty. As a result of this option, some SSI beneficiaries, who would otherwise lose Medicaid coverage due to a medical CDR or non-medical redetermination, would continue to be covered. In addition, some of the coverage costs for these individuals will be eligible for the enhanced Federal matching rate, resulting in higher Federal Medicaid costs in those States.

Health Care Fraud and Abuse Control Program (HCFAC).—The Budget proposes base and cap adjustment funding levels over the next 10 years and continues the program integrity cap adjustment through 2025. In order to maintain the same level of effort throughout the Budget window, the Budget proposes that the base amount increase annually at the rate of inflation in the current services baseline over the 10-year period. The cap adjustment is set at the levels specified under BBEDCA for 2021 and then increases annually based on inflation from 2022 through 2030. The mandatory savings from both the base and cap adjustment amounts are included in the Medicare and Medicaid baselines.

The discretionary base funding of $311 million plus an additional $6 million adjustment for inflation and cap adjustment of $496 million for HCFAC activities in 2021 are designed to reduce the Medicare improper payment rate, support the Health Care Fraud Prevention & Enforcement Action Team (HEAT) initiative, and reduce Medicaid improper payment rates. The investment will also allow CMS to deploy innovative efforts that focus on improving the analysis and application of data, including state-of-the-art predictive modeling capabilities, in order to prevent potentially wasteful, abusive, or fraudulent payments before they occur. The funding is to be allocated among CMS, the Health and Human Services Office of Inspector General, and the Department of Justice.

Over 2021 through 2030, as reflected in Table 10-1, this $5.8 billion investment in HCFAC cap adjustment funding will generate approximately $12.0 billion in savings to Medicare and Medicaid. This results in net deficit reduction of $6.1 billion over the 10-year period, reflecting prevention and recoupment of improper payments made to providers, as well as recoveries related to civil and criminal penalties. For HCFAC program integrity efforts, CMS actuaries conservatively estimate approximately $2 is saved or averted for every additional $1 spent.

Reemployment Services and Eligibility Assessments (RESEA).—The BBA of 2018 established a new adjustment to the discretionary caps for program integrity efforts targeted at Unemployment Insurance. Like the SSA and HCFAC cap adjustments, the RESEA cap adjustment is permitted up to a maximum amount specified in the law if the underlying appropriations bill first funds a base level of $117 million for Unemployment Insurance program integrity activities. While the discretionary caps are in statute through 2021, the law allows for the adjustment for congressional budget enforcement procedures through 2027; the Budget proposes levels at the same amount. Program integrity funding in 2028 through 2030 continues at level that results from applying the rate of inflation in the current services baseline to the 2027 amount. Table 10-1 shows the mandatory savings of $5.4 billion over 10 years, which includes an estimated $1.7 billion reduction in State unemployment taxes. When netted against the discretionary costs for the cap adjustment funding, the 10-year net savings for the program is $771 million.

Proposed Adjustment Pursuant to BBEDCA, Internal Revenue Service (IRS) Program Integrity.— The Budget proposes to establish and fund a new adjustment to the discretionary caps for IRS program integrity activities starting in 2021, as shown in Table 10-2. The IRS base appropriation funds current tax administration activities, including all tax enforcement and compliance program activities, in the Enforcement and

Table 10–2. PROPOSED PROGRAM INTEGRITY CAP ADJUSTMENT FOR THE INTERNAL REVENUE SERVICE (IRS)

(Budget authority/outlays/receipts in millions of dollars)

	2021	2022	2023	2024	2025	2026	2027	2028	2029	2030	10-year Total
Proposed Adjustment Pursuant to the BBEDCA, as amended [1]:											
Enforcement Base (budget authority)	9,176	9,461	9,760	10,070	10,391	10,720	11,062	11,415	11,779	12,163	105,997
Cap Adjustment:											
Budget Authority	400	828	1,173	1,524	1,878	1,993	1,993	2,004	2,013	2,023	15,829
Outlays	353	757	1,110	1,459	1,810	1,948	1,971	1,983	1,992	2,002	15,385
Receipt Savings from Discretionary Program Integrity Base Funding and Cap Adjustments: [2]											
Enforcement Base [3]	57,500	57,500	57,500	57,500	57,500	57,500	57,500	57,500	57,500	57,500	575,000
Cap Adjustment [4]	264	542	3,106	5,158	7,356	9,682	12,005	12,974	13,813	14,495	79,395
Net Savings from Proposed IRS Cap Adjustment: [1,2]	−89	−215	1,996	3,699	5,546	7,734	10,034	10,991	11,820	12,493	64,010

[1] The Budget proposes discretionary caps and cap adjustments through 2025 and levels from 2026 through 2030.

[2] Savings for IRS are revenue increases rather than spending reductions. They are shown as negatives for presentation and netting against outlays.

[3] No official estimate for 2021 enforcement revenue has been produced, so this figure is an approximation and included only for illustrative purposes.

[4] The IRS cap adjustment funds increases for existing enforcement initiatives and activities and new initiatives. The IRS enforcement program helps maintain the more than $3.6 trillion in taxes paid each year without direct enforcement measures. The cost increases will help maintain the base revenue while generating additional revenue through targeted program investments. The activities and new initiatives funded out of the cap adjustment will yield more than $79 billion in savings over ten years. Aside from direct enforcement revenue, the deterrence impact of these activities suggests the potential for even greater savings.

Operations Support accounts. The additional $400 million cap adjustment in 2021 funds new and continuing investments in expanding and improving the effectiveness and efficiency of the IRS's tax enforcement program. The activities are estimated to generate $79 billion in additional revenue over 10 years and cost approximately $15 billion, resulting in an estimated net savings of almost $64 billion. Once the new enforcement staff are trained and become fully operational these initiatives are expected to generate roughly $5 in additional revenue for every $1 in IRS expenses. Notably, the ROI is likely understated because it only includes amounts received; it does not reflect the effect that enhanced enforcement has on deterring noncompliance. This indirect deterrence helps to ensure the continued payment of over $3.6 trillion in taxes paid each year without direct enforcement measures.

Disaster Relief Funding

Section 251(b)(2)(D) of BBEDCA includes a provision to adjust the discretionary caps for appropriations that the Congress designates in statute as providing for disaster relief. "Disaster relief" is defined as activities carried out pursuant to a determination under section 102(2) of the Robert T. Stafford Disaster Relief and Emergency Assistance Act (42 U.S.C. 5122(2)) for major disasters declared by the President. Prior to enactment of the Consolidated Appropriations Act of 2018 (CAA of 2018; Public Law 115-141), BBEDCA set an annual limit for the adjustment (or funding ceiling) that was calculated by adding the average funding provided for disaster relief over the previous 10 years (excluding the highest and lowest years) plus any portion of the ceiling for the previous year that was not appropriated (or carryover). If the carryover from one year was not used in the subsequent year, it would not carry forward for a second year. This led to precipitous decline in the funding ceiling as higher disaster funding years began to fall out of the 10-year average formula. The ceiling fell from a high of $18,430 million in 2015 to a low of $7,366 million in 2018. The "use or lose" aspect of the carryover discouraged judicious use of the cap adjustment funding and the Administration proposed to work with the Congress in its 2018 and 2019 Budgets to address the declining ceiling.

To address the declining ceiling, Division O of the CAA of 2018 amended BBEDCA to stabilize the disaster formula by redefining the calculation beginning in fiscal year 2019. Under the new revised calculation, the funding ceiling is determined by adding three pieces: 1) the same 10-year average as calculated under the previous formula; 2) a portion of discretionary amounts appropriated to address Stafford Act disasters that were designated as emergency requirements pursuant to BBEDCA; and 3) the cumulative net carryover from 2018 and all subsequent fiscal years. With respect to the portion of emergency funding, the new calculation permits an adjustment of five percent of the total appropriations (net of any rescissions) that were provided after 2011 (or in the previous 10 years, whichever is less) as emergency requirements pursuant to section 251(b)(2)(A)(i) of BBEDCA for Stafford Act emergencies. On April 23, 2018, OMB released the

OMB Report on Disaster Relief Funding to the Committees on Appropriations and the Budget of the U.S. House of Representatives and the Senate, 2018[1] which specified the methodology and criteria OMB is using for estimating the emergency appropriations for Stafford Act disasters that will apply in the new formula. Furthermore, the final piece of this change effectively allows any unused carryover to continue to be factored into each funding ceiling until it is used.

As required by law, OMB included in its Sequestration Update Report for 2020 a preview estimate of the 2020 adjustment for disaster relief. In this report, the ceiling for the disaster relief adjustment in 2020 was calculated to be $17,503 million. This ceiling was calculated by adding together the three components under the new formula: the 10-year average ($7,944 million); 5 percent of Stafford Act emergencies since 2012 ($6,594 million); and carryover from the previous year ($2,965 million). In final 2020 appropriations Acts, the Congress had provided appropriations for the full amount available in 2020 with $17,352 million for the Federal Emergency Management Agency's Disaster Relief Fund (DRF) and $151 million for the Small Business Administration's Disaster Loans Program Account.

OMB must include in its Sequestration Update Report for 2021 a preview estimate of the ceiling on the adjustment for disaster relief funding. This estimate will contain the same components discussed above. At the time of the Budget, based on final 2020 appropriations, OMB estimates the total adjustment available for disaster funding for 2021 at $15,285 million. This ceiling estimate is based on these three components under the current formula: the 10-year average ($8,691 million); 5 percent of Stafford Act emergencies since 2012 ($6,594 million); and carryover from the previous year ($0). Any revisions necessary to account for any changes in 2020 appropriations will be included in the 2021 Sequestration Update Report.

In the 2021 Budget, the Administration is requesting $5,060 million in funding for FEMA's DRF to cover the costs of Presidentially declared major disasters, including identified costs for previously declared catastrophic events (defined by FEMA as events with expected costs that total more than $500 million) and the estimated annual cost of non-catastrophic events expected to obligate in 2021. The Administration's request addresses the significant and unprecedented recovery needs of the recent hurricanes and wildfires that have devastated our Nation. Consistent with past practice, the 2021 request level does not seek to pre-fund anticipated needs in other programs arising out of disasters that have yet to occur. As additional information about the need to fund prior or future disasters becomes available, additional requests, in the form of either 2020 supplemental appropriations (designated as either disaster relief or emergency requirements pursuant to BBEDCA), or amendments to the Budget, may be transmitted.

Under the principles outlined above, the Administration does not have adequate information about known or fu-

---

[1] The report is available on the OMB website: *https://www.whitehouse.gov/omb/legislative/omb-reports/*.

ture requirements necessary to estimate the total amount that will be requested in future years as disaster relief. Accordingly, the Budget does not explicitly request to use the BBEDCA disaster designation in any year after the budget year. Instead, a placeholder for disaster relief is included in each of the outyears that is equal to the 2021 request level ($5,060 million). This funding level does not reflect a specific request but a placeholder amount that, along with other outyear appropriations levels, will be decided on an annual basis as part of the normal budget development process.

Disaster Spending Challenges and Reforms.—The special treatment of disaster assistance in BBEDCA was intended to support greater discipline and transparency on Federal spending, while at the same time acknowledging the unpredictable nature of disasters. However, because substantial amounts of disaster spending are routinely designated as emergency funding under BBEDCA rather than making appropriate tradeoffs within the disaster cap, these objectives are often compromised. Since 2005, Federal disaster assistance has totaled at least $450 billion[2], with nearly half of that amount provided by the Congress within the last five years. In fiscal years 2017 and 2018 alone, the Congress provided $104 billion as emergency funding for disasters declared pursuant to the Stafford Act outside of the disaster relief cap adjustment. The current trajectory of Federal disaster spending—carried out through an overlapping and complex web of programs across 17 departments and agencies—is unsustainable and at times wasteful. A comprehensive examination of all Federal disaster relief and recovery programs is urgently needed to consider how the Nation can best (1) speed up recovery and improve long-term outcomes for individuals and communities, (2) balance stakeholder incentives with responsibilities for creating and assuming risk, and (3) reduce costs to the Federal Government and taxpayers. The Administration is wrestling with these challenges, and the 2021 Budget proposes select programmatic reforms that will begin to move disaster recovery programs toward a more fiscally sustainable solution.

One program that is illustrative of these problems is the Department of Housing and Urban Development Community Development Block Grant for Disaster Recovery (CDBG-DR). Since 2005, the Congress has appropriated over $80 billion for disaster-related activities. However, the significant overlap between CDBG-DR funded activities and other Federal disaster programs creates operational and planning inefficiencies, promotes perverse incentives that lead to wasteful spending and inequities, and causes unnecessary confusion for stakeholders (e.g., disaster survivors). For example, there are over a dozen Federal disaster programs deployed to address housing-related needs—each with different processes, funding limits, requirements, timelines, and involving different agencies at both the Federal and local levels. While CDBG-DR funding is intended for long-term recovery needs, the unpredictability of the amount, purpose, timing for when the Congress will provide fund-

ing, and the lack of regulations do not allow grantees to responsibly plan or act quickly. A reexamination of the CDBG-DR program, its role in disaster recovery, and its impact on Federal disaster spending is past due.

The Budget supports certain regulatory and legislative changes to help decrease Federal liabilities from the Federal Emergency Management Agency's (FEMA) Disaster Relief Fund (DRF). Specifically, the Budget supports phasing out Federal spending on certain public buildings and equipment following a disaster under FEMA's Public Assistance program. FEMA's current program is a no-limit, no-premium insurance policy for State and local governments, which disincentivizes self-protection and burdens taxpayers with the risky decisions made by State and local governments. Eliminating this assistance will encourage State and local governments to more responsibly manage their risk, including better land management and planning, purchasing insurance, and/or investing in mitigation. This is projected to result in approximately $895 million in savings to taxpayers a year. In addition, the Budget supports a non-Federal cost-share of 25 percent for FEMA's Individuals and Households Program. This is projected to result in $383 million in savings to taxpayers a year. Lastly, the Budget supports a regulatory change, which adjusts the per capita indicator to account for years where the indicator was not adjusted for inflation (from 1986-1999). This would increase the per capita indicator to $2.30. The regulation will also increase the $1 million minimum threshold for inflation to $1.509 million, correcting retroactively for the years during which the indicator was not adjusted for inflation. This is projected to save taxpayers $263 million a year.

Wildfire Suppression Operations at the Departments of Agriculture and the Interior

Wildfires naturally occur on public lands throughout the country. The cost of fighting wildfires has increased due to landscape conditions resulting from drought, pest and disease damage, overgrown forests, expanding residential and commercial development near the borders of public lands, and program management decisions. When these costs exceed the funds appropriated, the Federal Government covers the shortfall through transfers from other land management programs. For example, in 2018, Forest Service wildfire suppression spending reached a record $2.6 billion, necessitating transfers of $720 million from other non-fire programs. Historically, these transfers have been repaid in subsequent appropriations; however, "fire borrowing" impedes the missions of land management agencies to reduce the risk of catastrophic fire and restore and maintain healthy functioning ecosystems.

To create funding certainty in times of wildfire disasters, the CAA of 2018 enacted a new cap adjustment, which began in 2020, and the Administration proposes using it again in this Budget. The adjustment is permitted so long as a base level of funding for wildfire suppression operations is funded in the underlying appropriations bill under the caps. The base level is defined as being equal to average cost over 10 years for wildfire suppression operations that was requested in the President's 2015 Budget.

---

[2] *https://www.gao.gov/assets/710/702173.pdf.*

These amounts have been determined to be $1,011 million for the Department of Agriculture's Forest Service and $384 million for the Department of the Interior (DOI). The 2021 Budget requests these base amounts for wildfire suppression and seeks the full $2,350 million adjustment authorized in BBEDCA for 2021 with $2,040 million included for Forest Service and $310 million included for DOI. Providing the full level authorized in 2021 will ensure that adequate resources are available to fight wildland fires, protect communities, and safeguard human life during the most severe wildland fire season.

For the years after 2021, the Administration does not have sufficient information about future wildfire suppression needs and, therefore, includes a placeholder in the 2021 Budget for wildfire suppression in each of the outyears that is equal to the current 2021 request. Actual funding levels, up to but not exceeding the authorized cap adjustments, will be decided on an annual basis as part of the normal budget process.

Limits on Changes in Mandatory Spending in Appropriations Acts (CHIMPs)

The discretionary spending caps in place since the enactment of the BCA in 2011 have been circumvented annually in appropriations bills through the use of changes in mandatory programs, or CHIMPs, that have no net outlay savings to offset increases in discretionary spending.

There can be programmatic reasons to make changes to mandatory programs on annual basis in the annual appropriations bills. However, many enacted CHIMPs do not result in actual spending reductions. In some cases, the budget authority reduced in one year may become available again the following year, allowing the same reduction to be taken year after year. In other cases, the reduction comes from a program that never would have spent its funding anyway. In both of these cases, under current scoring rules, reductions in budget authority from such CHIMPs can be used to offset appropriations in other programs, which results in an overall increase in Federal spending. In such cases, CHIMPs are used as a tool to work around the constraints imposed by the discretionary budget enforcement caps.

The Administration supports limiting and ultimately phasing out the use of CHIMPs with no outlay savings. In support of this, the 2021 Budget proposes reforms to certain mandatory programs which have been the target of CHIMPs in the past, including the Department of Justice's Crime Victims Fund and the Department of Agriculture's Section 32 program. One goal of these reforms is to reduce the availability of CHIMPs by setting funding levels in permanent law rather than through annual appropriations Acts. For example, the appropriations Acts will no longer be able to claim billions in discretionary offsets from temporarily blocking the same funding in the Crime Victims Fund year after year. In addition, the Budget proposes permanent reductions to the Department of Health and Human Services' Children's Health Insurance Program to ensure that these amounts cannot be used as discretionary offsets in future fiscal years.

Limit on Discretionary Advance Appropriations

An advance appropriation first becomes available for obligation one or more fiscal years beyond the year for which the appropriations act is passed. Budget authority is recorded in the year the funds become available for obligation, not in the year the appropriation is enacted.

There are legitimate policy reasons to use advance appropriations to fund programs. However, advance appropriations can also be used in situations that lack a programmatic justification, as a gimmick to make room for expanded funding within the discretionary spending limits on budget authority for a given year under BBEDCA. For example, some education grants are forward funded (available beginning July 1 of the fiscal year) to provide certainty of funding for an entire school year, since school years straddle Federal fiscal years. This funding is recorded in the budget year because the funding is first legally available in that fiscal year. However, $22.6 billion of this funding is advance appropriated (available beginning three months later, on October 1) rather than forward funded. Prior Congresses increased advance appropriations and decreased the amounts of forward funding as a gimmick to free up room in the budget year without affecting the total amount available for a coming school year. This gimmick works because the advance appropriation is not recorded in the budget year but rather the following fiscal year. However, it works only in the year in which funds switch from forward funding to advance appropriations; that is, it works only in years in which the amounts of advance appropriations for such "straddle" programs are increased.

To curtail this gimmick, which allows over-budget funding in the budget year and exerts pressure for increased funding in future years by committing upfront a portion of the total budget authority limits under the discretionary caps in BBEDCA in those years, congressional budget resolutions since 2001 have set limits on the amount of advance appropriations. When the congressional limit equals the amount that had been advance appropriated in the most recent appropriations bill, there is no additional room to switch forward funding to advance appropriations, and so no room for this particular gimmick to operate in that year's budget.

The Budget includes $28,709 million in advance appropriations for 2022 and freezes them at this level in subsequent years. In this way, the Budget does not employ this potential gimmick. Moreover, the Administration supports limiting advance appropriations to the proposed level for 2022, below the limits included in sections 203 and 206 for the Senate and the House, respectively, of title II of the Bipartisan Budget Act of 2019. Those limits apply only to the accounts explicitly specified in the Congressional Record by the Chairs of the Committees on the Budget, as referenced in BBA of 2019.

Outside of these limits, the Administration would allow discretionary advance appropriations for veterans medical care, as is required by the Veterans Health Care Budget Reform and Transparency Act (Public Law 111-81). The veterans medical care accounts in the

Department of Veterans Affairs (VA) currently comprise Medical Services, Medical Support and Compliance, Medical Facilities, and Medical Community Care. The level of advance appropriations funding for veterans medical care is largely determined by the VA's Enrollee Health Care Projection Model. This actuarial model projects the funding requirement for over 90 types of healthcare services, including primary care, specialty care, and mental health. The remaining funding requirement is estimated based on other models and assumptions for services such as readjustment counseling and special activities. VA has included detailed information in its Congressional Budget Justifications about the overall 2022 veterans medical care funding request.

For a detailed table of accounts that have received discretionary and mandatory advance appropriations since 2019 or for which the Budget requests advance appropriations for 2022 and beyond, please refer to the Advance Appropriations chapter in the *Appendix*.

Statutory PAYGO

The Statutory Pay-As-You-Go Act of 2010 (PAYGO Act; Public Law 111-139) requires that, subject to specific exceptions, all legislation enacted during each session of the Congress changing taxes or mandatory expenditures and collections not increase projected deficits.

The Act established 5- and 10-year scorecards to record the budgetary effects of legislation; these scorecards are maintained by OMB and are published on the OMB web site. The Act also established special scorekeeping rules that affect whether all estimated budgetary effects of PAYGO bills are entered on the scorecards. Changes to off-budget programs (Social Security and the Postal Service) do not have budgetary effects for the purposes of PAYGO and are not counted. Provisions designated by the Congress in law as emergencies appear on the scorecards, but the effects are subtracted before computing the scorecard totals.

In addition to the exemptions in the PAYGO Act itself, the Congress has enacted laws affecting revenues or direct spending with a provision directing that the budgetary effects of all or part of the law be held off of the PAYGO scorecards. In the most recently completed congressional session, six pieces of legislation were enacted with such a provision.

The requirement of budget neutrality is enforced by an accompanying requirement of automatic across-the-board cuts in selected mandatory programs if enacted legislation, taken as a whole, does not meet that standard. If the annual report filed by OMB after the end of a congressional session shows net costs—that is, more costs than savings—in the budget-year column of either the 5- or 10-year scorecard, OMB is required to prepare, and the President is required to issue, a sequestration order implementing across-the-board cuts to non-exempt

mandatory programs in an amount sufficient to offset the net costs on the PAYGO scorecards. The list of exempt programs and special sequestration rules for certain programs are contained in sections 255 and 256 of BBEDCA.

As was the case during an earlier PAYGO enforcement regime in the 1990s, the PAYGO sequestration has not been required since the PAYGO Act reinstated the statutory PAYGO requirement. Since PAYGO was reinstated, OMB's annual PAYGO reports showed net savings in the budget year column of both the 5- and 10-year scorecards. For the first session of the 116th Congress, the most recent session, enacted legislation placed costs of $514 million in each year of the 5-year scorecard and $657 million in each year of the 10-year scorecard. However, the budget year balance on each of the PAYGO scorecards is zero because two laws, the Bipartisan Budget Act of 2019 (Public Law 116-37), and the Further Additional Continuing Appropriations Act, 2020, and Further Health Extenders Act of 2019 (Public Law 116-69), directed changes to the balances of the scorecards. Public Law 116-37 removed all balances included on the scorecards at the time of enactment, and Public Law 116-69 shifted the debits on both scorecards from fiscal year 2020 to fiscal year 2021. Consequently, no PAYGO sequestration was required in 2020 and the 2021 column of the 10-year PAYGO scorecard reflects a debit of $1,314 million.[3]

There are limitations to Statutory PAYGO's usefulness as a budget enforcement tool. In the past, the scorecards have carried large surpluses from year to year, giving the Congress little incentive to limit costly spending. Some costs, such as changes to the Postal Service or increases to debt service, are ignored. The frequent exemption of budgetary effects from the PAYGO scorecards by the Congress also suggests the PAYGO regime has been ineffective at controlling deficits. In the coming year the Administration looks forward to working with the Congress to rein in the deficit by exploring budget enforcement tools, including reforms to PAYGO.

Administrative PAYGO

In addition to enforcing budget discipline on enacted legislation, the Administration reinvigorated the Executive Branch's review of agency administrative actions that affect mandatory spending. Executive Order 13893, "Increasing Government Accountability for Administrative Actions by Reinvigorating Administrative PAYGO" requires agencies to offset the cost of administrative actions that would increase mandatory spending with other actions that would comparably reduce spending. Exceptions to this requirement are limited—according to the EO, the OMB Director may waive Administrative PAYGO requirements if it is necessary for the delivery of essential services, for effective program delivery, or because it is otherwise warranted by the public interest.

---

[3] OMB's annual PAYGO reports and other explanatory material about the PAYGO Act are available on OMB's website at *https://www.whitehouse.gov/omb/paygo/*.

II. BUDGET PRESENTATION

Highway Trust Fund Spending and 10-Year Transportation Reauthorization

The Budget proposes a 10-year surface transportation reauthorization plan that includes $75 billion in new spending above current law levels, along with a variety of proposals to offset the cost of the gap between new spending levels and receipts projected to support that spending from the Highway Trust Fund (HTF). Under BBEDCA baseline rules, the Budget shows outlays supported by HTF receipts inflating at the current services level. However, that presentation masks the reality that the HTF has a structural insolvency. The BBEDCA baseline results in a presentation that overestimates the amount of spending the HTF could support. In order to support the current services level of spending the HTF needs an additional $185 billion. Surface transportation reauthorizations have recently paid for this insolvency gap through transfers of cash from the General Fund, offset by cuts to mandatory spending and increases in certain receipts. The Administration supports working with the Congress to use a combination of Budget proposal to pay for the $261 billion gap between projected Highway Trust Fund (HTF) revenues and proposed spending levels.

The Highway Revenue Act of 1956 (Public Law 84-627) introduced the HTF to accelerate the development of the Interstate Highway System. In the 1970s, the HTF's scope was expanded to include expenditures on mass transit. In 1982, a permanent Mass Transit Account within the HTF was created. HTF programs are treated as hybrids for budget enforcement purposes: contract authority is classified as mandatory, while outlays are controlled by obligation limitations in appropriations acts and are therefore classified as discretionary. Broadly speaking, this framework evolved as a mechanism to ensure that collections into the HTF (e.g., motor fuel taxes) were used to pay only for programs that benefit surface transportation users, and that funding for those programs would generally be commensurate with collections. Deposits to the HTF through the 1990s were historically more than sufficient to meet the surface transportation funding needs.

However, by the 2000s, deposits into the HTF began to level off as vehicle fuel efficiency continued to improve. At the same time, the investment needs continued to rise as the infrastructure, much of which was built in the 1960s and 1970s, deteriorated and required recapitalization. The cost of construction also generally increased. The Federal motor fuel tax rates have stayed constant since 1993. By 2008, balances that had been building in the HTF were spent down. The 2008-2009 recession and rising gasoline prices had led to a reduction in the consumption of fuel resulting in the HTF reaching the point of insolvency for the first time. The Congress responded by providing the first in a series of General Fund transfers to the HTF to maintain solvency.

The passage of the Fixing America's Surface Transportation Act (FAST Act; Public Law 114-94), shored up the HTF and maintained the hybrid budgetary treatment through 2020. The FAST Act did not significantly amend transportation-related taxes or HTF authorization provisions beyond extending the authority to collect and spend revenue. The Congress retained the Federal fuel tax rate at 18.4 cents per gallon for gasoline and 24.4 cents for diesel. To maintain HTF solvency, the FAST Act transferred $70 billion from the General Fund into the HTF, offset by savings in other mandatory programs. Since 2008, HTF tax revenues have been supplemented by $140 billion in General Fund transfers. The last year of the FAST Act's authorization is 2020. The Administration looks forward to working with the Congress to responsibly pay for the needed increases in surface transportation spending by enacting the Administration's 10-year reauthorization levels with a combination of Budget savings proposals.

Adjustments to BBEDCA Baseline: Extension of Revenue Provisions

In order to provide a more realistic outlook for the deficit under current policies, the Budget presents the Administration's budget proposals relative to a baseline that makes an adjustments to the statutory baseline defined in BBEDCA by extending certain revenue provisions. Section 257 of BBEDCA provides the rules for constructing the baseline used by the Executive and Legislative Branches for scoring and other legal purposes. The adjustments made by the Administration are not intended to replace the BBEDCA baseline for these purposes, but rather are intended to make the baseline a more useful benchmark for assessing the deficit outlook and the impact of budget proposals.

The Tax Cuts and Jobs Act provided comprehensive tax reform for individuals and corporations. The Administration's adjusted baseline assumes permanent extension of the individual income tax and estate and gift tax provisions enacted in that Act that are currently set to expire at the end of 2025. These expirations were included in the tax bill not because these provisions were intended to be temporary, but in order to comply with reconciliation rules in the Senate. Assuming extension of these provisions in the adjusted baseline presentation results in reductions in governmental receipts and increases in outlays for refundable tax credits of $1,372.1 billion over the 2025-2030 period relative to the BBEDCA baseline. This yields a more realistic depiction of the outlook for receipts and the deficit than a strictly current law baseline in which these significant tax cuts expire.

Pell Grants

The Pell Grant program includes features that make it unlike other discretionary programs including that Pell Grants are awarded to all applicants who meet income and other eligibility criteria. This section provides some background on the unique nature of the Pell Grant program and explains how the Budget accommodates changes in discretionary costs.

Under current law, the Pell program has several notable features:

- The Pell Grant program acts like an entitlement program, such as the Supplemental Nutrition Assistance Program or Supplemental Security Income, in which everyone who meets specific eligibility requirements and applies for the program receives a benefit. Specifically, Pell Grant costs in a given year are determined by the maximum award set in statute, the number of eligible applicants, and the award for which those applicants are eligible based on their needs and costs of attendance. The maximum Pell award for the academic year 2020-2021 is $6,345, of which $5,285 was established in discretionary appropriations and the remaining $1,060 in mandatory funding is provided automatically by the College Cost Reduction and Access Act as amended (CCRAA).

- The cost of each Pell Grant is funded by discretionary budget authority provided in annual appropriations acts, along with mandatory budget authority provided not only by the CCRAA, and the BCA, but also by amendments to the Higher Education Act of 1965 contained in the 2011 and 2012 appropriations acts. There is no programmatic difference between the mandatory and discretionary funding.

- If valid applicants are more numerous than expected, or if these applicants are eligible for higher awards than anticipated, the Pell Grant program will cost more than projected at the time of the appropriation. If the costs during one academic year are higher than provided for in that year's appropriation, the Department of Education funds the extra costs with the subsequent year's appropriation.[4]

---

[4]   This ability to "borrow" from a subsequent appropriation is

- To prevent deliberate underfunding of Pell costs, in 2006 the congressional and Executive Branch scorekeepers agreed to a special scorekeeping rule for Pell. Under this rule, the annual appropriations bill is charged with the full Congressional Budget Office estimated cost of the Pell Grant program for the budget year, plus or minus any cumulative shortfalls or surpluses from prior years. This scorekeeping rule was adopted by the Congress as §406(b) of the Concurrent Resolution on the Budget for Fiscal Year 2006 (H. Con. Res. 95, 109th Congress).

Given the nature of the program, it is reasonable to consider Pell Grants an individual entitlement for purposes of budget analysis and enforcement. The discretionary portion of the award funded in annual appropriations Acts counts against the discretionary spending caps pursuant to section 251 of BBEDCA and appropriations allocations established annually under §302 of the Congressional Budget Act.

The total cost of Pell Grants can fluctuate from year to year, even with no change in the maximum Pell Grant award, because of changes in enrollment, college costs, and student and family resources. In general, the de-

---

unique to the Pell program. It comes about for two reasons. First, like many education programs, Pell is "forward-funded"—the budget authority enacted in the fall of one year is intended for the subsequent academic year, which begins in the following July. Second, even though the amount of funding is predicated on the expected cost of Pell during one academic year, the money is made legally available for the full 24-month period covering the current fiscal year and the subsequent fiscal year. This means that, if the funding for an academic year proves inadequate, the following year's appropriation will legally be available to cover the funding shortage for the first academic year. The 2021 appropriation, for instance, will support the 2021-2022 academic year beginning in July 2021 but will become available in October 2020 and can therefore help cover any shortages that may arise in funding for the 2020-2021 academic year.

Table 10–3. DISCRETIONARY PELL FUNDING NEEDS
Dollars in billions

Discretionary Pell Funding Needs (Baseline)

	2021	2022	2023	2024	2025	2026	2027	2028	2029	2030
Estimated Program Cost for $5,285 Maximum Award	24.3	24.8	25.4	26.0	26.5	27.2	27.8	28.4	29.1	29.7
Cumulative Incoming Surplus	9.8	....	....	....	....	....	....	....	....	....
Mandatory Budget Authority Available	1.2	1.2	1.2	1.2	1.2	1.2	1.2	1.2	1.2	1.2
Total Additional Budget Authority Needed	13.4	23.6	24.2	24.8	25.4	26.0	26.6	27.3	27.9	28.6
Fund Pell at 2020 Enacted Level	22.5	22.5	22.5	22.5	22.5	22.5	22.5	22.5	22.5	22.5
Surplus/Funding Gap from Prior Year	N/A	9.1	7.9	6.2	3.8	0.9	−2.6	−6.7	−11.5	−16.9
Cumulative Surplus/Discretionary Funding Gap (−)	9.1	7.9	6.2	3.8	0.9	−2.6	−6.7	−11.5	−16.9	−23.0

Effect of 2021 Budget Policies

	2021	2022	2023	2024	2025	2026	2027	2028	2029	2030
Expand Pell to Short-Term Programs	−0.1	−0.1	−0.2	−0.2	−0.2	−0.2	−0.2	−0.2	−0.2	−0.2
Make Incarcertaed Students Eligible for Pell Grants	−0.1	−0.1	−0.1	−0.1	−0.1	−0.1	−0.1	−0.1	−0.1	−0.1
Fund Iraq-Afghanistan Service Grants through Pell	−*	−*	−*	−*	−*	−*	−*	−*	−*	−*
Reduce Improper Payments in Pell Grants	*	*	*	*	*	*	*	*	*	*
Mandatory Funding Shift[1]	−*	−0.1	−0.1	−0.1	−0.1	−0.1	−0.1	−0.1	−0.1	−0.1
Surplus/Funding Gap from Prior Year	N/A	8.9	7.4	5.4	2.7	−0.5	−4.4	−8.9	−14.0	−19.8
Cumulative Surplus/Discretionary Funding Gap (−)	8.9	7.4	5.4	2.7	−0.5	−4.4	−8.9	−14.0	−19.8	−26.2

N/A = Not applicable
* $50 million or less.
[1] Some budget authority, provided in previous legislation and classified as mandatory but used to meet discretionary Pell grant program funding needs, will be reallocated to support new costs associated with the mandatory add-on.

mand for and costs of the program are countercyclical to the economy; more people go to school during periods of higher unemployment, but return to the workforce as the economy improves. In fact, the program experienced a spike in enrollment and costs during the most recent recession, reaching a peak of 9.4 million students in 2011. This spike required temporary mandatory or emergency appropriations to fund the program well above the level that could have been provided as a practical matter by the regular discretionary appropriation. Enrollment and costs declined continuously from 2011 to 2016, and the funding provided over that time has lasted longer than anticipated. Recent changes to the program expanded the amount of aid available to students, including the enactment of Year-Round Pell and increases to the maximum award. As a result, total program costs increased in the 2017-18 award year for the first time since the recession, and remained relatively steady in 2018 and 2019. The Budget projects enrollment to increase by about two percent over the course of the ten year budget window. Nevertheless, assuming no changes in current policy, the 2021 Budget baseline expects program costs to stay within available resources, which include the discretionary appropriation, budget authority carried forward from the previous year, and extra mandatory funds, until 2026 (see Table 10-3). These estimates have changed significantly from year to year, which illustrates continuing uncertainty about Pell program costs, and the year in which a shortfall will reemerge.

The 2021 Budget reflects the Administration's commitment to ensuring students receive the maximum Pell Grant for which they are eligible, and to expanding options available to pursuing postsecondary education and training. First, the Budget provides sufficient resources to fully fund Pell Grants in the award years covered by the budget year, and subsequent years, including the funds needed to continue support of Year-Round Pell. The Budget provides $22.5 billion in discretionary budget authority in 2020, the same as the 2019 enacted appropriation. Level-funding Pell in 2020, combined with available budget authority from the previous year and mandatory funding provided in previous legislation, provides $8.6 billion more than is needed to fully fund the program in the 2020-21 award year.

With significant budget authority still available in the program, the Budget also proposes legislative changes to provide more postsecondary pathways by expanding Pell Grant eligibility to high-quality short-term training programs. This will help low-income or out-of-work individuals access training programs that can equip them with skills to secure well-paying jobs in high-demand fields more quickly than traditional 2-year or 4-year degree programs. Further, to support returning citizens by improving employment outcomes and reducing recidivism, the Budget makes Pell Grants available to certain incarcerated students in Federal and State prisons. The Budget also proposes moving Iraq and Afghanistan Service Grants into the Pell program, which will exempt those awards from cuts due to sequestration and streamline the administration of the programs. Together, these three policies increase future discretionary Pell program costs by $2.7 billion over 10 years (see Table 10–3). Finally, the Budget includes a proposal to reduce the risk of improper payments in the program (see the Payment Integrity chapter for more detail). With these reforms, the Pell program still is expected to have sufficient discretionary funds until 2025.

Gross Versus Net Reductions in Joint Committee Sequestration

The net realized savings from Joint Committee mandatory sequestration are less than the intended savings amounts as a result of peculiarities in the BBEDCA sequestration procedures. The 2021 Budget shows the net effect of Joint Committee sequestration reductions by accounting for reductions in 2021, and each outyear, that remain in the sequestered account and are anticipated to become newly available for obligation in the year after sequestration, in accordance with section 256(k)(6) of BBEDCA. The budget authority and outlays from these "pop-up" resources are included in the baseline and policy estimates and amount to a cost of $1.5 billion in 2021. Additionally, the Budget annually accounts for lost savings that results from the sequestration of certain interfund payments, which produces no net deficit reduction. Such amount is $880 million in 2021.

Fannie Mae and Freddie Mac

The Budget continues to present Fannie Mae and Freddie Mac, the housing Government-sponsored enterprises (GSEs) currently in Federal conservatorship, as non-Federal entities. However, Treasury equity investments in the GSEs are recorded as budgetary outlays, and the dividends on those investments are recorded as offsetting receipts. In addition, the budget estimates reflect collections from the 10 basis point increase in GSE guarantee fees that was enacted under the Temporary Payroll Tax Cut Continuation Act of 2011 (Public Law. 112-78). The baseline also reflects collections from a 4.2 basis point set-aside on each dollar of unpaid principal balance of new business purchases authorized under the Housing and Economic Recovery Act of 2008 (Public Law 111-289) to be remitted to several Federal affordable housing programs; the Budget proposes to eliminate the 4.2 basis point set-aside and discontinue funding for these programs. The GSEs are discussed in more detail in Chapter 18, "Credit and Insurance."

Postal Service Reforms

The Administration proposes reform of the Postal Service, necessitated by the serious financial condition of the Postal Service Fund. The proposals are discussed in the Postal Service and General Services Administration sections of the *Appendix*.

The Postal Service is designated in statute as an off-budget independent establishment of the Executive Branch. This designation and budgetary treatment was most recently mandated in 1989, in part to reflect the policy agreement that the Postal Service should pay for its own costs through its own revenues and should operate more like an independent business entity. Statutory requirements on Postal Service expenses and restrictions that impede the Postal Service's ability to adapt to the ongoing evolution to paperless written communications have made those goals increasingly difficult to achieve. To address its current financial and structural challenges, the Administration proposes reform measures to ensure that the Postal Service funds existing commitments to current and former employees from business revenues, not taxpayer funds. To reflect the Postal Service's practice since 2012 of using defaults to on-budget accounts to continue operations, despite losses, the Administration's baseline now reflects probable defaults to on-budget accounts. This treatment allows for a clearer presentation of the Postal Service's likely actions in the absence of reform and more realistic scoring of reform proposals, with improvements in the Postal Service's finances reflected through lower defaults, and added costs for the Postal Service reflected as higher defaults. Under current scoring rules, savings from reform for the Postal Service affect the unified deficit but do not affect the PAYGO scorecard. Savings to on-budget accounts through lower projected defaults affect both the PAYGO scorecard and the unified deficit.

Fair Value for Credit Programs

Fair value is an approach to measuring the cost of Federal direct loan and loan guarantee programs that would align budget estimates with the market value of Federal assistance, typically by including risk premiums observed in the market. Under current budget rules, the cost of Federal credit programs is measured as the net present value of the estimated future cash flows resulting from a loan or loan guarantee discounted at Treasury interest rates. These rules are defined in law by the Federal Credit Reform Act of 1990 (FCRA). In recent years, some analysts have argued that fair value estimates would better capture the true costs imposed on taxpayers from Federal credit programs and would align with private sector standard practices for measuring the value of loans and loan guarantees. The Congressional Budget Office (CBO), for instance, has stated that fair value would be a more comprehensive measure of the cost of Federal credit programs. The Concurrent Resolution on the Budget for Fiscal Year 2018 (H. Con. Res. 71) also included language requiring CBO to produce fair value scores alongside FCRA scores upon request. The Administration supports proposals to improve the accuracy of cost estimates and is open to working with the Congress and knowledgeable members of the public to address any conceptual and implementation challenges necessary to implement fair value estimates for Federal credit programs.

III. BUDGET REFORM PROPOSALS

Discretionary Spending Limits

The BBEDCA baseline extends enacted appropriations at the account level assuming the rate of inflation for current services but allowances are included to bring total base discretionary funding in line with the BBEDCA caps for 2021. The BCA had required reductions to the discretionary caps in accordance with Joint Committee enforcement procedures but the BBA of 2019 effectively cancelled any further Joint Committee reductions for the discretionary caps in 2021. For 2021, the Budget proposes no change to the BBA of 2019 cap levels and budgets to the base cap for defense programs. For non-defense, however, the Administration would seek to begin rebalancing Federal responsibilities by budgeting to $590 billion—the original BCA level for 2021—instead of the 2019 BBA level of $626.5 billion. While no change is proposed to the current non-defense cap in 2021, proposing funding below the cap supports the Administration's principle that caps are ceilings for spending and not floors.

The 2021 Budget demonstrates that non-defense programs can be easily funded at a level that is five-percent below the legal limit set in the BBA for 2020 and about six-percent below the BBA limit for 2021. After 2021, the Administration would support new caps through 2025 at the levels in the 2021 Budget. These levels would codify a shift in resources from non-defense programs by instituting a 2-penny reduction to non-defense programs while increasing the defense category by about 2 percent to fully resource the 2018 National Defense Strategy. A four-year extension of the caps is a reasonable time limit and it would be prudent to revisit any further extension at that time based on the Nation's fiscal situation. Therefore, the Budget sets placeholder levels for 2026 through 2030 that project current policies with defense programs held flat at the 2025 level while non-defense programs continue the 2-penny reduction for the remainder of the budget window. The discretionary cap policy levels are reflected in Table S–7 of the main *Budget* volume.

Federal Capital Revolving Fund

The structure of the Federal budget and budget enforcement requirements can create hurdles to funding large-dollar capital investments that are handled differently at the State and local government levels. Expenditures for capital investment are combined with operating expenses in the Federal unified budget. Both kinds of expenditures must compete for limited funding within the discretionary caps. Large-dollar Federal capital investments can be squeezed out in this competition, forcing agency managers to turn to operating leases to meet long-term Federal requirements. These alternatives are more expensive than ownership over the long-term because: (1) Treasury can always borrow at lower interest rates; and (2) to avoid triggering scorekeeping and recording requirements for capital leases, agencies sign shorter-term consecutive leases of the same space. For example, the cost of two consecutive 15-year leases for a building can far exceed its fair market value, with the Government paying close to 180 percent of the value of the building. Alternative financing proposals typically run up against scorekeeping and recording rules that appropriately measure cost based on the full amount of the Government's obligations under the contract, which further constrains the ability of agency managers to meet capital needs.

In contrast, State and local governments separate capital investment from operating expenses. They are able to evaluate, rank, and finance proposed capital investments in separate capital budgets, which avoids direct competition between proposed capital acquisitions and operating expenses. If capital purchases are financed by borrowing, the associated debt service is an item in the operating budget. This separation of capital spending from operating expenses works well at the State and local government levels because of conditions that do not exist at the Federal level. State and local governments are required to balance their operating budgets, and their ability to borrow to finance capital spending is subject to the discipline of private credit markets that impose higher interest rates for riskier investments. In addition, State and local governments tend to own capital that they finance. In contrast, the Federal Government does not face a balanced budget requirement, and Treasury debt has historically been considered the safest investment regardless of the condition of the Federal balance sheet. Also, the bulk of Federal funding for capital is in the form of grants to lower levels of Government or to private entities, and it is difficult to see how non-federally owned investment can be included in a capital budget.

To deal with the drawbacks of the current Federal approach, the Budget proposes: (1) to create a Federal Capital Revolving Fund (FCRF) to fund large-dollar, federally owned, civilian real property capital projects; and (2) provide specific budget enforcement rules for the FCRF that would allow it to function, in effect, like State and local government capital budgets. This proposal incorporates principles that are central to the success of capital budgeting at the State and local level—a limit on total funding for capital investment, annual decisions on the allocation of funding for capital projects, and spreading the acquisition cost over 15 years in the discretionary operating budgets of agencies that purchase the assets. As part of the overall 2021 Budget infrastructure initiative, the FCRF would be capitalized initially by a $10 billion mandatory appropriation, and scored with anticipated outlays over the 10-year window for the purposes of pay-as-you-go budget enforcement rules. Balances in the FCRF would be available for transfer to purchasing agencies to fund large-dollar capital acquisitions only to the extent projects are designated in advance in appropriations Acts and the agency receives a discretionary appropriation for the first of a maximum of 15 required annual repayments. If these two conditions are met, the FCRF would transfer funds to the purchasing agency to cover the full cost to acquire the capital asset. Annual discretionary repayments by purchasing agencies would replenish the FCRF and would become available to fund additional capital projects. Total annual capital purchases would be limited to the lower of $2.5 billion or the balance in the FCRF, including annual repayments.

The Budget uses the FCRF concept to fund the expansion and remaining renovation, estimated at $294 million for the Department of Commerce National Institute of Standards and Technology (NIST) to do advance precision

Chart 10–1. SCORING OF $294 MILLION NIST CONSTRUCTION PROJECT USING THE FEDERAL CAPITAL REVOLVING FUND

Federal Capital Revolving Fund		
	Year 1	Years 2-15
Mandatory:		
Transfer to purchasing agency to buy building.............................	294	
Purchasing agency repayments....	-20	-274

Purchasing Agency		
	Year 1	Years 2-15
Mandatory:		
Collection of transfer from Federal Capital Revolving Fund...................	-294	
Payment to buy building...................	294	
Discretionary:		
Repayments to Federal Capital Revolving Fund...................	20	274

Total Government-Wide Deficit Impact			
	Year 1	Years 2-15	Total
Mandatory:			
Purchase building.............................	294		294
Collections from purchasing agency................	-20	-274	-294
Discretionary:			
Purchasing agency repayments.........................	20	274	294
Total Government-wide..	294	---	294

measurement tools and technologies for a variety of scientific endeavors at Building One on the Boulder Colorado campus. In accordance with the principles and design of the FCRF, the 2021 budget requests appropriations language designating the NIST expansion and renovation as a project to be funded out of the FCRF, which is housed within the General Services Administration, along with 1/15 of the full purchase price, or $19.6 million for the first year repayment back to the FCRF. The FCRF account is displayed funding the NIST project in 2021 and a total of $15 billion worth of Federal buildings projects using the initial $10 billion in mandatory appropriations and, starting in 2026, $5 billion from offsetting collections from annual project repayments.

The flow of funds for the expansion and renovation of a NIST research building with a $294 million cost and the proposed scoring are illustrated in Chart 10–1. Current budget enforcement rules would require the entire $294 million to be scored as discretionary budget authority in the first year, which would negate the benefit of the FCRF and leave agencies and policy makers facing the same trade-off constraints. As shown in Chart 10–1, under this proposal, transfers from the FCRF to agencies to fund capital projects, $294 million in the case of the NIST project, and the actual execution by agencies would be scored as direct spending (shown as mandatory in Chart 10–1), while agencies would use discretionary appropriations to fund the annual repayments to the FCRF, or $19.6 million for the NIST building construction first year repayment. The proposal allocates the costs between direct spending and discretionary spending—the up-front cost of capital investment would already be reflected in the baseline as direct spending once the FCRF is enacted with $10 billion in mandatory capital. This scoring approves a total capital investment upfront, keeping individual large projects from competing with annual operating expenses in the annual appropriations process. On the discretionary side of the budget the budgetary trade off would be locking into the incremental annual cost of repaying the FCRF over 15-years. Knowing that future discretionary appropriations will have to be used to repay the FCRF would provide an incentive for agencies, OMB, and the Congress to select projects with the highest mission criticality and returns. OMB would review agencies' proposed projects for inclusion in the President's Budget, as shown with the NIST request, and the Appropriations Committees would make final allocations by authorizing projects in annual appropriations Acts and providing the first year of repayment. This approach would allow for a more effective capital planning process for the Government's largest civilian real property projects, and is similar to capital budgets used by State and local governments.

Further Adjustments to the Proposed Discretionary Caps for Employer-Employee Share of Federal Employee Retirement

The Budget includes a proposal that starts in 2022 to reduce the contributions of Federal agencies to the retirement plans of civilian employees. The Budget proposes to reallocate the costs of Federal employee retirement by charging equal shares of employees' accruing retirement costs to employees and employers. The Budget takes the estimated reductions in the share of employee retirement paid by Federal agencies out of the proposed non-defense levels starting in 2022. Additionally, the discretionary non-defense levels proposed in the 2021 Budget for the 2022 through 2030 period are reduced further to account for the reduction in discretionary costs. This proposal starts at a reduction of discretionary budget authority of $6.3 billion in 2022 and totals $81.9 billion in reduced discretionary spending over the 2022 to 2030 period.

IMF Quota Subscription and Increase in the New Arrangements to Borrow

As part of a broader set of reforms at the International Monetary Fund (IMF), the Administration supports a proposal to extend and increase U.S. participation in of the IMF's New Arrangements to Borrow (NAB). Because U.S. participation in the NAB constitutes an exchange of monetary assets, the Administration does not score them as budget authority or outlays, and they are not included in the total funding requested by the Administration. Budget authority is the authority to enter into obligations that are liquidated by outlays, and U.S. transactions with the IMF do not result in outlays. The Administration's position follows the recommendation made by the 1967 President's Commission on Budget Concepts that "Subscriptions, drawings, and other transactions reflecting net changes in the U.S. position with the International Monetary Fund should be excluded from budget receipts and expenditures."[5] There is little basis for treating IMF quota subscriptions or NAB increases differently from other financial asset exchanges, such as deposits of cash in Treasury's accounts at the Federal Reserve Bank or purchases of gold, which are not recorded as either budget authority or outlays.

Estimating the Impacts of Debt Service

New legislation that affects direct spending and revenue will also indirectly affect interest payments on the Federal debt. These effects on interest payments can cause a significant budgetary impact; however, they are not captured in cost estimates that are required under the PAYGO Act, nor are they typically included in estimates of new legislation that are produced by the Congressional Budget Office. The Administration believes that cost estimates of new legislation could be improved by incorporating information on the effects of interest payments and looks forward to working with the Congress in making reforms in this area.

Funds for Reducing Discretionary Spending

Discretionary spending caps can be an important tool to rein in Government spending. Since the discretionary spending caps were reinstated in 2013 as part of the Budget Control Act of 2011, these caps have not been exceeded, an indication that avoiding a discretionary sequestration is a powerful discretionary budget enforce-

---

[5] Report of the President's Commission on Budget Concepts, Washington, D.C., October 1967, p.31.

ment tool. While spending caps are effective, in that they require the Administration and the Congress to balance competing tradeoffs for limited Federal funds, these caps are usually treated as a floor rather than as a ceiling. If the caps were considered a ceiling, annual discretionary choices could include spending levels below the cap, as proposed by the Administration in prior years and in this Budget for 2021. The 2021 Budget does not change the caps set in the BBA of 2019 but makes choices that bring non-defense spending levels to an amount that is about $30 billion (or nearly six percent) below the 2021 non-defense current law cap.

The Administration is interested in proposals that help the Congress consider proposals to reduce spending below the discretionary caps. For instance, the 2019 House Financial Services and General Government bill included the Fund for America's Kids and Grandkids to set aside $585 million under the Committee's 2019 congressional allocation that would be spent only if deficits were certified at zero. Using funds such as these promotes transparency about the choice between deficit reduction and additional spending. The Administration is supportive of creating such reserve funds in the coming years.

Outlay Caps and Benchmarks

The Budget achieves balance in fifteen years due to proposals to reform healthcare; eliminate wasteful spending in Medicare and other programs; reform student loans, disability programs, and the welfare system; and reprioritize Government to focus on the most effective programs. While the Budget's policies help bring spending under control, additional efforts to control spending are needed. Several budget process reforms should be considered, including setting spending caps on mandatory outlays, and benchmarks against which spending can be measured to determine sustainable levels.

Outlay caps that are consistent with the historical average as a share of gross domestic product (GDP), post-World War II levels could be enforced with sequestration across programs similar to other budget enforcement regimes. An outlay cap on mandatory spending would complement discretionary caps, which have been in place since 2013. The Budget proposes to continue discretionary caps through 2025 at declining levels and declining levels through 2030. Additional program and cost-cutting reforms such as those in the Budget would be necessary to bring outlays to or below the historical average as a share of GDP, post-World War II.

In addition to the Administration's policies, a fiscal rule, or benchmark, that limits total Federal spending to an amount representing affordability would embody fiscal responsibility and bring transparency to reasonable limits on the growth of spending. Such a fiscal rule would provide a benchmark with which to evaluate future Federal spending paths and is a helpful tool to objectively limit the growth of spending to a more reasonable and sustainable level.

FEDERAL RECEIPTS

11. GOVERNMENTAL RECEIPTS

A simpler, fairer, and more efficient tax system is critical to growing the economy and creating jobs. The enactment of the Tax Cuts and Jobs Act (Public Law 115–97) in 2017 reformed the Nation's outdated, overly complex, and burdensome tax system to unleash America's economy, and create millions of new, better-paying jobs that enable American workers to meet their families' needs. This Act, the first comprehensive tax reform in a genera-

tion, streamlines the tax system and ends special interest tax breaks and loopholes, ensuring that all Americans will be treated fairly by the tax system, not just the wealthy. This chapter presents the Budget's estimates of taxes and governmental receipts including the effects of tax legislation enacted in 2019, discusses the provisions of those enacted laws, and explains the Administration's additional receipt proposals.

Table 11–1.   RECEIPTS BY SOURCE—SUMMARY
(In billions of dollars)

	2019 Actual	Estimate										
		2020	2021	2022	2023	2024	2025	2026	2027	2028	2029	2030
Individual income taxes	1,717.9	1,812.0	1,931.7	2,048.4	2,184.5	2,345.7	2,505.4	2,678.7	2,862.3	3,040.1	3,228.4	3,425.7
Corporation income taxes	230.2	263.6	284.1	323.8	382.5	426.5	447.9	435.3	430.9	443.1	446.1	453.2
Social insurance and retirement receipts	1,243.4	1,312.0	1,373.6	1,448.1	1,521.0	1,603.7	1,687.3	1,779.1	1,865.5	1,972.2	2,066.2	2,168.4
(On-budget)	(329.1)	(345.0)	(362.6)	(383.4)	(405.3)	(429.3)	(453.5)	(478.9)	(503.1)	(531.6)	(556.6)	(582.5)
(Off-budget)	(914.3)	(967.1)	(1,011.0)	(1,064.7)	(1,115.7)	(1,174.4)	(1,233.8)	(1,300.2)	(1,362.4)	(1,440.6)	(1,509.6)	(1,586.0)
Excise taxes	99.5	94.6	87.2	89.0	90.4	95.1	95.2	96.8	98.4	99.1	102.2	105.4
Estate and gift taxes	16.7	20.4	21.6	22.8	24.3	25.8	27.5	28.8	30.7	33.1	34.9	36.7
Customs duties	70.8	92.3	53.8	42.7	44.0	45.3	46.5	47.8	49.2	50.5	51.7	52.0
Miscellaneous receipts	85.8	111.3	111.3	110.7	112.4	114.5	114.4	115.4	118.5	123.6	129.6	136.3
Total, receipts	**3,464.2**	**3,706.3**	**3,863.3**	**4,085.7**	**4,359.1**	**4,656.5**	**4,924.3**	**5,182.0**	**5,455.4**	**5,761.5**	**6,059.1**	**6,377.7**
(On-budget)	(2,549.9)	(2,739.3)	(2,852.3)	(3,021.0)	(3,243.4)	(3,482.1)	(3,690.5)	(3,881.8)	(4,093.0)	(4,321.0)	(4,549.6)	(4,791.8)
(Off-budget)	(914.3)	(967.1)	(1,011.0)	(1,064.7)	(1,115.7)	(1,174.4)	(1,233.8)	(1,300.2)	(1,362.4)	(1,440.6)	(1,509.6)	(1,586.0)
Total receipts as a percentage of GDP	16.3	16.7	16.5	16.6	16.9	17.2	17.3	17.3	17.4	17.5	17.6	17.6

ESTIMATES OF GOVERNMENTAL RECEIPTS

Governmental receipts are taxes and other collections from the public that result from the exercise of the Federal Government's sovereign or governmental powers. The difference between governmental receipts and outlays is the surplus or deficit.

The Federal Government also collects income from the public through market-oriented activities. Collections from these activities are subtracted from gross outlays, rather than added to taxes and other governmental receipts, and are discussed in Chapter 12, "Offsetting Collections and Offsetting Receipts," in this volume.

Total governmental receipts (hereafter referred to as "receipts") are estimated to be $3,706.3 billion in 2020, an increase of $242.2 billion or 7.0 percent from 2019. The estimated increase in 2020 is largely due to increases in individual and corporation income taxes and social

insurance and retirement receipts. Receipts in 2020 are estimated to be 16.7 percent of Gross Domestic Product (GDP), which is higher than in 2019, when receipts were 16.3 percent of GDP.

Receipts are estimated to rise to $3,863.3 billion in 2021, an increase of $156.9 billion or 4.2 percent relative to 2020. Receipts are projected to grow at an average annual rate of 6.3 percent between 2021 and 2025, rising to $4,924.3 billion. Receipts are projected to rise to $6,377.7 billion in 2030, growing at an average annual rate of 5.3 percent between 2025 and 2030. This growth is largely due to assumed increases in incomes resulting from both real economic growth and inflation.

As a share of GDP, receipts are projected to decrease from 16.7 percent in 2020 to 16.5 percent in 2021, and to steadily increase to 17.6 percent of GDP by 2030.

LEGISLATION ENACTED IN 2019 THAT AFFECTS GOVERNMENTAL RECEIPTS

Five laws were enacted during 2019 that affect receipts. The major provisions of these laws that have a significant impact on receipts are described below.[1]

CONSOLIDATED APPROPRIATIONS ACT, 2019 (Public Law 116–6)

The Act, which was signed into law on February 15, 2019, provides authority to the Bureau of Engraving and Printing to construct a more efficient production facility. This reduces the cost incurred by the Federal Reserve for printing currency and therefore increases deposits of earnings by the Federal Reserve System to the Department of the Treasury.

TAXPAYER FIRST ACT (Public Law 116–25)

The Act, which was signed into law on July 1, 2019, revises management and oversight of the Internal Revenue Service (IRS), modernizes the IRS to help combat tax fraud and update information technology systems, and makes other changes to the Internal Revenue Code. The Act requires Treasury to make available, by January 1, 2023, an internet website or other electronic medium that would allow users to prepare and file Forms 1099; prepare forms for distribution to recipients other than the IRS; and maintain a record of completed, filed, and distributed Forms 1099.

FURTHER CONSOLIDATED APPROPRIATIONS ACT, 2020 (Public Law 116–94)

The Act, which was signed into law on December 20, 2019, included a number of health revenue provisions in addition to the Taxpayer Certainty and Disaster Tax Relief Act of 2019. Major provisions are described below.

Affordable Care Act.—The Act repeals three taxes established by the Patient Protections and Affordable Care Act: a tax on medical devices, a tax on high-cost employer sponsored health plans, and an annual fee for health insurance providers.

Patient-Centered Outcomes Research Trust Fund.—The Act extends the fees for health insurers and sponsors of self-insured health plans that are deposited into the Trust Fund until September 30, 2029.

Discharge of indebtedness on principal residence excluded from gross income.—Taxpayers are allowed a maximum exclusion from gross income of $2 million for any discharge of indebtedness income by reason of a discharge (in whole or part) of qualified principal residence indebtedness. The provision is effective for discharges of indebtedness after December 31, 2017. The Act extends the exclusion through December 31, 2020.

Mortgage insurance premiums treated as qualified residence interest.—Certain premiums paid or accrued for qualified mortgage insurance by a taxpayer during a taxable year in connection with acquisition in-

debtedness on a qualified residence of the taxpayer are treated as interest that is qualified residence interest and is therefore deductible. Qualified residence interest is interest on acquisition indebtedness and home equity indebtedness with respect to a principal residence and a second residence of the taxpayer. This deduction expired on December 31, 2017. The Act extends the deduction through December 31, 2020.

Reduction in medical expense deduction floor.—Under prior law, individuals could claim an itemized deduction for unreimbursed medical expenses, but only to the extent that such expenses exceed 10 percent of a taxpayer's adjusted gross income. For taxable years 2017 and 2018, the threshold was lowered to 7.5 percent. The Act extends the 7.5 percent threshold through taxable year 2020.

Expired provisions.—The Act extends through calendar year 2020 several expired tax provisions, including the Indian employment tax credit, the railroad maintenance tax credit, mine rescue team training and mine safety equipment tax credits, empowerment zone tax incentives, and the American Samoa economic development credit.

Credit for biodiesel and renewable diesel.—The Act extends through December 31, 2022, the $1.00 per gallon production tax credit for biodiesel and diesel fuel created from biomass and the 10 cents per gallon credit for small biodiesel producers. This credit expired after December 31, 2017.

Renewable energy production tax credit.—The Act extends through December 31, 2020, the period during which qualified facilities producing electricity from closed-loop biomass, open-loop biomass, geothermal energy, small irrigation power, municipal solid waste, and qualified hydropower can be placed in service for the purposes of the electricity production credit.

Excise tax credits for alternative fuel.—The Act extends through December 31, 2020, the 50-cents-per-gallon excise tax credit or payment for certain alternative fuel used as fuel in a motor vehicle, motor boat, or airplane, and the 50-cents-per-gallon credit for alternative fuel mixed with a traditional fuel (gasoline, diesel, or kerosene) for use as a fuel. The credits expired on December 31, 2017.

Expiring provisions.—The Act extends through calendar year 2020 other provisions expiring at the end of calendar year 2019, including the new markets tax credit, the employer credit for paid family and medical leave, and the Work Opportunity Credit.

Disaster tax relief.—The Act provides emergency tax relief for individuals living in "qualified disaster areas." This includes any area with respect to which a major disaster was Presidentially-declared, during the period beginning on January 1, 2018, and ending 60 days after the date of the enactment of the Act. This does not include the California wildfire disaster area.

Special disaster-related rules for use of retirement funds.—Prior law imposed penalties or other limitations on distributions from tax-preferred retirement plans. The

---

[1] In the discussions of enacted legislation, years referred to are calendar years, unless otherwise noted.

Act permits penalty-free withdrawals, up to $100,000, from retirement plans for individuals whose principal place of abode was located in the qualified disaster areas. In addition, individuals who make withdrawals for qualified disaster relief can, within a three-year period starting on the date of the withdrawal, make contributions back to the retirement savings account, not to exceed the amount withdrawn.

Employee retention credit for employers affected by qualified disasters.—The Act provides a tax credit for 40 percent of wages (up to $6,000 per employee) paid by a disaster-affected employer to an employee from a qualified disaster area. The credit applies to wages paid without regard to whether services associated with those wages were performed.

Other disaster tax relief provisions.—The Act also temporarily suspends limitations on the deduction for charitable contributions associated with qualified disaster relief; eliminates the requirements that personal casualty losses must exceed 10 percent of adjusted gross income to qualify for deduction; and allows taxpayers in designated disaster areas to refer to earned income from the immediately preceding year for purposes of determining the Earned Income Tax Credit and Child Tax Credit in tax year 2018. Additionally, the Act provides additional low-income housing credit allocations relating to qualified 2017 and 2018 California disasters.

Repeal of increase in unrelated business taxable income for certain fringe benefit expenses.—The Act repeals the requirement that the unrelated business taxation income of tax-exempt organizations is increased by expenses related to qualified transportation fringe benefits.

Table 11–2. ADJUSTMENTS TO THE BALANCED BUDGET AND EMERGENCY DEFICIT CONTROL ACT (BBEDCA) BASELINE ESTIMATES OF GOVERNMENTAL RECEIPTS

(In billions of dollars)

	2020	2021	2022	2023	2024	2025	2026	2027	2028	2029	2030	2021– 2025	2021– 2030
BBEDCA baseline receipts	3,706.4	3,860.4	4,082.7	4,349.6	4,641.7	4,921.3	5,316.1	5,681.5	6,008.7	6,319.1	6,651.6	21,855.7	51,832.7
Adjustments to BBEDCA baseline:													
Extend individual income tax provisions[1]	....	....	....	....	....	–17.5	–158.3	–241.8	–265.9	–279.5	–292.2	–17.5	–1,255.1
Extend estate and gift tax provisions	....	....	....	....	....	....	....	–12.8	–12.2	–12.8	–13.6	....	–51.5
Total, adjustments to BBEDCA baseline	....	....	....	....	....	–17.5	–158.3	–254.6	–278.1	–292.3	–305.8	–17.5	–1,306.6
Adjusted baseline receipts	3,706.4	3,860.4	4,082.7	4,349.6	4,641.7	4,903.9	5,157.8	5,426.9	5,730.6	6,026.8	6,345.8	21,838.2	50,526.1

[1] This provision affects both receipts and outlays. Only the receipt effect is shown here. The outlay effects are listed below:

	2020	2021	2022	2023	2024	2025	2026	2027	2028	2029	2030	2021– 2025	2021– 2030
Extend individual income tax provisions	....	....	....	....	....	....	0.2	15.7	15.8	16.7	17.0	....	65.5
Total, outlay effects of adjustments to BBEDCA baseline	....	....	....	....	....	....	0.2	15.7	15.8	16.7	17.0	....	65.5

ADJUSTMENTS TO THE BALANCED BUDGET AND EMERGENCY DEFICIT CONTROL ACT (BBEDCA) BASELINE

An important step in addressing the Nation's fiscal problems is to be upfront about them and to establish a baseline that provides a realistic measure of the deficit outlook before new policies are enacted. This Budget does so by adjusting the BBEDCA baseline to reflect the true cost of extending major tax policies that are scheduled to expire but that are likely to be extended. The BBEDCA baseline, which is commonly used in budgeting and is defined in statute, reflects, with some exceptions, the projected receipts level under current law.

However, current law includes a number of scheduled tax changes that the Administration believes are unlikely to occur and that prevent it from serving as a realistic benchmark for judging the effect of new legislation. These tax changes include expiration in 2025 of the individual income and estate and gift tax provisions enacted in the Tax Cuts and Jobs Act. This Budget uses an adjusted baseline that is intended to be more realistic by assuming permanent extension of those expiring provisions. This baseline does not reflect the President's policy proposals, but is rather a realistic and fair benchmark from which to measure the effects of those policies.

Extend individual income tax provisions.—The Administration's adjusted baseline projection assumes permanent extension of all individual income tax provisions in the Tax Cuts and Jobs Act that are currently set to expire on December 31, 2025.

Extend estate and gift tax provisions.—The Administration's adjusted baseline projection assumes permanent extension of the estate and gift tax parameters and provisions in effect for calendar year 2025.

BUDGET PROPOSALS

The 2021 Budget supports the extension of the individual and estate tax provisions of the Tax Cuts and Jobs Act beyond their expiration in 2025, as described above, to provide certainty for taxpayers and to support continued economic growth. The Budget's additional proposals affecting governmental receipts are as follows:

Eliminate Corporation for Travel Promotion.— The Administration proposes to eliminate funding for the Corporation for Travel Promotion (also known as Brand USA). The Budget extends the authorization for the Electronic System for Travel Authorization (ESTA) surcharge currently deposited in the Travel Promotion Fund and redirects the surcharge to the General Fund.

Establish Education Freedom Scholarships.—The Administration proposes to make available annually up to $5 billion worth of income tax credits for individual and corporate donations to State-identified nonprofit education scholarship granting organizations (SGOs). (Taxpayers who claim the credit will not be allowed to claim an itemized deduction for the same contribution.) States will decide family eligibility requirements and allowable uses of scholarship funds. Based on State rules, SGOs would use donated funds to provide families with Education Freedom Scholarships for a broad range of educational activities, including career and technical education, transportation, special education services, and tuition for private schools.

Give Medicare beneficiaries with high deductible health plans the option to make tax deductible contributions to health savings accounts or medical savings accounts.—Under current law, workers who are entitled to Medicare are not allowed to contribute to a health savings account (HSA), even if they are working and are enrolled in a qualifying health plan through their employer. The Administration proposes to allow Medicare-eligible workers who have a high-deductible health plan through their employer to contribute to an HSA. In addition, the Administration proposes to allow beneficiaries enrolled in Medicare medical savings account (MSA) plans to contribute to their MSAs, beginning in 2022, subject to the annual HSA contribution limits as determined by the Internal Revenue Service. Beneficiaries would also be allowed a one-time opportunity to roll over the funds from their private HSAs to their Medicare MSAs. Beneficiaries who enroll in MSA plans would not be allowed to purchase Medigap or other supplemental insurance. The Administration also proposes to align MSA plans more closely with conventional Medicare Advantage plans by allowing MSA plans to offer Part D benefits, exclude preventive services from being subject to the plan deductible, and offer mandatory supplemental benefits for their enrollees. Medicare would retain a portion of savings from these plans.

Provide tax exemption for Indian Health Service (IHS) Health Professions, NURSE Corps, and Native Hawaiian scholarship and loan repayment programs in return for obligatory service require-

ment.—The Administration proposes to allow scholarship funds for qualified tuition and related expenses received under the IHS Health Professions, NURSE Corps, and Native Hawaiian scholarships to be excluded from income. The Administration also proposes to allow students to exclude from gross income student loan amounts forgiven or repaid by the IHS Loan Repayment Program and NURSE Corps. Under current law, National Health Service Corps programs and Armed Forces Health Professions Scholarships are provided an exception to the general rule that scholarship amounts representing payment for work are considered ordinary income and therefore taxable. Furthermore, certain loans forgiven or repaid as part of certain State and profession-based loan programs are provided an exception from the general rule that loan amounts paid on another's behalf are taxable income. Eliminating the current tax burden on scholarship and loan repayment recipients would allow IHS and the Health Resources and Services Administration to leverage another tool to bolster their ongoing efforts to recruit and retain qualified healthcare providers and provide equity between participants in these programs and other similar programs currently receiving these tax benefits.

Reform medical liability.—The Administration proposes to reform medical liability beginning in 2021. This proposal has the potential to lower health insurance premiums, increasing taxable income and payroll tax receipts.

Establish Electronic Visa Update System (EVUS) user fee.—The Administration proposes to establish a user fee for EVUS, a U.S. Customs and Border Protection program to collect biographic and travel-related information from certain non-immigrant visa holders prior to traveling to the United States. The user fee would fund the costs of providing and administering the system.

Establish an immigration services surcharge.— The Administration proposes to add a 10-percent surcharge on all requests received by U.S. Citizenship and Immigration Services, including applications for citizenship and adjustment of status and petitions for temporary workers.

Increase worksite enforcement penalties.—The Administration proposes to increase by 35 percent all penalty amounts against employers who violate Immigration and Nationality Act provisions on the unlawful employment of aliens.

Provide paid parental leave benefits.—The Administration proposes establishing a new benefit within the Unemployment Insurance (UI) program to provide up to six weeks paid leave to mothers, fathers, and adoptive parents. States are responsible for adjusting their UI tax structures to maintain sufficient balances in their Unemployment Trust Fund accounts.

Establish Unemployment Insurance (UI) solvency standard.—The Administration proposes to set a minimum solvency standard to encourage States to maintain sufficient balances in their UI trust funds. States that are currently below this minimum standard are expected to increase their State UI taxes to build up their trust fund balances. States that do not build up sufficient reserves will be subject to Federal Unemployment Tax Act credit reductions, increasing Federal UI receipts.

Improve UI Insurance program integrity.—The Administration proposes a package of reforms to the UI program aimed at improving program integrity. These reforms are expected to reduce outlays in the UI program by reducing improper payments. In general, reduced outlays allow States to keep UI taxes lower, reducing overall receipts to the UI trust funds.

Subject Financial Research Fund (FRF) assessments to annual appropriations action.—Expenses of the Financial Stability Oversight Council (FSOC) and Office of Financial Research (OFR) are paid through the FRF, which is authorized to assess fees on certain bank holding companies and nonbank financial companies supervised by the Federal Reserve Board of Governors. The FRF was established by the Dodd-Frank Act and is managed by the Department of the Treasury. To improve their effectiveness and ensure greater accountability, the Budget proposes to subject the activities of FSOC and OFR to the appropriations process. In so doing, currently authorized assessments would, beginning in 2022, be reclassified as discretionary offsetting collections and set at a level determined by the Congress.

Provide discretionary funding for Internal Revenue Service (IRS) program integrity cap adjustment.—The Administration proposes to establish and fund a new adjustment to the discretionary caps for IRS program integrity activities starting in 2021. The IRS base funding within the discretionary caps funds current tax administration activities, including all tax enforcement and compliance program activities, in the Enforcement and Operations Support accounts at IRS. The additional $400 million cap adjustment in 2021 will fund new and continuing investments in expanding and improving the effectiveness and efficiency of the IRS's tax enforcement program. The activities are estimated to generate $79 billion in additional revenue over 10 years and cost approximately $15 billion, resulting in an estimated net savings of $64 billion. Once the new staff are trained and become fully operational, these initiatives are expected to generate roughly $5 in additional revenue for every $1 in IRS expenses. Notably, the return on investment is likely understated because it only includes amounts received; it does not reflect the effect enhanced enforcement has on deterring noncompliance. This indirect deterrence helps to ensure the continued payment of $3.6 trillion in taxes paid each year without direct enforcement measures.

Increase oversight of paid tax return preparers.—Paid tax return preparers have an important role in tax administration because they assist taxpayers in complying with their obligations under the tax laws. Incompetent and dishonest tax return preparers increase collection costs, reduce revenues, disadvantage taxpayers by potentially subjecting them to penalties and interest as a result of incorrect returns, and undermine confidence in the tax system. To promote high quality services from paid tax return preparers, the proposal would explicitly provide that the Secretary of the Treasury has the authority to regulate all paid tax return preparers.

Provide the IRS with greater flexibility to address correctable errors.—The Administration proposes to expand IRS authority to correct errors on taxpayer returns. Current statute only allows the IRS to correct errors on returns in certain limited instances, such as basic math errors or the failure to include the appropriate social security number or taxpayer identification number. This proposal would expand the instances in which the IRS could correct a taxpayer's return including cases where: (1) the information provided by the taxpayer does not match the information contained in Government databases or Form W-2, or from other third party databases as the Secretary determines by regulation; (2) the taxpayer has exceeded the lifetime limit for claiming a deduction or credit; or (3) the taxpayer has failed to include with his or her return certain documentation that is required to be included on or attached to the return. This proposal would make it easier for IRS to correct clear taxpayer errors, directly improving tax compliance and reducing EITC and other improper payments and freeing IRS resources for other enforcement activities.

Eliminate the qualified plug-in electric drive motor vehicle credit.—The Administration proposes to repeal the tax credit for vehicles placed in service after December 31, 2020. Current law provides a non-refundable tax credit of up to $7,500 to the purchaser of a qualified plug-in electric drive motor vehicle. The credit phases out for a manufacturer's vehicles over a one-year period beginning with the second calendar quarter after which the manufacturer has sold a cumulative 200,000 qualifying vehicles.

Repeal exclusion of utility conservation subsidies.—The Administration proposes to repeal the exclusion of utility conservation subsidies to non-business customers who invest in energy conservation measures. The current rate subsidies are equivalent to payments from the utility to its customer, but individuals are not taxed on the value of these subsidies.

Repeal accelerated depreciation for renewable energy property.—The Administration proposes to repeal accelerated (five-year) depreciation for renewable energy property. The cost recovery period for such property—including solar energy, wind energy, biomass, geothermal, combined heat and power, and geothermal heat pump property; fuel cells; and micro-turbines—would range from five to 20 years, depending on the specific activity of the taxpayer and the type of property in service after repeal. Qualifying properties would still be eligible for the bonus depreciation allowance included in the TCJA.

Repeal energy investment credit.—The Administration proposes to repeal the energy investment credit for property for which construction begins after December 31, 2020. The IRC currently provides a credit equal to a certain portion of the cost of solar energy property, geothermal electric property, qualified fuel cell power plants, small wind energy property, stationary micro-turbine power plants, geothermal heat pumps, and combined heat and power property.

Repeal credit for residential energy efficient property.—The Administration proposes to repeal the credit for residential energy efficient property for property placed in service after December 31, 2020. Currently, a credit is available for a portion of the purchase of qualified photovoltaic and solar water heating property, fuel cell power plants, geothermal heat pumps, and small wind property used in or placed on a residence.

Fund the Federal Payment Levy Program via collections.—The Administration proposes to allow the Bureau of Fiscal Service to retain a portion of the funds collected under the Bureau's Fiscal Levy Program which processes and collects delinquent tax debts. Delinquent taxpayers would still receive credit based on the full amount collected before any deduction for Fiscal Service's costs and would not be impacted by the proposal. By allowing the Fiscal Service to recover its costs from levy collections, this structure would reduce administrative and overhead costs for both the Fiscal Service and the IRS and is similar to how Fiscal Service recovers its costs for Federal non-tax and State debts.

Reform inland waterways financing.—The Administration proposes to reform the laws governing the Inland Waterways Trust Fund, including establishing a fee to increase the amount paid by commercial navigation users of the inland waterways. In 1986, the Congress provided that commercial traffic on the inland waterways would be responsible for 50 percent of the capital costs of the locks, dams, and other features that make barge transportation possible on the inland waterways. The additional revenue would help finance the users' share of future capital investments as well as 10 percent of the cost of operation and maintenance activities in these waterways to support economic growth. The current excise tax on diesel fuel used in inland waterways commerce will not produce sufficient revenue to cover these costs.

Increase employee contributions to the Federal Employees Retirement System (FERS).—The Administration proposes to increase Federal employee

Table 11-3. EFFECT OF BUDGET PROPOSALS

(In millions of dollars)

	2020	2021	2022	2023	2024	2025	2026	2027	2028	2029	2030	2021-2025	2021-2030
Eliminate BrandUSA; make savings available for deficit reduction	....	....	....	....	....	....	....	....	316	321	328	....	965
Establish Education Freedom Scholarships	....	−893	−4,847	−4,928	−5,006	−4,974	−5,036	−4,916	−4,934	−4,960	−4,994	−20,648	−45,488
Give Medicare beneficiaries with high deductible health plans the option to make tax deductible contributions to health savings accounts or medical savings accounts	....	−615	−1,095	−1,311	−1,536	−1,665	−1,827	−1,958	−2,025	−2,089	−2,154	−6,222	−16,275
Provide tax exemption for certain HRSA and IHS scholarship and loan repayment programs	....	−22	−28	−28	−28	−29	−29	−29	−29	−30	−30	−135	−282
Reform medical liability	....	19	101	233	394	575	879	1,124	1,235	1,317	1,398	1,322	7,275
Establish Electronic Visa Update System user fee	....	38	42	47	52	58	64	72	79	88	107	237	647
Establish an immigration services surcharge	....	389	398	407	416	426	436	446	456	466	477	2,036	4,317
Increase worksite enforcement penalties	....	13	14	15	15	15	15	15	15	15	15	72	147
Provide paid parental leave benefits [1]	....	....	....	504	755	833	909	978	1,047	1,107	1,164	2,092	7,297
Establish an Unemployment Insurance (UI) solvency standard [1]	....	....	....	537	944	1,453	775	991	1,217	1,487	138	2,934	7,542
Improve UI program integrity [1]	....	2	−8	−20	−37	−42	−20	−72	−132	−72	−164	−105	−565
Subject Financial Research Fund to appropriations [1]	....	....	−61	−61	−61	−61	−61	−61	−61	−61	−61	−244	−549
Implement tax enforcement program integrity cap adjustment	....	264	542	3,106	5,158	7,356	9,682	12,005	12,974	13,813	14,495	16,426	79,395
Increase oversight of paid tax return preparers	....	5	17	22	24	27	30	33	36	40	44	95	278
Provide more flexible authority for the Internal Revenue Service to address correctable errors	....	435	650	683	718	754	792	831	872	915	959	3,240	7,609
Repeal the qualified plug-in electric drive motor vehicle credit	....	136	476	401	326	263	245	238	195	154	143	1,602	2,577
Repeal exclusion of utility conservation subsidies	....	2	7	7	6	6	5	5	5	4	4	28	51
Repeal accelerated depreciation for renewable energy property	....	111	348	526	594	637	653	606	527	440	343	2,216	4,785
Repeal energy investment credit	−36	−39	125	643	872	1,092	1,143	1,099	1,012	927	880	2,693	7,754
Repeal credit for residential energy efficient property	....	955	273	68	....	....	....	....	....	....	....	1,296	1,296
Fund the Federal Payment Levy Program via collections	....	−22	−22	−22	−22	−22	−22	−22	−22	−22	−22	−110	−220
Reform inland waterways financing	....	180	180	180	180	180	180	180	180	180	180	900	1,800
Increase Employee Contributions to 50 percent of Cost, Phased in at 1 percent per Year	....	....	2,194	4,697	7,221	9,506	11,120	12,503	13,314	13,384	13,447	23,618	87,386
Implement Defined Contribution System for Term Employees	....	....	−34	−91	−92	−94	−96	−98	−100	−102	−104	−311	−811
Consolidate the Public Company Accounting Oversight Board [1]	....	....	−234	−243	−251	−260	−269	−279	−288	−298	−309	−988	−2,431
Eliminate allocations to the Housing Trust Fund and Capital Magnet Fund	....	45	106	91	78	79	80	81	82	83	85	399	810
Improve clarity in worker classification and information reporting requirements	....	−23	−27	−1	14	22	20	17	19	19	32	−15	92
Require Social Security Number (SSN) for Child Tax Credit, Earned Income Tax Credit, and credit for other dependents	....	1,927	3,890	3,982	4,114	4,295	4,510	4,745	4,999	5,263	5,558	18,208	43,283
Offset overlapping unemployment and disability payments [1]	....	....	....	−1	−7	−10	−12	−15	−18	−21	−25	−18	−109
Total, effect of mandatory proposals	**−36**	**2,907**	**3,007**	**9,443**	**14,841**	**20,420**	**24,166**	**28,519**	**30,971**	**32,368**	**31,934**	**50,618**	**198,576**

[1] Net of income offsets.

contributions to FERS, equalizing employee and employer contributions to FERS so that half of the normal cost would be paid by each. For some specific occupations, such as law enforcement officers and firefighters, the costs of their retirement packages necessitates a higher normal-cost percentage. For those specific occupations, this proposal would increase, but not equalize, employee contributions. This proposal brings Federal retirement benefits more in line with the private sector. This adjustment will reduce the long-term cost to the Federal Government by reducing the Government's contribution rate. To reduce the impact on employees, this proposal will be phased in, increasing employee contributions by one percentage point per year, and reducing employer contributions by one percentage point per year, until both are equalized.

Implement a defined contribution system for term employees.—The Administration proposes to provide new Federal term employees with a more generous TSP defined contribution plan, in lieu of participation in the FERS defined benefit plan. Term employees would receive a defined contribution that consists of an automatic 5-percent agency contribution to the Thrift Savings Plan, and up to 5 percent additional in matching contributions. These employees are currently provided a 1-percent automatic agency contribution to the Thrift Savings Plan and up to 4 percent additional in matching contributions. For certain term employees in the public safety field, the automatic Government contribution would consist of 7 percent of basic pay, with a Government match of up to 7 percent.

Consolidate the Public Company Accounting Oversight Board (PCAOB) into the Securities and Exchange Commission (SEC).—The Administration proposes to consolidate PCAOB authorities, responsibilities, and funding streams into the SEC beginning in 2022.

Eliminate allocations to the Housing Trust Fund and Capital Magnet Fund.—The Administration proposes to eliminate an assessment on Fannie Mae and Freddie Mac that is used to fund the Housing Trust Fund and Capital Magnet Fund, two Federal programs that support affordable low-income housing. The resulting increase in taxable income at Fannie Mae and Freddie Mac would increase governmental receipts.

Improve clarity in worker classification and information reporting requirements.—The Administration proposes to: (1) establish a new safe harbor that allows a service recipient to classify a service provider as an independent contractor and requires withholding of in-

dividual income taxes to this independent contractor at a rate of five percent on the first $20,000 of payments; and (2) raise the reporting threshold for payments to all independent contractors from $600 to $1,000, and reduce the reporting threshold for third-party settlement organizations from $20,000 and 200 transactions per payee to $1,000 without regard to the number of transactions. In addition, Form 1099-K would be required to be filed with the IRS by January 31 of the year following the year for which the information is being reported. The proposal increases clarity in the tax code, reduces costly litigation, and improves tax compliance.

Require a social security number (SSN) that is valid for work in order to claim Child Tax Credit (CTC), Earned Income Tax Credit (EITC), and/or Credit for Other Dependents (ODTC).—The Administration proposes requiring a SSN that is valid for work to claim the EITC, the CTC (both the refundable and non-refundable portion), and/or the ODTC for the taxable year. For all credits, this requirement would apply to taxpayers (including both the primary and secondary filer on a joint return) and all qualifying children or dependents. Under current law, taxpayers who do not have SSNs that are valid for work may claim the CTC as long as the qualifying child for whom the credit is claimed has a valid SSN. Furthermore, the ODTC, created by the Tax Cuts and Jobs Act, allows taxpayers whose dependents do not meet the requirements of the CTC—including the SSN requirement—to claim this non-refundable credit. This proposal would ensure that only individuals who are authorized to work in the United States could claim these credits by extending the SSN requirement for qualifying children to parents on the tax form for the CTC and instituting an SSN requirement for the ODTC. While this SSN requirement is already current law for the EITC, this proposal would also fix an administrative gap to strengthen enforcement of the provision.

Offset overlapping unemployment and disability payments.—The Administration proposes to close a loophole that allows individuals to receive both UI and Disability Insurance (DI) benefits for the same period of joblessness. The proposal would offset the DI benefit to account for concurrent receipt of UI benefits. Offsetting the overlapping benefits would discourage some individuals from applying for UI, reducing benefit outlays. The reduction in benefit outlays is accompanied by a reduction in States' UI tax receipts, which are held in the Unemployment Trust Fund.

Table 11–4. RECEIPTS BY SOURCE

(In millions of dollars)

Source	2019 Actual	Estimate										
		2020	2021	2022	2023	2024	2025	2026	2027	2028	2029	2030
Individual income taxes:												
Federal funds	1,717,857	1,812,049	1,928,842	2,047,306	2,181,006	2,340,090	2,497,381	2,667,957	2,848,821	3,025,513	3,212,834	3,409,105
Legislative proposal, not subject to PAYGO	....	....	264	542	3,045	5,061	7,225	9,586	11,894	12,850	13,666	14,431
Legislative proposal, subject to PAYGO	....	–9	2,572	570	498	522	825	1,165	1,558	1,693	1,863	2,153
Total, Individual income taxes ...	**1,717,857**	**1,812,040**	**1,931,678**	**2,048,418**	**2,184,549**	**2,345,673**	**2,505,431**	**2,678,708**	**2,862,273**	**3,040,056**	**3,228,363**	**3,425,689**
Corporation income taxes:												
Federal funds	230,245	263,669	284,395	324,020	382,207	426,039	447,325	434,724	430,367	442,679	445,747	452,936
Legislative proposal, not subject to PAYGO	....	....	45	175	162	151	154	157	160	164	167	171
Legislative proposal, subject to PAYGO	....	–27	–347	–360	113	268	425	395	348	306	214	88
Total, Corporation income taxes	**230,245**	**263,642**	**284,093**	**323,835**	**382,482**	**426,458**	**447,904**	**435,276**	**430,875**	**443,149**	**446,128**	**453,195**
Social insurance and retirement receipts (trust funds):												
Employment and general retirement:												
Old-age survivors insurance (off-budget) ...	770,282	826,613	864,414	910,350	954,044	1,004,346	1,055,142	1,111,776	1,164,892	1,231,783	1,290,813	1,355,888
Legislative proposal, not subject to PAYGO	....	....	–142	–192	–321	–389	–431	–306	–294	–308	–352	–153
Disability insurance (off-budget)	144,021	140,460	146,788	154,587	162,008	170,549	179,174	188,792	197,812	209,171	219,195	230,245
Legislative proposal, not subject to PAYGO	....	....	–24	–33	–54	–66	–73	–52	–50	–52	–60	–26
Hospital Insurance	277,572	292,144	308,122	325,713	342,623	361,431	380,402	401,489	421,830	446,898	469,480	494,463
Legislative proposal, not subject to PAYGO	....	....	....	....	–36	–60	–82	–60	–68	–76	–90	–40
Legislative proposal, subject to PAYGO ..	....	....	–83	–116	–119	–121	–111	–95	–82	–77	–76	–73
Railroad retirement:												
Social security equivalent account	2,259	2,347	2,525	2,595	2,675	2,756	2,838	2,920	3,005	3,088	3,175	3,261
Rail pension & supplemental annuity .	3,259	3,222	3,380	3,466	3,566	3,671	3,778	3,885	3,996	4,292	4,457	4,777
Total, Employment and general retirement	1,197,393	1,264,786	1,324,980	1,396,370	1,464,386	1,542,117	1,620,637	1,708,349	1,791,041	1,894,719	1,986,542	2,088,342
On-budget	(283,090)	(297,713)	(313,944)	(331,658)	(348,709)	(367,677)	(386,825)	(408,139)	(428,681)	(454,125)	(476,946)	(502,388)
Off-budget	(914,303)	(967,073)	(1,011,036)	(1,064,712)	(1,115,677)	(1,174,440)	(1,233,812)	(1,300,210)	(1,362,360)	(1,440,594)	(1,509,596)	(1,585,954)
Unemployment insurance:												
Deposits by States [1]	34,624	34,909	35,782	36,199	36,726	37,946	39,439	42,044	43,365	44,615	45,586	47,215
Legislative proposal, not subject to PAYGO	....	....	2	–5	–18	–33	–34	–3	–65	–135	–55	–166
Legislative proposal, subject to PAYGO ..	....	....	....	–4	622	922	1,011	1,099	1,180	1,255	1,323	1,383
Federal unemployment receipts [1]	6,438	7,015	7,158	7,300	7,447	7,604	7,769	7,938	8,109	8,286	8,468	8,516
Legislative proposal, subject to PAYGO	....	....	....	....	671	1,179	1,816	968	1,239	1,522	1,859	172
Railroad unemployment receipts [1]	131	80	91	200	231	144	78	95	150	179	152	123
Total, Unemployment insurance	41,193	42,004	43,033	43,690	45,679	47,762	50,079	52,141	53,978	55,722	57,333	57,243

Table 11–4. RECEIPTS BY SOURCE—Continued

(In millions of dollars)

Source	2019 Actual	Estimate										
		2020	2021	2022	2023	2024	2025	2026	2027	2028	2029	2030
Other retirement:												
Federal employees retirement - employee share	4,757	5,205	5,550	5,895	6,284	6,695	7,122	7,564	8,024	8,489	8,967	9,472
Legislative proposal, subject to PAYGO	....	....	....	2,160	4,606	7,129	9,412	11,024	12,405	13,214	13,282	13,343
Non-Federal employees retirement [2]	29	31	31	31	30	30	30	29	29	29	28	28
Total, Other retirement	4,786	5,236	5,581	8,086	10,920	13,854	16,564	18,617	20,458	21,732	22,277	22,843
Total, Social insurance and retirement receipts (trust funds)	**1,243,372**	**1,312,026**	**1,373,594**	**1,448,146**	**1,520,985**	**1,603,733**	**1,687,280**	**1,779,107**	**1,865,477**	**1,972,173**	**2,066,152**	**2,168,428**
On-budget	(329,069)	(344,953)	(362,558)	(383,434)	(405,308)	(429,293)	(453,468)	(478,897)	(503,117)	(531,579)	(556,556)	(582,474)
Off-budget	(914,303)	(967,073)	(1,011,036)	(1,064,712)	(1,115,677)	(1,174,440)	(1,233,812)	(1,300,210)	(1,362,360)	(1,440,594)	(1,509,596)	(1,585,954)
Excise taxes:												
Federal funds:												
Alcohol	9,992	9,670	10,055	10,140	10,096	10,068	10,016	10,127	10,276	10,467	10,686	10,939
Tobacco	12,457	12,333	11,860	11,748	11,755	11,626	11,547	11,480	11,387	11,306	11,224	11,136
Transportation fuels	−3,623	−10,995	−4,275	−3,757	−2,299	−971	−976	−979	−978	−976	−973	−969
Telephone and teletype services	436	387	342	300	235	203	174	147	124	103	85	70
Health insurance providers	9,590	15,398	....	....	....	....	....	....	....	....	....	....
Indoor tanning services	69	65	63	60	58	56	54	51	49	47	44	42
Medical devices	−64	....	....	....	....	....	....	....	....	....	....	....
Other Federal fund excise taxes	6,070	3,155	3,223	3,297	3,305	3,368	3,465	3,565	3,669	3,781	3,892	4,006
Total, Federal funds	34,927	30,013	21,268	21,788	23,150	24,350	24,280	24,391	24,527	24,728	24,958	25,224
Trust funds:												
Transportation	44,111	42,354	42,669	43,063	43,085	43,213	43,323	43,551	43,772	44,035	44,297	44,639
Airport and airway	15,976	17,040	17,987	18,933	19,940	21,123	22,270	23,453	24,664	25,944	27,461	28,879
Sport fish restoration and boating safety	574	577	582	586	592	597	602	608	613	619	625	630
Black lung disability insurance	217	322	215	164	165	166	167	167	167	167	170	173
Inland waterway	117	114	112	109	107	105	103	101	100	99	99	98
Oil spill liability	156	502	679	686	694	701	715	721	713	719	726	729
Vaccine injury compensation	280	303	309	313	318	320	321	326	330	336	340	346
Leaking underground storage tank	226	214	214	215	213	213	212	212	211	211	209	208
Supplementary medical insurance	2,437	2,800	2,800	2,800	1,686	3,914	2,800	2,800	2,800	1,686	2,800	3,914
Patient-centered outcomes research	431	354	371	388	409	431	453	476	499	524	550	578
Total, Trust funds	64,525	64,580	65,938	67,257	67,209	70,783	70,966	72,415	73,869	74,340	77,277	80,194
Total, Excise taxes	**99,452**	**94,593**	**87,206**	**89,045**	**90,359**	**95,133**	**95,246**	**96,806**	**98,396**	**99,068**	**102,235**	**105,418**
Estate and gift taxes:												
Federal funds	16,672	20,389	21,641	22,786	24,263	25,815	27,507	28,837	30,731	33,056	34,938	36,728
Total, Estate and gift taxes	**16,672**	**20,389**	**21,641**	**22,786**	**24,263**	**25,815**	**27,507**	**28,837**	**30,731**	**33,056**	**34,938**	**36,728**
Customs duties and fees:												
Federal funds	69,136	90,585	52,024	40,896	42,111	43,321	44,547	45,791	47,045	48,308	49,516	49,691
Trust funds	1,648	1,719	1,787	1,837	1,888	1,940	1,994	2,049	2,106	2,165	2,224	2,286
Total, Customs duties and fees	**70,784**	**92,304**	**53,811**	**42,733**	**43,999**	**45,261**	**46,541**	**47,840**	**49,151**	**50,473**	**51,740**	**51,977**
Miscellaneous receipts:												
Federal funds:												

Table 11–4. RECEIPTS BY SOURCE—Continued

(In millions of dollars)

Source	2019 Actual	Estimate										
		2020	2021	2022	2023	2024	2025	2026	2027	2028	2029	2030
Miscellaneous taxes	695	699	637	623	622	622	622	622	498	622	615	615
Deposit of earnings, Federal Reserve System	52,793	72,681	70,704	68,449	67,750	67,121	63,595	61,404	61,700	64,317	68,283	73,549
Legislative proposal, subject to PAYGO......	....	....	110	614	633	652	673	693	714	737	759	783
Transfers from the Federal Reserve	468	580	595	614	633	652	673	693	714	737	759	783
Legislative proposal, subject to PAYGO	....	....	−110	−614	−633	−652	−673	−693	−714	−737	−759	−783
Fees for permits and regulatory and judicial services	20,279	20,511	20,957	22,572	24,907	27,838	31,140	34,242	37,181	39,034	40,933	42,186
Legislative proposal, subject to PAYGO	....	....	427	76	79	83	88	93	99	420	432	456
Fines, penalties, and forfeitures	9,919	15,093	16,299	16,651	16,669	16,751	16,832	16,926	16,901	17,031	17,155	17,295
Legislative proposal, subject to PAYGO	....	....	13	14	15	15	15	15	15	15	15	15
Refunds and recoveries ..	−35	−35	−35	−35	−35	−35	−35	−35	−35	−35	−35	−35
Total, Federal funds	84,119	109,529	109,597	108,964	110,640	113,047	112,930	113,960	117,073	122,141	128,157	134,864
Trust funds:												
United Mine Workers of America, combined benefit fund	17	11	10	9	8	7	6	6	5	5	4	4
Defense cooperation	321	646	379	433	524	143	146	149	152	155	158	162
Inland waterways (Legislative proposal, subject to PAYGO)	....	....	180	180	180	180	180	180	180	180	180	180
Fines, penalties, and forfeitures	1,322	1,147	1,104	1,115	1,073	1,095	1,103	1,097	1,094	1,092	1,094	1,096
Total, Trust funds	1,660	1,804	1,673	1,737	1,785	1,425	1,435	1,432	1,431	1,432	1,436	1,442
Total, Miscellaneous receipts ...	**85,779**	**111,333**	**111,270**	**110,701**	**112,425**	**114,472**	**114,365**	**115,392**	**118,504**	**123,573**	**129,593**	**136,306**
Total, budget receipts	**3,464,161**	**3,706,327**	**3,863,293**	**4,085,664**	**4,359,062**	**4,656,545**	**4,924,274**	**5,181,966**	**5,455,407**	**5,761,548**	**6,059,149**	**6,377,741**
On-budget	(2,549,858)	(2,739,254)	(2,852,257)	(3,020,952)	(3,243,385)	(3,482,105)	(3,690,462)	(3,881,756)	(4,093,047)	(4,320,954)	(4,549,553)	(4,791,787)
Off-budget	(914,303)	(967,073)	(1,011,036)	(1,064,712)	(1,115,677)	(1,174,440)	(1,233,812)	(1,300,210)	(1,362,360)	(1,440,594)	(1,509,596)	(1,585,954)

[1] Deposits by States cover the benefit part of the program. Federal unemployment receipts cover administrative costs at both the Federal and State levels. Railroad unemployment receipts cover both the benefits and administrative costs of the program for the railroads.

[2] Represents employer and employee contributions to the civil service retirement and disability fund for covered employees of Government-sponsored, privately owned enterprises and the District of Columbia municipal government.

12. OFFSETTING COLLECTIONS AND OFFSETTING RECEIPTS

I. INTRODUCTION AND BACKGROUND

The Government records money collected in one of two ways. It is either recorded as a governmental receipt and included in the amount reported on the receipts side of the budget or it is recorded as an offsetting collection or offsetting receipt, which reduces (or "offsets") the amount reported on the outlay side of the budget. Governmental receipts are discussed in the previous chapter, "Governmental Receipts." The first section of this chapter broadly discusses offsetting collections and offsetting receipts. The second section discusses user charges, which consist of a subset of offsetting collections and offsetting receipts and a small share of governmental receipts. The third section describes the user charge proposals in the 2021 Budget.

Offsetting collections and offsetting receipts are recorded as offsets to spending so that the budget totals for receipts and (net) outlays reflect the amount of resources allocated by the Government through collective political choice, rather than through the marketplace.[1] This practice ensures that the budget totals measure the transactions of the Government with the public, and avoids the double counting that would otherwise result when one account makes a payment to another account and the receiving account then spends the proceeds. Offsetting receipts and offsetting collections are recorded in the budget in one of two ways, based on interpretation of laws and longstanding budget concepts and practice. They are offsetting collections when the collections are authorized to be credited to expenditure accounts. Otherwise, they are deposited in receipt accounts and called offsetting receipts.

There are two sources of offsetting receipts and offsetting collections: from the public and from other budget accounts. Like governmental receipts, offsetting receipts and offsetting collections from the public reduce the deficit or increase the surplus. In contrast, offsetting receipts and offsetting collections resulting from transactions with other budget accounts, called intragovernmental transactions, exactly offset the payments made by these accounts, with no net impact on the deficit or surplus.[2] In 2019, offsetting receipts and offsetting collections from the public were $545 billion, while receipts and collections from intragovernmental transactions were $1,187 billion, for a total of $1,733 billion Government-wide.

As described above, intragovernmental transactions are responsible for the majority of offsetting collections and offsetting receipts, when measured by the magnitude of the dollars collected. Examples of intragovernmental transactions include interest payments to funds that hold Government securities (such as the Social Security trust funds), general fund transfers to civilian and military retirement pension and health benefits funds, and agency payments to funds for employee health insurance and retirement benefits. Although receipts and collections from intragovernmental collections exactly offset the payments themselves, with no effect on the deficit or surplus, it is important to record these transactions in the budget to show how much the Government is allocating to fund various programs. For example, in the case of civilian retirement pensions, Government agencies make accrual payments to the Civil Service Retirement and Disability Fund on behalf of current employees to fund their future retirement benefits; the receipt of these payments to the Fund is shown in a single receipt account. Recording the receipt of these payments is important because it demonstrates the total cost to the Government today of providing this future benefit.

Offsetting receipts and collections from the public comprise approximately 31 percent of total offsetting collections and offsetting receipts, when measured by the magnitude of the dollars collected. Most of the funds collected through offsetting collections and offsetting receipts from the public arise from business-like transactions with the public. Unlike governmental receipts, which are derived from the Government's exercise of its sovereign power, these offsetting collections and offsetting receipts arise primarily from voluntary payments from the public for goods or services provided by the Government. They are classified as offsets to outlays for the cost of producing the goods or services for sale, rather than as governmental receipts. These activities include the sale of postage stamps, land, timber, and electricity; charging fees for services provided to the public (e.g., admission to National parks); and collecting premiums for healthcare benefits (e.g., Medicare Parts B and D). As described above, treating offsetting collections and offsetting receipts as offsets to outlays ensures the budgetary totals represent governmental rather than market activity.

A relatively small portion ($18.9 billion in 2019) of offsetting collections and offsetting receipts from the public is derived from the Government's exercise of its sovereign power. From a conceptual standpoint, these should be classified as governmental receipts. However, they are classified as offsetting rather than governmental receipts either because this classification has been specified in law or because these collections have traditionally been classi-

---

[1] Showing collections from business-type transactions as offsets on the spending side of the budget follows the concept recommended by the Report of the President's Commission on Budget Concepts in 1967 and is discussed in Chapter 8 of this volume, "Budget Concepts."

[2] For the purposes of this discussion, "collections from the public" include collections from non-budgetary Government accounts, such as credit financing accounts and deposit funds. For more information on these non-budgetary accounts, see Chapter 9, "Coverage of the Budget."

Table 12-1. OFFSETTING COLLECTIONS AND OFFSETTING RECEIPTS FROM THE PUBLIC
(In billions of dollars)

	Actual 2019	Estimate	
		2020	2021
Offsetting collections (credited to expenditure accounts):			
User charges:			
Postal Service stamps and other fees (off-budget)	71.3	72.8	74.5
Defense Commissary Agency	4.5	4.8	4.6
Employee contributions for employees and retired employees health benefits funds	16.6	17.8	18.6
Sale of energy:			
Tennessee Valley Authority	47.9	47.8	46.3
Bonneville Power Administration	3.6	3.9	3.9
Pension Benefit Guaranty Corporation fund	10.1	12.5	14.2
Deposit Insurance	8.1	6.1	12.6
All other user charges	41.7	47.1	47.1
Subtotal, user charges	203.8	212.9	221.6
Other collections credited to expenditure accounts:			
Commodity Credit Corporation fund	7.7	10.0	10.3
Supplemental Security Income (collections from the States)	2.6	2.6	2.6
Other collections	30.8	4.7	5.3
Subtotal, other collections	41.1	17.3	18.3
Subtotal, offsetting collections	244.9	230.2	239.9
Offsetting receipts (deposited in receipt accounts):			
User charges:			
Medicare premiums	108.0	119.6	124.3
Spectrum auction, relocation, and licenses	....	2.6	18.8
Outer Continental Shelf rents, bonuses, and royalties	4.7	2.9	3.3
Immigration fees	4.8	4.8	5.2
All other user charges	27.8	26.4	28.2
Subtotal, user charges deposited in receipt accounts	145.3	156.3	179.9
Other collections deposited in receipt accounts:			
Military assistance program sales	33.0	47.8	44.3
Interest received from credit financing accounts	43.2	53.5	53.5
Proceeds, GSE equity related transactions	15.3	....	2.9
Student loan receipt of negative subsidy and downward reestimates	12.0	12.4	10.4
All other collections deposited in receipt accounts	51.4	56.1	45.8
Subtotal, other collections deposited in receipt accounts	154.9	169.8	157.0
Subtotal, offsetting receipts	300.3	326.0	336.9
Total, offsetting collections and offsetting receipts from the public	545.2	556.3	576.8
Total, offsetting collections and offsetting receipts excluding off-budget	473.6	483.3	502.2
ADDENDUM:			
User charges that are offsetting collections and offsetting receipts [1]	349.1	369.2	401.5
Other offsetting collections and offsetting receipts from the public	196.0	187.1	175.3

[1] Excludes user charges that are classified on the receipts side of the budget. For total user charges, see Table 12–3.

fied as offsets to outlays. Most of the offsetting collections and offsetting receipts in this category derive from fees from Government regulatory services or Government licenses, and include, for example, charges for regulating the nuclear energy industry, bankruptcy filing fees, and immigration fees.[3]

The final source of offsetting collections and offsetting receipts from the public is gifts. Gifts are voluntary contributions to the Government to support particular purposes or reduce the amount of Government debt held by the public.

The spending associated with the activities that generate offsetting collections and offsetting receipts from the public is included in total or "gross outlays." Offsetting collections and offsetting receipts from the public are sub-

---

[3] This category of receipts is known as "offsetting governmental receipts." Some argue that regulatory or licensing fees should be viewed as payments for a particular service or for the right to engage in a particular type of business. However, these fees are conceptually much more similar to taxes because they are compulsory, and they fund activities that are intended to provide broadly dispersed benefits, such as protecting the health of the public. Reclassifying these fees as governmental

receipts could require a change in law, and because of conventions for scoring appropriations bills, would make it impossible for fees that are controlled through annual appropriations acts to be scored as offsets to discretionary spending.

Table 12–2. SUMMARY OF OFFSETTING RECEIPTS BY TYPE

(In millions of dollars)

Receipt Type	Actual 2019	Estimate					
		2020	2021	2022	2023	2024	2025
Intragovernmental	804,024	849,475	886,845	911,658	948,847	995,450	1,044,399
Receipts from non-Federal sources:							
Proprietary	287,507	310,379	303,515	322,148	337,776	352,428	373,024
Offsetting governmental	12,766	15,663	33,379	15,331	15,755	16,295	16,836
Total, receipts from non-Federal sources	300,273	326,042	336,894	337,479	353,531	368,723	389,860
Total Offsetting receipts	1,104,297	1,175,517	1,223,739	1,249,137	1,302,378	1,364,173	1,434,259

tracted from gross outlays to yield "net outlays," which is the most common measure of outlays cited and generally referred to as simply "outlays." For 2019, gross outlays were $6,181 billion, or 29.1 percent of GDP and offsetting collections and offsetting receipts were $1,733 billion, or 8.2 percent of GDP, resulting in net outlays of $4,448 billion or 21.0 percent of GDP. Government-wide net outlays reflect the Government's net disbursements to the public and are subtracted from governmental receipts to derive the Government's deficit or surplus. For 2019, governmental receipts were $3,464 billion, or 16.3 percent of GDP, and the deficit was $984 billion, or 4.6 percent of GDP.

Although both offsetting collections and offsetting receipts are subtracted from gross outlays to derive net outlays, they are treated differently when it comes to accounting for specific programs and agencies. Offsetting collections are usually authorized to be spent for the purposes of an expenditure account and are generally available for use when collected, without further action by the Congress. Therefore, offsetting collections are recorded as offsets to spending within expenditure accounts, so that the account total highlights the net flow of funds.

Like governmental receipts, offsetting receipts are credited to receipt accounts, and any spending of the receipts is recorded in separate expenditure accounts. As a result, the budget separately displays the flow of funds into and out of the Government. Offsetting receipts may or may not be designated for a specific purpose, depending on the legislation that authorizes their collection. If designated for a particular purpose, the offsetting receipts may, in some cases, be spent without further action by the Congress. When not designated for a particular purpose, offsetting receipts are credited to the general fund, which contains all funds not otherwise allocated and which is used to finance Government spending that is not financed out of dedicated funds. In some cases where the receipts are designated for a particular purpose, offsetting receipts are reported in a particular agency and reduce or offset the outlays reported for that agency. In other cases, the offsetting receipts are "undistributed," which means they reduce total Government outlays, but not the outlays of any particular agency.

Table 12–1 summarizes offsetting collections and offsetting receipts from the public. The amounts shown in the table are not evident in the commonly cited budget measure of outlays, which is already net of these collec-

tions and receipts. For 2021, the table shows that total offsetting collections and offsetting receipts from the public are estimated to be $576.8 billion or 2.5 percent of GDP. Of these, an estimated $239.9 billion are offsetting collections and an estimated $336.9 billion are offsetting receipts. Table 12–1 also identifies those offsetting collections and offsetting receipts that are considered user charges, as defined and discussed below.

As shown in the table, major offsetting collections from the public include proceeds from Postal Service sales, electrical power sales, loan repayments to the Commodity Credit Corporation for loans made prior to enactment of the Federal Credit Reform Act, and Federal employee payments for health insurance. As also shown in the table, major offsetting receipts from the public include premiums for Medicare Parts B and D, proceeds from military assistance program sales, rents and royalties from Outer Continental Shelf oil extraction, dividends on holdings of preferred stock of the Government-sponsored enterprises, and interest income.

Tables 12–2 and 12–3 provide further detail about offsetting receipts, including both offsetting receipts from the public (as summarized in Table 12–1) and intragovernmental transactions. Table 12–5, formerly printed in this chapter, and Table 12–6, "Offsetting Collections and Offsetting Receipts, Detail—FY 2021 Budget," which is a complete listing by account, are available on the internet at *https://www.whitehouse.gov/omb/analytical-perspec-*

Table 12–3. GROSS OUTLAYS, USER CHARGES, OTHER OFFSETTING COLLECTIONS AND OFFSETTING RECEIPTS FROM THE PUBLIC, AND NET OUTLAYS

(In billions of dollars)

	Actual 2019	Estimate	
		2020	2021
Gross outlays to the public	6,180.8	6,588.4	6,691.7
Offsetting collections and offsetting receipts from the public:			
User charges [1]	349.1	369.2	401.5
Other	196.0	187.1	175.3
Subtotal, offsetting collections and offsetting receipts from the public	545.2	556.3	576.8
Net outlays	4,448.3	4,789.7	4,829.4

[1] $5.0 billion of the total user charges for 2019 were classified as governmental receipts, and the remainder were classified as offsetting collections and offsetting receipts. $5.2 billion and $5.5 billion of the total user charges for 2020 and 2021 are classified as governmental receipts, respectively.

tives/. In total, offsetting receipts are estimated to be $1,223.7 billion in 2021; $886.8 billion are from intragovernmental transactions and $336.9 billion are from the public. The offsetting receipts from the public consist of proprietary receipts ($303.5 billion), which are those resulting from business-like transactions such as the sale of goods or services, and offsetting governmental receipts, which, as discussed above, are derived from the exercise of the Government's sovereign power and, absent a specification in law or a long-standing practice, would be classified on the receipts side of the budget ($33.4 billion).

II. USER CHARGES

User charges or user fees[4] refer generally to those monies that the Government receives from the public for market-oriented activities and regulatory activities. In combination with budget concepts, laws that authorize user charges determine whether a user charge is classified as an offsetting collection, an offsetting receipt, or a governmental receipt. Almost all user charges, as defined below, are classified as offsetting collections or offsetting receipts; for 2021, only an estimated 1.4 percent of user charges are classified as governmental receipts. As summarized in Table 12–3, total user charges for 2021 are estimated to be $407.1 billion with $401.5 billion being offsetting collections or offsetting receipts, and accounting for more than two-thirds of all offsetting collections and offsetting receipts from the public.[5]

Definition. In this chapter, user charges refer to fees, charges, and assessments levied on individuals or organizations directly benefiting from or subject to regulation by a Government program or activity, where the payers do not represent a broad segment of the public such as those who pay income taxes.

Examples of business-type or market-oriented user charges and regulatory and licensing user charges include those charges listed in Table 12–1 for offsetting collections and offsetting receipts. User charges exclude certain offsetting collections and offsetting receipts from the public, such as payments received from credit programs, interest, and dividends, and also exclude payments from one part of the Federal Government to another. In addition, user charges do not include dedicated taxes (such as taxes paid to social insurance programs or excise taxes on gasoline) or customs duties, fines, penalties, or forfeitures.

Alternative definitions. The definition for user charges used in this chapter follows the definition used in OMB Circular No. A–25, "User Charges," which provides policy guidance to Executive Branch Agencies on setting the amount for user charges. Alternative definitions may be used for other purposes. Much of the discussion of user charges below—their purpose, when they should be levied, and how the amount should be set—applies to these alternative definitions as well.

A narrower definition of user charges could be limited to proceeds from the sale of goods and services, excluding the proceeds from the sale of assets, and to proceeds that are dedicated to financing the goods and services being provided. This definition is similar to one the House of Representatives uses as a guide for purposes of committee jurisdiction. (See the Congressional Record, January 3, 1991, p. H31, item 8.) The definition of user charges could be even narrower by excluding regulatory fees and focusing solely on business-type transactions. Alternatively, the user charge definition could be broader than the one used in this chapter by including beneficiary- or liability-based excise taxes.[6]

What is the purpose of user charges? User charges are intended to improve the efficiency and equity of financing certain Government activities. Charging users for activities that benefit a relatively limited number of people reduces the burden on the general taxpayer, as does charging regulated parties for regulatory activities in a particular sector.

User charges that are set to cover the costs of production of goods and services can result in more efficient resource allocation within the economy. When buyers are charged the cost of providing goods and services, they make better cost-benefit calculations regarding the size of their purchase, which in turn signals to the Government how much of the goods or services it should provide. Prices in private, competitive markets serve the same purposes. User charges for goods and services that do not have special social or distributional benefits may also improve equity or fairness by requiring those who benefit from an activity to pay for it and by not requiring those who do not benefit from an activity to pay for it.

When should the Government impose a charge? Discussions of whether to finance spending with a tax or a fee often focus on whether the benefits of the activity accrue to the public in general or to a limited group of people. In general, if the benefits of spending accrue broadly to the public or include special social or distributional benefits, then the program should be financed by taxes paid by the public. In contrast, if the benefits accrue to a limited number of private individuals or organizations

---

[4] In this chapter, the term "user charge" is generally used and has the same meaning as the term "user fee." The term "user charge" is the one used in OMB Circular No. A–11, "Preparation, Submission, and Execution of the Budget"; OMB Circular No. A–25, "User Charges"; and Chapter 8 of this volume, "Budget Concepts." In common usage, the terms "user charge" and "user fee" are often used interchangeably, and in A Glossary of Terms Used in the Federal Budget Process, GAO provides the same definition for both terms.

[5] User charge totals presented in this chapter include collections from accounts classified as containing user fee data. OMB accounts are classified as containing user fee data if more than half of collections are estimated to include user charges. Consequently, totals may include collections that are not user charges in accounts that meet the threshold and exclude user charges in accounts that do not meet the threshold.

[6] Beneficiary- and liability-based taxes are terms taken from the Congressional Budget Office, The Growth of Federal User Charges, August 1993, and updated in October 1995. Gasoline taxes are an example of beneficiary-based taxes. An example of a liability-based tax is the excise tax that formerly helped fund the hazardous substance superfund in the Environmental Protection Agency. This tax was paid by industry groups to finance environmental cleanup activities related to the industry activity but not necessarily caused by the payer of the fee.

and do not include special social or distributional benefits, then the program should be financed by charges paid by the private beneficiaries. For Federal programs where the benefits are entirely public or entirely private, applying this principle can be relatively easy. For example, the benefits from national defense accrue to the public in general, and according to this principle should be (and are) financed by taxes. In contrast, the benefits of electricity sold by the Tennessee Valley Authority accrue primarily to those using the electricity, and should be (and predominantly are) financed by user charges.

In many cases, however, an activity has benefits that accrue to both public and private groups, and it may be difficult to identify how much of the benefits accrue to each. Because of this, it can be difficult to know how much of the program should be financed by taxes and how much by fees. For example, the benefits from recreation areas are mixed. Fees for visitors to these areas are appropriate because the visitors benefit directly from their visit, but the public in general also benefits because these areas protect the Nation's natural and historic heritage now and for posterity. For this reason, visitor recreation fees generally cover only part of the cost to the Government of maintaining the recreation property. Where a fee may be appropriate to finance all or part of an activity, the extent to which a fee can be easily administered must be considered. For example, if fees are charged for entering or using Government-owned land then there must be clear points of entry onto the land and attendants patrolling and monitoring the land's use.

What amount should be charged? When the Government is acting in its capacity as sovereign and where user charges are appropriate, such as for some regulatory activities, current policy supports setting fees equal to the full cost to the Government, including both direct and indirect costs. When the Government is not acting in its capacity as sovereign and engages in a purely business-type transaction (such as leasing or selling goods, services, or resources), market price is generally the basis for establishing the fee.[7] If the Government is engaged in a purely business-type transaction and economic resources are allocated efficiently, then this market price should be equal to or greater than the Government's full cost of production.

Classification of user charges in the budget. As shown in the note to Table 12–3, most user charges are classified as offsets to outlays on the spending side of the budget, but a few are classified on the receipts side of the budget. An estimated $5.5 billion in 2021 of user charges are classified on the receipts side and are included in the governmental receipts totals described in the previous chapter, "Governmental Receipts." They are classified as receipts because they are regulatory charges collected by the Federal Government by the exercise of its sovereign powers. Examples include filing fees in the United States courts and agricultural quarantine inspection fees.

The remaining user charges, an estimated $401.5 billion in 2021, are classified as offsetting collections and offsetting receipts on the spending side of the Budget. As discussed above in the context of all offsetting collections and offsetting receipts, some of these user charges are collected by the Federal Government by the exercise of its sovereign powers and conceptually should appear on the receipts side of the budget, but they are required by law or a long-standing practice to be classified on the spending side.

[7] Policies for setting user charges are promulgated in OMB Circular No. A–25: "User Charges" (July 8, 1993).

III. USER CHARGE PROPOSALS

As shown in Table 12–1, an estimated $221.6 billion of user charges for 2021 will be credited directly to expenditure accounts and will generally be available for expenditure when they are collected, without further action by the Congress. An estimated $179.9 billion of user charges for 2021 will be deposited in offsetting receipt accounts and will be available to be spent only according to the legislation that established the charges.

As shown in Table 12–4, the Administration is proposing new or increased user charges that would, in the aggregate, increase collections by an estimated $4.2 billion in 2021 and an average of $15.1 billion per year from 2022 through 2030. These estimates reflect only the amounts to be collected; they do not include related spending. Each proposal is classified as either discretionary or mandatory, as those terms are defined in the Balanced Budget and Emergency Deficit Control Act of 1985, as amended. "Discretionary" refers to user charges controlled through annual appropriations acts and generally under the jurisdiction of the appropriations committees in the Congress. "Mandatory" refers to user charges controlled by permanent laws and under the jurisdiction of the authorizing committees. These and other terms are discussed further in this volume in Chapter 8, "Budget Concepts."

A. Discretionary User Charge Proposals

1. Offsetting collections

Department of Health and Human Services

Food and Drug Administration (FDA): Increase export certification user fee cap. Firms exporting products from the United States are often asked by foreign customers or foreign governments to supply a "certificate" for products regulated by the FDA to document the product's regulatory or marketing status. The proposal increases the maximum user fee cap from $175 per export certification to $600 to meet FDA's true cost of issuing export certificates and to ensure better and faster service for American companies that request the service.

FDA: Establish over-the-counter monograph user fee. FDA currently regulates over-the-counter (OTC) products through a three-phase public rulemaking process to establish standards or drug monographs for an OTC therapeutic drug class. The proposal would provide additional resources and authorities to FDA to bring new OTC products into the market faster so that Americans will have greater access to a wider range of safe and effective OTC products.

FDA: Expand tobacco product user fee. Currently, FDA's regulation of all tobacco products is financed through user fees collected from six product categories: cigarettes, roll your own tobacco, snuff, chewing tobacco, cigars, and pipe tobacco. This proposal would expand FDA's tobacco user fees and include user fee assessments on e-cigarettes and other electronic nicotine delivery systems (ENDS) manufacturers, which currently do not pay user fees, and increase the current limitation on total tobacco user fee collections by $100 million in 2021. To ensure that resources keep up with new tobacco products, the proposal would also index future collections to inflation. The expansion of tobacco user fees will strengthen FDA's ability to respond to the growth of newer products such as e-cigarettes through investments in regulatory science, enforcement, and premarket review of product applications.

FDA: Establish innovative food products user fee. Innovative food products include new ingredients, methods, and food contact substances. Examples of new products include new proteins, new ingredients, and synthetic foods. Food contact substances include components of food packaging and food processing equipment that come in contact with food. This new fee will allow FDA to evaluate emerging products and technologies to ensure their safety and get them to the market in a timely manner, thus fostering innovation.

Health Resources and Services Administration: Establish 340B Program user fee. To improve the administration and oversight of the 340B Drug Discount Program, the Budget includes a new user charge to those covered entities participating in the program.

Department of Homeland Security

Transportation Security Administration (TSA): Increase aviation passenger security fee. Pursuant to the Bipartisan Budget Act (BBA) of 2013, the passenger security fee is $5.60 per one-way trip. The fee revenue offsets the TSA Operations and Support appropriation, provides $250 million to the Aviation Security Capital Fund, and provides deficit reduction. The 2021 Budget proposes to increase the passenger security fee from $5.60 to $6.60 in 2021, and from $6.60 to $8.25 starting in 2022 in order to raise revenue closer to the full cost of aviation security, which was the intent of the authorizing language. This proposal will increase offsetting collections by an estimated $22.3 billion between 2021 and 2030.

Department of State

Establish The National Museum of American Diplomacy rental fee. This new user fee will enable the Department of State to provide support, on a cost-recovery basis, to outside organizations for programs and conference activities held at The National Museum of American Diplomacy.

Department of Transportation

Federal Railroad Administration (FRA): Establish Railroad Safety Inspection fee. The FRA establishes and enforces safety standards for U.S. railroads. FRA's rail safety inspectors work in the field and oversee railroads' operating and management practices. The Administration is proposing that, starting in 2021, the railroads contribute to partially cover the cost of FRA's field inspections because railroads benefit directly from Government efforts to maintain high safety standards. The proposed fee would be similar to existing charges collected from other industries regulated by Federal safety programs.

Department of the Treasury

Subject Financial Research Fund (FRF) assessments to annual appropriations action. Expenses of the Financial Stability Oversight Council (FSOC) and Office of Financial Research (OFR) are paid through the FRF, which is authorized to assess fees on certain bank holding companies and nonbank financial companies supervised by the Federal Reserve Board of Governors. The FRF was established by the Dodd-Frank Act and is managed by the Department of the Treasury. To improve their effectiveness and ensure greater accountability, the Budget proposes to subject the activities of FSOC and OFR to the appropriations process. In so doing, currently authorized assessments would, beginning in 2022, be reclassified as discretionary offsetting collections and set at a level determined by the Congress.

Environmental Protection Agency (EPA)

Establish ENERGY STAR fee. The Administration proposes to collect fees to fund EPA's administration of the ENERGY STAR program. Energy Star is a voluntary certification program that aims to help businesses and individuals save money and protect the environment through improved energy efficiency. By administering the voluntary program through the collection of user fees, entities participating in Energy Star would directly pay for the services and benefits that the program provides. Product manufacturers who seek to label their products under the program would pay a modest fee that would recover the full costs of EPA's work to set voluntary energy efficiency standards and to process applications. Fee collections will begin after EPA undertakes a rulemaking process to determine which products would be covered by fees and the level of fees, and to ensure that a fee system would not discourage manufacturers from participating in the program or result in a loss of environmental benefits.

Establish oil and chemical facility compliance assistance fees. The Administration proposes to provide an optional service to oil and chemical facilities to help these facilities identify actions to comply with certain environmental laws and regulations. Upon payment of a fee, EPA would conduct an on-site walk-through of a facility and provide recommendations and best practices regarding how to comply with certain regulations under the Clean Air Act and the Federal Water Pollution Control Act. This service would initially be available to facilities that are responsible for preparing and implementing a Risk Management Plan, Spill Prevention Control and Countermeasure Plan, and/or Facility Response Plan. Facilities choosing to utilize this service would pay a modest fee that would recover the full costs of EPA's work in providing this compliance assistance service to that facility. Fee collections and program implementation will begin after EPA issues procedures for applying for the service and the collection and use of such fees.

Commodity Futures Trading Commission (CFTC)

Establish CFTC user fee. The Budget proposes an amendment to the Commodity Exchange Act authorizing CFTC to collect user fees to fund the Commission's activities, like other Federal financial and banking regulators. Fee funding would shift the costs of services provided by CFTC from the general taxpayer to the primary beneficiaries of CFTC oversight. Contingent upon enactment of legislation authorizing CFTC to collect fees, the Administration proposes that collections begin in 2021 to offset a portion of CFTC's annual appropriation.

Small Business Administration (SBA)

Establish an upfront administrative fee. The Administration proposes charging an upfront fee to recover the cost of administering SBA's Business Loan Programs. In 2021, fee collections would offset half of administrative expenses.

Social Security Administration

Establish replacement Social Security card fee. The Budget proposes to collect fees on replacement Social Security cards. First-time Social Security cards including cards issued at birth would not be subject to the fee. The new fee would offset some administrative costs of processing Social Security card requests. While having a Social Security Number is required for many public and private sector transactions, individuals rarely need to display the physical Social Security card.

2. Offsetting receipts

Department of State

Extend Western Hemisphere Travel Initiative surcharge. The Administration proposes to permanently extend the authority for the Department of State to collect the Western Hemisphere Travel Initiative surcharge. The surcharge was initially enacted by the Passport Services Enhancement Act of 2005 (P.L. 109–167) to cover the Department's costs of meeting increased demand for passports, which resulted from the implementation of the Western Hemisphere Travel Initiative.

Increase Border Crossing Card (BCC) fee. The Budget includes a proposal to allow the fee charged for BCC minor applicants to be set administratively, rather than statutorily, at one-half the fee charged for processing an adult border crossing card. Administrative fee setting will allow the fee to better reflect the associated cost of service, consistent with other fees charged for consular services. As a result of this change, annual BCC fee collections be-

ginning in 2021 are projected to increase by $13 million (from $3 million to $16 million).

Establish a Machine-Readable Visa (MRV) surcharge. The Administration proposes implementing a machine-readable visa (MRV) surcharge to fund certain services provided by the Bureau of Consular Affairs (CA). As required by law, CA provides some services without charging a fee such as certain visa activities for foreign officials and diplomatic staff as well as Iraqi and Afghan applicants. The Department currently relies on nonimmigrant visa fees to fund those services, but the Department anticipates fee collections will not sufficiently cover the costs of providing those services over the long-term.

B. Mandatory User Charge Proposals

1. Offsetting collections

Department of Health and Human Services

Pass Treasury collection fees for Centers for Medicare and Medicaid Services (CMS) overpayment collections on to debtor. The Budget proposes to pass Treasury fees for CMS overpayment collections onto the debtor. Currently CMS pays the fee from the overpayment amount resulting in CMS recouping less than the overpayment. This proposal would require the debtor to pay the collection fee on top of the overpayment amount owed to CMS, resulting in all of the overpayment going back into the trust funds.

Charge long term care facilities fees for revisit surveys. The Budget proposes to allow the Department of Health and Human Services to charge long-term care facilities fees for revisits required to validate correction of deficiencies identified during initial and recertification visits or facility-reported incidents. Fees would cover associated costs necessary to perform revisit surveys. This proposal incentivizes quality of care and resident well-being.

Department of Labor

Improve Pension Benefit Guaranty Corporation (PBGC) Multiemployer Program solvency. PBGC acts as a backstop to protect pension payments for workers whose pension plans have failed. Currently, PBGC's multiemployer pension insurance program is underfunded, and its liabilities far exceed its assets. PBGC receives no taxpayer funds, and its premiums are currently much lower than what a private financial institution would charge for insuring the same risk. PBGC's multiemployer program, which insures the pension benefits of over 10 million workers, is at risk of insolvency by 2025. As an important step to protect the pensions of these hardworking Americans, the Budget proposes to create a variable-rate premium (VRP) and exit premium in the multiemployer program. A multiemployer VRP would require plans to pay additional premiums based on their level of underfunding, up to a cap, as is done in the single-employer program. An exit premium, equal to ten times the VRP cap, would be assessed on employers that withdraw from the system. PBGC would have limited authority to design waivers for some or all of the newly assessed premiums if there is a substantial risk that the payment of premiums will accelerate plan insolvency, resulting in earlier financial assistance to the plan. This proposal would raise approximately $26 billion in premiums over the ten-year window. At this level of receipts, the program is more likely than not to remain solvent over the next 20 years, helping to ensure that there is a safety net available to workers whose multiemployer plans fail.

Reform PBGC's single-employer premiums. The financial condition of PBGC's single-employer program has improved in recent years, reflecting premium increases enacted by the Congress, a strong economy, and the absence of large claims. Under current law, for plan years beginning in 2020, the single-employer premium consists of a flat-rate premium of $83 per participant and a variable-rate premium of $45 per $1,000 of unfunded vested benefits. The variable-rate premium is capped at $561 per participant and the flat and variable rates and the cap are indexed to wages. The Budget proposes to pause the indexation of premium rates for three years so that the rates for the 2021, 2022, and 2023 plan years remain at the 2020 level. Indexation would resume for plan years beginning in 2024. The Budget also proposes to rebalance the single-employer premium structure by increasing the cap on the variable-rate premium. Recent increases in the variable-rate premium have resulted in more plans with very significant underfunding having their premiums limited by the cap, thereby eroding the premium incentive to improve funding of pensions. The Budget proposes to increase the cap to $900 per participant in order to help restore the incentive to better fund promised pensions.

2. Offsetting receipts

Department of Agriculture

Establish Food Safety and Inspection Service (FSIS) user fee. The Administration proposes establishing a Food Safety and Inspection Service (FSIS) user fee to cover the costs of domestic inspection activity and import re-inspection and most of the central operations costs for Federal, State, and international inspection programs for meat, poultry, and eggs. The user fee would not cover Federal functions such as investigation, enforcement, risk analysis, and emergency response. The Administration estimates this fee would increase the cost of meat, poultry, and eggs for consumers by less than one cent per pound. FSIS inspections benefit the meat, poultry, and egg industries. FSIS personnel are continuously present for all egg processing and domestic slaughter operations, inspect each livestock and poultry carcass, and inspect operations at meat and poultry processing establishments at least once per shift. The inspections cover microbiological and chemical testing as well as cleanliness and cosmetic product defects. The "inspected by USDA" stamp on meat and poultry labels increases consumer confidence in the product which may increase sales.

Establish Forest Service Mineral Program cost recovery fee. The Forest Service does not currently collect user fees to recover costs for special use permits to extract energy and hardrock mineral resources. The Administration proposes establishing fees to reduce the need for discretionary appropriations to fund permitting and oversight for surface extraction mining operations. For oil and gas resources, this proposal would bring Forest Service authorities in closer alignment with those of the Department of the Interior (DOI) where the Bureau of Land Management has responsibility for subsurface minerals below most Federal lands and collects permitting fees for oil and gas. For hardrock mining, if the fees are properly structured, they could provide additional resources to improve permitting times.

Department of Commerce

Lease shared secondary licenses. To promote efficient use of the electromagnetic spectrum, the Administration proposes to require the leasing of Federal spectrum through secondary licenses. Under this proposal, the National Telecommunications and Information Administration (NTIA) would be granted authority to lease access to Federal spectrum for commercial use on a non-interference basis with Federal primary users. Working with other Federal agencies, NTIA would negotiate sharing arrangements on behalf of the Federal Government and would seek to increase the efficiency of spectrum when possible without causing harmful interference to Federal users authorized to operate in the negotiated bands. In addition to Federal spectrum auctions, leases will provide another option for maximizing the economic value of this scarce spectrum resource. Significant resources will be required by NTIA and other Federal Agencies to negotiate and manage these spectrum leases. The cost of administering the program will be offset by a portion of the lease revenue. Therefore the proposal is conservatively estimated to generate approximately $670 million in net deficit reduction for taxpayers.

Department of Energy

Reform Power Marketing Administration (PMA) power rates. The PMAs sell wholesale electricity generated at dams owned and operated by the Army Corps of Engineers or the Bureau of Reclamation. The Flood Control Act of 1944 requires the PMAs to generate revenues to recover all costs, including annual operating and maintenance costs and the taxpayers' investment in the power portions of dams and in transmission lines. The PMAs recover these costs by establishing rates, charged to utility customers, based on the cost of providing this electricity. These rates are limited to recovering costs and there is limited Federal or State regulatory oversight to ensure these rates are efficient and justified. Current law permits the PMAs to defer repayment of prior capital investment by the taxpayers and creates economic inefficiencies. The vast majority of the Nation's electricity needs are met through for-profit Investor Owned Utilities, which are subject to state and/or Federal regulatory oversight in the establishment of rates. This proposal would change the statutory requirement that the PMA rates be based on recovering costs to a rate structure that could allow for faster recoupment of taxpayer investment and consideration of rates charged by comparable utilities.

Department of Homeland Security

Extend expiring Customs and Border Protection (CBP) fees. The Budget proposes to extend the Merchandise Processing Fee beyond its current expiration date of September 30, 2029 to September 30, 2030, and makes permanent the rate increase (from 0.21 percent ad valorem to 0.3464 percent ad valorem) enacted in section 503 of the U.S.-Korea Free Trade Agreement Implementation Act (P.L. 112–41). It also proposes to extend fees statutorily set under the Consolidated Omnibus Budget Reconciliation Act of 1985 (COBRA) and the Express Consignment Courier Facilities (ECCF) fee created under the Trade Act of 2002 beyond their current expiration date of September 30, 2029 to September 30, 2030.

Increase Customs user fees. The Budget proposes to increase COBRA and ECCF fees created under the Trade Act of 2002. COBRA created a series of user fees for air and sea passengers, commercial trucks, railroad cars, private aircraft and vessels, commercial vessels, dutiable mail packages, broker permits, barges and bulk carriers from Canada and Mexico, cruise vessel passengers, and ferry vessel passengers. This proposal will increase the COBRA customs user fees by $2 for certain air and sea passengers and increase all other COBRA rates and caps by proportionate amounts. This fee was last adjusted in April 2007, yet international travel volumes continue to grow and CBP costs for customs inspections continue to increase. As a result, CBP relies on its annually appropriated funds to support the difference between fee collections and the costs of providing customs inspectional services. The Government Accountability Office's most recent review of these COBRA user fees (July 2016) identified that CBP collected $686 million in COBRA/ECCF fees compared to $870 million in operating costs, exhibiting a recovery rate of 78 percent.[8] With the fee increase, CBP would potentially collect the same amount it incurs in COBRA/ECCF eligible costs in 2021. In addition, the proposal amends the statutory hierarchy of eligible reimbursable costs to prioritize the salaries of full-time inspection personnel within the hierarchy. CBP estimates raising the fee and changing the hierarchy could offset the cost of an estimated 1,700 Customs CBP Officers. The proposed legislation will close the gap between costs and collections, enabling CBP to provide improved inspectional services to those who pay this user fee.

Increase immigration user fees. This proposal will increase the Immigration Inspection User Fee (IUF) by $2 and eliminate a partial fee exemption for sea passengers arriving from the United States, Canada, Mexico, or adjacent islands. These two adjustments will result in a total fee of $9 for all passengers, regardless of mode of transportation or point of departure. This fee is paid by passengers and is used to recover some of the costs related to determining the admissibility of passengers entering the U.S. Specifically, the fees collected support immigration inspections, the maintenance and updating of systems to track criminal and illegal aliens in areas with high apprehensions, asylum hearings, and the repair and maintenance of equipment. This fee was last adjusted in November 2001, yet international travel volumes have grown significantly since that time and CBP costs for immigration inspections continue to increase. For example, 21.8 million international travelers visited the United States in 2001, compared with 77 million in 2015. As a result, CBP relies on annually appropriated funds to support the difference between fee collections and the costs of providing immigration inspection services. The Government Accountability Office's most recent review of IUF (July 2016) identified that CBP collected $728 million in IUF fees compared to $1,003 million in operating costs, exhibiting a recovery rate of 73 percent.[9] To prevent this gap from widening again in the future, the proposal will authorize CBP to adjust the fee without further statutory changes. CBP estimates raising the fee and lifting the exemption could offset the cost of an estimated 1,480 CBP Officers.

Department of Labor

Expand Foreign Labor Certification fees. The Budget proposes authorizing legislation to establish and retain fees to cover the costs of operating the foreign labor certification programs, which ensure that employers proposing to bring in immigrant workers have checked to ensure that American workers cannot meet their needs and that immigrant workers are being compensated appropriately and not disadvantaging American workers. The ability to charge fees for these programs would give the Department of Labor (DOL) a more reliable, workload-based source of funding for this function (as the Department of Homeland Security has), and would ultimately eliminate the need for discretionary appropriations. The proposal includes the following: 1) charge employer fees for its prevailing wage determinations; 2) charge employer fees for its permanent labor certification program; 3) charge employer fees for H–2B non-agricultural workers; 4) charge employer fees for CW–1 Northern Mariana Islands transitional workers; and 5) retain and adjust the H–2A agricultural worker application fees currently deposited into the General·Fund. The fee levels would be set via regulation to ensure that the amounts are subject to review. Given DOL Inspector General's important role in investigating fraud and abuse, the proposal also includes a mechanism to provide funding for the Inspector General's work to oversee foreign labor certification programs.

Increase H–1B ACWIA filing fee. The Budget proposes authorizing legislation to double the American Competitiveness and Workforce Improvement Act (ACWIA) fee for the H–1B visa program in order to help train domestic workers and close the skills gap. The increased fee revenue would provide additional funding for DOL's training grants to support apprenticeship

[8] GAO–16–443, Enhanced Oversight Could Better Ensure Programs Receiving Fees and Other Collections Use Funds Efficiently, *http://www.gao.gov/products/GAO–16–443*.

[9] GAO–16–443, Enhanced Oversight Could Better Ensure Programs Receiving Fees and Other Collections Use Funds Efficiently, *http://www.gao.gov/products/GAO–16–443*.

while creating a new funding source for the Department of Education's Career and Technical Education formula grant. Under the proposal, the prescribed allocations for DOL job training grants (50 percent) and foreign labor certifications (5 percent) would remain the same. The National Science Foundation's allocation for the Innovative Technology Experiences for Students and Teachers program (10 percent) would remain the same, while its allocation for STEM scholarships would decrease from 30 percent to 15 percent, a level that would nonetheless maintain absolute funding levels under current estimates. The proposal would initiate a new 15 percent allocation for the Department of Education's Career and Technical Education formula grant, which would provide additional support for technical training at the K–12 and community college levels. The remaining 5 percent would be maintained for Department of Homeland Security processing costs.

Department of the Treasury

Increase and extend guarantee fee charged by GSEs. The Temporary Payroll Tax Cut Continuation Act of 2011 (P.L. 112–78) required that Fannie Mae and Freddie Mac increase their credit guarantee fees on single-family mortgage acquisitions between 2012 and 2021 by an average of at least 0.10 percentage points. Revenues generated by this fee increase are remitted directly to the Treasury for deficit reduction. The Budget proposes to increase this fee by 0.10 percentage points for single-family mortgage acquisitions in 2021, and then extend the 0.20 percentage point fee for acquisitions through 2025.

C. User Charge Proposals that are Governmental Receipts

Department of Homeland Security

CBP: Establish user fee for Electronic Visa Update System. The Budget proposes to establish a user fee for the Electronic Visa Update System (EVUS), a CBP program to collect biographic and travel-related information from certain non-immigrant visa holders prior to traveling to the United States. This process will complement the existing visa application process and enhance CBP's ability to make pre-travel admissibility and risk deter-

minations. CBP proposes to establish a user fee to fund the costs of establishing, providing, and administering the system.

Department of the Treasury

Subject Financial Research Fund (FRF) assessments to annual appropriations action. As explained above in the section of discretionary use charge proposals, the Budget proposes to subject activities of the Financial Stability Oversight Council (FSOC) and the Office of Financial Research (OFR) to the appropriations process in order to improve their effectiveness and ensure greater accountability. As part of the proposal, currently authorized assessments would be reclassified as discretionary offsetting collections, resulting in a reduction in governmental receipts and an increase in discretionary offsetting collections.

Corps of Engineers—Civil Works

Reform inland waterways funding. The Administration proposes to reform the laws governing the Inland Waterways Trust Fund, including establishing an annual fee to increase the amount paid by commercial navigation users of the inland waterways. In 1986, the Congress provided that commercial traffic on the inland waterways would be responsible for 50 percent of the capital costs of the locks, dams, and other features that make barge transportation possible on the inland waterways. The additional revenue would help finance future capital investments, as well as 10 percent of the operation and maintenance cost, in these waterways to support economic growth. The current excise tax on diesel fuel used in inland waterways commerce will not produce the revenue needed to cover these costs.

Corporation for Travel Promotion (BrandUSA)

Eliminate BrandUSA; make savings available for deficit reduction. The Administration proposes to eliminate funding for the Corporation for Travel Promotion (also known as BrandUSA). The budget extends the authorization for the Electronic System for Travel Authorization (ESTA) surcharge currently deposited in the Travel Promotion Fund and redirects the surcharge to the General Fund.

Table 12–4.   USER CHARGE PROPOSALS IN THE FY 2021 BUDGET[1]

(Estimated collections in millions of dollars)

	2021	2022	2023	2024	2025	2026	2027	2028	2029	2030	2021-2025	2021-2030
OFFSETTING COLLECTIONS AND OFFSETTING RECEIPTS												
DISCRETIONARY:												
Offsetting collections												
Department of Health and Human Services												
Food and Drug Administration (FDA): Increase export certification user fee cap	4	4	4	4	4	4	4	4	4	4	20	40
FDA: Establish over-the-counter monograph user fee	28	30	31	33	35	36	38	40	42	44	157	357
FDA: Expand tobacco product user fee	100	120	141	162	184	207	230	253	277	302	707	1,976
FDA: Establish innovative food products user fee	28	28	28	28	28	28	28	28	28	28	140	280
Health Resources and Services Administration: Establish 340B Program user fee	24	24	24	24	24	24	24	24	24	24	120	240
Department of Homeland Security												
Transportation Security Administration: Increase aviation passenger security fee	618	2,226	2,270	2,316	2,362	2,409	2,457	2,506	2,557	2,608	9,792	22,329
Department of State												
Establish The National Museum of American Diplomacy rental fee	*	*	*	*	*	*	*	*	*	*	*	*
Department of Transportation												
Federal Railroad Administration: Establish Railroad Safety Inspection fee	50	80	80	80	80	80	80	80	80	80	370	770
Department of the Treasury												
Subject Financial Research Fund assessments to annual appropriations action	....	76	76	76	76	76	76	76	76	76	304	684
Environmental Protection Agency												
Establish ENERGY STAR fee	46	46	46	46	46	46	46	46	46	46	230	460
Establish chemical facility compliance assistance fee	20	20	20	20	20	20	20	20	20	20	100	200
Establish oil facility compliance assistance fee	10	10	10	10	10	10	10	10	10	10	50	100
Commodity Futures Trading Commission (CFTC)												
Establish CFTC user fee	77	77	77	77	77	77	77	77	77	77	385	770
Small Business Administration												
Establish an upfront administrative fee	80	80	80	80	80	80	80	80	80	80	400	800
Social Security Administration												
Establish replacement Social Security card fee	270	270	270	270	270	270	270	270	270	270	1,350	2,700
Offsetting receipts												
Department of State												
Extend Western Hemisphere Travel Initiative surcharge	483	483	483	483	483	483	483	483	483	483	2,415	4,830
Increase Border Crossing Card Fee	13	13	13	13	13	13	13	13	13	13	65	130
Establish a Machine-Readable Visa surcharge	....	....	248	248	248	248	248	248	248	248	744	1,984
Subtotal, discretionary user charge proposals	1,851	3,587	3,901	3,970	4,040	4,111	4,184	4,258	4,335	4,413	17,349	38,650
MANDATORY:												
Offsetting collections												
Department of Health and Human Services												
Pass Treasury collection fees for CMS overpayment collections on to debtor	20	20	20	20	20	20	20	20	20	20	100	200
Charge long term care facilities fees for revisit surveys	....	27	28	29	29	30	31	31	32	33	113	270
Department of Labor												
Improve Pension Benefit Guaranty Corporation (PBGC) Multiemployer Program solvency	....	2,619	2,694	2,968	2,835	2,929	3,003	3,033	3,080	3,129	11,116	26,290
Reform PBGC's single-employer premiums	....	1,524	419	51	–4,624	4,869	–61	–131	–195	–211	–2,630	1,641
Offsetting receipts												
Department of Agriculture												
Establish Food Safety and Inspection Service user fee	....	660	660	660	660	660	660	660	660	660	2,640	5,940
Establish Forest Service Mineral Program cost recovery fee	60	60	60	60	60	60	60	60	60	60	300	600

Table 12–4.   USER CHARGE PROPOSALS IN THE FY 2021 BUDGET[1]**—Continued**

(Estimated collections in millions of dollars)

	2021	2022	2023	2024	2025	2026	2027	2028	2029	2030	2021-2025	2021-2030
Department of Commerce												
Lease shared secondary licenses	50	55	55	60	65	70	70	80	80	85	285	670
Department of Energy												
Reform Power Marketing Administration power rates	587	601	618	635	652	674	692	709	1114	1139	3,093	7,421
Department of Homeland Security												
Extend expiring Customs and Border Protection fees	....	....	....	....	....	....	....	....	....	6,005	....	6,005
Increase Customs user fees	431	453	478	492	510	532	551	574	594	618	2,364	5,233
Increase immigration user fees	376	387	438	446	535	546	639	652	708	722	2,182	5,449
Department of Labor												
Expand Foreign Labor Certification fees	....	40	82	85	89	94	98	103	108	114	296	813
Increase H–1B ACWIA filing fee	389	389	389	389	389	389	389	389	389	389	1,945	3,890
Department of the Treasury												
Increase and extend guarantee fee charged by GSEs	202	1,053	2,250	3,588	4,644	5,291	5,123	4,587	4,075	3,625	11,737	34,438
Subtotal, mandatory user charge proposals	2,115	7,888	8,191	9,483	5,864	16,164	11,275	10,767	10,725	16,388	33,541	98,860
Subtotal, user charge proposals that are offsetting collections and offsetting receipts	3,966	11,475	12,092	13,453	9,904	20,275	15,459	15,025	15,060	20,801	50,890	137,510
GOVERNMENTAL RECEIPTS												
Department of Homeland Security												
CBP: Establish user fee for Electronic Visa Update System	38	42	47	52	58	64	72	79	88	107	237	647
Department of the Treasury												
Subject Financial Research Fund assessments to annual appropriations action	....	–75	–75	–75	–75	–75	–75	–75	–75	–75	–300	–675
Corps of Engineers - Civil Works												
Reform inland waterways funding	180	180	180	180	180	180	180	180	180	180	900	1,800
Corportation for Travel Promotion (BrandUSA)												
Eliminate BrandUSA; make savings available for deficit reduction	....	....	....	....	....	....	....	316	321	328	....	965
Subtotal, governmental receipts user charge proposals	218	147	152	157	163	169	177	500	514	540	837	2,737
Total, user charge proposals	**4,184**	**11,622**	**12,244**	**13,610**	**10,067**	**20,444**	**15,636**	**15,525**	**15,574**	**21,341**	**51,727**	**140,247**

[1] A positive sign indicates an increase in collections.

* $500,000 or less

13. TAX EXPENDITURES

The Congressional Budget Act of 1974 (P.L. 93–344) requires that a list of "tax expenditures" be included in the Budget. Tax expenditures are defined in the law as "revenue losses attributable to provisions of the Federal tax laws which allow a special exclusion, exemption, or deduction from gross income or which provide a special credit, a preferential rate of tax, or a deferral of tax liability." These exceptions may be viewed as alternatives to other policy instruments, such as spending or regulatory programs.

Identification and measurement of tax expenditures depends crucially on the baseline tax system against which the actual tax system is compared. The tax expenditure estimates presented in this document are patterned on a comprehensive income tax, which defines income as the sum of consumption and the change in net wealth in a given period of time.

An important assumption underlying each tax expenditure estimate reported below is that other parts of the Tax Code remain unchanged. The estimates would be different if tax expenditures were changed simultaneously because of potential interactions among provisions. For that reason, this document does not present a grand total for the estimated tax expenditures.

Tax expenditures relating to the individual and corporate income taxes are estimated for 2019–2029 using two methods of accounting: current tax receipt effects and present value effects. The present value approach provides estimates of the receipt effects for tax expenditures that generally involve deferrals of tax payments into the future.

TAX EXPENDITURES IN THE INCOME TAX

Tax Expenditure Estimates

All tax expenditure estimates and descriptions presented here are based upon current tax law enacted as of July 1, 2019, and reflect the economic assumptions from the Mid-Session Review of the 2020 Budget. In some cases, expired or repealed provisions are listed if their tax receipt effects occur in 2019 or later.

The total receipt effects for tax expenditures for 2019–2029 are displayed according to the Budget's functional categories in Table 13-1. Descriptions of the specific tax expenditure provisions follow the discussion of general features of the tax expenditure concept.

Two baseline concepts—the normal tax baseline and the reference tax law baseline—are used to identify and estimate tax expenditures.[1] For the most part, the two concepts coincide. However, items treated as tax expenditures under the normal tax baseline, but not the reference tax law baseline, are indicated by the designation "normal tax method" in the tables. The receipt effects for these items are zero using the reference tax law. The alternative baseline concepts are discussed in detail below.

Tables 13-2A and 13-2B report separately the respective portions of the total receipt effects that arise under the individual and corporate income taxes. The location of the estimates under the individual and corporate headings does not imply that these categories of filers benefit from the special tax provisions in proportion to the respective tax expenditure amounts shown. Rather, these breakdowns show the form of tax liability that the various provisions affect. The ultimate beneficiaries of corporate tax expenditures could be shareholders, employees, customers, or other providers of capital, depending on economic forces.

Table 13-3 ranks the major tax expenditures by the size of their 2020–2029 receipt effect. The first column provides the number of the provision in order to cross reference this table to Tables 13-1, 13-2A, and 13-2B, as well as to the descriptions below.

Interpreting Tax Expenditure Estimates

The estimates shown for individual tax expenditures in Tables 13-1 through 13-3 do not necessarily equal the increase in Federal receipts (or the change in the budget balance) that would result from repealing these special provisions, for the following reasons.

First, eliminating a tax expenditure may have incentive effects that alter economic behavior. These incentives can affect the resulting magnitudes of the activity, or the consequences of other tax provisions or Government programs. For example, if capital gains were taxed at higher ordinary income tax rates, capital gain realizations would be expected to decline, which could result in lower tax receipts depending on the elasticity of the capital gains tax rates. Such behavioral effects are not reflected in the estimates.

Second, tax expenditures are interdependent even without incentive effects. Repeal of a tax expenditure provision can increase or decrease the tax receipts associated with other provisions. For example, even if behavior does not change, repeal of an itemized deduction could increase the receipt costs from other deductions because

---

[1] These baseline concepts are thoroughly discussed in Special Analysis G of the 1985 Budget, where the former is referred to as the pre-1983 method and the latter the post-1982 method.

some taxpayers would be moved into higher tax brackets. Alternatively, repeal of an itemized deduction could lower the receipt cost from other deductions if taxpayers are led to claim the standard deduction instead of itemizing. Similarly, if two provisions were repealed simultaneously, the increase in tax liability could be greater or less than the sum of the two separate tax expenditures, because each is estimated assuming that the other remains in force. In addition, the estimates reported in Table 13-1 are the totals of individual and corporate income tax receipt effects reported in Tables 13-2A and 13-2B, and do not reflect any possible interactions between individual and corporate income tax receipts. For this reason, the estimates in Table 13-1 should be regarded as approximations.

Present-Value Estimates

The annual value of tax expenditures for tax deferrals is reported on a cash basis in all tables except Table 13-4. Cash-based estimates reflect the difference between taxes deferred in the current year and incoming receipts that are received due to deferrals of taxes from prior years. Although such estimates are useful as a measure of cash flows into the Government, they do not accurately reflect the true economic cost of these provisions. For example, for a provision where activity levels have changed over time, so that incoming tax receipts from past deferrals are greater than deferred receipts from new activity, the cash-basis tax expenditure estimate can be negative, despite the fact that in present-value terms current deferrals have a real cost to the Government (i.e., taxpayers). Alternatively, in the case of a newly enacted deferral provision, a cash-based estimate can overstate the real effect on receipts to the Government because the newly deferred taxes will ultimately be received.

Discounted present-value estimates of receipt effects are presented in Table 13-4 for certain provisions that involve tax deferrals or other long-term receipt effects. These estimates complement the cash-based tax expenditure estimates presented in the other tables.

The present-value estimates represent the receipt effects, net of future tax payments that follow from activities undertaken during calendar year 2019 which cause the deferrals or other long-term receipt effects. For instance, a pension contribution in 2019 would cause a deferral of tax payments on wages in 2019 and on pension fund earnings on this contribution (e.g., interest) in later years. In some future year, however, the 2019 pension contribution and accrued earnings will be paid out and taxes will be due; these receipts are included in the present-value estimate. In general, this conceptual approach is similar to the one used for reporting the budgetary effects of credit programs, where direct loans and guarantees in a given year affect future cash flows.

Tax Expenditure Baselines

A tax expenditure is an exception to baseline provisions of the tax structure that usually results in a reduction in the amount of tax owed. The Congressional Budget Act of 1974, which mandated the tax expenditure budget, did not specify the baseline provisions of the tax law. As noted previously, deciding whether provisions are exceptions, therefore, is a matter of judgment. As in prior years, most of this year's tax expenditure estimates are presented using two baselines: the normal tax baseline and the reference tax law baseline. Tax expenditures may take the form of credits, deductions, special exceptions and allowances.

The normal tax baseline is patterned on a practical variant of a comprehensive income tax, which defines income as the sum of consumption and the change in net wealth in a given period of time. The normal tax baseline allows personal exemptions, a standard deduction, and deduction of expenses incurred in earning income. It is not limited to a particular structure of tax rates, or by a specific definition of the taxpaying unit.

The reference tax law baseline is also patterned on a comprehensive income tax, but it is closer to existing law. Reference law tax expenditures are limited to special exceptions from a generally provided tax rule that serves programmatic functions in a way that is analogous to spending programs. Provisions under the reference tax law baseline are generally tax expenditures under the normal tax baseline, but the reverse is not always true.

Both the normal tax and reference tax law baselines allow several major departures from a pure comprehensive income tax. For example, under the normal tax and reference tax law baselines:

- Income is taxable only when it is realized in exchange. Thus, the deferral of tax on unrealized capital gains is not regarded as a tax expenditure. Accrued income would be taxed under a comprehensive income tax.

- There is a separate corporate income tax.

- Tax rates on noncorporate business income vary by level of income.

- Individual tax rates, including brackets, standard deduction, and personal exemptions, are allowed to vary with marital status.

- Values of assets and debt are not generally adjusted for inflation. A comprehensive income tax would adjust the cost basis of capital assets and debt for changes in the general price level. Thus, under a comprehensive income tax baseline, the failure to take account of inflation in measuring depreciation, capital gains, and interest income would be regarded as a negative tax expenditure (i.e., a tax penalty), and failure to take account of inflation in measuring interest costs would be regarded as a positive tax expenditure (i.e., a tax subsidy).

- The Base Erosion and Anti-Abuse Tax (BEAT) for multinational corporations is treated as a minimum tax and considered part of the rate structure.

Although the reference tax law and normal tax baselines are generally similar, areas of difference include:

Tax rates. The separate schedules applying to the various taxpaying units and the Alternative Minimum Tax are treated as part of the baseline rate structure under both the reference tax law and normal tax methods.

Income subject to the tax. Income subject to tax is defined as gross income less the costs of earning that income. Under the reference tax law, gross income does not include gifts defined as receipts of money or property that are not consideration in an exchange nor does gross income include most transfer payments from the Government.[2] The normal tax baseline also excludes gifts between individuals from gross income. Under the normal tax baseline, however, all cash transfer payments from the Government to private individuals are counted in gross income, and exemptions of such transfers from tax are identified as tax expenditures. The costs of earning income are generally deductible in determining taxable income under both the reference tax law and normal tax baselines.[3]

Capital recovery. Under the reference tax law baseline no tax expenditures arise from accelerated depreciation. Under the normal tax baseline, the depreciation allowance for property is computed using estimates of economic depreciation.

As previously illustrated in the 2020 Tax Expenditure Budget, provisions defined as tax expenditures in the Budget would be different if a pure comprehensive income tax were employed as the baseline. Similarly, they would also look quite different if a consumption tax were employed; the current income tax can be considered as a hybrid tax with income and consumption tax features. Comprehensive income, also called Haig-Simons income, is the real, inflation-adjusted accretions to wealth, accrued or realized. Using a comprehensive income tax baseline, the tax base can be larger than that considered here. A broad-based consumption tax is a combination of an income tax plus a deduction for net saving, or just consumption plus the change in net worth. Under this baseline, some of the current tax provisions would no longer be considered as tax expenditures (e.g., deductions for retirement savings). These alternative baselines are further discussed in the *Appendix.*

Descriptions of Income Tax Provisions

Descriptions of the individual and corporate income tax expenditures reported on in this document follow. These descriptions relate to current law as of July 1, 2019.

---

[2] Gross income does, however, include transfer payments associated with past employment, such as Social Security benefits.

[3] In the case of individuals who hold "passive" equity interests in businesses, the pro rata shares of sales and expense deductions reportable in a year are limited. A passive business activity is defined generally to be one in which the holder of the interest, usually a partnership interest, does not actively perform managerial or other participatory functions. The taxpayer may generally report no larger deductions for a year than will reduce taxable income from such activities to zero. Deductions in excess of the limitation may be taken in subsequent years, or when the interest is liquidated. In addition, costs of earning income may be limited under the Alternative Minimum Tax.

National Defense

1. ***Exclusion of benefits and allowances to Armed Forces personnel.***—Under the baseline tax system, all compensation, including dedicated payments and in-kind benefits, should be included in taxable income because they represent accretions to wealth that do not materially differ from cash wages. As an example, a rental voucher of $100 is (approximately) equal in value to $100 of cash income. In contrast to this treatment, certain housing and meals, in addition to other benefits provided military personnel, either in cash or in kind, as well as certain amounts of pay related to combat service, are excluded from income subject to tax.

International Affairs

2. ***Exclusion of income earned abroad by U.S. citizens.***—Under the baseline tax system, all compensation received by U.S. citizens and residents is properly included in their taxable income. It makes no difference whether the compensation is a result of working abroad or whether it is labeled as a housing allowance. In contrast to this treatment, U.S. tax law allows U.S. citizens and residents who live abroad, work in the private sector, and satisfy a foreign residency requirement to exclude up to $80,000, plus adjustments for inflation since 2004, in foreign earned income from U.S. taxes. In addition, if these taxpayers are provided housing by their employers, then they may also exclude the cost of such housing from their income to the extent that it exceeds 16 percent of the earned income exclusion limit. This housing exclusion is capped at 30 percent of the earned income exclusion limit, with geographical adjustments. If taxpayers do not receive a specific allowance for housing expenses, they may deduct housing expenses up to the amount by which foreign earned income exceeds their foreign earned income exclusion.

3. ***Exclusion of certain allowances for Federal employees abroad.***—In general, all compensation received by U.S. citizens and residents is properly included in their taxable income. It makes no difference whether the compensation is a result of working abroad or whether it is labeled as an allowance for the high cost of living abroad. In contrast to this treatment, U.S. Federal civilian employees and Peace Corps members who work outside the continental United States are allowed to exclude from U.S. taxable income certain special allowances they receive to compensate them for the relatively high costs associated with living overseas. The allowances supplement wage income and cover expenses such as rent, education, and the cost of travel to and from the United States.

4. ***Inventory property sales source rules exception.***—The United States generally taxes the worldwide income of U.S. persons and business entities. Under the baseline tax system, worldwide income forms the tax base of U.S. corporations. For foreign source income taxed by the United States, taxpayers receive a credit for foreign taxes paid which is limited to the pre-credit U.S. tax on

Table 13–1. ESTIMATES OF TOTAL INCOME TAX EXPENDITURES FOR FISCAL YEARS 2019–2029

(In millions of dollars)

	Total from corporations and individuals											
	2019	2020	2021	2022	2023	2024	2025	2026	2027	2028	2029	2020–29
National Defense												
1 Exclusion of benefits and allowances to Armed Forces personnel	12,460	12,910	11,660	11,700	12,080	12,560	13,090	13,660	14,270	14,910	15,600	132,440
International affairs:												
2 Exclusion of income earned abroad by U.S. citizens ...	6,930	7,280	7,640	8,020	8,420	8,840	9,290	9,750	10,240	10,750	11,290	91,520
3 Exclusion of certain allowances for Federal employees abroad	240	250	260	280	290	300	320	330	350	370	390	3,140
4 Inventory property sales source rules exception	0	0	0	0	0	0	0	0	0	0	0	0
5 Reduced tax rate on active income of controlled foreign corporations (normal tax method)...............	35,470	40,000	42,980	44,660	35,220	21,760	10,720	46,840	75,840	79,250	82,810	480,080
6 Deduction for foreign-derived intangible income dervied from trade or business within the United States	7,530	8,100	9,880	11,150	11,610	12,130	12,670	9,240	7,000	7,340	7,700	96,820
7 Interest Charge Domestic International Sales Corporations (IC-DISCs)	1,280	1,340	1,410	1,480	1,560	1,630	1,720	1,800	1,890	1,990	2,090	16,910
General science, space, and technology:												
8 Expensing of research and experimentation expenditures (normal tax method)	5,520	5,740	6,330	−19,090	−34,990	−25,630	−15,640	−4,940	0	0	0	−88,220
9 Credit for increasing research activities	15,300	16,810	18,380	19,890	21,370	22,900	24,450	26,040	27,650	29,310	31,030	237,830
Energy:												
10 Expensing of exploration and development costs, fuels ...	930	1,060	890	630	500	510	600	740	790	730	640	7,090
11 Excess of percentage over cost depletion, fuels	670	760	820	870	920	980	1,050	1,180	1,280	1,350	1,400	10,610
12 Exception from passive loss limitation for working interests in oil and gas properties	10	10	10	10	10	10	10	10	10	10	10	100
13 Capital gains treatment of royalties on coal	150	140	140	140	140	150	160	170	190	200	210	1,640
14 Exclusion of interest on energy facility bonds	10	10	10	10	10	10	10	10	10	10	10	100
15 Enhanced oil recovery credit	510	440	320	270	330	430	560	650	650	630	630	4,910
16 Energy production credit [1]	4,230	4,310	4,290	4,250	4,200	4,070	3,920	3,290	2,590	1,760	1,070	33,750
17 Marginal wells credit	110	80	100	100	80	40	10	0	0	0	0	410
18 Energy investment credit [1]	3,710	4,510	4,820	4,490	3,700	2,690	2,010	1,540	1,220	1,020	920	26,920
19 Alcohol fuel credits [2]	0	0	0	0	0	0	0	0	0	0	0	0
20 Bio-Diesel and small agri-biodiesel producer tax credits [3]	0	0	0	0	0	0	0	0	0	0	0	0
21 Tax credits for clean-fuel burning vehicles and refueling property	940	580	380	380	380	310	220	200	200	190	140	2,980
22 Exclusion of utility conservation subsidies	450	470	490	510	540	570	590	620	650	680	710	5,830
23 Credit for holding clean renewable energy bonds [4]	70	70	70	70	70	70	70	70	70	70	70	700
24 Credit for investment in clean coal facilities	20	10	20	40	80	100	90	80	90	50	50	610
25 Natural gas distribution pipelines treated as 15-year property	70	70	50	30	−10	−50	−80	−120	−140	−140	−140	−530
26 Amortize all geological and geophysical expenditures over 2 years	230	250	260	270	290	310	310	350	370	380	380	3,170
27 Allowance of deduction for certain energy efficient commercial building property	10	0	0	0	0	0	0	0	0	0	0	0
28 Credit for construction of new energy efficient homes .	50	10	10	0	0	0	0	0	0	0	0	20
29 Credit for residential energy efficient property	1,980	1,740	1,410	360	70	0	0	0	0	0	0	3,580
30 Qualified energy conservation bonds [5]	30	30	30	30	30	30	30	30	30	30	30	300
31 Advanced Energy Property Credit	10	10	10	10	10	10	10	10	10	10	10	100
32 Advanced nuclear power production credit	0	0	0	100	190	240	270	280	280	280	270	1,910
33 Reduced tax rate for nuclear decommissioning funds .	100	100	110	110	120	120	130	130	140	150	150	1,260
Natural resources and environment:												
34 Expensing of exploration and development costs, nonfuel minerals	170	180	160	110	90	90	100	130	140	120	110	1,230
35 Excess of percentage over cost depletion, nonfuel minerals	120	130	140	160	160	170	190	210	220	240	240	1,860
36 Exclusion of interest on bonds for water, sewage, and hazardous waste facilities	300	320	310	320	340	340	350	380	380	390	390	3,520
37 Capital gains treatment of certain timber income	150	140	140	140	140	150	160	170	190	200	210	1,640

Table 13–1. ESTIMATES OF TOTAL INCOME TAX EXPENDITURES FOR FISCAL YEARS 2019–2029—Continued

(In millions of dollars)

		Total from corporations and individuals											
		2019	2020	2021	2022	2023	2024	2025	2026	2027	2028	2029	2020–29
38	Expensing of multiperiod timber growing costs	40	40	60	60	70	70	70	80	90	90	90	720
39	Tax incentives for preservation of historic structures ...	830	730	690	680	790	970	1,100	1,200	1,250	1,270	1,300	9,980
40	Carbon oxide sequestration credit	70	90	120	140	170	220	270	310	320	340	350	2,330
41	Deduction for endangered species recovery expenditures	30	30	30	30	30	40	40	40	60	60	60	420
Agriculture:													
42	Expensing of certain capital outlays	40	90	110	130	140	140	150	180	200	210	220	1,570
43	Expensing of certain multiperiod production costs	250	270	280	290	310	320	340	420	460	480	490	3,660
44	Treatment of loans forgiven for solvent farmers	50	50	50	60	60	60	70	70	70	70	70	630
45	Capital gains treatment of certain agriculture income .	1,490	1,410	1,390	1,400	1,440	1,490	1,560	1,730	1,920	2,010	2,100	16,450
46	Income averaging for farmers	170	180	190	190	200	210	220	230	230	230	230	2,110
47	Deferral of gain on sale of farm refiners	15	15	15	15	15	20	20	20	20	20	25	185
48	Expensing of reforestation expenditures	40	40	60	60	70	70	70	80	90	90	90	720
Commerce and housing:													
	Financial institutions and insurance:												
49	Exemption of credit union income	1,911	1,764	1,587	1,756	1,935	2,019	2,191	2,494	2,661	2,761	2,710	21,878
50	Exclusion of life insurance death benefits	13,210	13,760	14,340	14,870	15,470	16,090	16,680	17,550	18,590	19,200	19,690	166,240
51	Exemption or special alternative tax for small property and casualty insurance companies	110	120	130	130	140	140	150	160	160	170	170	1,470
52	Tax exemption of insurance income earned by tax-exempt organizations	330	330	340	350	360	380	390	400	410	420	430	3,810
53	Exclusion of interest spread of financial institutions	2,190	1,120	1,160	1,200	1,240	1,280	1,330	1,400	1,470	1,510	1,560	13,270
	Housing:												
54	Exclusion of interest on owner-occupied mortgage subsidy bonds	790	840	840	860	910	940	950	1,020	1,050	1,050	1,060	9,520
55	Exclusion of interest on rental housing bonds	1,030	1,090	1,080	1,110	1,180	1,210	1,210	1,310	1,360	1,360	1,370	12,280
56	Deductibility of mortgage interest on owner-occupied homes	25,130	27,090	29,580	32,290	34,960	37,510	40,110	85,520	112,580	119,280	125,820	644,740
57	Deductibility of State and local property tax on owner-occupied homes [17]	6,010	6,270	6,650	7,030	7,400	7,740	8,090	39,930	58,030	61,630	65,340	268,110
58	Deferral of income from installment sales	1,460	1,480	1,520	1,560	1,620	1,700	1,780	1,860	1,960	2,050	2,150	17,680
59	Capital gains exclusion on home sales	43,610	45,750	48,040	50,330	52,670	55,090	57,650	64,840	70,000	73,110	76,230	593,710
60	Exclusion of net imputed rental income	121,320	125,990	130,430	134,570	138,710	142,840	147,500	189,930	200,620	211,550	212,650	1,634,790
61	Exception from passive loss rules for $25,000 of rental loss	6,070	6,430	6,780	7,110	7,470	7,860	8,500	9,410	9,780	10,140	10,490	83,970
62	Credit for low-income housing investments	8,760	9,110	9,360	9,580	9,790	10,010	10,240	10,520	10,800	11,100	11,390	101,900
63	Accelerated depreciation on rental housing (normal tax method)	8,000	8,370	8,800	9,290	9,870	10,550	11,310	14,300	16,500	17,650	18,800	125,440
	Commerce:												
64	Discharge of business indebtedness	10	40	40	30	20	20	20	40	50	50	50	360
65	Exceptions from imputed interest rules	50	60	60	70	70	70	80	90	100	110	120	830
66	Treatment of qualified dividends	31,100	31,530	32,410	33,700	35,470	37,640	40,160	45,540	51,160	54,430	57,970	420,010
67	Capital gains (except agriculture, timber, iron ore, and coal)	111,470	104,920	103,790	104,580	107,170	111,200	116,250	129,410	143,110	149,840	157,060	1,227,330
68	Capital gains exclusion of small corporation stock	1,240	1,410	1,530	1,640	1,750	1,850	1,930	2,000	2,080	2,160	2,250	18,600
69	Step-up basis of capital gains at death	49,980	51,750	53,640	56,200	59,130	62,650	66,360	70,340	74,740	79,640	84,860	659,310
70	Carryover basis of capital gains on gifts	3,650	3,150	3,010	2,940	2,870	2,830	2,780	2,770	2,600	2,460	2,480	27,890
71	Ordinary income treatment of loss from small business corporation stock sale	70	70	70	70	70	80	80	80	80	90	90	780
72	Deferral of gains from like-kind exchanges	2,850	2,980	3,140	3,290	3,460	3,630	3,810	4,000	4,190	4,400	4,660	37,560
73	Depreciation of buildings other than rental housing (normal tax method)	−1,510	−1,870	−2,340	−2,890	−3,460	−4,040	−4,510	−5,570	−6,450	−7,080	−7,760	−45,970
74	Accelerated depreciation of machinery and equipment (normal tax method)	49,280	43,460	40,610	38,030	22,830	4,660	−9,700	−24,360	−40,690	−32,810	−16,970	25,060
75	Expensing of certain small investments (normal tax method)	−1,950	−710	−10	440	3,200	6,540	9,370	14,490	18,870	18,080	16,130	86,400
76	Exclusion of interest on small issue bonds	100	110	110	120	120	130	130	130	140	140	140	1,270
77	Special rules for certain film and TV production	30	10	0	0	0	0	0	0	0	0	0	10

Table 13–1.   ESTIMATES OF TOTAL INCOME TAX EXPENDITURES FOR FISCAL YEARS 2019–2029—Continued

(In millions of dollars)

	Total from corporations and individuals											
	2019	2020	2021	2022	2023	2024	2025	2026	2027	2028	2029	2020–29
78 Allow 20-percent deduction to certain pass-through income	34,923	53,132	54,698	56,499	59,037	62,065	65,730	22,119	0	0	0	373,280
Transportation:												
79 Tonnage tax	80	90	90	90	100	100	110	110	120	130	130	1,070
80 Deferral of tax on shipping companies	10	10	10	10	10	10	10	10	10	10	10	100
81 Exclusion of reimbursed employee parking expenses .	2,250	2,270	2,400	2,510	2,560	2,610	2,700	2,780	2,860	2,940	3,020	26,650
82 Exclusion for employer-provided transit passes	380	380	420	440	450	480	510	540	570	600	640	5,030
83 Tax credit for certain expenditures for maintaining railroad tracks	40	30	20	20	10	10	0	0	0	0	0	90
84 Exclusion of interest on bonds for Highway Projects and rail-truck transfer facilities	170	170	160	160	140	140	130	130	120	110	110	1,370
Community and regional development:												
85 Investment credit for rehabilitation of structures (other than historic)	10	10	0	0	0	0	0	0	0	0	0	10
86 Exclusion of interest for airport, dock, and similar bonds	610	650	640	660	700	720	720	780	800	810	810	7,290
87 Exemption of certain mutuals' and cooperatives' income	90	90	100	100	100	100	110	110	110	110	120	1,050
88 Empowerment zones	60	40	20	10	10	10	10	10	10	10	0	130
89 New markets tax credit	1,320	1,280	1,210	1,090	880	570	290	80	–120	–250	–300	4,730
90 Credit to holders of Gulf Tax Credit Bonds.	150	150	140	140	140	130	120	120	110	90	80	1,220
91 Recovery Zone Bonds [6]	90	90	80	80	80	70	60	70	60	50	50	690
92 Tribal Economic Development Bonds	10	10	10	10	10	10	10	10	10	10	10	100
93 Opportunity Zones	2,720	3,620	2,650	2,450	1,870	1,920	1,780	–5,850	–8,700	520	700	960
94 Employee retention credit	350	70	50	50	40	40	30	30	30	10	10	360
Education, training, employment, and social services:												
Education:												
95 Exclusion of scholarship and fellowship income (normal tax method)	3,040	3,220	3,390	3,580	3,800	4,020	4,260	4,780	5,550	5,860	6,180	44,640
96 Tax credits and deductions for postsecondary education expenses [7]	17,380	16,390	16,310	16,290	16,340	16,280	16,230	16,270	17,000	16,950	16,930	164,990
97 Education Individual Retirement Accounts	40	40	40	40	40	40	40	40	40	40	40	400
98 Deductibility of student-loan interest	1,920	2,040	2,060	2,100	2,130	2,250	2,300	2,330	2,950	2,960	3,020	24,140
99 Qualified tuition programs	2,200	2,410	2,650	2,920	3,240	3,640	4,130	5,070	6,080	7,230	8,750	46,120
100 Exclusion of interest on student-loan bonds	190	200	200	200	220	220	220	240	260	250	250	2,260
101 Exclusion of interest on bonds for private nonprofit educational facilities	1,850	1,950	1,940	1,990	2,120	2,170	2,180	2,350	2,430	2,440	2,450	22,020
102 Credit for holders of zone academy bonds [8]	170	150	130	110	90	80	60	50	50	40	40	800
103 Exclusion of interest on savings bonds redeemed to finance educational expenses	30	30	40	40	40	40	40	50	50	50	50	430
104 Parental personal exemption for students age 19 or over	0	0	0	0	0	0	0	5,630	8,520	8,690	8,930	31,770
105 Deductibility of charitable contributions (education)	4,140	4,450	4,790	5,100	5,410	5,720	6,020	7,160	9,200	9,620	10,070	67,540
106 Exclusion of employer-provided educational assistance	880	930	980	1,040	1,090	1,150	1,210	1,420	1,560	1,630	1,710	12,720
107 Special deduction for teacher expenses	180	180	180	190	180	180	180	190	220	220	220	1,940
108 Discharge of student loan indebtedness	80	90	90	100	100	110	120	130	150	160	170	1,220
109 Qualified school construction bonds [9]	600	570	540	520	490	470	440	410	390	360	330	4,520
Training, employment, and social services:												
110 Work opportunity tax credit	1,760	1,280	560	340	250	190	150	110	90	60	50	3,080
111 Employer-provided child care exclusion	570	610	660	710	770	830	900	1,230	1,430	1,510	1,590	10,240
112 Employer-provided child care credit	20	20	20	20	20	20	20	20	20	20	30	210
113 Assistance for adopted foster children	590	620	660	700	750	800	850	900	960	1,020	1,080	8,340
114 Adoption credit and exclusion	700	770	790	830	860	880	900	910	920	930	940	8,730
115 Exclusion of employee meals and lodging (other than military)	5,100	5,240	5,420	5,620	5,830	6,070	6,450	7,580	8,270	8,620	9,010	68,110
116 Credit for child and dependent care expenses	4,260	4,360	4,440	4,540	4,690	4,780	4,890	5,100	5,320	5,390	5,400	48,910
117 Credit for disabled access expenditures	10	10	10	10	10	10	10	10	10	10	10	100

Table 13–1. ESTIMATES OF TOTAL INCOME TAX EXPENDITURES FOR FISCAL YEARS 2019–2029—Continued

(In millions of dollars)

		Total from corporations and individuals											
		2019	2020	2021	2022	2023	2024	2025	2026	2027	2028	2029	2020–29
118	Deductibility of charitable contributions, other than education and health	36,660	39,540	42,760	45,510	48,270	51,040	53,750	64,790	84,810	88,800	92,980	612,250
119	Exclusion of certain foster care payments	480	490	510	510	520	530	540	540	540	540	560	5,280
120	Exclusion of parsonage allowances	870	920	970	1,020	1,080	1,130	1,190	1,260	1,320	1,390	1,470	11,750
121	Indian employment credit	30	20	20	20	20	10	10	10	10	10	10	140
122	Credit for employer differential wage payments	0	10	10	10	10	10	10	20	20	20	20	140
Health:													
123	Exclusion of employer contributions for medical insurance premiums and medical care [10]	202,290	214,420	227,880	242,230	258,730	276,820	295,050	348,700	389,240	413,090	438,240	3,104,400
124	Self-employed medical insurance premiums	7,050	7,320	7,780	8,320	8,870	9,420	10,120	11,730	13,080	13,900	14,670	105,210
125	Medical Savings Accounts / Health Savings Accounts	7,880	8,510	9,110	9,800	10,380	10,900	11,410	12,970	14,100	14,680	15,350	117,210
126	Deductibility of medical expenses	6,500	6,640	7,310	8,140	9,050	10,030	11,090	17,270	21,690	23,780	25,990	140,990
127	Exclusion of interest on hospital construction bonds	2,660	2,820	2,790	2,870	3,060	3,120	3,150	3,390	3,500	3,520	3,540	31,760
128	Refundable Premium Assistance Tax Credit [11]	7,040	3,910	4,110	3,690	3,590	3,370	3,740	4,810	5,380	5,660	5,980	44,240
129	Credit for employee health insurance expenses of small business [12]	70	50	40	30	10	10	10	0	0	0	0	150
130	Deductibility of charitable contributions (health)	7,540	8,080	8,650	9,180	9,690	10,200	10,710	12,150	14,590	15,260	15,950	114,460
131	Tax credit for orphan drug research	1,550	1,870	2,280	2,770	3,370	4,090	4,970	6,040	7,340	8,920	10,860	52,510
132	Special Blue Cross/Blue Shield tax benefits	200	230	260	300	330	370	400	430	470	510	550	3,850
133	Tax credit for health insurance purchased by certain displaced and retired individuals [13]	10	0	0	0	0	0	0	0	0	0	0	0
134	Distributions from retirement plans for premiums for health and long-term care insurance	420	430	450	460	470	490	500	590	630	650	660	5,330
Income security:													
135	Child credit [14]	74,880	75,770	76,530	77,100	77,740	78,300	78,990	55,850	20,650	20,450	20,240	581,620
136	Exclusion of railroad retirement (Social Security equivalent) benefits	230	220	210	200	190	180	170	170	180	180	170	1,870
137	Exclusion of workers' compensation benefits	9,680	9,770	9,870	9,970	10,070	10,170	10,270	10,370	10,470	10,570	10,680	102,210
138	Exclusion of public assistance benefits (normal tax method)	660	680	690	710	730	760	780	790	810	820	750	7,520
139	Exclusion of special benefits for disabled coal miners	20	20	20	10	10	10	10	10	10	10	10	120
140	Exclusion of military disability pensions	150	160	160	160	160	170	170	190	200	200	210	1,780
	Net exclusion of pension contributions and earnings:												
141	Defined benefit employer plans	71,653	73,831	75,807	78,012	79,560	80,979	81,129	83,516	84,065	85,124	86,795	808,818
142	Defined contribution employer plans	75,680	83,520	90,680	100,410	109,170	117,650	125,990	149,560	162,650	173,070	184,180	1,296,880
143	Individual Retirement Accounts	20,520	21,650	22,760	23,990	25,490	27,220	29,300	33,310	36,390	39,840	43,430	303,380
144	Low and moderate income savers credit	1,180	1,180	1,180	1,220	1,220	1,210	1,240	1,350	1,350	1,340	1,330	12,620
145	Self-Employed plans	24,150	26,580	29,250	32,070	34,900	38,560	42,770	50,570	62,750	69,180	75,380	462,010
	Exclusion of other employee benefits:												
146	Premiums on group term life insurance	2,960	3,080	3,200	3,320	3,450	3,580	3,710	4,210	4,480	4,640	4,790	38,460
147	Premiums on accident and disability insurance	330	330	340	340	340	350	350	350	350	350	350	3,450
148	Income of trusts to finance supplementary unemployment benefits	30	30	40	40	50	50	50	60	60	60	60	500
149	Income of trusts to finance voluntary employee benefits associations	990	1,060	1,130	1,210	1,280	1,360	1,440	1,610	1,700	1,800	1,900	14,490
150	Special ESOP rules	2,100	2,150	2,210	2,260	2,320	2,370	2,430	2,480	2,550	2,600	2,670	24,040
151	Additional deduction for the blind	40	40	40	40	40	50	50	50	60	60	70	500
152	Additional deduction for the elderly	4,990	5,290	5,680	6,150	6,490	6,910	7,340	6,950	7,030	7,480	8,010	67,330
153	Tax credit for the elderly and disabled	0	0	0	0	0	0	0	0	0	0	0	0
154	Deductibility of casualty losses	0	0	0	0	0	0	0	380	600	640	680	2,300
155	Earned income tax credit [15]	2,700	2,660	2,700	2,770	2,840	2,920	3,010	3,080	10,490	10,730	11,070	52,270
Social Security:													
	Exclusion of Social Security benefits:												
156	Social Security benefits for retired and disabled workers and spouses, dependents and survivors	29,100	30,900	32,490	33,990	35,640	36,330	36,430	41,480	48,460	50,590	52,670	398,980
157	Credit for certain employer contributions to Social Security	1,420	1,480	1,540	1,610	1,680	1,730	1,800	1,870	1,930	1,990	2,060	17,690

Table 13–1. ESTIMATES OF TOTAL INCOME TAX EXPENDITURES FOR FISCAL YEARS 2019–2029—Continued

(In millions of dollars)

	Total from corporations and individuals											
	2019	2020	2021	2022	2023	2024	2025	2026	2027	2028	2029	2020–29
Veterans benefits and services:												
158 Exclusion of veterans death benefits and disability compensation	7,590	8,340	8,910	9,200	9,500	9,820	10,150	10,950	12,380	12,790	13,230	105,270
159 Exclusion of veterans pensions	240	240	250	250	260	260	260	280	310	320	320	2,750
160 Exclusion of G.I. bill benefits	1,460	1,530	1,590	1,650	1,720	1,780	1,850	2,010	2,290	2,370	2,470	19,260
161 Exclusion of interest on veterans housing bonds	50	60	50	50	50	50	50	60	60	60	60	550
General purpose fiscal assistance:												
162 Exclusion of interest on public purpose State and local bonds	23,210	24,580	24,340	25,010	26,710	27,270	27,480	29,560	30,560	30,710	30,840	277,060
163 Build America Bonds [16]	0	0	0	0	0	0	0	0	0	0	0	0
164 Deductibility of nonbusiness State and local taxes other than on owner-occupied homes [17]	4,430	7,110	7,510	7,920	8,310	8,660	8,990	78,340	117,330	124,170	131,130	499,470
Interest:												
165 Deferral of interest on U.S. savings bonds	850	840	840	830	820	810	800	790	840	860	880	8,310
Addendum: Aid to State and local governments:												
Deductibility of:												
Property taxes on owner-occupied homes	6,010	6,270	6,650	7,030	7,400	7,740	8,090	39,930	58,030	61,630	65,340	268,110
Nonbusiness State and local taxes other than on owner-occupied homes	4,430	7,110	7,510	7,920	8,310	8,660	8,990	78,340	117,330	124,170	131,130	499,470
Exclusion of interest on State and local bonds for:												
Public purposes	23,210	24,580	24,340	25,010	26,710	27,270	27,480	29,560	30,560	30,710	30,840	277,060
Energy facilities	10	10	10	10	10	10	10	10	10	10	10	100
Water, sewage, and hazardous waste disposal facilities	300	320	310	320	340	340	350	380	380	390	390	3,520
Small-issues	100	110	110	120	120	130	130	130	140	140	140	1,270
Owner-occupied mortgage subsidies	790	840	840	860	910	940	950	1,020	1,050	1,050	1,060	9,520
Rental housing	1,030	1,090	1,080	1,110	1,180	1,210	1,210	1,310	1,360	1,360	1,370	12,280
Airports, docks, and similar facilities	610	650	640	660	700	720	720	780	800	810	810	7,290
Student loans	190	200	200	200	220	220	220	240	260	250	250	2,260
Private nonprofit educational facilities	1,850	1,950	1,940	1,990	2,120	2,170	2,180	2,350	2,430	2,440	2,450	22,020
Hospital construction	2,660	2,820	2,790	2,870	3,060	3,120	3,150	3,390	3,500	3,520	3,540	31,760
Veterans' housing	50	60	50	50	50	50	50	60	60	60	60	550

[1] Firms can take an energy grant in lieu of the energy production credit or the energy investment credit for facilities whose construction began in 2009, 2010, or 2011. The effect of the grant on outlays (in millions of dollars) is as follows: $0 in 2019 and thereafter.

[2] The alternative fuel mixture credit results in a reduction in excise tax receipts (in millions of dollars) as follows: 2019 $500 and $0 thereafter.

[3] In addition, the biodiesel producer tax credit results in a reduction in excise tax receipts (in millions of dollars) as follows: 2019 $2,130 and $0 thereafter.

[4] In addition, the credit for holding clean renewable energy bonds has outlay effects of (in millions of dollars): 2019 $50; 2020 $50; 2021 $50; 2022 $50; 2023 $50; 2024 $50; 2025, $50; 2026 $50; 2017 $50; 2028 $50; and 2029 $50.

[5] In addition, the qualified energy conservation bonds have outlay effects of (in millions of dollars): 2019 $40; 2020 $40; 2021 $40; 2022 $40; 2023 $40; 2024 $40; 2025, $40; 2026 $40; 2027 $40; 2028 $40; and 2029 $40.

[6] In addition, recovery zone bonds have outlay effects (in millions of dollars) as follows: 2019 $290; 2020 $290; 2021 $290; 2022 $290; 2023 $290; 2024 $290; 2025, $290; 2026 $290; 2027 $290; 2028 $290; and 2029 $290.

[7] In addition, the tax credits for postsecondary education expenses have outlay effects of (in millions of dollars): 2019 $2,860; 2020 $3,990; 2021 $3,970; 2022 $3,960; 2023 $3,940; 2024 $3,920; 2025 $3,900; 2026 $3,870; 2027 $3,560; 2028 $3,540; and 2029 $3,530.

[8] In addition, the credit for holders of zone academy bonds has outlay effects of (in millions of dollars): 2019 $60; 2020 $60; 2021 $60; 2022 $60; 2023 $60; 2024 $60; 2025 $60; 2026 $60; 2027 $60; 2028 $60; and 2029 $60.

[9] In addition, the provision for school construction bonds has outlay effects of (in millions of dollars): 2019 $690; 2020 $730; 2021 $730; 2022 $730; 2023 $730; 2024 $730; 2025 $730; 2026 $730; 2027 $730; 2028 $730; and 2029 $730.

[10] In addition, the employer contributions for health have effects on payroll tax receipts (in millions of dollars) as follows: 2019 $136,720; 2020 $143,440; 2021 $150,600; 2022 $158,700; 2023 $168,530; 2024 $179,380; 2025 $189,830; 2026 $200,370; 2027 $211,510; 2028 $223,270; and 2029 $235,650.

[11] In addition, the premium assistance credit provision has outlay effects of (in millions of dollars) as follows: 2019 $44,320; 2020 $42,430; 2021 $42,400; 2022 $43,590; 2023 $44,600; 2024 $45,730; 2025 $47,310; 2026 $48,400; 2027 $50,020; 2028 $52,180; and 2029 $54,640.

[12] In addition, the small business credit provision has outlay effects (in millions of dollars) as follows: The outlays round down to zero.

[13] In addition, the effect of the health coverage tax credit on receipts has outlay effects of (in millions of dollars) 2019 $30; 2020 $10; and $0 thereafter.

[14] In addition, the effect of the child tax credit on receipts has outlay effects of (in millions of dollars): 2019 $40,110; 2020 $41,410; 2021 $45,190; 2022 $45,270; 2023 $46,460; 2024 $46,670; 2025 $46,870; 2026 $47,850; 2027 $29,900; 2028 $29,890; and 2029 $30,290.

Table 13–1.   ESTIMATES OF TOTAL INCOME TAX EXPENDITURES FOR FISCAL YEARS 2019–2029—Continued

(In millions of dollars)

The child tax credit line also includes the credit for other dependents (in millions of dollars): 2019 $9,520; 2020 $9,690; 2021 $9,820; 2022 $9,920; 2023 $10,100; 2024 $10,160; 2025 $10,180; 2026 $6,000; 2027 $0; 2028 $0; and 2029 $0.

[15] In addition, the earned income tax credit on receipts has outlay effects of (in millions of dollars): 2019 $ 65,600; 2020 $66,420; 2021 $66,940; 2022 $68,220; 2023 $69,460; 2024 $70,910; 2025 $72,240; 2026 $73,290; 2027 $66,960; 2028 $67,930; and 2029 $69,910.

[16] In addition, the Build America Bonds have outlay effects of (in millions of dollars): 2019 $3,160; 2020 $3,390; 2021 $3,390; 2022 $3,390; 2023 $3,390; 2024 $3,390; 2025 $3,390; 2026 $3,390; 2027 $3,390; 2028 $3,390; and 2029 $3,390.

[17] Because of interactions with the $10,000 cap on State and local tax deductions for the years 2018 through 2025, these estimates understate the combined effects of repealing deductions for both property taxes on owner occupied housing and other non-business taxes. The estimate of repealing both is (in millions of dollars): 2019 $16,340; 2020 $19,870; 2021 $21,400; 2022 $23,040; 2023 $24,650; 2024 $26,220; 2025 $27,830; 2026 $121,680; 2027 $175,210; 2028 $185,920; and 2029 $196,870.

Note: Provisions with estimates denoted normal tax method have no revenue loss under the reference tax law method.

All estimates have been rounded to the nearest $10 million. Provisions with estimates that rounded to zero in each year are not included in the table.

Table 13–2A. ESTIMATES OF TOTAL CORPORATE INCOME TAX EXPENDITURES FOR FISCAL YEARS 2019–2029

(In millions of dollars)

	Total from corporations											
	2019	2020	2021	2022	2023	2024	2025	2026	2027	2028	2029	2020–29
National Defense												
1 Exclusion of benefits and allowances to Armed Forces personnel	0	0	0	0	0	0	0	0	0	0	0	0
International affairs:												
2 Exclusion of income earned abroad by U.S. citizens	0	0	0	0	0	0	0	0	0	0	0	0
3 Exclusion of certain allowances for Federal employees abroad	0	0	0	0	0	0	0	0	0	0	0	0
4 Inventory property sales source rules exception	0	0	0	0	0	0	0	0	0	0	0	0
5 Reduced tax rate on active income of controlled foreign corporations (normal tax method)	35,470	40,000	42,980	44,660	35,220	21,760	10,720	46,840	75,840	79,250	82,810	480,080
6 Deduction for foreign-derived intangible income dervied from trade or business within the United States	7,530	8,100	9,880	11,150	11,610	12,130	12,670	9,240	7,000	7,340	7,700	96,820
7 Interest Charge Domestic International Sales Corporations (IC-DISCs)	0	0	0	0	0	0	0	0	0	0	0	0
General science, space, and technology:												
8 Expensing of research and experimentation expenditures (normal tax method)	4,310	4,650	5,240	−17,550	−28,450	−20,720	−12,470	−3,630	0	0	0	−72,930
9 Credit for increasing research activities	13,440	14,780	16,170	17,510	18,820	20,160	21,520	22,900	24,290	25,720	27,190	209,060
Energy:												
10 Expensing of exploration and development costs, fuels	210	240	200	140	110	110	130	150	150	140	120	1,490
11 Excess of percentage over cost depletion, fuels	430	480	520	550	580	620	660	710	750	790	820	6,480
12 Exception from passive loss limitation for working interests in oil and gas properties	0	0	0	0	0	0	0	0	0	0	0	0
13 Capital gains treatment of royalties on coal	0	0	0	0	0	0	0	0	0	0	0	0
14 Exclusion of interest on energy facility bonds	0	0	0	0	0	0	0	0	0	0	0	0
15 Enhanced oil recovery credit	480	420	300	260	310	410	530	610	620	600	590	4,650
16 Energy production credit [1]	3,170	3,230	3,220	3,190	3,150	3,050	2,940	2,470	1,940	1,320	800	25,310
17 Marginal wells credit	30	20	30	30	20	10	0	0	0	0	0	110
18 Energy investment credit [1]	2,820	3,430	3,670	3,420	2,820	2,050	1,530	1,170	930	780	700	20,500
19 Alcohol fuel credits [2]	0	0	0	0	0	0	0	0	0	0	0	0
20 Bio-Diesel and small agri-biodiesel producer tax credits [3]	0	0	0	0	0	0	0	0	0	0	0	0
21 Tax credits for clean-fuel burning vehicles and refueling property	280	160	120	120	110	80	50	50	50	40	30	810
22 Exclusion of utility conservation subsidies	20	20	20	20	20	20	20	20	20	20	20	200
23 Credit for holding clean renewable energy bonds [4]	20	20	20	20	20	20	20	20	20	20	20	200
24 Credit for investment in clean coal facilities	20	10	20	40	70	90	80	70	80	50	50	560
25 Natural gas distribution pipelines treated as 15-year property	70	70	50	30	−10	−50	−80	−120	−140	−140	−140	−530
26 Amortize all geological and geophysical expenditures over 2 years	120	130	130	140	150	160	160	170	180	180	180	1,580
27 Allowance of deduction for certain energy efficient commercial building property......	0	0	0	0	0	0	0	0	0	0	0	0
28 Credit for construction of new energy efficient homes ..	10	0	0	0	0	0	0	0	0	0	0	0
29 Credit for residential energy efficient property	0	0	0	0	0	0	0	0	0	0	0	0
30 Qualified energy conservation bonds [5]	10	10	10	10	10	10	10	10	10	10	10	100
31 Advanced Energy Property Credit	10	10	10	10	10	10	10	10	10	10	10	100
32 Advanced nuclear power production credit	0	0	0	100	190	240	270	280	280	280	270	1,910
33 Reduced tax rate for nuclear decommissioning funds ..	100	100	110	110	120	120	130	130	140	150	150	1,260
Natural resources and environment:												
34 Expensing of exploration and development costs, nonfuel minerals	40	40	40	20	20	20	20	30	30	20	20	260
35 Excess of percentage over cost depletion, nonfuel minerals	80	80	90	100	100	110	120	130	130	140	140	1,140
36 Exclusion of interest on bonds for water, sewage, and hazardous waste facilities	40	40	30	20	20	20	20	30	20	20	20	240
37 Capital gains treatment of certain timber income	0	0	0	0	0	0	0	0	0	0	0	0

Table 13–2A.   ESTIMATES OF TOTAL CORPORATE INCOME TAX EXPENDITURES FOR FISCAL YEARS 2019–2029—Continued

(In millions of dollars)

	Total from corporations											
	2019	2020	2021	2022	2023	2024	2025	2026	2027	2028	2029	2020–29
38 Expensing of multiperiod timber growing costs	0	0	10	10	10	10	10	10	10	10	10	90
39 Tax incentives for preservation of historic structures	650	580	550	540	640	780	880	960	990	1,010	1,030	7,960
40 Carbon oxide sequestration credit	70	90	120	140	170	220	270	310	320	340	350	2,330
41 Deduction for endangered species recovery expenditures	10	10	10	10	10	10	10	10	20	20	20	130
Agriculture:												
42 Expensing of certain capital outlays	20	20	10	10	10	10	10	10	10	10	10	110
43 Expensing of certain multiperiod production costs	10	10	10	10	10	10	10	10	10	10	10	100
44 Treatment of loans forgiven for solvent farmers	0	0	0	0	0	0	0	0	0	0	0	0
45 Capital gains treatment of certain agriculture income ..	0	0	0	0	0	0	0	0	0	0	0	0
46 Income averaging for farmers	0	0	0	0	0	0	0	0	0	0	0	0
47 Deferral of gain on sale of farm refiners	15	15	15	15	15	20	20	20	20	20	25	185
48 Expensing of reforestation expenditures	0	0	10	10	10	10	10	10	10	10	10	90
Commerce and housing:												
Financial institutions and insurance:												
49 Exemption of credit union income	1,911	1,764	1,587	1,756	1,935	2,019	2,191	2,494	2,661	2,761	2,710	21,878
50 Exclusion of life insurance death benefits	1,240	1,280	1,320	1,360	1,410	1,450	1,490	1,540	1,580	1,630	1,680	14,740
51 Exemption or special alternative tax for small property and casualty insurance companies	110	120	130	130	140	140	150	160	160	170	170	1,470
52 Tax exemption of insurance income earned by tax-exempt organizations	330	330	340	350	360	380	390	400	410	420	430	3,810
53 Exclusion of interest spread of financial institutions	0	0	0	0	0	0	0	0	0	0	0	0
Housing:												
54 Exclusion of interest on owner-occupied mortgage subsidy bonds	100	100	80	60	60	60	60	80	70	50	50	670
55 Exclusion of interest on rental housing bonds	130	130	100	80	80	80	70	100	90	70	70	870
56 Deductibility of mortgage interest on owner-occupied homes	0	0	0	0	0	0	0	0	0	0	0	0
57 Deductibility of State and local property tax on owner-occupied homes	0	0	0	0	0	0	0	0	0	0	0	0
58 Deferral of income from installment sales	0	0	0	0	0	0	0	0	0	0	0	0
59 Capital gains exclusion on home sales	0	0	0	0	0	0	0	0	0	0	0	0
60 Exclusion of net imputed rental income	0	0	0	0	0	0	0	0	0	0	0	0
61 Exception from passive loss rules for $25,000 of rental loss	0	0	0	0	0	0	0	0	0	0	0	0
62 Credit for low-income housing investments	8,320	8,650	8,890	9,100	9,300	9,510	9,730	9,990	10,260	10,540	10,820	96,790
63 Accelerated depreciation on rental housing (normal tax method)	1,190	1,280	1,380	1,480	1,590	1,720	1,850	2,000	2,160	2,320	2,480	18,260
Commerce:												
64 Discharge of business indebtedness	0	0	0	0	0	0	0	0	0	0	0	0
65 Exceptions from imputed interest rules	0	0	0	0	0	0	0	0	0	0	0	0
66 Treatment of qualified dividends	0	0	0	0	0	0	0	0	0	0	0	0
67 Capital gains (except agriculture, timber, iron ore, and coal)	0	0	0	0	0	0	0	0	0	0	0	0
68 Capital gains exclusion of small corporation stock	0	0	0	0	0	0	0	0	0	0	0	0
69 Step-up basis of capital gains at death	0	0	0	0	0	0	0	0	0	0	0	0
70 Carryover basis of capital gains on gifts	0	0	0	0	0	0	0	0	0	0	0	0
71 Ordinary income treatment of loss from small business corporation stock sale..	0	0	0	0	0	0	0	0	0	0	0	0
72 Deferral of gains from like-kind exchanges	1,000	1,040	1,100	1,150	1,210	1,270	1,330	1,400	1,460	1,530	1,650	13,140
73 Depreciation of buildings other than rental housing (normal tax method)	−490	−650	−850	−1,080	−1,310	−1,530	−1,690	−1,810	−1,950	−2,110	−2,290	−15,270
74 Accelerated depreciation of machinery and equipment (normal tax method)	27,120	23,290	21,200	19,440	11,200	−80	−9,460	−17,350	−24,470	−19,490	−10,820	−6,540
75 Expensing of certain small investments (normal tax method)	−180	−50	40	80	260	710	1,170	1,500	1,930	1,840	1,540	9,020
76 Exclusion of interest on small issue bonds	10	10	10	10	10	10	10	10	10	10	10	100
77 Special rules for certain film and TV production	20	10	0	0	0	0	0	0	0	0	0	10

Table 13–2A. ESTIMATES OF TOTAL CORPORATE INCOME TAX EXPENDITURES FOR FISCAL YEARS 2019–2029—Continued

(In millions of dollars)

	Total from corporations											
	2019	2020	2021	2022	2023	2024	2025	2026	2027	2028	2029	2020–29
78 Allow 20-percent deduction to certain pass-through income	0	0	0	0	0	0	0	0	0	0	0	0
Transportation:												
79 Tonnage tax	80	90	90	90	100	100	110	110	120	130	130	1,070
80 Deferral of tax on shipping companies	10	10	10	10	10	10	10	10	10	10	10	100
81 Exclusion of reimbursed employee parking expenses	−1,100	−1,190	−1,220	−1,280	−1,300	−1,340	−1,380	−1,420	−1,460	−1,500	−1,550	−13,640
82 Exclusion for employer-provided transit passes	−360	−400	−420	−460	−480	−500	−530	−560	−590	−620	−650	−5,210
83 Tax credit for certain expenditures for maintaining railroad tracks	30	20	10	10	10	10	0	0	0	0	0	60
84 Exclusion of interest on bonds for Highway Projects and rail-truck transfer facilities	40	40	40	40	30	30	30	30	30	20	20	310
Community and regional development:												
85 Investment credit for rehabilitation of structures (other than historic)	0	0	0	0	0	0	0	0	0	0	0	0
86 Exclusion of interest for airport, dock, and similar bonds	80	80	60	50	50	50	40	60	50	40	40	520
87 Exemption of certain mutuals' and cooperatives' income	90	90	100	100	100	100	110	110	110	110	120	1,050
88 Empowerment zones	50	30	20	10	10	10	10	10	10	10	0	120
89 New markets tax credit	1,290	1,250	1,180	1,070	860	550	280	70	−120	−250	−300	4,590
90 Credit to holders of Gulf Tax Credit Bonds.	20	20	10	10	10	10	10	10	10	0	0	90
91 Recovery Zone Bonds [6]	10	10	10	10	10	0	0	10	0	0	0	50
92 Tribal Economic Development Bonds	0	0	0	0	0	0	0	0	0	0	0	0
93 Opportunity Zones	1,270	1,270	1,070	870	740	730	690	−3,400	−2,340	210	290	130
94 Employee retention credit	250	50	40	40	30	30	20	20	20	10	10	270
Education, training, employment, and social services:												
Education:												
95 Exclusion of scholarship and fellowship income (normal tax method)	40	40	30	20	20	20	20	30	20	20	20	240
96 Tax credits and deductions for postsecondary education expenses [7]	0	0	0	0	0	0	0	0	0	0	0	0
97 Education Individual Retirement Accounts	0	0	0	0	0	0	0	0	0	0	0	0
98 Deductibility of student-loan interest	0	0	0	0	0	0	0	0	0	0	0	0
99 Qualified tuition programs	0	0	0	0	0	0	0	0	0	0	0	0
100 Exclusion of interest on student-loan bonds	20	20	20	10	20	10	10	20	20	10	10	150
101 Exclusion of interest on bonds for private nonprofit educational facilities	240	230	180	140	150	140	130	180	150	120	120	1,540
102 Credit for holders of zone academy bonds [8]	170	150	130	110	90	80	60	50	50	40	40	800
103 Exclusion of interest on savings bonds redeemed to finance educational expenses	0	0	0	0	0	0	0	0	0	0	0	0
104 Parental personal exemption for students age 19 or over	0	0	0	0	0	0	0	0	0	0	0	0
105 Deductibility of charitable contributions (education)	570	600	620	660	690	730	760	800	830	860	890	7,440
106 Exclusion of employer-provided educational assistance	0	0	0	0	0	0	0	0	0	0	0	0
107 Special deduction for teacher expenses	0	0	0	0	0	0	0	0	0	0	0	0
108 Discharge of student loan indebtedness	0	0	0	0	0	0	0	0	0	0	0	0
109 Qualified school construction bonds [9]	150	140	130	130	120	120	110	100	100	90	80	1,120
Training, employment, and social services:												
110 Work opportunity tax credit	1,310	910	420	270	200	150	120	90	70	50	40	2,320
111 Employer-provided child care exclusion	0	0	0	0	0	0	0	0	0	0	0	0
112 Employer-provided child care credit	20	20	20	20	20	20	20	20	20	20	30	210
113 Assistance for adopted foster children	0	0	0	0	0	0	0	0	0	0	0	0
114 Adoption credit and exclusion	0	0	0	0	0	0	0	0	0	0	0	0
115 Exclusion of employee meals and lodging (other than military)	−310	−330	−340	−360	−380	−400	−420	−440	−460	−480	−510	−4,120
116 Credit for child and dependent care expenses	0	0	0	0	0	0	0	0	0	0	0	0
117 Credit for disabled access expenditures	0	0	0	0	0	0	0	0	0	0	0	0

Table 13–2A. ESTIMATES OF TOTAL CORPORATE INCOME TAX EXPENDITURES FOR FISCAL YEARS 2019–2029—Continued

(In millions of dollars)

		Total from corporations										
		2019	2020	2021	2022	2023	2024	2025	2026	2027	2028	2029	2020–29
118	Deductibility of charitable contributions, other than education and health	1,160	1,210	1,250	1,300	1,350	1,400	1,460	1,520	1,580	1,640	1,700	14,410
119	Exclusion of certain foster care payments	0	0	0	0	0	0	0	0	0	0	0	0
120	Exclusion of parsonage allowances	0	0	0	0	0	0	0	0	0	0	0	0
121	Indian employment credit	10	10	10	10	10	0	0	0	0	0	0	40
122	Credit for employer differential wage payments	0	10	10	10	10	10	10	10	10	10	10	100
Health:													
123	Exclusion of employer contributions for medical insurance premiums and medical care [10]	0	0	0	0	0	0	0	0	0	0	0	0
124	Self-employed medical insurance premiums	0	0	0	0	0	0	0	0	0	0	0	0
125	Medical Savings Accounts / Health Savings Accounts .	0	0	0	0	0	0	0	0	0	0	0	0
126	Deductibility of medical expenses	0	0	0	0	0	0	0	0	0	0	0	0
127	Exclusion of interest on hospital construction bonds	340	340	260	210	210	200	190	270	220	170	180	2,250
128	Refundable Premium Assistance Tax Credit [11]	0	0	0	0	0	0	0	0	0	0	0	0
129	Credit for employee health insurance expenses of small business [12]	20	10	10	10	0	0	0	0	0	0	0	30
130	Deductibility of charitable contributions (health)	3,580	3,810	4,030	4,250	4,460	4,670	4,890	5,100	5,320	5,550	5,780	47,860
131	Tax credit for orphan drug research	1,530	1,850	2,250	2,740	3,330	4,040	4,920	5,980	7,270	8,840	10,760	51,980
132	Special Blue Cross/Blue Shield tax benefits	200	230	260	300	330	370	400	430	470	510	550	3,850
133	Tax credit for health insurance purchased by certain displaced and retired individuals [13]	0	0	0	0	0	0	0	0	0	0	0	0
134	Distributions from retirement plans for premiums for health and long-term care insurance	0	0	0	0	0	0	0	0	0	0	0	0
Income security:													
135	Child credit [14]	0	0	0	0	0	0	0	0	0	0	0	0
136	Exclusion of railroad retirement (Social Security equivalent) benefits	0	0	0	0	0	0	0	0	0	0	0	0
137	Exclusion of workers' compensation benefits	0	0	0	0	0	0	0	0	0	0	0	0
138	Exclusion of public assistance benefits (normal tax method)	0	0	0	0	0	0	0	0	0	0	0	0
139	Exclusion of special benefits for disabled coal miners ..	0	0	0	0	0	0	0	0	0	0	0	0
140	Exclusion of military disability pensions	0	0	0	0	0	0	0	0	0	0	0	0
	Net exclusion of pension contributions and earnings:												
141	Defined benefit employer plans	0	0	0	0	0	0	0	0	0	0	0	0
142	Defined contribution employer plans	0	0	0	0	0	0	0	0	0	0	0	0
143	Individual Retirement Accounts	0	0	0	0	0	0	0	0	0	0	0	0
144	Low and moderate income savers credit	0	0	0	0	0	0	0	0	0	0	0	0
145	Self-Employed plans	0	0	0	0	0	0	0	0	0	0	0	0
	Exclusion of other employee benefits:												
146	Premiums on group term life insurance	0	0	0	0	0	0	0	0	0	0	0	0
147	Premiums on accident and disability insurance	0	0	0	0	0	0	0	0	0	0	0	0
148	Income of trusts to finance supplementary unemployment benefits	0	0	0	0	0	0	0	0	0	0	0	0
149	Income of trusts to finance voluntary employee benefits associations	0	0	0	0	0	0	0	0	0	0	0	0
150	Special ESOP rules	1,970	2,020	2,070	2,120	2,170	2,220	2,270	2,320	2,380	2,430	2,490	22,490
151	Additional deduction for the blind	0	0	0	0	0	0	0	0	0	0	0	0
152	Additional deduction for the elderly	0	0	0	0	0	0	0	0	0	0	0	0
153	Tax credit for the elderly and disabled	0	0	0	0	0	0	0	0	0	0	0	0
154	Deductibility of casualty losses	0	0	0	0	0	0	0	0	0	0	0	0
155	Earned income tax credit [15]	0	0	0	0	0	0	0	0	0	0	0	0
Social Security:													
	Exclusion of Social Security benefits:												
156	Social Security benefits for retired and disabled workers and spouses, dependents and survivors	0	0	0	0	0	0	0	0	0	0	0	0
157	Credit for certain employer contributions to Social Security	500	530	570	610	650	680	720	760	790	830	870	7,010

Table 13–2A.   ESTIMATES OF TOTAL CORPORATE INCOME TAX EXPENDITURES FOR FISCAL YEARS 2019–2029—Continued

(In millions of dollars)

	Total from corporations											
	2019	2020	2021	2022	2023	2024	2025	2026	2027	2028	2029	2020–29
Veterans benefits and services:												
158 Exclusion of veterans death benefits and disability compensation	0	0	0	0	0	0	0	0	0	0	0	0
159 Exclusion of veterans pensions	0	0	0	0	0	0	0	0	0	0	0	0
160 Exclusion of G.I. bill benefits	0	0	0	0	0	0	0	0	0	0	0	0
161 Exclusion of interest on veterans housing bonds	10	10	0	0	0	0	0	0	0	0	0	10
General purpose fiscal assistance:												
162 Exclusion of interest on public purpose State and local bonds	2,990	2,930	2,240	1,790	1,870	1,780	1,650	2,320	1,930	1,500	1,530	19,540
163 Build America Bonds [16]	0	0	0	0	0	0	0	0	0	0	0	0
164 Deductibility of nonbusiness State and local taxes other than on owner-occupied homes	0	0	0	0	0	0	0	0	0	0	0	0
Interest:												
165 Deferral of interest on U.S. savings bonds	0	0	0	0	0	0	0	0	0	0	0	0
Addendum: Aid to State and local governments:												
Deductibility of:												
Property taxes on owner-occupied homes	0	0	0	0	0	0	0	0	0	0	0	0
Nonbusiness State and local taxes other than on owner-occupied homes	0	0	0	0	0	0	0	0	0	0	0	0
Exclusion of interest on State and local bonds for:												
Public purposes	2,990	2,930	2,240	1,790	1,870	1,780	1,650	2,320	1,930	1,500	1,530	19,540
Energy facilities	0	0	0	0	0	0	0	0	0	0	0	0
Water, sewage, and hazardous waste disposal facilities	40	40	30	20	20	20	20	30	20	20	20	240
Small-issues	10	10	10	10	10	10	10	10	10	10	10	100
Owner-occupied mortgage subsidies	100	100	80	60	60	60	60	80	70	50	50	670
Rental housing	130	130	100	80	80	80	70	100	90	70	70	870
Airports, docks, and similar facilities	80	80	60	50	50	50	40	60	50	40	40	520
Student loans	20	20	20	10	20	10	10	20	20	10	10	150
Private nonprofit educational facilities	240	230	180	140	150	140	130	180	150	120	120	1,540
Hospital construction	340	340	260	210	210	200	190	270	220	170	180	2,250
Veterans' housing	10	10	0	0	0	0	0	0	0	0	0	10

See Table 13-1 footnotes for specific table information

Table 13–2B. ESTIMATES OF TOTAL INDIVIDUAL INCOME TAX EXPENDITURES FOR FISCAL YEARS 2019–2029

(In millions of dollars)

	Total from individuals											
	2019	2020	2021	2022	2023	2024	2025	2026	2027	2028	2029	2020–29
National Defense												
1 Exclusion of benefits and allowances to Armed Forces personnel	12,460	12,910	11,660	11,700	12,080	12,560	13,090	13,660	14,270	14,910	15,600	132,440
International affairs:												
2 Exclusion of income earned abroad by U.S. citizens ...	6,930	7,280	7,640	8,020	8,420	8,840	9,290	9,750	10,240	10,750	11,290	91,520
3 Exclusion of certain allowances for Federal employees abroad	240	250	260	280	290	300	320	330	350	370	390	3,140
4 Inventory property sales source rules exception	0	0	0	0	0	0	0	0	0	0	0	0
5 Reduced tax rate on active income of controlled foreign corporations (normal tax method)	0	0	0	0	0	0	0	0	0	0	0	0
6 Deduction for foreign-derived intangible income dervied from trade or business within the United States	0	0	0	0	0	0	0	0	0	0	0	0
7 Interest Charge Domestic International Sales Corporations (IC-DISCs)	1,280	1,340	1,410	1,480	1,560	1,630	1,720	1,800	1,890	1,990	2,090	16,910)
General science, space, and technology:												
8 Expensing of research and experimentation expenditures (normal tax method)........................	1,210	1,090	1,090	–1,540	–6,540	–4,910	–3,170	–1,310	0	0	0	–15,290
9 Credit for increasing research activities	1,860	2,030	2,210	2,380	2,550	2,740	2,930	3,140	3,360	3,590	3,840	28,770
Energy:												
10 Expensing of exploration and development costs, fuels	720	820	690	490	390	400	470	590	640	590	520	5,600
11 Excess of percentage over cost depletion, fuels	240	280	300	320	340	360	390	470	530	560	580	4,130
12 Exception from passive loss limitation for working interests in oil and gas properties	10	10	10	10	10	10	10	10	10	10	10	100
13 Capital gains treatment of royalties on coal	150	140	140	140	140	150	160	170	190	200	210	1,640
14 Exclusion of interest on energy facility bonds	10	10	10	10	10	10	10	10	10	10	10	100
15 Enhanced oil recovery credit	30	20	20	10	20	20	30	40	30	30	40	260
16 Energy production credit [1]	1,060	1,080	1,070	1,060	1,050	1,020	980	820	650	440	270	8,440
17 Marginal wells credit	80	60	70	70	60	30	10	0	0	0	0	300
18 Energy investment credit [1]	890	1,080	1,150	1,070	880	640	480	370	290	240	220	6,420
19 Alcohol fuel credits [2]	0	0	0	0	0	0	0	0	0	0	0	0
20 Bio-Diesel and small agri-biodiesel producer tax credits [3]	0	0	0	0	0	0	0	0	0	0	0	0
21 Tax credits for clean-fuel burning vehicles and refueling property	660	420	260	260	270	230	170	150	150	150	110	2,170
22 Exclusion of utility conservation subsidies	430	450	470	490	520	550	570	600	630	660	690	5,630
23 Credit for holding clean renewable energy bonds [4]	50	50	50	50	50	50	50	50	50	50	50	500
24 Credit for investment in clean coal facilities	0	0	0	0	10	10	10	10	10	0	0	50
25 Natural gas distribution pipelines treated as 15-year property	0	0	0	0	0	0	0	0	0	0	0	0
26 Amortize all geological and geophysical expenditures over 2 years	110	120	130	130	140	150	150	180	190	200	200	1,590
27 Allowance of deduction for certain energy efficient commercial building property...............................	10	0	0	0	0	0	0	0	0	0	0	0
28 Credit for construction of new energy efficient homes .	40	10	10	0	0	0	0	0	0	0	0	20
29 Credit for residential energy efficient property	1,980	1,740	1,410	360	70	0	0	0	0	0	0	3,580
30 Qualified energy conservation bonds [5]	20	20	20	20	20	20	20	20	20	20	20	200
31 Advanced Energy Property Credit	0	0	0	0	0	0	0	0	0	0	0	0
32 Advanced nuclear power production credit	0	0	0	0	0	0	0	0	0	0	0	0
33 Reduced tax rate for nuclear decommissioning funds .	0	0	0	0	0	0	0	0	0	0	0	0
Natural resources and environment:												
34 Expensing of exploration and development costs, nonfuel minerals	130	140	120	90	70	70	80	100	110	100	90	970
35 Excess of percentage over cost depletion, nonfuel minerals	40	50	50	60	60	60	70	80	90	100	100	720
36 Exclusion of interest on bonds for water, sewage, and hazardous waste facilities	260	280	280	300	320	320	330	350	360	370	370	3,280
37 Capital gains treatment of certain timber income	150	140	140	140	140	150	160	170	190	200	210	1,640

Table 13–2B. ESTIMATES OF TOTAL INDIVIDUAL INCOME TAX EXPENDITURES FOR FISCAL YEARS 2019–2029—Continued

(In millions of dollars)

	Total from individuals											
	2019	2020	2021	2022	2023	2024	2025	2026	2027	2028	2029	2020–29
38 Expensing of multiperiod timber growing costs	40	40	50	50	60	60	60	70	80	80	80	630
39 Tax incentives for preservation of historic structures ...	180	150	140	140	150	190	220	240	260	260	270	2,020
40 Carbon oxide sequestration credit	0	0	0	0	0	0	0	0	0	0	0	0
41 Deduction for endangered species recovery expenditures	20	20	20	20	20	30	30	30	40	40	40	290
Agriculture:												
42 Expensing of certain capital outlays	20	70	100	120	130	130	140	170	190	200	210	1,460
43 Expensing of certain multiperiod production costs	240	260	270	280	300	310	330	410	450	470	480	3,560
44 Treatment of loans forgiven for solvent farmers	50	50	50	60	60	60	70	70	70	70	70	630
45 Capital gains treatment of certain agriculture income .	1,490	1,410	1,390	1,400	1,440	1,490	1,560	1,730	1,920	2,010	2,100	16,450
46 Income averaging for farmers	170	180	190	190	200	210	220	230	230	230	230	2,110
47 Deferral of gain on sale of farm refiners	0	0	0	0	0	0	0	0	0	0	0	0
48 Expensing of reforestation expenditures	40	40	50	50	60	60	60	70	80	80	80	630
Commerce and housing:												
Financial institutions and insurance:												
49 Exemption of credit union income	0	0	0	0	0	0	0	0	0	0	0	0
50 Exclusion of life insurance death benefits	11,970	12,480	13,020	13,510	14,060	14,640	15,190	16,010	17,010	17,570	18,010	151,500
51 Exemption or special alternative tax for small property and casualty insurance companies	0	0	0	0	0	0	0	0	0	0	0	0
52 Tax exemption of insurance income earned by tax-exempt organizations	0	0	0	0	0	0	0	0	0	0	0	0
53 Exclusion of interest spread of financial institutions	2,190	1,120	1,160	1,200	1,240	1,280	1,330	1,400	1,470	1,510	1,560	13,270
Housing:												
54 Exclusion of interest on owner-occupied mortgage subsidy bonds	690	740	760	800	850	880	890	940	980	1,000	1,010	8,850
55 Exclusion of interest on rental housing bonds	900	960	980	1,030	1,100	1,130	1,140	1,210	1,270	1,290	1,300	11,410
56 Deductibility of mortgage interest on owner-occupied homes	25,130	27,090	29,580	32,290	34,960	37,510	40,110	85,520	112,580	119,280	125,820	644,740
57 Deductibility of State and local property tax on owner-occupied homes	6,010	6,270	6,650	7,030	7,400	7,740	8,090	39,930	58,030	61,630	65,340	268,110
58 Deferral of income from installment sales	1,460	1,480	1,520	1,560	1,620	1,700	1,780	1,860	1,960	2,050	2,150	17,680
59 Capital gains exclusion on home sales	43,610	45,750	48,040	50,330	52,670	55,090	57,650	64,840	70,000	73,110	76,230	593,710
60 Exclusion of net imputed rental income	121,320	125,990	130,430	134,570	138,710	142,840	147,500	189,930	200,620	211,550	212,650	1,634,790
61 Exception from passive loss rules for $25,000 of rental loss	6,070	6,430	6,780	7,110	7,470	7,860	8,500	9,410	9,780	10,140	10,490	83,970
62 Credit for low-income housing investments	440	460	470	480	490	500	510	530	540	560	570	5,110
63 Accelerated depreciation on rental housing (normal tax method)	6,810	7,090	7,420	7,810	8,280	8,830	9,460	12,300	14,340	15,330	16,320	107,180
Commerce:												
64 Discharge of business indebtedness	10	40	40	30	20	20	20	40	50	50	50	360
65 Exceptions from imputed interest rules	50	60	60	70	70	70	80	90	100	110	120	830
66 Treatment of qualified dividends	31,100	31,530	32,410	33,700	35,470	37,640	40,160	45,540	51,160	54,430	57,970	420,010
67 Capital gains (except agriculture, timber, iron ore, and coal)	111,470	104,920	103,790	104,580	107,170	111,200	116,250	129,410	143,110	149,840	157,060	1,227,330
68 Capital gains exclusion of small corporation stock	1,240	1,410	1,530	1,640	1,750	1,850	1,930	2,000	2,080	2,160	2,250	18,600
69 Step-up basis of capital gains at death	49,980	51,750	53,640	56,200	59,130	62,650	66,360	70,340	74,740	79,640	84,860	659,310
70 Carryover basis of capital gains on gifts	3,650	3,150	3,010	2,940	2,870	2,830	2,780	2,770	2,600	2,460	2,480	27,890
71 Ordinary income treatment of loss from small business corporation stock sale	70	70	70	70	70	80	80	80	80	90	90	780
72 Deferral of gains from like-kind exchanges	1,850	1,940	2,040	2,140	2,250	2,360	2,480	2,600	2,730	2,870	3,010	24,420
73 Depreciation of buildings other than rental housing (normal tax method)	−1,020	−1,220	−1,490	−1,810	−2,150	−2,510	−2,820	−3,760	−4,500	−4,970	−5,470	−30,700
74 Accelerated depreciation of machinery and equipment (normal tax method)	22,160	20,170	19,410	18,590	11,630	4,740	−240	−7,010	−16,220	−13,320	−6,150	31,600
75 Expensing of certain small investments (normal tax method)	−1,770	−660	−50	360	2,940	5,830	8,200	12,990	16,940	16,240	14,590	77,380
76 Exclusion of interest on small issue bonds	90	100	100	110	110	120	120	120	130	130	130	1,170
77 Special rules for certain film and TV production	10	0	0	0	0	0	0	0	0	0	0	0

Table 13–2B. ESTIMATES OF TOTAL INDIVIDUAL INCOME TAX EXPENDITURES FOR FISCAL YEARS 2019–2029—Continued

(In millions of dollars)

	Total from individuals											
	2019	2020	2021	2022	2023	2024	2025	2026	2027	2028	2029	2020–29
78 Allow 20-percent deduction to certain pass-through income	34,923	53,132	54,698	56,499	59,037	62,065	65,730	22,119	0	0	0	373,280
Transportation:												
79 Tonnage tax	0	0	0	0	0	0	0	0	0	0	0	0
80 Deferral of tax on shipping companies	0	0	0	0	0	0	0	0	0	0	0	0
81 Exclusion of reimbursed employee parking expenses	3,350	3,460	3,620	3,790	3,860	3,950	4,080	4,200	4,320	4,440	4,570	40,290
82 Exclusion for employer-provided transit passes	740	780	840	900	930	980	1,040	1,100	1,160	1,220	1,290	10,240
83 Tax credit for certain expenditures for maintaining railroad tracks	10	10	10	10	0	0	0	0	0	0	0	30
84 Exclusion of interest on bonds for Highway Projects and rail-truck transfer facilities	130	130	120	120	110	110	100	100	90	90	90	1,060
Community and regional development:												
85 Investment credit for rehabilitation of structures (other than historic)	10	10	0	0	0	0	0	0	0	0	0	10
86 Exclusion of interest for airport, dock, and similar bonds	530	570	580	610	650	670	680	720	750	770	770	6,770
87 Exemption of certain mutuals' and cooperatives' income	0	0	0	0	0	0	0	0	0	0	0	0
88 Empowerment zones	10	10	0	0	0	0	0	0	0	0	0	10
89 New markets tax credit	30	30	30	20	20	20	10	10	0	0	0	140
90 Credit to holders of Gulf Tax Credit Bonds	130	130	130	130	130	120	110	110	100	90	80	1,130
91 Recovery Zone Bonds [6]	80	80	70	70	70	70	60	60	60	50	50	640
92 Tribal Economic Development Bonds	10	10	10	10	10	10	10	10	10	10	10	100
93 Opportunity Zones	1,450	2,350	1,580	1,580	1,130	1,190	1,090	−2,450	−6,360	310	410	830
94 Employee retention credit	100	20	10	10	10	10	10	10	10	0	0	90
Education, training, employment, and social services:												
Education:												
95 Exclusion of scholarship and fellowship income (normal tax method)	3,000	3,180	3,360	3,560	3,780	4,000	4,240	4,750	5,530	5,840	6,160	44,400
96 Tax credits and deductions for postsecondary education expenses [7]	17,380	16,390	16,310	16,290	16,340	16,280	16,230	16,270	17,000	16,950	16,930	164,990
97 Education Individual Retirement Accounts	40	40	40	40	40	40	40	40	40	40	40	400
98 Deductibility of student-loan interest	1,920	2,040	2,060	2,100	2,130	2,250	2,300	2,330	2,950	2,960	3,020	24,140
99 Qualified tuition programs	2,200	2,410	2,650	2,920	3,240	3,640	4,130	5,070	6,080	7,230	8,750	46,120
100 Exclusion of interest on student-loan bonds	170	180	180	190	200	210	210	220	240	240	240	2,110
101 Exclusion of interest on bonds for private nonprofit educational facilities	1,610	1,720	1,760	1,850	1,970	2,030	2,050	2,170	2,280	2,320	2,330	20,480
102 Credit for holders of zone academy bonds [8]	0	0	0	0	0	0	0	0	0	0	0	0
103 Exclusion of interest on savings bonds redeemed to finance educational expenses	30	30	40	40	40	40	40	50	50	50	50	430
104 Parental personal exemption for students age 19 or over	0	0	0	0	0	0	0	5,630	8,520	8,690	8,930	31,770
105 Deductibility of charitable contributions (education)	3,570	3,850	4,170	4,440	4,720	4,990	5,260	6,360	8,370	8,760	9,180	60,100
106 Exclusion of employer-provided educational assistance	880	930	980	1,040	1,090	1,150	1,210	1,420	1,560	1,630	1,710	12,720
107 Special deduction for teacher expenses	180	180	180	190	180	180	180	190	220	220	220	1,940
108 Discharge of student loan indebtedness	80	90	90	100	100	110	120	130	150	160	170	1,220
109 Qualified school construction bonds [9]	450	430	410	390	370	350	330	310	290	270	250	3,400
Training, employment, and social services:												
110 Work opportunity tax credit	450	370	140	70	50	40	30	20	20	10	10	760
111 Employer-provided child care exclusion	570	610	660	710	770	830	900	1,230	1,430	1,510	1,590	10,240
112 Employer-provided child care credit	0	0	0	0	0	0	0	0	0	0	0	0
113 Assistance for adopted foster children	590	620	660	700	750	800	850	900	960	1,020	1,080	8,340
114 Adoption credit and exclusion	700	770	790	830	860	880	900	910	920	930	940	8,730
115 Exclusion of employee meals and lodging (other than military)	5,410	5,570	5,760	5,980	6,210	6,470	6,870	8,020	8,730	9,100	9,520	72,230
116 Credit for child and dependent care expenses	4,260	4,360	4,440	4,540	4,690	4,780	4,890	5,100	5,320	5,390	5,400	48,910
117 Credit for disabled access expenditures	10	10	10	10	10	10	10	10	10	10	10	100

Table 13–2B. ESTIMATES OF TOTAL INDIVIDUAL INCOME TAX EXPENDITURES FOR FISCAL YEARS 2019–2029—Continued

(In millions of dollars)

		Total from individuals										
		2019	2020	2021	2022	2023	2024	2025	2026	2027	2028	2029	2020–29
118	Deductibility of charitable contributions, other than education and health	35,500	38,330	41,510	44,210	46,920	49,640	52,290	63,270	83,230	87,160	91,280	597,840
119	Exclusion of certain foster care payments	480	490	510	510	520	530	540	540	540	540	560	5,280
120	Exclusion of parsonage allowances	870	920	970	1,020	1,080	1,130	1,190	1,260	1,320	1,390	1,470	11,750
121	Indian employment credit	20	10	10	10	10	10	10	10	10	10	10	100
122	Credit for employer differential wage payments	0	0	0	0	0	0	0	10	10	10	10	40
Health:													
123	Exclusion of employer contributions for medical insurance premiums and medical care [10]	202,290	214,420	227,880	242,230	258,730	276,820	295,050	348,700	389,240	413,090	438,240	3,104,400
124	Self-employed medical insurance premiums	7,050	7,320	7,780	8,320	8,870	9,420	10,120	11,730	13,080	13,900	14,670	105,210
125	Medical Savings Accounts / Health Savings Accounts	7,880	8,510	9,110	9,800	10,380	10,900	11,410	12,970	14,100	14,680	15,350	117,210
126	Deductibility of medical expenses	6,500	6,640	7,310	8,140	9,050	10,030	11,090	17,270	21,690	23,780	25,990	140,990
127	Exclusion of interest on hospital construction bonds	2,320	2,480	2,530	2,660	2,850	2,920	2,960	3,120	3,280	3,350	3,360	29,510
128	Refundable Premium Assistance Tax Credit [11]	7,040	3,910	4,110	3,690	3,590	3,370	3,740	4,810	5,380	5,660	5,980	44,240
129	Credit for employee health insurance expenses of small business [12]	50	40	30	20	10	10	10	0	0	0	0	120
130	Deductibility of charitable contributions (health)	3,960	4,270	4,620	4,930	5,230	5,530	5,820	7,050	9,270	9,710	10,170	66,600
131	Tax credit for orphan drug research	20	20	30	30	40	50	50	60	70	80	100	530
132	Special Blue Cross/Blue Shield tax benefits	0	0	0	0	0	0	0	0	0	0	0	0
133	Tax credit for health insurance purchased by certain displaced and retired individuals [13]	10	0	0	0	0	0	0	0	0	0	0	0
134	Distributions from retirement plans for premiums for health and long-term care insurance	420	430	450	460	470	490	500	590	630	650	660	5,330
Income security:													
135	Child credit [14]	74,880	75,770	76,530	77,100	77,740	78,300	78,990	55,850	20,650	20,450	20,240	581,620
136	Exclusion of railroad retirement (Social Security equivalent) benefits	230	220	210	200	190	180	170	170	180	180	170	1,870
137	Exclusion of workers' compensation benefits	9,680	9,770	9,870	9,970	10,070	10,170	10,270	10,370	10,470	10,570	10,680	102,210
138	Exclusion of public assistance benefits (normal tax method)	660	680	690	710	730	760	780	790	810	820	750	7,520
139	Exclusion of special benefits for disabled coal miners	20	20	20	10	10	10	10	10	10	10	10	120
140	Exclusion of military disability pensions	150	160	160	160	160	170	170	190	200	200	210	1,780
	Net exclusion of pension contributions and earnings:												
141	Defined benefit employer plans	71,653	73,831	75,807	78,012	79,560	80,979	81,129	83,516	84,065	85,124	86,795	808,818
142	Defined contribution employer plans	75,680	83,520	90,680	100,410	109,170	117,650	125,990	149,560	162,650	173,070	184,180	1,296,880
143	Individual Retirement Accounts	20,520	21,650	22,760	23,990	25,490	27,220	29,300	33,310	36,390	39,840	43,430	303,380
144	Low and moderate income savers credit	1,180	1,180	1,180	1,220	1,220	1,210	1,240	1,350	1,350	1,340	1,330	12,620
145	Self-Employed plans	24,150	26,580	29,250	32,070	34,900	38,560	42,770	50,570	62,750	69,180	75,380	462,010
	Exclusion of other employee benefits:												
146	Premiums on group term life insurance	2,960	3,080	3,200	3,320	3,450	3,580	3,710	4,210	4,480	4,640	4,790	38,460
147	Premiums on accident and disability insurance	330	330	340	340	340	350	350	350	350	350	350	3,450
148	Income of trusts to finance supplementary unemployment benefits	30	30	40	40	50	50	50	60	60	60	60	500
149	Income of trusts to finance voluntary employee benefits associations	990	1,060	1,130	1,210	1,280	1,360	1,440	1,610	1,700	1,800	1,900	14,490
150	Special ESOP rules	130	130	140	140	150	150	160	160	170	170	180	1,550
151	Additional deduction for the blind	40	40	40	40	40	50	50	50	60	60	70	500
152	Additional deduction for the elderly	4,990	5,290	5,680	6,150	6,490	6,910	7,340	6,950	7,030	7,480	8,010	67,330
153	Tax credit for the elderly and disabled	0	0	0	0	0	0	0	0	0	0	0	0
154	Deductibility of casualty losses	0	0	0	0	0	0	0	380	600	640	680	2,300
155	Earned income tax credit [15]	2,700	2,660	2,700	2,770	2,840	2,920	3,010	3,080	10,490	10,730	11,070	52,270
Social Security:													
	Exclusion of Social Security benefits:												
156	Social Security benefits for retired and disabled workers and spouses, dependents and survivors	29,100	30,900	32,490	33,990	35,640	36,330	36,430	41,480	48,460	50,590	52,670	398,980
157	Credit for certain employer contributions to Social Security	920	950	970	1,000	1,030	1,050	1,080	1,110	1,140	1,160	1,190	10,680
Veterans benefits and services:													

Table 13–2B.   ESTIMATES OF TOTAL INDIVIDUAL INCOME TAX EXPENDITURES FOR FISCAL YEARS 2019–2029—Continued

(In millions of dollars)

	Total from individuals											
	2019	2020	2021	2022	2023	2024	2025	2026	2027	2028	2029	2020–29
158 Exclusion of veterans death benefits and disability compensation	7,590	8,340	8,910	9,200	9,500	9,820	10,150	10,950	12,380	12,790	13,230	105,270
159 Exclusion of veterans pensions	240	240	250	250	260	260	260	280	310	320	320	2,750
160 Exclusion of G.I. bill benefits	1,460	1,530	1,590	1,650	1,720	1,780	1,850	2,010	2,290	2,370	2,470	19,260
161 Exclusion of interest on veterans housing bonds	40	50	50	50	50	50	50	60	60	60	60	540
General purpose fiscal assistance:												
162 Exclusion of interest on public purpose State and local bonds	20,220	21,650	22,100	23,220	24,840	25,490	25,830	27,240	28,630	29,210	29,310	257,520
163 Build America Bonds [16]	0	0	0	0	0	0	0	0	0	0	0	0
164 Deductibility of nonbusiness State and local taxes other than on owner-occupied homes [17]	4,430	7,110	7,510	7,920	8,310	8,660	8,990	78,340	117,330	124,170	131,130	499,470
Interest:												
165 Deferral of interest on U.S. savings bonds	850	840	840	830	820	810	800	790	840	860	880	8,310
Addendum: Aid to State and local governments:												
Deductibility of:												
Property taxes on owner-occupied homes	6,010	6,270	6,650	7,030	7,400	7,740	8,090	39,930	58,030	61,630	65,340	268,110
Nonbusiness State and local taxes other than on owner-occupied homes	4,430	7,110	7,510	7,920	8,310	8,660	8,990	78,340	117,330	124,170	131,130	499,470
Exclusion of interest on State and local bonds for:												
Public purposes	20,220	21,650	22,100	23,220	24,840	25,490	25,830	27,240	28,630	29,210	29,310	257,520
Energy facilities	10	10	10	10	10	10	10	10	10	10	10	100
Water, sewage, and hazardous waste disposal facilities	260	280	280	300	320	320	330	350	360	370	370	3,280
Small-issues	90	100	100	110	110	120	120	120	130	130	130	1,170
Owner-occupied mortgage subsidies	690	740	760	800	850	880	890	940	980	1,000	1,010	8,850
Rental housing	900	960	980	1,030	1,100	1,130	1,140	1,210	1,270	1,290	1,300	11,410
Airports, docks, and similar facilities	530	570	580	610	650	670	680	720	750	770	770	6,770
Student loans	170	180	180	190	200	210	210	220	240	240	240	2,110
Private nonprofit educational facilities	1,610	1,720	1,760	1,850	1,970	2,030	2,050	2,170	2,280	2,320	2,330	20,480
Hospital construction	2,320	2,480	2,530	2,660	2,850	2,920	2,960	3,120	3,280	3,350	3,360	29,510
Veterans' housing	40	50	50	50	50	50	50	60	60	60	60	540

See Table 13-1 footnotes for specific table information

Table 13–3. INCOME TAX EXPENDITURES RANKED BY TOTAL FISCAL YEAR 2020–2029 PROJECTED REVENUE EFFECT

(In millions of dollars)

	Provision	2020	2021	2020–2029
123	Exclusion of employer contributions for medical insurance premiums	214,420	227,880	3,104,400
60	Exclusion of net imputed rental income	125,990	130,430	1,634,790
142	Defined contribution employer plans	83,520	90,680	1,296,880
67	Capital gains (except agriculture, timber, iron ore, and coal)	104,920	103,790	1,227,330
141	Defined benefit employer plans	73,831	75,807	808,818
69	Step-up basis of capital gains at death	51,750	53,640	659,310
56	Deductibility of mortgage interest on owner-occupied homes	27,090	29,580	644,740
118	Deductibility of charitable contributions, other than education and health	39,540	42,760	612,250
59	Capital gains exclusion on home sales	45,750	48,040	593,710
135	Child credit [14]	75,770	76,530	581,620
164	Deductibility of nonbusiness State and local taxes other than	7,110	7,510	499,470
5	Reduced tax rate on active income of controlled	40,000	42,980	480,080
145	Self-Employed plans	26,580	29,250	462,010
66	Treatment of qualified dividends	31,530	32,410	420,010
156	Social Security benefits for retired and disabled workers and spouses, dependents and survivors	30,900	32,490	398,980
78	Allow 20-percent deduction to certain pass-through income	53,132	54,698	373,280
143	Individual Retirement Accounts	21,650	22,760	303,380
162	Exclusion of interest on public purpose State and local bonds	24,580	24,340	277,060
57	Deductibility of State and local property tax on owner-occupied homes [17]	6,270	6,650	268,110
9	Credit for increasing research activities	16,810	18,380	237,830
50	Exclusion of life insurance death benefits	13,760	14,340	166,240
96	Tax credits and deductions for postsecondary education expenses [7]	16,390	16,310	164,990
126	Deductibility of medical expenses	6,640	7,310	140,990
1	Exclusion of benefits and allowances to Armed Forces personnel	12,910	11,660	132,440
63	Accelerated depreciation on rental housing (normal tax method)	8,370	8,800	125,440
125	Medical Savings Accounts / Health Savings Accounts	8,510	9,110	117,210
130	Deductibility of charitable contributions (health)	8,080	8,650	114,460
158	Exclusion of veterans death benefits and disability compensation	8,340	8,910	105,270
124	Self-employed medical insurance premiums	7,320	7,780	105,210
137	Exclusion of workers' compensation benefits	9,770	9,870	102,210
62	Credit for low-income housing investments	9,110	9,360	101,900
6	Deduction for foreign-derived intangible income dervied from	8,100	9,880	96,820
2	Exclusion of income earned abroad by U.S. citizens	7,280	7,640	91,520
75	Expensing of certain small investments (normal tax method)	–710	–10	86,400
61	Exception from passive loss rules for $25,000 of rental loss	6,430	6,780	83,970
115	Exclusion of employee meals and lodging (other than military)	5,240	5,420	68,110
105	Deductibility of charitable contributions (education)	4,450	4,790	67,540
152	Additional deduction for the elderly	5,290	5,680	67,330
131	Tax credit for orphan drug research	1,870	2,280	52,510
72	Deferral of gains from like-kind exchanges	2,980	3,140	37,560
155	Earned income tax credit [15]	2,660	2,700	52,270
116	Credit for child and dependent care expenses	4,360	4,440	48,910
99	Qualified tuition programs	2,410	2,650	46,120
95	Exclusion of scholarship and fellowship income (normal tax method)	3,220	3,390	44,640
128	Refundable Premium Assistance Tax Credit [11]	3,910	4,110	44,240
146	Premiums on group term life insurance	3,080	3,200	38,460
16	Energy production credit [1]	4,310	4,290	33,750
104	Parental personal exemption for students age 19 or over	0	0	31,770
127	Exclusion of interest on hospital construction bonds	2,820	2,790	31,760
70	Carryover basis of capital gains on gifts	3,150	3,010	27,890
18	Energy investment credit [1]	4,510	4,820	26,920
81	Exclusion of reimbursed employee parking expenses	2,270	2,400	26,650
74	Accelerated depreciation of machinery and equipment (normal tax method)	43,460	40,610	25,060
98	Deductibility of student-loan interest	2,040	2,060	24,140
150	Special ESOP rules	2,150	2,210	24,040
101	Exclusion of interest on bonds for private nonprofit educational facilities	1,950	1,940	22,020
49	Exemption of credit union income	1,764	1,587	21,878
160	Exclusion of G.I. bill benefits	1,530	1,590	19,260
68	Capital gains exclusion of small corporation stock	1,410	1,530	18,600

Table 13–3. INCOME TAX EXPENDITURES RANKED BY TOTAL FISCAL YEAR 2020–2029 PROJECTED REVENUE EFFECT—Continued

(In millions of dollars)

	Provision	2020	2021	2020–2029
157	Credit for certain employer contributions to Social Security	1,480	1,540	17,690
58	Deferral of income from installment sales	1,480	1,520	17,680
7	Interest Charge Domestic International Sales Corporations (IC-DISCs)	1,340	1,410	16,910
45	Capital gains treatment of certain agriculture income	1,410	1,390	16,450
149	Income of trusts to finance voluntary employee benefits associations	1,060	1,130	14,490
53	Exclusion of interest spread of financial institutions	1,120	1,160	13,270
106	Exclusion of employer-provided educational assistance	930	980	12,720
144	Low and moderate income savers credit	1,180	1,180	12,620
55	Exclusion of interest on rental housing bonds	1,090	1,080	12,280
120	Exclusion of parsonage allowances	920	970	11,750
11	Excess of percentage over cost depletion, fuels	760	820	10,610
111	Employer-provided child care exclusion	610	660	10,240
39	Tax incentives for preservation of historic structures	730	690	9,980
54	Exclusion of interest on owner-occupied mortgage subsidy bonds	840	840	9,520
114	Adoption credit and exclusion	770	790	8,730
113	Assistance for adopted foster children	620	660	8,340
165	Deferral of interest on U.S. savings bonds	840	840	8,310
138	Exclusion of public assistance benefits (normal tax method)	680	690	7,520
86	Exclusion of interest for airport, dock, and similar bonds	650	640	7,290
10	Expensing of exploration and development costs, fuels	1,060	890	7,090
22	Exclusion of utility conservation subsidies	470	490	5,830
134	Distributions from retirement plans for premiums for health	430	450	5,330
119	Exclusion of certain foster care payments	490	510	5,280
82	Exclusion for employer-provided transit passes	380	420	5,030
15	Enhanced oil recovery credit	440	320	4,910
89	New markets tax credit	1,280	1,210	4,730
109	Qualified school construction bonds [9]	570	540	4,520
132	Special Blue Cross/Blue Shield tax benefits	230	260	3,850
52	Tax exemption of insurance income earned by tax-exempt organizations	330	340	3,810
43	Expensing of certain multiperiod production costs	270	280	3,660
29	Credit for residential energy efficient property	1,740	1,410	3,580
36	Exclusion of interest on bonds for water, sewage, and hazardous waste facilities	320	310	3,520
147	Premiums on accident and disability insurance	330	340	3,450
26	Amortize all geological and geophysical expenditures over 2 years	250	260	3,170
3	Exclusion of certain allowances for Federal employees abroad	250	260	3,140
110	Work opportunity tax credit	1,280	560	3,080
21	Tax credits for clean-fuel burning vehicles and refueling property	580	380	2,980
159	Exclusion of veterans pensions	240	250	2,750
40	Carbon oxide sequestration credit	90	120	2,330
154	Deductibility of casualty losses	0	0	2,300
100	Exclusion of interest on student-loan bonds	200	200	2,260
46	Income averaging for farmers	180	190	2,110
107	Special deduction for teacher expenses	180	180	1,940
32	Advanced nuclear power production credit	0	0	1,910
136	Exclusion of railroad retirement (Social Security equivalent) benefits	220	210	1,870
35	Excess of percentage over cost depletion, nonfuel minerals	130	140	1,860
140	Exclusion of military disability pensions	160	160	1,780
13	Capital gains treatment of royalties on coal	140	140	1,640
37	Capital gains treatment of certain timber income	140	140	1,640
42	Expensing of certain capital outlays	90	110	1,570
51	Exemption or special alternative tax for small property and casualty	120	130	1,470
84	Exclusion of interest on bonds for Highway Projects and rail-truck transfer facilities	170	160	1,370
76	Exclusion of interest on small issue bonds	110	110	1,270
33	Reduced tax rate for nuclear decommissioning funds	100	110	1,260
34	Expensing of exploration and development costs, nonfuel minerals	180	160	1,230
90	Credit to holders of Gulf Tax Credit Bonds.	150	140	1,220
108	Discharge of student loan indebtedness	90	90	1,220
79	Tonnage tax	90	90	1,070
87	Exemption of certain mutuals' and cooperatives' income	90	100	1,050

Table 13–3. INCOME TAX EXPENDITURES RANKED BY TOTAL FISCAL YEAR 2020–2029 PROJECTED REVENUE EFFECT—Continued

(In millions of dollars)

Provision	2020	2021	2020–2029
93 Opportunity Zones	3,620	2,650	960
65 Exceptions from imputed interest rules	60	60	830
102 Credit for holders of zone academy bonds [8]	150	130	800
71 Ordinary income treatment of loss from small business corporation stock sale	70	70	780
38 Expensing of multiperiod timber growing costs	40	60	720
48 Expensing of reforestation expenditures	40	60	720
23 Credit for holding clean renewable energy bonds [4]	70	70	700
91 Recovery Zone Bonds [6]	90	80	690
44 Treatment of loans forgiven for solvent farmers	50	50	630
24 Credit for investment in clean coal facilities	10	20	610
161 Exclusion of interest on veterans housing bonds	60	50	550
151 Additional deduction for the blind	40	40	500
148 Income of trusts to finance supplementary unemployment benefits	30	40	500
103 Exclusion of interest on savings bonds redeemed to finance educational	30	40	430
41 Deduction for endangered species recovery expenditures	30	30	420
17 Marginal wells credit	80	100	410
97 Education Individual Retirement Accounts	40	40	400
94 Employee retention credit	70	50	360
64 Discharge of business indebtedness	40	40	360
30 Qualified energy conservation bonds [5]	30	30	300
112 Employer-provided child care credit	20	20	210
47 Deferral of gain on sale of farm refiners	15	15	185
129 Credit for employee health insurance expenses of small business [12]	50	40	150
121 Indian employment credit	20	20	140
122 Credit for employer differential wage payments	10	10	140
88 Empowerment zones	40	20	130
139 Exclusion of special benefits for disabled coal miners	20	20	120
31 Advanced Energy Property Credit	10	10	100
14 Exclusion of interest on energy facility bonds	10	10	100
80 Deferral of tax on shipping companies	10	10	100
92 Tribal Economic Development Bonds	10	10	100
117 Credit for disabled access expenditures	10	10	100
12 Exception from passive loss limitation for working interests in oil and gas properties	10	10	100
83 Tax credit for certain expenditures for maintaining railroad tracks	30	20	90
28 Credit for construction of new energy efficient homes	10	10	20
85 Investment credit for rehabilitation of structures (other than historic)	10	0	10
77 Special rules for certain film and TV production	10	0	10
27 Allowance of deduction for certain energy efficient commercial building property	0	0	0
133 Tax credit for health insurance purchased by certain displaced	0	0	0
4 Inventory property sales source rules exception	0	0	0
19 Alcohol fuel credits [2]	0	0	0
20 Bio-Diesel and small agri-biodiesel producer tax credits [3]	0	0	0
153 Tax credit for the elderly and disabled	0	0	0
163 Build America Bonds [16]	0	0	0
25 Natural gas distribution pipelines treated as 15-year property	70	50	−530
73 Depreciation of buildings other than rental housing (normal tax method)	−1,870	−2,340	−45,970
8 Expensing of research and experimentation expenditures (normal tax method)	5,740	6,330	−88,220

See Table 13-1 footnotes for specific table information

Table 13–4. PRESENT VALUE OF SELECTED TAX EXPENDITURES FOR ACTIVITY IN CALENDAR YEAR 2019

(In millions of dollars)

	Provision	2019 Present Value of Revenue Loss
8	Expensing of research and experimentation expenditures (normal tax method)	2,280
23	Credit for holding clean renewable energy bonds	0
10	Expensing of exploration and development costs - fuels	840
34	Expensing of exploration and development costs - nonfuels	150
38	Expensing of multiperiod timber growing costs	150
43	Expensing of certain multiperiod production costs - agriculture	–30
42	Expensing of certain capital outlays - agriculture	0
48	Expensing of reforestation expenditures	30
63	Accelerated depreciation on rental housing	9,370
73	Depreciation of buildings other than rental	–3,250
74	Accelerated depreciation of machinery and equipment	22,460
78	Expensing of certain small investments (normal tax method)	500
102	Credit for holders of zone academy bonds	160
62	Credit for low-income housing investments	10,190
99	Qualified tuition programs	4,870
141	Defined benefit employer plans	36,274
142	Defined contribution employer plans	95,050
143	Exclusion of IRA contributions and earnings	2,260
143	Exclusion of Roth earnings and distributions	5,220
143	Exclusion of non-deductible IRA earnings	620
145	Exclusion of contributions and earnings for Self-Employed plans	6,010
162	Exclusion of interest on public-purpose bonds	19,390
	Exclusion of interest on non-public purpose bonds	6,380
165	Deferral of interest on U.S. savings bonds	240

the foreign source income. In contrast, the sales source rules for inventory property under current law allow U.S. exporters to use more foreign tax credits by allowing the exporters to attribute a larger portion of their earnings to foreign sources than would be the case if the allocation of earnings was based on actual economic activity. This exception was repealed for tax years beginning after December 31, 2017. Under the new provision, gains, profits, and income from the sale or exchange of inventory property produced partly in, and partly outside, the United States is allocated and apportioned on the basis of the location of production with respect to the property.

5. *Reduced tax rate on active income of controlled foreign corporations.*—Under the baseline tax system, worldwide income forms the tax base of U.S. corporations. In contrast, U.S. tax law exempts or preferentially taxes certain portions of this income. Prior to the passage of the Tax Cuts and Jobs Act (TCJA) effective January 1, 2018, active foreign income was generally taxed only upon repatriation. TCJA changed these rules, so that certain active income (called "Global Intangible Low Tax Income" or "GILTI") is taxed currently, even if it is not distributed. However, U.S. corporations generally receive a 50 percent deduction from U.S. tax on their GILTI (the deduction decreases to 37.5 percent in 2026), resulting in a substantially reduced rate of tax. In addition, some active income is excluded from tax, and distributions out

of active income are no longer taxed upon repatriation. These reductions and exemptions from U.S. taxation are considered tax expenditures. However, U.S. shareholders of specified foreign corporations must include their pro rata share of accumulated post-1986 deferred foreign income (as of the last taxable year before January 1, 2018) in U.S. taxable income, and this inclusion acts as an offset to the reduced tax rate on CFC income in the years in which the payments are received.

6. *Deduction for foreign-derived intangible income derived from a trade or business within the United States.*—Under the baseline tax system, the United States taxes income earned by U.S. corporations from serving foreign markets (e.g., exports and royalties) at the full U.S. rate. After the passage of TCJA, domestic corporations are allowed a deduction equal to 37.5 percent of "foreign-derived intangible income," which is essentially income from serving foreign markets (defined on a formulaic basis). The deduction falls to 21.875 percent in 2026.

7. *Interest Charge Domestic International Sales Corporations (IC-DISCs).*—Under the baseline tax system, taxpayer earnings are subject to tax using the regular tax rates applied to all taxpayers. In contrast, IC-DISCs allow income from exports to be taxed at the qualified dividend rate of 20 percent.

General Science, Space, and Technology

8. **Expensing of research and experimentation expenditures (normal tax method).**—The baseline tax system allows a deduction for the cost of producing income. It requires taxpayers to capitalize the costs associated with investments over time to better match the streams of income and associated costs. Research and experimentation (R&E) projects can be viewed as investments because, if successful, their benefits accrue for several years. It is often difficult, however, to identify whether a specific R&E project is successful and, if successful, what its expected life will be. Because of this ambiguity, the reference tax law baseline system would allow expensing of R&E expenditures. In contrast, under the normal tax method, the expensing of R&E expenditures is viewed as a tax expenditure. The baseline assumed for the normal tax method is that all R&E expenditures are successful and have an expected life of five years. Current law requires R&E expenditures paid or incurred in taxable years beginning after December 31, 2021, to be capitalized and amortized over 5 years, while allowing R&E expenditures paid or incurred in prior taxable years to be expensed.

9. **Credit for increasing research activities.**—The baseline tax system would uniformly tax all returns to investments and not allow credits for particular activities, investments, or industries. In contrast, the Tax Code allows an R&E credit of up to 20 percent of qualified research expenditures in excess of a base amount. The base amount of the credit is generally determined by multiplying a "fixed-base percentage" by the average amount of the company's gross receipts for the prior four years. The taxpayer's fixed base percentage generally is the ratio of its research expenses to gross receipts for 1984 through 1988. Taxpayers can elect the alternative simplified credit regime, which equals 14 percent of qualified research expenses that exceed 50 percent of the average qualified research expenses for the three preceding taxable years.

Energy

10. **Expensing of exploration and development costs, fuels.**—Under the baseline tax system, the costs of exploring and developing oil and gas wells and coal mines or other natural fuel deposits would be capitalized and then amortized (or depreciated) over an estimate of the economic life of the property. This insures that the net income from the well or mine is measured appropriately each year. In contrast to this treatment, current law allows immediate deduction, i.e., expensing, of intangible drilling costs for successful investments in domestic oil and gas wells (such as wages, the cost of using machinery for grading and drilling, and the cost of unsalvageable materials used in constructing wells). Current law also allows immediate deduction of eligible exploration and development costs for domestic coal mines and other natural fuel deposits. Because expensing allows recovery of costs sooner, it is more advantageous to the taxpayer than amortization. Expensing provisions for exploration expenditures apply only to properties for which a deduc-tion for percentage depletion is allowable. For oil and gas wells, integrated oil companies may expense only 70 percent of intangible drilling costs and must amortize the remaining 30 percent over five years. Non-integrated oil companies may expense all such costs.

11. **Excess of percentage over cost depletion, fuels.**—The baseline tax system would allow recovery of the costs of developing certain oil, gas, and mineral fuel properties using cost depletion. Cost depletion is similar in concept to depreciation, in that the costs of developing or acquiring the asset are capitalized and then gradually reduced over an estimate of the asset's economic life, as is appropriate for measuring net income. In contrast, the Tax Code generally allows independent fuel producers and royalty owners to take percentage depletion deductions rather than cost depletion on limited quantities of output. Under percentage depletion, taxpayers deduct a percentage of gross income from fossil fuel production. In certain cases the deduction is limited to a fraction of the asset's net income. Over the life of an investment, percentage depletion deductions can exceed the cost of the investment. Consequently, percentage depletion may provide more advantageous tax treatment than would cost depletion, which limits deductions to an investment's cost.

12. **Exception from passive loss limitation for working interests in oil and gas properties.**—The baseline tax system accepts current law's general rule limiting taxpayers' ability to deduct losses from passive activities against nonpassive income (e.g., wages, interest, and dividends). Passive activities generally are defined as those in which the taxpayer does not materially participate, and there are numerous additional considerations brought to bear on the determination of which activities are passive for a given taxpayer. Losses are limited in an attempt to limit tax sheltering activities. Passive losses that are unused may be carried forward and applied against future passive income. An exception from the passive loss limitation is provided for a working interest in an oil or gas property that the taxpayer holds directly or through an entity that does not limit the liability of the taxpayer with respect to the interest. Thus, taxpayers can deduct losses from such working interests against nonpassive income without regard to whether they materially participate in the activity.

13. **Capital gains treatment of royalties on coal.**—The baseline tax system generally would tax all income under the regular tax rate schedule. It would not allow preferentially low tax rates to apply to certain types or sources of income. For individuals, tax rates on regular income vary from 10 percent to 39.6 percent in the budget window (plus a 3.8 percent surtax on high income taxpayers), depending on the taxpayer's income. In contrast, current law allows capital gains realized by individuals to be taxed at a preferentially low rate that is no higher than 20 percent (plus the 3.8 percent surtax). Certain sales of coal under royalty contracts qualify for taxation as capital gains rather than ordinary income, and so benefit from the preferentially low 20 percent maximum tax rate on capital gains.

14. ***Exclusion of interest on energy facility bonds.***—The baseline tax system generally would tax all income under the regular tax rate schedule. It would not allow preferentially low (or zero) tax rates to apply to certain types or sources of income. In contrast, the Tax Code allows interest earned on State and local bonds used to finance construction of certain energy facilities to be exempt from tax. These bonds are generally subject to the State private-activity-bond annual volume cap.

15. ***Enhanced oil recovery credit.***—A credit is provided equal to 15 percent of the taxpayer's costs for enhanced oil recovery on U.S. projects. The credit is reduced in proportion to the ratio of the reference price of oil for the previous calendar year minus $28 (adjusted for inflation from 1990) to $6.

16. ***Energy production credit.***—The baseline tax system would not allow credits for particular activities, investments, or industries. Instead, it generally would seek to tax uniformly all returns from investment-like activities. In contrast, the Tax Code provides a credit for certain electricity produced from wind energy, biomass, geothermal energy, solar energy, small irrigation power, municipal solid waste, or qualified hydropower and sold to an unrelated party. Wind facilities must have begun construction before January 1, 2020. Facilities that begin construction in 2017 receive 80 percent of the credit, facilities that begin construction in 2018 receive 60 percent of the credit, and facilities that begin construction in 2019 receive 40 percent of the credit. Qualified facilities producing electricity from sources other than wind must begin construction before January 1, 2018. In addition to the electricity production credit, an income tax credit is allowed for the production of refined coal for facilities placed in service before January 1, 2012. The Tax Code also provided an income tax credit for Indian coal facilities. The Indian coal facilities credit expired on December 31, 2017.

17. ***Marginal wells credit.***—A credit is provided for crude oil and natural gas produced from a qualified marginal well. A marginal well is one that does not produce more than 1,095 barrel-of-oil equivalents per year, with this limit adjusted proportionately for the number of days the well is in production. The credit is no more than $3.00 per barrel of qualified crude oil production and $0.50 per thousand cubic feet of qualified natural gas production. The credit for natural gas is reduced in proportion to the amount by which the reference price of natural gas at the wellhead for the previous calendar year exceeds $1.67 per thousand cubic feet and is zero for a reference price that exceeds $2.00. The credit for crude oil is reduced in proportion to the amount by which the reference price of oil for the previous calendar year exceeds $15.00 per barrel and is zero for a reference price that exceeds $18.00. All dollar amounts are adjusted for inflation from 2004.

18. ***Energy investment credit.***—The baseline tax system would not allow credits for particular activities, investments, or industries. Instead, it generally would seek to tax uniformly all returns from investment-like activities. However, the Tax Code provides credits for investments in solar and geothermal energy property, qualified fuel cell power plants, stationary microturbine power plants, geothermal heat pumps, small wind property and combined heat and power property. The credit is 30 percent for property that begins construction before 2020, 26 percent for property that begins construction in 2020, and 22 percent for property that begins construction in 2021 and in all cases that is placed in service before January 1, 2024. A 10 percent credit is available for geothermal or qualified solar property placed in service after December 31, 2023. Owners of renewable power facilities that qualify for the energy production credit may instead elect to take an energy investment credit at a rate specified by law.

19. ***Alcohol fuel credits.***—The baseline tax system would not allow credits for particular activities, investments, or industries. Instead, it generally would seek to tax uniformly all returns from investment-like activities. In contrast, the Tax Code provided an income tax credit for qualified cellulosic biofuel production which was renamed the Second Generation Biofuel Producer Tax Credit. This provision expired on December 31, 2017.

20. ***Bio-diesel and small agri-biodiesel producer tax credits.***—The baseline tax system would not allow credits for particular activities, investments, or industries. Instead, it generally would seek to tax uniformly all returns from investment-like activities. However, the Tax Code allowed an income tax credit for Bio-diesel and for Bio-diesel derived from virgin sources. In lieu of the Bio-diesel credit, the taxpayer could claim a refundable excise tax credit. In addition, small agri-biodiesel producers were eligible for a separate income tax credit for biodiesel production, and a separate credit was available for qualified renewable diesel fuel mixtures. This provision expired on December 31, 2017.

21. ***Tax credits for clean-fuel burning vehicles and refueling property.***—The baseline tax system would not allow credits for particular activities, investments, or industries. Instead, it generally would seek to tax uniformly all returns from investment-like activities. In contrast, the Tax Code allows credits for plug-in electric-drive motor vehicles, alternative fuel vehicle refueling property, two-wheeled plug-in electric vehicles, and fuel cell motor vehicles. These provisions, except for the plug-in electric-drive motor vehicle credit, expired after December 31, 2017.

22. ***Exclusion of utility conservation subsidies.***—The baseline tax system generally takes a comprehensive view of taxable income that includes a wide variety of (measurable) accretions to wealth. In certain circumstances, public utilities offer rate subsidies to non-business customers who invest in energy conservation measures. These rate subsidies are equivalent to payments from the utility to its customer, and so represent accretions to wealth, income that would be taxable to the customer under the baseline tax system. In contrast, the Tax Code exempts these subsidies from the non-business customer's gross income.

23. ***Credit for holding clean renewable energy bonds.***—The baseline tax system would uniformly tax all returns to investments and not allow credits for particu-

lar activities, investments, or industries. In contrast, the Tax Code provides for the issuance of Clean Renewable Energy Bonds that entitle the bond holder to a Federal income tax credit in lieu of interest. As of March 2010, issuers of the unused authorization of such bonds could opt to receive direct payment with the yield becoming fully taxable.

24. *Credit for investment in clean coal facilities.*—The baseline tax system would uniformly tax all returns to investments and not allow credits for particular activities, investments, or industries. In contrast, the Tax Code provides investment tax credits for clean coal facilities producing electricity and for industrial gasification combined cycle projects.

25. *Natural gas distribution pipelines treated as 15-year property.*—The baseline tax system allows taxpayers to deduct the decline in the economic value of an investment over its economic life. However, the Tax Code allows depreciation of natural gas distribution pipelines (placed in service between 2005 and 2011) over a 15 year period. These deductions are accelerated relative to deductions based on economic depreciation.

26. *Amortize all geological and geophysical expenditures over two years.*—The baseline tax system allows taxpayers to deduct the decline in the economic value of an investment over its economic life. However, the Tax Code allows geological and geophysical expenditures incurred in connection with oil and gas exploration in the United States to be amortized over two years for non-integrated oil companies, a span of time that is generally shorter than the economic life of the assets.

27. *Allowance of deduction for certain energy efficient commercial building property.*—The baseline tax system would not allow deductions in lieu of normal depreciation allowances for particular investments in particular industries. Instead, it generally would seek to tax uniformly all returns from investment-like activities. In contrast, the Tax Code allows a deduction for certain energy efficient commercial building property. The basis of such property is reduced by the amount of the deduction. This provision expired on December 31, 2017.

28. *Credit for construction of new energy efficient homes.*—The baseline tax system would not allow credits for particular activities, investments, or industries. Instead, it generally would seek to tax uniformly all returns from investment-like activities. However, the Tax Code allowed contractors a tax credit of $2,000 for the construction of a qualified new energy-efficient home that had an annual level of heating and cooling energy consumption at least 50 percent below the annual consumption under the 2006 International Energy Conservation Code. The credit equaled $1,000 in the case of a new manufactured home that met a 30 percent standard or requirements for EPA's Energy Star homes. This provision expired on December 31, 2017.

29. *Credit for residential energy efficient property.*—The baseline tax system would uniformly tax all returns to investments and not allow credits for particular activities, investments, or industries. However, the Tax Code provides a credit for the purchase of a qualified photovoltaic property and solar water heating property, as well as for fuel cell power plants, geothermal heat pumps, and small wind property used in or placed on a residence. The credit is 30 percent for property placed in service before January 1, 2020, 26 percent for property placed in service in 2020, and 22 percent for property placed in service in 2021.

30. *Credit for qualified energy conservation bonds.*—The baseline tax system would uniformly tax all returns to investments and not allow credits for particular activities, investments, or industries. However, the Tax Code provides for the issuance of energy conservation bonds which entitle the bond holder to a Federal income tax credit in lieu of interest. As of March 2010, issuers of the unused authorization of such bonds could opt to receive direct payment with the yield becoming fully taxable.

31. *Advanced energy property credit.*—The baseline tax system would not allow credits for particular activities, investments, or industries. However, the Tax Code provides a 30 percent investment credit for property used in a qualified advanced energy manufacturing project. The Department of the Treasury may award up to $2.3 billion in tax credits for qualified investments.

32. *Advanced nuclear power facilities production credit.*—The baseline tax system would not allow credits or deductions for particular activities, investments, or industries. Instead, it generally would seek to tax uniformly all returns from investment-like activities. In contrast, the Tax Code allows a tax credit equal to 1.8 cents times the number of kilowatt hours of electricity produced at a qualifying advanced nuclear power facility. A taxpayer may claim no more than $125 million per 1,000 megawatts of capacity. The Department of the Treasury may allocate up to 6,000 megawatts of credit-eligible capacity. Any unutilized national capacity limitation shall be allocated after December 31, 2020, according to prioritization rules set forth by statute.

33. *Reduced tax rate for nuclear decommissioning funds.*—The baseline tax system would uniformly tax all returns to investments and not allow special rates for particular activities, investments, or industries. In contrast, the Tax Code provides a special 20 percent tax rate for investments made by Nuclear Decommissioning Reserve Funds.

Natural Resources and Environment

34. *Expensing of exploration and development costs, nonfuel minerals.*—The baseline tax system allows the taxpayer to deduct the depreciation of an asset according to the decline in its economic value over time. However, certain capital outlays associated with exploration and development of nonfuel minerals may be expensed rather than depreciated over the life of the asset.

35. *Excess of percentage over cost depletion, nonfuel minerals.*—The baseline tax system allows the taxpayer to deduct the decline in the economic value of an investment over time. Under current law, however,

most nonfuel mineral extractors may use percentage depletion (whereby the deduction is fixed as a percentage of receipts) rather than cost depletion, with percentage depletion rates ranging from 22 percent for sulfur to 5 percent for sand and gravel. Over the life of an investment, percentage depletion deductions can exceed the cost of the investment. Consequently, percentage depletion may provide more advantageous tax treatment than would cost depletion, which limits deductions to an investment's cost.

36. *Exclusion of interest on bonds for water, sewage, and hazardous waste facilities.*—The baseline tax system generally would tax all income under the regular tax rate schedule. It would not allow preferentially low (or zero) tax rates to apply to certain types or sources of income. In contrast, the Tax Code allows interest earned on State and local bonds used to finance construction of sewage, water, or hazardous waste facilities to be exempt from tax. These bonds are generally subject to the State private-activity bond annual volume cap.

37. *Capital gains treatment of certain timber.*—The baseline tax system generally would tax all income under the regular tax rate schedule. It would not allow preferentially low tax rates to apply to certain types or sources of income. However, under current law certain timber sales can be treated as a capital gain rather than ordinary income and therefore subject to the lower capital-gains tax rate. For individuals, tax rates on regular income vary from 10 percent to 39.6 percent in the budget window (plus a 3.8 percent surtax on high income taxpayers), depending on the taxpayer's income. In contrast, current law allows capital gains to be taxed at a preferentially low rate that is no higher than 20 percent (plus the 3.8 percent surtax).

38. *Expensing of multi-period timber growing costs.*—The baseline tax system requires the taxpayer to capitalize costs associated with investment property. However, most of the production costs of growing timber may be expensed under current law rather than capitalized and deducted when the timber is sold, thereby accelerating cost recovery.

39. *Tax incentives for preservation of historic structures.*—The baseline tax system would not allow credits for particular activities, investments, or industries. However, expenditures to preserve and restore certified historic structures qualify for an investment tax credit of 20 percent for certified rehabilitation activities. The taxpayer's recoverable basis must be reduced by the amount of the credit. The credit must be claimed ratably over the five years after the property is placed in service, for property placed in service after December 31, 2017.

40. *Carbon oxide sequestration credit.*—The baseline tax system would uniformly tax all returns to investments and not allow credits for particular activities, investments, or industries. In contrast, the Tax Code allows a credit for qualified carbon oxide captured at a qualified facility and disposed of in secure geological storage. In addition, the provision allows a credit for qualified carbon oxide that is captured at a qualified facility and used as a tertiary injectant in a qualified enhanced oil or natural gas recovery project. The credit differs according to whether the carbon was captured using equipment which was originally placed in service before February 9, 2018, or thereafter.

41. *Deduction for endangered species recovery expenditures.*—The baseline tax system would not allow deductions in addition to normal depreciation allowances for particular investments in particular industries. Instead, it generally would seek to tax uniformly all returns from investment-like activities. In contrast, under current law farmers can deduct up to 25 percent of their gross income for expenses incurred as a result of site and habitat improvement activities that will benefit endangered species on their farm land, in accordance with site specific management actions included in species recovery plans approved pursuant to the Endangered Species Act of 1973.

Agriculture

42. *Expensing of certain capital outlays.*—The baseline tax system requires the taxpayer to capitalize costs associated with investment property. However, farmers may expense certain expenditures for feed and fertilizer, for soil and water conservation measures, and certain other capital improvements under current law.

43. *Expensing of certain multiperiod production costs.*—The baseline tax system requires the taxpayer to capitalize costs associated with an investment over time. However, the production of livestock and crops with a production period greater than two years is exempt from the uniform cost capitalization rules (e.g., for costs for establishing orchards or structure improvements), thereby accelerating cost recovery.

44. *Treatment of loans forgiven for solvent farmers.*—Because loan forgiveness increases a debtors net worth the baseline tax system requires debtors to include the amount of loan forgiveness as income or else reduce their recoverable basis in the property related to the loan. If the amount of forgiveness exceeds the basis, the excess forgiveness is taxable if the taxpayer is not insolvent. For bankrupt debtors, the amount of loan forgiveness reduces carryover losses, unused credits, and then basis, with the remainder of the forgiven debt excluded from taxation. Qualified farm debt that is forgiven, however, is excluded from income even when the taxpayer is solvent.

45. *Capital gains treatment of certain agriculture income.*—For individuals, tax rates on regular income vary from 10 percent to 39.6 percent in the budget window (plus a 3.8 percent surtax on high income taxpayers), depending on the taxpayer's income. The baseline tax system generally would tax all income under the regular tax rate schedule. It would not allow preferentially low tax rates to apply to certain types or sources of income. In contrast, current law allows capital gains to be taxed at a preferentially low rate that is no higher than 20 percent (plus the 3.8 percent surtax). Certain agricultural income, such as unharvested crops, qualify for taxation as capital gains rather than ordinary income, and so benefit from

the preferentially low 20 percent maximum tax rate on capital gains.

46. *Income averaging for farmers.*—The baseline tax system generally taxes all earned income each year at the rate determined by the income tax. However, taxpayers may average their taxable income from farming and fishing over the previous three years.

47. *Deferral of gain on sales of farm refiners.*— The baseline tax system generally subjects capital gains to taxes the year that they are realized. However, the Tax Code allows a taxpayer who sells stock in a farm refiner to a farmers' cooperative to defer recognition of the gain if the proceeds are re-invested in a qualified replacement property.

48. *Expensing of reforestation expenditures.*— The baseline tax system requires the taxpayer to capitalize costs associated with an investment over time. In contrast, the Tax Code provides for the expensing of the first $10,000 in reforestation expenditures with 7-year amortization of the remaining expenses.

Commerce and Housing

This category includes a number of tax expenditure provisions that also affect economic activity in other functional categories. For example, provisions related to investment, such as accelerated depreciation, could be classified under the energy, natural resources and environment, agriculture, or transportation categories.

49. *Exemption of credit union income.*—Under the baseline tax system, corporations pay taxes on their profits under the regular tax rate schedule. However, in the Tax Code the earnings of credit unions not distributed to members as interest or dividends are exempt from the income tax.

50. *Exclusion of life insurance death benefits.*—Under the baseline tax system, individuals and corporations would pay taxes on their income when it is (actually or constructively) received or accrued. Nevertheless, current law generally excludes from tax amounts received under life insurance contracts if such amounts are paid by reason of the death of the insured.

51. *Exclusion or special alternative tax for small property and casualty insurance companies.*—The baseline tax system would require corporations to pay taxes on their profits under the regular tax rate schedule. It would not allow preferentially low (or zero) tax rates to apply to certain types or sources of income. Under current law, however, stock non-life insurance companies are generally exempt from tax if their gross receipts for the taxable year do not exceed $600,000 and more than 50 percent of such gross receipts consist of premiums. Mutual non-life insurance companies are generally tax-exempt if their annual gross receipts do not exceed $150,000 and more than 35 percent of gross receipts consist of premiums. Also, non-life insurance companies with no more than a specified level of annual net written premiums generally may elect to pay tax only on their taxable investment income provided certain diversification requirements are met. The underwriting income (premiums, less insurance loss-

es and expenses) of electing companies is excluded from tax. The specified premium limit is indexed for inflation; for 2019, the premium limit was $2.3 million.

52. *Tax exemption of insurance income earned by tax-exempt organizations.*—Under the baseline tax system, corporations pay taxes on their profits under the regular tax rate schedule. The baseline tax system would not allow preferentially low (or zero) tax rates to apply to certain types or sources of income. Generally the income generated by life and property and casualty insurance companies is subject to tax, albeit under special rules. However, income from insurance operations conducted by such exempt organizations as fraternal societies, voluntary employee benefit associations, and others are exempt from tax.

53. *Exclusion of interest spread of financial institutions.*—The baseline tax system generally would tax all income under the regular tax rate schedule. It would not allow preferentially low (or zero) tax rates to apply to certain types or sources of income. Consumers pay for some deposit-linked services, such as check cashing, by accepting a below-market interest rate on their demand deposits. If they received a market rate of interest on those deposits and paid explicit fees for the associated services, they would pay taxes on the full market rate and (unlike businesses) could not deduct the fees. The Government thus foregoes tax on the difference between the risk-free market interest rate and below-market interest rates on demand deposits, which under competitive conditions should equal the value of deposit services.

54. *Exclusion of interest on owner-occupied mortgage subsidy bonds.*—The baseline tax system generally would tax all income under the regular tax rate schedule. It would not allow preferentially low (or zero) tax rates to apply to certain types or sources of income. In contrast, the Tax Code allows interest earned on State and local bonds used to finance homes purchased by first-time, low-to-moderate-income buyers to be exempt from tax. These bonds are generally subject to the State private-activity-bond annual volume cap.

55. *Exclusion of interest on rental housing bonds.*—The baseline tax system generally would tax all income under the regular tax rate schedule. It would not allow preferentially low (or zero) tax rates to apply to certain types or sources of income. In contrast, the Tax Code allows interest earned on State and local government bonds used to finance multifamily rental housing projects to be tax-exempt.

56. *Mortgage interest expense on owner-occupied residences.*—Under the baseline tax system, expenses incurred in earning income would be deductible. However, such expenses would not be deductible when the income or the return on an investment is not taxed. In contrast, the Tax Code allows an exclusion from a taxpayer's taxable income for the value of owner-occupied housing services and also allows the owner-occupant to deduct mortgage interest paid on his or her primary residence and one secondary residence as an itemized non-business deduction. In general, the mortgage interest deduction is limited to interest on debt no greater than the owner's basis in the residence, and is also limited to interest on debt of no more than $1 million. Interest on up to $100,000 of other debt secured by a lien on a principal or second residence is also deductible, irrespective of the purpose of borrowing, provided the total debt does not exceed the fair market value of the residence. As an alternative to the deduction, holders of qualified Mortgage Credit Certificates issued by State or local governmental units or agencies may claim a tax credit equal to a proportion of their interest expense. In the case of taxable years beginning after December 31, 2017, and before January 1, 2026, (1) the $1 million limit is reduced to $750,000 for indebtedness incurred after December 15, 2017, and (2) the deduction for interest on home equity indebtedness is disallowed.

57. ***Deduction for property taxes on real property.***—Under the baseline tax system, expenses incurred in earning income would be deductible. However, such expenses would not be deductible when the income or the return on an investment is not taxed. In contrast, the Tax Code allows an exclusion from a taxpayer's taxable income for the value of owner-occupied housing services and also allows the owner-occupant to deduct property taxes paid on real property. In the case of taxable years beginning after December 31, 2017, and before January 1, 2026, (1) the deduction for foreign real property taxes paid is disallowed and (2) the deduction for taxes paid in any taxable year, which includes the deduction for property taxes on real property, is limited to $10,000 ($5,000 in the case of a married individual filing a separate return).

58. ***Deferral of income from installment sales.***— The baseline tax system generally would tax all income under the regular tax rate schedule. It would not allow preferentially low (or zero) tax rates, or deferral of tax, to apply to certain types or sources of income. Dealers in real and personal property (i.e., sellers who regularly hold property for sale or resale) cannot defer taxable income from installment sales until the receipt of the loan repayment. Nondealers (i.e., sellers of real property used in their business) are required to pay interest on deferred taxes attributable to their total installment obligations in excess of $5 million. Only properties with sales prices exceeding $150,000 are includable in the total. The payment of a market rate of interest eliminates the benefit of the tax deferral. The tax exemption for nondealers with total installment obligations of less than $5 million is, therefore, a tax expenditure.

59. ***Capital gains exclusion on home sales.***—The baseline tax system would not allow deductions and exemptions for certain types of income. In contrast, the Tax Code allows homeowners to exclude from gross income up to $250,000 ($500,000 in the case of a married couple filing a joint return) of the capital gains from the sale of a principal residence. To qualify, the taxpayer must have owned and used the property as the taxpayer's principal residence for a total of at least two of the five years preceding the date of sale. In addition, the exclusion may not be used more than once every two years.

60. ***Exclusion of net imputed rental income.***— Under the baseline tax system, the taxable income of a taxpayer who is an owner-occupant would include the implicit value of gross rental income on housing services earned on the investment in owner-occupied housing and would allow a deduction for expenses, such as interest, depreciation, property taxes, and other costs, associated with earning such rental income. In contrast, the Tax Code allows an exclusion from taxable income for the implicit gross rental income on housing services, while in certain circumstances allows a deduction for some costs associated with such income, such as for mortgage interest and property taxes.

61. ***Exception from passive loss rules for $25,000 of rental loss.***—The baseline tax system accepts current law's general rule limiting taxpayers' ability to deduct losses from passive activities against nonpassive income (e.g., wages, interest, and dividends). Passive activities generally are defined as those in which the taxpayer does not materially participate, and there are numerous additional considerations brought to bear on the determination of which activities are passive for a given taxpayer. Losses are limited in an attempt to limit tax sheltering activities. Passive losses that are unused may be carried forward and applied against future passive income. In contrast to the general restrictions on passive losses, the Tax Code exempts certain owners of rental real estate activities from "passive income" limitations. The exemption is limited to $25,000 in losses and phases out for taxpayers with income between $100,000 and $150,000.

62. ***Credit for low-income housing investments.***—The baseline tax system would uniformly tax all returns to investments and not allow credits for particular activities, investments, or industries. However, under current law taxpayers who invest in certain low-income housing are eligible for a tax credit. The credit rate is set so that the present value of the credit is equal to at least 70 percent of the building's qualified basis for new construction and 30 percent for (1) housing receiving other Federal benefits (such as tax-exempt bond financing) or (2) substantially rehabilitated existing housing. The credit can exceed these levels in certain statutorily defined and State designated areas where project development costs are higher. The credit is allowed in equal amounts over 10 years and is generally subject to a volume cap.

63. ***Accelerated depreciation on rental housing.***—Under a comprehensive economic income tax, the costs of acquiring a building are capitalized and depreciated over time in accordance with the decline in the property's economic value due to wear and tear or obsolescence. This insures that the net income from the rental property is measured appropriately each year. Current law allows depreciation that is accelerated relative to economic depreciation. However, the depreciation provisions of the Tax Code are part of the reference tax law, and thus do not give rise to tax expenditures under reference tax law. Under normal tax baseline, in contrast, depreciation allowances reflect estimates of economic depreciation.

64. ***Discharge of business indebtedness.***—Under the baseline tax system, all income would generally be taxed under the regular tax rate schedule. The baseline tax system would not allow preferentially low (or zero) tax rates to apply to certain types or sources of income.

In contrast, the Tax Code allows an exclusion from a taxpayer's taxable income for any discharge of qualified real property business indebtedness by taxpayers other than a C corporation. If the canceled debt is not reported as current income, however, the basis of the underlying property must be reduced by the amount canceled.

65. *Exceptions from imputed interest rules.*— Under the baseline tax system, holders (issuers) of debt instruments are generally required to report interest earned (paid) in the period it accrues, not when received. In addition, the amount of interest accrued is determined by the actual price paid, not by the stated principal and interest stipulated in the instrument. But under current law, any debt associated with the sale of property worth less than $250,000 is exempted from the general interest accounting rules. This general $250,000 exception is not a tax expenditure under reference tax law but is under normal tax baseline. Current law also includes exceptions for certain property worth more than $250,000. These are tax expenditure under reference tax law and normal tax baselines. These exceptions include, sales of personal residences worth more than $250,000, and sales of farms and small businesses worth between $250,000 and $1 million.

66. *Treatment of qualified dividends.*—The baseline tax system generally would tax all income under the regular tax rate schedule. It would not allow preferentially low tax rates to apply to certain types or sources of income. For individuals, tax rates on regular income vary from 10 percent to 39.6 percent in the budget window (plus a 3.8 percent surtax on high income taxpayers), depending on the taxpayer's income. In contrast, under current law, qualified dividends are taxed at a preferentially low rate that is no higher than 20 percent (plus the 3.8 percent surtax).

67. *Capital gains (except agriculture, timber, iron ore, and coal).*—The baseline tax system generally would tax all income under the regular tax rate schedule. It would not allow preferentially low tax rates to apply to certain types or sources of income. For individuals, tax rates on regular income vary from 10 percent to 39.6 percent in the budget window (plus a 3.8 percent surtax on high income taxpayers), depending on the taxpayer's income. In contrast, under current law, capital gains on assets held for more than one year are taxed at a preferentially low rate that is no higher than 20 percent (plus the 3.8 percent surtax).

68. *Capital gains exclusion of small corporation stock.*—The baseline tax system would not allow deductions and exemptions or provide preferential treatment of certain sources of income or types of activities. In contrast, the Tax Code provided an exclusion of 50 percent, applied to ordinary rates with a maximum of a 28 percent tax rate, for capital gains from qualified small business stock held by individuals for more than 5 years; 75 percent for stock issued after February 17, 2009 and before September 28, 2010; and 100 percent for stock issued after September 27, 2010. A qualified small business is a corporation whose gross assets do not exceed $50 million as of the date of issuance of the stock.

69. *Step-up basis of capital gains at death.*— Under the baseline tax system, unrealized capital gains would be taxed when assets are transferred at death. It would not allow for exempting gains upon transfer of the underlying assets to the heirs. In contrast, capital gains on assets held at the owner's death are not subject to capital gains tax under current law. The cost basis of the appreciated assets is adjusted to the market value at the owner's date of death which becomes the basis for the heirs.

70. *Carryover basis of capital gains on gifts.*— Under the baseline tax system, unrealized capital gains would be taxed when assets are transferred by gift. In contrast, when a gift of appreciated asset is made under current law, the donor's basis in the transferred property (the cost that was incurred when the transferred property was first acquired) carries over to the donee. The carryover of the donor's basis allows a continued deferral of unrealized capital gains.

71. *Deferral of capital gains from like-kind exchanges.*—The baseline tax system generally would tax all income under the regular tax rate schedule. It would not allow preferentially low (or zero) tax rates, or deferral of tax, to apply to certain types or sources of income. In contrast, current law allows the deferral of accrued gains on assets transferred in qualified like-kind exchanges.

72. *Ordinary income treatment of loss from small business corporation stock sale.*—The baseline tax system limits to $3,000 the write-off of losses from capital assets, with carryover of the excess to future years. In contrast, the Tax Code allows up to $100,000 in losses from the sale of small business corporate stock (capitalization less than $1 million) to be treated as ordinary losses and fully deducted.

73. *Depreciation of buildings other than rental housing.*—Under a comprehensive economic income tax, the costs of acquiring a building are capitalized and depreciated over time in accordance with the decline in the property's economic value due to wear and tear or obsolescence. This insures that the net income from the property is measured appropriately each year. Current law allows depreciation deductions that differ from those under economic depreciation. However, the depreciation provisions of the Tax Code are part of the reference tax law, and thus do not give rise to tax expenditures under reference tax law. Under normal tax baseline, in contrast, depreciation allowances reflect estimates of economic depreciation.

74. *Accelerated depreciation of machinery and equipment.*—Under a comprehensive economic income tax, the costs of acquiring machinery and equipment are capitalized and depreciated over time in accordance with the decline in the property's economic value due to wear and tear or obsolescence. This insures that the net income from the property is measured appropriately each year. Current law allows depreciation deductions that are accelerated relative to economic depreciation. In particular, through 2022, 100 percent of the purchase cost of qualified property is eligible to be expensed immediately; this percentage phases out to zero through 2027. The depreciation provisions of the Tax Code are part of the reference tax law, and thus do not give rise to tax expenditures un-

der reference tax law. Under the normal tax baseline, in contrast, depreciation allowances reflect estimates of economic depreciation.

75. *Expensing of certain small investments.*— Under the reference tax law baseline, the costs of acquiring tangible property and computer software would be depreciated using the Tax Code's depreciation provisions. Under the normal tax baseline, depreciation allowances are estimates of economic depreciation. However, subject to investment limitations, the Tax Code allows up to $1 million (indexed for inflation) in qualifying investments in tangible property and certain computer software to be expensed rather than depreciated over time.

76. *Exclusion of interest on small issue bonds.*— The baseline tax system generally would tax all income under the regular tax rate schedule. It would not allow preferentially low (or zero) tax rates to apply to certain types or sources of income. In contrast, the Tax Code allows interest earned on small issue industrial development bonds (IDBs) issued by State and local governments to finance manufacturing facilities to be tax exempt. Depreciable property financed with small issue IDBs must be depreciated, however, using the straight-line method. The annual volume of small issue IDBs is subject to the unified volume cap discussed in the mortgage housing bond section above.

77. *Special rules for certain film and TV production.*— The baseline tax system generally would tax all income under the regular tax rate schedule. It would not allow deductions and exemptions or preferentially low (or zero) tax rates to apply to certain types or sources of income. In contrast, the Tax Code allowed taxpayers to deduct up to $15 million per production ($20 million in certain distressed areas) in non-capital expenditures incurred during the year. This provision expired at the end of 2016.

78. *Allow 20-percent deduction to certain pass-through income.*— The baseline tax system generally would tax all income under the regular tax rate schedule. It would not allow deductions and exemptions or preferentially low (or zero) tax rates to apply to certain types or sources of income. In contrast, for tax years 2018 to 2025, the Tax Code allows for a deduction equal to up to 20 percent of income attributable to domestic pass-through businesses, subject to certain limitations.

Transportation

79. *Tonnage tax.*— The baseline tax system generally would tax all profits and income under the regular tax rate schedule. U.S. shipping companies may choose to be subject to a tonnage tax based on gross shipping weight in lieu of an income tax, in which case profits would not be subject to tax under the regular tax rate schedule.

80. *Deferral of tax on shipping companies.*— The baseline tax system generally would tax all profits and income under the regular tax rate schedule. It would not allow preferentially low (or zero) tax rates to apply to certain types or sources of income. In contrast, the Tax Code allows certain companies that operate U.S. flag vessels to defer income taxes on that portion of their income used for shipping purposes (e.g., primarily construction, modernization and major repairs to ships, and repayment of loans to finance these investments).

81. *Exclusion of reimbursed employee parking expenses.*— Under the baseline tax system, all compensation, including dedicated payments and in-kind benefits, would be included in taxable income. Dedicated payments and in-kind benefits represent accretions to wealth that do not differ materially from cash wages. In contrast, the Tax Code allows an exclusion from taxable income for employee parking expenses that are paid for by the employer or that are received by the employee in lieu of wages. In 2018, the maximum amount of the parking exclusion is $260 per month. The tax expenditure estimate does not include any subsidy provided through employer-owned parking facilities. However, beginning in 2018, parking expenses are no longer deductible to employers (except Government).

82. *Exclusion for employer-provided transit passes.*— Under the baseline tax system, all compensation, including dedicated payments and in-kind benefits, would be included in taxable income. Dedicated payments and in-kind benefits represent accretions to wealth that do not differ materially from cash wages. In contrast, the Tax Code allows an exclusion from a taxpayer's taxable income for passes, tokens, fare cards, and vanpool expenses that are paid for by an employer or that are received by the employee in lieu of wages to defray an employee's commuting costs. Due to a parity to parking provision, the maximum amount of the transit exclusion is $260 per month in 2018. However, beginning in 2018, transit expenses are no longer deductible to employers (except Government).

83. *Tax credit for certain expenditures for maintaining railroad tracks.*— The baseline tax system would not allow credits for particular activities, investments, or industries. However, the Tax Code allowed eligible taxpayers to claim a credit equal to the lesser of 50 percent of maintenance expenditures and the product of $3,500 and the number of miles of railroad track owned or leased. This provision applies to maintenance expenditures in taxable years beginning before January 1, 2017.

84. *Exclusion of interest on bonds for Highway Projects and rail-truck transfer facilities.*— The baseline tax system generally would tax all income under the regular tax rate schedule. It would not allow preferentially low (or zero) tax rates to apply to certain types or sources of income. In contrast, the Tax Code provides for $15 billion of tax-exempt bond authority to finance qualified highway or surface freight transfer facilities.

Community and Regional Development

85. *Investment credit for rehabilitation of structures.*— The baseline tax system would uniformly tax all returns to investments and not allow credits for particular activities, investments, or industries. Under prior law, the Tax Code allowed a 10 percent investment tax credit for the rehabilitation of buildings that are used for business or productive activities and that were erected before 1936 for other than residential purposes. The taxpayer's recoverable basis must be reduced by the amount of the credit. The credit is repealed for rehabilitation expenditures incurred after December 31, 2017.

86. *Exclusion of interest for airport, dock, and similar bonds.*—The baseline tax system generally would tax all income under the regular tax rate schedule. It would not allow preferentially low (or zero) tax rates to apply to certain types or sources of income. In contrast, the Tax Code allows interest earned on State and local bonds issued to finance high-speed rail facilities and Government-owned airports, docks, wharves, and sport and convention facilities to be tax-exempt. These bonds are not subject to a volume cap.

87. *Exemption of certain mutuals' and cooperatives' income.*—Under the baseline tax system, corporations pay taxes on their profits under the regular tax rate schedule. In contrast, the Tax Code provides for the incomes of mutual and cooperative telephone and electric companies to be exempt from tax if at least 85 percent of their receipts are derived from patron service charges.

88. *Empowerment zones.*—The baseline tax system generally would tax all income under the regular tax rate schedule. It would not allow preferentially low tax rates to apply to certain types or sources of income, tax credits, and write-offs faster than economic depreciation. In contrast, the Tax Code allowed qualifying businesses in designated economically depressed areas to receive tax benefits such as an employment credit, increased expensing of investment in equipment, special tax-exempt financing, and certain capital gains incentives. A taxpayer's ability to accrue new tax benefits for empowerment zones expired on December 31, 2017.

89. *New markets tax credit.*—The baseline tax system would not allow credits for particular activities, investments, or industries. However, the Tax Code allows taxpayers who make qualified equity investments in a Community Development Entity (CDE), which then make qualified investments in low-income communities, to be eligible for a tax credit that is received over 7 years. The total equity investment available for the credit across all CDEs is generally $3.5 billion for each calendar year 2010 through 2019, the last year for which credit allocations are authorized.

90. *Credit to holders of Gulf and Midwest Tax Credit Bonds.*—The baseline tax system would not allow credits for particular activities, investments, or industries. Instead, under current law taxpayers that own Gulf and Midwest Tax Credit bonds receive a non-refundable tax credit rather than interest. The credit is included in gross income.

91. *Recovery Zone Bonds.*—The baseline tax system would not allow credits for particular activities, investments, or industries. In addition, it would tax all income under the regular tax rate schedule. It would not allow preferentially low (or zero) tax rates to apply to certain types or sources of income. In contrast, the Tax Code allowed local governments to issue up $10 billion in tax-

able Recovery Zone Economic Development Bonds in 2009 and 2010 and receive a direct payment from Treasury equal to 45 percent of interest expenses. In addition, local governments could issue up to $15 billion in tax exempt Recovery Zone Facility Bonds. These bonds financed certain kinds of business development in areas of economic distress.

92. *Tribal Economic Development Bonds.*—The baseline tax system generally would tax all income under the regular tax rate schedule. It would not allow preferentially low (or zero) tax rates to apply to certain types or sources of income. In contrast, the Tax Code was modified in 2009 to allow Indian tribal governments to issue tax exempt "tribal economic development bonds." There is a national bond limitation of $2 billion on such bonds.

93. *Opportunity Zones.*—The baseline tax system generally would tax all income under the regular tax rate schedule. It would not allow deferral or exclusion from income for investments made within certain geographic regions. In contrast, the Tax Code allows the temporary deferral of the recognition of capital gain if reinvested prior to December 31, 2026, in a qualifying opportunity fund which in turn invests in qualifying low-income communities designated as opportunity zones. For qualifying investments held at least 5 years, 10 percent of the deferred gain is excluded from income; this exclusion increases to 15 percent for investments held for at least 7 years. In addition, capital gains from the sale or exchange of an investment in a qualified opportunity fund held for at least 10 years are excluded from gross income. Opportunity zone designations expire on December 31, 2028.

94. *Employee Retention Credit.*—The baseline tax system would not allow credits for particular activities, investments, or industries. In contrast, the Tax Code provides employers located in certain presidentially declared disaster areas a 40 percent credit for up to $6,000 in wages paid to each eligible employee while the business was inoperable as a result of the disaster. Only wages paid after the disaster occurred and before January 1, 2018 are eligible for the credit. Employers must reduce their deduction for wages paid by the amount of the credit claimed.

Education, Training, Employment, and Social Services

95. *Exclusion of scholarship and fellowship income.*—Scholarships and fellowships are excluded from taxable income to the extent they pay for tuition and course-related expenses of the grantee. Similarly, tuition reductions for employees of educational institutions and their families are not included in taxable income. From an economic point of view, scholarships and fellowships are either gifts not conditioned on the performance of services, or they are rebates of educational costs. Thus, under the baseline tax system of the reference tax law method, this exclusion is not a tax expenditure because this method does not include either gifts or price reductions in a taxpayer's gross income. The exclusion, however, is considered a tax expenditure under the normal tax method,

which includes gift-like transfers of Government funds in gross income. (Many scholarships are derived directly or indirectly from Government funding.)

96. ***Tax credits for post-secondary education expenses.***—The baseline tax system would not allow credits for particular activities, investments, or industries. Under current law in 2019, however, there were two credits for certain post-secondary education expenses. The American Opportunity Tax Credit allows a partially refundable credit of up to $2,500 per eligible student for qualified tuition and related expenses paid during each of the first four years of the student's post-secondary education. The credit is phased out for taxpayers with modified adjusted gross income between $160,000 and $180,000 if married filing jointly ($80,000 and $90,000 for other taxpayers), not indexed. The Lifetime Learning Credit allows a non-refundable credit for 20 percent of an eligible student's qualified tuition and fees, up to a maximum credit per return of $2,000. In 2019, the credit is phased out ratably for taxpayers with modified AGI between $116,000 and $136,000 if married filing jointly ($58,000 and $68,000 for other taxpayers), indexed. The Lifetime Learning credit can be claimed in any year in which post-secondary education expenses are incurred. Only one credit can be claimed per qualifying student. Married individuals filing separate returns cannot claim either credit.

97. ***Education Individual Retirement Accounts (IRA).***—The baseline tax system generally would tax all income under the regular tax rate schedule. It would not allow preferentially low (or zero) tax rates to apply to certain types or sources of income. While contributions to an education IRA are not tax-deductible under current law, investment income earned by education IRAs is not taxed when earned, and investment income from an education IRA is tax-exempt when withdrawn to pay for a student's education expenses. The maximum annual contribution to an education IRA is $2,000 per beneficiary. In 2019, the maximum contribution is phased down ratably for taxpayers with modified AGI between $190,000 and $220,000 if married filing jointly ($95,000 and $110,000 for other taxpayers).

98. ***Deductibility of student loan interest.***—The baseline tax system accepts current law's general rule limiting taxpayers' ability to deduct non-business interest expenses. In contrast, taxpayers may claim an above-the-line deduction of up to $2,500 on interest paid on an education loan. In 2019, the maximum deduction is phased down ratably for taxpayers with modified AGI between $140,000 and $170,000 if married filing jointly ($70,000 and $85,000 for other taxpayers). Married individuals filing separate returns cannot claim the deduction.

99. ***Qualified tuition programs.***—The baseline tax system generally would tax all income under the regular tax rate schedule. It would not allow preferentially low (or zero) tax rates to apply to certain types or sources of income. Some States have adopted prepaid tuition plans, prepaid room and board plans, and college savings plans, which allow persons to pay in advance or save for college expenses for designated beneficiaries. Under current law, investment income, or the return on prepayments, is not taxed when earned, and is tax-exempt when withdrawn to pay for qualified expenses. Beginning in 2018, the definition of a qualified expense was expanded to include up to $10,000 per child per year of expenses for primary or secondary education, including tuition at religious schools.

100. ***Exclusion of interest on student-loan bonds.***—The baseline tax system generally would tax all income under the regular tax rate schedule. It would not allow preferentially low (or zero) tax rates to apply to certain types or sources of income. In contrast, interest earned on State and local bonds issued to finance student loans is tax-exempt under current law. The volume of all such private activity bonds that each State may issue annually is limited.

101. ***Exclusion of interest on bonds for private nonprofit educational facilities.***—The baseline tax system generally would tax all income under the regular tax rate schedule. It would not allow preferentially low (or zero) tax rates to apply to certain types or sources of income. In contrast, under current law interest earned on State and local government bonds issued to finance the construction of facilities used by private nonprofit educational institutions is not taxed.

102. ***Credit for holders of zone academy bonds.***—The baseline tax system would not allow credits for particular activities, investments, or industries. Under current law, however, financial institutions that own zone academy bonds receive a non-refundable tax credit rather than interest. The credit is included in gross income. Proceeds from zone academy bonds may only be used to renovate, but not construct, qualifying schools and for certain other school purposes. The total amount of zone academy bonds that may be issued was limited to $1.4 billion in 2009 and 2010. As of March 2010, issuers of the unused authorization of such bonds could opt to receive direct payment with the yield becoming fully taxable. An additional $0.4 billion of these bonds with a tax credit was authorized to be issued each year in 2011 through 2016.

103. ***Exclusion of interest on savings bonds redeemed to finance educational expenses.***—The baseline tax system generally would tax all income under the regular tax rate schedule. It would not allow preferentially low (or zero) tax rates to apply to certain types or sources of income. Under current law, however, interest earned on U.S. savings bonds issued after December 31, 1989, is tax-exempt if the bonds are transferred to an educational institution to pay for educational expenses. The tax exemption is phased out for taxpayers with AGI between $121,600 and $151,600 if married filing jointly ($81,100 and $96,100 for other taxpayers) in 2019.

104. ***Parental personal exemption for students age 19 or over.***—Under the baseline tax system, a personal exemption would be allowed for the taxpayer, as well as for the taxpayer's spouse and dependents who do not claim a personal exemption on their own tax returns. These exemptions are repealed for taxable years beginning after December 31, 2017, and before January 1, 2026. However, the definitions regarding eligibility for dependent exemptions for children (and qualifying relatives), which determine eligibility for a number of family-related

provisions, remain in place. These provisions include the new $500 credit for dependents other than qualifying children (Other Dependent Credit, or ODC). In general, to be considered a dependent child, a child would have to be under age 19. In contrast, the Tax Code allows taxpayers to consider their children aged 19 to 23 as dependents, as long as the children are full-time students and reside with the taxpayer for over half the year (with exceptions for temporary absences from home, such as for school attendance). Absent this provision, children over 18 would need to meet the more stringent rules for qualified relatives in order to qualify the taxpayer for certain benefits, including the ODC.

105. *Charitable contributions to educational institutions.*—The baseline tax system would not allow a deduction for personal expenditures. In contrast, the Tax Code provides taxpayers a deduction for contributions to nonprofit educational institutions that are similar to personal expenditures. Moreover, taxpayers who donate capital assets to educational institutions can deduct the asset's current value without being taxed on any appreciation in value. An individual's total charitable contribution generally may not exceed 50 percent (60 percent for tax years 2018 and 2025) of adjusted gross income; a corporation's total charitable contributions generally may not exceed 10 percent of pre-tax income.

106. *Exclusion of employer-provided educational assistance.*—Under the baseline tax system, all compensation, including dedicated payments and in-kind benefits, should be included in taxable income because it represent accretions to wealth that do not materially differ from cash wages. Under current law, however, employer-provided educational assistance is excluded from an employee's gross income, even though the employer's costs for this assistance are a deductible business expense. The maximum exclusion is $5,250 per taxpayer.

107. *Special deduction for teacher expenses.*— The baseline tax system would not allow a deduction for personal expenditures. In contrast, the Tax Code allowed educators in both public and private elementary and secondary schools, who worked at least 900 hours during a school year as a teacher, instructor, counselor, principal, or aide, to subtract up to $250 of qualified expenses, indexed to 2014, when determining their adjusted gross income (AGI).

108. *Discharge of student loan indebtedness.*— Under the baseline tax system, all compensation, including dedicated payments and in-kind benefits, should be included in taxable income. In contrast, the Tax Code allows certain professionals who perform in underserved areas or specific fields, and as a consequence have their student loans discharged, not to recognize such discharge as income.

109. *Qualified school construction bonds.*—The baseline tax system would not allow credits for particular activities, investments, or industries. Instead, it generally would seek to tax uniformly all returns from investment-like activities. In contrast, the Tax Code was modified in 2009 to provide a tax credit in lieu of interest to holders of qualified school construction bonds. The national volume limit is $22.4 billion over 2009 and 2010. As of March 2010, issuers of such bonds could opt to receive direct payment with the yield becoming fully taxable.

110. *Work opportunity tax credit.*—The baseline tax system would not allow credits for particular activities, investments, or industries. Instead, it generally would seek to tax uniformly all returns from investment-like activities. In contrast, the Tax Code provides employers with a tax credit for qualified wages paid to individuals. The credit applies to employees who began work on or before December 31, 2019 and who are certified as members of various targeted groups. The amount of the credit that can be claimed is 25 percent of qualified wages for employment less than 400 hours and 40 percent for employment of 400 hours or more. Generally, the maximum credit per employee is $2,400 and can only be claimed on the first year of wages an individual earns from an employer. However, the credit for long-term welfare recipients can be claimed on second year wages as well and has a $9,000 maximum. Also, certain categories of veterans are eligible for a higher maximum credit of up to $9,600. Employers must reduce their deduction for wages paid by the amount of the credit claimed.

111. *Employer-provided child care exclusion.*—Under the baseline tax system, all compensation, including dedicated payments and in-kind benefits, should be included in taxable income. In contrast, under current law up to $5,000 of employer-provided child care is excluded from an employee's gross income even though the employer's costs for the child care are a deductible business expense.

112. *Employer-provided child care credit.*—The baseline tax system would not allow credits for particular activities, investments, or industries. In contrast, current law provides a credit equal to 25 percent of qualified expenses for employee child care and 10 percent of qualified expenses for child care resource and referral services. Employer deductions for such expenses are reduced by the amount of the credit. The maximum total credit is limited to $150,000 per taxable year.

113. *Assistance for adopted foster children.*— Under the baseline tax system, all compensation, including dedicated payments and in-kind benefits, should be included in taxable income. Taxpayers who adopt eligible children from the public foster care system can receive monthly payments for the children's significant and varied needs and a reimbursement of up to $2,000 for nonrecurring adoption expenses; special needs adoptions receive the maximum benefit even if that amount is not spent. These payments are excluded from gross income under current law.

114. *Adoption credit and exclusion.*—The baseline tax system would not allow credits for particular activities. In contrast, taxpayers can receive a tax credit for qualified adoption expenses under current law. Taxpayers may also exclude qualified adoption expenses provided or reimbursed by an employer from income, subject to the same maximum amounts and phase-out as the credit. The same expenses cannot qualify for tax benefits under both programs; however, a taxpayer may use the

benefits of the exclusion and the tax credit for different expenses.

115. ***Exclusion of employee meals and lodging.***—Under the baseline tax system, all compensation, including dedicated payments and in-kind benefits, should be included in taxable income. Furthermore, all compensation would generally be deductible by the employer. In contrast, under current law employer-provided meals and lodging are excluded from an employee's gross income. Additionally, beginning in 2018, employers are allowed a deduction for 50 percent of the expenses of employer-provided meals. Employer-provided lodging is fully deductible by the employer, in general.

116. ***Credit for child and dependent care expenses.***—The baseline tax system would not allow credits for particular activities or targeted at specific groups. In contrast, the Tax Code provides a tax credit to parents who work or attend school and who have child and dependent care expenses. Expenditures up to a maximum $3,000 for one dependent and $6,000 for two or more dependents are eligible for the credit. The credit is equal to 35 percent of qualified expenditures for taxpayers with incomes of up to $15,000. The credit is reduced to a minimum of 20 percent by one percentage point for each $2,000 of income in excess of $15,000.

117. ***Credit for disabled access expenditures.***— The baseline tax system would not allow credits for particular activities, investments, or industries. In contrast, the Tax Code provides small businesses (less than $1 million in gross receipts or fewer than 31 full-time employees) a 50 percent credit for expenditures in excess of $250 to remove access barriers for disabled persons. The credit is limited to $5,000.

118. ***Deductibility of charitable contributions, other than education and health.***—The baseline tax system would not allow a deduction for personal expenditures including charitable contributions. In contrast, the Tax Code provides taxpayers a deduction for contributions to charitable, religious, and certain other nonprofit organizations. Taxpayers who donate capital assets to charitable organizations can deduct the assets' current value without being taxed on any appreciation in value. An individual's total charitable contribution generally may not exceed 50 percent (60 percent between 2018 and 2025) of adjusted gross income; a corporation's total charitable contributions generally may not exceed 10 percent of pre-tax income.

119. ***Exclusion of certain foster care payments.***— The baseline tax system generally would tax all income under the regular tax rate schedule. It would not allow preferentially low (or zero) tax rates to apply to certain types or sources of income. Foster parents provide a home and care for children who are wards of the State, under contract with the State. Under current law, compensation received for this service is excluded from the gross incomes of foster parents; the expenses they incur are nondeductible.

120. ***Exclusion of parsonage allowances.***—Under the baseline tax system, all compensation, including dedicated payments and in-kind benefits, would be included in taxable income. Dedicated payments and in-kind benefits represent accretions to wealth that do not differ materially from cash wages. In contrast, the Tax Code allows an exclusion from a clergyman's taxable income for the value of the clergyman's housing allowance or the rental value of the clergyman's parsonage.

121. ***Indian employment credit.***—The baseline tax system would not allow credits for particular activities, investments, or industries. Instead, it generally would seek to tax uniformly all returns from investment-like activities. In contrast, the Tax Code provides employers with a tax credit for qualified wages paid to employees who are enrolled members of Indian tribes. The amount of the credit that could be claimed is 20 percent of the excess of qualified wages and health insurance costs paid by the employer in the current tax year over the amount of such wages and costs paid by the employer in 1993. Qualified wages and health insurance costs with respect to any employee for the taxable year could not exceed $20,000. Employees have to live on or near the reservation where they work to be eligible for the credit. Employers must reduce their deduction for wages paid by the amount of the credit claimed. The credit does not apply to taxable years beginning after December 31, 2017.

122. ***Credit for employer differential wage payments.***—The baseline tax system would not allow credits for particular activities, investments, or industries. In contrast, the Tax Code provides employers with a 20 percent tax credit for eligible differential wages paid to employees who are members of the uniformed services while on active duty for more than 30 days. The amount of eligible differential wage payments made to a qualified employee in a taxable year is capped at $20,000. Employers must reduce their deduction for wages paid by the amount of the credit claimed.

Health

123. ***Exclusion of employer contributions for medical insurance premiums and medical care.***—Under the baseline tax system, all compensation, including dedicated payments and in-kind benefits, should be included in taxable income. In contrast, under current law, employer-paid health insurance premiums and other medical expenses (including long-term care or Health Reimbursement Accounts) are not included in employee gross income even though they are deducted as a business expense by the employee.

124. ***Self-employed medical insurance premiums.***—Under the baseline tax system, all compensation and remuneration, including dedicated payments and in-kind benefits, should be included in taxable income. In contrast, under current law self-employed taxpayers may deduct their family health insurance premiums. Taxpayers without self-employment income are not eligible for this special deduction. The deduction is not available for any month in which the self-employed individual is eligible to participate in an employer-subsidized health plan and the deduction may not exceed the self-employed individual's earned income from self-employment.

125. **Medical Savings Accounts and Health Savings Accounts.**—Under the baseline tax system, all compensation, including dedicated payments and in-kind benefits, should be included in taxable income. Also, the baseline tax system would not allow a deduction for personal expenditures and generally would tax investment earnings. In contrast, individual contributions to Archer Medical Savings Accounts (Archer MSAs) and Health Savings Accounts (HSAs) are allowed as a deduction in determining adjusted gross income whether or not the individual itemizes deductions. Employer contributions to Archer MSAs and HSAs are excluded from income and employment taxes. Archer MSAs and HSAs require that the individual have coverage by a qualifying high deductible health plan. Earnings from the accounts are excluded from taxable income. Distributions from the accounts used for medical expenses are not taxable. The rules for HSAs are generally more flexible than for Archer MSAs and the deductible contribution amounts are greater (in 2019, $3,350 for taxpayers with individual coverage and $6,750 for taxpayers with family coverage). Thus, HSAs have largely replaced MSAs.

126. **Deductibility of medical expenses.**—The baseline tax system would not allow a deduction for personal expenditures. In contrast, under current law personal expenditures for medical care (including the costs of prescription drugs) exceeding 7.5 percent of the taxpayer's adjusted gross income are deductible. For tax years beginning after 2012, only medical expenditures exceeding 10 percent of the taxpayer's adjusted gross income are deductible. However, for the years 2013, 2014, 2015 and 2016, if either the taxpayer or the taxpayer's spouse turned 65 before the end of the taxable year, the threshold remained at 7.5 percent of adjusted income. Beginning in 2017, the 10 percent threshold applied to all taxpayers, including those over 65.

127. **Exclusion of interest on hospital construction bonds.**—The baseline tax system generally would tax all income under the regular tax rate schedule. It would not allow preferentially low (or zero) tax rates to apply to certain types or sources of income. In contrast, under current law interest earned on State and local government debt issued to finance hospital construction is excluded from income subject to tax.

128. **Refundable Premium Assistance Tax Credit.**—The baseline tax system would not allow credits for particular activities or targeted at specific groups. In contrast, for taxable years ending after 2013, the Tax Code provides a premium assistance credit to any eligible taxpayer for any qualified health insurance purchased through a Health Insurance Exchange. In general, an eligible taxpayer is a taxpayer with annual household income between 100 percent and 400 percent of the Federal poverty level for a family of the taxpayer's size and that does not have access to affordable minimum essential healthcare coverage. The amount of the credit equals the lesser of (1) the actual premiums paid by the taxpayer for such coverage or (2) the difference between the cost of a statutorily-identified benchmark plan offered on the exchange and a required payment by the taxpayer that increases with income.

129. **Credit for employee health insurance expenses of small business.**—The baseline tax system would not allow credits for particular activities or targeted at specific groups. In contrast, the Tax Code provides a tax credit to qualified small employers that make a certain level of non-elective contributions towards the purchase of certain health insurance coverage for its employees. To receive a credit, an employer must have fewer than 25 full-time-equivalent employees whose average annual full-time-equivalent wages from the employer are less than $50,000 (indexed for taxable years after 2013). However, to receive a full credit, an employer must have no more than 10 full-time employees, and the average wage paid to these employees must be no more than $25,000 (indexed for taxable years after 2013). A qualifying employer may claim the credit for any taxable year beginning in 2010, 2011, 2012, and 2013 and for up to two years for insurance purchased through a Health Insurance Exchange thereafter. For taxable years beginning in 2010, 2011, 2012, and 2013, the maximum credit is 35 percent of premiums paid by qualified taxable employers and 25 percent of premiums paid by qualified tax-exempt organizations. For taxable years beginning in 2014 and later years, the maximum tax credit increases to 50 percent of premiums paid by qualified taxable employers and 35 percent of premiums paid by qualified tax-exempt organizations.

130. **Deductibility of charitable contributions to health institutions.**—The baseline tax system would not allow a deduction for personal expenditures including charitable contributions. In contrast, the Tax Code provides individuals and corporations a deduction for contributions to nonprofit health institutions. Tax expenditures resulting from the deductibility of contributions to other charitable institutions are listed under the education, training, employment, and social services function.

131. **Tax credit for orphan drug research.**—The baseline tax system would not allow credits for particular activities, investments, or industries. In contrast, under current law drug firms can claim a tax credit of 50 percent of the costs for clinical testing required by the Food and Drug Administration for drugs that treat rare physical conditions or rare diseases. This rate is modified to 25 percent by TCJA for expenditures incurred or paid in tax years beginning after December 31, 2017.

132. **Special Blue Cross/Blue Shield tax benefits.**—The baseline tax system generally would tax all profits under the regular tax rate schedule using broadly applicable measures of baseline income. It would not allow preferentially low tax rates to apply to certain types or sources of income. In contrast, certain Blue Cross and Blue Shield (BC/BS) health insurance providers and certain other health insurers are provided with special tax benefits, provided that their percentage of total premium revenue expended on reimbursement for clinical services provided to enrollees or for activities that improve healthcare quality is not less than 85 percent for the taxable year. A qualifying insurer may take as a deduction 100 percent

of any net increase in its unearned premium reserves, instead of the 80 percent allowed other insurers. A qualifying insurer is also allowed a special deduction equal to the amount by which 25 percent of its health-claim expenses exceeds its beginning-of-the-year accounting surplus. The deduction is limited to the insurer's taxable income determined without the special deduction.

133. Tax credit for health insurance purchased by certain displaced and retired individuals.—The baseline tax system would not allow credits for particular activities, investments, or industries. In contrast, the Tax Code provides a refundable tax credit of 72.5 percent for the purchase of health insurance coverage by individuals eligible for Trade Adjustment Assistance and certain Pension Benefit Guarantee Corporation pension recipients. This provision will expire on December 31, 2020.

134. Distributions from retirement plans for premiums for health and long-term care insurance.—Under the baseline tax system, all compensation, including dedicated and deferred payments, should be included in taxable income. In contrast, the Tax Code provides for tax-free distributions of up to $3,000 from governmental retirement plans for premiums for health and long term care premiums of public safety officers.

Income Security

135. Child credit.—The baseline tax system would not allow credits for particular activities or targeted at specific groups. Under current law, however, taxpayers with children under age 17 can qualify for a $2,000 per child partially refundable child credit. Up to $1,400 per child of unclaimed credit due to insufficient tax liability may be refundable—taxpayers may claim a refund for 15 percent of earnings in excess of a $2,500 floor, up to the lesser of the amount of unused credit or $1,400 per child. To be eligible for the child credit, the child must have a Social Security Number (SSN). A taxpayer may also claim a nonrefundable credit of $500 for each qualifying child not eligible for the $2,000 credit (those over sixteen and those without SSNs) and for each dependent relative. The total combined child and other dependent credit is phased out for taxpayers at the rate of $50 per $1,000 of modified AGI above $400,000 ($200,000 for single or head of household filers and $200,000 for married taxpayers filing separately). For tax years beginning after December 31, 2025, the credit returns to its pre-TCJA value of $1,000. At that time, up to the full value of the credit (subject to a phase-in of 15 percent of earnings in excess of $3,000) will be refundable and the $500 other dependent credit will expire. The credit will once again phase out at the rate of $50 per $1,000 of modified AGI above $110,000 ($75,000 for single or head of household filers and $55,000 for married taxpayers filing separately). The social security requirement will remain in place.

136. Exclusion of railroad Social Security equivalent benefits.—Under the baseline tax system, all compensation, including dedicated and deferred payments, should be included in taxable income. In contrast, the Social Security Equivalent Benefit paid to railroad retirees is not generally subject to the income tax unless the recipient's gross income reaches a certain threshold under current law. See provision number 156, Social Security benefits for retired workers, for discussion of the threshold.

137. Exclusion of workers' compensation benefits.—Under the baseline tax system, all compensation, including dedicated payments and in-kind benefits, should be included in taxable income. However, workers compensation is not subject to the income tax under current law.

138. Exclusion of public assistance benefits.—Under the reference tax law baseline, gifts and transfers are not treated as income to the recipients. In contrast, the normal tax method considers cash transfers from the Government as part of the recipients' income, and thus, treats the exclusion for public assistance benefits under current law as a tax expenditure.

139. Exclusion of special benefits for disabled coal miners.—Under the baseline tax system, all compensation, including dedicated payments and in-kind benefits, should be included in taxable income. However, disability payments to former coal miners out of the Black Lung Trust Fund, although income to the recipient, are not subject to the income tax.

140. Exclusion of military disability pensions.—Under the baseline tax system, all compensation, including dedicated payments and in-kind benefits, should be included in taxable income. In contrast, most of the military disability pension income received by current disabled military retirees is excluded from their income subject to tax.

141. Defined benefit employer plans.—Under the baseline tax system, all compensation, including deferred and dedicated payments, should be included in taxable income. In addition, investment income would be taxed as earned. In contrast, under current law certain contributions to defined benefit pension plans are excluded from an employee's gross income even though employers can deduct their contributions. In addition, the tax on the investment income earned by defined benefit pension plans is deferred until the money is withdrawn.

142. Defined contribution employer plans.—Under the baseline tax system, all compensation, including deferred and dedicated payments, should be included in taxable income. In addition, investment income would be taxed as earned. In contrast, under current law individual taxpayers and employers can make tax-preferred contributions to employer-provided 401(k) and similar plans (e.g. 403(b) plans and the Federal Government's Thrift Savings Plan). In 2019, an employee could exclude up to $19,000 of wages from AGI under a qualified arrangement with an employer's 401(k) plan. Employees age 50 or over could exclude up to $25,000 in contributions. The defined contribution plan limit, including both employee and employer contributions, is $56,000 in 2019. The tax on contributions made by both employees and employers and the investment income earned by these plans is deferred until withdrawn.

143. Individual Retirement Accounts (IRAs).—Under the baseline tax system, all compensation, including deferred and dedicated payments, should be included in taxable income. In addition, investment income would be taxed as earned. In contrast, under current law individual taxpayers can take advantage of traditional and Roth IRAs to defer or otherwise reduce the tax on the return to their retirement savings. The IRA contribution limit is $6,000 in 2019; taxpayers age 50 or over are allowed to make additional "catch-up" contributions of $1,000. Contributions to a traditional IRA are generally deductible but the deduction is phased out for workers with incomes above certain levels who, or whose spouses, are active participants in an employer-provided retirement plan. Contributions and account earnings are includible in income when withdrawn from traditional IRAs. Roth IRA contributions are not deductible, but earnings and withdrawals are exempt from taxation. Income limits also apply to Roth IRA contributions.

144. ***Low and moderate-income savers' credit.***—The baseline tax system would not allow credits for particular activities or targeted at specific groups. In contrast, the Tax Code provides an additional incentive for lower-income taxpayers to save through a nonrefundable credit of up to 50 percent on IRA and other retirement contributions of up to $2,000. This credit is in addition to any deduction or exclusion. The credit is completely phased out by $64,000 for joint filers, $48,000 for head of household filers, and $32,000 for other filers in 2019.

145. ***Self-employed plans.***—Under the baseline tax system, all compensation, including deferred and dedicated payments, should be included in taxable income. In addition, investment income would be taxed as earned. In contrast, under current law self-employed individuals can make deductible contributions to their own retirement plans equal to 25 percent of their income, up to a maximum of $56,000 in 2019. Total plan contributions are limited to 25 percent of a firm's total wages. The tax on the investment income earned by self-employed SEP, SIMPLE, and qualified plans is deferred until withdrawn.

146. ***Premiums on group term life insurance.***— Under the baseline tax system, all compensation, including deferred and dedicated payments, should be included in taxable income. In contrast, under current law employer-provided life insurance benefits are excluded from an employee's gross income (to the extent that the employer's share of the total costs does not exceed the cost of $50,000 of such insurance) even though the employer's costs for the insurance are a deductible business expense.

147. ***Premiums on accident and disability insurance.***—Under the baseline tax system, all compensation, including dedicated payments and in-kind benefits, should be included in taxable income. In contrast, under current law employer-provided accident and disability benefits are excluded from an employee's gross income even though the employer's costs for the benefits are a deductible business expense.

148. ***Exclusion of investment income from Supplementary Unemployment Benefit Trusts.***— Under the baseline tax system, all compensation, including dedicated payments and in-kind benefits, should be included in taxable income. In addition, invest-

ment income would be taxed as earned. Under current law, employers may establish trusts to pay supplemental unemployment benefits to employees separated from employment. Investment income earned by such trusts is exempt from taxation.

149. ***Exclusion of investment income from Voluntary Employee Benefit Associations trusts.***— Under the baseline tax system, all compensation, including dedicated payments and in-kind benefits, should be included in taxable income. Under current law, employers may establish associations, or VEBAs, to pay employee benefits, which may include health benefit plans, life insurance, and disability insurance, among other employee benefits. Investment income earned by such trusts is exempt from taxation.

150. ***Special Employee Stock Ownership Plan (ESOP) rules.***—ESOPs are a special type of tax-exempt employee benefit plan. Under the baseline tax system, all compensation, including dedicated payments and in-kind benefits, should be included in taxable income. In addition, investment income would be taxed as earned. In contrast, employer-paid contributions (the value of stock issued to the ESOP) are deductible by the employer as part of employee compensation costs. They are not included in the employees' gross income for tax purposes, however, until they are paid out as benefits. In addition, the following special income tax provisions for ESOPs are intended to increase ownership of corporations by their employees: (1) annual employer contributions are subject to less restrictive limitations than other qualified retirement plans; (2) ESOPs may borrow to purchase employer stock, guaranteed by their agreement with the employer that the debt will be serviced by his payment (deductible by him) of a portion of wages (excludable by the employees) to service the loan; (3) employees who sell appreciated company stock to the ESOP may defer any taxes due until they withdraw benefits; (4) dividends paid to ESOP-held stock are deductible by the employer; and (5) earnings are not taxed as they accrue.

151. ***Additional deduction for the blind.***—Under the baseline tax system, the standard deduction is allowed. An additional standard deduction for a targeted group within a given filing status would not be allowed. In contrast, the Tax Code allows taxpayers who are blind to claim an additional $1,650 standard deduction if single, or $1,300 if married in 2019.

152. ***Additional deduction for the elderly.***— Under the baseline tax system, the standard deduction is allowed. An additional standard deduction for a targeted group within a given filing status would not be allowed. In contrast, the Tax Code allows taxpayers who are 65 years or older to claim an additional $1,650 standard deduction if single, or $1,300 if married in 2019.

153. ***Tax credit for the elderly and disabled.***— Under the baseline tax system, a credit targeted at a specific group within a given filing status or for particular activities would not be allowed. In contrast, the Tax Code allows taxpayers who are 65 years of age or older, or who are permanently disabled, to claim a non-refundable tax credit equal to 15 percent of the sum of their earned and

retirement income. The amount to which the 15 percent rate is applied is limited to no more than $5,000 for single individuals or married couples filing a joint return where only one spouse is 65 years of age or older or disabled, and up to $7,500 for joint returns where both spouses are 65 years of age or older or disabled. These limits are reduced by one-half of the taxpayer's adjusted gross income over $7,500 for single individuals and $10,000 for married couples filing a joint return.

154. ***Deductibility of casualty losses.***—Under the baseline tax system, neither the purchase of property nor insurance premiums to protect the property's value are deductible as costs of earning income. Therefore, reimbursement for insured loss of such property is not included as a part of gross income, and uninsured losses are not deductible. In contrast, the Tax Code provides a deduction for uninsured casualty and theft losses of more than $100 each, to the extent that total losses during the year exceed 10 percent of the taxpayer's adjusted gross income. In the case of taxable years beginning after December 31, 2017, and before January 1, 2026, personal casualty losses are deductible only to the extent they are attributable to a federally declared disaster area.

155. ***Earned income tax credit (EITC).***—The baseline tax system would not allow credits for particular activities or targeted at specific groups. In contrast, the Tax Code provides an EITC to low-income workers at a maximum rate of 45 percent of income. In 2019, for a family with one qualifying child, the credit is 34 percent of the first $10,370 of earned income. The credit is 40 percent of the first $14,570 of income for a family with two qualifying children, and it is 45 percent of the first $14,570 of income for a family with three or more qualifying children. Low-income workers with no qualifying children are eligible for a 7.65 percent credit on the first $6,920 of earned income. The credit plateaus and then phases out with the greater of AGI or earnings at income levels and rates which depend upon how many qualifying children are eligible and marital status. In 2018, the phase-down for married filers begins at incomes $5,790 ($5,800 for filers without children) greater than for otherwise similar unmarried filers. Earned income tax credits in excess of tax liabilities owed through the individual income tax system are refundable to individuals. Beginning in 2018, the parameters of the EITC are indexed by the chained CPI, which results in a smaller inflation adjustment. This change is permanent.

Social Security

156. ***Social Security benefits for retired and disabled workers and spouses, dependents, and survivors.***—The baseline tax system would tax Social Security benefits to the extent that contributions to Social Security were not previously taxed. Thus, the portion of Social Security benefits that is attributable to employer contributions and to earnings on employer and employee contributions (and not attributable to employee contributions which are taxed at the time of contribution) would be subject to tax. In contrast, the Tax Code may not tax all of the Social Security benefits that exceed the beneficiary's contributions from previously taxed income. Actuarially, previously taxed contributions generally do not exceed 15 percent of benefits, even for retirees receiving the highest levels of benefits. Therefore, up to 85 percent of recipients' Social Security and Railroad Social Security Equivalent retirement benefits are included in (phased into) the income tax base if the recipient's provisional income exceeds certain base amounts. (Provisional income is equal to other items included in adjusted gross income plus foreign or U.S. possession income, tax-exempt interest, and one half of Social Security and Railroad Social Security Equivalent retirement benefits.) The untaxed portion of the benefits received by taxpayers who are below the income amounts at which 85 percent of the benefits are taxable is counted as a tax expenditure. Benefits paid to disabled workers and to spouses, dependents, and survivors are treated in a similar manner. Railroad Social Security Equivalent benefits are treated like Social Security benefits. See also provision number 136, Exclusion of railroad Social Security equivalent benefits.

157. ***Credit for certain employer Social Security contributions.***—Under the baseline tax system, employer contributions to Social Security represent labor cost and are deductible expenses. Under current law, however, certain employers are allowed a tax credit, instead of a deduction, against taxes paid on tips received from customers in connection with the providing, delivering, or serving of food or beverages for consumption. The tip credit equals the full amount of the employer's share of FICA taxes paid on the portion of tips, when added to the employee's non-tip wages, in excess of $5.15 per hour. The credit is available only with respect to FICA taxes paid on tips.

Veterans Benefits and Services

158. ***Exclusion of veterans death benefits and disability compensation.***—Under the baseline tax system, all compensation, including dedicated payments and in-kind benefits, should be included in taxable income because they represent accretions to wealth that do not materially differ from cash wages. In contrast, all compensation due to death or disability paid by the Veterans Administration is excluded from taxable income under current law.

159. ***Exclusion of veterans pensions.***—Under the baseline tax system, all compensation, including dedicated payments and in-kind benefits, should be included in taxable income because they represent accretions to wealth that do not materially differ from cash wages. Under current law, however, pension payments made by the Veterans Administration are excluded from gross income.

160. ***Exclusion of G.I. Bill benefits.***—Under the baseline tax system, all compensation, including dedicated payments and in-kind benefits, should be included in taxable income because they represent accretions to wealth that do not materially differ from cash wages.

Under current law, however, G.I. Bill benefits paid by the Veterans Administration are excluded from gross income.

161. ***Exclusion of interest on veterans housing bonds.***—The baseline tax system generally would tax all income under the regular tax rate schedule. It would not allow preferentially low (or zero) tax rates to apply to certain types or sources of income. In contrast, under current law, interest earned on general obligation bonds issued by State and local governments to finance housing for veterans is excluded from taxable income.

General Government

162. ***Exclusion of interest on public purpose State and local bonds.***—The baseline tax system generally would tax all income under the regular tax rate schedule. It would not allow preferentially low (or zero) tax rates to apply to certain types or sources of income. In contrast, under current law interest earned on State and local government bonds issued to finance public-purpose construction (e.g., schools, roads, sewers), equipment acquisition, and other public purposes is tax-exempt. Interest on bonds issued by Indian tribal governments for essential governmental purposes is also tax-exempt.

163. ***Build America Bonds.***—The baseline tax system would not allow credits for particular activities or targeted at specific groups. In contrast, the Tax Code in 2009 allowed State and local governments to issue taxable bonds through 2010 and receive a direct payment from Treasury equal to 35 percent of interest expenses. Alternatively, State and local governments could issue

taxable bonds and the private lenders receive the 35 percent credit which is included in taxable income.

164. ***Deductibility of nonbusiness State and local taxes other than on owner-occupied homes.***—Under the baseline tax system, a deduction for personal consumption expenditures would not be allowed. In contrast, the Tax Code allows taxpayers who itemize their deductions to claim a deduction for State and local income taxes (or, at the taxpayer's election, State and local sales taxes) and property taxes, even though these taxes primarily pay for services that, if purchased directly by taxpayers, would not be deductible. (The estimates for this tax expenditure do not include the estimates for the deductibility of State and local property tax on owner-occupied homes. See item 57.) In the case of taxable years beginning after December 31, 2017, and before January 1, 2026, (1) the deduction for foreign real property taxes paid is disallowed and (2) the deduction for taxes paid in any taxable year, which includes the deduction for property taxes on real property, is limited to $10,000 ($5,000 in the case of a married individual filing a separate return).

Interest

165. ***Deferral of interest on U.S. savings bonds.***—The baseline tax system would uniformly tax all returns to investments and not allow an exemption or deferral for particular activities, investments, or industries. In contrast, taxpayers may defer paying tax on interest earned on U.S. savings bonds until the bonds are redeemed.

APPENDIX A

Performance Measures and the Economic Effects of Tax Expenditures

The Government Performance and Results Act of 1993 (GPRA) directs Federal Agencies to develop annual and strategic plans for their programs and activities. These plans set out performance objectives to be achieved over a specific time period. Most of these objectives are achieved through direct expenditure programs. Tax expenditures—spending programs implemented through the tax code by reducing tax obligations for certain activities—contribute to achieving these goals in a manner similar to direct expenditure programs.

Tax expenditures by definition work through the tax system and, particularly, the income tax. Thus, they may be relatively advantageous policy approaches when the benefit or incentive is related to income and is intended to be widely available. Because there is an existing public administrative and private compliance structure for the tax system, income-based programs that require little oversight might be efficiently run through the tax system. In addition, some tax expenditures actually simplify the operation of the tax system (for example, the exclusion for up to $500,000 of capital gains on home sales). Tax expenditures also implicitly subsidize certain activities in a manner similar to direct expenditures. For example, exempting employer-sponsored health insurance from income taxation is equivalent to a direct spending subsidy equal to the forgone tax obligations for this type of compensation. Spending, regulatory, or tax-disincentive policies can also modify behavior, but may have different economic effects. Finally, a variety of tax expenditure tools can be used, e.g., deductions, credits, exemptions, deferrals, floors, ceilings, phase-ins, phase-outs, and these can be dependent on income, expenses, or demographic characteristics (age, number of family members, etc.). This wide range of policy instruments means that tax expenditures can be flexible and can have very different economic effects.

Tax expenditures also have limitations. In many cases they add to the complexity of the tax system, which raises both administrative and compliance costs. For example, personal exemptions, deductions, credits, and phase-outs can complicate filing and decision-making. The income tax system may have little or no contact with persons who have no or very low incomes, and does not require information on certain characteristics of individuals used in some spending programs, such as wealth or duration of employment. These features may reduce the effectiveness of tax expenditures for addressing socioeconomic disparities. Tax expenditures also generally do not enable the same degree of agency discretion as an outlay program. For example, grant or direct Federal service delivery programs can prioritize activities to be addressed with specific resources in a way that is difficult to emulate with tax expenditures.

Outlay programs have advantages where the direct provision of Government services is particularly warranted, such as equipping and maintaining the Armed Forces or administering the system of justice. Outlay programs may also be specifically designed to meet the needs of low-income families who would not otherwise be subject to income taxes or need to file a tax return. Outlay programs may also receive more year-to-year oversight and fine tuning through the legislative and executive budget process. In addition, many different types of spending programs include direct Government provision; credit programs; and payments to State and local governments, the private sector, or individuals in the form of grants or contracts, which provide flexibility for policy design. On the other hand, certain outlay programs may rely less directly on economic incentives and private-market provision than tax incentives, thereby reducing the relative efficiency of spending programs for some goals. Finally, spending programs, particularly on the discretionary side, may respond less rapidly to changing activity levels and economic conditions than tax expenditures.

Regulations may have more direct and immediate effects than outlay and tax-expenditure programs because regulations apply directly and immediately to the regulated party (i.e., the intended actor), generally in the private sector. Regulations can also be fine-tuned more quickly than tax expenditures because they can often be changed as needed by the Executive Branch without legislation. Like tax expenditures, regulations often rely largely on voluntary compliance, rather than detailed inspections and policing. As such, the public administrative costs tend to be modest relative to the private resource costs associated with modifying activities. Historically, regulations have tended to rely on proscriptive measures, as opposed to economic incentives. This reliance can diminish their economic efficiency, although this feature can also promote full compliance where (as in certain safety-related cases) policymakers believe that trade-offs with economic considerations are not of paramount importance. Also, regulations generally do not directly affect Federal outlays or receipts. Thus, like tax expenditures, they may escape the degree of scrutiny that outlay programs receive.

A Framework for Evaluating the Effectiveness of Tax Expenditures

Across all major budgetary categories—from housing and health to space, technology, agriculture, and national defense—tax expenditures make up a significant portion of Federal activity and affect every area of the economy. For these reasons, a comprehensive evaluation framework that examines incentives, direct results, and spillover effects will benefit the budgetary process by informing decisions on tax expenditure policy.

As described above, tax expenditures, like spending and regulatory programs, have a variety of objectives and economic effects. These include encouraging certain types of activities (e.g., saving for retirement or investing in certain sectors); increasing certain types of after-tax income (e.g., favorable tax treatment of Social Security income); and reducing private compliance costs and Government administrative costs (e.g., the exclusion for up to $500,000 of capital gains on home sales). Some of these objectives are well-suited to quantitative measurement and evaluation, while others are less well-suited.

Performance measurement is generally concerned with inputs, outputs, and outcomes. In the case of tax expenditures, the principal input is usually the revenue effect. Outputs are quantitative or qualitative measures of goods and services, or changes in income and investment, directly produced by these inputs. Outcomes, in turn, represent the changes in the economy, society, or environment that are the ultimate goals of programs. Evaluations assess whether programs are meeting intended goals, but may also encompass analyzing whether initiatives are superior to other policy alternatives.

The Administration is working toward examining the objectives and effects of the wide range of tax expenditures in our budget, despite challenges related to data availability, measurement, and analysis. Evaluations include an assessment of whether tax expenditures are achieving intended policy results in an efficient manner, with minimal burdens on individual taxpayers, consumers, and firms, and an examination of possible unintended effects and their consequences.

As an illustration of how evaluations can inform budgetary decisions, consider education and research investment credits.

Education. There are millions of individuals taking advantage of tax credits designed to help pay for educational expenses. There are a number of different credits available as well as other important forms of Federal support for higher education such as subsidized student loans and grants. An evaluation would explore the possible relationships between use of the credits and the use of student loans and grants, seeking to answer, for example, whether the use of credits reduces or increases the likelihood of students applying for loans. Such an evaluation would allow stakeholders to determine the need for programs— whether they involve tax credits, subsidized loans, or grants.

Investment. A series of tax expenditures reduce the cost of investment, both in specific activities such as research and experimentation, extractive industries, and certain financial activities, and more generally throughout the economy, through accelerated depreciation for plant and equipment. These provisions can be evaluated along a number of dimensions. For example, it is useful to consider the strength of the incentives by measuring their effects on the cost of capital (the return which investments must yield to cover their costs) and effective tax rates. The impact of these provisions on the amount of cor-

responding forms of investment (e.g., research spending, exploration activity, equipment) might also be estimated. In some cases, such as research, there is evidence that this private investment can provide significant positive externalities—that is, economic benefits that are not reflected in the market transactions between private parties. It could be useful to quantify these externalities and compare them with the size of tax expenditures. Measures could also indicate the effects on production from these investments such as numbers or values of patents, energy production and reserves, and industrial production. Issues to be considered include the extent to which the preferences increase production (as opposed to benefiting existing output) and their cost-effectiveness relative to other policies. Analysis could also consider objectives that are more difficult to measure but could be ultimate goals, such as promoting energy security or economic growth. Such an assessment is likely to involve tax analysis as well as consideration of non-tax matters such as market structure, scientific, and other information.

The tax proposals subject to these analyses include items that indirectly affect the estimated value of tax expenditures (such as changes in income tax rates), proposals that make reforms to improve tax compliance and administration, as well as proposals which would change, add, or delete tax expenditures.

Barriers to Evaluation. Developing a framework that is sufficiently comprehensive, accurate, and flexible is a significant challenge. Evaluations are constrained by the availability of appropriate data and challenges in economic modeling:

- Data availability—Data may not exist, or may not exist in an analytically appropriate form, to conduct rigorous evaluations of certain types of expenditures. For example, measuring the effects of tax expenditures designed to achieve tax neutrality for individuals and firms earning income abroad, and foreign firms could require data from foreign governments or firms which are not readily available.

- Analytical constraints—Evaluations of tax expenditures face analytical constraints even when data are available. For example, individuals might have access to several tax expenditures and programs aimed at improving the same outcome. Isolating the effect of a single tax credit is challenging absent a well-specified research design.

- Resources—Tax expenditure analyses are seriously constrained by staffing considerations. Evaluations typically require expert analysts who are often engaged in other areas of work related to the budget.

The Executive Branch is focused on addressing these challenges to lay the foundation for the analysis of tax expenditures comprehensively, alongside evaluations of the effectiveness of direct spending initiatives.

APPENDIX B

TAX EXPENDITURE PRESENTATION UNDER ALTERNATIVE BASELINES

The 2020 Budget provided a presentation of the Department of Treasury review of the tax expenditure budget. This appendix revisits the earlier review with a focus on current tax expenditures identified (1) using comprehensive income as a baseline tax system and (2) using a consumption tax as a baseline tax system.

The first section of this appendix compares major tax expenditures in the current budget to those implied by a comprehensive income baseline. This comparison includes a discussion of negative tax expenditures. The second section compares the major tax expenditures in the current budget to those implied by a consumption tax baseline, and also discusses negative tax expenditures.

DIFFERENCES BETWEEN OFFICIAL TAX EXPENDITURES AND THOSE BASED ONCOMPREHENSIVE INCOME

As discussed in the main body of the this chapter, official tax expenditures are measured relative to normal tax or reference tax law baselines that deviate from a uniform tax on a comprehensive concept of income. Consequently, tax expenditures identified in the budget can differ from those that would be identified if a comprehensive income tax were chosen as the baseline tax system. This appendix addresses this issue by comparing major tax expenditures listed in the current tax expenditure budget with those implied by a comprehensive income baseline. Many large tax expenditures would continue to be tax expenditures were the baseline taken to be comprehensive income, al-

Table 13–5. COMPARISON OF CURRENT TAX EXPENDITURES WITH THOSE IMPLIED BY A COMPREHENSIVE INCOME TAX[1]

Description	Revenue Effect 2029
A. Tax Expenditure Under a Comprehensive Income Tax	
Exclusion of net imputed rental income on owner-occupied housing	212,650
Defined contribution employer plans	184,180
Capital gains (except agriculture, timber, iron ore, and coal)	157,060
Reduced tax rate on active income of controlled foreign corporations	82,810
Capital gains exclusion on home sales	76,230
Defined benefit employer plans	86,795
Self-Employed plans	75,380
Individual Retirement Accounts	43,430
Exclusion of interest on public purpose State and local bonds	30,840
Exclusion of veterans death beenfits and disability compensation	13,230
Credit for low-income housing investments	11,390
Exclusion of workers' compensation benefits	10,680
B. Possibly a Tax Expenditure Under a Comprehensive Income Tax, But With Some Qualifications	
Deductibility of nonbusiness State and local taxes other than on owner-occupied homes	131,130
Deductibility of mortgage interest on owner-occupied homes	*125,820*
Step-up basis of capital gains at death	84,860
Deductibility of State and local property tax on owner-occupied homes	65,340
Exclusion of Social Security benefits for retired workers	52,670
Child credit	20,240
Earned income tax credit	11,070
C. Uncertain	
Exclusion of employer contributions for medical insurance premiums and medical care	438,240
Deductibility of charitable contributions, other than education and health	92,980
Deductibility of medical expenses	25,990
Deductibility of self-employed medical insurance premiums	14,670
D. Probably Not a Tax Expenditure Under a Comprehensive Income Tax	
Exception from passive loss rules for $25,000 of rental loss	10,490

[1] The measurement of certain tax expenditures under a comprehensive income tax baseline may differ from the official budget estimate even when the provision would be a tax expenditure under both baselines.
Source: Table 13–1, Tax Expenditure Budget.

Table 13–6.   COMPARISON OF CURRENT TAX EXPENDITURES WITH THOSE IMPLIED BY A COMPREHENSIVE CONSUMPTION TAX[1]

Description	Revenue Effect 2029
A. Tax Expenditure Under a Consumption Base	
Exclusion of net imputed rental income on owner-occupied housing	212,650
Exclusion of workers' compensation benefits	10,680
B. Probably a Tax Expenditure Under a Consumption Base	
Deductibility of mortgage interest on owner-occupied homes	125,820
Deductibility of nonbusiness State and local taxes other than on owner-occupied homes	131,130
Child credit	20,240
Exclusion of Social Security benefits for retired workers	52,670
Earned income tax credit	11,070
Exclusion of veterans death beenfits and disability compensation	13,230
C. Uncertain	
Exclusion of employer contributions for medical insurance premiums and medical care	438,240
Deductibility of charitable contributions, other than education and health	92,980
Deductibility of State and local property tax on owner-occupied homes	65,340
Deductibility of medical expenses	25,990
Deductibility of self-employed medical insurance premiums	14,670
Credit for low-income housing investments	11,390
D. Not a Tax Expenditure Under a Consumption Base	
Defined benefit employer plans	86,795
Defined contribution employer plans	184,180
Capital gains exclusion on home sales	76,230
Step-up basis of capital gains at death	84,860
Capital gains (except agriculture, timber, iron ore, and coal)	157,060
Exclusion of interest on public purpose State and local bonds	30,840
Self-Employed plans	75,380
Reduced tax rate on active income of controlled foreign corporations (normal tax method)	82,810
Individual Retirement Accounts	43,430
Exception from passive loss rules for $25,000 of rental loss	10,490

[1] The measurement of certain tax expenditures under a consumption tax baseline may differ from the official budget estimate even when the provision would be a tax expenditure under both baselines.

Source: Table 13–1, Tax Expenditure Budget.

though some would be smaller. A comprehensive income baseline would also result in a number of additional tax provisions being counted as tax expenditures.

Current budgetary practice excludes from the list of official tax expenditures those provisions that over-tax certain items of income. This exclusion conforms to the view that tax expenditures are substitutes for direct Government spending programs. However, this treatment gives a one-sided picture of how current law deviates from the baseline tax system. Relative to comprehensive income, a number of current tax provisions would be negative tax expenditures. Some of these also might be negative tax expenditures under the reference law or normal law baselines, expanded to admit negative tax expenditures.

Treatment of Major Tax Expenditures from the Current Budget under a Comprehensive Income Tax Baseline

Comprehensive income, also called Haig-Simons income, is the real, inflation adjusted, accretion to one's economic power arising between two points in time, e.g., the beginning and ending of the year. It includes all accretions to wealth, whether or not realized, whether or not related to a market transaction, and whether a return to capital or labor. Inflation adjusted capital gains (and losses) would be included in comprehensive income as they accrue. Business, investment, and casualty losses, including losses caused by depreciation, would be deducted. Implicit returns, such as those accruing to homeowners, also would be included in comprehensive income. A comprehensive income tax baseline would tax all sources of income once. Thus, it would not include a separate tax on corporate income that leads to the double taxation of corporate profits.

While comprehensive income can be defined on the sources side of the consumer's balance sheet, it sometimes is instructive to use the identity between the sources of wealth and the uses of wealth to redefine it as the sum of consumption during the period plus the change in net worth between the beginning and the end of the period.

Comprehensive income has some validity[4], but it suffers from a host of problems. These include conceptual ambiguities, some of which are discussed below, as well as practical problems in measurement and tax administration, e.g., how to implement a practicable deduction for economic depreciation or include in income the return earned on consumer durable goods, including housing, automobiles, and major appliances. Furthermore, comprehensive income does not necessarily represent an ideal tax base; efficiency or equity might be improved by deviating from this tax base, e.g., by reducing the tax rate on capital income in order to further spur economic growth. In addition, some elements of comprehensive income would be difficult or impossible to administer in a tax system.

Classifying individual tax provisions relative to a comprehensive income baseline is difficult, in part because of the ambiguity of the baseline. It also is difficult because of interactions between tax provisions (or their absence). These interactions mean that it may not always be appropriate to consider each provision in isolation. Nonetheless, Appendix Table 13-5 attempts such a classification for each of the 25 largest tax expenditures from the Budget.

We classify fifteen of the 25 items as tax expenditures under a comprehensive income base (those in panel A). Most of these give preferential tax treatment to the return on certain types of savings or investment. They are a result of the explicitly hybrid nature of the existing tax system, and arise out of policy decisions that reflect discomfort with the high tax rate on capital income that would otherwise arise under the current structure of the income tax. Even these relatively clear cut items, however, can raise ambiguities particularly in light of the absence of integration of the corporate and individual tax systems. In the presence of a corporate income tax, the reduction or elimination of an individual level tax on income from investment in corporate equities might not be a tax expenditure relative to a comprehensive income baseline. Rather, an individual income tax preference might undo the corporate tax penalty (i.e., the double tax). A similar line of reasoning could be used to argue that in the case of corporations, expensing[5] of R&E is not a tax expenditure because it serves to offset the corporate tax penalty.

The failure to tax net rental income from owner-occupied housing was considered as a tax expenditure for the first time in the 2006 Budget. Because net rental income (gross rents minus depreciation, interest, taxes, and other expenses) would be in the homeowner's tax base under a comprehensive income baseline, this item would be a tax expenditure relative to a comprehensive income baseline.

The exclusion of worker's compensation benefits also would be a tax expenditure under a comprehensive income baseline. For example, if a worker were to buy unemployment insurance himself, he would be able to deduct the premium (since it represents a reduction in net worth) but should include in income the benefit when paid (since it represents an increase in net worth).[6] If the employer pays the premium, the proper treatment would allow the employer a deduction and allow the employee to disregard the premium, but he would take the proceeds, if any, into income. Current law allows the employer to deduct the premium and excludes both the premium and the benefits from the employee's tax base.

Veteran's death and disability benefits may represent a tax expenditure. This is clearly the case to the extent that they are seen as deferred wages or as transfers. It also is the case to the extent that they are seen as insurance benefits, since the premiums, which come in the form of foregone wages, were not included in taxable income. [7]

Panel B deals with items that may be tax expenditures but that raise issues. Current law allows deductions for home mortgage interest and for property taxes on owner-occupied housing. The tax expenditure budget includes both of these deductions. From one perspective, these two deductions would not be considered tax expenditures relative to a comprehensive income base; this base would allow both deductions. However, this perspective ignores current law's failure to impute gross rental income. Conditional on this failure, the deductions for interest and property taxes might be viewed as inappropriate because they move the tax system away from rather than toward a comprehensive income base.[8] Indeed, the sum of the tax expenditure for these two deductions, plus the tax expenditure for the failure to include net rental income, sums to the tax expenditure for owner-occupied housing relative to a comprehensive income base. Consequently, there is an argument for classifying them as tax expenditures relative to a comprehensive income baseline.

The deduction of nonbusiness State and local taxes other than on owner-occupied homes also is included in this section. These taxes include income, sales, and property taxes. The stated justification for this tax expenditure is that, "Taxpayers may deduct State and local income taxes and property taxes even though these taxes primarily pay

---

[4] See, e.g., David F. Bradford, *Untangling the Income Tax* 15–31 (Harvard University Press 1986) and Richard Goode, *The Economic Definition of Income*, in *Comprehensive Income Taxation* 1–29 (Joseph Pechman ed., The Brookings Institution 1977).

[5] Expensing means immediate deduction. Proper income tax treatment requires capitalization followed by annual depreciation allowances reflecting the decay in value of the associated R&E spending.

[6] Suppose a taxpayer buys a one year term unemployment insurance policy at the beginning of the year. At that time he exchanges one asset, cash, for another, the insurance policy, so there is no change in net worth. But, at the end of the year, the policy expires and so is worthless, hence the taxpayer has a reduction in net worth equal to the premium. If the policy pays off during the year (i.e., the taxpayer has a work-related injury), then the taxpayer would include the proceeds in income because they represent an increase in his net worth.

[7] The treatment of insurance premiums and benefits is discussed more completely below.

[8] If there were no deduction for interest and property taxes, the tax expenditure base (i.e., the proper tax base minus the actual tax base) for owner-occupied housing would equal the homeowner's net rental income: gross rents minus (depreciation+interest+property taxes+other expenses). With the deduction for interest and property taxes, the tax expenditure base rises to gross rents minus (depreciation+other expenses).

for services that, if purchased directly by taxpayers, would not be deductible."[9] The idea is that these taxes represent (or serve as proxies for) consumption expenditures for which current law makes no imputations to income.[10]

In contrast to the view in the official Budget, the deduction for State and local taxes might not be a tax expenditure if the baseline were comprehensive income. Properly measured comprehensive income would include the value of State and local government benefits received, but would allow a deduction for State and local taxes paid.[11] Thus, in this sense the deductibility of State and local taxes may be consistent with the comprehensive income base, meaning it is not a tax expenditure. Nonetheless, imputing the value of State and local services is difficult and is not done under current law. Consequently, a deduction for taxes might sensibly be viewed as a tax expenditure relative to a comprehensive income baseline.[12]

To the extent that the personal and dependent care exemptions and the standard deduction properly remove from taxable income all expenditures that do not yield suitably discretionary consumption value, or otherwise appropriately adjust for differing taxpaying capacity, then the child care credit and the earned income tax credit would be tax expenditures. In contrast, a competing perspective views these credits as appropriate modifications that account for differing taxpaying capacity. Even accepting this competing perspective, however, one might question why these programs come in the form of credits rather than deductions.

The step-up of basis at death lowers the income tax on capital gains for those who inherit assets below what it would be otherwise. From that perspective it would be a tax expenditure under a comprehensive income baseline. Nonetheless, there are ambiguities. Under a comprehensive income baseline, all real inflation-adjusted gains would be taxed as accrued, so there would be no deferred unrealized gains on assets held at death.

The lack of full taxation of Social Security benefits also is listed in panel B. Consider first Social Security retirement benefits. To the extent that Social Security is viewed as a pension, a comprehensive income tax would include in income all contributions to Social Security retirement funds (payroll taxes) and tax accretions to value as they arise (inside build-up).[13] Benefits paid out of prior contributions and the inside build-up, however, would not be included in the tax base because the fall in the value of the individual's Social Security account would be offset by an increase in cash. In contrast, to the extent that Social Security is viewed as a transfer program, all contributions should be deductible from the income tax base and all benefits received should be included in the income tax base.

A similar analysis applies to Social Security benefits paid to dependents and survivors. If these benefits represent Government transfers, then they should be included in the tax base. If the taxpaying unit consists of the worker plus dependents and survivors, then to the extent that Social Security benefits represent payments from a pension, the annual pension earnings should be taxed in the same way that earnings accruing to retirees are taxed. However, benefits paid to dependents and survivors might be viewed as a gift or transfer from the decedent, in which case the dependents and survivors should pay tax on the full amount of the benefit received. (In this case the decedent or his estate should pay tax on the pension income as well, to the extent that the gift represents consumption rather than a reduction in net worth.) In addition, dependents' and survivors' benefits might be viewed in part as providing life insurance. In that case, the annual premiums paid each year, or the portion of Social Security taxes attributable to the premiums, should be deducted from income, since they represent a decline in net worth, while benefits should be included in income. Alternatively, taxing premiums and excluding benefits also would represent appropriate income tax policy. In contrast to any of these treatments, current law excludes one-half of Social Security contributions (employer-paid payroll taxes) from the base of the income tax, makes no attempt to tax accretions, and subjects some, but not all, benefits to taxation. The difference between current law's treatment of Social Security benefits and their treatment under a comprehensive income tax would qualify as a tax expenditure, but such a tax expenditure differs in concept from that included in the official budget. The tax expenditures in the official budget[14] reflect exemptions for lower income beneficiaries from the tax on 85 percent of Social Security benefits.[15] Historically, payroll taxes paid by the employee represented no more than 15 percent of the expected value of the retirement benefits received by a lower-earnings Social Security beneficiary. The 85 percent inclusion rate is intended to tax upon distribution the remaining amount of the retirement benefit payment, the portion arising from the payroll tax contributions made by employers, and the implicit return on the employee and employer contributions. Thus, the tax expenditure conceived and measured in the current budget is not intended to capture the deviation from a comprehensive income baseline, which would additionally account for

---

[9] Fiscal Year 2003 Budget of the United States Government, *Analytical Perspectives* 127 (U.S. Government Printing Office 2002).

[10] Property taxes on owner-occupied housing also might serve as a proxy for the value of untaxed local services provided to homeowners. As such, they would be listed in the tax expenditure budget (as configured, i.e., building on the estimate for the failure to tax net rents) twice, once because current law does not tax rental income and again as a proxy for Government services received. Property taxes on other consumer durables such as automobiles also might be included twice, owing to current law's exclusion from income of the associated service flow.

[11] U.S. Treasury, Blueprints for Basic Tax Reform (Washington, D.C.: U.S. Government Printing Office, 1977) p. 92.

[12] Under the normal tax method employed by the Joint Committee on Taxation, the value of some public assistance benefits provided by State Governments is included as a tax expenditure, thereby raising a potential double counting issue.

[13] As a practical matter, this may be impossible to do. Valuing claims subject to future contingencies is very difficult, as discussed in Bradford,

supra note 4, at 23–24.

[14] This includes the tax expenditure for benefits paid to workers, that for benefits paid to survivors and dependents, and that for benefits paid to dependents.

[15] The current budget does not include as a tax expenditure the absence of income taxation on the employer's contributions (payroll taxes) to Social Security retirement at the time these contributions are made.

the deferral of tax on the employer's contributions and on the rate of return (less an inflation adjustment attributable to the employee's payroll tax contributions). Rather, it is intended to approximate the taxation of private pensions with employee contributions made from after-tax income,[16] on the assumption that Social Security is comparable to such pensions. Hence, the official tax expenditure understates the tax advantage accorded Social Security retirement benefits relative to a comprehensive income baseline. To the extent that the benefits paid to dependents and survivors should be taxed as private pensions, the same conclusion applies: the official tax expenditure understates the tax advantage.

The deduction for U.S. production activities also raises problems. To the extent it is viewed as a tax break for certain qualifying businesses ("manufacturers"), it would be a tax expenditure. In contrast, the deduction may prove to be so broad that it is available to most U.S. businesses, in which case it might not be seen as a tax expenditure. Rather, it would represent a feature of the baseline tax rate system, because the deduction is equivalent to a lower tax rate. In addition, to the extent that it is viewed as providing relief from the double tax on corporate profits, it might not be a tax expenditure.

The next category (panel C) includes items whose treatment is less certain. The proper treatment of some of these items under a comprehensive income tax is ambiguous, while others perhaps serve as proxies for what would be a tax expenditure under a comprehensive income base.[17] Consider, for example, the items relating to charitable contributions. Under existing law, charitable contributions are deductible, and this deduction is considered on its face a tax expenditure in the current budget.[18]

The treatment of charitable donations, however, is ambiguous under a comprehensive income tax. If charitable contributions are a consumption item for the giver, then they are properly included in his taxable income; a deduction for contributions would then be a tax expenditure relative to a comprehensive income baseline. In contrast, charitable contributions could represent a transfer of purchasing power from the giver to the receiver. As such, they would represent a reduction in the giver's net worth, not an item of consumption, and so properly would be deductible, implying that current law's treatment is not a tax expenditure. At the same time, however, the value of the charitable benefits received is income to the recipient. Under current law, such income generally is not taxed,

and so represents a tax expenditure whose size might be approximated by the size of the donor's contribution.[19]

Medical expenditures may or may not be an element of income (or consumption). Some argue that medical expenditures don't represent discretionary spending, and so are not really consumption. Instead, they are a reduction of net worth and should be excluded from the tax base. In contrast, others argue that there is no way to logically distinguish medical care from other consumption items. Those who view medical spending as consumption point out that there is choice in many healthcare decisions, e.g., whether to go to the best doctor, whether to have voluntary surgical procedures, and whether to exercise and eat nutritiously so as to improve and maintain one's health and minimize medical expenditures. This element of choice makes it more difficult to argue, at least in many cases, that medical spending is more "necessary" than, or otherwise different from, other consumption spending.

The exemption of full taxation of Social Security benefits paid to the disabled also raises some issues. Social Security benefits for the disabled most closely resemble either Government transfers or insurance. A comprehensive income tax would require the worker to include the benefit fully in his income and would allow him to deduct associated Social Security taxes. If viewed as insurance, he also could include the premium (i.e., tax) and exclude the benefit. The deviation between such treatment and current law's treatment (described above) would be a tax expenditure under a comprehensive income baseline.

In contrast, as described above, the official tax expenditure measures the benefit of exemption for low-income beneficiaries from the tax on 85 percent of Social Security benefits. This measurement does not correspond closely to that required under a comprehensive income base. If the payment of the benefit is viewed as a transfer and divorced from the treatment of Social Security taxes, then the current tax expenditure understates the tax expenditure measured relative to a comprehensive income baseline. If the payment of the benefit is viewed as a transfer but the inability to deduct the employee's share of the Social Security tax is simultaneously considered, then it is less likely that the current tax expenditure overstates the tax expenditure relative to a comprehensive income baseline, and in some cases it may generate a negative tax expenditure. If the benefit is viewed as insurance and the tax as a premium, then the current tax expenditure overstates the tax expenditure relative to a comprehensive income baseline. Indeed, in the insurance model, the ability to exclude from tax only one-half of the premium might suggest that one-half of the payout should be taxed, so that the current tax rules impose a greater tax burden than that implied by a comprehensive income tax, i.e., a negative tax expenditure.[20]

The final category (panel D) includes items that would not be tax expenditures under a comprehensive income

---

[16] Private pensions allow the employee to defer tax on all inside build-up. They also allow the employee to defer tax on contributions made by the employer, but not on contributions made directly by the employee. Applying these tax rules to Social Security would require the employee to include in his taxable income benefits paid out of inside build-up and out of the employer's contributions, but would allow the employee to exclude from his taxable income benefits paid out of his own contributions.

[17] See, e.g., Goode, supra note 4, at 16–17; Bradford, supra note 4, at 19–21, 30–31.

[18] The item also includes gifts of appreciated property, at least part of which represents a tax expenditure relative to an ideal income tax, even if one assumes that charitable donations are not consumption.

[19] If recipients tend to be in lower tax brackets, then the tax expenditure is smaller than when measured at the donor's tax rates.

[20] In contrast, the passive loss rules themselves, which restrict the deduction of losses, would be a negative tax expenditure when compared to a comprehensive tax base.

tax base. A tax based on comprehensive income would allow all losses to be deducted. Hence, the exception from the passive loss rules would not be a tax expenditure.

Major Tax Expenditures under a Comprehensive Income Baseline That Are Excluded from the Current Budget

While most of the major tax expenditures in the current budget also would be tax expenditures under a comprehensive income base, there also are tax expenditures relative to this base that are not found on the existing tax expenditure list. These additional tax expenditures include the imputed return from certain consumer durables (e.g., automobiles); the imputed return to consumption of financial services (e.g., checking account services received in kind and paid for by accepting a below market interest rate on deposits); the difference between capital gains (and losses) as they accrue and capital gains as they are realized; private gifts and inheritances received; in-kind benefits from such Government programs as food-stamps; Medicaid and public housing; the value of payouts from insurance policies;[21] and benefits received from private charities. Under some ideas of a comprehensive income baseline, the value of leisure and of household production of goods and services also would be included as tax expenditures. The personal exemption and standard deduction also might be considered tax expenditures, although they can be viewed differently, e.g., as elements of the basic tax rate schedule. The foreign tax credit also might be a tax expenditure, since a deduction for foreign taxes, rather than a credit, would seem to measure the income of U.S. residents properly.

Negative Tax Expenditures

Under current budgetary practice, negative tax expenditures—tax provisions that raise rather than lower taxes—are excluded from the official tax expenditure list. This exclusion conforms with the view that tax expenditures are intended to be similar to Government spending programs.

If attention is expanded from a focus on spending-like programs to include any deviation from the baseline tax system, negative tax expenditures would be of interest. Relative to a comprehensive income baseline, there are a number of important negative tax expenditures, some of which also might be viewed as negative tax expenditures under an expanded interpretation of the normal or reference law baseline. The passive loss rules, restrictions on the deductibility of capital losses, and NOL carry-forward requirements each would generate a negative tax expenditure, since a comprehensive income tax would allow full deductibility of losses. If human capital were considered an asset, then its cost (e.g., certain education and training expenses, including perhaps the cost of college and professional school) should be amortizable, but it is not under current law.[22] Some restricted deductions under the indi-

vidual AMT might be negative tax expenditures as might the phase-out of personal exemptions and of itemized deductions. The inability to deduct consumer interest also might be a negative tax expenditure, as an interest deduction may be required to properly measure income, as seen by the equivalence between borrowing and reduced lending.[23]

Current tax law also fails to index for inflation interest receipts, capital gains, depreciation, and inventories. This failure leads to negative tax expenditures because comprehensive income would be indexed for inflation. Current law, however, also fails to index for inflation the deduction for interest payments; this represents a (positive) tax expenditure.

The issue of indexing also highlights that even if one wished to focus only on tax policies that are similar to spending programs, accounting for some negative tax expenditures may be required. For example, the net subsidy created by accelerated depreciation is properly measured by the difference between depreciation allowances specified under existing tax law and economic depreciation, which is indexed for inflation.[24]

DIFFERENCES BETWEEN OFFICIAL TAX EXPENDITURES AND TAX EXPENDITURES RELATIVE TO A CONSUMPTION BASE

This section compares tax expenditures listed in the official tax expenditure budget with those implied by a comprehensive consumption tax baseline. It first discusses some of the difficulties encountered in trying to compare current tax provisions to those that would be observed under a comprehensive consumption base. Next, it discusses which of the thirty largest official tax expenditures would be tax expenditures under the consumption tax baseline, concluding that about one-half of the top thirty official tax expenditures would remain tax expenditures under this baseline. Most of those that fall off the list are tax incentives for savings and investment.

The section next discusses some major differences between current law and a comprehensive consumption tax baseline that are excluded from the current list of tax expenditures. These differences include the consumption value of owner-occupied housing and other consumer durables, benefits from in-kind Government transfers, and gifts. It concludes with a discussion of negative tax expenditures relative to a consumption tax baseline.

Ambiguities in Determining Tax Expenditures Relative to a Consumption Tax Baseline

A broad-based consumption tax is a combination of an income tax plus a deduction for net savings. This

---

[21] To the extent that premiums are deductible.

[22] Current law offers favorable treatment to some education costs, thereby creating (positive) tax expenditures. Current law allows expens-

ing of that part of the cost of education and career training that is related to foregone earnings and this would be a tax expenditure under a comprehensive income baseline.

[23] See Bradford, supra note 4, at 41.

[24] Accelerated depreciation can be described as the equivalent of an interest free loan from the Government to the taxpayer. Under Federal budget accounting principles, such a loan would be treated as an outlay equal to the present value of the foregone interest.

follows from the definition of comprehensive income as consumption plus the change in net worth. It therefore seems straightforward to say that the current law's deviations from a consumption base are the sum of (a) tax expenditures on an income baseline associated with exemptions and deductions for certain types of income and (b) overpayments of tax, or negative tax expenditures, to the extent net savings is not deductible from the tax base. In reality, however, the situation is more complicated. A number of issues arise, some of which also are problems in defining a comprehensive income baseline, but seem more severe, or at least only more obvious, for the consumption tax baseline.

It is not always clear how to treat certain items under a consumption tax baseline. One problem is determining whether a particular expenditure is an item of consumption. Spending on medical care and charitable donations are two examples. The classification below suggests that medical spending and charitable contributions might be included in the definition of consumption, but also considers an alternative view.

There may be more than one way to treat various items under a consumption tax baseline. For example, a consumption tax baseline might ignore borrowing and lending by excluding from the borrower's tax base the proceeds from loans, denying the borrower a deduction for payments of interest and principal, and excluding interest and principal payments received from the lender's tax base. On the other hand, a consumption tax baseline might include borrowing and lending in the tax base by requiring the borrower to add the proceeds from loans in his tax base, allowing the lender to deduct loans from his tax base, allowing the borrower to deduct payments of principal and interest, and requiring the lender to include receipt of principal and interest payments. In present value terms, the two approaches are equivalent for both the borrower and the lender; in particular both allow the tax base to measure consumption and both impose a zero effective tax rate on interest income. But which approach is taken obviously has different implications (at least on an annual flow basis) for the treatment of many important items of income and expense, such as the home mortgage interest deduction. The classification below suggests that the deduction for home mortgage interest could be a tax expenditure, but takes note of alternative views.

Some exclusions of income are equivalent in many respects to a consumption tax baseline treatment that immediately deducts the cost of an investment while taxing the future cash-flow. For example, exempting investment income is equivalent to a consumption tax baseline treatment as far as the normal rate of return on new investment is concerned. This is because expensing generates a tax reduction that offsets in present value terms the tax paid on the investment's future normal returns. Expensing gives the income from a marginal investment a zero effective tax rate. However, a yield exemption approach differs from a consumption tax baseline as far as the distribution of income and Government receipts is concerned. Pure profits in excess of the normal rate of return would be taxed under a consumption tax baseline, because they are an element of cash-flow, but would not be taxed under a yield exemption tax system. Should exemption of certain kinds of investment income, and certain investment tax credits, be regarded as the equivalent of a consumption tax baseline treatment? The classification that follows takes a fairly broad view of this equivalence and considers many tax provisions that reduce or eliminate the tax on capital income to be roughly consistent with a broad-based consumption tax.

Looking at provisions one at a time can be misleading. The hybrid character of the existing tax system leads to many provisions that might make good sense in the context of a consumption tax baseline, but that generate inefficiencies because of the problem of the "uneven playing field" when evaluated within the context of the existing tax rules. It is not clear how these should be classified. For example, many saving incentives are targeted to specific tax favored sources of capital income. The inability to save on a similar tax-favored basis irrespective of the ultimate purpose to which the savings is applied potentially distorts economic choices in ways that would not occur under a broad-based consumption tax. As another example, under a consumption value-added tax (VAT) based on the destination principle, there would be a rebate of the VAT on exports and a tax on imports. Does this mean that the extraterritorial income exclusion (the successor of the Foreign Sales Corporation provision) is not a tax expenditure? Resolution comes down to judgments about how broad is broad enough to be considered general, or whether it even matters at all that a provision is targeted in some way. The classification that follows views many savings incentives, even if targeted, as roughly consistent with a broad-based consumption tax.

In addition, provisions can interact even once an appropriate treatment is determined. For example, suppose that it is determined that financial flows are out of the tax base. Then the deduction for home mortgage interest would seem to be a tax expenditure. However, this conclusion is cast into doubt because current law generally taxes interest income. When combined with the homeowners' deduction, this results in a zero tax rate on the interest flow, consistent with a consumption tax baseline treatment.

Capital gains would not be a part of a consumption tax baseline. Proceeds from asset sales and sometimes borrowing would be part of the cash-flow tax base, but, for transactions between domestic investors at a flat tax rate, would cancel out in the economy as a whole. How should existing tax expenditures related to capital gains be classified? The classification below generally views available capital gains tax breaks as consistent with a broad-based consumption tax because they lower the tax rate on capital income toward the zero rate that is consistent with a consumption-based tax.

Such considerations suggest that trying to compute the current tax baseline's deviations from "the" base of a consumption tax is impossible because deviations cannot be uniquely determined, making it very difficult to do a consistent accounting of the differences between the current tax base and a consumption base. Nonetheless, Appendix

Table 13-6 attempts a classification based on the judgments outlined above.

Treatment of Major Tax Expenditures under a Comprehensive Consumption Tax Baseline

As noted above, the major difference between a consumption tax baseline and a comprehensive income baseline is in the treatment of savings, or in the taxation of capital income. Consequently, many current tax expenditures related to preferential taxation of capital income would not be tax expenditures under a consumption tax baseline. However, preferential treatment of items of income that is unrelated to moderately broad-based savings or investment incentives would remain tax expenditures under a consumption tax baseline. In addition, several official tax expenditures relating to items of income and expense are difficult to classify properly, while others may serve as proxies for properly measured tax expenditures.

Appendix Table 13-6 shows 30 large official tax expenditures from the Budget classified according to whether they would be considered a tax expenditure under a consumption tax baseline. Two of the 30 items would likely be a tax expenditure (shown in panel A) under a consumption tax baseline, while an additional seven (those in panel B) probably would be tax expenditures.

A consumption tax baseline would include in the homeowner's tax base the value of the implicit (gross) rental income from owner-occupied housing. Net rental income is a component of this, and so would be included as a tax expenditure, relative to a consumption tax baseline.[25]

The exclusion of workers' compensation benefits allows an exclusion from income that is unrelated to investment, and so would be included in the base of a consumption tax.

Consider next the deductibility of home mortgage interest and of property taxes on owner-occupied housing. Both items would seem to be strong candidates for inclusion as a tax expenditure, given current law's failure to impute the consumption value of housing. That is, focusing on the homeowner's tax base, these deductions move the tax system away from rather than toward the proper treatment of housing services.[26]

However, with respect to the home mortgage interest deduction, some ambiguity is introduced by the taxation of interest income to lenders. In a sense, the homeowner's deduction offsets the lenders inclusion, leaving (for equal tax rates) no net tax due on the interest flow, as would be appropriate under a consumption tax baseline. Hence, from the perspective of the entire tax system, it is less clear that the home mortgage interest deduction represents a tax expenditure.[27]

Some ambiguity also is introduced by the variable treatment of financial flows possible under a consumption tax baseline. That is, the proper treatment of interest under a consumption tax baseline depends on whether financial flows are in or out of the consumption tax baseline. If the loans are taken into income (as they would be under some types of consumption taxes), then the associated interest and principal payments should be deductible, otherwise not.

With respect to property taxes on housing as well as other State and local taxes, some ambiguity arises because the tax might not represent consumption—it might be considered a reduction in net worth. Considered alone, this argument perhaps has some merit. However, there are two problems with this argument when viewed from the context of the entire tax system. First, the deduction for property taxes would seem to be inappropriate when there is no imputation for the associated consumption value, as discussed above. Second, the current tax system does not impute the consumption value of State and local services, and tax payments might serve as a proxy for that value, making their deduction unnecessary for the proper measurement of consumption.

The official tax expenditures for Social Security benefits reflects exceptions for low-income taxpayers from the general rule that 85 percent of Social Security benefits are included in the recipient's tax base. The 85 percent inclusion is intended as a simplified mechanism for taxing Social Security benefits as if the Social Security program were a private pension with employee contributions made from after-tax income. Under these tax rules, income earned on contributions made by both employers and employees benefits from tax deferral, but employer contributions also benefit because the employee may exclude them from his taxable income, while the employee's own contributions are included in his taxable income. These tax rules give the equivalent of consumption tax treatment, a zero effective tax rate on the return, to the extent that the original pension contributions are made by the employer, but give less generous treatment to the extent that the original contributions are made by the employee. Income earned on employee contributions is taxed at a low, but positive, effective tax rate. Based on historical calculations, the 85 percent inclusion reflects roughly the outcome of applying these tax rules to a lower-income earner when one-half of the contributions are from the employer and one-half from the employee.

The current tax expenditure measures a tax benefit relative to a baseline that is somewhere between a comprehensive income tax and a consumption tax. The properly measured tax expenditure relative to a consump-

---

[25] Suppose that the rental value of a house is $100 per year, and that depreciation is $20, interest is $15, property taxes are $10, and other expenses are $5. Net rental income is $50 (gross rents less all items of expense). Hence, net rental income is a component of the gross rent, which is the consumption value of the housing services. Under a real based cash flow tax, in which financial flows are outside the tax base, the homeowner's net tax base would be $85: gross rents minus (property taxes + other expenses), assuming that property taxes are viewed as a reduction in net worth and that he makes no new investment (which would be deductible).

[26] Using the figures from the example in the previous footnote, the homeowner would pay tax on gross rents minus property taxes minus other expenses, or on $85. If property taxes and mortgage interest were not deducted, then this would be the size of the tax expenditure. However, current law allows these deductions, which raises the tax expenditure base to $110.

---

[27] One must guard against double counting here, however, to the extent that current law's general taxation of capital income is calculated elsewhere in the tax expenditure budget as a negative tax expenditure.

tion tax baseline would include only those Social Security benefits that are accorded treatment more favorable than that implied by a consumption tax, which would correspond to including 50 percent of Social Security benefits in the recipient's tax base.

A similar analysis would apply to exclusion of Social Security benefits of dependents and retirees.

There is a strong case for viewing the child credit and the earned income tax credit as social welfare programs (transfers). As such, they would be tax expenditures relative to a consumption tax baseline. Nonetheless, these credits could alternatively be viewed as relieving tax on "nondiscretionary" consumption, and so not properly considered a tax expenditure.

The treatment of the items in panel C is less uncertain. Several of these items relate to the costs of medical care or to charitable contributions. As discussed in the previous section of the appendix, there is disagreement within the tax policy community over the extent to which medical care and charitable giving represent consumption items. Medical care is widely held to be consumption, except perhaps the medical care that actually raises, rather than simply sustains the individual's ability to work. Charitable giving, on the other hand, may be considered to be a reduction in net worth that should be excluded from the tax base because it does not yield direct satisfaction to taxpayer who makes the expenditure. In this case, the tax expenditure lies not with the individual making the charitable deduction, but with the exclusion from taxation of the amounts received by the recipient.

There also is the issue of how to tax medical insurance premiums. Under current law, employees do not have to include insurance premiums paid for by employers in their income. The self-employed also may exclude (via a deduction) medical insurance premiums from their taxable income. From some perspectives, these premiums should be in the tax base because they appear to represent consumption. Yet an alternative perspective would support excluding the premium from tax as long as the consumption tax base included the value of any medical services paid for by the insurance policy, because the premium equals the expected value of insurance benefits received. But even from this alternative perspective, the official tax expenditure might continue to be a tax expenditure under a consumption tax baseline because current law excludes the value of medical services paid with insurance benefits from the employee's taxable income.

If medical spending is not consumption, one approach to measuring the consumption base would ignore insurance, but allow the consumer to deduct the value of all medical services obtained. An alternative approach would allow a deduction for the premium but include the value of any insurance benefits received, while continuing to allow a deduction for a value of all medical services obtained. In either case, the official tax expenditure for the exclusion of employer provided medical insurance and expenses would not be a tax expenditure relative to a consumption tax baseline.

The extraterritorial income exclusion replaces the previous Foreign Sales Corporation program. It provides an exclusion from income for certain exports. To the extent that the program is viewed as a component of a destination-based VAT it might not be a tax expenditure. In addition, to the extent that the exclusion reduces the income tax bias against investment it might be consistent with consumption tax principles (i.e., a low tax rate on capital income).

The credit for low-income housing acts to lower the tax burden on qualified investment, and so from one perspective would not be a tax expenditure under a consumption tax baseline. However, in some cases the credit is too generous; it can give a negative tax on income from qualified investment rather than the zero tax called for under consumption tax principles. In addition, the credit is very narrowly targeted. Consequently, it could be considered a tax expenditure relative to a consumption tax baseline.

The final panel (D) shows items that are not likely to be tax expenditures under a consumption base. Most of these relate to tax provisions that eliminate or reduce the tax on various types of capital income because a zero tax on capital income is consistent with consumption tax principles.

The deduction for U.S. production activities is not classified as a tax expenditure. This reflects the view that it represents a widespread reduction in taxes on capital income or an offset to the corporate income tax. In contrast to this classification, however, it would be a tax expenditure to the extent that it is viewed as a targeted tax incentive.

The exception from the passive loss rules probably would not be a tax expenditure because proper measurement of income, and hence of consumption, requires full deduction of losses.

Major Tax Expenditures under a Consumption Tax That Are Excluded from the Current Budget

Several differences between current law and a consumption tax are left off the official tax expenditure list. Additional tax expenditures include the imputed consumption value from consumer durables and financial services received in kind, private gifts and inheritances received, possibly benefits paid by insurance policies, in-kind benefits from such Government programs as food-stamps, Medicaid, and public housing, and benefits received from charities. Under some ideas of a consumption tax baseline, the value of leisure and of household production of goods and services would be included as a tax expenditure.

A consumption tax baseline implemented as a tax on cash flows would tax all proceeds from sales of capital assets when consumed, rather than just capital gains; because of expensing, taxpayers effectively would have a zero basis. The proceeds from borrowing would be in the base of a consumption tax that also allowed a deduction for repayment of principal and interest, but are excluded from the current tax base. The deduction of business interest expense might be a tax expenditure, since under some forms of consumption taxation interest is neither deducted from the borrower's tax base nor included in the lender's tax base. The personal exemption and standard deduction also might be considered tax expenditures, although they can be viewed differently, e.g., as elements of the basic tax rate schedule.

Negative Tax Expenditures

Importantly, current law also deviates from a consumption tax baseline norm in ways that increase, rather than decrease, tax liability. These could be called negative tax expenditures. The official budget excludes negative tax expenditures on the theory that tax expenditures are intended to substitute for Government spending programs. Yet excluding negative tax expenditures gives a very one-sided look at the differences between the existing tax system and a consumption tax.

A large item on this list would be the inclusion of capital income in the current individual income tax base, including the income earned on inside-build up in Social Security accounts. Depreciation allowances, even if accelerated, would be a negative tax expenditure since consumption tax treatment generally would require expensing. Depending on the treatment of loans, the borrower's inability to deduct payments of principal and the lender's inability to deduct loans might be a negative tax expenditure. The passive loss rules and NOL carry-forward provisions also might generate negative tax expenditures, because the change in net worth requires a deduction for losses (consumption = income – the change in net worth). If human capital were considered an asset, then its cost (e.g., certain education and training expenses, including perhaps costs of college and professional school) should be expensed, but it is not under current law. Certain restrictions under the individual AMT as well as the phase-out of personal exemptions and of itemized deductions also might be considered negative tax expenditures. Under some views, the current tax treatment of Social Security benefits paid to the disabled would be a negative tax expenditure.

SPECIAL TOPICS

14. AID TO STATE AND LOCAL GOVERNMENTS

The analysis in this chapter focuses on Federal spending that is provided to State and local governments, U.S. territories, and American Indian Tribal governments to help fund programs administered by those entities and steps the Administration is taking to improve the management of these programs. This type of Federal spending is known as Federal grants-in-aid.

In 2019 the Federal Government spent $721 billion on aid to State and local governments. Spending on grants-in-aid was 3.4 percent of GDP in 2019. These funds support activities that touch every American, such as education, transportation infrastructure, workforce initiatives, community development, and homeland security. Over the past 30 years, spending for Federal grants-in-aid has increased as a percentage of Federal outlays from 10.7 percent in 1989 to 16.2 percent in 2019. Yet, grants for capital investment have remained under 3.0 percent of total spending, while payments for individuals have grown from 5.9 percent to 12.3 percent of total Federal outlays. Using 2012 constant dollars, grants for capital investment have decreased by $91 billion over the last 10 years, while payments for individuals have increased by $28 billion.[1]

The 2021 Budget recognizes a greater role for State and local governments and the private sector, and refocuses Federal grants to State and local governments on the highest priority areas for Federal support as part of the effort to restore Federal fiscal responsibility and right-size the role of the Federal Government. The 2021 Budget slows the growth of grant spending over the 10-year budget window and, in particular, starts to rein in the growth of Medicaid, which accounts for 55 percent of total grant spending to State and local governments. The Budget provides $810 billion in outlays for aid to State and local governments in 2021, an increase of 2.4 percent from spending in 2020, which is estimated to be $791 billion. Total Federal grant spending to State and local governments is estimated to be 3.4 percent of GDP in 2021 and 17 percent of total Federal outlays.

Background and Analysis

Federal grants are authorized by the Congress in statute, which then establishes the purpose of the grant and how it is awarded. Most often Federal grants-in-aid are awarded as direct cash assistance, but Federal grants-in-aid can also include payments for grants-in-kind—non-monetary aid, such as commodities purchased for the National School Lunch Program—and Federal revenues shared with State and local governments, such as funds distributed to State and local law enforcement agencies from Federal asset forfeiture programs.

In its 2019 State Expenditure Report, the National Association of State Budget Officers (NASBO) reports that 30.7 percent of total State spending, which is estimated to be about $2.1 trillion[2] in State fiscal year[3] 2019 came from Federal funds. "Total [F]ederal fund spending is estimated to have grown by 4.7 percent in fiscal 2019, 3.5 percent in fiscal 2018, and 2.5 percent in fiscal 2017."[4]

Table 14-1, below, shows Federal grants-in-aid spending by decade, actual spending in 2019, and estimated spending in 2020 and 2021.

The Federal budget classifies grants-in-aid by general area or function. Of the total proposed grant spending in 2021, 62 percent is for health programs, with most of the funding going to Medicaid. Beyond health programs, 14 percent of Federal aid is estimated to go to income security programs; 9 percent to transportation programs; 8 percent to education, training, and social services; and 7 percent for all other functions.

The Federal budget also classifies grant spending by BEA category—discretionary or mandatory.[5] Funding for discretionary grant programs is determined annually through appropriations acts. Outlays for discretionary grant programs account for 28 percent of total grant spending. Funding for mandatory programs is provided directly in authorizing legislation that establishes eligibility criteria or benefit formulas; funding for mandatory programs usually is not limited by the annual appropriations process. Outlays for mandatory grant programs account for 72 percent of total grant spending. Section B of Table 14-1 shows the distribution of grants between mandatory and discretionary spending.

In 2021, grants-in-aid provided from discretionary funding are estimated to have outlays of $231 billion, an increase of less than one percent from 2020. The three largest discretionary programs in 2021 are estimated to be Federal-aid Highways programs, with outlays of $46 billion; Tenant Based Rental Assistance, with outlays of $20 billion; and Education for the Disadvantaged, with outlays of $17 billion.[6]

---

[1] 2021 *Historical Tables*. Table 12.1 - Summary Comparison of Total Outlays for Grants to State and Local Governments: 1940 - 2025. *https://www.whitehouse.gov/omb/historical-tables/*.

[2] "2019 State Expenditure Report." National Association of State Budget Officers, 2019. p. 1, 3.

[3] According to "The Fiscal Survey of States" published by the National Association of State Budget Officers (Fall 2019, p. VI), "Forty-six States begin their fiscal years in July and end them in June. The exceptions are New York, which starts its fiscal year on April 1; Texas, with a September 1 start date; and Alabama and Michigan, which start their fiscal years on October 1."

[4] "2019 State Expenditure Report." National Association of State Budget Officers, 2019. p. 2.

[5] For more information on these categories, see Chapter 8, "Budget Concepts," in this volume.

[6] Obligation data by State for programs in each of these budget accounts may be found in the State-by-State tables included with other Budget materials on the OMB website.

Table 14–1. TRENDS IN FEDERAL GRANTS TO STATE AND LOCAL GOVERNMENTS

(Outlays in billions of dollars)

	Actual									Estimate	
	1960	1970	1980	1990	2000	2005	2010	2015	2019	2020	2021
A. Distribution of grants by function:											
Natural resources and environment	0.1	0.4	5.4	3.7	4.6	5.9	9.1	7.0	6.7	6.6	6.8
Agriculture	0.2	0.6	0.6	1.1	0.7	0.9	0.8	0.7	0.8	1.1	1.0
Transportation	3.0	4.6	13.0	19.2	32.2	43.4	61.0	60.8	65.6	68.3	71.0
Community and regional development	0.1	1.8	6.5	5.0	8.7	20.2	18.9	14.4	15.6	23.2	26.9
Education, training, employment, and social services	0.5	6.4	21.9	21.8	36.7	57.2	97.6	60.5	63.1	68.8	66.0
Health	0.2	3.8	15.8	43.9	124.8	197.8	290.2	368.0	442.3	485.7	499.0
Income security	2.6	5.8	18.5	36.9	68.7	90.9	115.2	101.1	112.6	117.0	116.9
Administration of justice	....	0.0	0.5	0.6	5.3	4.8	5.1	3.7	5.2	9.3	8.0
General government	0.2	0.5	8.6	2.3	2.1	4.4	5.2	3.8	4.2	4.8	4.2
Other	0.0	0.1	0.7	0.8	2.1	2.6	5.3	4.3	5.0	5.9	10.5
Total	**7.0**	**24.1**	**91.4**	**135.3**	**285.9**	**428.0**	**608.4**	**624.4**	**721.1**	**790.7**	**810.1**
B. Distribution of grants by BEA category:											
Discretionary	N/A	10.2	53.4	63.5	116.7	182.3	247.4	189.6	207.1	228.9	230.7
Mandatory	N/A	13.9	38.0	71.9	169.2	245.7	361.0	434.7	514.0	561.8	579.4
Total	**7.0**	**24.1**	**91.4**	**135.3**	**285.9**	**428.0**	**608.4**	**624.4**	**721.1**	**790.7**	**810.1**
C. Composition:											
Current dollars:											
Payments for individuals [1]	2.6	9.1	33.1	77.4	186.5	278.8	391.4	463.4	549.3	597.3	588.2
Physical capital [1]	3.3	7.1	22.6	27.2	48.7	60.8	93.3	77.2	80.8	87.3	97.3
Other grants	1.1	7.9	35.8	30.7	50.7	88.4	123.7	83.7	91.0	106.1	124.6
Total	**7.0**	**24.1**	**91.4**	**135.3**	**285.9**	**428.0**	**608.4**	**624.4**	**721.1**	**790.7**	**810.1**
Percentage of total grants:											
Payments for individuals [1]	37.4%	37.7%	36.2%	57.2%	65.3%	65.1%	64.3%	74.2%	76.2%	75.5%	72.6%
Physical capital [1]	47.3%	29.3%	24.7%	20.1%	17.0%	14.2%	15.3%	12.4%	11.2%	11.0%	12.0%
Other grants	15.3%	33.0%	39.1%	22.7%	17.7%	20.7%	20.3%	13.4%	12.6%	13.4%	15.4%
Total	**100.0%**	**100.0%**	**100.0%**	**100.0%**	**100.0%**	**100.0%**	**100.0%**	**100.0%**	**100.0%**	**100.0%**	**100.0%**
Constant (FY 2012) dollars:											
Payments for individuals [1]	16.0	44.0	81.8	123.4	239.6	322.6	408.5	447.9	499.8	531.6	511.8
Physical capital [1]	25.1	40.1	57.6	48.0	71.9	77.8	98.5	73.4	70.8	74.6	80.7
Other grants	13.7	67.6	144.4	67.5	77.6	111.1	130.5	78.4	78.6	89.3	101.9
Total	**54.8**	**151.7**	**283.7**	**238.9**	**389.1**	**511.6**	**637.6**	**599.6**	**649.3**	**695.6**	**694.4**
D. Total grants as a percent of:											
Federal outlays:											
Total	7.6%	12.3%	15.5%	10.8%	16.0%	17.3%	17.6%	16.9%	16.2%	16.5%	16.8%
Domestic programs [2]	18.0%	23.2%	22.2%	17.1%	22.0%	23.5%	23.4%	21.2%	21.0%	21.1%	21.5%
State and local expenditures	14.2%	19.4%	26.4%	18.0%	21.0%	22.9%	25.6%	23.9%	24.1%	N/A	N/A
Gross domestic product	1.3%	2.3%	3.3%	2.3%	2.8%	3.3%	4.1%	3.4%	3.4%	3.6%	3.5%
E. As a share of total State and local gross investments:											
Federal capital grants	24.1%	24.6%	34.5%	21.0%	21.3%	21.2%	26.8%	21.8%	19.4%	N/A	N/A
State and local own-source financing	75.9%	75.4%	65.5%	79.0%	78.7%	78.8%	73.2%	78.2%	80.6%	N/A	N/A
Total	**100.0%**	**100.0%**	**100.0%**	**100.0%**	**100.0%**	**100.0%**	**100.0%**	**100.0%**	**100.0%**		

N/A: Not available at publishing.

[1] Grants that are both payments for individuals and capital investment are shown under capital investment.

[2] Excludes national defense, international affairs, net interest, and undistributed offsetting receipts.

In 2021, outlays for mandatory grant programs are estimated to be $579 billion, an increase of 3.1 percent from spending in 2020, which is estimated to be $562 billion. Medicaid is by far the largest mandatory grant program with estimated outlays of $448 billion in 2021. After Medicaid, the three largest mandatory grant programs by outlays in 2021 are: Child Nutrition programs, which include the School Breakfast Program, the National School Lunch Program and others, $26 billion; the Temporary Assistance for Needy Families program, $16 billion; and the Children's Health Insurance Fund, $16 billion.[7]

---

[7] Obligation data by State for programs in each of these budget accounts may be found in the State-by-State tables included with other budget materials on the OMB web site.

Federal spending by State for major grants-in-aid may be found on the OMB website at *www.whitehouse.gov/omb/Analytical-Perspectives/*. This supplemental material includes two tables that summarize State-by-State spending for major grant programs, one summarizing obligations for each program by agency and bureau, and another summarizing total obligations across all programs for each State, followed by 35 individual tables showing State-by-State obligation data for each grant program. The programs shown in these State-by-State tables cover 95 percent of total grants-in-aid to State and local governments.

Below are highlights from the Budget listed by function followed by Table 14-2, which shows the Budget's funding level for grants in every Budget account, organized by functional category, BEA category, and by Federal Agency.

HIGHLIGHTS

Grants Management Reform

In addition to the 2021 Budget proposals highlighted below, the President's Management Agenda (PMA) includes "Results-Oriented Accountability for Grants," a Cross-Agency Priority (CAP) Goal, to tackle the challenges of administering grants while also ensuring that grants are achieving the desired results for American taxpayers. This goal outlines an ambitious vision to maximize the value of grant funding for aid to State and local governments, but also for grants to individuals and other non-government entities. The CAP goal recognizes that as the rate of Federal aid to State and local governments slows, it is essential that Federal dollars be delivered to intended recipients as efficiently and effectively as possible. It does so by developing data standards and common business applications and by applying a risk-based, data-driven framework that balances compliance requirements with a stronger emphasis on demonstrating successful results for the American taxpayer by ensuring an adequate accountability framework is in place. To achieve this vision, the Administration has outlined four key strategies: standardize the grants management business process and data; build shared IT infrastructure; manage risk; and achieve program goals and objectives. Since the release of the PMA in March 2018, the 2018 Single Audit Compliance Supplement was significantly streamlined, allowing for further opportunity to refine the 2019 Single Audit Compliance Supplement with an increased focus on compliance requirements that inform performance. The CAP goal team has also publicly released draft core grants management data standards for public comment. The final standards will help build future shared solutions that will increase access to and use of data to support powerful data analytics, setting the stage for risk-based performance management. More details regarding these accomplishments and other future milestones are available at *Performance.gov* (*https://www.performance.gov/*).

Natural Resources and Environment

The Budget includes $50 million for the Environmental Protection Agency to establish a new grant program to identify and help resolve environmental hazards in schools. Approximately 50 million American children spend their time in K-12 school facilities every day, and many of these buildings are old and contain environmental hazards that could pose a risk to children's health. Activities supported by this program will result in safer and healthier school environments for American children. The Budget also includes $55 million in funding for lead-focused grants as part of a newly proposed Lead Exposure Reduction Initiative, as well as more funds for Environmental Protection Agency grant programs established by the America's Water Infrastructure Act (AWIA), which will assist in sewer overflow prevention and water infrastructure workforce investment.

The Budget includes the elimination of Abandoned Mine Land economic development grants, and National Wildlife Refuge Fund payments to local governments, which fail to take into account the economic benefits refuges provide to communities. The Budget also proposes to eliminate funding for several lower priority grant and education programs within the National Oceanic and Atmospheric Administration, including Sea Grant, Coastal Zone Management Grants, and the Pacific Coastal Salmon Recovery Fund.

Agriculture

The Budget prioritizes competitive research through the Department of Agriculture's flagship grant program, the Agriculture and Food Research Initiative (AFRI). The Budget requests $700 million for AFRI, an increase of $285 million above the 2019 enacted level and maintains formula-based research and extension grants at the level requested in the 2020 Budget. In 2021, the Budget also invests in our Nation's aging research infrastructure by proposing $1.3 million for a new Agricultural Research Service research facility.

Transportation

The Budget continues to invest in competitive grant programs that partner with communities to deliver surface transportation projects with significant benefits. The Budget provides $1 billion to the Better Utilizing Investments to Leverage Development (BUILD) program, and $1 billion in discretionary resources to the Infrastructure for Rebuilding America (INFRA) program. These programs use competitive processes to target resources efficiently and effectively, and DOT will focus on strengthening these processes in 2020.

The Budget also provides $440 million in transitional grants for States and Amtrak to begin the process to restructure Amtrak's network. Amtrak's network has not been significantly modified since Amtrak's inception nearly 50 years ago, and long distance routes continually underperform, suffering from low ridership and large operating losses of roughly half a billion dollars annually.

Community and Regional Development

The Budget proposes $425 million within the Department of Housing and Urban Development (HUD) to promote healthy and lead-safe homes, $90 million above the 2020 enacted level. Research has shown that lead-based paint hazard control is an efficient and effective form of reducing and preventing lead exposure, generating high returns on investments due to increased lifetime earnings and reduced medical costs. This funding level also includes resources for enforcement, education, and research activities to further support this goal.

The Budget also helps to maintain and modernize rural utilities by providing critical support for infrastructure by funding water and wastewater grants within the Department of Agriculture. The Budget proposes $44 million for Agriculture's distance learning and telemedicine grants, of which 20 percent will be dedicated to projects that combat the opioids crisis. In addition, the Budget also proposes $30 million in community facilities grants, which can be used to support treatment centers and other community needs.

The Budget proposes a $418 million competitive National Security and Resilience grant program that would be rigorously evaluated to demonstrate how the Federal Emergency Management Agency is supporting communities to make the Nation safer and better prepared. The Budget eliminates the Community Development Block Grant Program and the Economic Development Administration, which provides small grants.

Education, Training, Employment, and Social Services

The Budget proposes to consolidate 29 elementary and secondary education programs into a single, $19 billion Elementary and Secondary Education for the Disadvantaged (ESED) block grant. The ESED block grant would significantly reduce burden and empower States and school districts to decide how best to use Federal funds to address local education needs and improve outcomes for all students. Funds would be allocated to districts through the Title I Grants to Local Educational Agencies formulas, ensuring Federal education funds continue to support school districts serving disadvantaged students. ESED funds could be used to support any of the activities authorized by the consolidated grant programs.

The Budget invests nearly $13 billion in Individuals with Disabilities Education Act (IDEA) Part B Grants to States, an increase of $100 million compared to the 2020 enacted level. This increase will provide more resources for States to provide special education and related services for over 7 million students with disabilities served by IDEA Part B. Additionally, the Budget continues to fund all other IDEA grant programs at the 2020 enacted levels.

The Budget proposes to restructure and streamline the TRIO and Gaining Early Awareness and Readiness for Undergraduate Programs (GEAR UP) programs by consolidating them into a $950 million State formula grant. These grants would support evidence-based postsecondary preparation programs designed to help low-income students progress through the pipeline from middle school to postsecondary opportunities. Given the statutory prohibition limiting the Department's ability to evaluate overall TRIO program effectiveness using the most rigorous methodologies, as well as budget constraints, the Budget supports a restructuring of the programs that leverages evidence-based activities and allows States more flexibility in meeting the unique needs of their students.

The Budget includes over $2 billion for Career and Technical Education, an $880 million increase compared to the 2020 enacted level. This amount includes $2 billion in discretionary funding and an estimated $117 million from H-1B visa fees. The recently reauthorized program helps ensure students have access to technical training including work-based learning during high school and a wide array of post-secondary options including certificate programs, community colleges, and apprenticeships.

The Budget eliminates 11 ineffective or duplicative programs including Federal Supplemental Educational Opportunity Grants.

Health

As part of the Ending the HIV Epidemic initiative, the Budget includes $302 million for the Health Resources and Services Administration to deliver additional care and treatment for people living with HIV through the Ryan White HIV/AIDS Program and to supply testing, evaluation, prescription of PrEP, and associated medical costs for people who are at risk for HIV infections through the Health Centers program. The Budget also prioritizes the reauthorization of the Ryan White program to ensure Federal funds are allocated to address the changing landscape of HIV across the United States.

The Budget invests $5 billion in HHS to combat the opioid epidemic, making makes critical investments in surveillance, prevention, treatment, access to overdose reversal drugs, recovery support services, and research. This funding includes $1.6 billion, an $85 million increase, for State Opioid Response (SOR) grants, which supports prevention, treatment, and recovery support services.

The Budget invests in Certified Community Behavioral Health Centers (CCBHC) expansion grants, and extends the CCBHC Medicaid demonstrations through 2021. These activities make it easier for individuals with mental illness and their families to navigate the healthcare system and get services that they need. In addition, the Budget includes $125 million to help schools, community organizations, first responders, and other entities identify mental health issues and help affected youth and other individuals get the treatment they need. In addition, some individuals with serious mental illness need hospitalization, yet there are not always enough inpatient beds to serve them. The Budget provides targeted flexibility to States to provide inpatient mental health services to Medicaid beneficiaries with serious mental illness.

The Budget also supports the President's health reform vision, which will prioritize Federal resources for the most vulnerable. Medicaid reform would restore balance, flexibility, integrity, and accountability to the State-Federal partnership. Spending would grow at a more sustainable rate by ending the financial bias that currently favors able-bodied working-age adults over the truly vulnerable.

In addition, Budget will empower States with additional tools to strengthen and modernize their Medicaid programs. The Budget will give States additional flexibility around benefits and cost-sharing, such as increasing copayments for non-emergency use of the emergency department to encourage appropriate use of healthcare resources, as well as allowing States to consider personal savings and other assets when determining Medicaid eligibility. Additionally, the Budget would allow States to streamline appeals processes and delegate authority to another entity to help eliminate duplicative appeals and reduce beneficiary confusion. The Budget also extends support for States to enhance their use of Home and Community Based Services (HCBS) through a permanent Money Follows the Person option. This option would continue to give States flexibility to provide additional transitional services to promote care in the community and provide enhanced funding for States with high rates of institutionalization to make necessary structural changes. Further, the Budget will bolster the safety net available to States experiencing Children's Health Insurance Program (CHIP) funding shortfalls, while eliminating funding streams that do not support children's health.

Addressing Medicaid improper payments and fraud is a key priority for the Administration. The Budget will ensure sound stewardship of taxpayer dollars by strengthening CMS's ability to address weaknesses in provider screening, enrollment, and identification, and beneficiary eligibility determinations, the leading causes of Medicaid improper payments. The Budget will increase CMS oversight by requiring Medicaid and CHIP providers to undergo centralized CMS screening and increase State accountability by strengthening CMS's flexibility to ensure Federal recovery of overpayments due to incorrect eligibility determinations. The Budget also takes numerous steps to cut wasteful Medicaid spending. The Budget proposes eliminating loopholes that some States use to shift and increase costs to Federal taxpayers, and ensuring that State Medicaid supplemental payments to hospitals and other providers are supported by robust and timely data. The Budget also extends current law reductions in Medicaid disproportionate share hospital payments.

Income Security

The Budget invests in a better future for Americans with a proposal to provide paid leave to new mothers and fathers, including adoptive parents, so all families can afford to take time to recover from childbirth and bond with a new child. The proposal would allow States to establish paid parental leave programs in a way that is most appropriate for their workforce and economy. The Budget proposes to combat improper payments in the Unemployment Insurance (UI) program by providing grants to States to combat the top two root causes of improper payments in their programs. The Budget also reduces waste, fraud, and abuse in the UI program with a package of program integrity proposals. These proposals would require States to use the tools already at their disposal for combatting improper payments while expanding their authority to spend certain UI program funds on activities that reduce waste, fraud, and abuse in the system. The Budget also supports the UI Integrity Center of Excellence, which is developing a data hub to allow States to access a fraud analytics database to identify fraud as effectively as possible.

Within HUD, the Housing Voucher and project-based rental assistance (PBRA) programs benefit from leveraging both public and private financing to invest in long-term affordable housing stock. To advance this objective, the Budget requests $100 million for the Rental Assistance Demonstration, which supports the redevelopment of Public Housing units through conversion to Housing Voucher and PBRA units. Additional authorities in the Public Housing program, such as repositioning certain troubled public housing assets, would also assist in this effort. Recognizing this shift and that State and local governments should bear greater responsibility in providing affordable housing, the Budget does not request funding for the Public Housing Capital Fund.

The Budget also eliminates the HOME Investment Partnership Program, which has not been authorized since 1994. State and local governments are better positioned to more comprehensively address the unique market challenges and local policies that lead to affordable housing problems. The Budget provides $2.8 billion for the Homeless Assistance Grant (HAG) programs to continue supporting approximately 1.1 million individuals who experience homelessness each year. HAG primarily funds the Continuum of Care (CoC) program, which provides competitive funding to support coordinated and locally driven community-based networks of programs to prevent and address homelessness across the Nation. Within this total, the Budget requests $280 million for Emergency Solutions Grants to support emergency shelter, rapid re-housing, and homelessness prevention. The Administration will also begin a new initiative to reduce unsheltered homelessness, targeted to select cities that have experienced the largest increase in unsheltered homelessness in recent years.

The Budget continues bold proposals to reform work requirements for able-bodied adults participating in the Supplemental Nutrition Assistance program (SNAP) to promote self-sufficiency. This proposal would streamline SNAP work requirements and apply them consistently to able-bodied adults ages 18 to 65, unless they qualify for specific exemptions. Under the proposal, adults would be required to work at least 80 hours per month in order to receive SNAP benefits. The Budget also combines the traditional SNAP Electronic Benefits Transfer benefits with "Harvest Boxes" of 100 percent American-grown foods provided directly to households—ensuring that Americans in need have access to a nutritious diet while significantly reducing the cost to taxpayers. States would maintain the ability to provide choice to their participants, including by using innovative approaches for the inclusion of fresh products. To bolster State program integrity initiatives, the Budget also includes proposals to reserve benefits for those most in need, promote efficiency in State operations, and strengthen program integrity and oversight, including through enhanced use of data matching.

The Budget improves consistency between work requirements in federally funded public assistance programs, including Medicaid and Temporary Assistance for Needy Families (TANF), by requiring that able-bodied, working-age individuals find employment, train for work, or volunteer (community service) in order to receive welfare benefits.

The Budget also supports States in providing key services to children and youth by increasing State flexibilities and reducing administrative burdens in foster care. These child welfare reforms focus on preventing the need for foster care unless absolutely necessary to ensure families can remain intact. In addition, the Budget promotes evidence-building and innovation to strengthen America's safety net, proposes improvements to the TANF program, and supports efforts to get noncustodial parents to work. Further, the Budget proposes a $1 billion one-time investment for States to build the supply of care and stimulate employer investment in child care and funds child care and early learning to help families access and afford the care they need, and maintains funding for Head Start and the Child Care and Development Block Grant at HHS. Together, these proposals reflect the Administration's commitment to helping low-income families end dependency on Government benefits and promote the principle that gainful employment is the best pathway to financial self-sufficiency and family well-being.

Administration of Justice

The Budget also supports key State and local assistance programs, including $412 million for the Byrne Justice Assistance Grants Program, which provides State and local governments with crucial Federal funding to prevent and control crime. In addition, the Budget provides $40 million for the Project Safe Neighborhoods program, which leverages Federal, State, and local partnerships to address gang violence and gun crime. An additional $97 million is provided for programs supporting research and innovation for law enforcement, including $44 million for the National Institute of Justice, $43 million for the Bureau of Justice Statistics, and $10 million for Coverdell Forensic Science Grants. The Budget further reflects the Administration's commitment to support rural communities by providing $56 million to grant programs specifically targeted to those communities. Finally, the Budget supports critical programs designed to address domestic violence, dating violence, sexual assault, and stalking by providing $499 million in Violence Against Women Act funding. In addition, through State and local assistance programs, the Budget provides $88 million for the Second Chance Act Grant program to reduce recidivism and help returning citizens lead productive lives. In addition, the Budget includes $361 million for opioid-related State and local assistance including $160 million for the Comprehensive Opioid Abuse Program to support treatment and recovery, diversion, and alternatives to incarceration programs; $132 million for Drug Courts, Mental Health Courts, and Veterans Treatment Courts; $30 million for Residential Substance Abuse Treatment; $30 million for Prescription Drug Monitoring Programs; and $9 million for Opioid-Affected Youth.

OTHER SOURCES OF INFORMATION ON FEDERAL GRANTS-IN-AID

A number of other sources provide State-by-State spending data and other information on Federal grants, but may use a broader definition of grants beyond what is included in this chapter.

The website *Grants.gov* is a primary source of information for communities wishing to apply for grants and other financial assistance. *Grants.gov* hosts all open notices of opportunities to apply for Federal grants.

The *System for Award Management* hosted by the General Services Administration contains detailed Assistance Listings (formally known as the Catalog of Federal Domestic Assistance) of grant and other financial assistance programs; discussions of eligibility criteria, application procedures, and estimated obligations; and related information. The *Assistance Listings* are available on the internet at *https://beta.sam.gov*.

Current and updated grant receipt information by State and local governments and other non-Federal entities can be found on *USASpending.gov*. This public website includes additional detail on Federal spending, including contract and loan information.

The Federal Audit Clearinghouse maintains an online database (*https://harvester.census.gov/facweb/*) that pro-

vides public access to audit reports conducted under OMB guidance located at 2 CFR part 200, Uniform Administrative Requirements, Cost Principles, and Audit Requirements for Federal Awards. Information is available for each audited entity, including the amount of Federal money expended by program and whether there were audit findings.

The Bureau of Economic Analysis, in the Department of Commerce, produces the monthly *Survey of Current Business*, which provides data on the National income and product accounts (NIPA), a broad statistical concept encompassing the entire economy. These accounts, which are available at *bea.gov/national*, include data on Federal grants to State and local governments.

In addition, information on grants and awards can be found through individual Federal Agencies' websites:

- USDA Current Research Information System, *https://cris.nifa.usda.gov/*

- DOD Medical Research Programs, *https://cdmrp.army.mil/search.aspx*

- Department of Education, Institute of Education Sciences, Funded Research Grants and Contracts, *https://www2.ed.gov/fund/grants-apply.html*

- Department of Health and Human Services (HHS) Grants, *https://www.hhs.gov/grants/grants/index.html*

- HHS Tracking Accountability in Government Grants System (TAGGS), *https://taggs.hhs.gov/Advanced-Search.cfm*

- National Institutes of Health (NIH) Grants and Funding, *https://grants.nih.gov/funding/index.htm*

- Department of Housing and Urban Development Grants, *https://www.hud.gov/program-offices/spm/geomgmt/grantsinfe*

- Department of Justice Grants, *https://www.justice.gov/grants*

- Department of Labor Employment and Training Administration (ETA), Grants Awarded, *https://www.doleta.gov/grants/grants_awarded.cfm*

- Department of Transportation Grants, *https://www.transportation.gov/grants*

- Environmental Protection Agency (EPA), *https://www.epa.gov/grants*

- National Library of Medicine (NLM), Health Services Research Projects in Progress (HSRProj), *https://wwwcf.nlm.nih.gov/hsr_project/home_proj.cfm*

- National Science Foundation (NSF) Awards, *https://www.nsf.gov/awardsearch/*

- Small Business Innovation Research (SBIR) and Small Business Technology Transfer (STTR) Awards, *https://www.sbir.gov/sbirsearch/award/all*

Table 14–2. FEDERAL GRANTS TO STATE AND LOCAL GOVERNMENTS—BUDGET AUTHORITY AND OUTLAYS

(In millions of dollars)

Function, Category, Agency, and Program	Budget Authority			Outlays		
	2019 Actual	2020 Estimate	2021 Estimate	2019 Actual	2020 Estimate	2021 Estimate
Energy						
Discretionary:						
Department of Energy:						
Energy Programs:						
Energy Efficiency and Renewable Energy	351	397	....	278	375	370
Mandatory:						
Tennessee Valley Authority:						
Tennessee Valley Authority Fund	541	538	526	541	538	526
Total, Energy	**892**	**935**	**526**	**819**	**913**	**896**
Natural Resources and Environment						
Discretionary:						
Department of Agriculture:						
Farm Service Agency:						
Grassroots Source Water Protection Program	7	7	....	7	7	....
Natural Resources Conservation Service:						
Watershed Rehabilitation Program	12	28	....	19	18	....
Watershed and Flood Prevention Operations	315	979	34	122	379	13
Forest Service:						
State and Private Forestry	271	271	175	163	322	320
Department of Commerce:						
National Oceanic and Atmospheric Administration:						
Operations, Research, and Facilities	87	90	....	97	100	....
Pacific Coastal Salmon Recovery	65	65	....	65	87	76
Department of the Interior:						
Office of Surface Mining Reclamation and Enforcement:						
Regulation and Technology	69	44	44	59	51	46
Abandoned Mine Reclamation Fund	115	115	....	40	62	67
United States Geological Survey:						
Surveys, Investigations, and Research	4	7	....	4	7	....
United States Fish and Wildlife Service:						
Cooperative Endangered Species Conservation Fund	45	36	–8	39	30	44
State Wildlife Grants	64	68	31	64	71	73
National Park Service:						
National Recreation and Preservation	64	71	34	60	77	55
Land Acquisition and State Assistance	134	140	....	56	77	118
Historic Preservation Fund	153	119	41	67	157	149
Environmental Protection Agency:						
State and Tribal Assistance Grants	4,543	4,246	2,721	3,826	2,833	3,387
Hazardous Substance Superfund	250	250	250	199	244	267
Leaking Underground Storage Tank Trust Fund	83	83	40	78	78	69
Total, discretionary	**6,281**	**6,619**	**3,362**	**4,965**	**4,600**	**4,684**
Mandatory:						
Department of Agriculture:						
Farm Service Agency:						
Grassroots Source Water Protection Program	5	....	....	....	5	....
Department of Commerce:						
National Oceanic and Atmospheric Administration:						
Gulf Coast Ecosystem Restoration Science, Observation, Monitoring, and Technology	6	6	7	4	6	5
Department of the Interior:						
Bureau of Land Management:						
Miscellaneous Permanent Payment Accounts	41	49	27	40	49	29
Office of Surface Mining Reclamation and Enforcement:						

Table 14–2. FEDERAL GRANTS TO STATE AND LOCAL GOVERNMENTS—BUDGET AUTHORITY AND OUTLAYS—Continued

(In millions of dollars)

Function, Category, Agency, and Program	Budget Authority			Outlays		
	2019 Actual	2020 Estimate	2021 Estimate	2019 Actual	2020 Estimate	2021 Estimate
Payments to States in Lieu of Coal Fee Receipts	....	....	....	12	10	10
Abandoned Mine Reclamation Fund	188	129	137	151	198	191
United States Fish and Wildlife Service:						
Federal Aid in Wildlife Restoration	734	665	811	762	784	828
Cooperative Endangered Species Conservation Fund	70	66	73	70	66	73
Coastal Impact Assistance	−15	....	....	1	1	1
Sport Fish Restoration	451	459	480	427	455	494
National Park Service:						
Land Acquisition and State Assistance	76	115	120	2	39	74
Departmental Offices:						
National Forests Fund, Payment to States	5	12	13	4	12	13
Leases of Lands Acquired for Flood Control, Navigation, and Allied Purposes	44	29	32	44	29	32
States Share from Certain Gulf of Mexico Leases	215	370	352	215	370	352
Corps of Engineers--Civil Works:						
South Dakota Terrestrial Wildlife Habitat Restoration Trust Fund	3	3	3	1	3	3
Total, mandatory	**1,823**	**1,903**	**2,055**	**1,733**	**2,027**	**2,105**
Total, Natural Resources and Environment	**8,104**	**8,522**	**5,417**	**6,698**	**6,627**	**6,789**
Agriculture						
Discretionary:						
Department of Agriculture:						
National Institute of Food and Agriculture:						
Extension Activities	452	470	....	453	592	324
National Institute of Food and Agriculture	....	....	811	....	....	308
Research and Education Activities	357	357	....	297	432	245
Agricultural Marketing Service:						
Payments to States and Possessions	1	1	1	1	1	1
Farm Service Agency:						
State Mediation Grants	4	6	7	4	3	7
Total, discretionary	**814**	**834**	**819**	**755**	**1,028**	**885**
Mandatory:						
Department of Agriculture:						
Agricultural Marketing Service:						
Payments to States and Possessions	85	80	85	73	77	83
Total, Agriculture	**899**	**914**	**904**	**828**	**1,105**	**968**
Commerce and Housing Credit						
Discretionary:						
Department of Commerce:						
National Oceanic and Atmospheric Administration:						
Fisheries Disaster Assistance	165	....	....	39	125	125
Mandatory:						
Department of Commerce:						
National Telecommunications and Information Administration:						
State and Local Implementation Fund	....	....	....	9	25	2
Department of the Treasury:						
Departmental Offices:						
State Small Business Credit Initiative	....	....	....	....	2	....
Federal Communications Commission:						
Universal Service Fund	1,633	1,713	1,802	2,113	2,272	1,974
Total, mandatory	**1,633**	**1,713**	**1,802**	**2,122**	**2,299**	**1,976**
Total, Commerce and Housing Credit	**1,798**	**1,713**	**1,802**	**2,161**	**2,424**	**2,101**

Table 14–2.　FEDERAL GRANTS TO STATE AND LOCAL GOVERNMENTS—BUDGET AUTHORITY AND OUTLAYS—Continued

(In millions of dollars)

Function, Category, Agency, and Program	Budget Authority			Outlays		
	2019 Actual	2020 Estimate	2021 Estimate	2019 Actual	2020 Estimate	2021 Estimate
Transportation						
Discretionaryⁱ						
Department of Transportation:						
Office of the Secretary:						
National Infrastructure Investments	875	975	975	351	842	1,256
Nationally Significant Freight Projects	....	....	990	....	....	....
Federal Aviation Administration:						
Payment to Grants-in-aid for Airports	500	400	....	500	400	....
Grants-in-aid for Airports (Airport and Airway Trust Fund)	....	....	....	3,303	3,309	3,382
Grants-in-aid for Airports (Airport and Airway Trust Fund) (non-add obligation limitations) [1]	*3,350*	*3,350*	*3,350*	....	....	....
Federal Highway Administration:						
Emergency Relief Program	1,650	....	....	767	759	703
Highway Infrastructure Programs	3,250	2,166	....	568	783	1,302
Appalachian Development Highway System	....	....	−12	6	17	10
Federal-aid Highways	....	....	....	43,040	43,840	45,587
Federal-aid Highways (non-add obligation limitations) [1]	*44,085*	*44,692*	*48,682*	....	....	....
Miscellaneous Appropriations	....	−20	−82	13	17	13
Miscellaneous Highway Trust Funds	....	....	−44	9	12	6
Federal Motor Carrier Safety Administration:						
Motor Carrier Safety Grants	....	....	....	316	420	378
Motor Carrier Safety Grants (non-add obligation limitations) [1]	*383*	*391*	*403*	....	....	....
National Highway Traffic Safety Administration:						
Highway Traffic Safety Grants	....	....	....	637	708	671
Highway Traffic Safety Grants (non-add obligation limitations) [1]	*715*	*724*	*647*	....	....	....
Federal Railroad Administration:						
Northeast Corridor Improvement Program	....	....	....	1	9	10
Capital and Debt Service Grants to the National Railroad Passenger Corporation	....	....	....	2	2	....
Restoration and Enhancement Grants	5	2	....	....	2	1
Magnetic Levitation Technology Deployment Program	10	2	....	....	....	....
Rail Safety Technology Program	....	....	−1	....	....	....
Railroad Safety Grants	....	....	....	16	19	9
Grants to the National Railroad Passenger Corporation	....	....	....	....	....	3
Intercity Passenger Rail Grant Program	....	....	−10	1	10	1
Rail Line Relocation and Improvement Program	....	....	−13	....	2	1
Capital Assistance for High Speed Rail Corridors and Intercity Passenger Rail Service	....	....	−55	26	85	61
Next Generation High-speed Rail	....	....	−3	....	1	....
Pennsylvania Station Redevelopment Project	....	....	....	15	3	2
National Network Transformation Grants	....	....	545	....	....	545
Northeast Corridor Grants to the National Railroad Passenger Corporation	647	697	323	646	697	324
National Network Grants to the National Railroad Passenger Corporation	1,285	1,294	608	1,284	1,295	611
Federal-State Partnership for State of Good Repair	396	198	....	....	....	125
Consolidated Rail Infrastructure and Safety Improvements	252	322	327	5	13	110
Federal Transit Administration:						
Washington Metropolitan Area Transit Authority	150	150	150	159	109	114
Formula Grants	−47	....	−2	9	45	....
Capital Investment Grants	2,553	1,978	1,889	1,826	2,323	2,638
Public Transportation Emergency Relief Program	11	....	....	615	1,005	877
Transit Formula Grants	....	....	....	10,500	10,596	11,321
Transit Formula Grants (non-add obligation limitations) [1]	*11,013*	*11,450*	*12,346*	....	....	....
Pipeline and Hazardous Materials Safety Administration:						
Pipeline Safety	53	76	76	46	66	77
Trust Fund Share of Pipeline Safety	8	8	8	9	9	8
Total, discretionary	**11,598**	**8,248**	**5,669**	**64,670**	**67,398**	**70,146**
Total, obligation limitations (non-add) [1]	*59,546*	*60,607*	*65,428*	....	....	....

Table 14–2. FEDERAL GRANTS TO STATE AND LOCAL GOVERNMENTS—BUDGET AUTHORITY AND OUTLAYS—Continued

(In millions of dollars)

Function, Category, Agency, and Program	Budget Authority			Outlays		
	2019 Actual	2020 Estimate	2021 Estimate	2019 Actual	2020 Estimate	2021 Estimate
Mandatory:						
Department of Homeland Security:						
United States Coast Guard:						
Boat Safety	117	117	117	104	105	114
Department of Transportation:						
Federal Aviation Administration:						
Grants-in-aid for Airports (Airport and Airway Trust Fund)	3,690	3,579	3,175	....	....	....
Federal Highway Administration:						
Federal-aid Highways	44,399	44,970	49,421	728	731	742
Miscellaneous Appropriations	135	80	....	135	80	....
Federal Motor Carrier Safety Administration:						
Motor Carrier Safety Grants	382	388	403	....	....	....
National Highway Traffic Safety Administration:						
Highway Traffic Safety Grants	653	661	584	....	....	....
Federal Transit Administration:						
Transit Formula Grants	10,985	11,422	12,321	....	....	....
Total, mandatory	**60,361**	**61,217**	**66,021**	**967**	**916**	**856**
Total, Transportation	**71,959**	**69,465**	**71,690**	**65,637**	**68,314**	**71,002**
Community and Regional Development						
Discretionary:						
Department of Agriculture:						
Rural Utilities Service:						
Distance Learning, Telemedicine, and Broadband Program	279	348	292	147	99	352
Rural Water and Waste Disposal Program Account	613	654	614	522	900	1,049
Rural Housing Service:						
Rural Community Facilities Program Account	200	49	60	48	41	65
Rural Business-Cooperative Service:						
Rural Business Program Account	65	72	7	65	88	44
Department of Commerce:						
Economic Development Administration:						
Economic Development Assistance Programs	852	276	–38	221	565	510
Department of Homeland Security:						
Federal Emergency Management Agency:						
Federal Assistance	2,739	2,963	2,341	1,350	2,238	2,128
State and Local Programs	....	....	....	903	209	222
Disaster Relief Fund	6,383	17,563	5,653	6,735	10,953	12,298
Department of Housing and Urban Development:						
Community Planning and Development:						
Community Development Fund	7,473	3,425	....	5,178	7,427	9,573
Community Development Loan Guarantees Program Account	....	....	....	1	2	....
Brownfields Redevelopment	....	....	....	....	2	2
Office of Lead Hazard Control and Healthy Homes:						
Lead Hazard Reduction	279	290	360	95	178	212
Department of the Interior:						
Bureau of Indian Affairs:						
Operation of Indian Programs	149	178	178	149	178	180
Indian Guaranteed Loan Program Account	11	11	1	9	11	1
Denali Commission	22	15	....	16	44	27
Total, discretionary	**19,065**	**25,844**	**9,468**	**15,439**	**22,935**	**26,663**
Mandatory:						
Department of Housing and Urban Development:						
Community Planning and Development:						
Neighborhood Stabilization Program	....	....	....	20	59	59

Table 14–2.   FEDERAL GRANTS TO STATE AND LOCAL GOVERNMENTS—BUDGET AUTHORITY AND OUTLAYS—Continued

(In millions of dollars)

Function, Category, Agency, and Program	Budget Authority			Outlays		
	2019 Actual	2020 Estimate	2021 Estimate	2019 Actual	2020 Estimate	2021 Estimate
Department of the Interior:						
Bureau of Indian Affairs:						
Indian Guaranteed Loan Program Account	18	35	....	18	35	....
Department of the Treasury:						
Fiscal Service:						
Gulf Coast Restoration Trust Fund	315	339	351	88	188	171
Total, mandatory	**333**	**374**	**351**	**126**	**282**	**230**
Total, Community and Regional Development	**19,398**	**26,218**	**9,819**	**15,565**	**23,217**	**26,893**
Education, Training, Employment, and Social Services						
Discretionary:						
Department of Education:						
Office of Elementary and Secondary Education:						
Improving Elementary and Secondary Education	....	....	6,841	....	....	274
Indian Education	175	174	174	162	216	174
Impact Aid	1,441	1,481	1,406	1,417	1,375	1,440
Safe Schools and Citizenship Education	193	210	....	160	199	185
Education for the Disadvantaged	16,494	16,944	10,841	16,203	17,637	16,521
School Improvement Programs	5,102	5,274	2,066	4,616	5,146	5,200
Office of Innovation and Improvement:						
Innovation and Improvement	931	987	....	857	1,353	953
Office of English Language Acquisition:						
English Language Acquisition	686	732	....	702	746	712
Office of Special Education and Rehabilitative Services:						
Special Education	13,264	13,674	13,774	12,978	13,562	13,644
Rehabilitation Services	86	87	64	87	81	74
Office of Career, Technical, and Adult Education:						
Career, Technical and Adult Education	1,904	1,940	2,619	1,782	1,872	1,960
Office of Postsecondary Education:						
Higher Education	360	365	....	348	408	363
Institute of Education Sciences	26	26	....	25	25	21
Disaster Education Recovery	160	....	....	368	518	563
Department of Health and Human Services:						
Administration for Children and Families:						
Promoting Safe and Stable Families	100	93	60	61	92	77
Children and Families Services Programs	11,923	12,519	11,498	11,240	11,730	12,183
Administration for Community Living:						
Aging and Disability Services Programs	1,843	1,829	1,710	1,917	2,102	1,889
Department of the Interior:						
Bureau of Indian Affairs:						
Operation of Indian Programs	94	....	....	90	68	2
Bureau of Indian Education:						
Operation of Indian Education Programs	....	94	94	....	38	66
Department of Labor:						
Employment and Training Administration:						
Training and Employment Services	2,790	3,091	2,980	2,684	3,020	3,071
State Unemployment Insurance and Employment Service Operations	364	81	81	53	76	74
Unemployment Trust Fund	1,088	1,102	1,102	979	1,107	1,114
Corporation for National and Community Service:						
Operating Expenses	538	15	15	262	270	133
Corporation for Public Broadcasting	465	465	30	465	465	30
District of Columbia:						
District of Columbia General and Special Payments:						
Federal Payment for Resident Tuition Support	40	40	....	40	40	....

Table 14–2. FEDERAL GRANTS TO STATE AND LOCAL GOVERNMENTS—BUDGET AUTHORITY AND OUTLAYS—Continued

(In millions of dollars)

Function, Category, Agency, and Program	Budget Authority			Outlays		
	2019 Actual	2020 Estimate	2021 Estimate	2019 Actual	2020 Estimate	2021 Estimate
Federal Payment for School Improvement	53	53	90	53	53	90
Institute of Museum and Library Services:						
Office of Museum and Library Services: Grants and Administration	224	229	....	210	299	170
National Endowment for the Arts:						
Grants and Administration	49	52	....	48	52	34
Total, discretionary	**60,393**	**61,557**	**55,445**	**57,807**	**62,550**	**61,017**
Mandatory:						
Department of Education:						
Office of Special Education and Rehabilitative Services:						
Rehabilitation Services	3,304	3,397	3,668	3,032	3,683	3,543
Office of Career, Technical, and Adult Education:						
Career and Technical Education State Grants, H–1B Funded	....	....	117	....	....	6
Department of Health and Human Services:						
Administration for Children and Families:						
Promoting Safe and Stable Families	489	995	565	421	607	801
Social Services Block Grant	1,680	1,685	....	1,646	1,715	352
Department of Labor:						
Employment and Training Administration:						
TAA Community College and Career Training Grant Fund	....	....	....	18	....	....
Federal Unemployment Benefits and Allowances	401	410	300	182	213	266
Total, mandatory	**5,874**	**6,487**	**4,650**	**5,299**	**6,218**	**4,968**
Total, Education, Training, Employment, and Social Services	**66,267**	**68,044**	**60,095**	**63,106**	**68,768**	**65,985**
Health						
Discretionary:						
Department of Agriculture:						
Food Safety and Inspection Service:						
Salaries and Expenses	56	56	56	52	54	56
Department of Health and Human Services:						
Health Resources and Services Administration:						
Health Resources and Services	2,914	2,935	2,910	3,009	3,236	3,011
Indian Health Service:						
Payments for Tribal Leases	....	....	101	....	....	101
Contract Support Costs	799	855	855	830	877	892
Centers for Disease Control and Prevention:						
CDC-wide Activities and Program Support	3,346	3,437	3,437	1,162	1,197	1,009
Substance Abuse and Mental Health Services Administration	4,846	4,906	4,768	3,679	5,506	5,055
Departmental Management:						
Public Health and Social Services Emergency Fund	265	276	258	254	260	269
Department of Labor:						
Occupational Safety and Health Administration:						
Salaries and Expenses	112	182	170	112	182	170
Mine Safety and Health Administration:						
Salaries and Expenses	11	11	11	11	11	11
Total, discretionary	**12,349**	**12,658**	**12,566**	**9,109**	**11,323**	**10,574**
Mandatory:						
Department of Health and Human Services:						
Health Resources and Services Administration:						
Maternal, Infant, and Early Childhood Home Visiting Programs	400	376	400	384	386	392
Centers for Medicare and Medicaid Services:						
Rate Review Grants	....	....	....	17	13	5
Affordable Insurance Exchange Grants	....	....	....	4	....	....
Cost-sharing Reductions	....	1,266	1,307	....	1,266	1,307
Grants to States for Medicaid	411,084	422,175	450,174	409,421	447,241	448,145

Table 14–2. FEDERAL GRANTS TO STATE AND LOCAL GOVERNMENTS—BUDGET AUTHORITY AND OUTLAYS—Continued

(In millions of dollars)

Function, Category, Agency, and Program	Budget Authority			Outlays		
	2019 Actual	2020 Estimate	2021 Estimate	2019 Actual	2020 Estimate	2021 Estimate
Payments to Hospitals	....	....	17,500	....	....	17,500
Children's Health Insurance Fund	20,539	20,530	22,103	17,689	17,654	15,778
State Grants and Demonstrations	392	260	91	378	437	429
Child Enrollment Contingency Fund	4,635	4,429	5,128	3	310	....
Departmental Management:						
Pregnancy Assistance Fund	23	....	....	21	25	1
Department of the Treasury:						
Internal Revenue Service:						
Refundable Premium Tax Credit	6,036	6,071	4,863	5,298	7,023	4,863
Total, mandatory	**443,109**	**455,107**	**501,566**	**433,215**	**474,355**	**488,420**
Total, Health	**455,458**	**467,765**	**514,132**	**442,324**	**485,678**	**498,994**
Income Security						
Discretionary:						
Department of Agriculture:						
Food and Nutrition Service:						
Commodity Assistance Program	324	344	81	366	362	205
Special Supplemental Nutrition Program for Women, Infants, and Children (WIC)	5,574	5,000	4,252	5,314	5,029	4,412
Department of Health and Human Services:						
Administration for Children and Families:						
Low Income Home Energy Assistance	3,653	3,740	....	3,695	3,757	1,296
Refugee and Entrant Assistance	515	524	524	515	496	434
Payments to States for the Child Care and Development Block Grant	5,276	5,814	5,814	3,906	5,283	6,348
Department of Homeland Security:						
Federal Emergency Management Agency:						
Federal Assistance	150	125	....	99	151	130
Emergency Food and Shelter	....	....	....	13	3	....
Department of Housing and Urban Development:						
Public and Indian Housing Programs:						
Moving to Work	....	....	5,185	....	....	4,322
Public Housing Fund	4,548	4,487	3,444	4,458	4,520	3,656
Revitalization of Severely Distressed Public Housing (HOPE VI)	....	....	....	13	18	1
Native Hawaiian Housing Block Grant	2	2	....	1	3	3
Tenant Based Rental Assistance	22,687	23,920	18,897	22,208	24,349	19,792
Public Housing Capital Fund	2,741	2,839	....	2,150	2,418	2,553
Native American Programs	753	824	600	657	641	685
Housing Certificate Fund	....	....	....	....	6	10
Choice Neighborhoods Initiative	150	175	....	109	168	179
Self-Sufficiency Programs	80	130	190	71	78	112
Rental Assistance Demonstration	....	....	100	....	....	100
Community Planning and Development:						
Homeless Assistance Grants	1,406	1,481	1,479	1,149	1,201	1,390
Home Investment Partnership Program	1,250	1,350	....	939	1,104	1,214
Housing Opportunities for Persons with AIDS	393	410	330	358	387	429
Permanent Supportive Housing	....	....	....	....	5	....
Housing Programs:						
Project-based Rental Assistance	245	345	345	245	272	260
Department of Labor:						
Employment and Training Administration:						
Unemployment Trust Fund	2,534	2,559	2,671	3,038	2,602	2,973
Total, discretionary	**52,281**	**54,069**	**43,912**	**49,304**	**52,853**	**50,504**
Mandatory:						
Department of Agriculture:						
Agricultural Marketing Service:						

Table 14–2. FEDERAL GRANTS TO STATE AND LOCAL GOVERNMENTS—BUDGET AUTHORITY AND OUTLAYS—Continued

(In millions of dollars)

Function, Category, Agency, and Program	Budget Authority			Outlays		
	2019 Actual	2020 Estimate	2021 Estimate	2019 Actual	2020 Estimate	2021 Estimate
Funds for Strengthening Markets, Income, and Supply (section 32)	1,069	1,167	283	843	947	83
Food and Nutrition Service:						
Supplemental Nutrition Assistance Program	7,405	7,270	7,270	7,100	6,975	7,121
Commodity Assistance Program	24	24	25	19	24	25
Child Nutrition Programs	23,310	23,788	25,673	23,247	22,797	25,872
Department of Health and Human Services:						
Administration for Children and Families:						
Payments to States for Child Support Enforcement and Family Support Programs	4,322	4,402	4,458	4,117	4,324	4,370
Contingency Fund	608	608	....	600	608	....
Payments for Foster Care and Permanency	8,559	9,388	10,060	8,599	9,389	9,955
Child Care Entitlement to States	2,917	2,917	4,212	3,244	2,961	3,231
Temporary Assistance for Needy Families	16,734	16,736	15,242	15,493	16,103	15,712
Total, mandatory	**64,948**	**66,300**	**67,223**	**63,262**	**64,128**	**66,369**
Total, Income Security	**117,229**	**120,369**	**111,135**	**112,566**	**116,981**	**116,873**
Social Security						
Mandatory:						
Social Security Administration:						
Federal Disability Insurance Trust Fund	4	8	7	14	12	10
Veterans Benefits and Services						
Discretionary:						
Department of Veterans Affairs:						
Veterans Health Administration:						
Medical Community Care	1,256	1,515	1,639	1,256	1,515	1,639
Medical Services	654	640	640	654	640	696
Departmental Administration:						
Grants for Construction of State Extended Care Facilities	150	90	90	91	333	320
Grants for Construction of Veterans Cemeteries	45	45	45	49	91	58
Total, discretionary	**2,105**	**2,290**	**2,414**	**2,050**	**2,579**	**2,713**
Total, Veterans Benefits and Services	**2,105**	**2,290**	**2,414**	**2,050**	**2,579**	**2,713**
Administration of Justice						
Discretionary:						
Department of Housing and Urban Development:						
Fair Housing and Equal Opportunity:						
Fair Housing Activities	65	70	65	60	65	68
Department of Justice:						
Legal Activities and U.S. Marshals:						
Assets Forfeiture Fund	21	21	21	21	20	21
Drug Enforcement Administration:						
High Intensity Drug Trafficking Areas Program	....	....	254	....	....	62
Office of Justice Programs:						
Research, Evaluation, and Statistics	70	17	17	4	4	4
State and Local Law Enforcement Assistance	605	605	605	1,049	918	917
Juvenile Justice Programs	279	229	229	231	248	256
Community Oriented Policing Services	250	292	....	184	211	261
Violence against Women Prevention and Prosecution Programs	461	500	....	479	462	342
Equal Employment Opportunity Commission:						
Salaries and Expenses	30	31	28	45	46	40
Federal Drug Control Programs:						
High Intensity Drug Trafficking Areas Program	258	285	....	245	338	171
State Justice Institute:						
Salaries and Expenses	6	7	8	4	11	7
Total, discretionary	**2,045**	**2,057**	**1,227**	**2,322**	**2,323**	**2,149**

Table 14–2.   FEDERAL GRANTS TO STATE AND LOCAL GOVERNMENTS—BUDGET AUTHORITY AND OUTLAYS—Continued

(In millions of dollars)

Function, Category, Agency, and Program	Budget Authority			Outlays		
	2019 Actual	2020 Estimate	2021 Estimate	2019 Actual	2020 Estimate	2021 Estimate
Mandatory:						
Department of Justice:						
Legal Activities and U.S. Marshals:						
Assets Forfeiture Fund	347	306	315	349	337	341
Office of Justice Programs:						
Crime Victims Fund	2,700	7,166	906	2,300	6,533	5,358
Department of the Treasury:						
Departmental Offices:						
Treasury Forfeiture Fund	160	196	195	190	98	102
Total, mandatory	**3,207**	**7,668**	**1,416**	**2,839**	**6,968**	**5,801**
Total, Administration of Justice	**5,252**	**9,725**	**2,643**	**5,161**	**9,291**	**7,950**
General Government						
Discretionary:						
Department of the Interior:						
United States Fish and Wildlife Service:						
National Wildlife Refuge Fund	13	13	....	13	13	....
Insular Affairs:						
Assistance to Territories	75	75	53	60	98	79
Department-Wide Programs:						
Payments in Lieu of Taxes	....	....	442	....	....	442
District of Columbia:						
District of Columbia Courts:						
Federal Payment to the District of Columbia Courts	258	250	268	239	253	267
Federal Payment for Defender Services in District of Columbia Courts	46	46	46	43	52	50
District of Columbia General and Special Payments:						
Federal Support for Economic Development and Management Reforms in the District	14	15	6	14	15	6
Election Assistance Commission:						
Election Security Grants	....	425	....	1	425	....
Total, discretionary	**406**	**824**	**815**	**370**	**856**	**844**
Mandatory:						
Department of Agriculture:						
Forest Service:						
Forest Service Permanent Appropriations	290	281	269	278	269	281
Department of Energy:						
Energy Programs:						
Payments to States under Federal Power Act	4	5	5	....	9	5
Department of the Interior:						
Office of Surface Mining Reclamation and Enforcement:						
Payments to States in Lieu of Coal Fee Receipts	103	42	45	57	134	142
United States Fish and Wildlife Service:						
National Wildlife Refuge Fund	9	8	8	10	9	9
Departmental Offices:						
Mineral Leasing and Associated Payments	2,152	1,772	1,810	2,152	1,772	1,810
National Petroleum Reserve, Alaska	15	14	17	15	14	17
Payment to Alaska, Arctic National Wildlife Refuge	....	473	251	....	473	251
Geothermal Lease Revenues, Payment to Counties	4	4	....	4	4	....
Insular Affairs:						
Assistance to Territories	28	28	28	24	22	26
Payments to the United States Territories, Fiscal Assistance	331	302	302	331	302	302
Department-Wide Programs:						
Payments in Lieu of Taxes	516	500	....	516	500	....
Department of the Treasury:						
Alcohol and Tobacco Tax and Trade Bureau:						

Table 14–2. FEDERAL GRANTS TO STATE AND LOCAL GOVERNMENTS—BUDGET AUTHORITY AND OUTLAYS—Continued

(In millions of dollars)

Function, Category, Agency, and Program	Budget Authority			Outlays		
	2019 Actual	2020 Estimate	2021 Estimate	2019 Actual	2020 Estimate	2021 Estimate
Internal Revenue Collections for Puerto Rico	445	453	459	445	453	459
District of Columbia:						
District of Columbia Courts:						
District of Columbia Crime Victims Compensation Fund	6	6	6	9	6	6
Total, mandatory	**3,903**	**3,888**	**3,200**	**3,841**	**3,967**	**3,308**
Total, General Government	**4,309**	**4,712**	**4,015**	**4,211**	**4,823**	**4,152**
Allowances						
Mandatory:						
Allowances:						
Infrastructure Initiative	....	....	189,990	....	....	4,750
Total, Grants	**753,674**	**780,680**	**974,589**	**721,140**	**790,732**	**810,076**
Discretionary	**167,853**	**175,397**	**135,697**	**207,108**	**228,945**	**230,674**
Transportation obligation limitations (non-add) [1]	*59,546*	*60,607*	*65,428*	....	....	....
Mandatory	**585,821**	**605,283**	**838,892**	**514,032**	**561,787**	**579,402**

[1] Mandatory contract authority provides budget authority for these programs, but program levels are set by discretionary obligation limitations in appropriations bills and outlays are recorded as discretionary. This table shows the obligation limitations as non-additive items to avoid double counting. For all surface transportation programs subject to reauthorization, the Budget includes placeholder funding levels for 2010 that do not represent Administration policy.

15. INFORMATION TECHNOLOGY

Federal Information Technology (IT) provides Americans with important services and information and is the foundation of how Government serves the public in the digital age. The President proposes spending over $92 billion on IT at agencies[1], which will be used to deliver critical citizen services, keep sensitive data and systems secure, and to further the vision of modern Government. The Budget also supports the IT Modernization (Modernize IT to Increase Productivity and Security) Cross Agency Priority (CAP) Goal of the President's Management Agenda (PMA)[2], Federal laws that enable agency technology planning, oversight, funding, and accountability practices, and Office of Management and Budget (OMB) guidance to agencies on the strategic use of IT to enable mission outcomes. It also supports the modernization of antiquated and often unsecured legacy systems; agency migration to secure, cost-effective commercial cloud solutions, and shared services; the recruitment, retention, and reskilling of the Federal technology and cybersecurity workforce to ensure higher value service delivery; and the reduction of cybersecurity risk across the Federal enterprise. These investments will, in alignment with the PMA, focus on addressing root cause structural issues, promoting stronger collaboration and coordination among Federal Agencies, and addressing capability challenges that have impeded the Government's technology vision. This analysis excludes information on classified IT investments by the Department of Defense.

Federal Spending on IT

As shown in Table 15-1, the Federal Government Budget for IT at agencies is estimated to be $92 billion in 2021. This figure is an increase from the estimate reported for 2020. Table 15-2 displays IT spending for civilian agencies. The Department of Homeland Security (DHS) is the largest civilian agency in IT spending, while the bottom five agencies represent 1.1 percent of Federal civilian IT spending. Chart 15-1 shows trending information for Federal civilian IT spending from 2011 forward.[3]

IT Investments Overview

The 2021 Budget includes funding for 8,645 investments at agencies. These investments support three main functions: mission delivery; IT infrastructure, IT security, and IT management; and administrative services and mission support (see Chart 15-2). As Chart 15-3 shows, IT investments can vary widely in size and scope. As a result, the largest 100 investments at civilian agencies account for 42 percent of Federal IT spending.

Of those 8,645 IT investments, 591 are considered major IT investments. As outlined in OMB Circular A-11 and FY 2021 Capital Planning and Investment Control (CPIC) Guidance, agencies determine if an IT investment is classified as major based on whether the associated investment has significant program or policy implications; has high executive visibility; has high development, operating, or maintenance costs; or requires special management attention because of its importance to the mission or function of the agency. For all major IT investments, agencies are required by CPIC Guidance to submit Business Cases, which provide additional transparency regarding the cost, schedule, risk, and performance data related to its spending.

OMB requires that agency Chief Information Officers (CIOs) provide risk ratings for all major IT investments on the IT Dashboard website on a continuous basis and assess how risks for major development efforts are being addressed and mitigated. The agency CIO rates each investment based on his or her best judgment, using a set of pre-established criteria. As a rule, the evaluation should reflect the CIO's assessment of the investment's ability to accomplish defined security, efficiency, mission, and/or service goals as of the time of the Budget release. Chart 15-4 summarizes the CIO risk ratings for all major civilian IT investments Government-wide. The IT Dashboard shows slight decreases in the general health of IT investments across Government, as denoted by the decreased proportion of CIO-rated "Green" ("Low Risk" to "Moderately Low Risk") investments. "Green" investments comprised 35 percent of all rated investments in 2020 compared to 41 percent in 2019, reflecting the increased complexity of initiatives (assessments based on total life cycle of investments).

The remainder of this chapter describes important aspects of the latest initiatives undertaken with respect to Federal IT policies and projects, addressing a variety of topics. In the important area of cybersecurity policy and spending, however, the reader is referred to Chapter 19 of this volume, entitled "Cybersecurity Funding." This chapter addresses the important area of the protection of Federal systems and data, including those which have personally identifiable information, and the Continuous Diagnostics and Mitigation (CDM) program -- a dynamic approach to fortifying the cybersecurity of Government networks and systems.

---

[1] The scope of the analysis in this chapter refers to agencies represented on the IT Dashboard, located at *https://www.itdashboard.gov/*.

[2] See *https://www.perfomance.gov/*.

[3] Note that as of the 2020 CPIC guidance, IT related grants made to State and local governments are no longer included in agency IT investment submissions.

Table 15–1. FEDERAL IT SPENDING
(In millions of dollars)

	FY 2019	FY 2020	FY 2021
Civilian Agencies	51,877	52,925	53,358
Department of Defense	36,906	39,057	38,815
Total	**88,783**	**91,982**	**92,174**

Note: This analysis excludes Department of Defense classified spending.

Cloud Adoption

The Administration last year issued the Federal Cloud Computing Strategy, now commonly referred to as the "Cloud Smart" strategy. This is a significant update to the "Cloud First" strategy released in 2007. Cloud Smart emphasizes the need for application-specific business case analysis to determine the best solution and computing environment. The strategy describes three pillars for successful cloud adoption: a risk-based security approach, improved Federal procurement guidance, and the continued development of the Federal IT workforce. OMB, the CIO Council, GSA, and other agency partners have made significant progress in satisfying the 22 actions outlined in the strategy that will accelerate the adoption of cloud technologies.

The PMA set a goal that 95 percent of civilian Government employee email boxes will be serviced by a cloud-based service. At the end of 2019, 76 percent of email inboxes at Federal civilian CFO Act agencies are now hosted on cloud services, up 10 percent from 2018. This transition improves the efficiency of Government business and communication.

The Cloud Smart policy also directed that agencies complete an Application Rationalization to create an outlook for application disposition, transition to cloud and inform plans for data center closure and optimization. The Agency Application Rationalization plan provides a roadmap to prioritize, navigate and manage risk for ongoing modernization efforts.

As agencies plan their modernization, there are activities directed by OMB, the 21st Century Idea Act, and the CIO council that advance the use of and effectiveness of digital service delivery across all agencies. The activities specific to enhancement of digital service capabilities and user-center design have been a focus in previous years and continue to be a priority focus in the initiatives planned for 2021.

Data Center Optimization Initiative (DCOI)

In addition to the Cloud Smart strategy, OMB updated the companion Data Center Optimization Initiative (DCOI) policy in 2019. This update refocused data center optimization on the applications and data rather than just IT infrastructure. Agencies are to consider the applications' total cost of ownership, security requirements and mission mandates when determining future IT infrastructure optimization efforts. The updated DCOI policy also clarifies both the criteria by which a data center is reportable to OMB, and the criteria that may exempt some data centers from closure. This change in policy re-

Table 15–2. ESTIMATED FY 2021 CIVILIAN FEDERAL IT SPENDING AND PERCENTAGE BY AGENCY
(In millions of dollars)

Agency	FY 2021	Percent of Total
Department of Veterans Affairs	$7,761	14.5%
Department of Homeland Security	$7,298	13.7%
Department of Health and Human Services	$6,422	12.0%
Department of the Treasury	$5,107	9.6%
Department of Transportation	$3,392	6.4%
Department of Justice	$3,265	6.1%
Department of Energy	$2,847	5.3%
Department of Commerce	$2,634	4.9%
Department of State	$2,634	4.9%
Department of Agriculture	$2,372	4.4%
National Aeronautics and Space Administration ...	$2,154	4.0%
Social Security Administration	$1,940	3.6%
Department of the Interior	$1,390	2.6%
Department of Education	$887	1.7%
Department of Labor	$784	1.5%
General Services Administration	$638	1.2%
Department of Housing and Urban Development ..	$409	0.8%
Environmental Protection Agency	$353	0.7%
U.S. Army Corps of Engineers	$247	0.5%
U.S. Agency for International Development	$222	0.4%
Nuclear Regulatory Commission	$141	0.3%
Office of Personnel Management	$130	0.2%
National Science Foundation	$127	0.2%
Small Business Administration	$108	0.2%
National Archives and Records Administration	$99	0.2%
Total	**$53,358**	**100.0%**

Note: This analysis excludes the Department of Defense.

duced the number of Federal data centers reported on the Federal IT Dashboard (https://itdashboard.gov/). Using the adjusted criteria, Federal Agencies have closed 4,247 data centers for a cumulative cost savings or avoidance of $2.2 billion since 2010.

Enterprise Infrastructure Solutions

Federal cloud adoption is underpinned by the modernization of Government communications networks. OMB has designated the GSA Enterprise Infrastructure Solutions (EIS) contract as "Best-in-Class" or the preferred Government-wide solution to leverage the Government's buying power for telecommunications and IT infrastructure requirements. As Federal Agencies transition to the EIS contract they are taking the opportunity to develop a holistic approach toward cloud infrastructure, enhanced mobility, automation, satellite communications, and security. EIS is the only Federal network services contract to include both OMB policy directives and DHS cybersecurity requirements. Through aggregated Federal buying, EIS can deliver a monthly savings of 16-21 percent. Modern, secure, and cost-effective communications networks are enabling Federal Agencies to continue to adopt a modern IT infrastructure and improve citizen services.

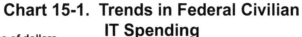

Chart 15-1. Trends in Federal Civilian IT Spending

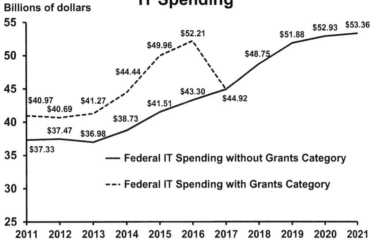

Billions of dollars

$40.97	$52.21
$40.69	$49.96
$37.47	$44.44

— Federal IT Spending without Grants Category

--- Federal IT Spending with Grants Category

$37.33, $37.47, $36.98, $38.73, $41.51, $43.30, $44.92, $48.75, $51.88, $52.93, $53.36

$40.97, $40.69, $41.27, $44.44, $49.96, $52.21

2011 2012 2013 2014 2015 2016 2017 2018 2019 2020 2021

Notes: Investments labeled as "Part 06 – Grants to State and Local IT Investments" were excluded from 2011 – 2015 figures. Investments labeled "Part 04 - Grants and Other Transferred Funding" were excluded in 2016 figures. The 2017 – 2020 estimates did not include these types of investments.

Improving the IT Workforce

Maintaining and securing Federal IT requires a large, highly capable IT workforce. A current focus for policies guiding the strengthening of the Federal IT workforce, stemming from the President's Management Agenda, is the direction given to Federal Agencies to build a workforce able to leverage data as a strategic asset to grow the economy, increase the effectiveness of the Federal Government, facilitate oversight, and promote transparency.

To accomplish this goal, agencies need a workforce highly skilled in the technology, methodologies, and theory of data science. These individuals blend disciplines including mathematics, statistics, and computer science, and need to be able to adapt and develop their skills in a rapidly-changing field. To date, the Government has taken steps to expand the data science workforce, including efforts to establish a dedicated data scientist occupational series to reflect the unique qualifications and skills of the data science workforce. In addition, the Administration has provided training and other professional development opportunities for data scientists to build data literacy and capacity Government-wide.

The President's Budget continues to invest in the data science, data-skilled workforce, to make the Government an attractive employer for top-tier talent, improve our ability to oversee and administer Government-wide programs, and to better deliver services to the American people. A highly skilled data science workforce is essential for the Government's ability to innovate in artificial intelligence and machine learning. Agencies need staff who understand these technologies, both to generate the foundational data needed for them to operate, as well as to manage the automated services to ensure they are accu-

rate, fair, and aligned to the needs of the Government and the American people. Agencies also need cross-functional data scientists who can work in areas like financial management, acquisition, and privacy protections, to drive value across a range of Government domains. Ultimately, a strong cadre of data scientists will allow the Government to run more efficiently and effectively, and drive more user-centric services to the American people.

Shared Services

On April 26, 2019, OMB issued OMB M-19-16[4] establishing a new approach to shared services called Sharing Quality Services (SQS). The memo created a new governance structure leveraging the agencies leadership to help drive and champion these changes. During the summer of 2019, the Administration refreshed the Shared Services Governance Board (SSGB), now comprised of representatives from all the Government-wide councils, and created a new SQS Senior Accountable Point of Contact (SAPOC) group to coordinate actions across the agency to support adoption of the shared service strategies and to be the voice of the Government customer.

In the evolving Shared Service environment, Quality Service Management Offices (QSMOs) will manage the marketplace of solutions for a defined mission-support function. QSMO planning and formal designation of QSMOs already spans the 2019 and 2020 fiscal years. During the preparation for the 2021 Budget, three agencies prepared and presented plans for future services. In addition, exploration and analysis of standards for additional mission support areas will occur in 2020 and 2021. This multiyear journey of agency customer-led,

---

[4] *M-19-16, Centralized Mission Support Capabilities for the Federal Government.*

Chart 15-2. 2021 Federal Civilian IT Investment Portfolio Summary

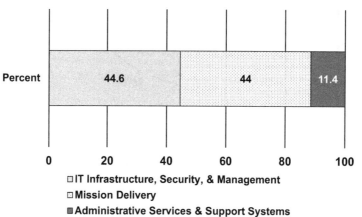

Percent   44.6   44   11.4

0   20   40   60   80   100

☐ IT Infrastructure, Security, & Management
☐ Mission Delivery
■ Administrative Services & Support Systems

Government-wide identification of standards, alignment of modern services, and introduction of enhanced capabilities will lead the way to transform the Federal Government through improved mission support service quality, and decreased total cost of services, across the Federal enterprise.

United States Digital Service

Americans expect and deserve their interactions with the Federal Government to be simple, fast, and responsive. The United States Digital Service (USDS) is enhancing the Federal Government's most critical public-facing digital services through design and technology expertise. USDS recruits some of the country's top technical talent and partners directly with Federal Agencies to ensure that critical services reach the public. USDS projects not only provide the public with better digital services, but also help streamline agency processes and save taxpayer dollars.

To successfully modernize technical systems, USDS developed a new approach through the Digital Services Playbook.[5] A main element of USDS' approach is to understand what people need. Historically, the Government developed products without regard to how the American people would actually interact with those products. For instance, USDS supported the VA in developing and rolling out the new *VA.gov*, which consolidates the most important information for veterans and places it in one location. Veterans can now update their contact information in one place without having to worry about making the same change in disparate systems. Since the redesign and relaunch of *VA.gov*, 684,000 veterans updated their profiles in 2019, a 479 percent increase over a year prior. USDS continues to collaborate with the VA on

_____
[5] See *https://playbook.cio.gov/*.

Chart 15-3. Percentage of 2021 Federal Civilian IT Spending by Number of Investments

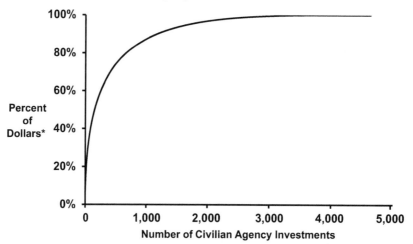

Percent of Dollars*

Number of Civilian Agency Investments

*Percent of Dollars Represented by Largest Investments, Progressing to Smallest Investments

Chart 15-4. CIO Risk Ratings for Federal Civilian Major IT Investments

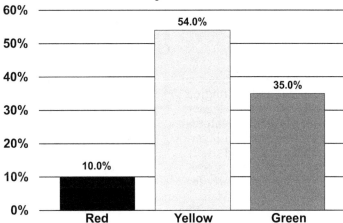

enhancing veterans' access to benefits and services, seeing significant increases in application submissions for healthcare, burials, and education benefits through the site. USDS has a number of similar projects across the Federal Government that not only help update and modernize legacy systems, but also change the culture of how the Government thinks about providing services to the American people.

USDS implements modern best practices that can be replicated across agencies. For instance, USDS is assisting the VA and Centers for Medicare and Medicaid Services (CMS) migrate to the cloud. Both of these agencies are also at the forefront of leveraging industry standard technology known as application programming interfaces (APIs) that allow software to interact with other software. At the 2019 Blue Button 2.10 Developers Conference on July 30, the CMS USDS team launched Data at the Point of Care (DPC), a pilot API program. The DPC API gives some doctors and healthcare providers access to Medicare claims data, which may improve patient healthcare and overall customer experience. Under DPC, healthcare providers will have access to patient health histories, providing insight into other treatments they may be receiving. Medicare recipients may have more time with their doctors to address current health needs, and better, more coordinated healthcare.

In addition, USDS is working with OMB and OPM to pilot a new way to assess qualifications within the competitive service, with the goal of ensuring only qualified candidates make it to hiring managers for review. The two pilots conducted at DOI and HHS were highly successful, resulting in 20 selections to positions that had previously been advertised with no successful selections, and five additional agencies are moving toward piloting the process. USDS is working with OPM to prototype and test technology to help SMEs to engage in parts of this process.

USDS is also helping drive the adoption and implementation of information security best practices. In a combined project with GSA, USDS launched *Login.gov* that makes managing Federal benefits, services, and applications easier and more secure through the use of modern identity management solutions such as two-factor authentication. *Login.gov* scaled to over 18 million users, and continues to grow as it is adopted by additional agencies.

Current Federal procurement practices largely do not provide the flexibility required to buy and deliver modern digital services. Meanwhile, the pace of technological change continues to accelerate, while citizen demand for Federal digital services increases. To meet this demand, the Office of Federal Procurement Policy (OFPP) and USDS developed a training program to enhance digital services acquisition expertise across agencies. Graduates of the training receive the Federal Acquisition Certification in Contracting Core-Plus Specialization in Digital Services (FAC-C-DS). As of December 2019, more than 300 people have graduated from the training program, and several agencies are running the training program internally, including the VA, DOE, and DHS. In addition, there are three companies now providing open enrollment courses for others interested in taking the training.

IPv6

The Federal Government is continuing its transition to the new version of Internet Protocol, called IPv6 -- the international standard enabling interoperability for all devices connected to the global internet. The protocol used for the last 30 years (IPv4) is at the point where its pool of available addresses is reaching virtual exhaustion. While stop-gap measures have served to extend IPv4's viability thus far, it is imperative that IPv6, with its vastly larger address space, sees widespread adoption in the near future. This will accommodate internet growth and innovation, giving better support to mobility, security, and virtualized network services. The Federal Government has been leading on policies to move the vendor community and Federal Agencies forward on the path to IPv6 adoption for the last 15 years, pushing network operators, software vendors, service providers, and other private sector actors toward adoption of the latest IPv6 industry standards – mirroring the same transitions seen across the world. The Federal Government will continue to migrate its information services and networks until an IPV6-only environment is achieved.

IT Modernization

Due to the complexity of the IT landscape, agencies are often inefficient in acquiring, developing, and managing Federal IT investments. This is largely due to both legacy and internally developed, non-standards based systems designed to perform only one function rather than leveraging commercial off the shelf technologies that largely enable more efficient use of Federal technical resources. These legacy and high-customized systems are costly for the Federal Government to maintain and secure.

The Administration continues to pursue its IT Modernization CAP Goal, with its three-pronged approach focusing on enhancing Federal IT and digital services, reducing cybersecurity risks to the Federal mission, and building a modern IT and cybersecurity workforce. Federal Agencies are increasing efforts to modernize their IT in a way that will enhance mission effectiveness and reduce mission risks through a series of complementary initiatives that have and will continue to drive sustained change in Federal technology, deployment, security, and service delivery. Though a substantial amount of work is still required, below are several specific detailed efforts of the Administration's IT modernization strategy.

OMB continues to support the adoption and evolution of the Federal Information Technology Acquisition Reform Act (FITARA)[6] to provide agency CIOs with the authority, accountability, and support to deliver IT services across their agency enterprise. OMB continues to work with the Congress and the Government Accountability Office to improve the technology areas reflected in the FITARA Scorecard to ensure consistent, effective metrics-based evaluation of agency progress and outcomes. Through the Chief Information Officers Council (CIO Council), OMB and agency CIOs will direct discreet projects, coordination efforts, and focused problem solving initiatives to unleash the effectiveness of technical capabilities within agencies to deliver on missions and improve citizen services.

Leveraging Data as a Strategic Asset

On June 4, 2019, the Administration released the first comprehensive Federal Data Strategy[7] for managing and using Federal data. The Strategy is comprised of a mission statement, 10 guiding principles, and 40 best practices. The related first annual action plan includes 20 actions comprised of foundational steps and Administrative priorities to implement the Strategy. The Strategy and 2020 Action Plan are available on *https://strategy.data.gov*.

On July 10, 2019, the Administration released the first memorandum of guidance[8] related to implementing the Foundations for Evidence-based Policymaking Act, outlining the personnel and planning guidance needed to begin implementation of the Evidence Act's provisions. The guidance includes requiring all agencies to designate a Chief Data Officer and establish a Data Governance Body.

- The Budget supports the Foundations for Evidence-based Policymaking Act and the Federal Data Strategy by funding a U.S. Federal Data Service within the Department of Commerce. The Budget helps implement the OPEN Government Data Act by supporting the Federal Data Catalogue and related data services within the General Services Administration.

- The Budget supports the Federal Geographic Data Committee's work to improve management of geospatial data and implement the provisions of the Geospatial Data Act.

- The Budget includes technology investments that further enhance protection of data and foundational capabilities for management of data access and use.

Artificial Intelligence

The age of artificial intelligence (AI) is here, and has transformative potential for a wide spectrum of Federal missions ranging from healthcare to transportation to manufacturing. Recognizing the importance of American leadership in AI to maintaining the economic and National security of the United States, Federal Agencies have been directed by Executive Order 13859, "Maintaining American Leadership in Artificial Intelligence," issued on February 11, 2019, to support AI by prioritizing AI investments in their Research and Development (R&D) programs. To maintain America's AI advantage, Federal Agencies are to focus on two distinct areas. The first area of focus is internal—Federal use of AI to better achieve agency missions and serve citizens. The second focus area is external – including provision of data and related resources to support the private sector and academia in their efforts to harness AI. In both of the these areas, the Administration's policies and strategies aim to accelerate AI innovation to increase our prosperity, enhance our National/economic security, and improve our quality of life.

Agencies are now directed to include support to academia and the private sector via public-private partnerships for AI, to make Federal data, models, and computing resources available to researchers, to establish guidance for AI development and use across economic sectors, and to support programs to prepare our workforce with the skills needed to adapt and thrive in this new

---

[6] National Defense Authorization Act for Fiscal Year 2015, Title VIII, Subtitle D, H.R. 3979.

[7] *M-19-18, Federal Data Strategy – A Framework for Consistency*

[8] *M-19-23, Phase 1 Implementation of the Foundations for Evidence-Based Policymaking Act of 2018: Learning Agendas, Personnel, and Planning Guidance*

age of AI. All of this should be aligned with promotion of an international environment that supports AI R&D, and opens markets for American AI industries, while also ensuring that the technology is developed in a manner consistent with America's values and interests. Internal to the Federal Government, agencies are encouraged to deploy AI to improve service delivery, realizing efficiencies allowing the redeployment of resources to further enhance agency performance.

Private sector companies with Federal support are leveraging AI today to improve outcomes. Two examples include financial and food security. In financial services, the Securities and Exchange Commission (SEC) is implementing machine learning algorithms to monitor and detect potential investment market misconduct. Additionally, in September 2019, the Consumer Financial Protection Bureau (CFPB) issued new policies that allow for an increased use of data and machine learning algorithms in financial products and services. This drives competition that lowers prices and provides consumers with more and better products and services. The U.S. Department of Agriculture (USDA) is conducting research and development to use machine learning and AI to create better crop yield models, based on weather data and analysis. These efforts will help rural America thrive, and promote more efficient and profitable agricultural production. Finally, the United States Postal Service (USPS) is deploying an AI capability in 192 mail processing and sorting centers to increase package data processing by a factor of 10. This improvement would not be possible without the machine learning capabilities this technology delivers.

Technology Modernization Fund

The Technology Modernization Fund (TMF) is an innovative funding vehicle that gives agencies additional ways to deliver services to the American public more quickly, to better secure sensitive systems and data, and to use taxpayer dollars more efficiently.[9] The mission of the TMF is to enable agencies to accelerate transformation of the way they use technology to deliver their mission and services to the American public in an effective, efficient, and secure manner. Agencies must apply to and compete for TMF funds. Effective evaluation, selection, and monitoring of approved projects by the TMF Board provides strong incentives for agencies to develop comprehensive, high quality modernization plans. Funds are distributed in an incremental manner, tied to milestones and objectives. Agencies that receive funds from the TMF work with GSA and OMB to ensure that projects make maximum use of commercial products and services in their planning and execution, and that TMF funds will be repaid over a period not to exceed five years. Payback is achieved through cost savings and cost avoidance generated by the initiative. In addition, funding transfer increments are tied to successful delivery of initiative products or achievement of milestones thus tying budget costs to the results delivered. Successful projects will operate as proofs of concept and will provide valuable insights to the Board, which may recommend prioritizing the selection of more comprehensive modernization projects that can serve the interests of the Executive Branch as a whole. This Budget includes additional TMF funding to meet the demand generated by agencies and to invest strategically in modernizing agency systems through commercial solutions and improving the adoption and delivery of shared services.

Since its start in March 2019, the Technology Modernization Fund (TMF) Board has awarded nine initiatives a total of approximately $90 Million. In 2020, two new modernization projects have been approved for funding. The Equal Employment Opportunity Commission received $4 million to accelerate the modernization of its core Charge and Case Management System and the U.S. Department of Agriculture received an award to overhaul its antiquated, mostly paper-based Specialty Crops inspection system. These two proposals both have key elements in common: they are each systems with thousands of customer touchpoints throughout the Nation, and both Agencies are leveraging innovative commercial capabilities to enable their respective digital transformations. In addition, both projects are using TMF funds to enhance the speed at which improved citizen services are delivered. The TMF awards and Agency use of working capital approaches, are levers to accelerate modernization across Government in a manner that demonstrates efficient management of taxpayer resources.

---

[9] See *https://tmf.cio.gov/*.

16. FEDERAL INVESTMENT

Federal investment is the portion of Federal spending of taxpayer money intended to yield long-term benefits for the economy and the Nation that would be greater than if that money had been allocated in the private sector. It promotes improved efficiency within Federal agencies, as well as growth in the national economy by increasing the overall stock of capital. Investment spending can take the form of direct Federal spending or grants to State and local governments.[1] It can be designated for physical capital—a tangible asset or the improvement of that asset—that increases production over a period of years or increases value to the Government. It can also be for research and development, education, or training, all of which are intangible, but can still increase income in the future or provide other long-term benefits.

Most presentations in this volume combine investment spending with spending intended for current use. This chapter focuses solely on Federal and federally financed investment. It provides a comprehensive picture of Federal spending for physical capital, research and development, and education and training. The analysis in this chapter disregards spending for non-investment activities, and therefore, provides only a partial picture of Federal support for specific national needs, such as defense, which also include current use spending.

Total Federal investment spending was $558 billion in 2019. It is expected to increase by 20 percent in 2020 to $667 billion. The Budget proposes a 9 percent decrease from 2020 for a total of $609 billion in 2021.

---

[1] For more information on Federal grants to State and local governments see Chapter 14, "Aid to State and Local Governments," in this volume.

DESCRIPTION OF FEDERAL INVESTMENT

The budget uses a relatively broad definition of investment. It defines Federal investment as encompassing spending for research, development, education, and training as well as physical assets such as land, structures, infrastructure, and major equipment. It also includes spending regardless of the ultimate ownership of the resulting asset, or the purpose it serves. For the purposes of this definition, however, Federal investment does not include "social investment" items like healthcare or social services where it is difficult to separate out the degree to which the spending provides current versus future benefits. The distinction between investment spending and current outlays is a matter of judgment, but the definition used for the purposes of this analysis has remained consistent over time and is useful for historical comparisons.[2]

Investment in physical assets can be for the construction or improvement of buildings, structures, and infrastructure or for the development or acquisition of major equipment. The broader research and development category includes spending on the facilities in which these activities occur, major equipment for the conduct of research and development, as well as spending for basic and applied research, and experimental development.[3] Investment in education and training includes vocational rehabilitation, programs for veterans, funding for school systems and higher education, and agricultural extension services. This category excludes training for military personnel or other individuals in Government service.

The budget further classifies investments as either grants to State and local governments (e.g. for highways or education), or "direct Federal programs." This "direct Federal" category consists primarily of spending for assets owned by the Federal Government, such as weapons systems and buildings, but also includes grants to private organizations and individuals for investment, such as capital grants to Amtrak, Pell Grants, and higher education loans to individuals. For grants made to State and local governments, it is the recipient jurisdiction, not the Federal Government that ultimately determines whether the money is used to finance investment or current purposes. This analysis classifies outlays based on the category in which the recipient jurisdictions are expected to spend a majority of the money. General purpose fiscal assistance is classified as current spending, although in practice, some may be spent by recipient jurisdictions on investment.

Additionally, in this analysis, Federal investment includes credit programs that are for investment purposes. When direct loans and loan guarantees are used to fund investment, the subsidy value is included as investment. The subsidies are classified according to their program purpose, such as construction, or education and training.

This discussion presents spending for gross investment, without adjusting for depreciation.

Composition of Federal Investment Outlays

Major Federal Investment

The composition of major Federal investment outlays is summarized in Table 16–1. The categories include major public physical investment, the conduct of research and

---

[2] Historical figures on investment outlays beginning in 1940 may be found in the Budget's historical tables. The historical tables are available at *https://www.whitehouse.gov/omb/historical-tables/*.

[3] A more thorough discussion of research and development funding may be found in Chapter 17, "Research and Development," in this volume.

Table 16–1.   COMPOSITION OF FEDERAL INVESTMENT OUTLAYS

(In billions of dollars)

Federal Investment	Actual 2019	Estimate	
		2020	2021
Major public physical capital investment:			
Direct Federal:			
National defense	163.0	177.2	192.4
Non-defense	35.9	46.6	45.8
Subtotal, direct major public physical capital investment	198.9	223.8	238.2
Grants to State and local governments	80.8	87.3	97.3
Subtotal, major public physical capital investment	279.7	311.1	335.4
Conduct of research and development:			
National defense	56.0	65.8	64.9
Non-defense	67.7	73.8	75.6
Subtotal, conduct of research and development	123.6	139.6	140.5
Conduct of education and training:			
Grants to State and local governments	58.8	64.2	62.5
Direct Federal	94.0	149.4	68.4
Subtotal, conduct of education and training	152.8	213.5	130.9
Total, major Federal investment outlays	**556.2**	**664.3**	**606.8**
MEMORANDUM			
Major Federal investment outlays:			
National defense	219.0	243.1	257.3
Non-defense	337.2	421.2	349.6
Total, major Federal investment outlays	556.2	664.3	606.8
Miscellaneous physical investment:			
Commodity inventories	−1.1	−0.7	−1.2
Other physical investment (direct)	2.5	3.9	3.7
Total, miscellaneous physical investment	1.4	3.2	2.5
Total, Federal investment outlays, including miscellaneous physical investment	557.6	667.4	609.4

development, and the conduct of education and training. Total major Federal investment outlays were $556 billion in 2019. They are estimated to increase 19 percent to $664 billion in 2020, and decrease by 9 percent to $607 billion in 2021. For 2019 through 2021, defense investment outlays comprise about 40 percent of total major Federal investment while non-defense investment comprises around 60 percent. In 2020, defense investment outlays are expected to increase by $24 billion, 11 percent, while non-defense investment outlays are expected to increase by $84 billion, 25 percent. In 2021, the Budget requests a defense investment increase of another $14 billion, or 5.9 percent, over 2020 and a decrease in non-defense investment of $72 billion, or 17 percent. The major factors contributing to these changes are described below.

Major Federal investment outlays will comprise an estimated 13 percent of total Federal outlays in 2021 and 2.6 percent of the Nation's gross domestic product. Budget authority and outlays for major Federal investment by subcategory may be found in Table 16–2 at the end of this chapter.

Physical investment. Outlays for major public physical capital (hereafter referred to as "physical investment outlays") were $280 billion in 2019 and are estimated to increase by 11 percent to $311 billion in 2020. In 2021, outlays for physical investment are estimated to increase

by 8 percent to $335 billion. Physical investment outlays are for construction and renovation, the development or purchase of major equipment, and the purchase or sale of land and structures. Around two-thirds of these outlays are for direct physical investment by the Federal Government, with the remainder being grants to State and local governments for physical investment.

Direct physical investment outlays by the Federal Government are primarily for national defense. Defense outlays for physical investment are estimated to be $192 billion in 2021, $15 billion higher than in 2020 due to increases for the conduct of research and development.

Outlays for direct physical investment for non-defense purposes are estimated to be $46 billion in 2021, a decrease of 2 percent from 2020. Outlays for 2021 include $25 billion for construction and renovation, about the same as 2020. This amount includes funds for construction and renovation of veterans' hospitals and Indian Health Service hospitals and clinics; water, power, and natural resources projects of the Corps of Engineers, and the Bureau of Reclamation within the Department of the Interior; energy projects of the Power Marketing Administrations within the Department of Energy, and the Tennessee Valley Authority; construction of office buildings by the General Services Administration; construction for the administration of justice programs (largely in Customs and Border Protection within the Department of Homeland Security); construction for embassy security; facilities for space and science programs of the National Aeronautics and Space Administration, Department of Energy, and National Science Foundation; and Postal Service facilities.

Outlays for grants to State and local governments for physical investment are estimated to be $97 billion in 2021, an 11 percent increase over the 2020 estimate of $87 billion. Grants for physical investment fund transportation programs, sewage treatment plants, community and regional development, public housing, and other State and tribal assistance. The increase in 2021 is mostly accounted for by the $5 billion in spending proposed by the Infrastructure Initiative.

Conduct of research and development. Outlays for the conduct of research and development were $124 billion in 2019. Outlays are estimated to increase by 13 percent to $140 billion in 2020, and increase by less than 1 percent in 2021. Nearly half of research and development outlays are for national defense, a trend which has remained consistent over the past decade. Much of this year's increase is due to an $8 billion increase in research and development within military programs accompanied by smaller increases in defense-related research and development at the Department of Energy. Physical investment for research and development facilities and equipment is included in the physical investment category.

Non-defense outlays for the conduct of research and development are estimated to be $76 billion in 2021, $2 billion higher than 2020. Most investments in this area are funded through programs in the National Institutes of Health, the National Aeronautics and Space Administration, the National Science Foundation, and the Department of Agriculture.

A discussion of research and development funding can be found in Chapter 17, "Research and Development," in this volume.

Conduct of education and training. Outlays for the conduct of education and training were $153 billion in 2019. Outlays are estimated to increase by 40 percent to $214 billion in 2020, and decrease by 39 percent in 2021 to $131 billion. Grants to State and local governments for this category are estimated to be $62 billion in 2021, 48 percent of the total. They include education programs for the disadvantaged and individuals with disabilities, early care and education programs, training programs in the Department of Labor, and other education programs. Direct Federal education and training outlays in 2021 are estimated to be $68 billion, which is a decrease of $81 billion, or 54 percent, from 2020 primarily due to a one-time upward reestimate in 2020 in the Federal Direct Student Loan program. Programs in this category primarily consist of aid for higher education through student financial assistance, loan subsidies, and veterans' education, training, and rehabilitation. This category does not include outlays for education and training of Federal civilian and military employees. Outlays for education and training that are for physical investment and for research and development are in the categories for physical investment and the conduct of research and development.

Miscellaneous Physical Investment

In addition to the categories of major Federal investment, several miscellaneous categories of investment outlays are shown at the bottom of Table 16–1. These items, all for physical investment, are generally unrelated to improving Government operations or enhancing economic activity.

Outlays for commodity inventories are for the purchase or sale of agricultural products pursuant to farm price support programs and other commodities. Sales are estimated to exceed purchases by $3 billion in 2021.

Outlays for other miscellaneous physical investment are estimated to be $4 billion in 2021. This category consists entirely of direct Federal outlays and includes primarily conservation programs.

Detailed Table on Investment Spending

Table 16-2 provides data on budget authority as well as outlays for major Federal investment, divided according to grants to State and local governments and direct Federal spending. Miscellaneous investment is not included because it is generally unrelated to improving Government operations or enhancing economic activity.

Table 16–2. FEDERAL INVESTMENT BUDGET AUTHORITY AND OUTLAYS: GRANT AND DIRECT FEDERAL PROGRAMS

(In millions of dollars)

Description	Budget Authority			Outlays		
	2019 Actual	2020 Estimate	2021 Estimate	2019 Actual	2020 Estimate	2021 Estimate
GRANTS TO STATE AND LOCAL GOVERNMENTS						
Major public physical investment:						
Construction and rehabilitation:						
Transportation:						
Highways	49,226	46,983	49,283	45,235	46,207	48,363
Mass transportation	13,652	13,550	14,358	13,109	14,078	14,950
Rail transportation	2,590	2,513	1,176	1,996	2,136	1,257
Air and other transportation	5,065	4,954	5,140	4,154	4,551	4,638
Subtotal, transportation	70,533	68,000	69,957	64,494	66,972	69,208
Other construction and rehabilitation:						
Pollution control and abatement	4,114	3,804	2,655	3,403	2,637	3,092
Community and regional development	9,504	4,781	1,003	6,166	9,306	11,541
Housing assistance	4,896	5,190	600	3,869	4,357	4,635
Other	1,344	2,115	190,694	914	1,828	6,158
Subtotal, other construction and rehabilitation	19,858	15,890	194,952	14,352	18,128	25,426
Subtotal, construction and rehabilitation	90,391	83,890	264,909	78,846	85,100	94,634
Other physical assets	2,449	2,433	2,119	1,944	2,225	2,643
Subtotal, major public physical investment	**92,840**	**86,323**	**267,028**	**80,790**	**87,325**	**97,277**
Conduct of research and development:						
Agriculture	357	357	363	297	432	405
Other	186	193	27	51	57	25
Subtotal, conduct of research and development	**543**	**550**	**390**	**348**	**489**	**430**
Conduct of education and training:						
Elementary, secondary, and vocational education	40,480	41,546	37,888	39,381	42,766	41,767
Higher education	400	405	....	388	448	363
Research and general education aids	764	772	30	748	841	255
Training and employment	3,191	3,501	3,397	2,884	3,233	3,343
Social services	13,858	14,545	13,772	12,649	13,791	14,113
Agriculture	452	470	448	453	592	472
Other	1,872	1,935	2,024	2,323	2,493	2,174
Subtotal, conduct of education and training	**61,017**	**63,174**	**57,559**	**58,826**	**64,164**	**62,487**
Subtotal, grants for investment	**154,400**	**150,047**	**324,977**	**139,964**	**151,978**	**160,194**
DIRECT FEDERAL PROGRAMS						
Major public physical investment:						
Construction and rehabilitation:						
National defense:						
Military construction and family housing	11,339	16,472	6,597	7,024	7,564	10,928
Atomic energy defense activities and other	1,820	1,936	1,765	1,411	1,847	1,728
Subtotal, national defense	13,159	18,408	8,362	8,435	9,411	12,656
Non-defense:						
International affairs	1,373	1,090	996	895	1,378	1,372
General science, space, and technology	1,965	2,011	1,610	1,606	1,991	1,971
Water resources projects	4,964	4,524	3,436	2,891	2,942	2,740
Other natural resources and environment	1,742	1,529	1,278	1,204	1,671	1,767
Energy	2,005	3,209	−1,980	2,067	2,809	3,014
Postal service	857	958	1,223	647	757	938
Transportation	791	590	61	185	158	374
Veterans hospitals and other health facilities	6,189	4,643	4,987	3,585	4,550	4,302
Administration of justice	3,660	3,331	2,503	1,079	2,524	3,229
GSA real property activities	1,851	986	12,126	1,211	1,860	2,484
Other construction	4,203	3,322	1,461	3,412	3,663	2,307
Subtotal, non-defense	29,600	26,193	27,701	18,782	24,303	24,498
Subtotal, construction and rehabilitation	42,759	44,601	36,063	27,217	33,714	37,154

Table 16–2. FEDERAL INVESTMENT BUDGET AUTHORITY AND OUTLAYS: GRANT AND DIRECT FEDERAL PROGRAMS—Continued

(In millions of dollars)

Description	Budget Authority			Outlays		
	2019 Actual	2020 Estimate	2021 Estimate	2019 Actual	2020 Estimate	2021 Estimate
Acquisition of major equipment:						
National defense:						
Department of Defense	176,808	179,947	175,105	154,407	167,404	179,246
Atomic energy defense activities	641	709	730	220	458	484
Subtotal, national defense	177,449	180,656	175,835	154,627	167,862	179,730
Non-defense:						
General science and basic research	665	584	478	515	588	496
Postal service	1,119	5,160	2,174	772	1,544	1,896
Air transportation	3,743	3,787	3,807	3,529	4,123	4,107
Water transportation (Coast Guard)	2,691	1,753	1,547	1,485	2,352	2,231
Other transportation (railroads)	2	2	....	2	2	....
Hospital and medical care for veterans	2,683	2,251	3,465	1,976	2,984	3,167
Federal law enforcement activities	1,195	1,879	1,715	1,008	1,625	1,460
Department of the Treasury (fiscal operations)	347	323	437	380	367	415
National Oceanic and Atmospheric Administration	1,690	1,355	1,431	1,351	2,022	1,576
Other	4,819	5,135	5,658	5,744	6,354	5,748
Subtotal, non-defense	18,954	22,229	20,712	16,762	21,961	21,096
Subtotal, acquisition of major equipment	196,403	202,885	197,547	171,389	189,823	200,826
Purchase or sale of land and structures:						
National defense	–35	–35	–34	–52	–25	–26
Natural resources and environment	342	312	91	241	258	256
Other	155	159	157	129	28	–44
Subtotal, purchase or sale of land and structures	462	436	214	318	261	186
Subtotal, major public physical investment	**239,624**	**247,922**	**232,824**	**198,924**	**223,798**	**238,166**
Conduct of research and development:						
National defense:						
Defense military	54,669	62,691	59,831	50,952	58,738	57,688
Atomic energy and other	6,870	7,291	7,319	5,008	7,073	7,239
Subtotal, national defense	61,539	69,982	67,150	55,960	65,811	64,927
Non-defense:						
International affairs	235	226	73	235	226	226
General science, space, and technology:						
NASA	10,016	13,428	12,656	9,792	12,267	12,063
National Science Foundation	5,923	6,129	5,805	5,273	5,414	5,816
Department of Energy	5,045	5,325	4,734	4,503	5,102	5,084
Subtotal, general science, space, and technology	20,984	24,882	23,195	19,568	22,783	22,963
Energy	4,212	4,323	1,958	3,493	3,455	3,446
Transportation:						
Department of Transportation	875	936	566	803	928	650
NASA	565	575	630	558	558	581
Other transportation	24	23	35	36	23	27
Subtotal, transportation	1,464	1,534	1,231	1,397	1,509	1,258
Health:						
National Institutes of Health	36,929	39,323	36,650	33,879	36,481	38,592
Other health	1,858	1,186	832	1,461	802	835
Subtotal, health	38,787	40,509	37,482	35,340	37,283	39,427
Agriculture	1,849	1,935	1,967	1,612	2,032	2,320
Natural resources and environment	2,477	2,501	1,781	2,348	2,464	1,947
National Institute of Standards and Technology	625	657	560	671	677	627
Hospital and medical care for veterans	1,370	1,313	1,351	1,205	1,304	1,326
All other research and development	1,564	1,556	1,417	1,443	1,586	1,587
Subtotal, non-defense	73,567	79,436	71,015	67,312	73,319	75,127
Subtotal, conduct of research and development	**135,106**	**149,418**	**138,165**	**123,272**	**139,130**	**140,054**

Table 16–2.   FEDERAL INVESTMENT BUDGET AUTHORITY AND OUTLAYS: GRANT AND DIRECT FEDERAL PROGRAMS—Continued

(In millions of dollars)

Description	Budget Authority			Outlays		
	2019 Actual	2020 Estimate	2021 Estimate	2019 Actual	2020 Estimate	2021 Estimate
Conduct of education and training:						
Elementary, secondary, and vocational education	1,392	1,460	1,127	1,309	1,194	1,137
Higher education	70,755	125,123	41,229	70,477	124,106	43,575
Research and general education aids	2,331	2,430	2,293	2,324	2,309	2,297
Training and employment	2,642	2,309	1,824	2,239	2,457	2,088
Health	2,043	2,172	1,318	1,906	2,053	1,896
Veterans education, training, and rehabilitation	10,080	14,317	12,830	13,433	14,649	15,048
General science and basic research	910	935	919	811	876	929
National defense	....	....	....	2	....	....
International affairs	713	743	322	668	711	567
Other	1,111	1,036	843	845	997	898
Subtotal, conduct of education and training	**91,977**	**150,525**	**62,705**	**94,014**	**149,352**	**68,435**
Subtotal, direct Federal investment	**466,707**	**547,865**	**433,694**	**416,210**	**512,280**	**446,655**
Total, Federal investment	**621,107**	**697,912**	**758,671**	**556,174**	**664,258**	**606,849**

17. RESEARCH AND DEVELOPMENT

Over the past 70 years, America has emerged as the unquestioned global leader in science and technology (S&T). Nearly uninterrupted growth in combined public, private, academic, and nonprofit research and development (R&D) investment—together with the freedom to chase bold ideas; a diverse, highly-skilled, and entrepreneurial U.S. workforce; and world class universities and Federal and National laboratories—have resulted in the discoveries and innovations that have fueled improvements in national health, prosperity, and security. Today, the world is faced with extraordinary opportunities and profound challenges that require U.S. leadership. From leveraging international R&D collaborations and partnerships, to countering global threats to our economic and national security, to navigating the impact of technology both at home and in the workplace, we must commit to taking the wise and bold steps necessary to ensure America remains the global S&T leader for generations to come.

The Administration is deeply committed to this important goal by investing $142.2 billion in Federal R&D. For 2021, the Administration is prioritizing the science and technology that underpin the Industries of the Future (IotF)—artificial intelligence (AI), quantum information science (QIS), 5G/advanced communications, biotechnology, and advanced manufacturing. Relative to the 2020 President's Budget, this includes major increases in QIS and non-defense AI R&D as part of a commitment to double Federal AI and QIS R&D investments by 2022. R&D investments in AI and QIS, in particular, act as innovation multipliers and employment drivers, not only by promoting S&T progress across many disciplines, but also by helping to build a highly-skilled American workforce. Other IotF areas, such as biotechnology and advanced manufacturing, are poised for potentially transformative advances. Together, IotF investments are vital to the Nation's global competitiveness and the health, prosperity, and security of the American people.

These and other high priority investments, combined with thoughtful reallocations in lower priority areas, will revolutionize our ability to solve previously intractable problems, foster new industries and jobs, and keep the American people safe while remaining responsible stewards of taxpayer dollars. Table 17-1 shows a breakout of 2021 R&D funding.

Table 17–1.   TOTAL FEDERAL R&D FUNDING BY AGENCY AT THE BUREAU OR ACCOUNT LEVEL
(Mandatory and Discretionary Budget Authority [1,2], Dollar Amounts In Millions)

	2019 Actual	2020 Estimate [3]	2021 Proposed	Dollar Change: 2020 to 2021	Percent Change: 2020 to 2021
By Agency					
Agriculture	3,026	2,941	2,769	−172	−6%
Agriculture Research Service	1,702	1,625	1,435	−190	−12%
Animal and Plant Health Inspection Service	39	40	40	0	0%
Economic Research Service	88	85	62	−23	−27%
Forest Service	306	309	255	−54	−17%
National Agricultural Statistics Service	9	9	9	0	0%
National Institute of Food and Agriculture	882	873	968	95	11%
Commerce	1,959	1,948	1,506	−442	−23%
Bureau of the Census	122	155	163	8	5%
National Institute of Standards and Technology	763	807	653	−154	−19%
National Oceanic and Atmospheric Administration	1,066	978	678	−300	−31%
National Telecommunications and Information Administration	8	8	12	4	50%
Defense [4]	54,691	64,544	59,831	−4,713	−7%
Military Construction	22	1,853	0	−1,853	−100%
Military Personnel	441	437	447	10	2%
Defense Health Program	1,716	1,979	308	−1,671	−84%
Research, Development, Test, and Evaluation	52,512	60,275	59,076	−1,199	−2%
Education	248	259	230	−29	−11%
Institute of Education Sciences	230	241	213	−28	−12%

Table 17–1. TOTAL FEDERAL R&D FUNDING BY AGENCY AT THE BUREAU OR ACCOUNT LEVEL—Continued

(Mandatory and Discretionary Budget Authority [1,2], Dollar Amounts In Millions)

	2019 Actual	2020 Estimate [3]	2021 Proposed	Dollar Change: 2020 to 2021	Percent Change: 2020 to 2021
Office of Innovation and Improvement	0	1	0	–1	–100%
Office of Postsecondary Education	1	1	1	0	0%
Office of Special Education and Rehabilitative Services	14	14	14	0	0%
Office of Career, Technical, and Adult Education	3	2	2	0	0%
Energy	18,271	19,219	16,051	–3,168	–16%
Fossil Energy Research and Development	682	709	696	–13	–2%
Science	6,640	6,924	5,760	–1,164	–17%
Electricity	136	155	175	20	13%
Nuclear Energy	1,293	1,161	1,082	–79	–7%
Energy Efficiency and Renewable Energy	1,796	2,054	672	–1,382	–67%
Advanced Research Projects Agency--Energy	366	425	–311	–736	–173%
Cybersecurity, Energy Security, and Emergency Response	49	36	62	26	72%
Defense Environmental Cleanup	25	30	28	–2	–7%
National Nuclear Security Administration	7,280	7,723	7,885	162	2%
Power Marketing Administration	4	2	2	0	0%
Environmental Protection Agency	489	492	318	–174	–35%
Science and Technology	473	473	299	–174	–37%
Hazardous Substance Superfund	15	18	18	0	0%
Inland Oil Spill Programs	1	1	1	0	0%
Health and Human Services	38,511	40,818	37,875	–2,943	–7%
Administration for Children and Families	5	5	4	–1	–20%
Centers for Disease Control and Prevention	466	435	435	0	0%
Centers for Medicare and Medicaid Services	20	20	20	0	0%
Departmental Management	7	18	18	0	0%
Food and Drug Administration	491	410	410	0	0%
Health Resources and Services Administration	23	23	23	0	0%
National Institutes of Health [5]	37,499	39,907	36,965	–2,942	–7%
Homeland Security	668	532	450	–82	–15%
Science and Technology	510	422	357	–65	–15%
Transportation Security Administration	21	23	30	7	30%
United States Coast Guard	4	1	10	9	900%
United States Secret Service	3	11	0	–11	–100%
Management Directorate	3	0	0	0	0%
U.S. Customs and Border Protection	67	0	0	0	0%
Cybersecurity and Infrastructure Security Agency	13	14	6	–8	–57%
Countering Weapons of Mass Destruction Office	47	61	47	–14	–23%
Interior	958	973	725	–248	–25%
Bureau of Land Management	25	21	21	0	0%
Bureau of Reclamation	129	115	76	–39	–34%
Bureau of Safety and Environmental Enforcement	27	27	25	–2	–7%
Department-Wide Programs	3	3	3	0	0%
National Park Service	27	26	26	0	0%
Office of Surface Mining Reclamation and Enforcement	1	1	1	0	0%
United States Fish and Wildlife Service	15	15	15	0	0%
United States Geological Survey	640	660	460	–200	–30%
Bureau of Ocean Energy Management	86	100	93	–7	–7%
Bureau of Indian Affairs	5	5	5	0	0%
National Aeronautics and Space Administration	10,698	14,057	13,334	–723	–5%
Science	6,154	7,019	6,261	–758	–11%
Aeronautics	565	575	630	55	10%
Low Earth Orbit and Spaceflight Operations	1,586	1,551	1,496	–55	–4%
Safety, Security and Mission Services	272	237	245	8	3%
Deep Space Exploration Systems	1,288	3,576	3,139	–437	–12%
Construction and Environmental Compliance and Restoration	117	54	48	–6	–11%

Table 17–1.   TOTAL FEDERAL R&D FUNDING BY AGENCY AT THE BUREAU OR ACCOUNT LEVEL—Continued

(Mandatory and Discretionary Budget Authority [1,2], Dollar Amounts In Millions)

	2019 Actual	2020 Estimate [3]	2021 Proposed	Dollar Change: 2020 to 2021	Percent Change: 2020 to 2021
Exploration Technology	716	1,045	1,515	470	45%
National Science Foundation	6,586	6,752	6,328	–424	–6%
Research and Related Activities	5,823	6,033	5,613	–420	–7%
Education and Human Resources	467	476	485	9	2%
Major Research Equipment and Facilities Construction	296	243	230	–13	–5%
Transportation	1,071	1,134	594	–540	–48%
Federal Aviation Administration	501	533	447	–86	–16%
Federal Highway Administration	375	404	0	–404	–100%
Federal Motor Carrier Safety Administration	9	9	12	3	33%
Federal Railroad Administration	45	44	45	1	2%
Federal Transit Administration	28	36	33	–3	–8%
National Highway Traffic Safety Administration	76	68	19	–49	–72%
Office of the Secretary	13	16	14	–2	–13%
Pipeline and Hazardous Materials Safety Administration	24	24	24	0	0%
Smithsonian Institution	339	330	328	–2	–1%
Veterans Affairs	1,370	1,313	1,351	38	3%
Medical Care Support	591	563	563	0	0%
Medical and Prosthetic Research	779	750	788	38	5%

[1] This table shows funding levels for Departments or Independent agencies with more than $200 million in R&D activities in 2021.

[2] The Experimental Development definition is used in this table across all three fiscal years.

[3] The FY 2020 Estimate column applies the main FY 2021 President's Budget volume approach of using FY 2020 enacted appropriations.

[4] Totals for Experimental Development spending in FY 2019-2021 do not include the DOD Budget Activity 07 (Operational System Development) due to changes in the definition of development. These funds are requested in the FY 2021 Budget request and support the development efforts to upgrade systems that have been fielded or have received approval for full rate production and anticipate production funding in the current or subsequent fiscal year.

[5] NIH includes Agency for Healthcare Research and Quality (AHRQ) funding as the FY 2021 Budget proposes that AHRQ be consolidated within NIH as a new institute.

I. PRIORITIES FOR FEDERAL RESEARCH AND DEVELOPMENT

The President's Budget provides support for Federal R&D to keep America prosperous, resilient, healthy, and safe. This section highlights key R&D priorities in the 2021 Budget, with a focus on strategic investments in AI, QIS, and national security.

American Leadership in the Industries of the Future

America's multisector U.S. R&D enterprise continues to enable the Nation to pursue, realize, and lead in critical and emerging areas of S&T. Private industry working in a robust free market can bring the best ideas forward, leading to new and better products and processes and in some cases creating entirely new industries. These innovations often start with Federal contributions in early-stage R&D, particularly in S&T areas that require sustained support before becoming ready for private sector investment. Beginning in 2017, the Administration identified several S&T areas critical to advancing America's leadership in the IotF and since then has made R&D investments, and enacted several key policies, to realize their full promise to improve the prosperity, health, and security of the American people.

Artificial intelligence (AI) is transforming every segment of American life, with applications ranging from medical diagnostics and precision agriculture, to autonomous transportation, job reskilling and upskilling and

national defense, and beyond. The Administration has taken a forward-looking approach to fortify American leadership in AI, including considerations about its effective and trustworthy use. In 2019, the President signed an Executive Order launching the American AI Initiative, the national AI strategy of the United States, which is taking a multipronged approach to accelerating our national leadership in AI. The Administration also released the National AI R&D Strategic Plan: 2019 Update to define priority areas of Federal investment in AI R&D, and the 2016-2019 Progress Report on Advancing AI R&D to document the depth and breadth of agency investments that are transforming the state of the field, consistent with the strategic research plan. The 2021 Budget includes a major increase in non-defense AI funding compared to the 2020 Budget and is on a path to double Government-wide spending on AI R&D by 2022. The Budget includes over $850 million for AI R&D at the National Science Foundation (NSF), which represents a 70-plus percent increase over the 2020 Budget. This increase will advance NSF's ability to invest in both core and AI-related research, and it will enable NSF to create several National AI Research Institutes, in collaboration with the Departments of Agriculture, Homeland Security, Transportation, and Veterans Affairs. These institutes serve as focal points for multisector, multidisciplinary research and workforce efforts among academia, industry,

Federal agencies, and nonprofits, helping to ensure that America remains the global AI leader.

QIS promises to enable new technologies and opportunities for the Nation over the next two decades. Researchers will be able to tackle previously unsolvable problems and explore new domains of communication, sensing, and computation. QIS will improve our industrial base, creating new jobs and entirely new industries in the process, while helping keep America safe. Recognizing the potential of QIS, in late 2018 the President signed into law the National Quantum Initiative Act. The 2021 Budget greatly bolsters Federal QIS R&D funding with aggregate investment across key agencies increasing by over 50 percent compared to the 2020 Budget on the path to doubling by 2022. NSF investment will more than double with an additional $120 million supporting the National Quantum Initiative. The Department of Energy (DOE) will bolster quantum information efforts at the national laboratories and in academia and industry with an approximate increase of $75 million. Additional efforts at the National Institute for Standards and Technology (NIST) will ensure the standards and science for engineering quantum systems can progress while enabling supporting technology from industrial investments. Expanded QIS defense and intelligence R&D will enable new applications and improve industrial engagement while sustaining their multi-decade effort to encourage quantum information science and technology. Initial funding is included to allow NASA to explore the potential for a space-based quantum entanglement experiment.

The Administration is also prioritizing other S&T areas critical to American leadership in IotF. Advanced manufacturing—which includes both new manufacturing methods and the production of new products enabled by cutting-edge technologies—is an engine of America's economic power and a pillar of its national security. For example, NIST will invest $20 million for a new Manufacturing USA Institute—a public-private partnership that brings together industry, academia, and Government partners to nurture manufacturing innovation and accelerate commercialization. In addition, the 2021 Budget puts an additional $100 million into the Department of Agriculture's flagship competitive grants program (AFRI), which will be invested in artificial intelligence and machine learning to promote advanced manufacturing in the food and agricultural sciences, as well as continue efforts in robotics and application of big data required for future advancements in precision agriculture. In terms of biotechnology, the Budget will support AFRI's continued investments in areas such as gene editing to improve production traits and enhance resistance to disease in crops and livestock. Finally, though not categorized as R&D, investments in STEM education and workforce are critical to creating a diverse, highly skilled, and entrepreneurial workforce that can discover, invent, build, and transform the Industries of the Future. The 2021 Budget will help empower the workforce of the future by investing an additional $50 million at NSF compared to the 2020 Budget Request on education and workforce development for AI and QIS, with focused efforts in outreach to community colleges, Historically Black Colleges and Universities, and Minority Serving Institutions.

American Security

The 2018 National Defense Strategy calls for leadership in research, technology, invention, and innovation to "ensure we will be able to fight and win the wars of the future." As adversaries leverage emerging and disruptive technologies to threaten the Nation, it is imperative that we invest in R&D to remain at the leading edge of S&T, maintain military superiority, remain agile in the face of existing and new threats, and keep the American people safe. The President's 2021 Budget continues to prioritize R&D in technologies that contribute to the security of the American people. The Department of Defense (DOD) will invest more than $59 billion in research, engineering, and prototyping activities in 2021 to enable advanced military capabilities that will help meet emerging threats and protect American security into the future, including offensive and defensive hypersonic weapons capabilities, resilient national security space systems, and modernized and flexible strategic and nonstrategic nuclear deterrent capabilities.

In addition to DOD funding, the 2021 Budget also supports critical investments to protect the Nation. For instance, at the Department of Homeland Security, the 2021 Budget requests $83 million in R&D funding to further detect and defend against radiological, nuclear, chemical, and biological threats; $44 million in R&D to improve resilience to natural disasters and physical threats, for first responder technologies and public safety, and for fundamental R&D to ensure cross-border threat screening and supply chain defense; and $38 million for cybersecurity R&D. To enhance border security, the 2021 Budget will invest $89 million in R&D for air security technologies, to gain efficiencies in immigration service technology, and for ensuring the security of land and maritime borders.

American Space Exploration and Commercialization

In December 2017, the President signed Space Policy Directive 1 which called for the "United States [to] lead the return of humans to the Moon for long-term exploration and utilization". Subsequently in March 2019, the Vice President on behalf of the President declared "it is the stated policy of this [A]dministration and the United States of America to return American astronauts to the Moon within the next five years." Given these policy objectives, the 2021 Budget focuses R&D efforts to accomplish the goal of sustainable deep space exploration, starting with the lunar surface with an eye to Mars.

Within the 2021 Budget, a substantial commitment is made to promote innovation, such as the Lunar Surface Innovation Initiative. Technologies are prioritized that enable a sustainable presence on the lunar surface that also feed forward directly to Mars including in-situ resource utilization, cryogenic fuel storage and management, surface excavation, manufacturing and construction, and advanced space power (e.g. small nuclear fission reactors).

A robust and competitive commercial space sector is vital to continued progress in space and will enable the expansion of America's economic sphere of influence to low Earth orbit, the Moon and then beyond. To that end, space exploration activities will focus on maximizing public-private partnerships. Allowing American industry to innovate will benefit the American taxpayer by increasing the capability of private companies to provide quality space services but at a lower cost.

II. FEDERAL R&D DATA

R&D is the collection of efforts directed toward gaining greater knowledge or understanding and applying knowledge toward the production of useful materials, devices, and methods. R&D investments can be characterized as basic research, applied research, development, R&D equipment, or R&D facilities. The Office of Management and Budget (OMB) has used those or similar categories in its collection of R&D data since 1949. Starting with the 2018 Budget, OMB implemented a refinement to the categories by more narrowly defining "development" as "experimental development" to better align with the data collected by the National Science Foundation on its multiple R&D surveys, and to be consistent with international standards. An explanation of this change is included below. Please note that R&D crosscuts in specific topical areas as mandated by law will be reported separately in forthcoming Supplements to the President's 2021 Budget.

Background on Federal R&D Funding

More than 20 Federal agencies fund R&D in the United States. The character of the R&D that these agencies fund depends on the mission of each agency and on the role of R&D in accomplishing it. Table 17-2 shows agency-by-agency spending on basic research, applied research, experimental development, and R&D equipment and facilities.

Basic research is systematic study directed toward a fuller knowledge or understanding of the fundamental aspects of phenomena and of observable facts without specific applications toward processes or products in mind. Basic research, however, may include activities with broad applications in mind.

Applied research is systematic study to gain knowledge or understanding necessary to determine the means by which a recognized and specific need may be met.

Experimental development is creative and systematic work, drawing on knowledge gained from research and practical experience, which is directed at producing new products or processes or improving existing products or processes. Like research, experimental development will result in gaining additional knowledge.

Research and development equipment includes acquisition or design and production of movable equipment, such as spectrometers, research satellites, detectors, and other instruments. At a minimum, this category includes programs devoted to the purchase or construction of R&D equipment.

Research and development facilities include the acquisition, design, and construction of, or major repairs or alterations to, all physical facilities for use in R&D activities. Facilities include land, buildings, and fixed capital equipment, regardless of whether the facilities are to be used by the Government or by a private organization, and regardless of where title to the property may rest. This category includes such fixed facilities as reactors, wind tunnels, and particle accelerators.

Comprehensive Government-wide efforts are currently underway to increase the accuracy and consistency of the R&D budget via a collaborative community of practice of Federal agencies, which have been working to identify best practices and standards for the most accurate classification and reporting of R&D activities. For example, to better align with National Science Foundation R&D surveys and international standards, starting with the 2018 Budget OMB narrowed the definition of development to "experimental development." This definition, unlike the previous definition of development, excludes user demonstrations of a system for a specific use case and pre-production development (i.e., non-experimental work on a product or system before it goes into full production). Because of this earlier change, the experimental development amounts reported are significantly lower than the development amounts shown in past Budgets.

Table 17–2.   FEDERAL RESEARCH AND DEVELOPMENT SPENDING
(Mandatory and Discretionary Budget Authority [1], Dollar Amounts In Millions)

	2019 Actual	2020 Estimate [2]	2021 Proposed	Dollar Change: 2020 to 2021	Percent Change: 2020 to 2021
By Agency					
Defense [4]	54,691	64,544	59,831	−4,713	−7%
Health and Human Services	38,511	40,818	37,875	−2,943	−7%
Energy	18,271	19,219	16,051	−3,168	−16%
NASA	10,698	14,057	13,334	−723	−5%
National Science Foundation	6,586	6,752	6,328	−424	−6%
Agriculture	3,026	2,941	2,769	−172	−6%
Commerce	1,959	1,948	1,506	−442	−23%
Veterans Affairs	1,370	1,313	1,351	38	3%
Transportation	1,071	1,134	594	−540	−48%
Interior	958	973	725	−248	−25%
Homeland Security	668	532	450	−82	−15%
Smithsonian Institution	339	330	328	−2	−1%
Environmental Protection Agency	489	492	318	−174	−35%
Education	248	259	230	−29	−11%
Other	1,249	661	495	−166	−25%
TOTAL [3]	**140,134**	**155,973**	**142,185**	**−13,788**	**−9%**
Basic Research					
Defense	2,492	2,628	2,331	−297	−11%
Health and Human Services	19,082	20,492	19,154	−1,338	−7%
Energy	5,103	5,514	5,461	−53	−1%
NASA	4,948	6,880	6,110	−770	−11%
National Science Foundation	5,139	5,322	5,018	−304	−6%
Agriculture	1,213	1,264	1,256	−8	−1%
Commerce	232	242	208	−34	−14%
Veterans Affairs	600	559	576	17	3%
Transportation	0	16	18	2	13%
Interior	80	82	65	−17	−21%
Homeland Security	42	47	27	−20	−43%
Smithsonian Institution	269	276	281	5	2%
Environmental Protection Agency	....	....	....	....	....
Education	60	70	70	0	0%
Other	56	68	63	−5	−7%
SUBTOTAL	**39,316**	**43,460**	**40,638**	**−2,822**	**−6%**
Applied Research					
Defense	6,071	6,288	5,506	−782	−12%
Health and Human Services	19,110	20,026	18,336	−1,690	−8%
Energy	8,318	8,351	6,526	−1,825	−22%
NASA	2,743	3,002	3,409	407	14%
National Science Foundation	784	807	787	−20	−2%
Agriculture	1,126	1,154	1,150	−4	−0%
Commerce	976	1,046	809	−237	−23%
Veterans Affairs	738	725	745	20	3%
Transportation	705	736	314	−422	−57%
Interior	710	717	533	−184	−26%
Homeland Security	203	165	71	−94	−57%
Smithsonian Institution	....	....	....	....	....
Environmental Protection Agency	415	416	250	−166	−40%
Education	118	126	117	−9	−7%
Other	947	371	252	−119	−32%
SUBTOTAL	**42,964**	**43,930**	**38,805**	**−5,125**	**−12%**
Experimental Development3					
Defense [4]	46,106	53,775	51,994	−1,781	−3%

Table 17–2. FEDERAL RESEARCH AND DEVELOPMENT SPENDING—Continued

(Mandatory and Discretionary Budget Authority [1], Dollar Amounts In Millions)

	2019 Actual	2020 Estimate [2]	2021 Proposed	Dollar Change: 2020 to 2021	Percent Change: 2020 to 2021
Health and Human Services	76	35	35	0	0%
Energy	2,606	2,982	1,935	−1,047	−35%
NASA	2,890	4,121	3,767	−354	−9%
National Science Foundation	....	....	....	....	....
Agriculture	165	176	172	−4	−2%
Commerce	267	263	200	−63	−24%
Veterans Affairs	32	29	30	1	3%
Transportation	326	344	234	−110	−32%
Interior	162	172	125	−47	−27%
Homeland Security	356	320	329	9	3%
Smithsonian Institution	....	....	....	....	....
Environmental Protection Agency	74	76	68	−8	−11%
Education	70	63	43	−20	−32%
Other	239	222	180	−42	−19%
SUBTOTAL	**53,369**	**62,578**	**59,112**	**−3,466**	**−6%**
Facilities and Equipment					
Defense	22	1,853	0	−1,853	−100%
Health and Human Services	243	265	350	85	32%
Energy	2,244	2,372	2,129	−243	−10%
NASA	117	54	48	−6	−11%
National Science Foundation	663	623	523	−100	−16%
Agriculture	522	347	191	−156	−45%
Commerce	484	397	289	−108	−27%
Veterans Affairs	....	....	....	....	....
Transportation	40	38	28	−10	−26%
Interior	6	2	2	0	0%
Homeland Security	67	0	23	23	....
Smithsonian Institution	70	54	47	−7	−13%
Environmental Protection Agency	....	....	....	....	....
Education	....	....	....	....	....
Other	7	0	0	0	0%
SUBTOTAL	**4,485**	**6,005**	**3,630**	**−2,375**	**−40%**

[1] This table shows funding levels for Departments or Independent agencies with more than $200 million in R&D activities in 2021.

[2] The FY 2020 Estimate column applies the main FY 2021 President's Budget volume approach of using FY 2020 enacted appropriations.

[3] The total uses the Experimental Development definition across the three fiscal years.

[4] The totals for Experimental Development spending in FY 2019-2021 do not include the DOD Budget Activity 07 (Operational System Development) due to changes in the definition of development. These funds are requested in the FY 2021 Budget request and support the development efforts to upgrade systems that have been fielded or have received approval for full rate production and anticipate production funding in the current or subsequent fiscal year.

III. OTHER SOURCES OF FEDERAL SUPPORT FOR R&D

The President's 2021 Budget seeks to build on strong private sector R&D investment by prioritizing Federal investments in areas that industry is not likely to support in comparison to later-stage applied research and development that the private sector is better equipped to pursue. This complementary relationship is enhanced by public-private partnerships. Partnerships between Federal departments and agencies and industry and multisector partnerships facilitated by Federal funding can serve as force multipliers, enabling partnering organizations to achieve higher returns on investment, create efficiencies, and advance their respective missions. In addition, a key means of stimulating private sector investment and bridging Federal Government research with industry development is through the transfer of technology. Federal technology transfer seeks to help domestic companies develop and commercialize products derived from Government-funded R&D, which can lead to greater productivity from U.S. R&D investments and ultimately promote the Nation's economic growth. Recognizing the benefits of this mechanism, the 2021 Budget sustains funding for technology transfer efforts where appropriate. In addition, the Administration is working to enable and enhance the Federal Government's transition of discoveries from laboratory to market through a Cross-Agency Priority Goal under the President's Management Agenda.

Because much of the federally funded R&D is conducted outside of the Government, the Administration seeks to reduce the associated workload on funding recipients and partners in order to promote greater effectiveness and efficiency in our Federal spending. A significant effort to reduce the administrative and regulatory workload associated with Federal R&D funding is currently underway through an interagency working group on research regulation (as required by the Research and Development Efficiency Act). More broadly, beyond just R&D, the Administration is working under a President's Management Agenda Cross-Agency Priority Goal to reduce administrative burdens for all Federal grant recipients and promoting results-oriented accountability.

The Federal Government also stimulates private investment in R&D through tax preferences. Historically, dating back to the 1950s, the private sector has performed the majority of U.S. R&D. As of 2018, it is estimated that businesses performed 73 percent of total U.S. R&D.[1] Businesses have also been a predominant source of U.S. R&D funding since the 1980s with an estimated $404.2 billion invested by this sector in 2018, which accounts for about 70 percent of total U.S. funding.[2] The research and experimentation (R&E) tax credit, which was made permanent through the Protecting Americans from Tax Hikes Act of 2015 (P.L. 114-113) and modified in the Tax Cut and Jobs Act of 2017 (P.L. 115-97), essentially provides a credit to qualified research expenses. R&E tax credit claims have at least doubled over the past two decades, growing from an estimated $4.4 billion in 1997 to $12.6 billion in 2014.[3] The manufacturing and the professional, scientific, and technical services sectors account for about 70 percent of total claims in 2014.

---

[1] NSF National Center for Science and Engineering Statistics (Jan 2020). National Patterns of R&D Resources: 2017-2018 Data Update. NSF 20-307.

[2] NSF National Center for Science and Engineering Statistics (Jan 2020). National Patterns of R&D Resources: 2017-2018 Data Update. NSF 20-307.

[3] IRS Statistics of Income Division (Nov 2019). SOI Tax Statistics – Corporate Research Credit.

18.   CREDIT AND INSURANCE

The Federal Government offers direct loans and loan guarantees to support a wide range of activities including home ownership, student loans, small business, farming, energy, infrastructure investment, and exports. In addition, Government-sponsored enterprises (GSEs) operate under Federal charters for the purpose of enhancing credit availability for targeted sectors. Through its insurance programs, the Federal Government insures deposits at depository institutions, guarantees private-sector defined-benefit pensions, and insures against some other risks such as flood and terrorism.

This chapter discusses the roles of these diverse programs. The first section discusses individual credit programs and GSEs. The second section reviews Federal deposit insurance, pension guarantees, disaster insurance, and insurance against terrorism and other security-related risks. This year's chapter includes a brief analysis of the Troubled Asset Relief Program (TARP), which was previously contained in a separate chapter. The last section discusses "fair value" cost estimates for Federal credit programs.

I. CREDIT IN VARIOUS SECTORS

Housing Credit Programs

Through housing credit programs, the Federal Government promotes homeownership among various target groups, including low- and moderate-income people, veterans, and rural residents. In times of economic crisis, the Federal Government's role and target market can expand dramatically.

Federal Housing Administration

The Federal Housing Administration (FHA) guarantees mortgage loans to provide access to homeownership for people who may have difficulty obtaining a conventional mortgage. FHA has been a primary facilitator of mortgage credit for first-time and minority homebuyers, a pioneer of products such as the 30-year self-amortizing mortgage, and a vehicle to enhance credit for many low- to moderate-income households. One of the major benefits of an FHA-insured mortgage is that it provides a homeownership option for borrowers who can make only a modest down-payment, but show that they are creditworthy and have sufficient income to afford the house they want to buy. In 2019, 83 percent of FHA purchase mortgages were obtained by first-time homebuyers. Of all FHA loans (purchase and refinance), 33 percent served minority borrowers and 58 percent served low- to moderate-income borrowers.

In addition to traditional single-family "forward" mortgages, FHA insures "reverse" mortgages for seniors and loans for the construction, rehabilitation, and refinancing of multifamily housing, hospitals and other healthcare facilities.

FHA and the Single-Family Mortgage Market

FHA's share of the mortgage market tends to fluctuate with economic conditions and other factors. In the early 2000s, FHA's market presence diminished greatly as low interest rates increased the affordability of mortgage financing and more borrowers used emerging non-prime mortgage products, including subprime and Alt-A mortgages. Many of these products had risky and hard-to-understand features such as low "teaser rates" offered for periods as short as the first two years of the mortgage, high loan-to-value ratios (with some mortgages exceeding the value of the house), and interest-only loans with balloon payments that require full payoff at a set future date. The Alt-A mortgage made credit easily available by waiving documentation of income or assets. This competition eroded the market share by dollar volume of FHA's single-family purchase and refinance loans, reducing it from 9 percent in 2000 to less than 2 percent in 2005. [1]

During the financial crisis, starting at the end of 2007, the availability of credit guarantees from the FHA and Government National Mortgage Association (which supports the secondary market for federally-insured housing loans by guaranteeing securities backed by mortgages guaranteed by FHA, VA, and USDA) was an important factor countering the tightening of private-sector credit. FHA's share of the mortgage market increased to a peak of 18 percent in 2009. Since then, FHA market share has declined (12 percent in 2018) but remains higher than it was in the early 2000s.

FHA Home Equity Conversion Mortgages

Home Equity Conversion Mortgages (HECMs) are designed to support aging in place by enabling elderly homeowners to borrow against the equity in their homes without having to make repayments during their lifetime (unless they move, refinance or fail to meet certain requirements). A HECM is also known as a "reverse" mortgage because the change in home equity over time is generally the opposite of a forward mortgage. While a traditional forward mortgage starts with a small amount of equity and builds equity with amortization of the loan,

---

[1]   FHA market share is reported by calendar year throughout this section.

a HECM starts with a large equity cushion that declines over time as the loan accrues interest and premiums. The risk of HECMs is therefore weighted toward the end of the mortgage, while forward mortgage risk is concentrated in the first 10 years.

FHA Mutual Mortgage Insurance (MMI) Fund

FHA guarantees for forward and reverse mortgages are administered under the Mutual Mortgage Insurance (MMI) Fund. At the end of 2019, the MMI Fund had $1,288 billion in total mortgages outstanding and a capital ratio of 4.84 percent, remaining above the 2 percent statutory minimum for the fifth straight year and increasing from the 2018 level of 2.76 percent. Although its financial condition has improved, the HECM portfolio continues to have a negative impact on the MMI Fund, offsetting the positive capital position of the forward mortgage portfolio. While the 2019 capital ratio for forward mortgages was 5.44 percent, the HECM portfolio had a capital ratio of –9.22 percent. For more information on the financial status of the MMI Fund, please see the Annual Report to Congress Regarding the Financial Status of the FHA Mutual Mortgage Insurance Fund, Fiscal Year 2019.[2]

Since 2018, FHA has implemented several policies to reduce risk to the MMI Fund and protect taxpayers, including lowering the maximum loan-to-value (LTV) ratio for cash-out refinances, increasing the share of higher-risk loans referred to manual underwriting, lowering the share of home equity a homeowner can borrow against in the HECM program and requiring a second appraisal for certain HECM transactions.

FHA's new origination volume in 2019 was $215 billion for forward mortgages and $11 billion for HECMs, and the Budget projects $200 billion and $11 billion, respectively, for 2021.

FHA Multifamily and Healthcare Guarantees

In addition to the single-family mortgage insurance provided through the MMI Fund, FHA's General Insurance and Special Risk Insurance (GISRI) loan programs continue to facilitate the construction, rehabilitation, and refinancing of multifamily housing, hospitals and other healthcare facilities. The credit enhancement provided by FHA enables borrowers to obtain long-term, fixed-rate financing, which mitigates interest rate risk and facilitates lower monthly mortgage payments. This can improve the financial sustainability of multifamily housing and healthcare facilities and may also translate into more affordable rents/lower healthcare costs for consumers.

GISRI's new origination loan volume for all programs in 2019 was $18 billion and the Budget projects $20 billion for 2021. The total amount of guarantees outstanding on mortgages in the FHA GISRI Fund were $162 billion at the end of 2019.

VA Housing Loan Program

The Department of Veterans Affairs (VA) assists veterans, members of the Selected Reserve, and active duty personnel in purchasing homes in recognition of their service to the Nation. The VA housing loan program effectively substitutes the Federal guarantee for the borrower's down payment, making the lending terms more favorable than loans without a VA loan guarantee. VA does not guarantee the entire mortgage loan to veterans but provides a 100 percent guarantee on the first 25 percent of losses upon default. In 2019, mortgage interest rates remained low and the strong economy provided opportunities for returning veterans to purchase homes. VA guaranteed a total of 624,546 new purchase home loans in 2019, providing approximately $43.5 billion in guarantees. Additionally, 94,861 veteran borrowers lowered interest rates on their home mortgages through refinancing. VA provided approximately $40 billion in guarantees to assist 610,513 borrowers in 2018. That followed $47 billion and 740,389 borrowers in 2017.

VA, in cooperation with VA-guaranteed loan servicers, also assists borrowers through home retention options and alternatives to foreclosure. VA intervenes when needed to help veterans and service members avoid foreclosure through loan modifications, special forbearances, repayment plans, and acquired loans, as well as assistance to complete compromised sales or deeds-in-lieu of foreclosure. These joint efforts helped resolve over 87 percent of defaulted VA-guaranteed loans and assisted over 101,000 veterans retain homeownership or avoid foreclosure in 2019. These efforts resulted in $2.63 billion in avoided guaranteed claim payments.

Rural Housing Service

The Rural Housing Service (RHS) at the U.S. Department of Agriculture (USDA) offers direct and guaranteed loans to help very-low- to moderate-income rural residents buy and maintain adequate, affordable housing. RHS housing loans and loan guarantees differ from other Federal housing loan programs in that they are means-tested, making them more accessible to low-income, rural residents. The single family housing guaranteed loan program is designed to provide home loan guarantees for moderate-income rural residents whose incomes are between 80 percent and 115 percent (maximum for the program) of area median income.

Historically, RHS has offered both direct and guaranteed homeownership loans. In recent years, the portfolio has shifted to more efficient loan guarantees, an indication the direct loan program has achieved its goal of graduating borrowers to commercial credit and lowering costs to the taxpayer. The single family housing guaranteed loan program was authorized in 1990 at $100 million and has grown into a $24 billion loan program annually. The shift to guaranteed lending is in part attributable to the mortgage banking industry offering historically low mortgage rates, resulting in instances where the average 30-year fixed commercial mortgage rate has been at or below the average borrower rate for the RHS single family direct loan. Furthermore, financial markets have become more efficient and have increased the reach of mortgage credit to lower credit qualities and incomes. The number of rural areas isolated from broad credit availability has

---

[2] https://www.hud.gov/sites/dfiles/Housing/documents/2019FHAAnnualReportMMIFund.pdf

shrunk as access to high speed broadband has increased and correspondent lending has grown.

Education Credit Programs

The Department of Education (ED) direct student loan program is one of the largest Federal credit programs with $1.165 trillion in Direct Loan principal outstanding at the end of 2019. The Federal student loan programs provide students and their families with the funds to help meet postsecondary education costs. Because funding for the loan programs is provided through mandatory budget authority, student loans are considered separately for budget purposes from other Federal student financial assistance programs (which are largely discretionary), but should be viewed as part of the overall Federal effort to expand access to higher education.

Loans for higher education were first authorized under the William D. Ford program—which was included in the Higher Education Act of 1965. The direct loan program was authorized by the Student Loan Reform Act of 1993 (Public Law 103–66). The enactment of the Student Aid and Fiscal Responsibility Act (SAFRA) of 2010 (Public Law 111–152) ended the guaranteed loan program (FFEL). On July 1, 2010, ED became the sole originator of Federal student loans through the Direct Loan program.

Under the current direct loan program, the Federal Government partners with over 6,000 institutions of higher education, which then disburse loan funds to students. Loans are available to students and parents of students regardless of income and only the Parent PLUS program includes a minimal credit check. There are three types of Direct Loans: Federal Direct Subsidized Stafford Loans, Federal Direct Unsubsidized Stafford Loans, and Federal Direct PLUS Loans, each with different terms. The Federal Government does not charge interest while the borrowers are in school and during certain deferment periods for Direct Subsidized Stafford loans—which are available only to undergraduate borrowers from low and moderate income families.

The Direct Loan program offers a variety of repayment options including income-driven repayment ones for all student borrowers. Depending on the plan, monthly payments are capped at no more than 10 or 15 percent of borrower discretionary income with any remaining balance after 20 or 25 years forgiven. In addition, under current law, borrowers working in public service professions while making 10 years of qualifying payments are eligible for Public Service Loan Forgiveness (PSLF).

The 2021 President's Budget includes several policy proposals for this program. For a detailed description of these proposals, please see the Federal Direct Student Loan Program Account section of the Budget *Appendix*.

Small Business and Farm Credit Programs

The Government offers direct loans and loan guarantees to small businesses and farmers, who may have difficulty obtaining credit elsewhere. It also provides guarantees of debt issued by certain investment funds that invest in small businesses. Two GSEs, the Farm Credit System and the Federal Agricultural Mortgage Corporation, increase liquidity in the agricultural lending market.

Small Business Administration

The Congress created the U.S. Small Business Administration (SBA) in 1953 as an independent agency of the Federal Government to aid, counsel, assist and protect the interests of small business concerns; preserve free competitive enterprise; and maintain and strengthen the overall economy of the Nation. The SBA began making direct business loans and guaranteeing bank loans to small business owners, and providing inexpensive and immediate disaster relief to those hard-hit by natural disasters. By 1958, The Investment Company Act had established the Small Business Investment Company (SBIC) Program, under which the SBA continues to license, regulate, and guarantee funds for privately-owned and operated venture capital investment firms. The SBA continues to complement credit markets by guaranteeing credit-worthy small business borrowers access to affordable credit provided through private lenders when they cannot obtain financing on reasonable terms or conditions elsewhere.

The SBA has grown significantly since its creation, both in terms of its total assistance provided and its array of programs offered to micro-entrepreneurs and small business owners. From its Washington, D.C. headquarters, it leverages its field personnel and diverse network of private sector and nonprofit partners across each U.S. State and territory. The SBA ensures that small businesses across America have the tools and resources needed to start and develop their operations, drive U.S. competitiveness, help grow the economy, and promote economic security.

In 2019, the SBA provided $21.5 billion in loan guarantees to assist small business owners with access to affordable capital through its largest program, the 7(a) General Business Loan Guarantee program. This program provides access to financing for general business operations, such as operating and capital expenses. Through the 504 Certified Development Company (CDC) and Refinance Programs, the SBA also supported about $5.0 billion in guaranteed loans for fixed-asset financing and the opportunity for small businesses to refinance existing 504 CDC loans. These programs enable small businesses to secure financing for assets such as machinery and equipment, construction, and commercial real estate, and to take advantage of current low interest rates and free up resources for expansion.

The SBA also creates opportunities for very small and emerging businesses to grow. Through the 7(m) Direct Microloan program, which supports non-profit intermediaries that provide loans of up to $50,000 to rising entrepreneurs, the SBA provided $42 million in direct lending to the smallest of small businesses and startups. By supporting innovative financial instruments such as the SBA's SBIC program that partners with private investors to finance small businesses through professionally managed investment funds, the SBA supported $1.6 billion in venture capital investments in small businesses in 2019.

SBA continues to be a valuable source for American communities who need access to low-interest loans to recovery quickly in the wake of disaster. In 2019, the SBA delivered $1.4 billion in disaster relief lending to businesses, homeowners, renters, and property owners.

For a detailed description of the 2021 President's Budget policy proposals for these programs, please see the SBA Business Loans Program Account and Disaster Loans Program Account sections of the Budget *Appendix*.

Community Development Financial Institutions

Since its creation in 1994, the Department of the Treasury's Community Development Financial Institutions (CDFI) Fund has—through different grant, loan, and tax credit programs—worked to expand the availability of credit, investment capital, and financial services for underserved people and communities by supporting the growth and capacity of a national network of CDFIs, investors, and financial service providers. Today, there are over 1,000 Certified CDFIs nationwide, including a variety of loan funds, community development banks, credit unions, and venture capital funds. CDFI certification also enables some non-depository financial institutions to apply for financing programs offered by certain Federal Home Loan Banks.

Unlike other CDFI Fund programs, the CDFI Bond Guarantee Program (BGP)—enacted through the Small Business Jobs Act of 2010—does not offer grants, but is instead a Federal credit program. The BGP was designed to provide CDFIs greater access to low-cost, long-term, fixed-rate capital.

Under the BGP, Treasury provides a 100-percent guarantee on long-term bonds of at least $100 million issued to qualified CDFIs, with a maximum maturity of 30 years. To date, Treasury has issued $1.6 billion in bond guarantee commitments to 25 CDFIs, $1.1 billion of which has been disbursed to help finance affordable housing, charter schools, commercial real estate, community healthcare facilities and other eligible uses in 27 States and the District of Columbia. The Budget continues to propose reforms such as eliminating the requirement for a relending account, which adds unnecessary cost and complexity to the program

Farm Service Agency

Farm operating loans were first offered in 1937 by the newly created Farm Security Administration to assist family farmers who were unable to obtain credit from a commercial source to buy equipment, livestock, or seed. Farm ownership loans were authorized in 1961 to provide family farmers with financial assistance to purchase farmland. Presently, the Farm Service Agency (FSA) assists low-income family farmers in starting and maintaining viable farming operations. Emphasis is placed on aiding beginning and socially disadvantaged farmers.

Legislation mandates that a portion of appropriated funds are set-aside for exclusive use by underserved groups.

FSA offers operating loans and ownership loans, both of which may be either direct or guaranteed loans. Operating loans provide credit to farmers and ranchers for annual production expenses and purchases of livestock, machinery, and equipment, while farm ownership loans assist producers in acquiring and developing their farming or ranching operations. As a condition of eligibility for direct loans, borrowers must be unable to obtain private credit at reasonable rates and terms. As FSA is the "lender of last resort," default rates on FSA direct loans are generally higher than those on private-sector loans. FSA-guaranteed farm loans are made to more creditworthy borrowers who have access to private credit markets. Because the private loan originators must retain 10 percent of the risk, they exercise care in examining the repayment ability of borrowers. The subsidy rates for the direct programs fluctuate largely because of changes in the interest component of the subsidy rate. Since the early 1990's, the majority of FSA loan assistance has been guaranteed rather than direct lending.

In 2019, FSA provided loans and loan guarantees to more than 32,000 family farmers totaling $5.7 billion. In recent years, FSA assistance has been at record levels from a downturn in the agricultural economy. The average size of farm ownership loans remained consistent over the past few years, with new customers receiving the bulk of the direct loans. Direct and guaranteed loan programs provided assistance totaling $2.7 billion to more than 18,300 beginning farmers although the number of beginning farmer loans decreased slightly by seven percent. The majority of assistance provided in the operating loan program during 2019 was to beginning farmers. Sixty-two percent of direct operating loans were made to beginning farmers. A beginning farmer is an individual or entity who: has operated a farm for not more than 10 years; substantially participates in the operation; and for farm ownership loans, the applicant cannot own a farm greater than 30 percent of the average size farm in the county, at time of application. If the applicant is an entity, all members must be related by blood or marriage, and all entity members must be eligible beginning farmers.

Loans for socially disadvantaged farmers totaled $789 million, of which $506 million was in the farm ownership program and $283 million in the farm operating program. Lending to minority and women farmers was a significant portion of overall assistance provided, with $789 million in loans and loan guarantees provided to more than 6,550 farmers. Loan assistance provided to beginning and socially disadvantaged farmers increased in 2019 compared to 2018, fulfilling an initiative of the Department to expand lending to underserved groups as a percentage of total loans made.

The FSA Microloan program increases overall direct and guaranteed lending to small niche producers and minorities. This program dramatically simplifies application procedures for small loans and implement more flexible eligibility and experience requirements. Demand for the micro-loan program continues to grow while delinquencies and defaults remain at or below those of the regular FSA operating loan program.

Energy and Infrastructure Credit Programs

The Department of Energy (DOE) administers three credit programs: Title XVII (a loan guarantee program to support innovative energy technologies), the Advanced Technology Vehicle Manufacturing loan program (a direct loan program to support advanced automotive technologies), and the Tribal Energy Loan Guarantee Program (a loan guarantee program to support tribal energy development). Title XVII of the Energy Policy Act of 2005 (Public Law 109–58) authorizes DOE to issue loan guarantees for projects that employ innovative technologies to reduce air pollutants or man-made greenhouse gases. The Congress provided DOE $4 billion in loan volume authority in 2007, and the 2009 Consolidated Appropriations Act provided an additional $47 billion in loan volume authority, allocated as follows: $18.5 billion for nuclear power facilities, $2 billion for "front-end" nuclear enrichment activities, $8 billion for advanced fossil energy technologies, and $18.5 billion for energy efficiency, renewable energy, and transmission and distribution projects. The 2011 appropriations reduced the available loan volume authority for energy efficiency, renewable energy, and transmission and distribution projects by $17 billion and provided $170 million in credit subsidy to support renewable energy or energy efficient end-use energy technologies, $9 million of which was subsequently repurposed for the Tribal Energy Loan Guarantee Program in 2017 appropriations. From 2014 to 2015, DOE issued three loan guarantees totaling over $8 billion to support the construction of two new commercial nuclear power reactors. In 2019, DOE issued an additional $3.7 billion to support completion of the nuclear power project.

The American Reinvestment and Recovery Act of 2009 (Public Law 111–5) amended the program's authorizing statute and provided $2.5 billion in credit subsidy to support loan guarantees on a temporary basis for commercial or advanced renewable energy systems, electric power transmission systems, and leading edge biofuel projects. Authority for the temporary program to extend new loans expired September 30, 2011. Prior to expiration, DOE issued loan guarantees to 28 projects totaling over $16 billion in loan volume. Four projects withdrew prior to any disbursement of funds.

Section 136 of the Energy Independence and Security Act of 2007 (Public Law 110–140) authorizes DOE to issue loans to support the development of advanced technology vehicles and qualifying components. In 2009, the Congress appropriated $7.5 billion in credit subsidy to support a maximum of $25 billion in loans under ATVM. From 2009 to 2011, DOE issued five loans totaling over $8 billion to support the manufacturing of advanced technology vehicles. DOE has not issued any ATVM loans since 2011.

Title XXVI of the Energy Policy Act of 1992, as amended (Public Law 102-486, Public Law 109-58) authorizes DOE to guarantee up to $2 billion in loans to Indian tribes for energy development. In 2017, the Congress appropriated $8.5 million in credit subsidy to support tribal energy development. DOE issued a solicitation in 2018, but has not yet issued any loan guarantees under this authority.

Electric and Telecommunications Loans

Rural Utilities Service (RUS) programs of the USDA provide grants and loans to support the distribution of rural electrification, telecommunications, distance learning, and broadband infrastructure systems.

In 2019, RUS delivered $5.77 billion in direct electrification loans (including $4.99 billion in FFB Electric Loans, $750 million in electric underwriting, and $34.2 million rural energy savings loans), $181.5 million in direct telecommunications loans, and $47.8 million in direct broadband loans.

USDA Rural Infrastructure and Business Development Programs

USDA, through a variety of Rural Development (RD) programs, provides grants, direct loans, and loan guarantees to communities for constructing facilities such as healthcare clinics, police stations, and water systems, as well as to assist rural businesses and cooperatives in creating new community infrastructure (e.g., educational and healthcare networks) and to diversify the rural economy and employment opportunities. In 2019, RD provided $853 million in Community Facility (CF) direct loans, which are for communities of 20,000 or less. The CF programs have the flexibility to finance more than 100 separate types of essential community infrastructure that ultimately improve access to healthcare, education, public safety and other critical facilities and services. RD also provided $1.8 billion in water and wastewater (W&W) direct loans, and guaranteed $1.2 billion in rural business loans, which will help create and save jobs in rural America. The 2018 Farm Bill gave CF and W&W loan guarantees new authorization to serve communities of 50,000 or less and allowed the programs to charge a fee to offset the loan subsidy cost. RD began executing the programs with the new authorities in 2020.

Water Infrastructure

The Environmental Protection Agency's (EPA) Water Infrastructure Finance and Innovation Act (WIFIA) program accelerates investment in the Nation's water infrastructure by providing long-term, low-cost supplemental loans for projects of regional or national significance. During 2019, EPA solicited the second round of loans, selecting thirty-nine entities with projects in sixteen States to apply for up to $5 billion in WIFIA loans. Those projects will leverage more than $5 billion in private capital, in addition to other funding sources, to help finance a total of over $10 billion in water infrastructure investments. The selected projects demonstrate the broad range of project types that the WIFIA program can finance, including wastewater, drinking water, stormwater, and water recycling projects.

Transportation Infrastructure

The Department of Transportation (DOT) administers credit programs that fund critical transportation infrastructure projects, often using innovative financing methods. The two predominant programs are the Transportation Infrastructure Finance and Innovation Act (TIFIA) and the Railroad Rehabilitation and Improvement Financing (RRIF) loan programs. DOT's Build America Bureau administers these programs, as well as Private Activity Bonds (PABs) and the Nationally Significant Freight and Highway Projects (INFRA) grant program, all under one roof. The Bureau serves as the single point of contact for States, municipalities, and other project sponsors looking to utilize Federal transportation expertise, apply for Federal transportation credit and grant programs, and explore ways to access private capital in public-private partnerships. For the first time, the 2021 Budget will reflect the TIFIA and RRIF programs' accounts in the Office of the Secretary, where the Bureau is housed, rather than in the Federal Highway Administration and Federal Railroad Administration.

Established by the Transportation Equity Act of the 21st century (TEA–21) (Public Law 105–178) in 1998, the TIFIA program is designed to fill market gaps and leverage substantial private co-investment by providing supplemental and subordinate capital to projects of national or regional significance. Through TIFIA, DOT provides three types of Federal credit assistance to highway, transit, rail, and intermodal projects: direct loans, loan guarantees, and lines of credit.

TIFIA can help advance qualified, large-scale projects that otherwise might be delayed or deferred because of size, complexity, or uncertainty over the timing of revenues at a relatively low budgetary cost. Each dollar of subsidy provided for TIFIA can provide approximately $14 in credit assistance, and leverage additional non-Federal transportation infrastructure investment. The Fixing America's Surface Transportation (FAST) Act of 2015 (Public Law 114–94) authorizes $300 million for TIFIA in 2020.

DOT has also provided direct loans and loan guarantees to railroads since 1976 for facilities maintenance, rehabilitation, acquisitions, and refinancing. Federal assistance was created to provide financial assistance to the financially-challenged portions of the rail industry. However, following railroad deregulation in 1980, the industry's financial condition began to improve, larger railroads were able to access private credit markets, and interest in Federal credit support began to decrease.

Also established by TEA–21 in 1998, the RRIF program provides loans or loan guarantees with an interest rate equal to the Treasury rate for similar-term securities. TEA–21 also stipulates that non-Federal sources pay the subsidy cost of the loan (a "Credit Risk Premium"), thereby allowing the program to operate without Federal subsidy appropriations. The RRIF program assists projects that improve rail safety, enhance the environment, promote economic development, or enhance the capacity of the national rail network. While refinancing existing debt is an eligible use of RRIF proceeds, capital investment projects that would not occur without a RRIF loan are prioritized. Since its inception, over $6.3 billion in direct loans have been made under the RRIF program.

The FAST Act included programmatic changes to enhance the RRIF program to mirror the qualities of TIFIA, including broader eligibility, a loan term that can be as long as 35 years from project completion, and a fully subordinated loan under certain conditions. Additionally, in 2016 the Congress appropriated $1.96 million to assist Class II and Class III Railroads in preparing and applying for direct loans and loan guarantees.

In the Consolidated Appropriations Act, 2018 (Public Law 115-141), for the first time in RRIF's history, the Congress appropriated $25 million in subsidy budget authority for direct loans and loan guarantees to the RRIF program. This appropriation allows DOT to issue RRIF loans without requiring credit risk premiums from borrowers to cover the subsidy costs of the loans.

International Credit Programs

Through 2020, seven Federal agencies—USDA, the Department of Defense, the Department of State, the Department of the Treasury, the Agency for International Development (USAID), the Export-Import Bank (ExIm), and the International Development Finance Corporation (DFC)—provide direct loans, loan guarantees, and insurance to a variety of private and sovereign borrowers. These programs are intended to level the playing field for U.S. exporters, deliver robust support for U.S. goods and services, stabilize international financial markets, enhance security, and promote sustainable development. The Better Utilization of Investments Leading to Development (BUILD) Act of 2018 (Public Law 115-254), discussed further below, made significant changes to modernize and consolidate several of these functions to promote efficiency and transparency.

Federal export credit programs counter official financing that foreign governments around the world, largely in Europe and Japan, but also increasingly in emerging markets such as China and Brazil, provide their exporters, usually through export credit agencies (ECAs). The U.S. Government has worked since the 1970's to constrain official credit support through a multilateral agreement in the Organization for Economic Cooperation and Development (OECD). This agreement has established standards for Government-backed financing of exports. In addition to ongoing work in keeping these OECD standards up-to-date, the U.S. Government established the International Working Group (IWG) on Export Credits to set up a new framework that will include China and other non-OECD countries, which until now have not been subject to export credit standards. The process of establishing these new standards, which is not yet complete, advances a congressional mandate to reduce subsidized export financing programs.

Export Support Programs

When the private sector is unable or unwilling to provide financing, the Export-Import Bank, the U.S. ECA, fills the gap for American businesses by equipping them with the financing support necessary to level the playing field against foreign competitors. ExIm support includes direct loans and loan guarantees for creditworthy foreign buyers to help secure export sales from U.S. exporters, as well as working capital guarantees and export credit insurance to help U.S. exporters secure financing for overseas sales. USDA's Export Credit Guarantee Programs (also known as GSM programs) similarly help to level the playing field. Like programs of other agricultural exporting nations, GSM programs guarantee payment from countries and entities that want to import U.S. agricultural products but cannot easily obtain credit. The GSM 102 program provides guarantees for credit extended with short-term repayment terms not to exceed 18 months.

Exchange Stabilization Fund

Consistent with U.S. obligations in the International Monetary Fund regarding global financial stability, the Exchange Stabilization Fund managed by the Department of the Treasury may provide loans or credits to a foreign entity or government of a foreign country. A loan or credit may not be made for more than six months in any 12-month period unless the President gives the Congress a written statement that unique or emergency circumstances require that the loan or credit be for more than six months.

Sovereign Lending and Guarantees

The U.S. Government can extend short-to-medium-term loan guarantees that cover potential losses that might be incurred by lenders if a country defaults on its borrowings; for example, the U.S. may guarantee another country's sovereign bond issuance. The purpose of this tool is to provide the Nation's sovereign international partners access to necessary, urgent, and relatively affordable financing during temporary periods of strain when they cannot access such financing in international financial markets, and to support critical reforms that will enhance long term fiscal sustainability, often in concert with support from international financial institutions such as the International Monetary Fund. The long term goal of sovereign loan guarantees is to help lay the economic groundwork for the Nation's international partners to graduate to an unenhanced bond issuance in the international capital markets. For example, as part of the U.S. response to fiscal crises, the U.S. Government has extended sovereign loan guarantees to Tunisia, Jordan, Ukraine, and Iraq to enhance their access to capital markets, while promoting economic policy adjustment.

Development Programs

Credit is an important tool in U.S. bilateral assistance to promote sustainable development. On January 2, 2020, the U.S. International Development Finance Corporation (DFC) launched to consolidate, modernize, and reform the U.S. Government's "development finance" capabilities. The DFC provides loans, guarantees, and other investment tools such as equity and political risk insurance to facilitate and incentivize private-sector investment in emerging markets that will have positive developmental impact, meet national security objectives, and open markets for U.S. trade. Through the DFC's equity program, the U.S. Government will partner with allies and deliver financially-sound alternatives to State-led initiatives from countries like China.

The Government-Sponsored Enterprises (GSEs)

Fannie Mae and Freddie Mac

The Federal National Mortgage Association, or Fannie Mae, created in 1938, and the Federal Home Loan Mortgage Corporation, or Freddie Mac, created in 1970, were established to support the stability and liquidity of a secondary market for residential mortgage loans. Fannie Mae's and Freddie Mac's public missions were later broadened to promote affordable housing. The Federal Home Loan Bank (FHLB) System, created in 1932, is comprised of eleven individual banks with shared liabilities. Together they lend money to financial institutions—mainly banks and thrifts—that are involved in mortgage financing to varying degrees, and they also finance some mortgages using their own funds. The mission of the FHLB System is broadly defined as promoting housing finance, and the System also has specific requirements to support affordable housing.

Together these three GSEs currently are involved, in one form or another, with approximately half of residential mortgages outstanding in the U.S. today.

History of the Conservatorship of Fannie Mae and Freddie Mac and Budgetary Effects

Growing stress and losses in the mortgage markets in 2007 and 2008 seriously eroded the capital of Fannie Mae and Freddie Mac. Legislation enacted in July 2008 strengthened regulation of the housing GSEs through the creation of the Federal Housing Finance Agency (FHFA), a new independent regulator of housing GSEs, and provided the Department of the Treasury with authorities to purchase securities from Fannie Mae and Freddie Mac.

On September 6, 2008, FHFA placed Fannie Mae and Freddie Mac under Federal conservatorship. In its Strategic Plan for the Conservatorships of Fannie Mae and Freddie Mac, updated in 2019, FHFA outlined three key objectives for conservatorship: 1) focus on the GSEs' core mission responsibilities to foster competitive, liquid, efficient, and resilient national housing finance markets that support sustainable homeownership and affordable rental housing; 2) operate in a safe and sound manner appropriate for entities in conservatorship; and 3) prepare for the GSEs' eventual exits from conservatorship.

On September 7, 2008, the U.S. Treasury launched various programs to provide temporary financial support to Fannie Mae and Freddie Mac under the temporary authority to purchase securities. Treasury entered into agreements with Fannie Mae and Freddie Mac to make investments in senior preferred stock in each GSE in order to ensure that each company maintains a positive net worth. Based on the financial results reported by each company as of December 31, 2012, the cumulative funding commitment through these Preferred Stock Purchase Agreements (PSPAs) with Fannie Mae and Freddie Mac was set at $445.5 billion. In total, as of December 31, 2019, $191.5 billion has been invested in Fannie Mae and Freddie Mac.

The PSPAs also require that Fannie Mae and Freddie Mac pay quarterly dividends to Treasury, equal to the GSE's positive net worth above a minimum capital reserve amount for each company. Through December 31, 2019, the GSEs have paid a total of $301.0 billion in dividend payments to Treasury on the senior preferred stock. The Budget estimates additional dividend receipts of $150.6 billion from January 1, 2020, through 2030.

The Temporary Payroll Tax Cut Continuation Act of 2011 (Public Law 112–78) required that Fannie Mae and Freddie Mac increase their credit guarantee fees on single-family mortgage acquisitions between 2012 and 2021 by an average of at least 0.10 percentage point. Revenues generated by this fee increase are remitted directly to the Treasury for deficit reduction and are not included in the PSPA amounts. The Budget proposes to increase this fee by 0.10 percentage point for single-family mortgage acquisitions in 2021, and then extend the 0.20 percentage point fee for acquisitions through 2025. This proposal will help to level the playing field for private lenders seeking to compete with Fannie Mae and Freddie Mac. With this proposal, combined with the existing authority under the Temporary Pay-roll Tax Cut Continuation Act, the Budget estimates resulting deficit reductions of $88.4 billion from 2012 through 2030.

In addition, in 2014 FHFA directed Fannie Mae and Freddie Mac to set aside 0.042 percentage point for each dollar of the unpaid principal balance of new business purchases (including but not limited to mortgages purchased for securitization) in each year to fund several Federal affordable housing programs created by Housing and Economic Recovery act of 2008, including the Housing Trust Fund and the Capital Magnet Fund. These set-asides were suspended by FHFA in November 2008 and reinstated effective January 1, 2015. The 2021 Budget again proposes to eliminate the 0.042 percentage point set-aside and discontinue funding for these funds, resulting in an increase to the estimated PSPA dividends.

Future of the Housing Finance System

On March 27, 2019, the President issued a Presidential Memorandum directing the Departments of the Treasury and HUD to reform the housing finance system to reduce taxpayer risks, expand the private sector's role, modernize Government housing programs, and make sustainable home ownership for American families our benchmark of success. On September 5, 2019, Treasury and HUD published plans with legislative and administrative recommendations to accomplish the goals set forth in the Presidential Memorandum. Treasury's plan made rec-

ommendations to define a limited role for the Federal Government in the housing finance system, enhance taxpayer protections against future bailouts, and promote private sector competition in the housing finance system. Additionally, Treasury made recommendations and listed preconditions for ending the GSEs' conservatorships. HUD's plan made recommendations to refocus FHA to its core mission, protect taxpayers, modernize FHA and Ginnie Mae, and provide liquidity to the housing finance system.

The Administration's preference is to work with the Congress to enact comprehensive housing finance reform legislation. Legislation could achieve lasting structural reform that tailors explicit Government support of the secondary market and eliminates the GSEs' competitive advantages over private-sector entities. At the same time, the Administration believes that reform can and should proceed, and pending legislation, it will continue to support the administrative actions described in the plans. Any reform of the housing system likely will impact 2021 Budget projections in ways that cannot be estimated at this time.

The Farm Credit System (Banks and Associations)

The Farm Credit System (FCS or System) is a Government-sponsored enterprise (GSE) composed of a nationwide network of borrower-owned cooperative lending institutions originally authorized by the Congress in 1916. The FCS's mission continues to be providing sound and dependable credit to American farmers, ranchers, producers or harvesters of aquatic products, their cooperatives, and farm-related businesses. The institutions serve rural America by providing financing for rural residential real estate, rural communication, energy and water infrastructure, and agricultural exports. In addition, maintaining special policies and programs for the extension of credit to young, beginning, and small farmers and ranchers is a legislative mandate for the System.

The financial condition of the System's banks and associations remains fundamentally sound. The ratio of capital to assets remained stable at 17.6 percent on September 30, 2019, compared with 17.4 percent on September 30, 2018. Capital consisted of $57.2 billion that is available to absorb losses. For the first nine months of calendar year 2019, net income equaled $4.1 billion compared with $4.0 billion for the same period of the previous year.

Over the 12-month period ending September 30, 2019, System assets grew 5.7 percent, primarily due to higher cash and investment balances and increased real estate mortgage loans from continued demand by new and existing customers. During the same period, nonperforming assets as a percentage of loans and other property owned was unchanged at 0.92 percent.

The number of FCS institutions continues to decrease because of consolidation. As of September 30, 2019, the System consisted of four banks and 68 associations, compared with seven banks and 104 associations in September 2002. Of the 72 FCS banks and associations rated, 65 of them had one of the top two examination ratings (1 or 2 on a 1 to 5 scale) and accounted for 97.7 percent of gross

Systems assets. Seven FCS institutions had a rating of 3 or lower.

From 2017 to 2018, dollar volume outstanding for total System loans grew by 3.2 percent. Loan dollar volume outstanding to young farmers grew by 6.2 percent, to beginning farmers by 4.5 percent, and to small farmers by 1.8 percent.

While the dollar volume of loans outstanding grew, the number of total System loans outstanding declined by 9.5 percent. The number of loans outstanding to young farmers declined by 5.3 percent, to beginning farmers by 3.8 percent, and to small farmers by 6.8 percent. The decreases in the number of loans were primarily due to the way System institutions had been tracking loan participations—which are loans that are shared by two or more institutions. Young, beginning, and small farmers are not mutually exclusive groups and, thus, cannot be added across categories.

The System's overall new loan dollar volume increased by 12.2 percent in 2018. New loan dollar volume to young farmers increased by 7.6 percent, to beginning farmers by 7.1 percent, and to small farmers by 6.8 percent.

For total System loans, the number of new loans made in 2018 declined by 21.4 percent compared with 2017. The number of loans to young farmers declined by 17.7 percent, to beginning farmers by 15.5 percent, and to small farmers by 16.1 percent.

The loans to young farmers in 2018 represented 18.1 percent of all loans the System made during the year and 11.4 percent of the dollar volume of loans made. The loans made to beginning farmers in 2018 represented 24.2 percent of all System loans made during the year and 15.6 percent of the dollar volume of loans made. The loans in 2018 to small farmers represented 44.6 percent of all loans made during the year and 14.6 percent of the dollar volume of loans made.

The System, while continuing to record strong earnings and capital growth, remains exposed to a variety of risks associated with its portfolio concentration in agriculture and rural America. In 2019, continued pressure on grain and soybean prices due to large supplies relative to demand, along with trade issues, has stressed less efficient producers and those with significant leverage are feeling financial pressure or renting a large share of their acreage. Producers most vulnerable to financial stress are farmers with crop losses (particularly corn and soybeans in parts of the Midwest in 2019) in combination with today's weaker prices. Another segment under stress is smaller or higher-cost dairy farms despite an improvement in milk prices. Amid the challenging economic environment, the combination of farm commodity programs, disaster assistance, crop insurance, and the 2018 and 2019 Market Facilitation Program payments is supporting the U.S. farm sector.

The general economy continues to expand slowly, which benefits demand for high-value agricultural products as well as the housing-related sectors such as timber and nurseries. Overall, the agricultural sector remains subject to risks such as changes in farmland values, which have declined since 2014 in the Midwest; continued volatility in commodity prices; and weather-related catastrophes.

Federal Agricultural Mortgage Corporation (Farmer Mac)

Farmer Mac was established in 1988 as a federally chartered instrumentality of the United States and an institution of the System to facilitate a secondary market for farm real estate and rural housing loans. Farmer Mac is not liable for any debt or obligation of the other System institutions, and no other System institutions are liable for any debt or obligation of Farmer Mac. The Farm Credit System Reform Act of 1996 expanded Farmer Mac's role from a guarantor of securities backed by loan pools to a direct purchaser of mortgages, enabling it to form pools to securitize. The Food, Conservation, and Energy Act of 2008 expanded Farmer Mac's program authorities by allowing it to purchase and guarantee securities backed by rural utility loans made by cooperatives.

Farmer Mac continues to meet core capital and regulatory risk-based capital requirements. As of September 30, 2019, Farmer Mac's total outstanding program volume (loans purchased and guaranteed, standby loan purchase commitments, and AgVantage bonds purchased and guaranteed) amounted to $20.9 billion, which represents an increase of 7.1 percent from the level a year ago. Of total program activity, $17.0 billion were on-balance sheet loans and guaranteed securities, and $3.9 billion were off-balance-sheet obligations. Total assets were $21.3 billion, with non-program investments (including cash and cash equivalents) accounting for $3.7 billion of those assets. Farmer Mac's net income attributable to common stockholders ("net income") for the first three quarters of calendar year 2019 was $64.6 million. Net income decreased compared to the same period in 2018 during which Farmer Mac reported net income of $75.3 million.

II. INSURANCE PROGRAMS

Deposit Insurance

Federal deposit insurance promotes stability in the U.S. financial system. Prior to the establishment of Federal deposit insurance, depository institution failures often caused depositors to lose confidence in the banking system and rush to withdraw deposits. Such sudden withdrawals caused serious disruption to the economy. In 1933, in the midst of the Great Depression, a system of Federal deposit insurance was established to protect depositors and to prevent bank failures from causing widespread disruption in financial markets.

Today, the Federal Deposit Insurance Corporation (FDIC) insures deposits in banks and savings associations (thrifts) using the resources available in its Deposit Insurance Fund (DIF). The National Credit Union

Administration (NCUA) insures deposits (shares) in most credit unions through the National Credit Union Share Insurance Fund (SIF). (Some credit unions are privately insured.) As of September 30, 2019, the FDIC insured $7.7 trillion of deposits at 5,265 commercial banks and thrifts, and the NCUA insured nearly $1.2 trillion of shares at 5,281 credit unions.

Since its creation, the Federal deposit insurance system has undergone many reforms. As a result of the 2008 financial crisis, several reforms were enacted to protect both the immediate and longer-term integrity of the Federal deposit insurance system. The Helping Families Save Their Homes Act of 2009 (P.L. 111–22) provided NCUA with tools to protect the SIF and the financial stability of the credit union system. Notably, the Act:

- Established the Temporary Corporate Credit Union Stabilization Fund (TCCUSF), allowing NCUA to segregate the losses of corporate credit unions and providing a mechanism for assessing those losses to federally insured credit unions over an extended period of time; On September 28, 2017, the NCUA Board voted unanimously to close the TCCUSF effective October 1, 2017, ahead of its sunset date of June 30, 2021, the assets and liabilities of the TCCUSF were distributed into the SIF;

- Provided flexibility to the NCUA Board by permitting use of a restoration plan to spread insurance premium assessments over a period of up to eight years, or longer in extraordinary circumstances, if the SIF equity ratio fell below 1.2 percent; and

- Permanently increased the Share Insurance Fund's borrowing authority to $6 billion.

The Dodd-Frank Wall Street Reform and Consumer Protection (Dodd-Frank) Act of 2010 (P.L. 111–203) established new DIF reserve ratio requirements. The Act requires the FDIC to achieve a minimum DIF reserve ratio (ratio of the deposit insurance fund balance to total estimated insured deposits) of 1.35 percent by 2020, up from 1.15 percent in 2016. On September 30, 2018, the DIF reserve ratio reached 1.36 percent. In addition to raising the minimum reserve ratio, the Dodd-Frank Act also:

- Eliminated the FDIC's requirement to rebate premiums when the DIF reserve ratio is between 1.35 and 1.5 percent;

- Gave the FDIC discretion to suspend or limit rebates when the DIF reserve ratio is 1.5 percent or higher, effectively removing the 1.5 percent cap on the DIF; and

- Required the FDIC to offset the effect on small insured depository institutions (defined as banks with assets less than $10 billion) when setting assessments to raise the reserve ratio from 1.15 to 1.35 percent. In implementing the Dodd-Frank Act, the FDIC issued a final rule setting a long-term (i.e., beyond 2028) reserve ratio target of 2 percent, a goal that FDIC considers necessary to maintain a positive fund balance during economic crises while permitting steady long-term assessment rates that provide transparency and predictability to the banking sector.

The Dodd-Frank Act also permanently increased the insured deposit level to $250,000 per account at banks or credit unions insured by the FDIC or NCUA.

Recent Fund Performance

As of September 30, 2019, the FDIC DIF balance stood at $108.9 billion, a one-year increase of $8.7 billion. The growth in the DIF balance is primarily a result of assessment revenue inflows. The reserve ratio on September 30, 2019, was 1.41 percent.

As of September 30, 2019, the number of insured institutions on the FDIC's "problem list" (institutions with the highest risk ratings) totaled 55, which represented a decrease of nearly 94 percent from December 2010, the peak year for bank failures during the financial crisis. Furthermore, the assets held by problem institutions were nearly 88 percent below the level in December 2009, the peak year for assets held by problem institutions.

The NCUA-administered SIF ended September 2019 with assets of $16.7 billion and an equity ratio of 1.33 percent. On September 28, 2017, NCUA raised the normal operating level of the SIF equity ratio to 1.39 percent and lowered it to 1.38 percent in December 2018. If the ratio exceeds the normal operating level, a distribution is normally paid to insured credit unions to reduce the equity ratio.

The health of the credit union industry has markedly improved since the financial crisis. As of September 30, 2019, NCUA reserved $116 million in the SIF to cover potential losses, a decrease of 26 percent from the $156 million reserved as of September 30, 2018. The ratio of insured shares in problem institutions to total insured shares decreased slightly from 0.91 percent in September 2018 to 0.84 percent in September 2019. This is a significant reduction from a high of 5.7 percent in December 2009.

Restoring the Deposit Insurance Funds

Pursuant to the Dodd-Frank Act, the restoration period for the FDIC's DIF reserve ratio to reach 1.35 percent was extended to 2020. (Prior to the Act, the DIF reserve ratio was required to reach the minimum target of 1.15 percent by the end of 2016.) On March 25, 2016, the FDIC published a final rule to implement this requirement no later than 2019. The Dodd-Frank Act placed the responsibility for the cost of increasing the reserve ratio to 1.35 percent on large banks (generally, those with $10 billion or more in assets). FDIC regulations provided that when the reserve ratio exceeds 1.35 percent, surcharges on insured depository institutions (IDIs) with total consolidated assets of $10 billion or more would cease. The last surcharge was collected in December 2018. As of June 30, 2019, the reserve ratio reached 1.38 percent for the first time, resulting in small IDIs receiving assessment credits for the portion of their assessments that contributed to the growth in the reserve ratio from 1.15 to 1.35 percent. Under a final rule adopted at the FDIC November 2019 board meeting, these credits will continue to be provided to small IDIs until they have received the equivalent of their full contributions, so long as the reserve ratio is in excess of 1.35 percent. Any remaining credits not applied to banks' assessments after four quarters in June 2020 are expected to be disbursed to small IDIs in a one-time lump sum payment.

Budget Outlook

The Budget estimates DIF net outlays of -$53.2 billion over the current 10-year budget window (2021–2030). This $53.2 billion in net inflows to the DIF is a $12.7 billion reduction of net inflows over the previous 10-year window (2020–2029) for the 2020 President's Budget. Growth in the DIF balance and in the size of the banking sector accounted for most of this change, as the latest public data on the banking industry led to minimal changes in projections of failed assets as a share of the banking system, or to the receivership proceeds, resolution outlays, and premiums necessary to reach the long-run DIF target of 1.5 percent. Although the FDIC has authority to borrow up to $100 billion from Treasury to maintain sufficient DIF balances, the Budget does not anticipate FDIC utilizing its borrowing authority because the DIF is projected to maintain positive operating cash flows over the entire 10-year budget horizon.

Pension Guarantees

The Pension Benefit Guaranty Corporation (PBGC) insures the pension benefits of workers and retirees in covered defined-benefit pension plans. PBGC operates two legally distinct insurance programs: single-employer plans and multiemployer plans.

Single-Employer Program

Under the single-employer program, PBGC pays benefits, up to a guaranteed level, when a company's plan closes without enough assets to pay future benefits. PBGC's claims exposure is the amount by which guaranteed benefits exceed assets in insured plans. In the near term, the risk of loss stems from financially distressed firms with underfunded plans. In the longer term, loss exposure results from the possibility that well-funded plans become underfunded due to inadequate contributions, poor investment results, or increased liabilities, and that the healthy firms sponsoring those plans become distressed.

PBGC monitors companies with underfunded plans and acts to protect the interests of the pension insurance program's stakeholders where possible. Under its Early Warning Program, PBGC works with companies to strengthen plan funding or otherwise protect the insurance program from avoidable losses. However, PBGC's authority to manage risks to the insurance program is limited. Most private insurers can diversify or reinsure their catastrophic risks as well as flexibly price these risks. Unlike private insurers, Federal law does not al-low PBGC to deny insurance coverage to a defined-benefit plan or adjust premiums according to risk. Both types of PBGC premiums—the flat rate (a per person charge paid by all plans) and the variable rate (paid by underfunded plans) are set in statute.

Claims against PBGC's insurance programs are highly variable. One large pension plan termination may result in a larger claim against PBGC than the termination of many smaller plans. The future financial health of the PBGC will continue to depend largely on the termination of a limited number of very large plans.

Single employer plans generally provide benefits to the employees of one employer. When an underfunded single employer plan terminates, usually through the bankruptcy process, PBGC becomes trustee of the plan, applies legal limits on payouts, and pays benefits. The amount of benefit paid is determined after taking into account (a) the benefit that a beneficiary had accrued in the terminated plan, (b) the availability of assets from the terminated plan to cover benefits, and (c) the legal maximum benefit level set in statute. In 2020, the maximum annual payment guaranteed under the single-employer program was $69,750 for a retiree aged 65.

Multiemployer Plans

Multiemployer plans are collectively bargained pension plans maintained by one or more labor unions and more than one unrelated employer, usually within the same or related industries. PBGC's role in the multiemployer program is more like that of a re-insurer; if a company contributing to a multiemployer plan fails, its liabilities are assumed by the other employers in the plan, not by PBGC. PBGC becomes responsible for insurance coverage when the plan runs out of money to pay benefits at the statutorily guaranteed level, which usually occurs after most or all contributing employers have withdrawn from the plan, leaving the plan without sufficient income. PBGC provides insolvent multiemployer plans with financial assistance in the form of loans sufficient to pay guaranteed benefits and administrative expenses. Since multiemployer plans do not receive PBGC assistance until their assets are fully depleted, financial assistance is almost never repaid. Benefits under the multiemployer program are calculated based on the benefit that a participant would have received under the insolvent plan, subject to the legal multiemployer maximum set in statute. The maximum guaranteed amount depends on the participant's years of service and the rate at which benefits are accrued. For example, for a participant with 30 years of service, PBGC guarantees 100 percent of the pension benefit up to a yearly amount of $3,960. If the pension exceeds that amount, PBGC guarantees 75 percent of the rest of the pension benefit up to a total maximum guarantee of $12,870 per year. This limit has been in place since 2001 and is not adjusted for inflation or cost-of-living increases.

In recent years, many multiemployer pension plans have become severely underfunded as a result of unfavorable investment outcomes, employers withdrawing from plans, and demographic challenges. In 2001, only 15 plans covering about 80,000 participants were under 40 percent funded using estimated market rates. By 2016, this had grown to over 350 plans covering over 4 million participants. While many plans have benefited from an improving economy and will recover, about 14 percent of all participants in the multiemployer system are in plans projected to become insolvent within twenty years.

As of September 30, 2019, the single-employer program reported a positive net position of $8.7 billion, while the multiemployer program reported a long-term actuarial deficit of $65.2 billion. The challenges facing the multiemployer program are immediate. In its 2019 Annual Report, PBGC reported that it had just $2.9 billion in accumulated assets from premium payments made by multiemployer plans, which it projected would be depleted by 2025. If the program runs out of cash, the only funds available to support benefits would be the premiums that continue to be paid by remaining plans; this could result in benefits being cut much more deeply, to a small fraction of current guarantee levels.

Premiums

PBGC's combined liabilities exceeded assets by $56.5 billion at the end of fiscal year 2019. While the single-employer program's financial position is projected to continue improving over the next 10 years, in part because the Congress has raised premiums in that program several times, the multiemployer program is projected to run out of funds in 2025. Particularly in the multiemployer program, premium rates remain much lower than what a private financial institution would charge for insuring the same risk and well below what is needed to ensure PBGC's solvency.

The Budget includes two policy proposals to reform PBGC premiums. For an in-depth discussion of these proposals, please see the Labor chapter of the Budget *Appendix*.

Disaster Insurance

Flood Insurance

The Federal Government provides flood insurance through the National Flood Insurance Program (NFIP), which is administered by the Department of Homeland Security (DHS) Federal Emergency Management Agency (FEMA). Flood insurance is available to homeowners, renters, businesses, and State and local governments in communities that have adopted and enforce minimum floodplain management measures. Coverage is limited to buildings and their contents. At the end of 2019, the program had over five million policies worth $1.31 trillion in force in more than 22,000 communities. The program is currently authorized until September 30, 2020.

The Congress established NFIP in 1968 to make flood insurance coverage widely available, to combine a program of insurance with flood mitigation measures to reduce the Nation's risk of loss from floods, and to reduce Federal disaster-assistance expenditures on flood losses. The NFIP requires participating communities to adopt

certain land use ordinances consistent with FEMA's floodplain management regulations and take other mitigation efforts to reduce flood-related losses in high flood hazard areas ("Special Flood Hazard Areas") identified through partnership with FEMA, States, and local communities. These efforts have resulted in substantial reductions in the risk of flood-related losses nationwide. However, structures built prior to flood mapping and NFIP floodplain management requirements are eligible for discounted premiums. Currently, FEMA estimates that approximately 20 percent of the total policies in force pay less than fully actuarial rates while continuing to be at relatively high risk of flooding.

FEMA's Community Rating System offers discounts on policy premiums in communities that adopt and enforce more stringent floodplain land use ordinances than those identified in FEMA's regulations and/or engage in mitigation activities beyond those required by the NFIP. The discounts provide an incentive for communities to implement new flood protection activities that can help save lives and property when a flood occurs. Further, NFIP offers flood mitigation assistance grants for planning and carrying out activities to reduce the risk of flood damage to structures covered by NFIP, which may include demolition or relocation of a structure, elevation or flood-proofing a structure, and community-wide mitigation efforts that will reduce future flood claims for the NFIP. In particular, flood mitigation assistance grants targeted toward repetitive and severe repetitive loss properties not only help owners of high-risk property, but also reduce the disproportionate drain these properties cause on the National Flood Insurance Fund.

Due to the catastrophic nature of flooding, with hurricanes Harvey, Katrina, and Sandy as notable examples, insured flood damages can far exceed premium revenue and deplete the program's reserves. On those occasions, the NFIP exercises its borrowing authority through the Treasury to meet flood insurance claim obligations. While the program needed appropriations in the early 1980s to repay the funds borrowed during the 1970's, it was able to repay all borrowed funds with interest using only premium dollars between 1986 and 2004. In 2005, however, Hurricanes Katrina, Rita, and Wilma generated more flood insurance claims than the cumulative number of claims paid from 1968 to 2004. Hurricane Sandy in 2012 generated $8.8 billion in flood insurance claims. As a result, in 2013 the Congress increased the borrowing authority for the fund to $30.425 billion. After the estimated $2.4 billion and $670 million in flood insurance claims generated by the Louisiana flooding of August 2016 and Hurricane Matthew in October 2016, respectively, the NFIP used its borrowing authority again, bringing the total outstanding debt to Treasury to $24.6 billion.

In the fall 2017, Hurricanes Harvey and Irma struck the southern coast of the United States, resulting in catastrophic flood damage across Texas, Louisiana, and Florida. To pay claims, NFIP exhausted all borrowing authority. The Congress provided $16 billion in debt cancellation to the NFIP, bringing its debt to $20.525 billion. To pay Hurricane Harvey flood claims, NFIP also received more than $1 billion in reinsurance payments as a result of transferring risk to the private reinsurance market at the beginning of 2017. FEMA continues to mature its reinsurance program and transfer additional risk to the private market.

In July 2012, resulting largely from experiences during Hurricanes Katrina, Rita, and Wilma in 2005, the Biggert Waters Flood Insurance Reform Act of 2012 (Public Law 112–141; BW–12) was signed into law. In addition to re-authorizing the NFIP for five years, the bill required the NFIP generally to move to full risk-based premium rates and strengthened the NFIP financially and operationally. In 2013, the NFIP began phasing in risk-based premiums for certain properties, as required by the law, and began collecting a policyholder Reserve Fund assessment that is available to meet the expected future obligations of the flood insurance program.

In March 2014, largely in reaction to premium increases initiated by BW–12, the Homeowner Flood Insurance Affordability Act of 2014 (HFIAA) was signed into law, further reforming the NFIP and revising many sections of BW–12. Notably, HFIAA repealed and adjusted many of the major premium increases introduced by BW–12 and required retroactive refunds of collected BW–12 premium increases, introduced a phase-in to higher full-risk premiums for structures newly mapped into the Special Flood Hazard Area until full-risk rates are achieved, and created an Office of the Flood Insurance Advocate. HFIAA also introduced a fixed annual surcharge of $25 for primary residents and $250 for all other policies to be deposited into the Reserve Fund. In 2019, FEMA began utilizing its administrative authority to accelerate the premium increases required by BW-12 and HFIAA so that policy-holders recognize the flood risk they face and to encourage financial soundness of the program. Beginning in October 2021, NFIP will begin charging policyholders based on its new rating system that are fairer, easier to understand, and better reflect a property's unique flood risk.

The 2018-2022 FEMA Strategic Plan creates a shared vision for the NFIP and other FEMA programs to build a more prepared and resilient Nation. The Strategic Plan sets out three overarching goals: Building a culture of preparedness, Readying the Nation for catastrophic events, and reducing the complexity of FEMA. While the NFIP supports all three goals, it is central to building a culture of preparedness. To that end, FEMA is pursuing initiatives including:

1. Providing products that clearly and accurately communicate flood risk;

2. Helping individuals, businesses, and communities understand their risks and the available options like the NFIP to best manage those risks;

3. Transforming the NFIP into a simpler, customer-focused program that policyholders value and trust; and

4. Doubling the number of properties covered by flood insurance (either the NFIP or private insurance) by 2022.

Crop Insurance

Subsidized Federal crop insurance, administered by USDA's Risk Management Agency (RMA) on behalf of the Federal Crop Insurance Corporation (FCIC), assists farmers in managing yield and revenue shortfalls due to bad weather or other natural disasters. The program is a cooperative partnership between the Federal Government and the private insurance industry. Private insurance companies sell and service crop insurance policies. The Federal Government, in turn, pays private companies an administrative and operating (A&O) expense subsidy to cover expenses associated with selling and servicing these policies. The Federal Government also provides re-insurance through the Standard Reinsurance Agreement (SRA) and pays companies an "underwriting gain" if they have a profitable year. For the 2021 Budget, the payments to the companies are projected to be $2.5 billion in combined subsidies. The Federal Government also subsidizes premiums for farmers as a way to encourage farmers to participate in the program.

The most basic type of crop insurance is catastrophic coverage (CAT), which compensates the farmer for losses in excess of 50 percent of the individual's average yield at 55 percent of the expected market price. The CAT premium is entirely subsidized, and farmers pay only an administrative fee. Higher levels of coverage, called "buy-up," are also available. A portion of the premium for buy-up coverage is paid by FCIC on behalf of producers and varies by coverage level – generally, the higher the coverage level, the lower the percent of premium subsidized. The remaining (unsubsidized) premium amount is owed by the producer and represents an out-of-pocket expense.

For 2019, the 10 principal crops (barley, corn, cotton, grain sorghum, peanuts, potatoes, rice, soybeans, tobacco, and wheat) accounted for over 78 percent of total liability, and approximately 86 percent of the total U.S. planted acres of those 10 crops were covered by crop insurance. Producers can purchase both yield and revenue-based insurance products which are underwritten on the basis of a producer's actual production history (APH). Revenue insurance programs protect against loss of revenue resulting from low prices, low yields, or a combination of both. Revenue insurance has enhanced traditional yield insurance by adding price as an insurable component.

In addition to price and revenue insurance, FCIC has made available other plans of insurance to provide protection for a variety of crops grown across the United States. For example, "area plans" of insurance offer protection based on a geographic area (most commonly, a county), and do not directly insure an individual farm. Often, the loss trigger is based on an index, such as a rainfall or vegetative index, which is established by a Government entity (for example, NOAA or USGS). One such plan is the pilot Rainfall and Vegetation Index plan, which insures against a decline in an index value covering Pasture, Rangeland, and Forage. These pilot programs meet the needs of livestock producers who purchase insurance for protection from losses of forage produced for grazing or harvested for hay. In 2019, there were 32,086 Rainfall Index policies earning premiums, covering over 140 million acres of pasture, rangeland and forage. In 2019, there was about $260 million in liability for those producers who purchased livestock coverage and $5.88 billion in liability for those producers who purchased coverage for milk.

A crop insurance policy also contains coverage compensating farmers when they are prevented from planting their crops due to weather and other perils. When an insured farmer is unable to plant the planned crop within the planting time period because of excessive drought or moisture, the farmer may file a prevented planting claim, which pays the farmer a portion of the full coverage level. It is optional for the farmer to plant a second crop on the acreage. If the farmer does, the prevented planting claim on the first crop is reduced and the farmer's APH is recorded for that year. If the farmer does not plant a second crop, the farmer gets the full prevented planting claim, and the farmer's APH is held harmless for premium calculation purposes the following year. Buy-up coverage for prevented planting is limited to 5 percent.

RMA is continuously working to develop new products and to expand or improve existing products in order to cover more agricultural commodities through internal development, and through the section 508(h) authority in the Federal Crop Insurance Act, where the private sector is allowed to develop and submit new concepts for policies or plan of insurance. In 2019, RMA added new coverage for hybrid vegetable seed, white and waxy corn, and increased caps on livestock insurance products. RMA also took numerous actions in response to the flooding disaster affecting the Midwest including deferring the accrual of interest for premium payments for several months, allowing for additional time to report acreage in affected States, and delivery of disaster funding via the private delivery system. In particular, RMA, via Approved Insurance Providers, directly paid an additional 10 percent to 15 percent (totaling roughly $600 million) to insureds on eligible preventing planting indemnities under the authority and funding of the Disaster Relief Act, 2019. This was on top of a record $4.3 billion in claims relating to preventing planting in 2019. For more information and additional crop insurance program details, please reference RMA's website *www.rma.usda.gov*.

Farm Credit System Insurance Corporation (FCSIC)

Although not specifically disaster-related, FCSIC, an independent Government-controlled corporation, ensures the timely payment of principal and interest on FCS obligations on which the System banks are jointly and severally liable. On September 30, 2019, the assets in the Insurance Fund totaled $5.1 billion. As of September 30, 2019, the Insurance Fund as a percentage of adjusted insured debt was 2.08 percent. This was slightly above the statutory secure base amount of 2.00 percent. As of September 30, 2019, outstanding insured System obligations increased 5.2 percent compared with that of September 30, 2018, from $268.6 billion to $282.6 billion.

Insurance against Security-Related Risks

Terrorism Risk Insurance

The Terrorism Risk Insurance Program (TRIP) was authorized by the Terrorism Risk Insurance Act of 2002 to ensure the continued availability of property and casualty insurance following the terrorist attacks of September 11, 2001. TRIP's initial three-year authorization established a system of shared public and private compensation for insured property and casualty losses arising from certified acts of foreign terrorism.

TRIP was originally intended to be temporary, but has been repeatedly extended, and is currently set to expire on December 31, 2027, after it was reauthorized by the Terrorism Risk Insurance Program Reauthorization Act of 2019 (P.L. 116-94). The prior reauthorization, the Terrorism Risk Insurance Extension Act of 2015 (P.L. 114–1), made several program changes to reduce potential Federal liability. Over the first five of those extension years, the loss threshold that triggers Federal assistance is increased by $20 million each year to $200 million in 2020, and the Government's share of losses above the deductible decreases from 85 to 80 percent over the same period. The 2015 extension also required Treasury to recoup 140 percent of all Federal payments made under the program up to a mandatory recoupment amount, which increased by $2 billion each year until 2019 when the threshold was set at $37.5 billion. Since January 1, 2020, the mandatory recoupment amount has been indexed to a running three-year average of the aggregate insurer deductible of 20 percent of direct-earned premiums.

The Budget baseline includes the estimated Federal cost of providing terrorism risk insurance, reflecting current law. Using market data synthesized through a proprietary model, the Budget projects annual outlays and recoupment for TRIP. While the Budget does not forecast any specific triggering events, the Budget includes estimates representing the weighted average of TRIP payments over a full range of possible scenarios, most of which include no notional terrorist attacks (and therefore no TRIP payments), and some of which include notional terrorist attacks of varying magnitudes. On this basis, the Budget projects net spending of $256 million over the 2021–2025 period and $394 million over the 2021–2030 period.

Aviation War Risk Insurance

In December 2014, the Congress sunset the premium aviation war risk insurance program, thereby sending U.S. air carriers back to the commercial aviation insurance market for all of their war risk insurance coverage. The non-premium program is authorized through December 31, 2018. It provides aviation insurance coverage for aircraft used in connection with certain Government contract operations by a department or agency that agrees to indemnify the Secretary of Transportation for any losses covered by the insurance.

III. BUDGETARY EFFECTS OF THE TROUBLED ASSET RELIEF PROGRAM (TARP)

This section provides analysis consistent with Sections 202 and 203 of the Emergency Economic Stabilization Act (EESA) of 2008 (P.L. 110-343), including estimates of the cost to taxpayers and the budgetary effects of TARP transactions as reflected in the Budget. This section also explains the changes in TARP costs, and includes alternative estimates as prescribed under EESA. Under EESA, Treasury has purchased different types of financial instruments with varying terms and conditions.[3] The Budget reflects the costs of these instruments using the methodology as provided by Section 123 of EESA.

The estimated costs of each transaction reflect the underlying structure of the instrument. TARP financial instruments have included direct loans, structured loans, equity, loan guarantees, and direct incentive payments. The costs of equity purchases, loans, guarantees, and loss sharing are the net present value of cash flows to and from the Government over the life of the instrument, per the Federal Credit Reform Act (FCRA) of 1990; as amended (2 U.S.C. 661 et seq.), with an EESA-required adjustment to the discount rate for market risks. Costs for the incentive payments under TARP housing programs, other than loss sharing under the Federal Housing Administration (FHA) Refinance program, involve financial instruments without any provision for future returns and are recorded on a cash basis.[4] For further discussion of market-risk adjustments, please see the following section about fair value budgeting.

Tables 18–11 through 18–17 are available online. Table 18–11 summarizes the cumulative and anticipated activity under TARP, and the estimated lifetime budgetary cost reflected in the Budget, compared to estimates from the 2020 Budget. The direct impact of TARP on the deficit is projected to be $31.9 billion, down $0.6 billion from the $32.5 billion estimate in the 2020 Budget. The total programmatic cost represents the lifetime net present value cost of TARP obligations from the date of disbursement, which is now estimated to be $50.7 billion, a figure that excludes interest on reestimates.[5]

Table 18–12 shows the current value of TARP assets through the actual balances of TARP financing accounts as of the end of each fiscal year through 2019, and pro-

jected balances for each subsequent year through 2030.[6] Based on actual net balances in financing accounts at the end of 2009, the value of TARP assets totaled $129.9 billion. As of September 30, 2019, total TARP net asset value has decreased to -$46 million. This negative balance is due to a one-time recovery in excess of last year's estimated asset value. Updated estimates reflect a positive balance in the financing accounts in 2020. The overall balance of the financing accounts is estimated to continue falling as TARP investments continue to wind down.

Table 18-13 shows the estimated impact of TARP activity on the deficit, debt held by the public and gross Federal debt following the methodology required by EESA. Direct activity under TARP is expected to increase the 2020 deficit by $1.8 billion, the major components being:

- Outlays for TARP housing programs are estimated at $920 million in 2020.

- Administrative expense outlays for TARP are estimated at $47 million in 2020.

- Outlays for the Special Inspector General for TARP are estimated at $31 million in 2020.

- TARP reestimates and interest on reestimates will decrease the deficit by $67.8 million in 2020.

- The projected net financing account interest paid to Treasury at market risk adjusted rates is less than $1 million in 2020.

- Debt service is estimated at $815 million for 2020 and then expected to increase to $1.8 billion by 2030, largely due to outlays for TARP housing programs. Total debt service will continue over time after TARP winds down, due to the financing of past TARP costs.

Debt net of financial assets due to TARP is estimated to be $36.3 billion as of the end of 2020. This is $0.1 billion lower than the projected debt held net of financial assets for 2020 that was reflected in the 2020 Budget.

Table 18-14 reflects the estimated effects of TARP transactions on the deficit and debt, as calculated on a cash basis. Under cash basis reporting, the 2020 deficit would be $58 million higher than the $1.8 billion estimate now reflected in the Budget. However, the impact of TARP on the Federal debt, and on debt held net of financial assets, is the same on a cash basis as under FCRA and therefore these data are not repeated in Table 18–14.

Table 18-15 shows detailed information on upward and downward reestimates to program costs. The current reestimate of $68 million reflects a decrease in estimated TARP costs from the 2020 Budget. This decrease was due in large part to improved market conditions and continued progress winding down TARP investments over the past year.

---

[3] For a more detailed analysis of the assets purchased through TARP and its budgetary effects, please see the "Budgetary Effect of the Troubled Asset Relief Program chapter included in the *Analytical Perspectives* volume of prior budgets.

[4] Section 123 of EESA provides Treasury the authority to record TARP equity purchases pursuant to FCRA, with required adjustments to the discount rate for market risks. The HHF and Making Home Affordable (MHA) program involve the purchase of financial instruments that have no provision for repayment or other return on investment, and do not constitute direct loans or guarantees under FCRA. Therefore these purchases are recorded on a cash basis. Administrative expenses for TARP are recorded under the Office of Financial Stability and the Special Inspector General for TARP on a cash basis, consistent with other Federal administrative costs, but are recorded separately from TARP program costs.

[5] With the exception of MHA and HHF, all the other TARP investments are reflected on a present value basis pursuant to FCRA and EESA.

[6] Reestimates for TARP are calculated using actual data through September 30, 2019, and updated projections of future activity. Thus, the full impacts of TARP reestimates are reflected in the 2020 financing account balances.

The 2021 Budget, as shown in table 18–16, reflects a total TARP deficit impact of $31.9 billion. This is a decrease of $0.6 billion from the 2020 Budget projection of $32.5 billion. The estimated 2020 TARP deficit impact reflected in Table 18–16 differs from the programmatic cost of $50.7 billion in the Budget because the deficit impact includes $18.8 billion in cumulative downward adjustments for interest on subsidy reestimates. See footnote 2 in Table 18–16.

Table 18–17 compares the OMB estimate for TARP's deficit impact to the deficit impact estimated by CBO in its "Report on the Troubled Asset Relief Program—April 2019."[7]

CBO estimates the total cost of TARP at $31 billion, based on estimated lifetime TARP disbursements of $443 billion. The Budget reflects a total deficit cost of $32 billion, based estimated disbursements of $445 billion. CBO and OMB cost estimates for TARP have generally converged over time as TARP equity programs have wound down.

_____

[7] Available at: www.cbo.gov/system/files/2019-04/55124-TARP_April2019.pdf

IV. SPECIAL TOPICS

FAIR VALUE BUDGETING FOR CREDIT PROGRAMS

As described in Section 1, the Federal Government utilizes a wide array of loan and loan guarantee programs to deliver services to the American people. Accurately estimating the costs of these programs is critical to ensuring that the Budget reflects the true position of the Federal Government, as well as how policymakers are allocating limited resources across competing needs and priorities.

The way that the Budget accounts for the costs of the loan and loan guarantees programs has changed over time in order to improve the accuracy and utility of cost estimates. Prior to 1990, budgeting for loans was done on a cash basis, meaning that the budgetary costs of a direct loan or loan guarantee was the net cash flows for that fiscal year. The Federal Credit Reform Act of 1990 (FCRA) updated this approach by requiring cost estimates for these programs to reflect the estimated lifetime costs of loans and loan guarantees up front on a net present value basis. This required policy officials to budget for those lifetime costs when making programmatic decisions. While this approach provides a more realistic portrayal of the costs of the Federal credit programs, it can be challenging to determine the present value of projected cash flows that can extend far into the future and may be highly uncertain.

The Administration supports proposals to improve the accuracy of cost estimates that are consistent with the original goals of FCRA—specifically, to provide better information on the costs of credit programs and improve resource allocation by placing them on a comparable basis to other forms of Federal spending.

One proposal that has recently gained some support is a "fair value" approach. Fair value is an alternative approach to measuring the cost of Federal direct loan and loan guarantee programs that would align budget estimates with the market value of Federal assistance, typically by including risk premiums observed in the market. Further, fair value would require programs to incorporate non-diversifiable, project-specific risks inherent to such loans or guarantees. Several outside experts have argued that the Federal Government should utilize fair value to estimate the cost of direct and guaranteed loans. The Congressional Budget Office (CBO), for instance, has stated that fair value would be a more comprehensive measure of the cost of Federal credit programs.[8] Prior Congressional Budget Resolutions have also endorsed fair value, and the Congress has periodically required fair value estimates in legislation for particular programs. Notably, the Emergency Economic Stabilization Act (EESA) of 2008 (P.L. 110– 343), as amended, required costs for Treasury's Troubled Asset Relief Program (TARP) to be estimated on a net present value, adjusted to reflect a premium for market risk.

Properly estimating the cost of providing credit assistance, as opposed to other forms of financial assistance such as grants, is an important consideration to policymakers as they allocate spending among programs. The ability to offer credit assistance on more generous terms than the most efficient private sector participants, fueled by the Federal Government's advantage in a lower cost of borrowing, can cause price distortions in the marketplace. While there is a conceptual debate about whether the Federal Government should be influenced by the same market risks as individual taxpayers, it is generally true that direct loans and loan guarantees are expected to perform worse when macroeconomic conditions are declining, and will be exposed to certain risks that are inherent to the project and not able to be diversified away. Therefore, any pricing differences may incentivize policymakers to choose for the Government to hold direct loan assets or be exposed to loan guarantee liabilities when individual taxpayers would not do so.

But while fair value analysis offers some useful insights and helps inform decision-making for specific programs, the Governmental Accountability Office (GAO) and others have noted that fair value may impose implementation costs and challenges, and that these challenges would need to be carefully addressed in order to prevent the distortion of credit estimates. Further, fair value cost estimates would reflect non-cash costs in the Budget, raising concerns about consistency and transparency.

The sections below will discuss cost estimation methods under FCRA and a fair value approach, analyze the differences between recent FCRA and fair value cost es-

_____

[8] https://www.cbo.gov/system/files/2019-05/55278-FairValue2020.pdf

timates, and describe the conceptual and implementation challenges that need to be addressed.

Methodology for Estimating Costs under FCRA and Fair Value

Costs under FCRA

Before FCRA, the budget reflected the cash flows of loans and loan guarantees in the years that they occurred. The cost of new direct loans was greatly overstated—appropriations were required for the full face value of loans and did not consider expected repayment over time. In contrast, new loan guarantees appeared to not have a cost, and there was no requirement to set aside a reserve to cover anticipated losses. FCRA greatly improved the accuracy of cost estimates by capturing the lifetime expected cash flows for loans and loan guarantees up front. Under FCRA, the subsidy cost is equal to the net present value of the cash flows to and from the Government, netting out expected losses from default or other adverse events. The present value is estimated using the Government's cost of funds, as reflected in Treasury rates, to discount these cash flows.

Costs under Fair Value[9]

In contrast to FCRA where estimated cash flows are discounted by the Government's cost of funds (Treasury rates), under fair value cash flows would typically reflect estimated market-determined rates for the characteristics of the loan or loan guarantee (comparable market rates), instead of Treasury rates. A fair value cost estimate for loan guarantees would require determining the value that a private guarantor would charge for bearing the risk of providing the guarantee, or which a private lender would be willing to pay for the guarantee itself— a potentially more challenging task than calculating the private sector's discount rate for direct loans. Comparable market rates would need to be derived or estimated from available market data, and applied to cash flows. Discount rates would vary across programs, and in some cases by individual loan or guarantee. Because fair value estimates reflect market-determined rates that reflect the uncertainty associated with loan performance and other factors not included in FCRA estimates, fair value costs would be higher.

Budgetary Cost Estimates under FCRA and Fair Value

The Report of the 1967 President's Commission on Budget Concepts stressed the need to—amongst other purposes—provide accurate and transparent costs to the Government, allocate resources to serve national objectives, and provide the public with information about the Government's impact on the national economy. In order to present the budget on a truly comprehensive basis, the Commission evaluated the need to provide separate, substantive information on loan programs as distinct from other forms of expenditures. FCRA costs reflect estimated cash flows, including expected losses due to default and other adverse events. Actual experience may deviate from initial estimates; however, through the reestimates the subsidy costs are ultimately tied to actual cash flows and these reestimates help agencies learn from past experience to improve techniques for generating new estimates. In some instances, however, this has the impact of generally shifting cash flows upwards by changing the calculation from an overall expected estimate of cash flows, including project risks, to a "modal" estimate—i.e., the specific single path of cash flow that is most likely to occur. As the latter approach does not include information of the probability of all other outcomes, from a discounted cash flow perspective this can result in underestimation of costs. As a measure of expected budgetary cost ex-post (i.e. once the risk has been resolved in default or repayment), FCRA estimates have been fairly accurate overall, although not always on a program-by-program basis. Net lifetime reestimates of subsidy cost for credit programs[10] over the 27 years that FCRA has been in place are $113.8 billion upward—less than one percent of the $11.8 trillion in face value of loans and guarantees made under FCRA, or 2.7 percent of the $4.1 trillion currently outstanding.

However, there are additional costs beyond those captured under FCRA that could be reflected in the budget. Fair value cost estimates include the same underlying credit risk assumptions as FCRA estimates, and add an additional premium above the expected costs. Those costs could include certain factors such as the administrative costs which are budgeted separately under FCRA, a liquidity premium, and a component related to the exemption of Treasuries from the State income tax.

Producing a fair value cost estimates that isolates the market risk premium would need to disaggregate those other costs not currently specifically measured in FCRA estimates. CBO and others have produced numerous estimates over the last several years which can provide a starting point for developing an appropriate methodology for budget execution. On a FCRA basis, Federal credit programs in the 2020 Budget are expected to save $12 billion; by contrast, CBO's analysis on a fair value basis shows that these programs are expected to cost $35 billion.[11] The biggest driver of this difference is student loans, which accounts for $4.1 billion of savings under FCRA but which CBO estimates would cost $17.7 billion on a fair value basis. These differences may assist policy makers in their examination of these programs and let taxpayers know the true added cost or savings over time.

---

[9] Pages 393-398 of the *Analytical Perspectives* volume of the 2013 Budget include more discussion of the issues raised in this section and the following section on Implementation.

[10] Excludes the Troubled Asset Relief Program and the International Monetary Fund increases provided in the 2009 Supplemental Appropriations Act, where reestimates reflect the return of a market risk adjustment premium. Also excludes reestimates from the Small Business Lending Fund, an equity program presented on a FCRA basis pursuant to legislation.

[11] https://www.cbo.gov/system/files/2019-05/55278-FairValue2020.pdf (ibid 10) CBO's analysis includes Fannie Mae and Freddie Mac as Federal entities. Please see Chapter 9 Coverage of the Budget for an analysis of why the Administration does not include these entities.

Conceptual and Implementation Challenges of Fair Value

There are both conceptual and practical implementation issues that need to be addressed prior to moving to a fair value methodology. Key issues include:

- **Determining the right valuation methods across agencies with vastly different credit programs.**

Fair-value estimates require analysts to make judgments about discount rates for each program, which could create inconsistencies in the estimates of costs from program to program. Guidance would need to be developed that determined the appropriate granularity of market risk premia for specific programs and sectors, and to ensure that similarly situated programs are using similar market premia assumptions. This could be especially challenging for programs where costs are estimated based on individual borrower characteristics (i.e. credit-worthiness, industry, collateral value, fee structure, and loan maturity).

While it may be relatively easier to adjust the discount rate methodology for direct loan programs, developing fair value estimates for guaranteed loan programs is more complex. Rather than computing cash flows to and from the Government—for example, guarantee fees received and default claims disbursed—agencies would instead need to determine the value that market participants would assign to the guarantee itself. There is additional complexity in determining the appropriate estimation methodology for direct loans or loan guarantees where market data is limited, or where a non-Federal counterpart does not exist in the market.

- **Ensuring that estimates are transparent to policymakers and the public.**

Changes in risk premia over time could create considerable swings in mandatory outlays and receipts, or make it challenging to determine the effects of modifying existing programs. These swings could be difficult to communicate to policymakers and the public, and create confusion over whether changes in program costs are due to identifiable, actionable policy decisions or because of outside market factors. In addition to the challenges of creating initial estimates, market-risk adjusted discounting for the reestimate process would need to be reconciled with the intragovernmental cash flow accounting process established by FCRA.

- **Managing the additional volatility of fair value estimates on the Federal Budget process.**

Fair-value cost estimates would be somewhat more volatile over time because of changes in market conditions—although factors that also affect FCRA estimates would continue to be the main cause of volatility. Favorable decreases in market risk might encourage policymakers to expand programs—only to see those market conditions change the next year. Conversely, unfavorable increases

in market risk incentivize policymakers to constrain programs that are otherwise fundamentally sound.

Because fair value would reflect additional non-cash costs in the Budget, care would need to be taken to ensure that savings from changes to credit programs are not overstated. Further, decisions will need to be made whether to retroactively apply fair value estimates to currently outstanding loan programs, or to only apply fair value estimates to future activity.

- **Updating the various statutes, standards, and guidance that currently govern credit programs.**

There is an entire infrastructure surrounding the current FCRA approach that would need to overhauled. The Administration would also need to work with the audit and accounting community to make appropriate updates to various Federal accounting standards, implementation manuals, and associated guidance.

- **Obtaining necessary financial and human resources.**

Depending on the specifics of a fair value proposal, the issues described above could require a significant investment in resources to implement at OMB, Treasury, and the various Federal credit agencies. A key issue would be the Government's ability to recruit and train staff to develop the necessary infrastructure for implementation. In implementing current FCRA requirements, some Federal credit programs have faced significant administrative challenges in hiring staff with the right technical skill sets, and developing critical management infrastructure, including financial accounting systems, monitoring, and modeling capabilities. For example: the shift to fair value would likely require OMB to develop new discounting software to capture additional data points to ensure an appropriate level of transparency for budgetary and financial statement accounting. Fair value will likely place greater demands on agencies in all of these areas.

Summary

The Administration supports proposals to improve the accuracy of program cost estimates and is open to working with the Congress and knowledgeable members of the public to address any conceptual and implementation challenges necessary to develop fair value estimates for Federal credit programs in an efficient manner. Fair value cost of estimates for Federal credit programs have the potential to capture elements of program costs that are not included in FCRA-based cost estimates. The Budget is more informative when it shows the direct cost to the Government in an accurate and transparent manner, as well as the economic costs imposed on taxpayers for extending credit assistance. Further, other alternatives to fair value budgeting should also be evaluated—including greater investment in improving FCRA cost estimates, and strengthened cost-benefit analyses at the program level.

Chart 18-1. Face Value of Federal Credit Outstanding

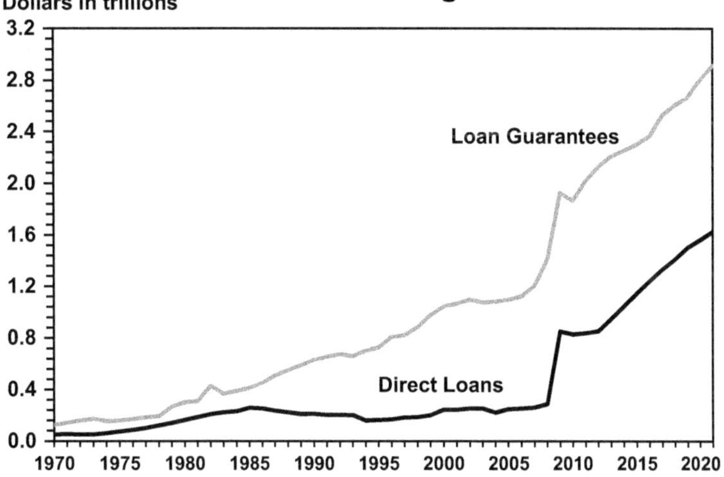

Dollars in trillions

Table 18–1. PROJECTED COSTS OF FEDERAL CREDIT PROGRAMS UNDER FCRA AND FAIR VALUE IN 2020 [1]

	Number of Programs	Obligations or Commitments (Billions of dollars)	Subsidy Rate (Percent) Fair Value		Subsidy (Billions of dollars)	
			FCRA Estimate	Fair-Value Estimate	FCRA Estimate	Fair-Value Estimate
By Department or Agency						
Housing and Urban Development	17	245	−3.0	2.9	−7.3	7.1
Veterans Affairs	5	126	0.6	2.3	0.7	2.9
Education	7	102	−4.0	17.3	−4.1	17.7
Agriculture	26	44	−0.1	2.7	**	1.2
Small Business Administration	7	44	*	9.5	**	4.1
Export-Import Bank	4	22	−5.1	−1.8	−1.1	−0.4
International Assistance	9	13	−2.6	3.9	−0.3	0.5
Transportation	2	5	5.0	25.7	0.2	1.2
Other	7	3	2.1	20.5	0.1	0.6
All Departments and Agencies	**84**	**603**	**−2.0**	**5.8**	**−11.8**	**35.0**

* Denotes less than 0.05%.
** Denotes less than $50 million.

Table 18–2. ESTIMATED FUTURE COST OF OUTSTANDING FEDERAL CREDIT PROGRAMS[1]

(In billions of dollars)

Program	Outstanding 2018	Estimated Future Costs of 2018 Outstanding[2]	Outstanding 2019	Estimated Future Costs of 2019 Outstanding[2]
Direct Loans:[2]				
Federal Student Loans	1,122	64	1,203	154
Education Temporary Student Loan Purchase Authority	57	*	53	7
Farm Service Agency, Rural Development, Rural Housing	58	3	60	4
Rural Utilities Service and Rural Telephone Bank	53	2	53	2
Housing and Urban Development	31	15	38	17
Export-Import Bank	19	2	16	1
Advanced Technology Vehicle Manufacturing, Title 17 Loans	14	1	15	*
Transportation Infrastructure Finance and Innovation Act Loans	15	*	19	–1
Disaster Assistance	9	2	10	2
International Assistance	8	4	9	5
Other direct loan programs[3]	23	6	23	6
Total direct loans	1,410	99	1,498	197
Guaranteed Loans:[2]				
FHA Mutual Mortgage Insurance Fund	1,265	14	1,288	–2
Department of Veterans Affairs (VA) Mortgages	664	9	713	8
Federal Student Loan Guarantees	157	3	141	5
FHA General and Special Risk Insurance Fund	158	5	163	5
Farm Service Agency, Rural Development, Rural Housing	149	1	151	1
Small Business Administration (SBA) Business Loan Guarantees[4]	129	3	130	2
Export-Import Bank	42	1	34	1
International Assistance	26	4	25	3
Other guaranteed loan programs[3]	16	1	16	1
Total guaranteed loans[4]	2,606	39	2,662	22
Total Federal credit	**4,016**	**138**	**4,160**	**220**

* $500 million or less.

[1] Future costs represent balance sheet estimates of allowance for subsidy cost, liabilities for loan guarantees, and estimated uncollectible principal and interest.

[2] Excludes loans and guarantees by deposit insurance agencies and programs not included under credit reform, such as Tennessee Valley Authority loan guarantees. Defaulted guaranteed loans that result in loans receivable are included in direct loan amounts.

[3] As authorized by the statute, table includes TARP and SBLF equity purchases. Future costs for TARP are calculated using the discount rate required by the Federal Credit Reform Act adjusted for market risks, as directed in legislation.

[4] To avoid double-counting, outstandings for GNMA and SBA secondary market guarantees, and TARP FHA Letter of Credit program are excluded from the totals.

Table 18–3. DIRECT LOAN SUBSIDY RATES, BUDGET AUTHORITY, AND LOAN LEVELS, 2019–2021

(Dollar amounts in millions)

Agency and Program Account	2019 Actual			2020 Enacted			2021 Proposed		
	Subsidy rate [1]	Subsidy budget authority	Loan levels	Subsidy rate [1]	Subsidy budget authority	Loan levels	Subsidy rate [1]	Subsidy budget authority	Loan levels
Agriculture:									
Agricultural Credit Insurance Fund Program Account	0.99	27	2,633	2.03	82	4,070	−1.52	−70	4,641
Farm Storage Facility Loans Program Account	−0.52	−2	236	−0.23	−1	309	−0.88	−3	309
Rural Electrification and Telecommunications Loans Program Account ..	−3.63	−216	5,962	−2.42	−103	4,253	−1.94	−88	4,529
Distance Learning, Telemedicine, and Broadband Program	19.53	9	48	28.71	103	358	26.75	90	335
Rural Water and Waste Disposal Program Account	−0.27	−3	1,092	4.56	66	1,447	−1.53	−19	1,270
Rural Community Facilities Program Account	−7.61	−59	774	−4.96	−124	2,500	−6.56	−164	2,500
Multifamily Housing Revitalization Program Account	49.99	22	45	56.78	16	28	....	....	....
Rural Housing Insurance Fund Program Account	8.63	99	1,146	10.44	113	1,086	−2.46	−*	2
Rural Microenterprise Investment Program Account	9.52	*	3	14.88	2	13	....	....	....
Intermediary Relending Program Fund Account	22.01	4	19	27.63	4	19	....	....	....
Rural Economic Development Loans Program Account	13.35	6	48	16.78	8	48	....	....	....
Commerce:									
Fisheries Finance Program Account	−9.04	−2	19	−2.66	−9	321	−9.65	−11	124
Education:									
College Housing and Academic Facilities Loans Program Account	8.08	18	221	9.50	32	341	7.96	18	220
TEACH Grant Program Account	28.37	29	102	28.93	29	99	27.44	28	101
Federal Direct Student Loan Program Account	−1.15	−1,646	143,749	5.89	8,473	143,780	−5.76	−8,327	144,609
Energy:									
Title 17 Innovative Technology Loan Guarantee Program	−2.85	−105	3,703	....	....	....	....	....	....
Homeland Security:									
Disaster Assistance Direct Loan Program Account	95.13	37	39	74.61	116	155	76.25	36	47
Housing and Urban Development:									
FHA-Mutual Mortgage Insurance Program Account	0.00	....	1	0.00	....	1	0.00	....	1
FHA-General and Special Risk Program Account	−14.38	−98	623	....	....	....	....	....	....
State:									
Repatriation Loans Program Account	40.45	1	3	41.34	1	2	55.45	1	2
Transportation:									
Federal-aid Highways	2.48	38	1,535	....	....	....	....	....	....
Railroad Rehabilitation and Improvement Program	−1.04	−10	914	0.00	....	600	0.00	....	600
TIFIA Highway Trust Fund Program Account	....	....	....	2.84	272	9,577	0.97	311	32,062
Treasury:									
Community Development Financial Institutions Fund Program Account .	−4.75	−5	100	2	1	507	[2]0.00	....	300
Veterans Affairs:									
Veterans Housing Benefit Program Fund	−5.30	−4	71	8.72	7	88	−22.12	−22	99
Native American Veteran Housing Loan Program Account	−9.59	−1	6	−4.07	−1	14	−17.37	−3	15
Environmental Protection Agency:									
Water Infrastructure Finance and Innovation Program Account	0.82	21	2,524	2	55	6,044	[2]1.08	20	1,845
International Assistance Programs:									
Foreign Military Financing Loan Program Account	....	....	....	....	....	....	[2]0.00	....	4,000
Overseas Private Investment Corporation Program Account	−5.90	−79	1,496	−13.99	−7	110	....	....	....
United States International Development Finance Corporation	....	....	....	−11.65	−332	2,770	[2]1.37	−60	4,350
Small Business Administration:									
Disaster Loans Program Account	12.29	173	1,406	13.62	150	1,100	8.92	98	1,100
Business Loans Program Account	8.77	4	42	9.29	5	50	8.99	4	41
Export-Import Bank of the United States:									
Export-Import Bank Loans Program Account	−13.59	−681	5,009	....	....	....	....	....	....
Total	N/A	−2,423	173,569	N/A	8,958	179,690	N/A	−8,161	203,102

N/A = Not applicable

* $500,000 or less

[1] Additional information on credit subsidy rates is contained in the Federal Credit Supplement.

[2] Rate reflects notional estimate. Estimates will be determined at the time of execution and will reflect the terms of the contracts and other characteristics.

Table 18–4. LOAN GUARANTEE SUBSIDY RATES, BUDGET AUTHORITY, AND LOAN LEVELS, 2019–2021

(Dollar amounts in millions)

Agency and Program	2019 Actual			2020 Enacted			2021 Proposed		
	Subsidy rate [1]	Subsidy budget authority	Loan levels	Subsidy rate [1]	Subsidy budget authority	Loan levels	Subsidy rate [1]	Subsidy budget authority	Loan levels
Agriculture:									
Agricultural Credit Insurance Fund Program Account	0.23	7	3,107	0.38	22	5,762	0.44	25	5,880
Commodity Credit Corporation Export Loans Program Account	–0.22	–5	2,024	–0.39	–22	5,500	–0.40	–22	5,500
Rural Water and Waste Disposal Program Account	0.38	*	11	0.14	*	57	0.12	*	67
Rural Community Facilities Program Account	2.89	5	187	–0.51	–3	500	–0.74	–4	500
Rural Housing Insurance Fund Program Account	–0.75	–114	15,026	–0.60	–105	17,409	–0.74	–127	17,063
Rural Business Program Account	2.32	31	1,343	2.05	28	1,390	0.83	14	1,704
Rural Energy for America Program	4.46	9	206	3.53	24	672	....	....	....
Biorefinery Assistance Program Account	25.03	94	375	14.93	45	303	16.16	65	400
Health and Human Services:									
Health Center Facility Loan Guarantee Program	....	....	....	2.57	2	60	2.78	2	66
Housing and Urban Development:									
Indian Housing Loan Guarantee Fund Program Account	0.26	1	548	0.11	1	600	0.30	1	600
Native Hawaiian Housing Loan Guarantee Fund Program Account	–0.32	–*	16	–0.34	–*	16	–0.15	–*	15
Native American Housing Block Grant	11.26	2	13	6.25	2	17	6.39	1	20
Community Development Loan Guarantees Program Account	0.00	....	59	–0.01	–*	100	....	....	....
FHA-Mutual Mortgage Insurance Program Account	–3.05	–6,887	225,571	–2.13	–4,665	218,615	–3.31	–6,976	210,728
FHA-General and Special Risk Program Account	–2.79	–480	17,169	–3.12	–637	20,432	–2.39	–474	19,753
Interior:									
Indian Guaranteed Loan Program Account	5.34	6	106	5.56	10	183	....	....	....
Veterans Affairs:									
Veterans Housing Benefit Program Fund	0.07	131	187,409	–0.30	–512	170,737	–0.50	–714	142,877
International Assistance Programs:									
Foreign Military Financing Loan Program Account	....	....	....	....	....	....	0.00	....	4,000
Loan Guarantees to Israel Program Account	0.00	....	2,000	0.00	....	500	0.00	....	500
Development Credit Authority Program Account	2.19	22	1,006	....	....	....	....	....	....
Overseas Private Investment Corporation Program Account	–11.41	–415	3,633	–9.51	–9	55	....	....	....
United State International Development Finance Corporation	....	....	....	....	....	....	[2]–2.26	–57	2,506
Small Business Administration:									
Business Loans Program Account	0.00	....	28,071	0.20	99	49,000	[2]0.00	....	42,500
Export-Import Bank of the United States:									
Export-Import Bank Loans Program Account	–0.19	–6	3,206	–4.87	–1,121	23,030	–4.97	–1,037	20,875
Total	N/A	**–7,599**	**491,086**	N/A	**–6,841**	**514,938**	N/A	**–9,303**	**475,554**
ADDENDUM: SECONDARY GUARANTEED LOAN COMMITMENT LIMITATIONS									
Government National Mortgage Association:									
Guarantees of Mortgage-backed Securities Loan Guarantee Program Account	–0.44	–1,987	451,555	–0.29	–1,183	408,000	–0.31	–1,207	389,237
Small Business Administration:									
Secondary Market Guarantee Program	0.00	....	8,498	0.00	....	12,000	0.00	....	13,000
Total, secondary guarantee loan commitments	N/A	**–1,987**	**460,053**	N/A	**–1,183**	**420,000**	N/A	**–1,207**	**402,237**

N/A = Not applicable.
* $500,000 or less
[1] Additional information on credit subsidy rates is contained in the Federal Credit Supplement.
[2] Rate reflects notional estimate. Estimates will be determined at the time of execution and will reflect the terms of the contracts and other characteristics.

Table 18–5.   SUMMARY OF FEDERAL DIRECT LOANS AND LOAN GUARANTEES[1]

(In billions of dollars)

	Actual								Estimate	
	2012	2013	2014	2015	2016	2017	2018	2019	2020	2021
Direct Loans:										
Obligations	191.1	174.4	174.0	181.3	175.6	180.0	169.7	173.6	179.7	203.1
Disbursements	170.0	157.5	155.4	161.4	158.5	164.4	151.9	150.8	154.5	164.0
Budget authority:										
New subsidy budget authority[2]	−27.2	−29.8	−22.4	4.9	−9.0	−1.0	−2.4	−1.2	9.5	−8.2
Reestimated subsidy budget authority[2,3]	16.8	−19.7	−0.8	10.1	8.0	32.5	−10.3	29.9	67.1	....
Total subsidy budget authority	**−10.4**	**−49.4**	**−23.2**	**15.1**	**−1.1**	**31.5**	**−12.8**	**28.7**	**76.5**	**−8.2**
Loan guarantees:										
Commitments[4]	479.7	536.6	350.8	478.3	537.6	530.2	461.7	491.1	517.6	476.8
Lender disbursements[4]	444.3	491.3	335.6	461.6	517.6	520.6	465.1	482.7	488.4	464.1
Budget authority:										
New subsidy budget authority[2]	−6.9	−17.9	−13.7	−11.9	−7.5	−8.8	−5.4	−9.6	−8.0	−10.7
Reestimated subsidy budget authority[2,3]	−4.9	20.8	1.2	−1.1	−13.6	16.8	9.4	−20.2	−15.9	....
Total subsidy budget authority	**−11.8**	**2.8**	**−12.5**	**−13.1**	**−21.1**	**8.0**	**4.0**	**−29.8**	**−23.9**	**−10.7**

[1] As authorized by statute, table includes TARP and SBLF equity purchases, and International Monetary Fund (IMF) transactions resulting from the 2009 Supplemental Appropriations Act.

[2] Credit subsidy costs for TARP and IMF transactions are calculated using the discount rate required by the Federal Credit Reform Act adjusted for market risks, as directed in legislation.

[3] Includes interest on reestimate.

[4] To avoid double-counting, the face value of GNMA and SBA secondary market guarantees and the TARP FHA Letter of Credit program are excluded from the totals.

19. CYBERSECURITY FUNDING

Cybersecurity is an important component of the Administration's IT modernization efforts, and the President remains dedicated to securing the Federal enterprise from cyber-related threats. Assessments of the Federal Government's overall cybersecurity risk continue to find the Federal enterprise to be threatened. Cybersecurity budgetary priorities will continue to seek to reduce this risk, based on data-driven, risk-based assessments of the threat environment and the current Federal cybersecurity posture. The President's Budget includes approximately $18.8 billion for cybersecurity funding, which supports the protection of Federal information systems and our Nation's most valuable information including the personal information of the American public. The 2021 Budget funds activities in support of Executive Order 13800, "Strengthening the Cybersecurity of Federal Networks and Critical Infrastructure,"[1] the outcomes of the Report to the President on Federal IT Modernization, the Modernize IT to Increase Productivity and Security (IT Modernization) Cross Agency Priority (CAP) Goal of the President's Management Agenda (PMA),[2] and the National Cybersecurity Strategy.[3]

National Cybersecurity Strategy

In September 2018, the White House released the National Cyber Strategy, which reinforces ongoing work and provides strategic direction for the Federal Government to take action on short and long-term improvements to cybersecurity for the Government and critical infrastructure. The National Cyber Strategy recognizes that private and public entities have struggled to secure their systems as adversaries have increased the frequency and sophistication of their malicious cyber activities, and directs the Federal Government to do its part to ensure a secure cyber environment for our Nation.

Supply Chain Risk Management

In 2019, as part of the National Cyber Strategy and with the passage of the SECURE Technology Act, agencies are required to assess the risks to their respective information and communications technology supply chains. In addition to agency Supply Chain Risk Management (SCRM) programs, enterprise wide risk is being addressed through the Federal Acquisition Security Council (FASC). The FASC will make recommendations on po-

tential exclusion and removal orders to the Secretaries of Defense and Homeland Security as well as the Director of National Intelligence to address risk to each of their enterprises. These critical steps help agencies safeguard information and communication technology from emerging threats and support the need to establish standards for the acquisition community around SCRM.

Trusted Internet Connections

On September 12, 2019, OMB updated the Trusted Internet Connection (TIC) initiative after more than a decade. The updated policy allows industry to propose, and agencies to adopt, new solutions to take advantage of modern internet capabilities.

Leading up to the release of the new policy, the Small Business Administration (SBA) and the Department of Energy (DOE) worked with OMB and the Department of Homeland Security (DHS) to pilot selected solutions. The success of these pilots shows that solutions using current technologies can continue progress on goals outlined a decade ago. The technologies used DOE's pilot increased the flexibility and reach of the agency users so they are no longer required to be tethered to DOE's Federal computing network. DOE's mobile device users were able to directly access their cloud based systems, saving tax payer funds necessary to support some of DOE's Government operations. SBA's pilot helped transform the Agency's technology platform and improve the ability to scale up. SBA leveraged the technologies used in their TIC pilot in 2018 to help the Agency to rapidly scale up to support victims of natural disasters.

Continuous Diagnostic and Mitigation

Prior to the establishment of the Continuous Diagnostics and Mitigation (CDM) program at the Department of Homeland Security (DHS), Federal Agencies inconsistently implemented Information Security Continuous Monitoring (ISCM) policies. The CDM Program provides a dynamic approach for baselining ISCM efforts: DHS's CDM program provides Federal Agencies with the tools, integration services, and dashboards necessary for identifying cybersecurity risks on a continuous basis. This near real-time monitoring enhances agencies' ability to prioritize cybersecurity risks, enabling cybersecurity personnel to mitigate the most significant problems first. The CDM program also provides DHS with a Federal enterprise view of the cyber threat landscape through the Federal CDM Dashboard that receives summary data from all Federal Agency Dashboards. The CDM objectives are to reduce agency-specific security threats; increase visibility into the Federal enterprise cybersecurity posture;

---

[1] *https://www.whitehouse.gov/presidential-actions/presidential-executive-order-strengthening-cybersecurity-federal-networks-critical-infrastructure/*.

[2] See *https://www.perfomance.gov/*.

[3] *https://www.whitehouse.gov/wp-content/uploads/2018/09/National-Cyber-Strategy.pdf*.

improve Federal cybersecurity response capabilities; and streamline Federal Information Security Modernization Act of 2014 (FISMA) reporting.

To further support the CDM program, the Fiscal Year 2019-2020 Guidance on Federal Information Security and Privacy Management Requirements (M-20-04) requires Federal Agencies to provide sufficient justification prior to purchasing and using tools purchased outside of the CDM acquisition vehicles. Additionally, M-20-04 requires that Federal Agencies fund long-term operations and mainte-nance (e.g., licensing costs) of their CDM-related tools and capabilities as CDM-specific line items in their annual congressional budget justification documents.

Federal Information Security Modernization Act

FISMA designates OMB as responsible for oversee-ing Federal Agencies' information security and privacy practices and for developing and directing implementa-tion of policies and guidelines that support and sustain those practices. The President's Budget provides funding for agencies to implement cybersecurity defenses that are necessary to protect the data of the American people and sensitive national security information.

These cybersecurity defenses include key capabili-ties identified as targets for progress in the President's Management Agenda. For example, as of October 2019 all 23 of the civilian CFO Act agencies reported the ability to remotely wipe agency-owned mobile devices of agency data in the event that they are lost or stolen. Additional details on these Government-wide targets can be found on *perfor-mance.gov*. Furthermore, OMB leverages a quarterly Risk Management Assessment (RMA) process to help agencies understand and decrease their cybersecurity risk by fo-cusing on high priority controls, tracking improvements over time. A complete set of agency cybersecurity perfor-mance summaries, which provide a high-level overview of RMA and Inspector General ratings, will be available in the forthcoming annual FISMA report.

Data Collection Methodology and Adjustments

Section 630 of the Consolidated Appropriations Act, 2017 (P.L. 115–31) amended 31 U.S.C. § 1105 (a)(35) to require that an analysis of Federal cybersecurity funding be incorporated into the President's Budget. The Federal spending estimates in this analysis utilize funding and programmatic information collected on the Executive Branch's cybersecurity efforts, including cybersecurity activities and funding for all Federal Agencies, not just those carried out by DHS and DOD.

Agencies provide funding data at a level of detail suf-ficient to consolidate information to determine total governmental spending on cybersecurity. OMB provided the following guidance to agencies regarding the reporting of cybersecurity budget information for each fiscal year (FY): FY 2019 Actual levels should reflect the actual bud-getary resources available for that year, FY 2020 Estimate levels should reflect the estimated budgetary resources

available that year, and FY 2021 levels should reflect the President's Budget. Agencies were directed to coordinate responses between their Chief Financial Officers, Chief Information Officers, and Chief Information Security Officers.

Cybersecurity Workforce

FISMA requires every Federal Agency to protect its information and information systems against an ever-changing array of cybersecurity threats. The Federal cybersecurity workforce is responsible for staying abreast of the latest threat intelligence, developing new and inno-vative ways to protect Federal information resources, and administering the tools that identify and protect against cyber attacks. However, the Federal Government is not alone in needing to protect and defend against these threats, and the demand for cyber professionals through-out the American economy exceeds the supply. This makes it critical for the Government to continue investing in new ways to recruit and retain cybersecurity talent. These challenges are addressed in both the Administration's "Delivering Government Solutions in the 21st Century" paper on "Solving the Federal Cybersecurity Workforce Shortage," as well as as well as Executive Order 13800 on America's Cybersecurity Workforce.

Over the last year, the Administration has seen success in programs like the Federal Cybersecurity Reskilling Academy, which showed that agencies can reskill exist-ing employees to fill critically needed skills gaps. The Administration also piloted a new hiring process that will allow agencies to better evaluate the capabilities of applicants to highly technical positions, such as in the cybersecurity field, accelerating the hiring process and improving agencies' ability to find and hire the best can-didates. These types of programs are the innovative work that the Federal Government needs to remain a competi-tive employer for our highest-need skillsets.

The President's Budget continues to build on these successes, investing in additional reskilling, as well as professional development for the existing cybersecu-rity workforce. Through centralized programs at the Cybersecurity and Infrastructure Security Agency de-signed to benefit all agencies, as well as making targeted investments in individual agencies' workforce budgets, the Administration is committed to an enterprise-wide effort to build a workforce to protect and defend the Government's information assets. There are multiple programs across agencies which address recruitment, retention, reskilling, and overall advancement of cyber skills in the American workforce. The 2021 Budget also supports efforts to develop technical skills within the na-tional workforce through educational programs, science and technology research, and grants to STEM fields.

Federal Budget Authority

The President's Budget includes $18.8 billion of budget authority for cybersecurity-related activities, consistent with the 2020 estimate. Due to the sensitive nature of some activities, this amount does not represent the entire cyber budget.

Agencies estimated cybersecurity budget authority for 2021 reflects planned investments to protect information and information systems commensurate with the risk and magnitude of potential harm. However, a number of agencies also have cybersecurity-related spending that is not dedicated to the protection of their own networks, serving instead a broader cybersecurity mission. For instance, there are a number of programs that provide tools and capabilities Government-wide, such as DHS's Continuous Diagnostics and Mitigation (CDM) program. Additionally, numerous programs exist that further enhance national and Federal cybersecurity focused on areas such as standards, research, and the investigation of cyber-crimes rather than specific technical capabilities.

Table 19-1 provides an overview of civilian CFO Act Agency cybersecurity spending as aligned to the NIST Cybersecurity Framework functions, Identify, Protect, Detect, Respond, and Recover. Table 19-2 provides an agency level view of cybersecurity spending.

Table 19–1. NIST FRAMEWORK FUNCTION CIVILIAN CFO ACT AGENCY FUNDING TOTALS
(In millions of dollars)

NIST Framework Function	FY 2021
Identify	2,461
Protect	2,740
Detect	918
Respond	2,189
Recover	206
Total	**8,514**

Note: This analysis excludes Department of Defense spending.

Non-Federal Cybersecurity Spending

While it is difficult to estimate how much the U.S. private sector spends on cybersecurity, the research firm Gartner releases routine estimates of cybersecurity spending globally and forecasts that cybersecurity spending is anticipated to reach $170.4 billion in 2022.[4] The International Data Corporation predicts that information security spending would increase worldwide by 10.7 percent in 2019 to $106.6 billion, forecasting that it could reach an estimated $151.2 billion in 2023.[5]

Additional Information

The President's Budget is also required to include an analysis of fee-based cybersecurity costs as well as gross and net appropriations or obligational authority and outlays. Agencies have not historically reported their cybersecurity budgets in this manner, and OMB continues to work with the broader Federal community to capture this information in a way that is helpful to both agencies and the Congress.

[4] Source: Gartner, "Forecast Analysis: Information Security, Worldwide, 2Q18 Update," September 14, 2018, at *https://www.gartner.com/en/documents/3889055*.

[5] Source: International Data Corporation, "New IDC Spending Guide Sees Solid Growth Ahead for Security Products and Services," October 16, 2019, at *https://www.idc.com/getdoc.jsp?containerId=prUS45591619*.

Table 19–2. CYBERSECURITY FUNDING BY AGENCY
(In millions of dollars)

Organization	FY 2019	FY 2020	FY 2021
CFO Act Agencies	**$16,552.7**	**$18,398.1**	**$18,360.4**
Department of Agriculture	$208.2	$231.2	$230.1
Department of Commerce	$446.4	$514.3	$378.1
Department of Defense	$8,527.0	$10,075.0	$9,846.0
Department of Education	$119.0	$166.2	$162.6
Department of Energy	$578.4	$550.4	$665.6
Department of Health and Human Services	$512.5	$475.7	$519.4
Department of Homeland Security	$2,590.8	$2,574.1	$2,604.3
Department of Housing and Urban Development	$60.8	$68.2	$69.0
Department of Justice	$837.2	$900.5	$929.2
Department of Labor	$86.6	$92.2	$89.1
Department of State	$381.5	$405.8	$488.6
Department of the Interior	$103.8	$121.4	$133.3
Department of the Treasury	$510.8	$588.4	$688.8
Department of Transportation	$216.4	$262.1	$249.2
Department of Veterans Affairs	$491.7	$524.6	$460.4
Environmental Protection Agency	$42.1	$32.5	$46.8
General Services Administration	$72.6	$82.4	$79.2
National Aeronautics and Space Administration	$167.6	$166.6	$163.8
National Science Foundation	$246.4	$226.3	$212.0
Nuclear Regulatory Commission	$28.8	$27.5	$26.9
Office of Personnel Management	$40.9	$47.1	$53.8
Small Business Administration	$16.3	$15.7	$16.1
Social Security Administration	$204.0	$207.6	$205.0
U.S. Agency for International Development	$62.6	$42.5	$43.3
Non-CFO Act Agencies	**$384.3**	**$393.6**	**$418.4**
Access Board	$0.8	$0.6	$0.6
American Battle Monuments Commission	$0.4	$0.8	$1.3
Armed Forces Retirement Home	$0.3	$0.3	$0.3
Chemical Safety and Hazard Investigation Board	$0.8	$0.8	$2.7
Commission on Civil Rights	$0.4	$0.4	$0.5
Commodity Futures Trading Commission	$7.6	$10.8	$11.0
Consumer Product Safety Commission	$3.0	$2.9	$4.3
Corporation for National and Community Service	$3.0	$3.2	$3.2
Council of the Inspectors General on Integrity and Efficiency	$0.6	$0.6	$0.6
Court Services and Offender Supervision Agency for the District	$3.4	$3.5	$3.5
Defense Nuclear Facilities Safety Board	$1.8	$2.3	$2.3
Equal Employment Opportunity Commission	$4.0	$3.9	$2.5
Export-Import Bank of the United States	$3.4	$3.1	$3.2
Farm Credit Administration	$3.0	$3.3	$3.5
Federal Communications Commission	$15.3	$12.0	$13.9
Federal Deposit Insurance Corporation	$109.8	$109.8	$109.8
Federal Election Commission	$1.0	$1.0	$1.0
Federal Financial Institutions Examination Council	$0.1	$0.1	$0.1
Federal Labor Relations Authority	*	*	*
Federal Maritime Commission	$0.1	$0.1	$0.2
Federal Retirement Thrift Investment Board	$66.2	$66.1	$77.4
Federal Trade Commission	$11.4	$12.3	$12.6
Gulf Coast Ecosystem Restoration Council	$0.2	$0.2	$0.2
Institute of Museum and Library Services	$0.3	$0.3	$0.3
International Assistance Programs	$16.7	$17.6	$17.6
African Development Foundation	$1.0	$1.0	$1.0
Inter-American Foundation	$0.4	$0.4	$0.4
Millennium Challenge Corporation	$1.6	$1.7	$1.5
Overseas Private Investment Corporation	$1.7	$2.0	$2.3
Peace Corps	$10.9	$11.2	$11.2

Table 19–2. CYBERSECURITY FUNDING BY AGENCY—Continued

(In millions of dollars)

Organization	FY 2019	FY 2020	FY 2021
Trade and Development Agency	$1.1	$1.3	$1.3
International Trade Commission	$3.0	$4.2	$5.4
Marine Mammal Commission	$0.1	$0.1	$0.1
Merit Systems Protection Board	$0.2	$1.0	$1.0
Morris K. Udall and Stewart L. Udall Foundation	*	*	*
National Archives and Records Administration	$9.7	$7.7	$7.8
National Credit Union Administration	$6.7	$7.4	$7.3
National Endowment for the Arts	$2.2	$1.6	$1.4
National Endowment for the Humanities	$1.1	$1.1	$1.1
National Gallery of Art	$2.0	$2.0	$2.0
National Labor Relations Board	$2.1	$2.2	$2.3
National Transportation Safety Board	$1.0	$1.5	$1.5
Nuclear Waste Technical Review Board	$0.3	$0.3	$0.3
Occupational Safety and Health Review Commission	$1.3	$1.3	$1.3
Office of Government Ethics	$0.3	$0.4	$0.4
Office of Special Counsel	$0.3	$0.3	$0.4
Postal Regulatory Commission	$0.2	$0.6	$0.7
Presidio Trust	$0.7	$0.7	$0.7
Privacy and Civil Liberties Oversight Board	$1.4	$1.4	$1.4
Securities and Exchange Commission	$38.3	$41.8	$46.6
Selective Service System	$4.1	$2.5	$2.0
Smithsonian Institution	$7.8	$8.7	$10.3
Surface Transportation Board	$1.8	$0.9	$0.9
Tennessee Valley Authority	$21.0	$21.6	$21.6
U.S. Agency for Global Media	$8.1	$7.9	$7.3
U.S. Army Corps of Engineers	$15.2	$18.8	$20.3
United States Holocaust Memorial Museum	$1.4	$1.6	$1.7
United States Institute of Peace	$0.3	$0.3	$0.3
Total	**$16,936.9**	**$18,791.6**	**$18,778.8**

* $50 thousand or less

20. FEDERAL DRUG CONTROL FUNDING

The 2021 Budget supports $35.7 billion for National Drug Control Program agencies to implement the Administration's drug control policies. The funding requested by each Department and agency in the National Drug Control Program is included in the table below.

Table 20–1.   DRUG CONTROL FUNDING FY 2019—FY 2021

(Dollars in millions)

Department/Agency	FY 2019 Final	FY 2020 Enacted	FY 2021 President's Budget
Department of Agriculture:			
U.S. Forest Service	14.800	14.800	14.800
Office of Rural Development	16.000	0.000	6.200
Total USDA	**30.800**	**14.800**	**21.000**
Court Services and Offender Supervision Agency for D.C.	**53.367**	**49.310**	**56.213**
Department of Defense:			
Defense Security Cooperation Agency [1]	167.805	173.661	173.661
Drug Interdiction and Counterdrug Activities (incl. OPTEMPO, and OCO) [2,3]	3,602.513	1,140.159	865.509
Defense Health Program	75.431	99.766	89.744
Total DOD	**3,845.749**	**1,413.586**	**1,128.914**
Department of Education:			
Office of Elementary and Secondary Education [4]	**57.547**	**58.759**	**100.000**
Federal Judiciary:	**1,129.049**	**1,179.874**	**1,230.404**
Department of Health and Human Services:			
Administration for Children and Families	40.000	30.000	60.000
Centers for Disease Control and Prevention (incl. DFC in FY 2021) [5]	475.579	475.579	575.579
Centers for Medicare and Medicaid Services	8,160.000	8,550.000	9,020.000
Health Resources and Services Administration	665.000	655.000	655.000
Indian Health Service	117.447	118.533	118.007
National Institute on Alcohol Abuse and Alcoholism	57.570	59.919	54.508
National Institute on Drug Abuse	1,408.216	1,457.724	1,431.770
Substance Abuse and Mental Health Services Administration [6]	4,140.271	4,158.346	4,003.328
Total HHS	**15,064.083**	**15,505.101**	**15,918.192**
Department of Homeland Security:			
Customs and Border Protection	3,566.169	3,761.469	3,447.641
Federal Emergency Management Agency	13.500	13.500	5.864
Federal Law Enforcement Training Center	50.665	54.760	57.336
Immigration and Customs Enforcement	560.797	598.529	673.889
U.S. Coast Guard	1,559.671	1,836.755	1,825.839
Total DHS	**5,750.802**	**6,265.013**	**6,010.569**
Department of Housing and Urban Development:			
Office of Community Planning and Development	**544.968**	**575.360**	**576.752**
Department of the Interior:			
Bureau of Indian Affairs	17.966	17.966	17.966
Bureau of Land Management	5.100	5.100	5.100
National Park Service	3.450	3.450	3.187
Total DOI	**26.516**	**26.516**	**26.253**
Department of Justice:			
Assets Forfeiture Fund	222.760	236.313	243.235
Bureau of Prisons	3,527.527	3,600.605	3,592.583
Criminal Division	37.989	42.573	44.795

Table 20–1.   DRUG CONTROL FUNDING FY 2019—FY 2021—Continued

(Dollars in millions)

Department/Agency	FY 2019 Final	FY 2020 Enacted	FY 2021 President's Budget
Drug Enforcement Administration (incl. HIDTA in FY 2021) [7]	2,661.117	2,702.646	3,113.304
Organized Crime Drug Enforcement Task Forces	560.000	550.458	585.145
Office of Justice Programs	510.350	551.692	429.743
U.S. Attorneys	81.389	89.164	94.854
United States Marshals Service	851.391	875.673	932.970
Total DOJ	**8,452.523**	**8,649.124**	**9,036.629**
Department of Labor:			
Employment and Training Administration	6.000	26.000	26.000
Office of Workers' Compensation Programs	7.769	7.769	7.769
Total DOL	**13.769**	**33.769**	**33.769**
Office of National Drug Control Policy:			
Operations	18.400	18.400	16.400
High Intensity Drug Trafficking Areas Program [7]	280.000	285.000	0.000
Other Federal Drug Control Programs [5]	118.327	121.715	12.432
Total ONDCP	**416.727**	**425.115**	**28.832**
Department of State: [8]			
Bureau of International Narcotics and Law Enforcement Affairs	412.537	381.595	441.358
United States Agency for International Development	78.500	70.518	79.000
Total DOS	**491.037**	**452.113**	**520.358**
Department of the Transportation:			
Federal Aviation Administration	32.256	35.435	38.035
National Highway Traffic Safety Administration	18.919	6.700	6.700
Total DOT	**51.175**	**42.135**	**44.735**
Department of the Treasury:			
Internal Revenue Service	**61.833**	**60.257**	**60.257**
Department of Veterans Affairs:			
Veterans Health Administration	**818.318**	**850.595**	**902.988**
Total Federal Drug Budget [9]	**$36,808.263**	**$35,601.427**	**$35,695.865**

[1] Due to the Defense Wide Review, FY 2021 estimates were not available. The FY 2020 level was used as an estimated baseline for FY 2021.

[2] FY 2019 includes $2.5 billion reprogrammed from other DOD programs for barrier construction to block drug smuggling corridors along the U.S. southwest border in support of the Department of Homeland Security (DHS) under 10 U.S.C. §284(b)(7).

[3] The FY 2021 request does not include any OCO funding for the Drug Interdiction and Counter-Drug Activities, Defense account.

[4] The Administration estimates that approximately .5 percent of the total funding for Elementary and Secondary Education's Disadvantaged Block Grant proposed in the FY 2021 Budget. It is not meant to indicate an amount of funding required by the Department of Education to be committed to drug prevention programming by State or Local Education Authorities. In the out-years, ONDCP will work the Department to refine the estimate.

[5] The FY 2021 funding level for CDC includes $100 million for the Drug-Free Communities (DFC) program. For FY 2019 and FY 2020, DFC is included under the Office of National Drug Control Policy heading.

[6] Includes budget authority and funding through evaluation set-aside authorized by Section 241 of the Public Health Service (PHS) Act.

[7] The FY 2021 funding level for DEA includes $254 million for the High Intensity Drug Trafficking Areas (HIDTA) program. For FY 2019 and FY 2020, HIDTA is included under the Office of National Drug Control Policy heading.

[8] Funding for FY 2020 and FY 2021 is a mechanical calculation that does not reflect decisions on funding priorities.

[9] Detail may not sum to total due to rounding.

TECHNICAL BUDGET ANALYSES

21. CURRENT SERVICES ESTIMATES

Current services, or "baseline," estimates are designed to provide a benchmark against which Budget proposals can be measured. A baseline is not a prediction of the final outcome of the annual budget process, nor is it a proposed budget. It can be a useful tool in budgeting, however. It can be used as a benchmark against which to measure the magnitude of the policy changes in the President's Budget or other budget proposals, and it can also be used to warn of future problems if policy is not changed, either for the Government's overall fiscal health or for individual tax and spending programs.

Ideally, a current services baseline would provide a projection of estimated receipts, outlays, deficits or surpluses, and budget authority reflecting this year's enacted policies and programs for each year in the future. Defining this baseline is challenging because funding for many programs in operation today expires within the 10-year budget window. Most significantly, funding for discretionary programs is provided one year at a time in annual appropriations acts. Mandatory programs are not generally subject to annual appropriations, but many operate under multiyear authorizations that expire within the budget window. The framework used to construct the baseline must address whether and how to project

forward the funding for these programs beyond their scheduled expiration dates.

Since the early 1970s, when the first requirements for the calculation of a "current services" baseline were enacted, OMB has constructed the baseline using a variety of concepts and measures. Throughout the 1990s, OMB calculated the baseline using a detailed set of rules in the Balanced Budget and Emergency Deficit Control Act of 1985 (BBEDCA), as amended by the Budget Enforcement Act of 1990 (BEA; P.L. 101-508). Although BBEDCA's baseline rules lapsed for a period when the enforcement provisions of the BEA expired in 2002, budget practitioners continued to adhere to them. The Budget Control Act of 2011 (BCA; P.L. 112-25) formally reinstated the BEA's baseline rules.

The Administration believes adjustments to the BBEDCA baseline are needed to better represent the deficit outlook under current policy and to serve as a more appropriate benchmark against which to measure policy changes. These adjustments allow the baseline to provide a more realistic outlook for tax receipts than a baseline following the BBEDCA rules. These baseline adjustments are discussed in more detail below. Table 21–1 shows estimates of receipts, outlays, and deficits under

Table 21–1. CATEGORY TOTALS FOR THE ADJUSTED BASELINE
(In billions of dollars)

	2019	2020	2021	2022	2023	2024	2025	2026	2027	2028	2029	2030
Receipts	3,464	3,706	3,860	4,083	4,350	4,642	4,904	5,158	5,427	5,731	6,027	6,346
Outlays:												
Discretionary:												
Defense	676	713	753	769	782	797	812	829	850	870	891	913
Non-defense	661	724	733	748	758	774	784	801	816	835	853	873
Subtotal, discretionary	1,338	1,438	1,486	1,516	1,541	1,571	1,596	1,630	1,665	1,705	1,744	1,786
Mandatory:												
Social Security	1,038	1,092	1,151	1,217	1,287	1,362	1,442	1,526	1,615	1,709	1,807	1,909
Medicare	644	694	746	828	847	864	973	1,043	1,114	1,273	1,222	1,399
Medicaid and CHIP	427	465	468	490	519	545	575	614	649	687	731	769
Other mandatory	626	726	644	677	681	682	721	767	790	850	830	899
Subtotal, mandatory	2,735	2,977	3,010	3,212	3,334	3,453	3,711	3,950	4,168	4,520	4,590	4,976
Net interest	375	376	379	401	434	469	518	575	633	686	731	775
Total, outlays	4,448	4,791	4,875	5,130	5,308	5,493	5,826	6,154	6,466	6,911	7,065	7,538
Unified deficit(+)/surplus(-)	984	1,085	1,014	1,047	958	851	922	997	1,039	1,180	1,038	1,192
On-budget	(992)	(1,092)	(1,006)	(1,025)	(919)	(799)	(852)	(922)	(949)	(1,082)	(917)	(1,052)
Off-budget	(–8)	(–7)	(8)	(22)	(39)	(53)	(69)	(74)	(90)	(99)	(121)	(140)
Memorandum:												
BBEDCA baseline deficit	984	1,085	1,014	1,047	958	851	904	836	761	871	705	836
Extension of expiring tax provisions	....	....	....	....	....	....	17	158	270	294	309	323
Related debt service	....	....	....	....	....	....	*	2	8	16	24	34
Adjusted baseline deficit	984	1,085	1,014	1,047	958	851	922	997	1,039	1,180	1,038	1,192

*Less than $500 million.

the Administration's adjusted baseline for 2019 through 2030.[1] The table also shows the Administration's estimates by major component of the budget. The estimates are based on the economic assumptions underlying the Budget, which, as discussed later in this chapter, were developed on the assumption that the Administration's budget proposals will be enacted. OMB maintains a memorandum bank to detail the adjustments made to the BBEDCA baseline to produce this adjusted baseline.

Conceptual Basis for Estimates

Receipts and outlays are divided into two categories that are important for calculating the baseline: those controlled by authorizing legislation (receipts and direct or mandatory spending) and those controlled through the annual appropriations process (discretionary spending). Different estimating rules apply to each category.

Direct spending and receipts.—Direct spending includes the major entitlement programs, such as Social Security, Medicare, Medicaid, Federal employee retirement, unemployment compensation, and the Supplemental Nutrition Assistance Program (SNAP). It also includes such programs as deposit insurance and farm price and income supports, where the Government is legally obligated to make payments under certain conditions. Taxes and other receipts are like direct spending in that they involve ongoing activities that generally operate under permanent or long-standing authority, and the underlying statutes generally specify the tax rates or benefit levels that must be collected or paid, and who must pay or who is eligible to receive benefits.

The baseline generally—but not always—assumes that receipts and direct spending programs continue in the future as specified by current law. The budgetary effects of anticipated regulatory and administrative actions that are permissible under current law are also reflected in the estimates. BBEDCA requires several exemptions to this general rule, and the Administration's adjusted baseline also provides exceptions to produce a more realistic deficit outlook. Exceptions in BBEDCA and the Administration's adjusted baseline are described below:

- Expiring excise taxes dedicated to a trust fund are assumed to be extended at the rates in effect at the time of expiration. During the projection period of 2020 through 2030, the taxes affected by this exception are:
  - taxes deposited in the Airport and Airway Trust Fund, which expire on September 30, 2023;
  - taxes deposited in the Oil Spill Liability Trust Fund, which expire on December 31, 2020;
  - taxes deposited in the Patient-Centered Outcomes Research Trust Fund, which expire on September 30, 2029;

  - taxes deposited in the Sport Fish Restoration and Boating Resources Trust Fund, which expire on September 30, 2020; and
  - taxes deposited in the Highway Trust Fund and the Leaking Underground Storage Tank Trust Fund, which expire on September 30, 2022.

- While BBEDCA requires the extension of trust fund excise taxes, it otherwise bases the receipt estimates on current law. Individual income tax and estate tax provisions of the recently enacted Tax Cuts and Jobs Act that expire after tax year 2025 are assumed to expire according to current law in the BBEDCA baseline. However, the Administration's adjusted baseline extends these provisions permanently. This results in a more realistic outlook for receipts and the deficit, reflecting the likely extension of these provisions.

- Expiring authorizations for direct spending programs that were enacted on or before the date of enactment of the Balanced Budget Act of 1997 are assumed to be extended if their current year outlays exceed $50 million. For example, even though the Environmental Quality Incentives Program, which was authorized prior to the Balanced Budget Act of 1997, continues only through 2023 under current law, the baseline estimates assume continuation of this program through the projection period, because the program's current year outlays exceed the $50 million threshold.[2]

Discretionary spending.—Discretionary programs differ in one important aspect from direct spending programs: the Congress provides spending authority for almost all discretionary programs one year at a time. The spending authority is normally provided in the form of annual appropriations. Absent appropriations of additional funds in the future, discretionary programs would cease to operate after existing balances were spent. If the baseline were intended strictly to reflect current law, then a baseline would reflect only the expenditure of remaining balances from appropriations laws already enacted. Instead, the BBEDCA baseline provides a mechanical definition to reflect the continuing costs of discretionary programs. Under BBEDCA, the baseline estimates for discretionary programs in the current year are based on that year's enacted appropriations, or on the annualized levels provided by a continuing resolution if final full-year appropriations have not been enacted. For the budget year and beyond, the spending authority in the current year is adjusted for inflation, using specified inflation rates.[3] The definition attempts to keep discretionary spending for each program roughly level in real terms.

---

[1] The estimates are shown on a unified budget basis; i.e., the off-budget receipts and outlays of the Social Security trust funds and the Postal Service Fund are added to the on-budget receipts and outlays to calculate the unified budget totals.

[2] If enacted after the Balanced Budget Act of 1997 (P.L. 105-33), programs that are expressly temporary in nature expire in the baseline as provided by current law, even if their current year outlays exceed the $50 million threshold.

[3] The Administration's baseline uses the inflation rates for discretionary spending required by BBEDCA. This requirement results in an overcompensation in the calculation for Federal pay as a result of the calendar-year timing of Federal pay adjustments. Updating the calcula-

BBEDCA also imposes caps through 2021 on budget authority for the defense function and for the aggregate of the non-defense functions. These caps were initially established by the BCA, and subsequent legislation later amended the levels of the caps for each year. The most recent budget deal, the Bipartisan Budget Act of 2019 (BBA of 2019; P.L. 116–37), set new caps for 2020 and 2021, which are the last years for which caps were originally set in the BCA. The baseline includes allowances that bring the inflated baseline calculated for individual discretionary accounts to the level of the defense and non-defense caps for 2021. After 2021, these allowances assume that discretionary spending grows with inflation from the 2021 cap levels.

BBEDCA allows for adjustments to the discretionary caps for disaster relief spending, emergency requirements, Overseas Contingency Operations (OCO), wildfire suppression, certain program integrity activities, and the 2020 Census. The adjustments are permitted provided that such funding is designated in legislation by the Congress and, where appropriate, subsequently so by the President. Current adjustments include the following:

- Disaster relief, emergency requirements, and wildfire suppression.—The BBEDCA baseline projects forward $17.5 billion of funding designated for disaster relief pursuant to Stafford Act declarations for the Department of Homeland Security and the Small Business Administration in 2020. While this funding is increased thereafter by the BBEDCA inflation rates, an allowance is included to reduce the funding stream to the projected funding ceiling for 2021 that is determined for such appropriations by a formula included in BBEDCA. The baseline also inflates a net $8.5 billion of enacted emergency funding provided mostly to the Departments of Defense and Health and Human Services for expenses related to disaster relief, including from recent major hurricanes, flooding, and earthquakes occurring in 2019 as well as for procurement of Ebola medical countermeasures. Finally, the baseline also includes the nearly $2.3 billion provided in the 2020 Interior and Environment Appropriations Act for wildfire suppression activities at the Departments of Agriculture (Forest Service) and the Interior. The wildfire suppression amounts are inflated at the BBEDCA inflation rates.

- OCO.—The BBEDCA baseline reflects the $79.5 billion level of OCO appropriations enacted in the 2020 appropriations Acts inflated at the BBEDCA inflation rates.

- Program integrity activities.—The baseline assumes enacted levels provided in the 2020 Labor, HHS, and Education Appropriations Act for the program integrity cap adjustments authorized in BBEDCA through 2021, and inflates those amounts after the cap adjustments expire in 2021. Additionally, the baseline assumes savings in mandatory benefit pay-

ments from enacting the program integrity cap adjustments at their full levels after 2020.

- 2020 Census.—The BBA of 2019 created a new cap adjustment for any appropriation provided for the Periodic Censuses and Programs account in the Bureau of the Census for the 2020 Census. The adjustment is limited to $2.5 billion and is for 2020 only. The 2020 Commerce, Justice, and Science Appropriations Act provided the $2.5 billion adjustment for 2020 and the baseline inflates this amount at BBEDCA inflation rates. However, since the cap adjustment was only for 2020, the baseline counts the inflated amount toward the non-defense cap in 2021.

In addition to the cap adjustments specified in BBEDCA, the 21st Century Cures Act permitted funds to be appropriated each year and not count toward the discretionary caps so long as the appropriations were specified for the authorized purposes. These amounts are included in the baseline outside of the discretionary cap totals and adjusted for inflation in the budget year and beyond.

Joint Committee Enforcement.—The Joint Select Committee process under the BCA stipulated that, absent intervening legislation, enforcement procedures would be invoked annually through 2021 to reduce the levels of discretionary and mandatory spending to accomplish certain deficit reduction. The BBEDCA baseline includes the effects of the across-the-board reductions ("sequestration") already invoked by Joint Committee sequestration orders for 2013 through 2020, as well as the sequestration order for mandatory spending for 2021 issued with the transmittal of the 2021 Budget.[4] As required by current law, the BBEDCA baseline also includes the extension of sequestration of mandatory spending through 2029 at the rate required for 2021.[5] For discretionary programs, there is no longer any adjustment required under current law for Joint Committee enforcement as the BBA of 2019 effectively cancelled any discretionary cap reductions that would have taken effect in 2021.

Economic Assumptions

As discussed above, an important purpose of the baseline is to serve as a benchmark against which policy proposals are measured. By convention, the President's Budget constructs baseline and policy estimates under the same set of economic and technical assumptions.

---

tion to address this annual timing discrepancy would have only a small effect on the discretionary baseline.

[4] The effects of past sequestration reductions are reflected in the detailed schedules for the affected budget accounts, while the 2021 reductions are reflected in allowance accounts due to the timing of the preparation of the detailed budget estimates and the issuance of the 2021 sequestration order. See Chapter 10, "Budget Process," of this volume for a more thorough discussion of the Joint Committee sequestration procedures.

[5] Since enactment of the BCA, the Congress has extended sequestration of mandatory spending through a series of amendments to section 251A of BBEDCA (2 U.S.C. 901a). Most recently, the Bipartisan Budget Act of 2019 (P.L. 116–37) extended it through 2029. This legislation also specified, for 2029, that spending for the Medicare program should be reduced by 4.0 percent for the first half of the sequestration period and zero for the second half.

Table 21–2.   SUMMARY OF ECONOMIC ASSUMPTIONS

(Fiscal years; in billions of dollars)

	2019	2020	2021	2022	2023	2024	2025	2026	2027	2028	2029	2030
Gross Domestic Product (GDP):												
Levels, in billions of dollars:												
Current dollars	21,216	22,211	23,353	24,543	25,791	27,104	28,473	29,884	31,343	32,875	34,480	36,164
Real, chained (2012) dollars	18,961	19,469	20,069	20,675	21,299	21,942	22,597	23,248	23,904	24,578	25,271	25,984
Percent change, year over year:												
Current dollars	4.3	4.7	5.1	5.1	5.1	5.1	5.0	5.0	4.9	4.9	4.9	4.9
Real, chained (2012) dollars	2.4	2.7	3.1	3.0	3.0	3.0	3.0	2.9	2.8	2.8	2.8	2.8
Inflation measures (percent change, year over year):												
GDP chained price index	1.9	2.0	2.0	2.0	2.0	2.0	2.0	2.0	2.0	2.0	2.0	2.0
Consumer price index (all urban)	1.9	2.2	2.3	2.3	2.3	2.3	2.3	2.3	2.3	2.3	2.3	2.3
Unemployment rate, civilian (percent)	3.7	3.5	3.6	3.8	3.9	4.0	4.0	4.0	4.0	4.0	4.0	4.0
Interest rates (percent):												
91-day Treasury bills	2.1	1.4	1.5	1.5	1.6	1.7	2.0	2.2	2.4	2.5	2.5	2.5
10-year Treasury notes	2.2	2.0	2.2	2.5	2.7	3.0	3.1	3.1	3.1	3.2	3.2	3.2
MEMORANDUM:												
Related program assumptions:												
Automatic benefit increases (percent):												
Social security and veterans pensions	2.8	1.6	2.4	2.3	2.3	2.3	2.3	2.3	2.3	2.3	2.3	2.3
Federal employee retirement	2.8	1.6	2.4	2.3	2.3	2.3	2.3	2.3	2.3	2.3	2.3	2.3
Supplemental Nutrition Assistance Program	....	....	1.3	2.2	2.3	2.3	2.3	2.3	2.3	2.3	2.3	2.3
Insured unemployment rate	1.2	1.1	1.2	1.2	1.2	1.2	1.2	1.2	1.2	1.2	1.2	1.2

These assumptions are developed on the basis that the President's Budget proposals will be enacted.

While this estimating approach has the virtue of simplicity, it offers an incomplete view of the effects of proposals, because it fails to capture the fact that the economy and the budget interact. Government tax and spending policies can influence prices, economic growth, consumption, savings, and investment. In turn, changes in economic conditions due to the enactment of proposals affect tax receipts and spending, including for unemployment benefits, entitlement payments that receive automatic cost-of-living adjustments (COLAs), income support programs for low-income individuals, and interest on the Federal debt.

Because of these interactions, it would be reasonable, from an economic perspective, to assume different economic paths for the baseline projection and the President's Budget. However, this would greatly complicate the process of producing the Budget, which normally includes a large number of proposals that could have potential economic feedback effects. Agencies would have to produce two sets of estimates for programs sensitive to economic assumptions even if those programs were not directly affected by any proposal in the Budget. Using different economic assumptions for baseline and policy estimates would also diminish the value of the baseline estimates as a benchmark for measuring proposed policy changes, because it would be difficult to separate the effects of proposed policy changes from the effects of different economic assumptions. Using the same economic assumptions for the baseline and the President's Budget eliminates this potential source of confusion.

The economic assumptions underlying the Budget and the Administration's baseline are summarized in Table 21–2. The economic outlook underlying these assumptions is discussed in greater detail in Chapter 2 of this volume.

Major Programmatic Assumptions

A number of programmatic assumptions must be made to calculate the baseline estimates. These include assumptions about annual cost-of-living adjustments in the indexed programs and the number of beneficiaries who will receive payments from the major benefit programs. Assumptions about various automatic cost-of-living-adjustments are shown in Table 21–2, and assumptions about baseline caseload projections for the major benefit programs are shown in Table 21–3. These assumptions affect baseline estimates of direct spending for each of these programs, and they also affect estimates of the discretionary baseline for a limited number of programs. For the administrative expenses for Medicare, Railroad Retirement, and unemployment insurance, the discretionary baseline is increased (or decreased) for changes in the number of beneficiaries in addition to the adjustments for inflation described earlier. Although these adjustments are applied at the account level, they have no effect in the aggregate because discretionary baseline levels are constrained to the BBEDCA caps.

It is also necessary to make assumptions about the continuation of expiring programs and provisions. As explained above, in the baseline estimates provided here, expiring excise taxes dedicated to a trust fund

Table 21–3. BASELINE BENEFICIARY PROJECTIONS FOR MAJOR BENEFIT PROGRAMS
(Annual average, in thousands)

	Actual 2019	Estimate										
		2020	2021	2022	2023	2024	2025	2026	2027	2028	2029	2030
Farmers receiving Federal payments	1,470	1,465	1,460	1,455	1,450	1,445	1,440	1,435	1,430	1,425	1,420	1,415
Federal direct student loans	7,825	7,927	7,987	8,072	8,153	8,243	8,315	8,366	8,407	8,435	8,465	8,493
Federal Pell Grants	6,673	6,834	6,975	7,117	7,276	7,427	7,582	7,744	7,905	8,102	8,259	8,427
Medicaid/Children's Health Insurance Program [1]	79,589	79,347	79,157	79,277	81,419	82,106	82,848	83,587	84,234	84,991	85,024	85,529
Medicare-eligible military retiree health benefits	2,438	2,461	2,482	2,505	2,524	2,549	2,576	2,601	2,623	2,643	2,656	2,656
Medicare [2]:												
Hospital insurance	60,616	61,954	63,484	65,148	66,797	68,410	70,049	71,682	73,258	74,774	76,202	77,508
Supplementary medical insurance:												
Part B	55,925	57,164	58,653	60,251	61,840	63,404	64,973	66,529	68,045	69,501	70,897	72,178
Part D	46,851	48,185	49,583	51,079	52,558	53,981	55,386	56,743	58,048	59,308	60,502	61,601
Prescription Drug Plans and Medicare:												
Advantage Prescription Drug Plans	45,431	46,907	48,461	50,108	51,606	53,006	54,387	55,720	57,002	58,239	59,412	60,491
Retiree Drug Subsidy	1,421	1,278	1,122	971	952	975	999	1,023	1,046	1,069	1,090	1,110
Managed Care Enrollment [3]	22,530	24,165	25,417	26,404	27,268	28,154	29,056	29,941	30,791	31,601	32,366	33,073
Railroad retirement	507	501	494	488	480	473	466	458	451	444	437	430
Federal civil service retirement	2,723	2,751	2,778	2,805	2,831	2,852	2,873	2,895	2,917	2,938	2,958	2,976
Military retirement	2,321	2,332	2,342	2,352	2,360	2,388	2,392	2,394	2,396	2,394	2,391	2,388
Unemployment insurance	5,132	5,054	5,449	5,624	5,781	5,885	5,953	5,997	6,022	6,046	6,065	6,080
Supplemental Nutrition Assistance Program	37,612	37,961	36,880	34,980	33,373	32,955	32,685	32,588	32,146	31,864	31,781	31,368
Child nutrition	34,717	35,140	35,567	35,929	36,225	36,526	36,831	37,139	37,451	37,768	38,089	38,410
Foster care, Adoption Assistance and Guardianship Assistance	704	795	867	984	1,083	1,186	1,302	1,422	1,552	1,694	1,852	2,006
Supplemental security income (SSI):												
Aged	1,114	1,112	1,112	1,116	1,123	1,135	1,151	1,168	1,184	1,200	1,216	1,231
Blind/disabled	6,842	6,811	6,763	6,741	6,738	6,745	6,759	6,769	6,777	6,789	6,804	6,824
Total, SSI	7,957	7,923	7,875	7,857	7,861	7,880	7,910	7,937	7,961	7,989	8,020	8,055
Child care and development fund [4]	2,198	2,293	2,391	2,344	2,332	2,157	2,052	1,991	1,934	1,877	1,822	1,770
Social security (OASDI):												
Old age and survivors insurance	53,100	54,520	55,867	57,232	58,643	60,103	61,535	62,941	64,327	65,803	67,201	68,501
Disability insurance	10,114	9,973	9,900	9,851	9,808	9,791	9,826	9,877	9,943	9,936	9,931	9,941
Total, OASDI	63,214	64,493	65,767	67,083	68,451	69,894	71,361	72,818	74,270	75,739	77,132	78,442
Veterans compensation:												
Veterans	4,852	5,089	5,268	5,426	5,579	5,729	5,875	6,016	6,151	6,282	6,408	6,531
Survivors (non-veterans)	430	443	456	471	488	506	526	547	570	593	618	643
Total, Veterans compensation	5,282	5,532	5,724	5,897	6,067	6,235	6,401	6,563	6,721	6,875	7,026	7,174
Veterans pensions:												
Veterans	248	237	231	228	226	226	228	230	231	233	234	236
Survivors (non-veterans)	185	167	161	159	160	161	161	162	163	164	165	166
Total, Veterans pensions	433	404	392	387	386	387	389	392	394	397	399	402

[1] Medicaid enrollment excludes territories.
[2] Medicare figures (Hospital Insurance, Part B, and Part D) do not sum to total Medicare enrollment due to enrollment in multiple programs.
[3] Enrollment figures include only beneficiaries who receive both Part A and Part B services through managed care.
[4] These levels include children served through CCDF (including TANF transfers) and through funds spent directly on child care in the Social Services Block Grant and TANF programs.

are extended at current rates. In general, mandatory programs with spending of at least $50 million in the current year are also assumed to continue, unless the programs are explicitly temporary in nature. Table 21–4, available at *https://www.whitehouse.gov/omb/analytical-perspectives/*, provides a listing of mandatory programs and taxes assumed to continue in the baseline after their expiration.[6] Many other important assump-

tions must be made in order to calculate the baseline estimates. These include the timing and content of regulations that will be issued over the projection period, the use of administrative discretion under current law, and other assumptions about the way programs operate, including administrative actions covered by Executive

and Afghanistan and other recurring international activities, are assumed to continue, and are therefore not presented in Table 21-4.

[6] All discretionary programs with enacted appropriations in the current year, including costs for overseas contingency operations in Iraq

Table 21–5.   RECEIPTS BY SOURCE IN THE PROJECTION OF ADJUSTED BASELINE

(In billions of dollars)

	2019 Actual	Estimate										
		2020	2021	2022	2023	2024	2025	2026	2027	2028	2029	2030
Individual income taxes	1,717.9	1,812.0	1,928.8	2,047.3	2,181.0	2,340.1	2,497.4	2,668.0	2,848.8	3,025.5	3,212.8	3,409.1
Corporation income taxes	230.2	263.7	284.4	324.0	382.2	426.0	447.3	434.7	430.4	442.7	445.7	452.9
Social insurance and retirement receipts	1,243.4	1,312.0	1,373.8	1,446.3	1,515.6	1,595.2	1,675.8	1,766.5	1,851.2	1,956.8	2,050.3	2,154.0
On-budget	(329.1)	(345.0)	(362.6)	(381.4)	(399.6)	(420.3)	(441.5)	(466.0)	(488.5)	(515.9)	(540.3)	(567.9)
Off-budget	(914.3)	(967.1)	(1,011.2)	(1,064.9)	(1,116.1)	(1,174.9)	(1,234.3)	(1,300.6)	(1,362.7)	(1,441.0)	(1,510.0)	(1,586.1)
Excise taxes	99.5	94.6	87.2	89.0	90.4	95.1	95.2	96.8	98.4	99.1	102.2	105.4
Estate and gift taxes	16.7	20.4	21.6	22.8	24.3	25.8	27.5	28.8	30.7	33.1	34.9	36.7
Customs duties	70.8	92.3	53.8	42.7	44.0	45.3	46.5	47.8	49.2	50.5	51.7	52.0
Miscellaneous receipts	85.8	111.3	110.7	110.4	112.2	114.2	114.1	115.1	118.2	123.0	129.0	135.7
Total, receipts	**3,464.2**	**3,706.4**	**3,860.4**	**4,082.7**	**4,349.6**	**4,641.7**	**4,903.9**	**5,157.8**	**5,426.9**	**5,730.6**	**6,026.8**	**6,345.8**
On-budget	(2,549.9)	(2,739.3)	(2,849.2)	(3,017.7)	(3,233.6)	(3,466.8)	(3,669.5)	(3,857.2)	(4,064.2)	(4,289.6)	(4,516.8)	(4,759.7)
Off-budget	(914.3)	(967.1)	(1,011.2)	(1,064.9)	(1,116.1)	(1,174.9)	(1,234.3)	(1,300.6)	(1,362.7)	(1,441.0)	(1,510.0)	(1,586.1)

Order 13893, "Increasing Government Accountability for Administrative Actions by Reinvigorating Administrative PAYGO" (2019). Table 21–4 lists many of these assumptions and their effects on the baseline estimates. The list is not intended to be exhaustive; the variety and complexity of Government programs are too great to provide a complete list. Instead, the table shows some of the more important assumptions.

Current Services Receipts, Outlays, and Budget Authority

Receipts.—Table 21–5 shows the Administration's baseline receipts by major source. Table 21–6 shows the scheduled increases in the Social Security taxable earnings base, which affect both payroll tax receipts for the program and the initial benefit levels for certain retirees.

Outlays.—Table 21–7 shows the growth from 2020 to 2021 and average annual growth over the five-year and ten-year periods for certain discretionary and major mandatory programs. Tables 21–8 and 21–9 show the Administration's baseline outlays by function and by agency, respectively. A more detailed presentation of these outlays (by function, category, subfunction, and program) is available on the internet as part of Table 21–12 at *https://www.whitehouse.gov/omb/analytical-perspectives/*.

Budget authority.—Tables 21–10 and 21–11 show estimates of budget authority in the Administration's baseline by function and by agency, respectively. A more detailed presentation of this budget authority with program-level estimates is also available on the internet as part of Table 21–12 at *https://www.whitehouse.gov/omb/analytical-perspectives/*.

Table 21–6.   EFFECT ON RECEIPTS OF CHANGES IN THE SOCIAL SECURITY TAXABLE EARNINGS BASE

(In billions of dollars)

	2021	2022	2023	2024	2025	2026	2027	2028	2029	2030
Social security (OASDI) taxable earnings base increases:										
$137,700 to $142,200 on Jan. 1, 2021	2.5	6.5	7.2	8.0	8.8	9.7	10.7	11.8	13.0	14.3
$142,200 to $147,900 on Jan. 1, 2022	....	3.4	8.5	9.4	10.3	11.4	12.6	13.9	15.3	16.9
$147,900 to $154,500 on Jan. 1, 2023	....	....	4.0	9.9	11.0	12.1	13.4	14.9	16.3	18.0
$154,500 to $162,000 on Jan. 1, 2024	....	....	....	4.5	11.4	12.5	13.8	15.4	16.9	18.7
$162,000 to $169,800 on Jan. 1, 2025	....	....	....	....	4.7	11.8	13.1	14.5	16.0	17.7
$169,800 to $177,600 on Jan. 1, 2026	....	....	....	....	....	4.7	11.9	13.2	14.5	16.0
$177,600 to $186,000 on Jan. 1, 2027	....	....	....	....	....	....	5.1	12.9	14.2	15.7
$186,000 to $194,700 on Jan. 1, 2028	....	....	....	....	....	....	....	5.4	13.4	14.8
$194,700 to $203,700 on Jan. 1, 2029	....	....	....	....	....	....	....	....	5.6	13.9
$203,700 to $213,300 on Jan. 1, 2030	....	....	....	....	....	....	....	....	....	6.0

Table 21–7. CHANGE IN OUTLAY ESTIMATES BY CATEGORY IN THE ADJUSTED BASELINE

(In billions of dollars)

	2020	2021	2022	2023	2024	2025	2026	2027	2028	2029	2030	Change 2020 to 2021 Amount	Change 2020 to 2021 Percent	Change 2020 to 2025 Amount	Change 2020 to 2025 Average annual rate	Change 2020 to 2030 Amount	Change 2020 to 2030 Average annual rate
Outlays:																	
Discretionary:																	
Defense	713	753	769	782	797	812	829	850	870	891	913	39	5.5%	98	2.6%	200	2.5%
Non-defense	724	733	748	758	774	784	801	816	835	853	873	8	1.2%	60	1.6%	149	1.9%
Subtotal, discretionary	1,438	1,486	1,516	1,541	1,571	1,596	1,630	1,665	1,705	1,744	1,786	48	3.3%	159	2.1%	349	2.2%
Mandatory:																	
Farm programs	30	21	20	21	19	19	19	18	18	18	18	–9	–30.2%	–11	–8.7%	–12	–5.1%
GSE support	–4	–7	–21	–21	–20	–19	–18	–18	–18	–18	–18	–3	67.9%	–15	35.3%	–14	15.4%
Medicaid	447	452	474	502	526	556	594	628	665	711	754	5	1.0%	109	4.4%	307	5.4%
Other health care	120	106	105	110	115	120	126	130	137	141	143	–14	–11.5%	*	0.1%	23	1.8%
Medicare	694	746	828	847	864	973	1,043	1,114	1,273	1,222	1,399	53	7.6%	279	7.0%	705	7.3%
Federal employee retirement and disability	155	160	171	171	171	182	187	192	204	197	208	5	3.3%	27	3.2%	53	3.0%
Unemployment compensation	27	29	31	33	35	37	38	40	42	44	46	2	7.3%	9	6.0%	19	5.3%
Other income security programs	272	277	284	286	287	293	311	315	329	328	338	4	1.6%	20	1.5%	66	2.2%
Social Security	1,092	1,151	1,217	1,287	1,362	1,442	1,526	1,615	1,709	1,807	1,909	60	5.5%	351	5.7%	818	5.7%
Veterans programs	125	135	154	154	152	176	186	197	224	204	233	10	8.4%	51	7.1%	108	6.4%
Other mandatory programs	126	73	65	61	61	63	66	66	70	71	83	–53	–41.9%	–64	–13.0%	–43	–4.1%
Undistributed offsetting receipts	–107	–134	–116	–117	–120	–129	–127	–130	–134	–137	–137	–27	25.3%	–22	3.9%	–30	2.5%
Subtotal, mandatory	2,977	3,010	3,212	3,334	3,453	3,711	3,950	4,168	4,520	4,590	4,976	33	1.1%	734	4.5%	2,000	5.3%
Net interest	376	379	401	434	469	518	575	633	686	731	775	3	0.9%	142	6.6%	399	7.5%
Total, outlays	4,791	4,875	5,130	5,308	5,493	5,826	6,154	6,466	6,911	7,065	7,538	84	1.7%	1,035	4.0%	2,747	4.6%

*Less than $500 million.

Table 21–8.   OUTLAYS BY FUNCTION IN THE ADJUSTED BASELINE

(In billions of dollars)

Function	2019 Actual	Estimate										
		2020	2021	2022	2023	2024	2025	2026	2027	2028	2029	2030
National Defense:												
Department of Defense—Military	654.0	689.6	729.0	746.3	759.0	773.2	786.9	803.4	823.7	843.7	864.0	885.1
Other	32.0	34.9	37.2	36.5	37.1	37.7	38.3	39.1	39.9	40.6	41.5	42.3
Total, National Defense	686.0	724.5	766.1	782.7	796.1	810.9	825.3	842.4	863.6	884.4	905.4	927.4
International Affairs	52.7	58.3	63.8	57.0	59.5	60.3	60.4	61.5	62.6	64.0	65.4	66.6
General Science, Space, and Technology	32.4	35.0	36.7	38.6	40.0	40.3	41.1	41.9	42.4	43.3	44.2	45.2
Energy	5.0	4.6	8.1	7.1	5.6	5.0	4.2	6.0	5.9	8.4	8.9	9.3
Natural Resources and Environment	37.8	42.8	47.4	51.5	51.6	53.3	51.8	52.2	52.7	53.6	54.5	55.3
Agriculture	38.3	38.3	28.9	28.5	29.5	27.4	27.3	27.1	26.8	27.2	27.0	27.1
Commerce and Housing Credit	−25.7	0.7	8.8	−1.7	−2.6	−0.2	3.3	6.5	7.6	8.1	9.1	9.7
On-Budget	(−24.6)	(0.6)	(7.6)	(−4.2)	(−3.6)	(−0.4)	(3.1)	(6.2)	(7.3)	(7.8)	(8.8)	(9.4)
Off-Budget	(−1.1)	(0.1)	(1.1)	(2.5)	(1.0)	(0.3)	(0.3)	(0.3)	(0.3)	(0.3)	(0.3)	(0.3)
Transportation	97.1	101.6	105.5	108.5	110.7	113.0	115.3	116.2	118.4	122.6	126.2	129.3
Community and Regional Development	26.9	30.3	36.3	44.5	39.2	41.9	40.4	41.5	39.6	39.8	38.6	39.2
Education, Training, Employment, and Social Services	136.8	195.5	122.0	120.9	127.6	131.5	135.7	138.7	141.8	144.6	147.2	149.9
Health	584.8	640.1	635.6	657.7	691.7	723.3	759.3	804.4	845.2	890.3	942.4	989.9
Medicare	651.0	699.3	752.7	835.3	854.9	872.3	981.5	1,051.1	1,123.1	1,282.0	1,231.2	1,408.8
Income Security	514.8	529.3	546.5	566.2	572.4	576.6	595.5	622.6	635.0	664.1	660.1	684.4
Social Security	1,044.4	1,097.2	1,157.0	1,223.3	1,293.4	1,369.3	1,449.2	1,533.3	1,622.0	1,717.0	1,815.4	1,917.3
On-Budget	(36.1)	(39.3)	(43.1)	(46.9)	(50.9)	(55.3)	(60.2)	(73.1)	(82.0)	(88.9)	(96.2)	(104.0)
Off-Budget	(1,008.3)	(1,057.9)	(1,113.9)	(1,176.4)	(1,242.6)	(1,314.0)	(1,389.0)	(1,460.2)	(1,540.0)	(1,628.1)	(1,719.2)	(1,813.3)
Veterans Benefits and Services	199.8	215.1	236.7	261.1	263.8	264.8	290.9	304.8	319.0	349.1	332.7	364.5
Administration of Justice	65.7	79.6	77.8	76.7	77.2	77.6	78.8	80.6	82.6	84.6	86.6	94.6
General Government	23.4	29.5	28.1	27.5	28.3	28.6	29.4	30.0	30.3	31.6	32.3	33.4
Net Interest	375.2	376.2	379.5	401.4	433.5	468.6	517.9	574.5	632.8	686.2	731.1	775.0
On-Budget	(457.7)	(455.2)	(455.1)	(472.5)	(500.7)	(533.7)	(580.8)	(636.9)	(696.5)	(750.1)	(793.8)	(836.5)
Off-Budget	(−82.5)	(−79.0)	(−75.7)	(−71.1)	(−67.2)	(−65.1)	(−62.9)	(−62.4)	(−63.7)	(−63.9)	(−62.7)	(−61.4)
Allowances	....	*	−28.8	−40.8	−47.2	−51.1	−52.5	−54.1	−55.1	−56.1	−56.5	−52.2
Undistributed Offsetting Receipts:												
Employer share, employee retirement (on-budget)	−72.8	−79.9	−90.4	−90.9	−90.8	−93.1	−95.4	−97.7	−100.0	−102.5	−104.8	−103.8
Employer share, employee retirement (off-budget)	−18.1	−19.1	−19.9	−20.6	−21.2	−21.7	−22.6	−23.3	−24.0	−24.9	−25.4	−26.4
Rents and royalties on the Outer Continental Shelf	−6.2	−4.9	−5.1	−4.7	−5.1	−5.4	−5.7	−5.9	−6.1	−6.4	−6.5	−6.7
Sale of major assets	....	....	....	....	....	....	....	....	....	....	....	....
Other undistributed offsetting receipts	−1.2	−3.1	−18.7	−*	−0.1	−0.1	−5.6	−*	−*	−*	−*	−*
Total, Undistributed Offsetting Receipts	−98.2	−107.0	−134.1	−116.2	−117.1	−120.3	−129.3	−126.9	−130.2	−133.8	−136.8	−136.9
On-Budget	(−80.1)	(−87.9)	(−114.2)	(−95.6)	(−96.0)	(−98.6)	(−106.7)	(−103.6)	(−106.2)	(−108.8)	(−111.4)	(−110.5)
Off-Budget	(−18.1)	(−19.1)	(−19.9)	(−20.6)	(−21.2)	(−21.7)	(−22.6)	(−23.3)	(−24.0)	(−24.9)	(−25.4)	(−26.4)
Total	**4,448.3**	**4,790.9**	**4,874.7**	**5,129.7**	**5,308.0**	**5,492.9**	**5,825.5**	**6,154.4**	**6,466.2**	**6,910.9**	**7,065.0**	**7,537.9**
On-Budget	(3,541.7)	(3,831.1)	(3,855.2)	(4,042.5)	(4,152.8)	(4,265.5)	(4,521.8)	(4,779.6)	(5,013.5)	(5,371.4)	(5,433.6)	(5,812.0)
Off-Budget	(906.6)	(959.8)	(1,019.5)	(1,087.2)	(1,155.2)	(1,227.5)	(1,303.7)	(1,374.8)	(1,452.6)	(1,539.5)	(1,631.4)	(1,725.9)

*Less than $500 million.

Table 21–9. OUTLAYS BY AGENCY IN THE ADJUSTED BASELINE

(In billions of dollars)

Agency	2019 Actual	Estimate										
		2020	2021	2022	2023	2024	2025	2026	2027	2028	2029	2030
Legislative Branch	5.0	6.0	5.5	5.6	5.7	5.9	6.0	6.2	6.4	6.5	6.7	6.9
Judicial Branch	8.0	8.6	8.9	9.1	9.3	9.6	9.9	10.1	10.4	10.7	11.0	11.2
Agriculture	150.1	154.6	147.4	147.6	149.9	149.3	151.6	154.5	156.8	160.3	163.5	163.5
Commerce	11.3	17.1	17.3	18.2	17.1	17.3	17.6	18.1	18.5	19.0	19.5	20.0
Defense—Military Programs	654.0	689.6	736.7	757.8	772.6	788.1	803.1	820.7	842.1	863.1	884.4	906.7
Education	104.4	159.3	85.2	83.5	89.8	93.4	97.1	99.5	102.2	104.3	106.2	108.2
Energy	28.9	34.4	38.8	38.0	37.3	37.0	36.6	38.6	39.2	42.2	43.2	44.0
Health and Human Services	1,213.8	1,321.4	1,387.0	1,502.1	1,555.6	1,602.4	1,746.9	1,861.3	1,973.2	2,176.2	2,187.2	2,377.5
Homeland Security	57.7	62.2	66.2	71.4	69.0	73.8	75.3	77.8	79.5	82.4	85.0	92.8
Housing and Urban Development	29.2	36.0	53.4	54.9	54.9	54.5	53.1	53.6	51.3	51.5	50.4	50.7
Interior	13.9	17.5	17.0	17.3	17.7	18.0	18.1	18.4	18.8	19.3	19.8	20.3
Justice	35.1	45.3	43.1	42.0	41.3	40.9	41.4	42.3	43.4	44.5	45.7	46.9
Labor	35.8	36.4	37.9	41.4	44.6	48.0	45.4	58.4	56.6	59.6	62.6	65.6
State	28.0	32.2	30.9	32.2	32.7	32.9	33.6	34.2	35.0	35.7	36.6	37.4
Transportation	80.7	84.7	88.9	91.7	93.5	95.4	97.2	97.6	99.2	101.7	103.9	106.2
Treasury	689.5	701.0	689.7	693.9	728.0	767.6	820.6	876.1	959.4	1,023.6	1,069.2	1,122.6
Veterans Affairs	199.6	214.3	236.2	260.6	263.3	264.3	290.4	304.3	318.5	348.6	332.1	364.0
Corps of Engineers—Civil Works	6.5	5.5	7.0	11.0	10.4	11.4	9.7	9.5	9.3	9.0	8.9	9.0
Other Defense Civil Programs	60.9	64.5	65.3	73.0	69.3	66.1	74.2	79.1	79.1	87.4	78.4	85.3
Environmental Protection Agency	8.1	7.5	8.5	8.9	9.3	9.6	9.8	10.1	10.3	10.6	10.9	10.8
Executive Office of the President	0.4	0.4	0.4	0.4	0.4	0.5	0.5	0.5	0.5	0.5	0.5	0.6
General Services Administration	−1.1	1.2	0.4	0.8	−0.3	−0.1	−*	−*	−*	*	*	*
International Assistance Programs	23.6	25.7	32.6	24.6	26.3	26.7	26.2	26.7	27.1	27.7	28.3	28.6
National Aeronautics and Space Administration	20.2	21.5	22.5	23.1	23.8	24.4	24.9	25.5	26.0	26.6	27.2	27.8
National Science Foundation	7.3	7.5	8.1	8.7	9.2	9.4	9.5	9.6	9.4	9.6	9.8	10.0
Office of Personnel Management	103.1	106.4	110.0	114.6	119.2	124.1	128.6	133.7	138.6	144.2	149.6	154.9
Small Business Administration	0.5	−0.2	1.1	1.0	1.0	1.1	1.1	1.1	1.1	1.2	1.2	1.2
Social Security Administration	1,101.8	1,155.2	1,216.2	1,288.3	1,355.8	1,428.7	1,514.6	1,600.5	1,691.0	1,792.6	1,882.8	1,991.6
On-Budget	(93.6)	(97.3)	(102.3)	(111.9)	(113.2)	(114.7)	(125.6)	(140.3)	(150.9)	(164.5)	(163.6)	(178.3)
Off-Budget	(1,008.3)	(1,057.9)	(1,113.9)	(1,176.4)	(1,242.6)	(1,314.0)	(1,389.0)	(1,460.2)	(1,540.0)	(1,628.1)	(1,719.2)	(1,813.3)
Other Independent Agencies	19.9	27.5	29.8	33.6	35.4	37.9	41.3	43.9	45.3	46.4	47.8	49.8
On-Budget	(21.0)	(27.4)	(28.7)	(31.1)	(34.4)	(37.6)	(41.1)	(43.6)	(45.0)	(46.1)	(47.6)	(49.5)
Off-Budget	(−1.1)	(0.1)	(1.1)	(2.5)	(1.0)	(0.3)	(0.3)	(0.3)	(0.3)	(0.3)	(0.3)	(0.3)
Allowances	....	*	−43.0	−69.8	−79.7	−85.8	−89.7	−94.5	−98.2	−102.5	−116.7	−81.9
Undistributed Offsetting Receipts	−247.8	−252.6	−274.4	−255.6	−254.5	−259.7	−268.9	−263.0	−283.8	−291.4	−290.8	−294.2
On-Budget	(−147.2)	(−154.4)	(−178.9)	(−163.9)	(−166.1)	(−172.8)	(−183.4)	(−177.3)	(−196.1)	(−202.6)	(−202.7)	(−206.4)
Off-Budget	(−100.6)	(−98.2)	(−95.5)	(−91.7)	(−88.4)	(−86.9)	(−85.5)	(−85.7)	(−87.7)	(−88.8)	(−88.1)	(−87.7)
Total	**4,448.3**	**4,790.9**	**4,874.7**	**5,129.7**	**5,308.0**	**5,492.9**	**5,825.5**	**6,154.4**	**6,466.2**	**6,910.9**	**7,065.0**	**7,537.9**
On-Budget	(3,541.7)	(3,831.1)	(3,855.2)	(4,042.5)	(4,152.8)	(4,265.5)	(4,521.8)	(4,779.6)	(5,013.5)	(5,371.4)	(5,433.6)	(5,812.0)
Off-Budget	(906.6)	(959.8)	(1,019.5)	(1,087.2)	(1,155.2)	(1,227.5)	(1,303.7)	(1,374.8)	(1,452.6)	(1,539.5)	(1,631.4)	(1,725.9)

*Less than $500 million.

Table 21–10.   BUDGET AUTHORITY BY FUNCTION IN THE ADJUSTED BASELINE

(In billions of dollars)

Function	2019 Actual	Estimate 2020	2021	2022	2023	2024	2025	2026	2027	2028	2029	2030
National Defense:												
Department of Defense—Military	712.6	721.5	729.9	747.4	765.4	783.4	802.3	821.6	841.6	862.1	883.2	904.8
Other	33.2	35.6	35.8	36.5	37.2	37.9	38.7	39.5	40.3	41.1	41.9	42.8
Total, National Defense	745.7	757.2	765.7	783.9	802.5	821.3	841.0	861.0	881.9	903.2	925.1	947.5
International Affairs	78.6	58.8	64.4	68.1	70.7	72.7	73.9	75.3	76.6	77.9	79.3	80.7
General Science, Space, and Technology	35.6	37.1	38.0	38.8	39.6	40.5	41.3	42.2	43.1	44.0	45.0	45.9
Energy	6.8	6.8	8.4	7.4	6.4	5.8	4.9	6.6	6.6	8.9	9.6	9.8
Natural Resources and Environment	46.5	47.7	47.8	49.3	50.9	52.1	53.0	54.2	55.3	56.6	57.9	59.1
Agriculture	41.7	41.6	29.6	27.3	27.9	27.5	27.5	27.3	27.1	27.5	27.4	27.4
Commerce and Housing Credit	6.4	23.3	23.6	12.0	13.7	17.0	21.3	24.4	26.3	27.9	29.4	30.9
On-Budget	(6.4)	(23.0)	(23.3)	(11.7)	(13.4)	(16.7)	(21.0)	(24.1)	(26.0)	(27.7)	(29.2)	(30.6)
Off-Budget	(−0.1)	(0.3)	(0.3)	(0.3)	(0.3)	(0.3)	(0.3)	(0.3)	(0.3)	(0.3)	(0.3)	(0.3)
Transportation	106.3	101.8	104.3	105.5	106.7	107.9	109.2	110.5	111.8	114.9	116.6	118.1
Community and Regional Development	31.5	32.1	32.9	33.9	35.9	36.5	37.0	37.6	38.2	38.9	39.6	40.2
Education, Training, Employment, and Social Services	141.0	195.9	122.2	124.4	129.0	133.3	137.7	140.9	144.0	146.8	149.4	152.1
Health	608.9	628.7	655.0	674.7	704.0	729.8	768.7	813.3	853.9	899.5	948.3	1,000.1
Medicare	702.1	753.7	804.8	835.0	855.1	872.5	981.6	1,051.2	1,123.2	1,281.9	1,228.0	1,416.1
Income Security	539.2	542.6	554.9	573.5	583.0	592.9	611.5	628.2	644.5	666.5	674.5	690.3
Social Security	1,047.0	1,102.1	1,162.7	1,228.9	1,299.5	1,375.9	1,456.1	1,540.6	1,629.8	1,725.1	1,823.8	1,925.9
On-Budget	(36.1)	(39.3)	(43.1)	(46.9)	(50.9)	(55.3)	(60.2)	(73.1)	(82.0)	(88.9)	(96.2)	(104.0)
Off-Budget	(1,010.9)	(1,062.8)	(1,119.5)	(1,181.9)	(1,248.6)	(1,320.6)	(1,395.8)	(1,467.4)	(1,547.8)	(1,636.2)	(1,727.6)	(1,822.0)
Veterans Benefits and Services	194.8	214.4	238.6	252.8	266.6	280.1	293.9	308.0	322.4	338.2	353.9	361.7
Administration of Justice	69.3	69.3	78.0	75.3	77.0	77.6	79.7	81.5	83.5	85.5	87.6	95.6
General Government	25.1	26.5	28.2	28.2	28.8	29.5	30.2	31.0	31.8	32.6	33.4	34.3
Net Interest	375.9	375.5	379.5	401.4	433.5	468.6	517.9	574.5	632.8	686.2	731.1	775.1
On-Budget	(458.4)	(454.5)	(455.1)	(472.5)	(500.7)	(533.7)	(580.8)	(636.9)	(696.5)	(750.1)	(793.8)	(836.5)
Off-Budget	(−82.5)	(−79.0)	(−75.7)	(−71.1)	(−67.2)	(−65.1)	(−62.9)	(−62.4)	(−63.7)	(−63.9)	(−62.7)	(−61.4)
Allowances	....	*	−50.4	−50.1	−51.7	−52.8	−53.9	−55.1	−55.7	−56.7	−57.1	−48.8
Undistributed Offsetting Receipts:												
Employer share, employee retirement (on-budget)	−72.8	−79.9	−90.4	−90.9	−90.8	−93.1	−95.4	−97.7	−100.0	−102.5	−104.8	−103.8
Employer share, employee retirement (off-budget)	−18.1	−19.1	−19.9	−20.6	−21.2	−21.7	−22.6	−23.3	−24.0	−24.9	−25.4	−26.4
Rents and royalties on the Outer Continental Shelf	−6.2	−4.9	−5.1	−4.7	−5.1	−5.4	−5.7	−5.9	−6.1	−6.4	−6.5	−6.7
Sale of major assets	....	....	....	....	....	....	....	....	....	....	....	....
Other undistributed offsetting receipts	−1.2	−3.1	−18.7	−*	−0.1	−0.1	−5.6	−*	−*	−*	−*	−*
Total, Undistributed Offsetting Receipts	−98.2	−107.0	−134.1	−116.2	−117.1	−120.3	−129.3	−126.9	−130.2	−133.8	−136.8	−136.9
On-Budget	(−80.1)	(−87.9)	(−114.2)	(−95.6)	(−96.0)	(−98.6)	(−106.7)	(−103.6)	(−106.2)	(−108.8)	(−111.4)	(−110.5)
Off-Budget	(−18.1)	(−19.1)	(−19.9)	(−20.6)	(−21.2)	(−21.7)	(−22.6)	(−23.3)	(−24.0)	(−24.9)	(−25.4)	(−26.4)
Total	**4,704.1**	**4,908.0**	**4,954.0**	**5,154.0**	**5,362.0**	**5,568.2**	**5,903.2**	**6,226.1**	**6,546.8**	**6,971.8**	**7,165.9**	**7,625.3**
On-Budget	(3,793.8)	(3,943.1)	(3,929.7)	(4,063.5)	(4,201.5)	(4,334.2)	(4,592.6)	(4,844.0)	(5,086.4)	(5,424.3)	(5,526.2)	(5,890.8)
Off-Budget	(910.3)	(964.9)	(1,024.3)	(1,090.5)	(1,160.5)	(1,234.1)	(1,310.6)	(1,382.1)	(1,460.4)	(1,547.6)	(1,639.8)	(1,734.5)
MEMORANDUM												
Discretionary Budget Authority:												
National Defense	718.8	746.0	752.7	770.7	789.2	808.2	827.8	847.6	868.3	889.3	911.0	933.2
International Affairs	56.3	55.8	57.2	58.4	59.7	61.0	62.3	63.6	65.0	66.4	67.8	69.3
Domestic	601.4	615.0	598.1	613.0	628.2	644.0	659.8	676.1	692.9	710.1	727.7	745.8
Total, Discretionary	1,376.5	1,416.8	1,408.0	1,442.2	1,477.1	1,513.2	1,549.9	1,587.3	1,626.2	1,665.8	1,706.5	1,748.3

*Less than $500 million.

Table 21–11. BUDGET AUTHORITY BY AGENCY IN THE ADJUSTED BASELINE
(In billions of dollars)

Agency	2019 Actual	Estimate										
		2020	2021	2022	2023	2024	2025	2026	2027	2028	2029	2030
Legislative Branch	5.1	5.3	5.5	5.6	5.8	6.0	6.1	6.3	6.4	6.6	6.8	7.0
Judicial Branch	8.1	8.4	8.8	9.0	9.3	9.5	9.8	10.0	10.3	10.6	10.9	11.1
Agriculture	166.7	162.0	150.9	150.7	152.9	155.1	157.8	161.1	163.4	166.8	170.4	168.5
Commerce	12.5	15.5	16.2	16.6	17.0	17.4	17.9	18.4	18.8	19.3	19.8	20.4
Defense—Military Programs	712.6	721.5	743.4	761.7	780.6	799.5	819.4	839.8	860.8	882.4	904.5	927.3
Education	106.2	159.0	85.2	87.0	90.9	94.6	98.3	100.9	103.7	105.8	107.7	109.8
Energy	32.3	37.3	38.1	37.8	37.6	38.0	37.6	39.6	40.4	43.2	44.4	45.0
Health and Human Services	1,284.0	1,366.2	1,458.2	1,517.7	1,566.4	1,608.4	1,755.6	1,869.6	1,981.3	2,185.5	2,192.7	2,387.2
Homeland Security	62.8	66.0	68.3	70.8	73.8	75.4	76.9	78.6	80.3	83.8	85.9	93.7
Housing and Urban Development	56.8	52.7	56.7	57.7	58.7	59.6	60.7	61.7	62.7	63.8	64.9	66.0
Interior	15.9	18.4	17.0	17.1	17.6	18.0	18.3	18.7	19.1	19.7	20.2	20.5
Justice	34.7	36.9	44.2	40.1	41.1	40.9	42.1	43.1	44.2	45.3	46.5	47.7
Labor	42.3	42.5	45.0	47.2	49.7	52.0	54.0	56.2	58.3	60.5	62.8	65.2
State	30.4	30.6	31.4	32.1	32.8	33.5	34.3	35.1	35.9	36.7	37.5	38.3
Transportation	88.7	86.1	88.1	88.8	89.4	90.1	90.9	91.6	92.4	93.1	93.9	94.8
Treasury	700.2	699.9	690.3	695.6	728.6	768.8	821.9	877.8	961.6	1,025.3	1,071.1	1,124.2
Veterans Affairs	194.2	214.0	238.1	252.4	266.1	279.6	293.4	307.5	321.9	337.6	353.4	361.2
Corps of Engineers—Civil Works	10.2	7.6	7.8	8.0	8.2	8.4	8.6	8.8	9.1	9.3	9.5	9.7
Other Defense Civil Programs	61.2	64.3	65.5	67.9	69.5	71.7	74.5	79.4	79.4	81.5	84.9	85.5
Environmental Protection Agency	9.2	9.0	9.2	9.4	9.7	9.9	10.2	10.4	10.6	10.9	11.2	11.4
Executive Office of the President	0.4	0.4	0.4	0.4	0.4	0.5	0.5	0.5	0.5	0.5	0.6	0.6
General Services Administration	−0.2	−1.1	0.3	0.3	0.3	0.3	0.3	0.3	0.3	0.3	0.4	0.4
International Assistance Programs	46.3	27.3	31.9	34.7	36.6	37.8	38.2	38.8	39.2	39.8	40.3	40.8
National Aeronautics and Space Administration	21.5	22.6	23.1	23.6	24.1	24.7	25.2	25.8	26.4	27.0	27.6	28.2
National Science Foundation	8.2	8.4	8.6	8.8	9.0	9.1	9.3	9.5	9.7	9.9	10.1	10.3
Office of Personnel Management	104.9	108.7	113.0	117.6	122.4	127.3	132.1	137.1	142.3	147.6	153.4	158.8
Small Business Administration	−0.1	−0.2	1.0	1.0	1.1	1.1	1.1	1.1	1.2	1.2	1.2	1.2
Social Security Administration	1,105.0	1,160.6	1,219.7	1,293.9	1,361.8	1,435.3	1,521.5	1,607.8	1,698.7	1,800.7	1,891.2	2,000.3
On-Budget	(94.1)	(97.8)	(100.2)	(112.0)	(113.2)	(114.7)	(125.7)	(140.4)	(150.9)	(164.6)	(163.6)	(178.4)
Off-Budget	(1,010.9)	(1,062.8)	(1,119.5)	(1,181.9)	(1,248.6)	(1,320.6)	(1,395.8)	(1,467.4)	(1,547.8)	(1,636.2)	(1,727.6)	(1,822.0)
Other Independent Agencies	31.8	30.8	35.2	38.4	41.3	44.1	47.9	50.2	51.6	53.3	55.0	57.0
On-Budget	(31.9)	(30.6)	(34.9)	(38.1)	(41.0)	(43.8)	(47.6)	(49.9)	(51.3)	(53.0)	(54.7)	(56.7)
Off-Budget	(−0.1)	(0.3)	(0.3)	(0.3)	(0.3)	(0.3)	(0.3)	(0.3)	(0.3)	(0.3)	(0.3)	(0.3)
Allowances	....	*	−72.7	−82.3	−86.0	−88.8	−92.3	−96.6	−99.9	−104.4	−121.7	−72.5
Undistributed Offsetting Receipts	−247.8	−252.6	−274.4	−255.6	−254.5	−259.7	−268.9	−263.0	−283.8	−291.4	−290.8	−294.2
On-Budget	(−147.2)	(−154.4)	(−178.9)	(−163.9)	(−166.1)	(−172.8)	(−183.4)	(−177.3)	(−196.1)	(−202.6)	(−202.7)	(−206.4)
Off-Budget	(−100.6)	(−98.2)	(−95.5)	(−91.7)	(−88.4)	(−86.9)	(−85.5)	(−85.7)	(−87.7)	(−88.8)	(−88.1)	(−87.7)
Total	**4,704.1**	**4,908.0**	**4,954.0**	**5,154.0**	**5,362.0**	**5,568.2**	**5,903.2**	**6,226.1**	**6,546.8**	**6,971.8**	**7,165.9**	**7,625.3**
On-Budget	(3,793.8)	(3,943.1)	(3,929.7)	(4,063.5)	(4,201.5)	(4,334.2)	(4,592.6)	(4,844.0)	(5,086.4)	(5,424.3)	(5,526.2)	(5,890.8)
Off-Budget	(910.3)	(964.9)	(1,024.3)	(1,090.5)	(1,160.5)	(1,234.1)	(1,310.6)	(1,382.1)	(1,460.4)	(1,547.6)	(1,639.8)	(1,734.5)

*Less than $500 million.

22.   TRUST FUNDS AND FEDERAL FUNDS

As is common for State and local government budgets, the budget for the Federal Government contains information about collections and expenditures for different types of funds. This chapter presents summary information about the transactions of the two major fund groups used by the Federal Government, trust funds and Federal funds. It also presents information about the income and outgo of the major trust funds and certain Federal funds that are financed by dedicated collections in a manner similar to trust funds.

The Federal Funds Group

The Federal funds group includes all financial transactions of the Government that are not required by law to be recorded in trust funds. It accounts for a larger share of the budget than the trust funds group.

The Federal funds group includes the "general fund," which is used for the general purposes of Government rather than being restricted by law to a specific program. The general fund is the largest fund in the Government and it receives all collections not dedicated for some other fund, including virtually all income taxes and many excise taxes. The general fund is used for all programs that are not supported by trust, special, or revolving funds.

The Federal funds group also includes special funds and revolving funds, both of which receive collections that are dedicated by law for specific purposes. Where the law requires that Federal fund collections be dedicated to a particular program, the collections and associated disbursements are recorded in special fund receipt and expenditure accounts.[1] An example is the portion of the Outer Continental Shelf mineral leasing receipts deposited into the Land and Water Conservation Fund. Money in special fund receipt accounts must be appropriated before it can be obligated and spent. The majority of special fund collections are derived from the Government's power to impose taxes or fines, or otherwise compel payment, as in the case of the Crime Victims Fund. In addition, a significant amount of collections credited to special funds is derived from certain types of business-like activity, such as the sale of Government land or other assets or the use of Government property. These collections include receipts from timber sales and royalties from oil and gas extraction.

Revolving funds are used to conduct continuing cycles of business-like activity. Revolving funds receive proceeds from the sale of products or services, and these proceeds finance ongoing activities that continue to provide products or services. Instead of being deposited in receipt accounts, the proceeds are recorded in revolving fund expenditure accounts. The proceeds are generally available for obligation and expenditure without further legislative action. Outlays for programs with revolving funds are reported both gross and net of these proceeds; gross outlays include the expenditures from the proceeds and net program outlays are derived by subtracting the proceeds from gross outlays. Because the proceeds of these sales are recorded as offsets to outlays within expenditure accounts rather than receipt accounts, the proceeds are known as "offsetting collections."[2] There are two classes of revolving funds in the Federal funds group. Public enterprise funds, such as the Postal Service Fund, conduct business-like operations mainly with the public. Intragovernmental funds, such as the Federal Buildings Fund, conduct business-like operations mainly within and between Government agencies.

The Trust Funds Group

The trust funds group consists of funds that are designated by law as trust funds. Like special funds and revolving funds, trust funds receive collections (frequently these collections are dedicated payroll taxes, excise taxes, or user fees), that are dedicated by law for specific purposes. Trust funds (particularly for social insurance or benefit programs) are commonly designed to link benefits and costs of a program more closely and an attempt to create fiscal discipline in certain programs. Some of the larger trust funds are used to budget for social insurance programs, such as Social Security, Medicare, and unemployment compensation. Unfortunately, many of these funds are expected to be depleted in the next 15 years. In the past, the Congress has taken action to increase a trust fund's revenue or reduce its outgo. Other large trust funds are used to budget for military and Federal civilian employees' retirement benefits, highway and transit construction and maintenance, and airport and airway development and maintenance. There are a few trust revolving funds that are credited with collections earmarked by law to carry out a cycle of business-type operations. There are also a few small trust funds that have been established to carry out the terms of a conditional gift or bequest. In total there are 14 major trust fund programs (including Social Security, Medicare, and the Highway Trust Fund), and over 100 additional trust funds in the 2021 Budget.

There is no substantive difference between special funds in the Federal funds group and trust funds, or between revolving funds in the Federal funds group and

---

[1] There are two types of budget accounts: expenditure (or appropriation) accounts and receipt accounts. Expenditure accounts are used to record outlays and receipt accounts are used to record governmental receipts and offsetting receipts. For further detail on expenditure and receipt accounts, see Chapter 8, "Budget Concepts," in this volume.

[2] See Chapter 12 in this volume for more information on offsetting collections and offsetting receipts.

trust revolving funds. Whether a particular fund is designated in law as a trust fund is, in many cases, arbitrary. For example, the National Service Life Insurance Fund is a trust fund, but the Servicemen's Group Life Insurance Fund is a Federal fund, even though both receive dedicated collections from veterans and both provide life insurance payments to veterans' beneficiaries.

The Federal Government uses the term "trust fund" differently than the way in which it is commonly used. In common usage, the term is used to refer to a private fund that has a beneficiary who owns the trust's income and may also own the trust's assets. A custodian or trustee manages the assets on behalf of the beneficiary according to the terms of the trust agreement, as established by a trustor. Neither the trustee nor the beneficiary can change the terms of the trust agreement; only the trustor can change the terms of the agreement. In contrast, the Federal Government owns and manages the assets and the earnings of most Federal trust funds and can unilaterally change the law to raise or lower future trust fund collections and payments or change the purpose for which the collections are used. Only a few small Federal trust funds are managed pursuant to a trust agreement whereby the Government acts as the trustee; even then the Government generally owns the funds and has some ability to alter the amount deposited into or paid out of the funds.

Deposit funds, which are funds held by the Government as a custodian on behalf of individuals or a non-Federal entity, are similar to private-sector trust funds. The Government makes no decisions about the amount of money placed in deposit funds or about how the proceeds are spent. For this reason, these funds are not classified

Table 22–1. RECEIPTS, OUTLAYS AND SURPLUS OR DEFICIT BY FUND GROUP

(In billions of dollars)

	2019 Actual	Estimate					
		2020	2021	2022	2023	2024	2025
Receipts:							
Federal funds cash income:							
From the public	2,507.0	2,665.5	2,777.4	2,947.6	3,133.3	3,351.1	3,546.5
From trust funds	1.0	0.9	1.0	1.0	1.1	1.2	1.2
Total, Federal funds cash income	2,508.0	2,666.4	2,778.4	2,948.7	3,134.4	3,352.2	3,547.8
Trust funds cash income:							
From the public	1,502.4	1,597.1	1,662.6	1,745.1	1,830.2	1,930.5	2,030.3
From Federal funds:							
Interest	149.6	145.6	140.6	140.4	139.2	142.3	143.8
Other	613.9	659.7	697.6	720.7	756.4	798.2	844.4
Total, Trust funds cash income	2,265.9	2,402.4	2,500.8	2,606.3	2,725.8	2,870.9	3,018.6
Offsetting collections from the public and offsetting receipts:							
Federal funds	−355.0	−340.2	−358.1	−382.0	−367.2	−373.6	−385.2
Trust funds	−954.7	−1,022.3	−1,057.8	−1,087.3	−1,134.0	−1,193.0	−1,256.9
Total, offsetting collections from the public and offsetting receipts	−1,309.7	−1,362.5	−1,415.9	−1,469.3	−1,501.2	−1,566.6	−1,642.1
Unified budget receipts:							
Federal funds	2,153.0	2,326.2	2,420.3	2,566.7	2,767.2	2,978.7	3,162.6
Trust funds	1,311.2	1,380.1	1,443.0	1,519.0	1,591.9	1,677.9	1,761.7
Total, unified budget receipts	3,464.2	3,706.3	3,863.3	4,085.7	4,359.1	4,656.5	4,924.3
Outlays:							
Federal funds cash outgo	3,604.9	3,861.9	3,842.9	3,926.0	3,958.4	4,022.9	4,131.6
Trust funds cash outgo	2,153.2	2,290.3	2,402.4	2,548.7	2,648.1	2,752.2	2,961.3
Offsetting collections from the public and offsetting receipts:							
Federal funds	−355.0	−340.2	−358.1	−382.0	−367.2	−373.6	−385.2
Trust funds	−954.7	−1,022.3	−1,057.8	−1,087.3	−1,134.0	−1,193.0	−1,256.9
Total, offsetting collections from the public and offsetting receipts	−1,309.7	−1,362.5	−1,415.9	−1,469.3	−1,501.2	−1,566.6	−1,642.1
Unified budget outlays:							
Federal funds	3,249.8	3,521.7	3,484.8	3,544.0	3,591.2	3,649.3	3,746.4
Trust funds	1,198.5	1,268.0	1,344.6	1,461.4	1,514.1	1,559.1	1,704.4
Total, unified budget outlays	4,448.3	4,789.7	4,829.4	5,005.4	5,105.3	5,208.5	5,450.8
Surplus or deficit(−):							
Federal funds	−1,096.9	−1,195.5	−1,064.5	−977.3	−824.0	−670.7	−583.8
Trust funds	112.7	112.1	98.4	57.6	77.7	118.8	57.3
Total, unified surplus/deficit(−)	−984.2	−1,083.4	−966.1	−919.8	−746.3	−551.9	−526.5

Note: Receipts include governmental, interfund, and proprietary, and exclude intrafund receipts (which are offset against intrafund payments so that cash income and cash outgo are not overstated).

as Federal trust funds, but are instead considered to be non-budgetary and excluded from the Federal budget.[3]

The income of a Federal Government trust fund must be used for the purposes specified in law. The income of some trust funds, such as the Federal Employees Health Benefits fund, is spent almost as quickly as it is collected. In other cases, such as the military and Federal civilian employees' retirement trust funds, the trust fund income is not spent as quickly as it is collected. And finally, in some cases the income (including intragovernmental interest income) is not sufficient to cover all of the expenditures in a given year. For funds that have a surplus of income over outgo, the surplus adds to the trust fund's balance, which is available for future expenditures. The balances are generally required by law to be invested in Federal securities issued by the Department of the Treasury.[4] The National Railroad Retirement Investment Trust is a rare example of a Government trust fund authorized to invest balances in equity markets.

A trust fund normally consists of one or more receipt accounts (to record income) and an expenditure account (to record outgo). However, a few trust funds, such as the Veterans Special Life Insurance fund, are established by law as trust revolving funds. Such a fund is similar to a revolving fund in the Federal funds group in that it may consist of a single account to record both income and outgo. Trust revolving funds are used to conduct a cycle of business-type operations; offsetting collections are credited to the funds (which are also expenditure accounts) and the funds' outlays are displayed net of the offsetting collections.

In recent years, there has been discussion of funding shortfalls in specific trust funds through general fund transfers, indicating that trust fund income and outgo are not balanced over the long-term and more fundamental program changes may be necessary. The approach of general fund transfers weakens the integrity of trust funds and undermines the budgetary and accounting treatment of trust funds.

Income and Outgo by Fund Group

Table 22–1 shows income, outgo, and the surplus or deficit by fund group and in the aggregate (netted to avoid double-counting) from which the total unified budget receipts, outlays, and surplus or deficit are derived. Income consists mostly of governmental receipts (derived from governmental activity, primarily income, payroll, and excise taxes). Income also includes offsetting receipts, which include proprietary receipts (derived from business-like transactions with the public), interfund collections (derived from payments from a fund in one fund group to a fund in the other fund group), and gifts. Outgo consists of payments made to the public or to a fund in the other fund group.

Two types of transactions are treated specially in the table. First, income and outgo for each fund group exclude all transactions that occur between funds within the same fund group.[5] These intrafund transactions constitute outgo and income for the individual funds that make and collect the payments, but they are offsetting within the fund group as a whole. The totals for each fund group measure only the group's transactions with the public and the other fund group. Second, outgo is calculated net of the collections from Federal sources that are credited to expenditure accounts (which, as noted above, are referred to as offsetting collections); the spending that is financed by those collections is included in outgo and the collections from Federal sources are subsequently subtracted from outgo.[6] Although it would be conceptually correct to add interfund offsetting collections from Federal sources to income for a particular fund, this cannot be done at the present time because the budget data do not provide this type of detail. As a result, both interfund and intrafund offsetting collections from Federal sources are offset against outgo in Table 22–1 and are not shown separately.

The vast majority of the interfund transactions in the table are payments by the Federal funds to the trust funds. These payments include interest payments from the general fund to the trust funds for interest earned on trust fund balances invested in interest-bearing Treasury securities. The payments also include payments by Federal agencies to Federal employee benefits trust funds and Social Security trust funds on behalf of current employees and general fund transfers to employee retirement trust funds to amortize the unfunded liabilities of these funds. In addition, the payments include general fund transfers to the Supplementary Medical Insurance trust fund for the cost of Medicare Parts B (outpatient and physician benefits) and D (prescription drug benefits) that is not covered by premiums or other income from the public.

In addition to investing their balances with the Treasury, some funds in the Federal funds group and most trust funds are authorized to borrow from the general fund of the Treasury.[7] Similar to the treatment of funds invested with the Treasury, borrowed funds are not recorded as receipts of the fund or included in the income of the fund. Rather, the borrowed funds finance outlays

---

[3] Deposit funds are discussed briefly in Chapter 9 of this volume, "Coverage of the Budget."

[4] Securities held by trust funds (and by other Government accounts), debt held by the public, and gross Federal debt are discussed in Chapter 4 of this volume, "Federal Borrowing and Debt."

[5] For example, the railroad retirement trust funds pay the equivalent of Social Security benefits to railroad retirees in addition to the regular railroad pension. These benefits are financed by a payment from the Federal Old-Age and Survivors Insurance trust fund to the railroad retirement trust funds. The payment and collection are not included in Table 22–1 so that the total trust fund income and outgo shown in the table reflect transactions with the public and with Federal funds.

[6] Collections from non-Federal sources are shown as income and spending that is financed by those collections is shown as outgo. For example, postage stamp fees are deposited as offsetting collections in the Postal Service Fund. As a result, the Fund's income reported in Table 22–1 includes postage stamp fees and the Fund's outgo is gross disbursements, including disbursements financed by those fees.

[7] For example, the Unemployment Trust Fund is authorized to borrow from the general fund for unemployment benefits; the Bonneville Power Administration Fund, a revolving fund in the Department of Energy, is authorized to borrow from the general fund; and the Black Lung Disability Trust Fund, a trust fund in the Department of Labor, is authorized to receive appropriations of repayable advances from the general fund, which constitute a form of borrowing.

Table 22–2. COMPARISON OF TOTAL FEDERAL FUND AND TRUST FUND RECEIPTS TO UNIFIED BUDGET RECEIPTS, FISCAL YEAR 2019

(In billions of dollars)

Gross Federal fund and Trust fund cash income:	
Federal funds	2,870.1
Trust funds	2,326.6
Total, gross Federal fund and Trust fund cash income	5,196.7
Deduct: intrabudgetary offsetting collections (from funds within same fund group):	
Federal funds	–329.5
Trust funds	–53.8
Subtotal, intrabudgetary offsetting collections	–383.3
Deduct: intrafund receipts (from funds within same fund group):	
Federal funds	–32.6
Trust funds	–6.9
Subtotal, intrafund receipts	–39.5
Federal fund and Trust fund cash income net of intrabudgetary offsetting collections and intrafund receipts:	
Federal funds	2,508.0
Trust funds	2,265.9
Total, Federal fund and Trust fund cash income net of intrafund receipts	4,773.9
Deduct: offsetting collections from the public:	
Federal funds	–222.9
Trust funds	–22.1
Subtotal, offsetting collections from the public	–244.9
Deduct other offsetting receipts:	
Federal fund receipts from Trust funds	–1.0
Trust fund receipts from Federal funds:	
Interest in receipt accounts	–149.6
General fund payments to Medicare Parts B and D	–333.7
Employing agencies' payments for pensions, Social Security, and Medicare	–83.0
General fund payments for unfunded liabilities of Federal employees' retirement funds	–132.0
Transfer of taxation of Social Security and RRB benefits to OASDI, HI, and RRB	–60.6
Other receipts from Federal funds	–4.5
Subtotal, Trust fund receipts from Federal funds	–763.5
Proprietary receipts:	
Federal funds	–119.6
Trust funds	–167.9
Subtotal, proprietary receipts	–287.5
Offsetting governmental receipts:	
Federal funds	–11.6
Trust funds	–1.2
Subtotal, offsetting governmental receipts	–12.8
Subtotal, other offsetting receipts	–1,064.8
Unified budget receipts:	
Federal funds	2,153.0
Trust funds	1,311.2
Total, unified budget receipts	3,464.2
Memoradum:	
Gross receipts:[1]	
Federal funds	2,317.7
Trust funds	2,250.7
Total, gross receipts	4,568.5

[1] Gross income excluding offsetting collections.

by the fund in excess of available receipts. Subsequently, any excess fund receipts are transferred from the fund to the general fund in repayment of the borrowing. The repayment is not recorded as an outlay of the fund or included in fund outgo. This treatment is consistent with the broad principle that borrowing and debt redemption are not budgetary transactions but rather a means of financing deficits or disposing of surpluses.[8]

Some income in both Federal funds and trust funds consists of offsetting receipts.[9] Offsetting receipts are not considered governmental receipts (such as taxes), but they are instead recorded on the outlay side of the budget.[10] Expenditures resulting from offsetting receipts are recorded as gross outlays and the collections of offsetting receipts are then subtracted from gross outlays to derive net outlays. Net outlays reflect the Government's net transactions with the public.

As shown in Table 22–1, 38 percent of all governmental receipts were deposited in trust funds in 2019 and the remaining 62 percent of governmental receipts were deposited in Federal funds, which, as noted above, include the general fund. As noted above, most outlays between the trust fund and Federal fund groups (interfund outlays) flow from Federal funds to trust funds, rather than from trust funds to Federal funds. As a result, while trust funds account for 27 percent of total 2019 outlays, they account for 33 percent of 2019 outlays net of interfund transactions.

Because the income for Federal funds and trust funds recorded in Table 22–1 includes offsetting receipts and offsetting collections from the public, offsetting receipts and offsetting collections from the public must be deducted from the two fund groups' combined gross income in order to reconcile to total governmental receipts in the unified budget. Similarly, because the outgo for Federal funds and trust funds in Table 22–1 consists of outlays gross of offsetting receipts and offsetting collections from the public, the amount of the offsetting receipts and offsetting collections from the public must be deducted from the sum of the Federal funds' and the trust funds' gross outgo in order to reconcile to total (net) unified budget outlays. Table 22–2 reconciles, for fiscal year 2019, the gross total of all trust fund and Federal fund receipts with the receipt total of the unified budget.

Income, Outgo, and Balances of Trust Funds

Table 22–3 shows, for the trust funds group as a whole, the funds' balance at the start of each year, income and outgo during the year, and the end-of-year balance. Income and outgo are divided between transactions with the public and transactions with Federal funds. Receipts

---

[8] Borrowing and debt repayment are discussed in Chapter 4 of this volume, "Federal Borrowing and Debt," and Chapter 8 of this volume, "Budget Concepts."

[9] Interest on borrowed funds is an example of an intragovernmental offsetting receipt and Medicare Part B's premiums are an example of offsetting receipts from the public.

[10] For further discussion of offsetting receipts, see Chapter 12 of this volume, "Offsetting Collections and Offsetting Receipts."

from Federal funds are divided between interest and other interfund receipts.

The definitions of income and outgo in this table differ from those in Table 22–1 in one important way. Trust fund collections that are offset against outgo (offsetting collections from Federal sources) within expenditure accounts instead of being deposited in separate receipt accounts are classified as income in this table, but not in Table 22–1. This classification is consistent with the definitions of income and outgo for trust funds used elsewhere in the budget. It has the effect of increasing both income and outgo by the amount of the offsetting collections from Federal sources. The difference was approximately $54 billion in 2019. Table 22–3, therefore, provides a more complete summary of trust fund income and outgo.

The trust funds group ran a surplus of $113 billion in 2019, and is expected to continue to run surpluses over the next several years. The resulting growth in trust fund balances continues a trend that has persisted over the past several decades.

The size of the trust fund balances is largely the consequence of the way some trust funds are financed. Some of the larger trust funds (primarily Social Security and the Federal retirement funds) are fully or partially advance funded, with collections on behalf of individual participants received by the funds years earlier than when the associated benefits are paid. For example, under the Federal military and civilian retirement programs, Federal agencies and employees together are required to pay the retirement trust funds an amount equal to accruing retirement benefits. Since many years pass between the time when benefits are accrued and when they are paid, the trust funds accumulate substantial balances over time. [11]

Due to advance funding and economic growth (both real and nominal), trust fund balances increased from $205 billion in 1982 to $5.3 trillion in 2019. Based on the estimates in the 2021 Budget, which include the effect of the Budget's proposals, the balances are estimated to increase by approximately 10 percent by the year 2025, rising to $5.8 trillion. Almost all of these balances are invested in Treasury securities and earn interest.

From the perspective of the trust fund, these balances are assets that represent the value, in today's dollars, of past taxes, fees, and other income from the public and from other Government accounts that the trust fund has received in excess of past spending. Trust fund assets held in Treasury securities are legal claims on the Treasury, similar to Treasury securities issued to the public. Like all other fund assets, these are available to the fund for future benefit payments and other expenditures. From the perspective of the Government as a whole, however,

---

[11] Until the 1980s, most trust funds operated on a pay-as-you-go basis as distinct from a pre-funded basis. Taxes and fees were set at levels sufficient to finance current program expenditures and administrative expenses, and to maintain balances generally equal to one year's worth of expenditures (to provide for unexpected events). As a result, trust fund balances tended to grow at about the same rate as the funds' annual expenditures. In the 1980s, pay-as-you-go financing was replaced by full or partial advance funding for some of the larger trust funds. The Social Security Amendments of 1983 (P.L. 98-21) raised payroll taxes above the levels necessary to finance then-current expenditures. Legislation enacted in the mid-1980s established the requirement for full accrual basis funding of Federal military and civilian retirement benefits.

Table 22–3. INCOME, OUTGO, AND BALANCES OF TRUST FUNDS GROUP

(In billions of dollars)

	2019 Actual	Estimate					
		2020	2021	2022	2023	2024	2025
Balance, start of year	5,187.9	5,300.1	5,412.4	5,510.8	5,568.4	5,646.1	5,764.9
Adjustments to balances	0.2	....	....	....	....	....	....
Total balance, start of year	5,188.1	5,300.1	5,412.4	5,510.8	5,568.4	5,646.1	5,764.9
Income:							
Governmental receipts	1,311.2	1,380.1	1,443.0	1,519.0	1,591.9	1,677.9	1,761.7
Offsetting governmental	1.2	0.1	0.1	0.1	0.1	0.1	0.1
Proprietary	189.3	216.5	219.1	225.6	237.8	252.0	268.1
From Federal funds:							
Interest	151.8	147.8	142.7	142.5	141.5	144.6	146.3
Other	666.1	716.9	754.0	779.4	816.7	860.9	910.0
Total income during the year	2,319.7	2,461.4	2,558.8	2,666.5	2,787.8	2,935.5	3,086.1
Outgo (–)	–2,207.0	–2,349.3	–2,460.4	–2,608.9	–2,710.1	–2,816.8	–3,028.7
Change in fund balance:							
Surplus or deficit(–):							
Excluding interest	–39.1	–35.7	–44.3	–84.9	–63.8	–25.9	–88.9
Interest	151.8	147.8	142.7	142.5	141.5	144.6	146.3
Subtotal, surplus or deficit (–)	112.7	112.1	98.4	57.6	77.7	118.8	57.3
Borrowing, transfers, lapses, & other adjustments	–0.7	0.2	0.1	....	....	....	....
Total change in fund balance	112.1	112.3	98.5	57.6	77.7	118.8	57.3
Balance, end of year	5,300.1	5,412.4	5,510.8	5,568.4	5,646.1	5,764.9	5,822.2

Note: In contrast to Table 22–1, income also includes income that is offset within expenditure accounts as offsetting collections from Federal sources, instead of being deposited in receipt accounts.

the trust fund balances do not represent net additions to the Government's balance sheet. The trust fund balances are assets of the agencies responsible for administering the trust fund programs and liabilities of the Department of the Treasury. These assets and liabilities cancel each other out in the Government-wide balance sheet. The effects of Treasury debt held by trust funds and other Government accounts are discussed further in Chapter 4 of this volume, "Federal Borrowing and Debt."

Although total trust fund balances are growing, the balances of some major individual funds are declining. Social Security and Medicare face particular challenges due to the decline in the ratio of active workers paying payroll taxes relative to retired workers receiving Social Security and Medicare benefits. Within the 2019-2025 window presented in Table 22–3, the Social Security and Medicare trust funds will begin to run deficits and their balances will consequently begin to fall. In the longer run, absent changes in the laws governing these programs, the funds will become unable to meet their obligations in full. For further discussion of the longer-term outlook of Social Security and Medicare, and the Federal budget as a whole, see Chapter 3 of this volume, "Long-Term Budget Outlook."

Table 22–4 shows estimates of income, outgo, surplus or deficit, and balances for 2019 through 2025 for the major trust funds. With the exception of transactions between trust funds, the data for the individual trust funds are conceptually the same as the data in Table 22–3 for the trust funds group. As explained previously, transactions between trust funds are shown as outgo of the fund that makes the payment and as income of the fund that collects it in the data for an individual trust fund, but the collections are offset against outgo in the data for the trust fund group as a whole.

As noted above, trust funds are funded by a combination of payments from the public and payments from Federal funds, including payments directly from the general fund and payments from agency appropriations. Similarly, the fund outgo amounts in Table 22–4 represent both outflows to the public—such as for the provision of benefit payments or the purchase of goods or services—and outflows to other Government accounts—such as for reimbursement for services provided by other agencies or payment of interest on borrowing from Treasury.

Because trust funds and Federal special and revolving funds conduct transactions both with the public and with other Government accounts, the surplus or deficit of an individual fund may differ from the fund's impact on the surplus or deficit of the Federal Government. Transactions with the public affect both the surplus or deficit of an individual fund and the Federal Government surplus or deficit. Transactions with other Government accounts affect the surplus or deficit of the particular fund. However, because that same transaction is offset in another Government account, there is no net impact on the total Federal Government surplus or deficit.

A brief description of the major trust funds is given below; additional information for these and other trust funds can be found in the Status of Funds tables in the Budget *Appendix*.

- Social Security Trust Funds: The Social Security trust funds consist of the Old Age and Survivors Insurance (OASI) trust fund and the Disability Insurance (DI) trust fund. The trust funds are funded by payroll taxes from employers and employees, interest earnings on trust fund balances, Federal agency payments as employers, and a portion of the income taxes paid on Social Security benefits.

- Medicare Trust Funds: Like the Social Security trust funds, the Medicare Hospital Insurance trust fund is funded by payroll taxes from employers and employees, Federal agency payments as employers, and a portion of the income taxes paid on Social Security benefits. The HI trust fund also receives transfers from the general fund of the Treasury for certain HI benefits and premiums from certain voluntary participants. The other Medicare trust fund, Supplementary Medical Insurance (SMI), finances Part B (outpatient and physician benefits) and Part D (prescription drug benefits). SMI receives premium payments from covered individuals, transfers from States toward Part D benefits, excise taxes on manufacturers and importers of brand-name prescription drugs, and transfers from the general fund of the Treasury for the portion of Part B and Part D costs not covered by premiums or transfers from States. In addition, like other trust funds, these two trust funds receive interest earnings on their trust fund balances.

- Highway Trust Fund: The fund finances Federal highway and transit infrastructure projects, as well as highway and vehicle safety activities. The Highway Trust Fund is financed by Federal motor fuel taxes and associated fees, and, in recent years, by general fund transfers, as those taxes and fees have been inadequate to support current levels of investment.

- Unemployment Trust Fund: The Unemployment Trust Fund is funded by Federal and State taxes on employers, payments from Federal agencies, taxes on certain employees, and interest earnings on trust fund balances. Unemployment insurance is administered largely by the States, following Federal guidelines. The Unemployment Trust Fund is composed of individual accounts for each State and several Federal accounts, including accounts related to the separate unemployment insurance program for railroad employees.

- Civilian and military retirement trust funds: The Civil Service Retirement and Disability Fund is funded by employee and agency payments, general fund transfers for the unfunded portion of retirement costs, and interest earnings on trust fund balances. The Military Retirement Fund likewise is funded by payments from the Department of Defense, general fund transfers for unfunded retirement costs, and interest earnings on trust fund balances.

Table 22–5 shows income, outgo, and balances of two Federal funds that are designated as special funds. These funds are similar to trust funds in that they are financed by dedicated receipts, the excess of income over outgo is invested in Treasury securities, the interest earnings add to fund balances, and the balances remain available to cover future expenditures. The table is illustrative of the Federal funds group, which includes many revolving funds and special funds.

Table 22–4. INCOME, OUTGO, AND BALANCES OF MAJOR TRUST FUNDS
(In billions of dollars)

	2019 Actual	Estimate					
		2020	2021	2022	2023	2024	2025
Airport and Airway Trust Fund							
Balance, start of year	17.0	17.9	17.7	17.8	18.8	20.7	23.6
Adjustments to balances	....	....	....	....	....	....	....
Total balance, start of year	17.0	17.9	17.7	17.8	18.8	20.7	23.6
Income:							
Governmental receipts	16.0	17.0	18.0	18.9	19.9	21.1	22.3
Offsetting governmental	....	....	....	....	....	....	....
Proprietary	*	0.1	0.1	0.1	0.1	0.1	0.1
Intrabudgetary:							
Intrafund	....	....	....	....	....	....	....
Interest	0.3	0.4	0.4	0.4	0.4	0.4	0.5
Other intrabudgetary	0.6	0.4	*	*	*	*	*
Total income during the year	16.9	18.0	18.5	19.4	20.4	21.7	22.9
Outgo (–)	–16.0	–18.2	–18.3	–18.4	–18.5	–18.8	–18.7
Change in fund balance:							
Surplus or deficit(–):							
Excluding interest	0.6	–0.7	–0.2	0.6	1.5	2.5	3.6
Interest	0.3	0.4	0.4	0.4	0.4	0.4	0.5
Subtotal, surplus or deficit (–)	0.9	–0.2	0.1	1.0	1.9	2.9	4.2
Borrowing, transfers, lapses, & other adjustments	....	....	....	....	....	....	....
Total change in fund balance	0.9	–0.2	0.1	1.0	1.9	2.9	4.2
Balance, end of year	17.9	17.7	17.8	18.8	20.7	23.6	27.7
Civil Service Retirement and Disability Fund							
Balance, start of year	923.0	939.7	959.1	981.3	991.9	1,001.1	1,010.6
Adjustments to balances	–*	....	....	....	....	....	....
Total balance, start of year	923.0	939.7	959.1	981.3	991.9	1,001.1	1,010.6
Income:							
Governmental receipts	4.7	5.2	5.5	8.0	10.8	13.8	16.5
Offsetting governmental	....	....	....	....	....	....	....
Proprietary	....	....	....	....	....	....	....
Intrabudgetary:							
Intrafund	....	....	....	....	....	....	....
Interest	25.6	25.4	24.7	24.1	23.9	24.4	25.4
Other intrabudgetary	75.3	80.7	85.9	74.4	72.4	71.2	69.9
Total income during the year	105.6	111.3	116.1	106.5	107.1	109.3	111.8
Outgo (–)	–88.9	–91.9	–93.9	–96.0	–97.9	–99.8	–101.7
Change in fund balance:							
Surplus or deficit(–):							
Excluding interest	–8.8	–6.0	–2.5	–13.6	–14.6	–14.8	–15.2
Interest	25.6	25.4	24.7	24.1	23.9	24.4	25.4
Subtotal, surplus or deficit (–)	16.7	19.4	22.2	10.6	9.2	9.5	10.2
Borrowing, transfers, lapses, & other adjustments	*	....	....	....	....	....	....
Total change in fund balance	16.7	19.4	22.2	10.6	9.2	9.5	10.2
Balance, end of year	939.7	959.1	981.3	991.9	1,001.1	1,010.6	1,020.8
Employees and Retired Employees Health Benefits Funds							
Balance, start of year	27.4	27.5	28.5	29.8	31.1	32.5	33.7
Adjustments to balances	–0.1	....	....	....	....	....	....

Table 22–4.   INCOME, OUTGO, AND BALANCES OF MAJOR TRUST FUNDS—Continued

(In billions of dollars)

	2019 Actual	Estimate					
		2020	2021	2022	2023	2024	2025
Total balance, start of year	27.3	27.5	28.5	29.8	31.1	32.5	33.7
Income:							
Governmental receipts	....	....	....	....	....	....	....
Offsetting governmental	....	....	....	....	....	....	....
Proprietary	16.6	17.8	18.6	19.5	20.7	22.0	23.1
Intrabudgetary:							
Intrafund	....	....	....	....	....	....	....
Interest	0.6	0.6	0.5	0.5	0.6	0.6	0.7
Other intrabudgetary	38.4	40.0	41.5	43.6	44.9	47.0	49.6
Total income during the year	55.6	58.5	60.6	63.6	66.2	69.6	73.4
Outgo (–)	–55.3	–57.5	–59.3	–62.3	–64.9	–68.4	–71.9
Change in fund balance:							
Surplus or deficit(–):							
Excluding interest	–0.3	0.4	0.7	0.8	0.7	0.6	0.8
Interest	0.6	0.6	0.5	0.5	0.6	0.6	0.7
Subtotal, surplus or deficit (–)	0.2	1.0	1.3	1.4	1.4	1.2	1.5
Borrowing, transfers, lapses, & other adjustments	–*	....	*	....	....	....	....
Total change in fund balance	0.2	1.0	1.3	1.4	1.4	1.2	1.5
Balance, end of year	27.5	28.5	29.8	31.1	32.5	33.7	35.2
Employees Life Insurance Fund							
Balance, start of year	46.5	47.7	49.2	50.6	52.0	53.6	55.2
Adjustments to balances	*	....	....	....	....	....	....
Total balance, start of year	46.5	47.7	49.2	50.6	52.0	53.6	55.2
Income:							
Governmental receipts	....	....	....	....	....	....	....
Offsetting governmental	....	....	....	....	....	....	....
Proprietary	3.0	3.2	3.2	3.3	3.4	3.5	3.6
Intrabudgetary:							
Intrafund	....	....	....	....	....	....	....
Interest	0.9	1.1	1.0	1.0	1.1	1.1	1.2
Other intrabudgetary	0.6	0.6	0.6	0.6	0.6	0.7	0.7
Total income during the year	4.5	4.8	4.9	4.9	5.1	5.3	5.4
Outgo (–)	–3.3	–3.4	–3.4	–3.5	–3.6	–3.6	–3.7
Change in fund balance:							
Surplus or deficit(–):							
Excluding interest	0.4	0.4	0.4	0.4	0.5	0.5	0.5
Interest	0.9	1.1	1.0	1.0	1.1	1.1	1.2
Subtotal, surplus or deficit (–)	1.3	1.5	1.4	1.4	1.5	1.6	1.7
Borrowing, transfers, lapses, & other adjustments	....	....	....	....	....	....	....
Total change in fund balance	1.3	1.5	1.4	1.4	1.5	1.6	1.7
Balance, end of year	47.7	49.2	50.6	52.0	53.6	55.2	56.9
Foreign Military Sales Trust Fund							
Balance, start of year	33.6	32.5	33.1	25.7	27.0	27.0	26.2
Adjustments to balances	....	....	....	....	....	....	....
Total balance, start of year	33.6	32.5	33.1	25.7	27.0	27.0	26.2

Table 22–4. INCOME, OUTGO, AND BALANCES OF MAJOR TRUST FUNDS—Continued

(In billions of dollars)

	2019 Actual	Estimate					
		2020	2021	2022	2023	2024	2025
Income:							
Governmental receipts	....	....	....	....	....	....	....
Offsetting governmental	....	....	....	....	....	....	....
Proprietary	33.0	47.8	44.3	42.2	40.9	40.3	40.1
Intrabudgetary:							
Intrafund	....	....	....	....	....	....	....
Interest	....	....	....	....	....	....	....
Other intrabudgetary	....	....	....	....	....	....	....
Total income during the year	33.0	47.8	44.3	42.2	40.9	40.3	40.1
Outgo (–)	–34.0	–47.2	–51.8	–40.9	–41.0	–41.0	–40.7
Change in fund balance:							
Surplus or deficit(–):							
Excluding interest	–1.0	0.6	–7.5	1.3	–*	–0.7	–0.6
Interest	....	....	....	....	....	....	....
Subtotal, surplus or deficit (–)	–1.0	0.6	–7.5	1.3	–*	–0.7	–0.6
Borrowing, transfers, lapses, & other adjustments	–*	....	....	....	....	....	....
Total change in fund balance	–1.0	0.6	–7.5	1.3	–*	–0.7	–0.6
Balance, end of year	32.5	33.1	25.7	27.0	27.0	26.2	25.6
Foreign Service Retirement and Disability Fund							
Balance, start of year	19.2	19.3	19.7	20.2	20.6	21.0	21.4
Adjustments to balances	–*	....	....	....	....	....	....
Total balance, start of year	19.2	19.3	19.7	20.2	20.6	21.0	21.4
Income:							
Governmental receipts	*	*	*	*	*	*	*
Offsetting governmental	....	....	....	....	....	....	....
Proprietary	....	....	....	....	....	....	....
Intrabudgetary:							
Intrafund	*	*	*	*	*	*	*
Interest	0.6	0.6	0.6	0.6	0.6	0.6	0.6
Other intrabudgetary	0.5	0.8	0.8	0.8	0.9	0.9	0.9
Total income during the year	1.1	1.4	1.4	1.5	1.5	1.5	1.5
Outgo (–)	–1.0	–1.0	–1.0	–1.0	–1.1	–1.1	–1.1
Change in fund balance:							
Surplus or deficit(–):							
Excluding interest	–0.4	–0.1	–0.2	–0.2	–0.2	–0.2	–0.2
Interest	0.6	0.6	0.6	0.6	0.6	0.6	0.6
Subtotal, surplus or deficit (–)	0.1	0.4	0.4	0.4	0.4	0.4	0.4
Borrowing, transfers, lapses, & other adjustments	....	....	....	....	....	....	....
Total change in fund balance	0.1	0.4	0.4	0.4	0.4	0.4	0.4
Balance, end of year	19.3	19.7	20.2	20.6	21.0	21.4	21.7
Highway Trust Fund							
Balance, start of year	44.5	32.9	18.1	1.4	–17.9	–39.5	–63.4
Adjustments to balances	....	....	....	....	....	....	....
Total balance, start of year	44.5	32.9	18.1	1.4	–17.9	–39.5	–63.4
Income:							
Governmental receipts	44.1	42.4	42.7	43.1	43.1	43.2	43.3

Table 22–4. INCOME, OUTGO, AND BALANCES OF MAJOR TRUST FUNDS—Continued

(In billions of dollars)

	2019 Actual	Estimate					
		2020	2021	2022	2023	2024	2025
Offsetting governmental	*	*	*	*	*	*	*
Proprietary	0.1	....	....	....	....	....	....
Intrabudgetary:							
Intrafund	....	....	....	....	....	....	....
Interest	0.8	0.4	0.1	*	....	....	....
Other intrabudgetary	0.1	0.4	0.4	0.4	0.4	0.4	0.4
Total income during the year	45.2	43.1	43.2	43.5	43.5	43.6	43.7
Outgo (–)	–56.4	–57.9	–59.9	–62.7	–65.2	–67.5	–69.9
Change in fund balance:							
Surplus or deficit(–):							
Excluding interest	–12.0	–15.2	–16.8	–19.2	–21.7	–23.8	–26.2
Interest	0.8	0.4	0.1	*	....	....	....
Subtotal, surplus or deficit (–)	–11.2	–14.8	–16.7	–19.2	–21.7	–23.8	–26.2
Borrowing, transfers, lapses, & other adjustments	–0.4	....	–*	....	....	....	....
Total change in fund balance	–11.6	–14.8	–16.8	–19.2	–21.7	–23.8	–26.2
Balance, end of year	32.9	18.1	1.4	–17.9	–39.5	–63.4	–89.5
Medicare: Hospital Insurance (HI) Trust Fund							
Balance, start of year	203.2	198.9	189.7	190.7	191.8	202.9	226.9
Adjustments to balances	*	....	....	....	....	....	....
Total balance, start of year	203.2	198.9	189.7	190.7	191.8	202.9	226.9
Income:							
Governmental receipts	278.4	292.8	308.6	326.2	343.0	361.8	380.8
Offsetting governmental	....	....	....	....	....	....	....
Proprietary	10.5	10.9	11.0	11.2	11.5	11.9	12.3
Intrabudgetary:							
Intrafund	....	....	....	....	....	....	....
Interest	7.0	6.2	6.0	5.6	5.4	5.4	5.7
Other intrabudgetary	29.7	33.3	35.7	38.7	41.8	45.1	48.9
Total income during the year	325.6	343.0	361.4	381.7	401.7	424.3	447.7
Outgo (–)	–329.8	–352.3	–360.3	–380.6	–390.7	–400.2	–439.1
Change in fund balance:							
Surplus or deficit(–):							
Excluding interest	–11.2	–15.4	–4.9	–4.5	5.6	18.6	2.8
Interest	7.0	6.2	6.0	5.6	5.4	5.4	5.7
Subtotal, surplus or deficit (–)	–4.3	–9.2	1.0	1.1	11.1	24.0	8.6
Borrowing, transfers, lapses, & other adjustments	–0.1	....	....	....	....	....	....
Total change in fund balance	–4.3	–9.2	1.0	1.1	11.1	24.0	8.6
Balance, end of year	198.9	189.7	190.7	191.8	202.9	226.9	235.5
Medicare: Supplementary Insurance (SMI) Trust Fund							
Balance, start of year	96.9	104.1	109.3	105.9	77.9	74.0	103.1
Adjustments to balances	....	....	....	....	....	....	....
Total balance, start of year	96.9	104.1	109.3	105.9	77.9	74.0	103.1
Income:							
Governmental receipts	2.4	2.8	2.8	2.8	1.7	3.9	2.8
Offsetting governmental	....	....	....	....	....	....	....
Proprietary	121.0	132.4	137.9	145.2	156.9	170.1	184.8

Table 22–4.   INCOME, OUTGO, AND BALANCES OF MAJOR TRUST FUNDS—Continued

(In billions of dollars)

	2019 Actual	Estimate					
		2020	2021	2022	2023	2024	2025
Intrabudgetary:							
Intrafund	....	....	....	....	....	....	....
Interest	2.7	1.2	1.4	2.2	3.7	4.4	4.9
Other intrabudgetary	333.7	361.6	377.7	400.9	427.1	457.7	491.4
Total income during the year	459.8	498.0	519.8	551.1	589.4	636.2	683.8
Outgo (–)	–452.7	–492.8	–523.1	–579.1	–593.3	–607.2	–684.8
Change in fund balance:							
Surplus or deficit(–):							
Excluding interest	4.4	4.0	–4.7	–30.1	–7.6	24.6	–5.8
Interest	2.7	1.2	1.4	2.2	3.7	4.4	4.9
Subtotal, surplus or deficit (–)	7.1	5.2	–3.3	–28.0	–3.9	29.0	–1.0
Borrowing, transfers, lapses, & other adjustments	–*	....	....	....	....	....	....
Total change in fund balance	7.1	5.2	–3.3	–28.0	–3.9	29.0	–1.0
Balance, end of year	104.1	109.3	105.9	77.9	74.0	103.1	102.1
Military Retirement Fund							
Balance, start of year	735.2	818.5	906.6	1,001.0	1,095.6	1,198.5	1,312.3
Adjustments to balances	–*	....	....	....	....	....	....
Total balance, start of year	735.2	818.5	906.6	1,001.0	1,095.6	1,198.5	1,312.3
Income:							
Governmental receipts	....	....	....	....	....	....	....
Offsetting governmental	....	....	....	....	....	....	....
Proprietary	....	....	....	....	....	....	....
Intrabudgetary:							
Intrafund	....	....	....	....	....	....	....
Interest	27.4	29.2	28.3	32.9	34.3	37.9	39.5
Other intrabudgetary	116.5	122.1	130.9	133.6	137.6	141.6	145.7
Total income during the year	143.9	151.3	159.2	166.5	171.8	179.5	185.2
Outgo (–)	–60.7	–63.1	–64.8	–72.0	–68.9	–65.7	–72.9
Change in fund balance:							
Surplus or deficit(–):							
Excluding interest	55.8	59.0	66.0	61.7	68.7	75.9	72.8
Interest	27.4	29.2	28.3	32.9	34.3	37.9	39.5
Subtotal, surplus or deficit (–)	83.2	88.2	94.4	94.6	102.9	113.8	112.2
Borrowing, transfers, lapses, & other adjustments	*	....	....	....	....	....	....
Total change in fund balance	83.2	88.2	94.4	94.6	102.9	113.8	112.2
Balance, end of year	818.5	906.6	1,001.0	1,095.6	1,198.5	1,312.3	1,424.5
Railroad Retirement Trust Funds							
Balance, start of year	24.6	23.3	20.9	19.4	18.1	17.0	15.9
Adjustments to balances	*	....	....	....	....	....	....
Total balance, start of year	24.6	23.3	20.9	19.4	18.1	17.0	15.9
Income:							
Governmental receipts	5.5	5.6	5.9	6.1	6.2	6.4	6.6
Offsetting governmental	....	....	....	....	....	....	....
Proprietary	*	....	....	....	....	....	....
Intrabudgetary:							
Intrafund	4.9	5.3	5.0	5.2	5.3	5.3	5.3

Table 22–4. INCOME, OUTGO, AND BALANCES OF MAJOR TRUST FUNDS—Continued

(In billions of dollars)

	2019 Actual	Estimate					
		2020	2021	2022	2023	2024	2025
Interest	0.7	0.5	0.5	0.5	0.6	0.6	0.6
Other intrabudgetary	0.9	0.8	0.9	0.9	0.9	1.0	1.0
Total income during the year	12.0	12.2	12.3	12.7	13.0	13.3	13.5
Outgo (–)	–13.4	–14.6	–13.8	–14.0	–14.2	–14.3	–14.5
Change in fund balance:							
Surplus or deficit(–):							
Excluding interest	–2.0	–2.9	–2.0	–1.8	–1.7	–1.6	–1.6
Interest	0.7	0.5	0.5	0.5	0.6	0.6	0.6
Subtotal, surplus or deficit (–)	–1.4	–2.4	–1.5	–1.3	–1.2	–1.1	–1.0
Borrowing, transfers, lapses, & other adjustments	0.1	....	....	....	....	....	....
Total change in fund balance	–1.3	–2.4	–1.5	–1.3	–1.2	–1.1	–1.0
Balance, end of year	23.3	20.9	19.4	18.1	17.0	15.9	14.8
Social Security: Disability Insurance (DI) Trust Fund							
Balance, start of year	93.1	96.4	94.8	98.0	106.2	118.8	135.8
Adjustments to balances	–*	....	....	....	....	....	....
Total balance, start of year	93.1	96.4	94.8	98.0	106.2	118.8	135.8
Income:							
Governmental receipts	144.0	140.5	146.8	154.6	162.0	170.5	179.1
Offsetting governmental	....	....	....	....	....	....	....
Proprietary	0.1	0.1	0.1	0.1	0.1	0.1	0.1
Intrabudgetary:							
Intrafund	....	....	....	....	....	....	....
Interest	2.9	2.8	2.8	2.6	2.7	3.0	3.4
Other intrabudgetary	4.0	4.4	4.6	4.9	5.0	5.3	5.6
Total income during the year	151.1	147.8	154.3	162.2	169.8	178.8	188.2
Outgo (–)	–147.8	–149.5	–151.2	–153.9	–157.1	–161.9	–168.0
Change in fund balance:							
Surplus or deficit(–):							
Excluding interest	0.4	–4.5	0.3	5.6	10.0	14.0	16.8
Interest	2.9	2.8	2.8	2.6	2.7	3.0	3.4
Subtotal, surplus or deficit (–)	3.3	–1.7	3.1	8.2	12.7	16.9	20.2
Borrowing, transfers, lapses, & other adjustments	....	0.1	*	....	....	....	....
Total change in fund balance	3.3	–1.6	3.2	8.2	12.7	16.9	20.2
Balance, end of year	96.4	94.8	98.0	106.2	118.8	135.8	156.0
Social Security: Old Age and Survivors Insurance (OASI) Trust Fund							
Balance, start of year	2,801.1	2,804.3	2,813.0	2,803.3	2,776.5	2,727.4	2,660.6
Adjustments to balances	....	....	....	....	....	....	....
Total balance, start of year	2,801.1	2,804.3	2,813.0	2,803.3	2,776.5	2,727.4	2,660.6
Income:							
Governmental receipts	770.3	826.6	864.3	910.2	953.7	1,004.0	1,054.7
Offsetting governmental	....	....	....	....	....	....	....
Proprietary	0.1	*	*	*	*	*	*
Intrabudgetary:							
Intrafund	....	....	....	....	....	....	....
Interest	79.6	76.2	72.9	68.4	64.5	62.2	59.5
Other intrabudgetary	50.2	54.0	58.4	62.7	67.0	71.7	77.2
Total income during the year	900.1	956.8	995.5	1,041.3	1,085.2	1,137.9	1,191.5

Table 22–4.   INCOME, OUTGO, AND BALANCES OF MAJOR TRUST FUNDS—Continued

(In billions of dollars)

	2019 Actual	Estimate					
		2020	2021	2022	2023	2024	2025
Outgo (–)	–896.8	–948.3	–1,005.3	–1,068.0	–1,134.4	–1,204.6	–1,277.4
Change in fund balance:							
Surplus or deficit(–):							
Excluding interest	–76.3	–67.7	–82.6	–95.2	–113.7	–128.9	–145.4
Interest	79.6	76.2	72.9	68.4	64.5	62.2	59.5
Subtotal, surplus or deficit (–)	3.2	8.5	–9.8	–26.7	–49.2	–66.8	–85.9
Borrowing, transfers, lapses, & other adjustments	....	0.1	*	....	....	....	....
Total change in fund balance	3.2	8.6	–9.7	–26.7	–49.2	–66.8	–85.9
Balance, end of year	2,804.3	2,813.0	2,803.3	2,776.5	2,727.4	2,660.6	2,574.7
Unemployment Trust Fund							
Balance, start of year	73.1	84.8	98.1	109.7	120.7	130.7	140.2
Adjustments to balances	....	....	....	....	....	....	....
Total balance, start of year	73.1	84.8	98.1	109.7	120.7	130.7	140.2
Income:							
Governmental receipts	41.2	42.0	43.0	43.7	45.7	47.8	50.1
Offsetting governmental	....	....	....	....	....	....	....
Proprietary	*	*	*	*	*	*	*
Intrabudgetary:							
Intrafund	....	....	....	....	....	....	....
Interest	1.8	2.1	2.4	2.7	3.0	3.1	3.4
Other intrabudgetary	0.4	0.4	0.4	0.5	0.5	0.5	0.5
Total income during the year	43.3	44.5	45.9	46.9	49.1	51.4	54.0
Outgo (–)	–31.3	–31.2	–34.3	–35.9	–39.1	–42.0	–44.0
Change in fund balance:							
Surplus or deficit(–):							
Excluding interest	10.2	11.2	9.2	8.2	7.1	6.3	6.6
Interest	1.8	2.1	2.4	2.7	3.0	3.1	3.4
Subtotal, surplus or deficit (–)	12.0	13.3	11.6	11.0	10.1	9.4	10.0
Borrowing, transfers, lapses, & other adjustments	–0.3	....	....	....	....	....	....
Total change in fund balance	11.7	13.3	11.6	11.0	10.1	9.4	10.0
Balance, end of year	84.8	98.1	109.7	120.7	130.7	140.2	150.2
All Other Trust Funds							
Balance, start of year	49.5	52.2	54.6	56.2	58.1	60.6	62.9
Adjustments to balances	0.3	....	....	....	....	....	....
Total balance, start of year	49.8	52.2	54.6	56.2	58.1	60.6	62.9
Income:							
Governmental receipts	4.5	5.3	5.4	5.5	5.7	5.4	5.5
Offsetting governmental	1.2	*	*	*	*	*	*
Proprietary	4.9	4.3	3.9	4.0	4.1	4.0	4.1
Intrabudgetary:							
Intrafund	0.1	....	....	....	....	....	....
Interest	1.0	1.1	1.1	0.9	0.9	0.9	0.9
Other intrabudgetary	15.3	17.3	16.0	17.3	17.5	18.0	18.2
Total income during the year	27.0	28.0	26.4	27.7	28.2	28.2	28.6
Outgo (–)	–24.6	–25.7	–24.8	–25.8	–25.6	–26.0	–25.5

Table 22–4.   INCOME, OUTGO, AND BALANCES OF MAJOR TRUST FUNDS—Continued

(In billions of dollars)

	2019 Actual	Estimate					
		2020	2021	2022	2023	2024	2025
Change in fund balance:							
Surplus or deficit(–):							
Excluding interest	1.4	1.2	0.6	1.0	1.6	1.4	2.2
Interest	1.0	1.1	1.1	0.9	0.9	0.9	0.9
Subtotal, surplus or deficit (–)	2.4	2.3	1.6	1.9	2.5	2.3	3.1
Borrowing, transfers, lapses, & other adjustments	*	–*	*	....	....	....	....
Total change in fund balance	2.4	2.3	1.7	1.9	2.5	2.3	3.1
Balance, end of year	52.2	54.6	56.2	58.1	60.6	62.9	66.0

* $50 million or less.

Table 22–5. INCOME, OUTGO, AND BALANCES OF SELECTED SPECIAL FUNDS

(In billions of dollars)

	2019 Actual	Estimate					
		2020	2021	2022	2023	2024	2025
Abandoned Mine Reclamation Fund							
Balance, start of year	2.8	2.7	2.6	2.4	2.1	1.9	1.6
Adjustments to balances	....	....	....	....	....	....	....
Total balance, start of year	2.8	2.7	2.6	2.4	2.1	1.9	1.6
Income:							
Governmental receipts	0.1	0.1	0.1	....	....	....	....
Offsetting governmental	....	....	....	....	....	....	....
Proprietary	....	....	....	....	....	....	....
Intrabudgetary:							
Intrafund	....	....	....	....	....	....	....
Interest	0.1	0.1	*	*	*	*	*
Other intrabudgetary	....	....	....	....	....	....	....
Total income during the year	0.2	0.2	0.2	*	*	*	*
Outgo (–)	–0.3	–0.3	–0.3	–0.3	–0.3	–0.3	–0.3
Change in fund balance:							
Surplus or deficit(–):							
Excluding interest	–0.1	–0.2	–0.2	–0.3	–0.3	–0.3	–0.3
Interest	0.1	0.1	*	*	*	*	*
Subtotal, surplus or deficit (–)	–0.1	–0.1	–0.2	–0.3	–0.3	–0.3	–0.2
Borrowing, transfers, lapses, & other adjustments	....	....	....	....	....	....	....
Total change in fund balance	–0.1	–0.1	–0.2	–0.3	–0.3	–0.3	–0.2
Balance, end of year	2.7	2.6	2.4	2.1	1.9	1.6	1.3
Department of Defense Medicare-Eligible Retiree Health Care Fund							
Balance, start of year	238.7	252.2	265.9	281.2	296.7	313.5	331.0
Adjustments to balances	....	....	....	....	....	....	....
Total balance, start of year	238.7	252.2	265.9	281.2	296.7	313.5	331.0
Income:							
Governmental receipts	....	....	....	....	....	....	....
Offsetting governmental	....	....	....	....	....	....	....
Proprietary	....	....	....	....	....	....	....
Intrabudgetary:							
Intrafund	13.5	14.7	15.5	16.2	16.9	17.6	18.4
Interest	10.5	10.2	11.5	11.4	12.7	13.3	13.2
Other intrabudgetary	....	....	....	....	....	....	....
Total income during the year	24.0	24.9	26.9	27.6	29.6	30.9	31.6
Outgo (–)	–10.5	–11.3	–11.6	–12.1	–12.8	–13.4	–14.2
Change in fund balance:							
Surplus or deficit(–):							
Excluding interest	3.0	3.4	3.8	4.1	4.1	4.2	4.2
Interest	10.5	10.2	11.5	11.4	12.7	13.3	13.2
Subtotal, surplus or deficit (–)	13.5	13.6	15.3	15.5	16.8	17.5	17.4
Borrowing, transfers, lapses, & other adjustments	....	....	....	....	....	....	....
Total change in fund balance	13.5	13.6	15.3	15.5	16.8	17.5	17.4
Balance, end of year	252.2	265.9	281.2	296.7	313.5	331.0	348.4

* $50 million or less.

23. COMPARISON OF ACTUAL TO ESTIMATED TOTALS

The Budget is required by statute to compare budget year estimates of receipts and outlays with the subsequent actual receipts and outlays for that year. This chapter meets that requirement by comparing the actual receipts, outlays, and deficit for 2018 with the current services estimates shown in the 2019 Budget, published in February 2018.[1] It also presents a more detailed comparison for mandatory and related programs, and reconciles the actual receipts, outlays, and deficit totals shown here with the figures for 2019 previously published by the Department of the Treasury.

Receipts

Actual receipts for 2019 were $3,464 billion, $40 billion more than the $3,424 billion current services estimate in the 2019 Budget, which was published in February 2018. As shown in Table 23–1, this increase was the net effect of legislative changes, economic conditions that differed from what had been expected, and technical factors that resulted in different tax liabilities and collection patterns than had been assumed.

Policy differences. Legislated tax changes enacted after February 2018 reduced 2019 receipts by a net $16 billion relative to the 2019 Budget current services estimate. An Act making further continuing appropriations

for the fiscal year ending September 30, 2018, and for other purposes (P.L. 115-120), extended for two years, through 2019, the moratorium on the 2.3% excise tax on the sale of medical devices, and suspended the annual fee on health insurance providers for one year. It was signed into law by the President on January 22, 2018, and accounted for almost all of the net reduction in receipts, reducing 2019 receipts by an estimated $13 billion. The Bipartisan Budget Act of 2018 (P.L. 115-123), provided tax relief to certain individuals and businesses in the areas affected by the California wildfires and areas affected by Hurricanes Harvey, Irma, and Maria; extended expiring provisions providing tax relief for families and individuals; incentives for growth, jobs, investment, and innovation; and incentives for energy production and conservation; and extended funding for the Children's Health Insurance Program and extended several Medicare provisions, among other health provisions. This Act was signed into law on February 9, 2018, and reduced 2018 receipts by an estimated $2 billion.

Economic differences. Differences between the economic assumptions upon which the current services estimates were based and actual economic performance increased 2019 receipts by a net $13 billion above the February 2018 current services estimate. Wage and salary income was higher in 2019 than initially projected, which increased individual income tax and social insurance receipts by $18 billion and $11 billion above the February 2018 estimate, respectively, and accounted for most of the net increase in receipts attributable to economic differences. Different economic factors than those assumed in February 2018 had a smaller effect on other sources of receipts, decreasing collections by a net $15 billion.

Technical factors. Technical factors increase receipts by a net $42 billion relative to the February 2018 current services estimate. These factors had the greatest effect on customs duties, increasing collections by $29 billion. Increases in individual income taxes, corporation

---

[1] The current services concept is discussed in Chapter 25, "Current Services Estimates." For mandatory programs and receipts, the February 2018 current services estimate was based on laws then in place, adjusted for certain expiring provisions. For discretionary programs, the current services estimate was based on the discretionary spending limits enacted in the Budget Control Act of 2011 (BCA). Spending for Overseas Contingency Operations, was estimated based on annualizing the amounts provided in the 2018 appropriations and increasing for inflation. The current services estimates also reflected the effects of discretionary and mandatory sequestration as required by the BCA following failure of the Joint Select Committee on Deficit Reduction to meet its deficit reduction target. For a detailed explanation of the 2018 estimate, see "Current Services Estimates," Chapter 23 in *Analytical Perspectives, Budget of the United States Government, Fiscal Year 2019*.

Table 23–1. COMPARISON OF ACTUAL 2019 RECEIPTS WITH THE INITIAL CURRENT SERVICES ESTIMATES
(In billions of dollars)

	Estimate (February 2018)	Changes			Total Changes	Actual
		Policy	Economic	Technical		
Individual income taxes	1,687	2	18	11	31	1,718
Corporation income taxes	225	–*	–6	11	5	230
Social insurance and retirement receipts	1,238	....	11	–5	6	1,243
Excise taxes	108	–17	–2	11	–8	99
Estate and gift taxes	17	....	1	–1	–*	17
Customs duties	44	–*	–2	29	27	71
Miscellaneous receipts	105	–*	–6	–14	–20	86
Total receipts	3,424	–16	13	42	40	3,464

* $500 million or less

income taxes, and excise tax receipts of $11 billion each accounted for most of the remaining changes in 2019 receipts attributable to technical factors, partially offset by a decrease in miscellaneous receipts of $14 billion. The models used to prepare the February 2018 estimates of individual and corporation income taxes were based on historical economic data and then-current tax and collections data that were all subsequently revised and account for the net increase in these two sources of receipts attributable to technical factors. New tariffs imposed on imports accounted for the increase in customs duties.

Outlays

Outlays for 2019 were $4,448 billion, $60 billion more than the $4,388 billion current services estimate in the 2019 Budget. Table 23–2 distributes the $60 billion net decrease in outlays among discretionary and mandatory programs and net interest.[2] The table also shows rough estimates according to three reasons for the changes: policy; economic conditions; and technical estimating differences, a residual.

Policy differences. Policy changes are the result of legislative actions that change spending levels, primarily through higher or lower appropriations or changes in authorizing legislation, which may themselves be in response to changed economic conditions. For 2019, policy changes increased outlays by $72 billion relative to the initial current services estimates, which included the impacts of Bipartisan Budget Act of 2018 (Public Law 115-123) and increased spending for disaster response and recovery efforts. P.L. 115-123 enacted an increase to the level of discretionary funding allowable for both defense and non-defense spending in 2018 and 2019. The combined policy changes from final 2018 and 2019 appropriations increased discretionary outlays by $56 billion. Policy changes increased mandatory outlays by a net

---

[2] Discretionary programs are controlled by annual appropriations, while mandatory programs are generally controlled by authorizing legislation. Mandatory programs are primarily formula benefit or entitlement programs with permanent spending authority that depends on eligibility criteria, benefit levels, and other factors.

$15 billion above current law, largely due to Public Laws 115-120 and 115-123 which funded the continuation of expiring health programs. Debt service costs associated with all policy changes increased outlays by less than $1 billion.

Economic and technical factors. Economic and technical estimating factors resulted in a net decrease in outlays of $12 billion. Technical changes result from changes in such factors as the number of beneficiaries for entitlement programs, crop conditions, or other factors not associated with policy changes or economic conditions. Defense discretionary spending increased relative to the current services estimate largely due to faster-than-estimated spending of new authority, while non-defense spending mainly decreased due to timing of the final enacted 2019 appropriations. Increases in discretionary outlays due to legislation, as discussed above, were offset by a $12 billion decrease in net outlays resulting from these technical changes. Outlays for mandatory programs decreased $11 billion due to economic and technical factors. There was a net decrease in outlays of $19 billion as a result of differences between actual economic conditions versus those forecast in February 2018. Outlays for Social Security were $8 billion lower than anticipated in the 2019 Budget largely due to lower-than-estimated number of beneficiaries and cost-of-living adjustments. Education, training, employment and social services programs were a combined $26 billion higher, offset by $15 billion lower income security programs outlays, the remaining changes were in veterans benefits and services, deposit insurance, and other programs. Outlays for net interest were approximately $11 billion higher due to economic and technical factors, primarily higher interest rates than originally assumed.

Deficit

The preceding two sections discussed the differences between the initial current services estimates and the actual Federal Government receipts and outlays for 2019. This section combines these effects to show the net deficit impact of these differences.

Table 23–2. COMPARISON OF ACTUAL 2019 OUTLAYS WITH THE INITIAL CURRENT SERVICES ESTIMATES

(In billions of dollars)

	Estimate (February 2018)	Changes Policy	Economic	Technical	Total Changes	Actual
Discretionary:						
Defense	637	31	....	8	39	676
Nondefense	656	25	....	−20	5	661
Subtotal, discretionary	1,293	56	....	−12	45	1,338
Mandatory:						
Social Security	1,047	....	4	−13	−8	1,038
Other programs	1,684	15	10	−13	12	1,697
Subtotal, mandatory	2,731	15	14	−25	4	2,735
Net interest	364	1	5	6	11	375
Total outlays	4,388	72	19	−31	60	4,448

* $500 million or less

Table 23–3. COMPARISON OF THE ACTUAL 2019 DEFICIT WITH THE INITIAL CURRENT SERVICES ESTIMATE

(In billions of dollars)

	Estimate (February 2018)	Changes			Total Changes	Actual
		Policy	Economic	Technical		
Receipts	3,424	−16	13	42	40	3,464
Outlays	4,388	72	19	−31	60	4,448
Deficit	964	88	6	−74	20	984

* $500 million or less

Note: Deficit changes are outlays minus receipts. For these changes, a positive number indicates an increase in the deficit.

As shown in Table 23–3, the 2019 current services deficit was initially estimated to be $964 billion. The actual deficit was $984 billion, which was a $20 billion increase from the initial estimate. Receipts were $40 billion higher and outlays were $60 billion higher than the initial estimate. The table shows the distribution of the changes according to the categories in the preceding two sections. The net effect of policy changes for receipts and outlays increased the deficit by $88 billion. Economic conditions that differed from the initial assumptions in February 2018 increased the deficit by $6 billion. Technical factors decreased the deficit by an estimated $74 billion.

Comparison of the Actual and Estimated Outlays for Mandatory and Related Programs for 2019

This section compares the original 2019 outlay estimates for mandatory and related programs in the current services estimates of the 2019 Budget with the actual outlays. Major examples of these programs include Social Security and Medicare benefits, Medicaid and unemployment compensation payments, and deposit insurance for banks and thrift institutions. This category also includes net interest outlays and undistributed offsetting receipts.

A number of factors may cause differences between the amounts estimated in the Budget and the actual mandatory outlays. For example, legislation may change benefit rates or coverage, the actual number of beneficiaries may differ from the number estimated, or economic conditions (such as inflation or interest rates) may differ from what was assumed in making the original estimates.

Table 23–4 shows the differences between the actual outlays for these programs in 2019 and the current services estimates included in the 2019 Budget. Actual outlays for mandatory spending and net interest in 2019 were $3,111 billion, which was $15 billion more than the current services estimate of $3,095 billion in February 2018.

As Table 23–4 shows, actual outlays for mandatory human resources programs were $2,800 billion, $7 billion higher than originally estimated. This increase was the net effect of legislative action, differences between actual and assumed economic conditions, differences between the anticipated and actual number of beneficiaries, and other technical differences. The overall increase in outlays for these programs was mainly driven by net upward reestimates in higher education programs due primarily to higher default and lower collection rates. This increase was partially offset by lower outlays in income security programs and veterans benefits and services. Mandatory

outlays for programs in functions outside human resources were $6 billion lower than originally estimated. Amongst these functions, the largest changes from the current services estimates were outlays for agriculture and mortgage credit programs. Agriculture outlays were $16 billion higher than originally estimated due to the Administration providing trade mitigation assistance to farmers. Downward re-estimates in Federal housing programs were the primary cause of lower than estimated mortgage credit program outlays.

Outlays for net interest were $375 billion, or $11 billion higher than the original estimate. As shown on Table 23–4, interest payments on Treasury debt securities increased by $14 billion. Interest earnings of trust funds increased by $6 billion, decreasing net outlays, while net outlays for other interest further increased net outlays by $4 billion.

Reconciliation of Differences with Amounts Published by the Treasury for 2019

Table 23-5 provides a reconciliation of the receipts, outlays, and deficit totals for 2019 published by the Department of the Treasury in the September 2019 Monthly Treasury Statement (MTS) and those published in this Budget. The Department of the Treasury made no adjustments to the estimates for the Combined Statement of Receipts, Outlays, and Balances. Additional adjustments for the 2021 Budget increased receipts by $1,965 million and increased outlays by $1,733 million. Some of these adjustments were for financial transactions that are not reported to the Department of the Treasury but are included in the Budget, including those for the Affordable Housing Program, the Electric Reliability Organization, the Federal Financial Institutions Examination Council Appraisal Subcommittee, Federal Retirement Thrift Investment Board Program Expenses, Medical Center Research Organizations, the Public Company Accounting Oversight Board, the Puerto Rico Oversight Board, the Securities Investor Protection Corporation, fees and payments related to the Standard Setting Body, and the United Mine Workers of America benefit funds. There was also an adjustment for the National Railroad Retirement Investment Trust (NRRIT), which relates to a conceptual difference in reporting. NRRIT reports to the Department of the Treasury with a one-month lag so that the fiscal year total provided in the Treasury Combined Statement covers September 2018 through August 2019. The Budget has been adjusted to reflect transactions that occurred during the actual fiscal year, which begins October 1. In addition, the Budget also reflects agency adjustments to 2019 outlays reported to Treasury after preparation of the Treasury Combined Statement. Finally, the adjustments account for differences in receipts or net outlays of the Departments of Homeland Security, Labor, Transportation and Treasury.

Table 23–4. COMPARISON OF ACTUAL AND ESTIMATED OUTLAYS FOR MANDATORY AND RELATED PROGRAMS UNDER CURRENT LAW

(In billions of dollars)

	2019		
	Estimate	Actual	Change
Mandatory outlays:			
Human resources programs:			
Education, training, employment, and social services:			
Higher Education	9	36	27
Other	7	6	–1
Total, education, training, employment, and social services	16	42	26
Health:			
Medicaid	420	409	–11
Other	96	109	13
Total, health	516	519	2
Medicare	640	644	4
Income security:			
Retirement and disability	153	153	–*
Unemployment compensation	29	27	–2
Food and nutrition assistance	95	88	–8
Other	180	175	–5
Total, income security	457	442	–15
Social security	1047	1038	–8
Veterans benefits and services:			
Income security for veterans	99	101	2
Other	17	14	–3
Total, veterans benefits and services	116	115	–2
Total, mandatory human resources programs	2,792	2,800	7
Other functions:			
Agriculture	15	32	16
International	7	*	–7
Mortgage credit	–23	–35	–12
Deposit insurance	–9	–8	1
Other advancement of commerce	15	21	6
Other functions	34	24	–10
Total, other functions	40	34	–6
Undistributed offsetting receipts:			
Employer share, employee retirement	–96	–87	9
Rents and royalties on the outer continental shelf	–4	–6	–2
Other undistributed offsetting receipts	–*	–5	–4
Total, undistributed offsetting receipts	–100	–98	2
Total, mandatory	2,731	2,735	4
Net interest:			
Interest on Treasury debt securities (gross)	559	573	14
Interest received by trust funds	–143	–150	–6
Other interest	–52	–48	4
Total, net interest	364	375	11
Total, outlays for mandatory and net interest	3,095	3,111	15

* $500 million or less

Table 23–5.   RECONCILIATION OF FINAL AMOUNTS FOR 2019

(In millions of dollars)

	Receipts	Outlays	Deficit
Totals published by Treasury (September MTS)	3,462,196	4,446,584	984,388
Miscellaneous Treasury adjustments	....	....	....
Totals published by Treasury in Combined Statement	3,462,196	4,446,584	984,388
Department of Homeland Security	....	1,360	1,360
Department of Labor	259	....	−259
Department of Transportation	440	....	−440
Department of the Treasury	98	....	−98
Affordable Housing Program	352	352	....
Electric Reliability Organization	100	100	....
Federal Financial Institutions Examination Council Appraisal Subcommittee	16	16	....
Federal Retirement Thrift Investment Board Program Expenses	....	−11	−11
Medical Center Research Organizations	....	−242	−242
National Railroad Retirement Investment Trust	....	−307	−307
Public Company Accounting Oversight Board	263	264	1
Puerto Rico Oversight Board	65	65	....
Securities Investor Protection Corporation	301	78	−223
Standard Setting Body	29	29	....
United Mine Workers of America benefit funds	17	17	....
Other	25	12	−13
Total adjustments, net	1,965	1,733	−232
Totals in the Budget	3,464,161	4,448,317	984,156
MEMORANDUM:			
Total change since year-end statement	1,965	1,733	−232